THE SOUTH AFRICAN BILL OF RIGHTS AND PLURALISM

A Comparative Perspective of Judicial Responses to Diversity

THE SOUTH AFRICAN BILL OF RIGHTS AND PLURALISM

A Comparative Perspective of Judicial Responses to Diversity

AUTHOR

Bertus de Villiers

juta

The South African Bill of Rights and Pluralism: A Comparative Perspective of Judicial Responses to Diversity

First published 2025

Juta and Company (Pty) Ltd
First Floor, Sunclare Building, 21 Dreyer Street, Claremont 7708
PO Box 14373, Lansdowne 7779, Cape Town, South Africa
www.juta.co.za

ISBN: 978 1 48515 385 6 (Print)
eISBN: 978 1 48515 449 5 (ePub)

Production Specialist: Valencia Wyngaard-Arenz
Editor: Rod Prodgers
Proofreader: James Ryan
Cover Designer: Drag and Drop (Jacques Nel)
Indexer: Lexinfo (Adami Geldenhuys)
Typesetter: Elinye Ithuba DTP Solutions

Typeset in Bembo Std Regular 11 pt on 14pt

Printed in South Africa by

CONTENTS

ABOUT THE AUTHOR

Bertus de Villiers is a Visiting Professor of the Law School of the University of Johannesburg. He is also a Fellow of the Alexander von Humboldt Foundation in Germany. Professor De Villiers has travelled widely and has undertaken research and lectured on constitutional and political developments in various countries. He has published extensively on a wide range of constitutional topics, in particular areas dealing with federalism, human rights, indigenous rights, minority rights and land reform.

His most notable books at the time of the drafting of the South African Constitution and more recently are:

At the time of the drafting of the South African Constitution

De Villiers, B. (1990) *Groepe: Meulsteen of Bousteen* RGN Uitgewers, Pretoria [Minorities: millstone or cornerstone]

De Villiers, B. (ed.) (1994) *The birth of a constitution* Juta, Cape Town

De Villiers, B. and R Licht (eds.) (1994) *South Africa's Crisis of Constitutional Democracy – Can the US Constitution Help?* Juta, Cape Town

Van Wyk, D.J., Dugard, B., De Villiers, D. Davis, D. (eds.) (1994) *Rights and constitutionalism in South Africa* Juta, Cape Town

De Villiers, B. (ed.) (1994) *Comparative federal experiences* Juta, Cape Town

De Villiers, B. (ed.) (1995) *Managing constitutional change* HSRC Publishers, Pretoria

De Villiers, B. (ed) (1997) *The rights of indigenous peoples – the quest for coexistence* HSRC Publishers, Pretoria

De Villiers, B. (ed.) (1998) *Institutional development in divided societies* HSRC Publishers, Pretoria (co-editor with A. Alen and F. Delmartino)

Recent books:

De Villiers, B., Marko, J., Palermo, F and Constantin, S. (eds.) (2021) *Litigating the rights of minorities and indigenous peoples in domestic and international courts* (Brill: Leiden)

De Villiers, B. (2022) *Navigating the unknown – essays on selected case studies about the rights of minorities* (Brill: Leiden)

De Villiers, B. (2023) *Indigenous rights in the modern era – regaining what has been lost* (Brill: Leiden)

De Villiers, B., Isra, S. and Mohammed, P.N. (eds.) (2024) *Courts and diversity: twenty years of the Constitutional Court of Indonesia* (Brill: Leiden)

Prof De Villiers can be contacted at bertusdv@uj.ac.au.

The Google profile of Prof De Villiers with a full list of his publications can be accessed at: https://scholar.google.com/citations?user=1hm8I8QAAAAJ&hl=en.

ACKNOWLEDGEMENT

I would like to express my deepest appreciation to the Alexander von Humboldt Stiftung for the generous and kind funding provided during my scientific journey that started many years ago. I am also indebted to the Law School of the University of Johannesburg for being there not only in my formative years as a student, but for so enthusiastically encouraging me as Visiting Professor. Written large across the pages of this book is the incredible help I have received from librarians Lizette van Zyl (University of Johannesburg), Jaya Ralph (Curtin University) and staff at the Max Planck Institute for Comparative Public Law and International Law in Heidelberg. In this modern age of self-search I have found the staff of these libraries indispensable and an ode to their profession. May they continue to help us for many years to quickly find relevant material. My thanks also to Director Prof Armin von Bogdandy and his predecessor directors at the Max Planck Institute for Comparative Public Law and International Law in Heidelberg, Germany, where I have since 1988 spent many cumulative years of research and *viel Spass* time. In Heidelberg I learnt the meaning of the following:

Es ist immer eine gute Zeit, eine gute Zeit zu haben!

I am keenly aware that with any publication, particularly one in comparative law, the author is vulnerable to changes of law in a case country. The information contained in this book is, to the best of my knowledge and efforts, contemporaneous up to March 2025.

ABBREVIATIONS

ACFC	Advisory Committee on the European Framework Convention
ACHPR	African Commission on Human and People's Rights
African Charter	African Charter on Human and Peoples' Rights
ANC	African National Congress
BVerfGE	*Bundesverfassungsgericht* (Constitutional Court of Germany)
CATSI Act	Aboriginal Corporations (Aboriginal and Torres Strait Islander) Act 2006
CERD	United Nations Committee on the Elimination of Racial Discrimination
CODESA	Convention for a Democratic South Africa
CONTRALESA	Congress of Traditional Leaders of South Africa
CJEU	Court of Justice of the European Union
Declaration on Minorities	UN Declaration on the Rights of Persons belonging to National or Ethnic, Religious and Linguistic Minorities
ECtHR	European Court of Human Rights
EFF	Economic Freedom Fighters
European Convention	European Convention on Human Rights
European Charter	European Charter for Regional or Minority Languages
EU	European Union
FCNM	Framework Convention for the Protection of National Minorities
FPIC	Free, prior, and informed consent
IACrtHR	Inter-American Court of Human Rights

ICESCR	International Covenant on Economic, Social and Cultural Rights
ICCPR	International Covenant on Civil and Political Rights
ILO 169	Indigenous and Tribal Peoples Convention, 1989 (No 169)
Ljubljana Guidelines	Ljubljana Guidelines on Integration of Diverse Societies
Lund Recommendations	Lund Recommendations on the Effective Participation of National Minorities in Public Life
MAT	Muslim Arbitration Tribunals
MPNF	Multi-Party Negotiation Forum
NP	National Party
PAC	Pan African Congress
UN	United Nations
UNDRIP	United Nations Declaration on the Rights of Indigenous Peoples
UNESCO	United Nations Educational, Scientific and Cultural Organization
UNHRC	United Nations Human Rights Council

DEDICATION

The secret of change is to focus all your energy not on fighting the old, but on building the new

– Socrates

Few people experience the joy to witness the conception, birth and 30-year celebration of a new constitution. I was privileged to witnesses the conception and birth (De Villiers 1994a) of the South African Constitution and now, in celebration of its 30th anniversary, I would like to make some observations on how it has fared as the foundational document of the country's new democracy in its response to the pluralism of the South African population.

I grew up as a child of the apartheid era. It was not by choice – that is where history placed me. It turned out to be a blessing for me. No professional experience I have had since can get close to the 1990–1996 exhilaration. But for me change started much earlier. At uni in the late 1970s change started for me. I embarked on a road to change the system, as many others had tried. Mine was a revolution from within. It is said that success has many fathers. There is indeed truth to this, as demonstrated by the numerous people of goodwill who contributed to the birth of democracy in South Africa – first through the interim Constitution of 1993, followed by the final Constitution in 1996. A country that, in all respects, was on the verge of massive civil unrest, if not outright civil war, pulled itself back from the abyss and negotiated, against all odds, a democratic Constitution within a remarkably short time. It was a home-grown product. Of course there were international inputs, but ultimately the Constitution was negotiated locally. It bears the imprint and sweat of many late hours of toil, accommodation, and compromise. Each compromise given is linked to another compromise received. The Constitution is a mosaic of give and take.

Three decades on, numerous critics assert they would have done a better job. Perhaps they are right. Or perhaps they are no different to any cynic, adept at convincing you that you either overpaid or received too little for an item.[1] Being

[1] The appropriateness of the 1993 and 1996 constitutional settlement continues to be the subject of heated political and scientific debate in South Africa. This book does not intend to deal with the merit of this ongoing discourse. It suffices to note that those on the right of the political spectrum are of the view that better protections for (Afrikaner) minority rights should have been negotiated, whereas those to the left of the spectrum feel that unjustifiable compromises were made to accommodate minority interests and property rights, and in doing so the negotiators of

outside of the cauldron of the 1990s makes the settlement susceptible to all types of criticism – some justifiable and some ill-informed and even irrational. Any constitutional settlement must be assessed within its context of birth. Critics often blame the Constitution for what, in effect, are failures of government – not shortcomings in the Constitution itself.

I see what arose from the 1990s as a truly transformative constitution. (De Villiers 2023a) To many of those involved, it was nothing short of a miracle that within three years after the unbanning of political organisations, an interim Constitution and government of national unity for a peaceful transition had been established.[2] Ultimately, in my view, the Constitution was a unique deal wrought from the hardest ore – a compromise that reflected and accommodated different histories, ideologies, agendas, objectives, fears and aspirations. It aligned with international norms and standards while drawing inspiration from comparative constitutional and political experiences. Moreover, it set a precedent for other

---

the liberation parties eroded the scope of the democratic government's power, slowed down land reform, and unduly restricted the popular will. Note, for example, the overview provided by Davis of the implementation of the Bill of Rights in which he concludes that the interpretation of the Constitution has served to restrict equality rather than enhance it, and to allow inequity rather than combat it. He says: 'Too little has been done to deconstruct the core of the South African legal system so as to embrace the challenges of a reconstitution of humanity and embrace the reassembling of the amputated parts of the South African body and thus also of the laws that have sustained dispossession and patterns of economic inequality that continue to run so markedly along race lines.' (Davis 2018, 372) On the other hand, Malan is of the view that the South African state is in a perilous condition of collapse: 'All three pillars of the South African unitary state are disintegrating. The state simply does not any longer have the monopoly on lawful violence. Lawful and unlawful non-state structures and formations with a capacity for violence are appearing everywhere, resulting in the criminal and security profile of the South African state increasingly becoming more fragmented and localised, with non-state structures taking over the function of maintaining safety and order to an ever-increasing extent. While the national infrastructure for an integrated countrywide economy has not disintegrated completely, it is in a state of decline. As a result, the idea of a countrywide South African economy is receding, with ever more local economies functioning increasingly more autonomously.' (Malan 2023)

[2] Many volumes have been written about the reasons why the conditions in South Africa became 'ripe' for negotiations in the early 1990s. Practically, when all the theories and speculations are peeled away, it was my personal observation that the parties simply realised that they were at a stalemate, which meant they could not achieve their objectives independently from one another. Negotiation was not their first choice; it was their last choice. Maharaj observes as follows: 'Once an armed stage is reached in any conflict, it becomes difficult to pull back. And the longer an armed struggle continues, the more difficult this becomes. In the case of an internal armed conflict, a process of negotiation is an essential step in finding a solution.' (Maharaj 2008, 14)

emerging and aspiring democracies. How often have I heard comments in the past 30 years by people from young and emerging democracies who had been inspired by the South African constitutional process.

In the implementation of the Constitution many mistakes have been made. However, these shortcomings are not the subject of this book. The drafters of the founding document cannot be faulted for the deficiencies and failures of consecutive governments and administrations. The responsibility for the governance process lies with those who have allowed corruption, facilitated nepotism, benefited from state capture, closed their eyes for the sake of collegiality and party loyalty, and enforced an ideologically inspired black economic empowerment programme that saw essential skills leave the economy and centuries of collective experience lying fallow. The lack of knowledge transfer has been breathtaking, perhaps unmatched in any of the post-1990 emerging democracies. Individuals are responsible for the state of the nation at its 30th celebration, not the Constitution. In this book I reflect critically on the positive achievements of a country that moved from legal darkness. I assess selected judgments of its highest courts in their dealing with the intricate issues of legal pluralism and the rights of minorities and indigenous groups comprising the diverse spectrum of South Africa's rainbow identities. I put those domestic jurisprudential developments in the context of international legal developments.

My interest in constitutional reforms started at university, at my alma mater, the University of Johannesburg (then the Rand Afrikaans University). There, in the early 1980s, we spent countless hours debating and reasoning whether and how our society could transition itself without collapsing into violence. The community I was born into held the power, but we recognised the necessity of sharing it for the sake of justice, peace, morality and stability. Top experts and speakers were regularly invited to our university during the late 1970s and 1980s to explain their ideas, share their experiences and impart their insights. At RAU-Island we could meet as young student leaders for days on end without external eyes or interference. I had the privilege of learning from a diverse range of perspectives, from Desmond Tutu's views on reconciliation to Samuel Huntington's messages on managing constitutional change and transition. Mangosuthu Buthelezi, who had to overcome the disappointment of rejection of the Indaba proposals. Dirk Mudge, on lessons from the Namibian democratisation and transition. Willem de Klerk, with his deep understanding of the Afrikaner heart, and Laurence Schlemmer, known for his lateral out-of-the-box thinking, were among those who left a lasting impact on me. Many a late-night conversation with Roelf Meyer about the practicalities of selling constitutional reform to a fearful white community clinging to power, and discussions with then rector Pieter De Lange, who was adept at anticipating challenges over the horizon, were particularly enlightening. Marinus Wiechers, one of the first contemporary Afrikaner constitutional free-thinkers, and George Barrie, who, along with Marinus, supervised my PhD on constitutional models and minority rights, played significant roles in my thinking.

Most important, my family, including my then girlfriend and now wife Corrien, and my best friends George Nell and Stephan Landman, who had to put up with me through my rebellious phase, but eventually embraced my new perspectives as their own. I dedicate this book to these individuals, as well as numerous others I haven't mentioned, all of whom had an indelible impact on my views and opinions during my student years.

My involvement with constitutional drafting started in the mid-1980s as a legal advisor at the Department of Constitutional Affairs, where, regardless of what many people may have thought at the time or even now, we had been given an open agenda to think creatively, develop constitutional models and consider ways to pursue constitutional reform in practice. Our small team was part of an inter-departmental task force known as *Operasie Skrik-vir-Niks* (Operation Scared of Nothing). How appropriate. In the mid-1980s we set the in-house groundwork for the unbanning of political organisations and the normalisation of politics, paving the way for a transition to constitutional democracy. A quantum leap was needed, not incremental reforms. We advised those *within* government, while also advising them about *changing* government. This was a unique and exhilarating experience, but at the same time risky and complex. We had free and open discussions and debates with Chris Heunis, Gerrit Viljoen, Roelf Meyer, Leon Wessels, Dawie de Villiers and FW De Klerk, to name a few. These were members of the deep Afrikaner and government establishment. It was never easy. Yet the level of openness would have astonished those who hadn't witnessed it firsthand. Under the leadership of technical experts, such as the strategist Fanie Cloete, drafter Rassie Malherbe, and advisor Fanie (SS) van der Merwe I honed my skills as an advisor *cum* free thinker, contributing both as part of the team and as an independent mind. As we travelled the world to meet constitutional experts and scholars in transitional politics, I learned how politics in plural societies across the world is the art of the possible, grounded in the ability to compromise. Moreover, for the first time, we met 'the other side'. It was delightful to explore common ground and share ideas as technical experts, all of us driven by a collective commitment to the betterment of South Africa. I also dedicate this book to them and others who had such a profound influence on my views and perspectives during my formative years as a young professional.

The events of February 2, 1990 – the announcements of the unbanning of political organisations, release of political prisoners and initiation of negotiations and transitional arrangements – forever changed us all. President FW de Klerk and the future President Nelson Mandela demonstrated a level of courage that few leaders, whether from minority groups or liberation movements worldwide, would have been willing to embrace. They placed themselves on a precipice, pledging to work together for the sake of a peaceful transition. Both faced the risk of rejection by their own. History is both kind and unkind to them. I thought they both displayed amazing courage and leadership. Both had taken a leap that placed them at risk of being despised by their own people, and hated by the other side. There was no guarantee it would work. On the contrary, the odds were heavily stacked against them. I remain saddened that they could not find the will or a way to cooperate with each other for longer after 1996.[3] They prevented a civil war, but they were unable to solidify the transition to peace through coalition, cooperation, and shared policies. They could (or should?) have laid the basis and political culture for a sustainable coalition government into the future. Ideally, they should have found a way to work together for another five years or more in the government of national unity, or by way of some informal coalition like the leaders of Switzerland had done for many years. Possibly South Africans were not ready for a coalition government. It is hard to say, but my sense remains that a golden opportunity to develop a transformative and accommodating political culture had been lost when the two of them parted ways.

I recall the excitement of my first meetings with members of the ANC constitutional team – Albie Sachs in London, Kader Asmal in Dublin, Dullah Omar in Cape Town, and Zola Skweyiya and Penuell Maduna at KwaMaritane in the Pilanesberg. Collaborating with Fink Haysom, we worked on drafting constitutional principles for provincial government and decentralisation. Sharing thoughts at the HSRC with Yvonne Mokgoro, Jabu Sindane, and Mandla Seleoane were highlights.

---

[3] Mr De Klerk and the National Party withdrew from the Government of National Unity on 30 June 1996.

I remember with fondness the first time I met Mr Mandela in 1991 at an ANC workshop on constitutional models. He called me aside and said in Afrikaans, '*kom ons drink koffie*' ('let's have a coffee'). What an experience it was! The pinnacle of it all was the meeting some months later with Mr Mandela and some of his key constitutional advisors at Shell House, Johannesburg at a presentation I made on options for provincial government, facilitated by Clive Menell and Frederick van Zyl Slabbert. (Expert Report Provinces 1993)

Later, in the post-1996 era, I worked with leaders such as Vincent Maphai, Jabu Sindane, Job Mokgoro and Mavuso Msimang in a shared commitment to implement what had been negotiated. To them and others who found peace after so many years of conflict, I also dedicate this book. From strangers to partners, colleagues and friends – we discovered a mutual dedication to South Africa. What they accomplished deserves nothing less than a collective Nobel Prize. It was truly amazing.

I feel honoured to have met so many constitutional experts from across the world who shared a passion for constitutionalism and the rule of law. It was as if fate had guided their careers to assist us at the southern tip of Africa. Rarely, if ever, had there been – or will there again be – such a confluence of experts in one country. These experts possessed scientific knowledge and skills that were pivotal to the negotiations. People such as Daniel Elazar, Ron Watts, Dennis Rondinelli, Arend Lijphart, Samuel Huntington, Donald Horowitz, Isawa Elaigwu, Uwe Leonardy, Andre Alen, John Kincaid and Frank Delmartino, and so many others, assisted us to design new institutions to accommodate the plurality of South Africa's society. I also dedicate this book to them – many of whom I initially met as experts but, over time, formed friendships with.[4]

Success has many fathers, and the Constitution's triumph is thanks to the multitude of people who played a role in its creation. It was not imposed by the United Nations. It was not left behind by a departing colonial power. It was not drafted by foreign experts in shady rooms who purport that 'universal norms' can be imposed on any country.[5] It was not copied from another nation.

---

[4] Nothing said in this book, including any individuals to whom I extend acknowledgment, suggests that I attempt to reflect their views. Nor does it imply that they endorse what I have said or written, or that they found my company as enjoyable as I found theirs. This is a one-sided acknowledgment of my professional and personal experiences and it is not intended to represent or embarrass any of the persons I mention.

[5] As observed by Venizelos, the purported universality of norms 'is neither a given nor self-evident.' (Venizelos 2024, 22)

It was produced by South Africans, for South Africans. Countless South African experts and ordinary citizens contributed their respective inputs. I experienced the amazing public interest through my involvement as an advisor to the committee on the demarcation of provinces where Flip Smit and Bax Nomvete guided the complexity of provincial demarcation. Hundreds, if not thousands, of submissions were made about provincial boundaries. It was a constitution that evolved through workshop after workshop, built on a foundation of compromise after compromise. The contemporary suggestions – by those who excel in revisionist history – that the Constitution was an elitist deal forced upon the populace, or that one side completely capitulated to the demands of the other, could not be further from the truth. Yes, the Constitution indeed had many fathers and mothers. To all of them, I dedicate this book.

Now, perhaps against all expectations, we celebrate the third decade of the Constitution. Not many of the emerging democratic constitutions of the 1990s have endured unscathed for 30 years. In fact, many of the international positive democratisation reforms of the 1990s have either lost momentum or are faltering. Violence and instability are always lurking. Waiting to pounce. As observed by Tazo in response to contemporary challenges experienced in Africa: '[T]he liberal nation-state model has proven incompatible with African composite societies. Hence the imperative need for African states to reconcile the organisation and functioning of the state with their own values, and thus forge a typically African constitutional identity.' (Tazo 2023)

The world is not in a good place. The worldwide democratic-induced stability and subsequent economic growth dreamt about in the 1990s remain elusive. Fundamental democratic freedoms, which were so widely accepted as established 'universal' norms during the 1990s, are being undermined and trampled. The international democratic wave (Huntington 1991) is losing impetus. The rule of law is (again) being threatened by the rule of might. According to a report by Freedom House, it was estimated that in 2022 around 60 countries experienced a decline in freedoms and democratic governance. (Repucci and Slipowitz 2022) Although the principles that guided the international wave of democratisation in the 1990s are so often being disregarded, not all hope is lost. According to the same report, South Africa was classified as 'free' among the 195 countries assessed. In South Africa, regardless of any criticism, the Constitution stands, the media is free, elections are peaceful and regular and, most importantly, the judiciary is (largely) independent. Government is held to account and complies with court orders. Constitutionalism has prevailed. Institutions are intact.

That said, appreciation for the achievements of the Constitution's drafters is diminishing. While in countries like the USA, India and Australia constitutional drafters are held in high regard, it seems that in South Africa critics from all sides are hastily working to diminish the constitutional legacy and thereby the Constitution itself. Doing so puts all at peril.

To all of those who have contributed to the *proper* management and defence of the Constitution, I dedicate this book. There is no guarantee for any constitution to survive. In fact, core aspects of the constitutional settlement of 1996 are being challenged. Corruption, maladministration, crime, inequality, racism, unimaginable societal violence and the collapse of many government services and public utilities are marring its 30th anniversary celebration. Social and economic inequalities are severe. Land reform has, at best, had limited success. Reconciliation is being tested. Institutions such as the judiciary are sought to be discredited. Race and ethnicity remain principal indicators of voting behaviour. The constitutional foundation discussed in this book is under scrutiny. Where we confronted the possibility of a civil war in the early 1990s, South Africa now faces the spectre of government fraction and endemic inefficiency. The dream of political alliances that would collaborate and govern based on a joint plan of action across racial boundaries remains a hope, regardless of cooperative efforts after the 2024 election.[6] Coalition government is not simple. Race remains, after three decades, *the* principal indicator of voting intention. It is not surprising that Davis and Klare hold the view that South Africa's 'constitutional experiment has fallen into a sorrowful state'. (Davis and Klare 2024) It is indeed a long walk to freedom.

In the next 30 years the Constitution looks headed towards rough seas.[7] The fabric of the Great Settlement of the 1990s is under challenge. The notion of liberal democratic values is in some quarters being criticised and trampled.

[6] The 2024 general election introduced a new era where one-party dominance at the national and provincial levels was for the first time replaced with multi-party governance and coalition. Coalition government is, however, as has been shown at local levels, no easy ride. The leadership and statesmanship required for coalition government would have to match the leadership that gave rise to the 1996 Constitution.

[7] The caution expressed by Habib shortly after the enactment of the interim constitution in 1993 remains relevant: 'The transition to democracy in South Africa and elsewhere does not simply involve an electoral event. Rather, democracy must be conceived as a process that often takes years to consolidate itself. The emergence of democratic possibilities in the country is by no means a guarantee for its continued existence. South Africa, like other nations, could easily succumb to the totalitarian impulses within its midst.' (Habib 1995, 69)

The personal linkage between new leaders and those of the Great Settlement is weakening. Inequality seems set to become an even greater stress factor in society. Without properly addressing inefficiencies in service delivery, essential services will collapse or the state will find itself competing with non-state actors seeking a form of do-it-yourself parallel state pursuant to functional autonomy. (De Villiers 2023c, 354) There is a strong likelihood that extra-parliamentary activities will become as important, if not more so, than parliamentary processes. This could shift power from a parliamentary democracy to a street-protest democracy, or new elitism where privatised delivery competes with and even replaces public services.

On the bright side, considering South Africa's successful transition from apartheid to democracy, there is hope that the country can also sustain constitutionalism and good governance for the next 30 years. Leadership of the calibre that made the transition in the 1990s possible will be essential for the next three decades. Socially South Africans have embraced a common flag and identity. The goodwill of South Africans towards each other is inspiring. A new generation of leaders now needs to embrace the Constitution and take ownership of it. Hopefully, this will not turn out to be easier said than done.

My wife, Corrien, has been an integral part of this entire journey. My primary school sweetheart from the age of 11, she has been my sounding board for many political arguments, ideas, propositions, disappointments, frustrations, struggles and jubilations. She has supported and encouraged me unwaveringly, and continues to do so, through all my work. To Corrien, and to Ronelia and Jacques – our kids who had to spend many nights without me from 1990 to 1996 when they were young – I dedicate this book.

Bertus de Villiers
13 March 2025

TABLE OF CASES

S

Y

W

EUROPEAN COURT OF HUMAN RIGHTS (ECtHR/ECHR)

A

B

C

P

R

S

T

V

W

Z

EUROPEAN UNION – COURT OF JUSTICE

GERMANY

INDIA

A

F

J

K

L

M

O

P

S

T

INDONESIA

D

S

ISRAEL

INTER-AMERICAN COURT OF HUMAN RIGHTS

K

M

S

X

KENYA

LESOTHO

MEXICO

NEW ZEALAND

L

W

NIGERIA

A

L

O

NORWAY

H

S

PERMANENT COURT OF INTERNATIONAL JUSTICE (PCIJ)

ROMANIA

RWANDA

SOUTH AFRICA

C

D

E

F

G

H

I

K

L

M

N

R

S

V

U

W

Z

UGANDA

UNITED KINGDOM

A

K

TABLE OF LEGISLATION AND INTERNATIONAL LEGAL INSTRUMENTS

NATIONAL LEGISLATION

NATIONAL LEGAL INSTRUMENTS

INTERNATIONAL AND REGIONAL LEGAL INSTRUMENTS

CHAPTER 1

DIVERSITY: A BEAUTIFUL DIFFICULTY

Our ability to reach unity in diversity will be the beauty and the test of civilization.

– Mahatma Gandhi

1.1 INTRODUCTION

South Africa is a microcosm of diversity – a rainbow nation. The diversity of the country is beautiful. But it also presents challenges. While South Africa is perhaps not the most ethnically diverse country in the world, compared to others such as India, Nigeria and Indonesia, its history makes it extremely complex to balance competing interests. The country's legacy of colonisation and apartheid left scars and practical socio-economic consequences that continue to reverberate intergenerationally. Its level of inequality, as measured by the Gini index, is one of the highest in the world. Its distribution of land ownership is highly skewed and disproportionate to the composition of the population. Its reconciliation process is continually being challenged, questioned and undermined, as is its much-lauded constitutional settlement often in the firing line. The level of crime makes you shudder. It is not a country with fertile conditions for democracy. That said, the poor levels of governance currently being endured by South Africa cannot be blamed on the Constitution. Instead, it is those responsible for implementing the Constitution who are principally at fault. It is important to recognise that no constitution is perfect or flawless, especially when scrutinised with the benefit of hindsight. Nonetheless, in many aspects the South African Constitution stands as a guiding light in comparative constitutional law. The inspiring transition process and the role of the country's courts in driving transformation and independence offer hope and inspiration to many other young and emerging democracies.

There are few challenges experienced by emerging and young democracies that are not mirrored in South Africa. The path of democratisation is not easy. In fact, many of the international democratisation efforts that commenced in the early 1990s, after the fall of the Berlin Wall, have faltered or are being challenged from within. South Africa is no different. The merits of the 1996 settlement are being questioned from all sides and both ends of the spectrum. Those who entered into the deal are being criticised for capitulating or selling out. Many of those who negotiated the deal are disappointed at the ineptitude of the Constitution's implementation, characterised by the practice of cancer-like corrosive corruption and nepotism. The institutions, along with the checks and balances, designed as part of the democratisation process are being described by some as obstacles rather than building blocks. The Trumpian penchant for ridiculing and eroding trust in the institutions of democracy is being used to great effect in South Africa as well as in many other young and aspiring democracies. This results in the destruction of public trust in the judiciary and other important democratic institutions. One thing is clear after 30 years of democracy: democracy is not a given. It is not an end point. It is an everlasting struggle. It is a work which has no completion date. If the USA with its centuries-old constitutional traditions is being forced back to the drawing board, and if liberal Europe continues its struggle against right-wing nationalism, and if the Middle East puts the world at risk with conflicts that predate us by millennia, then South Africa's ability to make its first constitution last for 30 years is no small achievement. But the walk to freedom is indeed a long one.

1.2 SUCCESS OR FAILURE?

Whether the South African democratisation process to date is considered a success, a failure, or somewhere in between, depends on the benchmarks used to judge it. If a peaceful transition of power, without any major violence or bloodshed taking place, is the benchmark, South Africa has performed extremely well. It has not turned into a state consumed by violence by citizens on citizens. Moreover, if the independence of the judiciary and the principle of constitutional supremacy are used as benchmarks, South Africa has outperformed many other democracies that emerged in the 1990s. For example, some of the new democracies of eastern Europe and Asia, which were conceived at the same time as the South African Constitution, have witnessed fierce attacks and governmental interference of various kinds on the judiciary. In contrast, if socio-economic transformation leading to greater equality among the population is used as yardstick, much remains to be done. In terms of socio-economic inequality, South Africa finds itself on a par with some of the world's poorest countries. If such levels of inequality persist together with failures in service delivery, the country's democratic foundations will surely be tested, even more so if the poor perceive their leaders to benefit from abusing and corrupting the system. If democratisation is measured by the quality of service delivery, tackling of crime and effectiveness of governance, the resulting assessment is substantially below par. Laudable constitutional rights and implied constitutional principles such as Ubuntu (Chapter 6) do not mean much for those navigating suburban roads pocked with endless potholes, for those living rough on the streets, for those who experience the most brutal crimes, or for those scared to venture out of their homes at night to enjoy the freedoms offered by the Constitution.

Success or failure is, therefore, a matter of perspective. However, given the tendency to focus on the half-empty glass, one might be left with a somewhat overly pessimistic view. In reality, though, there is from a comparative constitutional law perspective much to be optimistic about. One need only look at current world events and the slide away from democracy in many parts of the world to realise how well South Africa has done. While the USA was a benchmark for constitutional democracy in 1993, it now argues about the lawfulness of elections and has witnessed a violent invasion into the heart of democracy on Capitol Hill. Several democracies in central and eastern Europe are being challenged by undemocratic trends, with leaders willingly walking back into the arms of Communism. Many African states are challenged from within. South Africa in 2024 celebrated another general election without it being marred by violence, albeit that political parties such as the EFF and MKP are protagonists of parliamentary (majoritarianism) rather than constitutional sovereignty (constitutionalism). (Steytler 2024b)

Liberal democratic values and liberal forms of government cannot merely be transplanted from one setting to another. Even in the philosophical birthplace of so many liberal democratic ideas, its survival is not guaranteed. Western Europe is carrying a heavy burden of increasing radicalism; countries in central and eastern Europe are still finding their democratic feet; the Russian Federation has under Putin abdicated its efforts to democratise; and parts of Africa, the Middle East, Asia and South America are experiencing direct challenges to democracy. As observed by Tazo: '[T]he liberal nation-state model has proven incompatible with African composite societies. Hence the imperative need for African states to reconcile the organisation and functioning of the state with their own values, and thus forge a typically African constitutional identity.' (Tazo 2023)

Few in 1990 would have expected regular elections for 30 years in South Africa without violence. Few would have predicted the goodwill, love and patriotism that today exist between common people on the streets of South Africa. Nonetheless, valid concerns have been expressed that South Africa is drifting towards what has been called 'autocratic legalism'. This refers, as has happened in some central and eastern European states, to populist parties using its popular mandate, alone or in coalition, to erode or restrict fundamental rights and freedoms. (Davis 2023) As the adage goes, 'power tends to corrupt, and absolute power corrupts absolutely.'

1.3 DIVERSITY AND LEGAL PLURALISM

One of the major challenges that the negotiators had to deal with in drafting the Constitution was how to legally respond to and accommodate South Africa's population diversity and legal pluralism. Legal pluralism, according to the Constitutional Court of South Africa, is a reality and must be taken seriously by courts. (Alexkor case 2004, paras 45–51) With the benefit (and luxury) of hindsight, contemporary commentators often do not give adequate credit to those negotiators, considering the cauldron in which the Constitution was drafted. Critics tend to engage in revisionist history by critiquing the Constitution from the position of what they as critics would have *demanded*, rather than from the perspective of what could be *agreed*. Anyone can demand anything, but to reach a settlement requires statesmanship and compromise. Nowadays, demands are plentiful, while statesmanship has become rare. All sides in the 1990–1996 process sought different outcomes. Each party would have wanted their own position, ideally, to be endorsed. However, negotiations imply give and take – as epitomised by the 1996 Constitution. All the sides gave, and all the sides received in turn. The scale, overall, found a balance. The mere survival of the Constitution is living proof of the compromise it represents. While aspects of the Constitution could, of course, be improved, the same can be said of the constitutions of the USA, Canada, Australia, Germany, India and the United Kingdom, to name a few.

Comparative experiences show that, while many circumstances may give rise to a failure of democratisation, one of the most consistent factors to cause a failure is the inability of policymakers to adequately respond to societal plurality in general, and ethnocultural and indigenous diversity in particular. Many civil wars, as well as conditions of instability and violence, can be traced back to marginalised ethnocultural and indigenous groups seeking to be heard. Ethnocultural mobilisation remains one of the most effective and destructive powers in international politics. Even in stable democracies, such as Australia, New Zealand, Canada or those in western Europe, a significant challenge persists to *accommodate* ethnocultural and indigenous diversity within institutional design and political participation. A recent example of this was the rejection in 2023 by Australians of an amendment to the country's constitution which would have provided for an advisory Voice for Aboriginal people. (De Villiers 2024d) Similarly, voters in Chile rejected twice in as many years constitutional proposals to better recognise the rights of indigenous people. In New Zealand the interpretation of the Treaty of Waitangi remains politically sensitive. The internationally crafted constitution and much celebrated independence of South Sudan has suffered from ethnic and tribal disputes, and Sudan itself is marred by civil war. The finely balanced inter-ethnic federation of Ethiopia is challenged by civil war and unrest. The integrity of Spain remains under threat from separatists. The radical right causes fear and anxiety in the corridors of European powerbrokers. Ukraine would have to rebuild its relationship with marginalised minorities once the war ends. Indonesia works tirelessly to keep its ethno-plurality in containable limits.

It is not surprising that the United Nations, which consistently promotes the importance of individual rights, has acknowledged that successful and stable democratisation is closely linked to the successful accommodation of ethnic and indigenous plurality in ways other than just the rights of individuals. *Legally*, collective rights of a community present a challenge of definition and application, but *politically* it is sometimes the only way to secure stability. It is often not the right thing to accommodate minority interests, but it is the political expedient thing to do. Pragmatism rather than principle becomes the guide for the sake of stability.

The population plurality of South Africa presents itself in two material ways that also reflect international experiences: (a) the desire of communities to be effectively included in political processes; and (b) the desire of communities that have their unique laws, customs, cultures and traditions acknowledged by the state as lawful and legitimate. While the drafters of the Constitution created a legal framework in which these two desires can be accommodated, it is the courts that have been placed in a position to adjudicate disputes about the lawfulness of actions arising from minority customs, laws and traditions, as well as the viability of collective cultural, linguistic, religious and educational rights. The nature, extent and boundaries of legal pluralism are for the courts to determine, pursuant to constitutional principles of equality and non-discrimination within a sovereign state based on constitutionalism.

1.4 CONTEXT OF THE CONSTITUTION

In this book I invite readers on a journey that starts with the 1990–1996 constitution-drafting process and then meanders through various judgments, handed down by the courts over the past three decades, dealing with ethnocultural and indigenous diversity.[1] I commence with the constitution-drafting process because South Africa's achievements cannot be assessed in isolation from the 'Great Settlement' in 1996. Many of the adventurous critics today have lost sight of the events that framed the Constitution. Ignoring those events is akin to overlooking the impact of *The Federalist Papers* on American federalism, the great philosophical works of liberal democracies in Europe or the watershed events arising from the Reformation and Enlightenment.

The Constitution cannot be analysed (or criticised) in a vacuum. It is set within a context of compromise and nation-building. The Constitution must be interpreted with its transformative purpose in mind – not merely as a black letter document. (Davis and Klare 2024) It is intended to transform society, create greater equality, foster non-discrimination, and bring about socio-economic change. But it is also intended to reflect, accommodate and celebrate the plurality of the South African people. There is a risk that the accommodation of diversity objectives is being swept under the carpet of transformation. Two key ingredients that formed part of the Great Settlement were transformation and diversity. Only by reflecting on the core values that form the basis of the Constitution can one realistically assess the way the courts have responded to ethnocultural and indigenous plurality. It is therefore not only appropriate, but in fact essential to start any book that analyses and celebrates the first three decades of the Constitution with the conception and creation of the foundation document itself.

---

[1] I must emphasise that this book does not propose to undertake a comprehensive overview of the constitution-drafting process as was, for example done recently by Odendaal. (Odendaal 2023) My observations and comments are informed by personal experiences, contemporaneous engagements, and in-situ analysis, but I do not hesitate to acknowledge that reality is far more complex and nuanced than what can be encapsulated in a single book.

The journey starts by reflecting on the topic of legal pluralism and its impact on international literature and practice. The term 'legal pluralism' is overused and poorly defined. It is not a term of art with a settled meaning. In some respects, legal pluralism is used to describe any situation characterised by population pluralism and diversity. Doing this risks the term being used and abused by scholars to elevate any custom or tradition to a 'law' of equal standing with parliamentary laws. In fact, in some cases legal pluralism is used to challenge or undermine the legal system of the state and the international universality of rights. In the most extreme cases legal pluralism can be used to encourage secession and the forming of a new state or to lock individuals into social, cultural, religious and customary networks from which they cannot escape. I distinguish between state law and non-state law in the context of legal pluralism. For the sake of simplicity in this book *state law* refers to the legislation, executive Acts and common law that apply to an entire territory, as well as to all the persons residing therein. A person cannot opt out of state law, given that it binds all residents of a territorial jurisdiction. *Non-state law*, in contrast, refers to laws – not general customs, habits or traditions – that a community regards as binding and enforceable within the community, and are thus duly obeyed as if they were laws. Not all ethnocultural communities live in accordance with non-state law, but some religious groups, such as Muslims, Jews, Hindus and Orthodox Christians, have unique religious laws according to which they organise specific aspects of their lives. The same applies to many indigenous and tribal communities, which may adhere to unique non-state indigenous laws. Non-state law usually applies to persons rather than territories. Compliance with non-state law is by free association and individuals can opt out of non-state law (at least theoretically). While the theoretical accommodation of state law and non-state law may seem like a simple concept, it is not necessarily so. For example, many liberal democracies, particularly in Europe, struggle to find a balance between state law, non-state law and recognition of ethnocultural, religious and indigenous diversity. In this respect these countries may, ironically, benefit from South African jurisprudence.[2]

We revisit the constitution-drafting process of South Africa to specifically focus on the efforts undertaken to accommodate the ethnocultural and indigenous diversity of South Africa at the time of conception and birth of the

[2] Davies cautions that efforts to define the boundaries of law may soon become frustrated because of societal dynamics: '[D]efining law by reference to a limit, a boundary, or an essence only works up to a point because the "constitutive outside" never remains entirely outside – these boundaries are constantly being made and remade by actions and decisions.' (Davies 2024)

Constitution. The transition from the 1993 to the 1996 Constitutions remains unique in comparative law. Moreover, the Constitutional Principles enclosed in the 1993 Constitution played an unparalleled role to facilitate the transition from elite rule under the 1993 Constitution to majority rule under the 1996 Constitution. The essential Constitutional Principles on which I focus are those that relate to the accommodation of ethnocultural and indigenous diversity. These Principles reflect the realities against which the Constitution was drafted, the groundwork that had been laid for the transformation of South Africa and the compromises that had to be reached to achieve this. Contemporary criticism of the Constitution can only be considered credible if it acknowledges the nature of the compromise that underlies the founding document. I am not surprised that many of the fiercest contemporary critics of the Constitution were not around the table at the time of its drafting. They were not witness to the compromises that took place, and they were not exposed to the risk of civil war. To them, the mother document is seen merely as a piece of paper rather than a birth certificate. Considering this, it seems appropriate to commence this 30-year review of jurisprudence dealing with ethnocultural and indigenous diversity with consideration of the constitution-drafting process.

1.5 RELEVANCE OF INTERNATIONAL LAW

It is useful to reflect on the standards that have developed in international law concerning the rights and protections of ethnocultural and indigenous communities, as well as the impact these standards had on the negotiators of the Constitution during 1990–1996. These international standards also facilitate an assessment of the Constitution in contemporary circumstances and enable reflection on whether, then and now, the Constitution complies with universal norms concerning identity rights. This, in turn, contributes to an understanding of the context within which the Constitution is set, and specifically how the courts have attempted to respond to plurality. International law at the time of drafting caused both extremes of the political spectrum to revisit their position regarding ethnocultural and indigenous diversity: the National Party government of the day realised that race-based elitism under the banner of purported minority protection was not sustainable under international law; the ANC and others on the left realised that population plurality could not be ignored in constitutional design. Plurality is a force that will present itself in destruction unless it is harnessed by constitutional design and political leadership. I reflect on how the South African judiciary has been empowered to consider jurisprudential developments in international law and foreign state law in its deliberations. The courts have used this power to give content to the Bill of Rights, and in doing so they have also provided guidance to other countries. Judges, internationally, engage more than ever in citation of foreign case law. The world of the internet facilitates such comparisons. While intellectual exchanges of this nature are to be encouraged, I also point to the risk of judges using and abusing foreign case law to suit their own predispositions – potentially giving credibility to undisclosed biases – as well as the risk of comparing apples with oranges.

The interaction between the fundamental right of freedom of expression and limitations placed on this right with the aim of curbing hate speech is considered. Hate speech and speech that we hate can easily become confused, particularly in the context of cultural symbols and political slogans. Socially regarded hate speech is frequently not distinguished from what is legally regarded as hate speech. Critical or dislikable speech is often called hate speech in the media. Over recent years in South Africa, public discussion about the practical application of the hate speech test has been lively. If ever there was a factual situation that tested the theory and practice of the hate speech test, both in South Africa and internationally, it has been the so-called Old Flag cases (Old Flag case 2019; Old Flag appeal case 2023) and Kill the Boer cases. (Kill the Boer case 2011; Kill the Boer case 2022; Kill the Boer appeal case 2024) These two case scenarios encapsulate and reflect the complexity of South Africa's history – the narrative of the oppressor and the liberated, the differing perceptions of observers regarding speech, the interplay between remembering the past and pursuing reconciliation, the definition and application of hate speech, the sentiments of onlookers towards speech, the speaker's intent, the interaction between subjective and objective assessments of speech, the standard of proof for hate speech, the diverse interpretations of speech, the selective use or lack of use of Ubuntu to evaluate speech, the literal and figurative meanings of speech, the proportionality of a declaration of hate speech, and the potential benefits of considering international jurisprudence. The cases also highlight the notion that hate speech is principally local, circumstantial and time-bound. One can attempt to develop universal definitions or benchmarks for hate speech, but in the application of norms the local circumstances, history, conditions, context and events underlying the speech determine whether the speech meets the threshold of hate or whether it should be tolerated as freedom of expression. The universal principles demarcating the contours of hate speech may be relatively simple to express in terms of generality, but putting them into practice is not that straightforward. The Old Flag and Kill the Boer cases epitomise this complexity.

A fascinating aspect of jurisprudence it the elevation of the non-state, religious and customary-law concept of Ubuntu by the courts of South Africa to a legal term that has found application in many aspects of jurisprudence. Ubuntu, which finds its origin in African customary law, religion, and tradition, has been used to infuse new values into the Constitution and common law of South Africa. The concept has been given a raft of legal, social, psychological, spiritual and cultural meanings and applications, enabling it to be used (and perhaps abused) in many circumstances. Ubuntu has evolved into a mega-norm with practically no boundaries as it seeks to describe humaneness, social justice, reasonableness and fairness. The concept of Ubuntu, as discussed in this book, is distinctive for two main reasons: first, although the word appears in the languages of many African countries, it is only in South Africa that it has become a legal-philosophical term relied upon so extensively by the courts; and secondly, its application has become widespread in jurisprudence without any real scrutiny of whether this non-customary use of a deeply customary phrase is justified because of the inherent meaning underlying the term or whether it serves merely as a rationale for judges to validate their undisclosed biases behind an Ubuntu veil.

Ubuntu is essentially used in three different contexts: first, as a *source* of rights; secondly, as an instrument of statutory *interpretation*; and thirdly, as an *aide-memoire* that enables judges to explain their judgments to laypeople. It is apparent that Ubuntu, in effect, is used by courts to all aspects of society, and that it is used as a cornerstone to facilitate the ongoing transformation of South African society from apartheid to a free and democratic society. (De Villiers 2023a) The values espoused by Ubuntu may indeed have universal elements, but the use of the specific term, given its links to African values and religious systems, may also be perceived as alienating to parts of the community – particularly if Ubuntu is used selectively and in a discretionary and inconsistent manner. Critics have pointed out that the notion of community or group solidarity arising from Ubuntu may stand in contrast to liberal democratic principles of individual sovereignty and individual self-determination, while those seeking to protect minority rights may find a friend in the collective nature of Ubuntu. Moreover, the apparent subservient role of the individual to the community seemingly implied by Ubuntu may in turn erode fundamental freedoms and demand some form of group uniformity. Since Ubuntu is a culturally informed concept that lacks precise definition, the term could potentially be applied in situations for which it is not well suited, and its meaning may be influenced by the cultural and ideological background or biases of the judge relying on it.

The phrase 'free, prior and informed consent', and specifically what this entails for indigenous communities when their interests are affected, is increasingly used in South African and international jurisprudence. The 'right' of local communities in general, and indigenous communities in particular, to be consulted when their interests are impacted by legislation, administrative actions and private developments is becoming an integral component of contemporary democratic practices, particularly under the Constitution. Irrespective of whether consultation constitutes a justiciable right or merely a demand or expectation dressed up as a right, local communities are increasingly adamant about being heard when their interests are directly affected. Since the 1990s extra-parliamentary processes have intensified in importance, frequency, subject-matter and scope in South Africa. Whereas, under apartheid, extra-parliamentary processes were principally aimed at resistance and protest against the entire apartheid government, today these processes in South Africa are more sophisticated and community-based. This shift is due to the fact that numerous policy areas and issues may now be the target of protest. The judiciary is often called upon to intervene in such matters by adjudicating on the legality of parliamentary and administrative decisions. 'Lawfare' is becoming more common as citizens look to the courts for protection of their rights.[3] While street-based accountability and transparency beyond the sphere of parliamentary representation are now widely accepted as a new normal in South Africa,[4] I explore the extent, if any, to which indigenous people in South Africa must be specifically consulted when their rights to traditional lands are affected by legislation, government policies, administrative actions and other

[3] Henrico observes as follows about the growing trend of courts being used to litigate issues that ordinarily may fall within the sphere of other organs of government: 'However, a far more sinister phenomenon gripping South African jurisprudence is lawfare. When courts are used to resolve political spats, the real danger exists of the credibility and legitimacy of the judiciary being questioned. Is this, as opposed to judicial review in general or activism in particular, anathema to constitutionalism?' (Henrico 2023, 811) Justice Robert Beech-Jones of the High Court in Australia has cautioned that the increase in litigation in Australia is a symptom of distrust in the political process and the same distrust of politicians may also spill over to the judiciary. (Shanahan 2024)

[4] Note also how in Germany the notion of Citizen's Assemblies, as a form of direct democracy, is increasing in popularity. (Heidemann 2024) Also note in this respect the National Dialogue underway in South Africa to involve communities at all levels in discussions about essential policy issues. (Ramaphosa National Dialogue 2024)

developments. Is consultation with indigenous people merely part of a new set of standards for general community engagement, or does indigenous consultation entail a distinct and obligatory process? In international law, the phrase 'free, prior and informed consent' (FPIC) is often used to describe the involvement and inclusion of indigenous people in actions that affect them, particularly as these pertain to their rights to their traditional lands. The potential application of FPIC to the South African context raises several questions addressed in this chapter: What is the definition of indigenous people? What, if any, consultation rights can indigenous people claim pursuant to FPIC? What are the practical requirements that satisfy the legal obligation to consult with indigenous people? And, what are the effects of an absence of consultation or the withholding of consent by an indigenous community despite consultation having taken place?

One of the most complex and intriguing areas of pluralism is found in the interaction between religious legal pluralism and the liberal democratic, secular state. This is a particularly challenging area of legal pluralism because, among the various identities an individual may adhere to, religious codes often bear the closest resemblance to what can be considered non-state *law*. Religious codes are distinguishable from cultural or linguistic rules, practices and customs. While the latter are derived from intergenerational community practice, adherence and tradition, religious codes are derived from a perceived higher being – those laws are superhuman in origin; their source is divine law. Such codes predate the state and are not restricted to state territorial jurisdiction. While religious codes principally affect the private sphere, in some respects they may overlap with areas covered by state law. Like state law, religious codes demand compliance as if they have the status of law. The individual may thus get caught up between competing authorities – the divine and the secular – both of which possess established legal norms and mandate obedience. Ironically, many secular liberal democracies can gain insights from the way in which younger and emerging democracies have been dealing with this challenging issue. South Africa, having gained from the experiences of liberal democracies in the drafting of the Constitution, in return contributes internationally to the understanding of living with religious legal pluralism. Since its earliest years of new settler arrival South Africa has grappled with managing the reality of religious pluralism. The approach to religious pluralism in the country has frequently aligned with the prevailing political forces of the time. It is, therefore, not surprising that, since the enactment of the new Constitution, the approach to religious pluralism has been adjusted to reflect the values of constitutionalism. We reflect on the jurisprudence of the

Constitutional Court of South Africa, as well as that of the European Court of Human Rights, in an attempt to identify which norms, if any, exist to deal with and respond to religious legal pluralism. I comment particularly on the response of courts to Islamic religious traditions, such as the wearing of headscarves and marriages.

Consideration is given to the status of mother-tongue education in South Africa, how it was approached during the constitution-drafting process, international trends to mother-tongue teaching, and a reflection on the method adopted by South African courts to this important part of ethnocultural plurality. As explained, the courts may consider international law and foreign case law when interpreting the nature and scope of fundamental rights. Overviews of international law and selected foreign case law will hopefully assist to assess South African jurisprudence in the mother-tongue education debate. Likewise, the approaches adopted by South African courts may contribute to the development of international case law. Courts across the world are increasingly receptive to foreign municipal judgments and developments in international law – a concept referred to as '*Volkerrechtfreundlich*' (international law-friendly) by German theorists – demonstrating an element of reciprocity in jurisprudence. It is shown that the right to mother-tongue education is intrinsically linked to other identity rights such as culture, language, association, religion, self-determination, identity, family and script. These rights are interrelated and collectively represent identity rights aimed at acknowledging and protecting societal plurality. *Differentiation* among children based on language, culture or religion in education is tolerated, and even encouraged, by international law and jurisprudence in South Africa. However, if such differentiation results in unequal access to educational facilities or unequal treatment of children of ethnocultural communities, it is considered unjustified and regarded as *discrimination*.

An overview of indigenous customary law in South Africa highlights both its territorial and non-territorial nature in jurisdictional reach. It reflects on how the courts have responded to the official and dynamic (living) nature of customary law, recognising the weaknesses of such a binary distinction. A bird's eye view is then taken of the relevance and role of customary law in the constitution-drafting and certification process. The attempts to give statutory effect to customary law and to modernise it, such as through the Recognition of Customary Marriages Act, are considered. Finally, relevant jurisprudence from South Africa along with a few international case studies are analysed, aided by a set of questions that may help distil the core of jurisprudential thinking on the topic. The fundamental challenge of reconciling customary law with contemporary constitutionalism can be reduced into a simple question: Why should unequal treatment, discrimination or unjustified differentiation of individuals be tolerated just because it stems from customary law? Practically, why are the deaths of so many young men during initiation tolerated merely because it arises from custom? On the other hand, if customary law is entirely beholden to constitutional values, which in turn draw from universal human rights norms, does this not suggest that, eventually, customary law will regress to the *status quo ante* under apartheid, becoming a *de facto* secondary customary system entirely subservient to the Constitution and legislation enacted by Parliament aimed at regulating it? The ultimate consequence would be the erosion of customary *law* to the point where little, if anything, remains of it. In such a scenario customary habits and practices may survive, although not as part of a distinct legal system.

1.6 STRIKING A BALANCE

The South Africa courts have been remarkable in striking a balance between national uniformity and accommodation of ethnocultural and customary diversity. The courts do not always get it right, but courts never do. Comparative international jurisprudence highlights how challenging it is for courts to accommodate uniformity and diversity. Courts are in a never-ending endeavour to achieve those goals. South African courts are no different. Their interpreting of the Constitution is at best a journey and not a completely achieved objective. The jurisprudence of South Africa nevertheless makes for fascinating reading and the country has, as much as it took from international experiences during the drafting of the Constitution, also contributed to international jurisprudence in the management of the Constitution. The courts have demonstrated that diversity is a beautiful difficulty.

CHAPTER 2

PLURALISM IN LAW: PATHWAY TO THE RAINBOW NATION

We will all profit from a more diverse, inclusive society, understanding, accommodating, even celebrating our differences, while pulling together for the common good.

– Ruth Bader Ginsburg

2.1 INTRODUCTION

Pluralism generally is a catchword that describes the diversity of composition of a population. Legal pluralism refers, more specifically, to the presence of a variety of systems of law, customs, traditions and rules *with the force of law* that applies within the same territorial space. Pluralism as a sociological concept is not to be equated to legal pluralism. Pluralism in its general use implies the diversity of population with unique cultures, religions and languages, while legal pluralism indicates multiple *legal systems* within the same territory. Legal pluralism is as much an idea as an ideology, a norm and a social practice. (Neo 2020, 899)

All societies display elements of pluralism, but not all contain legal pluralism. No state legal system, regardless of its dominance, has been able to 'stamp out' all forms of law other than laws emanating from the state. (Tamanaha 2021, 209) In fact, Kaye expresses the opinion that until recently the notion of multiple sources of law was so 'commonplace' that it 'scarcely required a conceptual category to describe it'. (Kaye 2025, 86) The modern state often must cohabit with other laws of which it is not the author or source. It is the rule, rather than the exception, for modern states to have in their midst numerous and overlapping legal systems that may not be of the same hierarchy, but nevertheless demand adherence by followers. Pluralism of peoples, customs, traditions and ideas (not necessarily legal pluralism) has been described by the ECtHR as 'indissociable from a democratic society'. (Kokkinakis case 1993, para 31)[1]

Legal pluralism, according to the Constitutional Court of South Africa, is a reality and must be taken seriously by courts. (Alexkor case 2004, paras 45–51[2]) Tolerance and respect for pluralism and diversity are fundamental values of the South African Constitution that must be respected. (Prince case 2002, para 150) Pluralism in a sociological sense and as a legal reality is therefore accepted and endorsed in South African jurisprudence. But the discourse about legal pluralism is often a debate 'over the nature of historical analysis itself, and our attempts to make the past legible'. (Marglin and Letteney 2024, 152)

The question is not whether legal pluralism exists as a social phenomenon, but how the modern state – with its emphasis on universal individual rights, consistent norms and common identity – responds to legal pluralism. Not all ethnoculturally plural societies experience challenges associated with legal pluralism. South Africa is a plural society in its population composition *and* it is a society characterised by legal pluralism. Since European settlement in South Africa in 1652 the judiciary has applied Roman-Dutch Law, English Law, common law and, in certain circumstances, customary law. In addition,

---

[1] In the case of Fedotova the ECtHR emphasised that 'according to the court's case-law, this pluralism has to be accepted as a hallmark of democratic societies and the existing diversity of views among both Europeans and European States should be perceived not as a threat but as a source of enrichment'. (Fedotova case 2023, para 2.3) Notable is that the acceptance of pluralism as a sociological phenomenon is not to be confused with legal pluralism, which implies acceptance of a separate legal system within the same territory that may compete with the principal state legal system.

[2] The Alexkor case, which drew from international law and foreign law (e.g. Mabo), infused recognition of legal pluralism in South Africa and gave rise to domestic recognition of customary law in, for example, the Bhe case (2005); Cala Reserve case (2015); and Shilubana case (2008).

there were religious laws that were not applied by courts, yet they existed. Legal pluralism is not new to South Africa, but the impact of the Constitution on non-state legal systems is a work in progress.

Contemporary legal pluralism in South Africa finds its roots in indigenous law as well as in customs, religious orders and cultural customs and practices. (Rautenbach 2021b) Most notable is legal pluralism in the areas of customary law and religious law.[3] While legal pluralism has a simple logic to it, the literature has struggled to define the concept since it is capable of application to so many diverse situations. Although the Constitution 'marked the end of codification of intolerance' towards customary law (Dube 2022, 141), several questions remain about how to give effect to legal pluralism within the context of the universality of rights espoused by the Constitution. There is also concern that legal pluralism can easily become a sanitised version of apartheid where the rights of persons are determined by their ethnocultural, religious or customary status. (Mukaddam 2024, 143) For example, it is shown below that in the summer of 2024 around 30 young men died in the Eastern Cape province while undergoing initiation rituals. This was not front-page news. (Dorfling 2024b) If 30 young men had died in any other cultural, religious or secular event, there probably would have been public outrage and criminal prosecutions.

In this chapter we explore the concept of legal pluralism, examining the interaction between state law and non-state law, the practical application of legal pluralism and its relevance in the constitution-drafting process in South Africa.

2.2 WHAT IS LEGAL PLURALISM?

Legal pluralism is an expression undefined. It seeks to describe a social condition that exists, rather than to create a new reality. Jurisprudence responds to legal plurality – it does not create it. Courts may determine the hierarchy between different legal systems. Courts may, however, find themselves wedged between two divergent objectives: on the one hand, the stability and certainty of application of universal human rights norms, while on the other hand the plurality, diversity and uniqueness of community legal systems and practices (Kurnia and Melatyugra 2024, 499). In the most basic terms legal plurality refers

[3] See, for example, the recommendations from the South African Law Reform Commission about the recognition of Islamic personal laws by the legal and judicial system. (South African Law Commission 2000)

to 'the presence in a social field of more than one legal order'. (Griffiths 1986, 1)[4] Legal pluralism, along with the ethnocultural diversity and 'overlapping jurisdictions' underlying it, has been said to be among the 'most important challenges' to contemporary constitutionalism and the uniformity universality seeks to offer. (Pavel 2021, 143[5]) Indeed, in some respects, legal pluralism is the very antithesis of the uniformity sought to be provided by normative laws and rights. In the literature the use of the expression 'legal pluralism' is varied and dependent on the circumstances in which it is used. The concept seeks to describe a doctrine, an ideology,[6] a circumstance, a social reality, a human dynamic and a political objective, without being confined to the straitjacket of legal definition.

---

[4] Note, also, the debate in Europe in particular about 'constitutional pluralism', which implies a constitutional order that contains 'multiple claims of final authority'. (Capeta 2021, 149) In European Union law there is not a single European constitutional norm that supersedes the constitutional norms of the member states. European law is integrated within state constitutional law, but the source is that of a supra-national entity. The Court of Justice of the European Union (CJEU) is the final interpreter of EU law, but national courts, while respecting the judgments of the CJEU, do not regard themselves as bound by them. (Tamanaha 2021, 141) In regard to the judgments of the ECtHR, the approaches adopted by signatory states vary from viewing judgments as 'binding to respectful consideration but non-binding dialogue'. (Tamanaha 2021, 143)

[5] Pavel points to the inconsistencies that prevail, on the one hand, between the uniformity sought by international law and constitutionalism – whereby uniform norms are promoted – and, on the other hand, legal pluralism that supports a multiplicity of norms. (Pavel 2021, 148–49) Tusseau also observes that, according to one perspective, legal pluralism implies autonomy of a nature that 'excludes constitutionalism'. (Tusseau 2020, 12) Legal pluralism can therefore be a challenge to constitutionalism. Since legal pluralism may allow for, and even encourage, a diversity of norms, it does not demand or necessitate compliance with higher norms and orders for the betterment of the entire society. There is a strong group mentality underlying legal pluralism that may compete with individualism. Hence, there may not be a great difference between legal pluralism today and the absence of universal human rights norms in earlier centuries. At its most extreme, legal pluralism can be seen as an absence of a territorially defined political community with a shared set of beliefs, lifestyle and rules that are accepted as 'common ground' for all those who subscribe to the non-state legal system, effectively substituting any other legal system. (Croce and Goldoni 2020, 11)

[6] Griffiths refers to the 'ideology of legal centralism', which implies that 'law is and should be the law of the state, uniform for all persons, exclusive of any other law, and administered by a single set of state institutions'. (Griffiths 1986, 3) In line with this, the state is described by Griffiths as the sole source of laws, while other cultural, religious or indigenous customs and rules are not regarded as state laws, even if members of the respective communities may regard such community customs as 'laws'. This is, however, a rather one-dimensional approach to law, as has been shown by the South African judiciary in its acknowledgement of the plural and multidimensional nature of the South African legal system. The South African courts acknowledge, as outlined in greater detail in subsequent chapters (e.g. chapters 6, 8 and 10), that laws, customs,and rules do exist outside the sphere of state mono-legalism, and that these non-

Importantly, according to Pirie, is that 'different forms of law have existed through history and in different parts of the world, not all connected with a state or even centralized government'. (Pirie 2023, 20)

Legal pluralism, in its most basic form, refers to the presence of multiple legal systems within the same territorial jurisdiction. The different legal systems may cover the same social fields, separate social fields or overlapping social fields. In some respects the legal systems may even compete for sovereignty (and legitimacy) when it comes to their subjects (persons). For example, rules regarding marriage, cohabitation, inheritance or commercial dealings may diverge or even conflict between the legal systems. Religious or indigenous authorities may insist that their laws be adhered to rather than laws of the state. Büchler attempts to describe rather than define the complexity displayed by legal pluralism as follows:

> Legal pluralism refers to a plurality or multiplicity of norms within one legal order and to norms which coincide in the same social sphere and overlap in their approach to the same issues, people and territory. It is thus both an analytical framework and the cypher determining the simultaneous fragmentation, pluralisation, superposition and fusion of legal systems. (Büchler 2016, 80)

This creates for legal subjects the dilemma of which competing legal norms to follow. For courts, the challenge in turn is to determine when, if at all, to recognise or give effect to non-state laws and ascertain what the terms are of non-state law. The simplicity of 'one state, one law' is challenged by legal pluralism. This complexity is reflected in the proposition of Diala that 'modern states have lost absolute claims to normative sovereignty'. (Diala 2019, 3)

South Africa has a pluralist legal system, with the Constitution being the supreme law, but the Constitution recognises other laws, customs, traditions and practices within the social sphere of society. While the Constitution is supreme, the art is that some allowance should be made for the continued existence of legal plurality, otherwise the constitutional promise about maintenance of legal pluralism is an empty one. There is, in fact, a risk that constitutional norms may by way of judicial proclamation slowly erode or trump customary and religious law, with the effect that only unenforceable customs remain, and not 'laws'.

Pluralist legal systems are mostly characterised by a principal state law system that seeks to cover the entire field of legal interaction, while another system, a non-state law system, may regulate specific aspects of social, religious, customary

state laws could, in the appropriate circumstances, be taken into consideration by the courts, provided they do not offend the provisions of the Constitution. (Alexkor case 2004)

or cultural life. Examples of non-state laws include access to traditional lands, rules of marriage and unions, rules of inheritance and succession, rules for conflict resolution and diet, and penalties for minor criminal acts.[7] Does this imply that state law holds superiority or dominance over non-state law? Perhaps it does, or maybe it merely reflects a specific reality at a specific point in time concerning the power relationship and pragmatism between codes. Does it mean that, as time progresses, state law will gradually expand at the expense of non-state law? Perhaps, but this is not conclusive, as legal systems are dynamic, culture is constantly adjusting and adapting, and customs and roots are being rediscovered. While centralism, globalism and uniformity may be the flavour of today, legal pluralism and subsidiarity may be the flavour of days to come.

Notably, at least in some parts of the world, there has recently been an increase in religious association and thereby adherence to religious laws, often leading to civil disobedience of state laws. Liberal democratic states guard jealously their state law sovereignty. The ECtHR is a prime example of how, as expressed under the 'margin of appreciation',[8] European liberal democracies have been allowed to enact restrictions on the exercise of religious rights in different ways, regardless of the uniformity and universality sought through European human rights instruments.[9] In order for the margin of appreciation to be upheld, thereby rendering a restriction on a fundamental right as lawful, the restriction in question must be prescribed by law, pursue an enumerated public interest and be considered necessary in a democratic society. (Machnyikova 2005, 243)[10]

[7] Legal pluralism does not necessarily imply two competing legal systems of equal status in respect of every aspect of social life. Legal pluralism may pertain, rather, to specific rules, customs or laws that only affect a subset of the social life areas of a community. Examples may include inheritance arrangements, marriage, access to and use of land, and resolutions of family disputes, while for all other purposes the unified state laws are accepted.

[8] The concept of the 'margin of appreciation' was relied on in the Handyside case in 1976 when the ECtHR accepted that a state could place restrictions on a publication based on the mores of the state population, even if similar restrictions had not been imposed in other states under the European Convention. (Handyside case 1976) The ECtHR declared that 'the domestic margin of appreciation thus goes hand-in-hand with European supervision'. (Handyside case 1976, para 49)

[9] The result of the margin of appreciation's application is, however, that an 'illusive doctrine' with 'fuzzy contours' is utilised to determine the scope of and limitations to fundamental rights. (Sajo and Uitz 2020, 293) It must be noted that the concept of the margin of appreciation is widely used by the ECtHR to allow for state-based diversity in all areas of law, not only in the field of human rights.

[10] The notion of margin of appreciation has also been applied within domestic law to endorse the autonomy of a school to regulate its own affairs. For example, in the Michaela Community

Two South African judgments highlight this test: In the Gaum case in South Africa a decision that a marriage in the Dutch Reformed Church may only be between a man and woman was declared to be discriminatory and not mere differentiation. (Gaum case 2019)[11] In the Freedom of Religion case it was held that freedom of religion cannot be relied upon as a basis for a child to be subjected to corporal punishment. The court acknowledged that 'moderate and reasonable chastisement' finds its origin in religious and cultural practices (Freedom of Religion case 2019, para 62), but declared that the constitutional protections available to a child override whatever religious or cultural principle is sought to be relied on in support of such punishment. Furthermore, the court reasoned that alternative, non-violent mechanisms and options for discipline should be pursued if the best interests of the child are advanced. (Freedom of Religion case 2019, para 69) The court concluded that the common-law defence of moderate

---

case in the United Kingdom the decision of a school to adopt what was called a 'very high level of control over the behaviour of the pupils, underpinned by a strict approach to discipline; and an ethos which encourages pupils to see themselves as part of a team' was accepted as a basis on which to refuse a Muslim student permission to engage in public prayer at school. (Michaela Community case 2024, para 159) The court concluded that the restriction was proportionate and served a legitimate aim: 'The disadvantage to Muslim pupils at the School caused by the PRP is in my view outweighed by the aims which it seeks to promote in the interests of the School community as a whole, including Muslim pupils.' (Michaela Community case 2024, para 232)

[11] In the Gaum case a decision taken by the General Synod of the Dutch Reformed Church (NG Kerk) during November 2016 came under review. Every Dutch Reformed congregation was compelled to adhere to this decision because the General Synod is the body entrusted, according to art 42 of the *Kerkorde* (church order), with the competency to determine the church's communal identity in terms of the Bible, Creed, its Constitution, mission and policy. The 2016 decision's effect was to declare that a marriage in the NG Kerk was between a man and a woman. The 2016 decision would have reversed a prior 2015 decision that recognised the equality of all people, irrespective of their sexual orientation, and gave recognition to the status of civil unions between persons of the same sex that are characterised by love and fidelity. The 2015 decision also permitted ministers to solemnise such unions, but placed no positive duty on a minister of the church to do so. The 2015 decision furthermore removed the celibacy requirement for persons that are gay or lesbian to be ordained as a minister or elder in the church; such persons could thus be ordained as ministers or elders in the church. (Gaum case 2019, para 2) In 2016 the church sought to return to the traditional approach of a marriage being solely between a man and a woman. The court held that such a reversal would amount to discrimination under the Constitution, that the restriction was not protected by the right to religion, and that it could not be regarded as mere differentiation. (Gaum case 2019, para 68; 69) The court noted that even within the church, as far as its dogma is concerned, there were differences of opinion on this topic. The court declared that the decision by the church in 2016 to seek to reverse the 2015 decision amounted to discrimination and 'does not accommodate diversity'. (Gaum case 2019, para 82) The 2016 decision was duly declared unlawful. (Gaum case 2019, para 96)

and reasonable chastisement is not a valid constitutional defence against a charge of assault. (Freedom of Religion case 2019, para 73) In both these judgments the constitutionality of universal norms trumped the peculiarity of religious norms. But within the courts' consistency also hides an inconsistency, with indigenous initiation practices that are allowed to continue causing the deaths of many young men every year.

The threshold question that arises from legal pluralism is: What constitutes 'law'? There is no definitive answer to this question. Needham places the concept of law into a 'polythetic category'. (Needham 1975) This prompts another question about the content of legal plurality: Why is state law generally considered superior to non-state law? This chapter does not seek to engage in a philosophical discourse in response to these questions. It is adequate to acknowledge that those questions exist, and the response remains open ended. It is obvious that not all customs, practices and beliefs can be elevated to the status of 'law' principally because ordinary cultural customs are not intended to be binding law, there is not necessarily uniformity in customs, and there is not mandatory requirement or enforcement ability. But that being said, it is not unknown for a religious code such as Islam, Orthodox Christianity or the Jewish faith to refuse to submit in some respects to the supremacy of state courts. This highlights the phenomenon of a religious code treating its laws as sacrosanct and superior to those of the state.

In this book, when reference is made to non-state law, it is done so in the context of a rule of conduct, written or unwritten, that: (a) affects the rights and interests of those that accept it as law; (b) is observed by the members of an ethnocultural, religious or indigenous community as if the rule has legal effect; and (c) is capable of being enforced, formally or informally, by the community from which it originates on members of the community, but not on the broader public.

Legal pluralism in scientific literature may be a relatively new concept, but the phenomenon it seeks to describe is not new. In fact, community-based legal systems predate the state. (Holl 2025) Before the time of ancient state formation, and ever since, there have been countless examples of communities continuing to adhere to their own laws and customs, while also being subject to a state legal system. The origin of federal theory can be traced to the maintenance of a state-based legal order that may be inconsistent with the legal orders in other states within the federation. Even colonial powers with their emphasis on centralism rarely if ever sought to completely replace existing community and indigenous legal systems with their foreign laws. In some countries parliaments have even refrained from legislating on topics that fall within the customary and religious law of its citizens. For example, in a country with the rich diversity of India there is no uniform civil code to regulate all aspects of marriage, divorce or inheritance. (Acharya 2023)

Legal pluralism as a purported term of art entered scientific use since the 1970s and has become employed in a more general sense since the turn of the century. (Teubner and Bukovina 1997; Teubner 2012) Regardless of the term being widely in use, it often appears as a term of description rather than of definition. Legal pluralism may find expression easily, but 'there is no chance of defining it'. (Seinecke 2018, 21)

Tamanaha describes legal pluralism as a 'folly' that exhibits the appearance of a well-established theory of law, yet whose basic tenets remain unclear. (Tamanaha 1993) Praet states that the popularity of legal pluralism is an indication of the 'perceived failure of legal grand narratives such as the nation-state'. (Praet 2018, 31) To this there is an element of truth since the simplicity offered by the nation state is often not consistent with the complexity of legal pluralism. Griffiths says that legal pluralism is an attribute of a pluralistic society by which the origins of various legal systems within the same social field differ. (Griffiths 1986, 39) Sani calls literature seeking to encapsulate legal pluralism 'muddled in confusion'. (Sani 2020, 83) Neo, meanwhile, suggests that legal pluralism can be turned into a 'normative good' since it seeks to reflect the diversity of society. (Neo 2020, 899) Marglin and Letteny view legal pluralism as a 'provisional interpretive key that helps a historian make sense of novel information'. (Marglin and Letteney 2024, 153)

Legal pluralism, in essence, has become a generally used term, albeit in such different circumstances and contexts that the caution expressed (in another context) by Kelsen is worth noting, namely that 'different authors treat widely different problems under the same name, and that even one and the same author unconsciously uses the same word with several meanings'. (Kelsen 1945, 181)

Seinecke proposes that there are four 'family resemblances' that are common to the usage of legal pluralism: it refers to law that is not bound or defined by the state; an additional law to the law of the state exists; the different legal systems must interact; and the concept of legal pluralism implies a modification of state law and a strengthening of alternative, non-state law. Ultimately, though, legal pluralism is 'vague, open and highly contested'. (Seinecke 2018, 21)

2.3 PRACTICAL TYPOLOGY: STATE LAW AND NON-STATE LAW

While scientists struggle to define with any precision the nature and character of legal pluralism, for the purposes of this book I adopt a simple approach: laws, regulations, directives, judgments and administrative actions that arise from state agencies (principally from legislative and executive institutions and office bearers), at any level of government or by common law, are referred to as 'state law'. In contrast, the rules, customs, traditions and practices that arise from non-state entities, such as religious organisations, customary institutions or cultural customs and practices, are referred to as 'non-state law', *provided* the relevant community regards it as law.[12] Customs and practices not regarded as law are simply what they say – non-legal customs of a voluntary nature.

There is of course the risk that, by using the term non-state 'law', what otherwise constitutes a custom or practice may be wrongly categorised as having all the attributes of a 'law'.[13] This raises several questions about the nature of law, but these fall outside the scope of this chapter. (Hart 1961) It is, however, important to note that within ethnocultural and indigenous communities there are ordinary customs and practices that are adhered to but not regarded as 'law' by the community. Conversely, there may also be customs and practices within communities that do hold the status of 'law' among community members, even if they are not formally endorsed by the state. Ultimately, when viewed from the perspective of a non-state legal system, distinguishing between state law and non-state law is tenuous.

---

[12] I acknowledge that laws of various kinds may also be categorised in other ways. For example, Rautenbach speaks about legal positivism and legal centralism, whereby the former represents common law and other official laws as may originate from parliament, while the latter represents a central law-making body with unrecognised legal orders such as those of religions, not forming part of law. (Rautenbach 2021b, 6)

[13] It is incumbent on the South African courts to determine what is a mere *cultural custom* and what constitutes *customary law*. Customary law is a 'an independent source of norms within the legal system [of South Africa]. The Constitution, while giving force to indigenous law, makes it clear that such law is subject to the Constitution and has to be interpreted in the light of its values.' (Alexkor case 2004, para 51) At the same time it must be acknowledged that the purported distinction between state law and non-state law arises from a scientific background that is not necessarily shared by indigenous or religious communities. The mere act of categorisation may be in error without the test having been applied to the respective legal systems. Since the Constitution of South Africa recognises the equal status of customary law, one could argue that customary law through its constitutional recognition has the status of state law although it does not originate from parliament or the executive. But it also highlights the deficiency of categorisation of laws into state law and non-state law.

As alluded to above, the adopted typology of state law and non-state law is rudimentary. Nonetheless, for the purposes of this book this typology serves to explain that, regardless of the sovereignty of the constitution or of the legislative authority of parliament, there may be non-state laws that apply to the social field in which people find themselves and to which they adhere *as if* those laws are sovereign in nature to the exclusion of state laws.[14] While the state law authorities may not regard non-state customs and practices as 'laws' in the ordinary meaning of the word, to those that adhere to these non-state laws their effect is similar to that of a law of the state.[15] Courts face unique challenges when rules derived from non-state systems are invoked or referenced in litigation where, typically, only state laws are considered.[16]

State law and non-state law systems usually differ in hierarchy, in the sense that the state law system has sovereign, territorial application and is enforced by state agencies, while non-state laws have segmental, non-territorial application[17] to a

---

[14] Note, for example, how Aboriginal people in Australia speak about 'The Law' when they refer to traditional laws and customs, as well as to initiations pursuant to those customs. To those that adhere to The Law, customary law is the equivalent of state law. In Australia, as in many other countries where customary law is adhered to, there is often an urban–rural divide where persons from the same community accept or reject customary rules depending on where they reside. In rural areas, in particular, 'state legal systems are transplants that do not match the norms and understandings of many people within the society'. (Tamanaha 2021, 95)

[15] Note, for example, that many customary marriages in South Africa are not registered, albeit that those marriages can be registered pursuant to legislation that seeks to regulate customary marriages (Recognition Act 1998). Because of the complexities that often arise from the non-registration of customary marriages, Sibisi recommends that traditional leaders should play a greater role to officially record and register marriages over which they officiate. (Sibisi 2023, 531)

[16] Note in this respect how judges dealing with the legal system of the European Roma have responded to the relevance of Roma law to proceedings. According to Nafstad, judges tend to take note of Roma law to better understand the context of a dispute, but when the law is applied the uniform laws of the country are enforced. She says: 'Knowledge about Roma and about Roma law is of importance for several of the judges, but mostly as a basis for understanding the case and the involved persons better, as a tool to solve a problem. It does not imply that their cases should be treated in any other way than other cases. Among the judges, whether they had knowledge about Roma law or not, there is a strong emphasis and consensus on formal equality before the law.' (Nafstad 2018, 110)

[17] The notion of non-territoriality within the context of legal pluralism may, in some circumstances, coincide with the non-territorial self-government or autonomy sought by some ethnocultural or indigenous communities. As observed below, not all communities that adhere to non-state law desire self-government in a political sense. However, in some instances communities may seek institutional arrangements for self-government that are based on personal association rather than territorial jurisdiction. See, for example, non-territorial, self-governing, autonomy arrangements in Brussels, Schleswig-Holstein, Hungary, Estonia and South Tyrol.

specific subnational community and are usually enforced by means of informal – and not legal – community sanctions.[18] The legal systems also differ in origin and history, and may do so too in terms of level of detail and the extent to which they are codified. These differences notwithstanding, both state and non-state legal systems are perceived by their adherents as forms of 'law'.[19]

(De Villiers 2022b) See also the Noongar Settlement in Australia, in which extensive powers have been granted to the Aboriginal Noongar people by way of a settlement of their native title claim to self-determination in certain aspects of their social and cultural life (Noongar Package 2017) as well as indigenous communities in the USA and Canada that seek to expand their reserve-based governance functions over members of the community residing in urban areas. (Mathieu-Bedard 2017) Notable is also the Ngurrajuta Agreement in the Northern Territory of Australia, which envisages expanding of Aboriginal community control in a 10-year plan for projects that support training and pathways, housing development and management, community safety, family services and education which will be based on each community's priorities, needs and aspirations. (Ngurrajuta Local Decision Making Agreement 2024) The Ngurratjuta region identified six priority areas to be the focus of the Agreement, e.g. housing, municipal services, employment, educational attendance, welfare delivery, and economic development. The principle of self-determination for Aboriginal communities underpins the Agreement. (Ngurrajuta Local Decision Making Agreement 2024, para 2.2)

[18] The presence of numerous ethnocultural, indigenous and religious communities in a country does not necessarily imply that the legal system of the country is plural. For example, a country such as Australia is regarded, with the exception of some limited recognition of indigenous law, as mono-legal, or having a single legal system that applies to the entire territorial population. (Black 2010, 64) While this does not imply the absence of informal non-state customary and religious norms, it suggests that in general these norms are not recognised or enforced by the courts. Traditional forms of punishment, such as spearing, are applied in some traditional Aboriginal communities. Courts may take note of these customs, but they do not apply or condone them as if they were law originating from a non-state legal system. Those non-state laws are not recognised, enforced or supervised by the courts, and may even in some instances be criminalised by state law. There is, of course, a risk that informal legal systems exist 'underground', and individuals caught up in them may not receive adequate protection of their rights. (Black 2010, 65) However, if the state were to recognise multiple legal systems of which it is not the author, the risk of internal divisions and an erosion of uniform, state-legal standards could arise. Nonetheless, it must also be acknowledged that non-state legal systems, whether formal or informal, may also in time assimilate in some respects with the state legal system and ultimately apply national norms within a cultural context. (Cesari 2010) A non-state legal system, much like a state legal system, is subject to the dynamics of society, and it could conceivably adjust to changes in demands from its subjects.

[19] In some respects legal pluralism has become what is called in German a *Kampfbegriff*, a battle cry to mobilise the establishment of a new legal and social order, rather than just a description of an existing social reality. In this context what were once considered 'customs' and 'aspirations' have evolved into 'laws' and 'rights'. In some respects legal pluralism seeks to accord the status of a sovereign legal system to the customs and practices of a community. This raises, of course, the philosophical question – what is law and when does a custom become a law? Seinecke observes

2.4 SOVEREIGNTY OF STATE LAW OVER NON-STATE LAW

Generally, within the boundaries of a national territory there exists a predominant sovereign legal system derived from the constitution, parliamentary sovereignty, common law or a combination of these elements. Collectively the state, embodying these sources of law, is the sole creator, guardian and enforcer of laws. The laws emanating from this sovereign legal system are applicable to the entire population within the national territory. Adjacent to these laws, within the national territory, there may also exist additional legal systems, not authored by the state, which only affect specific segments of the population. Note, for example, how in South Africa the Constitution seeks to place indigenous customary law at the same level of other laws, save for it being subject to the Constitution (Chapter 10).[20] According to Diala, this supremacy of the Constitution over customary law makes a mockery of customary law as a separate legal system. (Diala 2019, 22) Meanwhile, in a federal-type system there may be asymmetrical state laws applied within certain states with special status.[21] While such decentralised laws remain state law, the localised laws may demonstrate a greater tolerance for,

---

that 'legal pluralism transforms social, economic, religious or other norms conceptually into law'. (Seinecke 2018, 28) By doing so, all rules that affect individuals are purported to be 'law' of the same genus, standard and enforceability. In its broadest context legal pluralism may perceive the state and state laws as hindrances to non-state community rights, rather than the state serving as a facilitator and guarantor for protecting those rights.

[20] Note that Manthwa seeks to draw a distinction between *indigenous* law and *customary* law: 'It must be stated that customary law differs from indigenous law as customary law emerges from the latter. Customary law is people's adaptation of indigenous law to socio-economic changes.' (Manthwa 2023, 662) The Constitution of South Africa does not draw a similar distinction. To the extent that Manthwa purports that adaptations to indigenous law should be seen as customary law, I take issue with the proposed approach since, as argued in chapter 10, all laws, including indigenous law and customary law, are by nature dynamic, living and open to adjustment. Indigenous law is therefore open to be living and adjustable in similar ways as any other legal system.

[21] The existence of regional and local laws that derive their authority from the constitution, or from decentralisation by the national parliament, is not generally regarded in the literature as an example of legal pluralism, given that those laws of subnational organs of state remain state laws. The challenge to precisely define legal pluralism is exemplified by the case of Aceh in Indonesia: if the acknowledgment and implementation of Sharia law by a decentralised region such as Aceh is not considered an example of legal pluralism, then what would qualify as such? Ryan refers to federal arrangements as an example of 'simple legal pluralism', since they involve two levels of government from which laws originate. (Ryan 2020, 526) He acknowledges, however, that the 'vexing questions' raised by pluralism about the interface between state-based and non-state-based norms continue to be the subject of ongoing discourse. Also note the opinion of McKerracher that Canadian federalism 'will lack legitimacy unless it can develop the capacity for reciprocal processes of external recognition with Indigenous legal orders'. (McKerracher 2023, 152)

and accommodation of, non-state law customs and practices (for example, in the Indonesian province of Aceh, which applies its own religious code). (De Villiers 2016b) In the case of Canada it has been proposed that 'the demand of relational legal pluralism for Canada's constitutional order is a federalism, or treaty federalism, that does not seek to subsume, deny or dominate Indigenous normativity'. (McKerracher 2023, 152)

An essential difference between state law and non-state law in this context is the notion of territoriality, whereby state law applies to all individuals within a territorial jurisdiction, whereas non-state law generally applies to individuals who associate with a particular community on a personal basis arising from freedom of association.[22] While individuals cannot opt out of state law, they can choose not to adhere to non-state law – at least in theory.

While non-state legal systems may not necessarily be recognised by the national legal system, from the perspective of those who live in accordance with and are subject to such non-state legal systems their rules are real and hold the force of law.[23] This typically pertains to matters such as family and personal law, marriage, access and management of land, inheritance, minor criminal matters and non-litigated dispute resolution.[24] In Indonesia, for example, the customary use of block voting in national elections by the so-called Big Man pursuant to the *noken* customary system has been accepted by the Constitutional Court as consistent with the Constitution regardless of its causing large numbers of voters to be disenfranchised. (De Villiers 2024a) A similar approach has been adopted in Mexico, where the indirect election of members of an indigenous community

---

[22] As explained in chapter 10, customary law often has a territorial and a non-territorial jurisdiction.

[23] Note, for example, how in the Bulelwa case the applicant relied on the processes of initiation and seclusion as a valid defence for failure to comply with court procedures. (Bulelwa case 2022) In that case Mathenjwa J recognised the customary concept of *ukuthwasa* to allow a stay of execution since the ancestral spirits have called a person into isolation and away from family. Manthwa describes the judgment as 'refreshing' since it was accepted that a traditional custom could be relied on in defence of a civil claim. (Manthwa 2023, 669)

[24] Note, for example, the discussion by Van der Schyff on the interaction between rituals related to the customary slaughter of animals in the Netherlands and state law legal standards for the humane slaughter of animals (Van der Schyff 2014), and the interaction between ritual slaughter and contemporary animal welfare. (Zoethout 2017) Also note the case of Muslims of Belgium in which the ECtRH upheld restrictions placed by Belgium on the slaughter of animals without prior stunning. (Muslims of Belgium case 2022) Wieshaider points out that the Court of Justice of the European Union has been inconsistent in its reasoning when it comes to regulating the slaughter of animals. (Wieshaider 2024)

at municipal level has been held to be consistent with the Constitution. (Indirect election case 2023)

The non-state legal system may be confined to the personal lives of individuals or it could extend to their public duties, rights and obligations. This sometimes leads to conflicts between adherence to non-state laws and the recognition of state laws, as seen, for example, in cases involving a traditional form of spearing or punishment according to customary law, or corporal punishment pursuant to religious law. (Jacobs 2021, Freedom of religion case 2019)[25]

The non-state legal systems do not primarily derive their existence from the constitution but, instead, originate from ancient laws, traditions and customs that are unique to a specific community. Non-state legal systems and laws often predate the modern state, but they may also have been introduced to the modern state by immigration from other states. Note, for example, migration patterns from Africa into Europe and to South Africa, where communities bring with them their religious and customary laws. The normative uniformity sought to be imposed by the state is therefore challenged by legal pluralism. According to Berman, the notion of the modern state and territorial sovereignty within which a single legal system reigns 'represents a retreat from the messy hybrid world of multiple, overlapping normative authority'. The state-centric view is nothing but a 'convenient fiction' that postulates the existence of a single, monist legal order. (Berman 2020, 6) The reality is that 'people are regulated by multiple different legal and quasi-legal regimes and that these regimes are sometimes associated with formal state law, but sometimes they are not'. (Berman 2020, 6)

Legal pluralism is therefore a term recently coined to describe a social reality that has existed since the formation of the modern state. There has always been some artificiality regarding the rigidity of the territorial boundaries associated with the modern state, and the uniformity of laws within such a national territory. Community boundaries are arguably more reflective of social reality, but for purposes of state formation reliance on community boundaries is too uncertain, poorly defined and flexible. Hence state borders are often rudimentary, arbitrary

[25] De Angelo and Tolino explain that Islam is different to other religions since 'it claims that its rules govern every aspect of a Muslim's life, *private and public*'. (emphasis added) (De Angelo and Tolino 2017, 147) In theory at least, the rules arising from Islam may find themselves in competition or conflict with state law as a parallel legal system attempting to regulate the same social field. This contrasts with other non-state religious and customary legal systems that generally acknowledge and accept the supremacy of the state law system, except in areas explicitly regulated by non-state law such as tribal systems. (Richardson 2019)

and not consistent with community residential patterns. This gives rise to communities that are split by national boundaries while they remain united in their customary and cultural laws. (De Villiers 2009) Community boundaries are typically not defined by territory but by freedom of association, making them more complex and dynamic, while the jurisdiction of community laws is often exercised on a personal rather than a territorial basis. At a practical level it may not be easy to determine if a person is part of a community or even, if so, whether the traditional laws and customs of that community apply to the individual concerned.

While constitutional lawyers and political scientists may find legal pluralism repugnant for its vagueness, the opposite perspective may also hold true. That is, legal centralism, mono-legalism and legal uniformity under a homogenous state are relatively recent creations that arguably erode full individual self-determination, whereas legal pluralism has deeper historical roots in human social organisation and better recognises the multiple identities of a person. Griffiths puts it as follows:

> Lawyers, but also social scientists, have suffered from a chronic inability to see that the legal reality of the modern state is not at all that of the tidy, consistent, organized ideals so nicely captured in the common identification of 'law' and 'legal system', but that legal reality is rather an unsystematic collage of inconsistent and overlapping parts, lending itself to no easy legal interpretation, morally and aesthetically offensive to the eye of the liberal idealist, and almost incomprehensible in its complexity to the would-be empirical student. (Griffiths 1986, 4)

2.5 APPLICATION OF LEGAL PLURALISM

Non-state legal systems may vary in scope and application. Legal pluralism seeks to elevate the customs and practices of the non-state system to 'law' that is recognised and even enforced by the state, as seen in examples like Aceh province in Indonesia and the elevation of customary law in the South African Constitution.[26] Legal pluralism often aims to integrate these laws into the legal framework of the national state. (Praet 2018, 30) But caution may have to be

[26] Anggraeni observes that, while legal pluralism is 'necessary' in Indonesia, it also 'results in tension and conflicts. Conflicts arise from the differences between legal systems and within a single legal system. Even within customary law, conflicts occur, such as between different customary laws within matrilineal, patrilineal, and parental kinship systems, particularly in inheritance distribution. Legal conflicts also arise when confronted with Islamic law, which is the affinity of Muslim society, and state law, which applies to all citizens.' (Anggraeni 2023, 43)

displayed because there may be disagreement within communities about the precise norms of non-state law. Since those customary rules are usually not codified, there may be disagreements within the same community about the content, nature, applicability and scope of customary laws. Note in this respect the Sengadi case, in which the court had to declare if the traditional handover of the bride to the bridegroom's family continued to be a customary lawful requirement for a valid marriage. The court answered in the negative, much to the dissatisfaction of critics. (Sengadi case 2019, para 42) Sibisi, for example, says that culturally the process of marriage is not complete without this ceremony and that empirical evidence does not support the finding that the important step can be waived. (Sibisi 2024, 935)

The question arises how courts should respond to non-state law. Generally speaking, non-state laws may be: (a) ignored by the courts on the basis of their being customs and practices rather than law; (b) used by the courts to supplement their interpretation of state laws by taking customs into account;[27] or (c) be declared by the courts as inconsistent with, or irrelevant to, state laws or universal norms.[28] The state may also enact laws to regulate, prohibit, criminalise, or restrict the application of non-state laws.

[27] The status of the non-state laws may vary from being entirely informal and little more than being the rules of a club or association, to being formally recognised and applied by the national courts. For example, note how in the Mexican state of Quintana Roo, Mayan customary law has been regarded as equal in stature to state law since 1997, whereas previously it had been treated as subordinate to state law. Before 1997 Mayan law was recognised but considered lower in stature than state law. Since 1997 customary law within the fields of criminal law, civil law and family matters is treated with the same status as state law. Individuals can now choose whether their dispute is determined pursuant to state law or customary law. (Hoekema 2017, 67) Within the context of Europe there is often ambivalence regarding preferences – whether to prioritise legal unity and consistency across all European states or to embrace legal pluralism and diversity within individual states. (Luts-Sootak et al 2018, 7) On the one hand, the appeal of universality of legal norms lies in its certainty and standardisation. On the other hand, legal pluralism implies diverse sources of law from various perspectives, challenging the universality of rights. Centrifugal and centripetal forces are operating within the same space of international law and constitutional law. In some respects the tension between such centrifugal and centripetal forces also exists within the state. While the courts represent the state and therefore uniform state law, a myriad other dispute and conflict resolution processes may coexist within the state without involving the courts. Law in contemporary society is therefore mostly pluralistic rather than monolithic. (Galanter 1981, 20)

[28] Note, for example, how South Africa and the Netherlands have adopted divergent approaches to the acceptance and regulation of Islamic finance. (Salah and Rautenbach 2015) Salah and Rautenbach conclude that the South African legal system, which reflects elements of state and non-state pluralism, 'seems to be more adaptable to the nature of Islamic finance'

Non-state laws may vary in the sanctions or remedies they offer.[29] Their enforceability may depend on the courts of the national legal system or on sanctions applicable solely to those within the specific community. Nevertheless, amid their diversity, non-state laws share a common characteristic – they are considered binding law for those who adhere to them. Non-state law is voluntary in nature, where individuals, theoretically at least, can reject it or the sanctions associated with it based on the freedom of association. In contrast, state law is mandatory and applies to all individuals within the national territory.

2.6 LEGAL PLURALISM: A HOUSE WITH MANY ROOMS

Legal pluralism suggests the coexistence of several legal systems concurrently, affecting the same individual, within the same space and related to the same subject-matter. Legal pluralism describes a situation where the hegemony of the state over what is deemed 'law' is challenged through the presence, recognition and accommodation of other, non-state, normative systems. Legal pluralism is sceptical of legal uniformity and 'critical of the tight coupling of law and state'. (Sani 2020, 83) The challenge for the state lies not in the informal existence of legal pluralism but to determine which subject-matters necessitate state law and uniformity within state boundaries and how these should be enforced in the face of possible conflicts with non-state laws. The state must also decide which, if any, subject-matters can be governed by non-state laws by way of a form of

and that the South African system has shown itself to be more adaptable to global financial developments that affect Islamic finance. (Salah and Rautenbach 2015, 515)

[29] For example, observe how in several South American states the customary-law systems of indigenous people are recognised by the state for application only to those communities that adhere to the customary law. This implies that within a specific social field state law and recognised customary law are potentially on an equal footing or customary law may even hold precedence. (Hoekema 2017, 69) Given that South African courts frequently acknowledge the existence of non-state laws and customs, a question arises within the context of the typology used: does the recognition of non-state law imply that it becomes a form of state law? This highlights the shortcomings and challenges associated with the legal typology of a complex social reality. I would suggest that a non-state law recognised by a court does not automatically become a state law, by reason that the state is not the author of that law. The source of the non-state law continues to be the customs of the community, exposing it to community dynamics and adjustments. However, in certain situations, such as in the case of Ubuntu, a non-state legal concept may be acknowledged, elevated and applied by the courts across the entire population, thereby acquiring the status of state law (Chapter 6). Furthermore, a customary law may be enacted into legislation, which renders it state law, as has happened in several African states where indigenous customary law has been codified (Chapter 10).

asymmetry where different legal rules apply to an individual dependent on the community with whom they associate. Legal pluralism therefore implies a house with 'many rooms'. (Galanter 1981)

Globalisation, with its emphasis on the universality and consistency of norms, has not led to the diminishment of legal plurality. Instead, globalisation has arguably heightened the need for and awareness and recognition of the rules subnational identities, minorities, indigenous people and communities. Among the consequences of the globalisation of rights is that, while state and international law are often perceived as guardians of individual fundamental rights, there is a simultaneous intensification of demands for subnational pluralism, often based on some form of collective rights. This reflects the desire of communities to live in accordance with and enforce their own legal rules,[30] as the universality of laws and rights is often perceived as insensitive and intolerant to the unique identities of individuals and the communities to whom they belong. There is, for example, evidence in Europe of grassroots resistance emerging among immigrant communities to the imposed uniformity of state law. It is not unknown that customary, religious or cultural identity is often favoured, particularly by immigrant communities, as a core principle of their societal organisation. The authority of the state to be the sole author of 'law' is thus being challenged by the reality of legal pluralism and the ongoing adherence to non-state laws.

2.7 STATE LAW AND NON-STATE LAW: VYING FOR SUPREMACY

Occasionally, state law and non-state law legal systems compete for supremacy. This may lead to discrimination,[31] conflict, violence, criminal prosecution,

[30] Brechin proposes that non-state legal systems, particularly in regard to their ability to be understood by a community and to resolve community conflicts, may sometimes be better suited for community needs, in that they are easier to access, cheaper and more conducive to dispute resolution in line with traditions, laws, customs and culture. (Brechin 2013, 294) Personal autonomy and self-determination are thereby enhanced since individuals can select the rules and forums by which specific aspects of their live are regulated. However, as Brechin acknowledges, personal choice is based on the presumption that the choice is indeed free and not mandated or enforced by a community on an unwilling or reluctant person. (Brechin 2013, 300) Note, for example, the Al Midani case, in which it was found that the parties had not consented to arbitration by the Sharia Council of London, thus rendering the orders made by the council invalid and legally unenforceable. (Al Midani case 1999) For an overview of Islamic councils in the UK, their operations, powers and functions outside the realm of state law, see Bowen. (Bowen 2016)

[31] Note, for example, the way the South African courts approached Muslim unions pre-1994, compared to post-1994. Pre-1994, the courts adopted and reflected the opinion of the dominant

asymmetry of a region or locality[32] or even secession – driven by the goal of establishing a new state with a reimagined state law legal order. (De Villiers, Isra, and Mochtar 2019)[33] Mostly, however, non-state legal systems find comfort in a *de facto* subservient status, whereby the universality of the predominant state law system is acknowledged (at least at a *de facto* level). Despite this accepted subservience, non-state laws may continue to apply within specific communities

white, Christian minority that polygynous unions are 'repugnant to the moral principles' of South Africa'. (Seedat case 1917, 307) In the Hassam case of 2009 the court revisited its condemnation and found that such a discriminatory approach to Muslim unions was 'no longer sustainable in the light of our Constitution'. (Hassam case 2009, para 20) This illustrates changing societal values, including evolving perceptions of non-state law, that must be considered by courts in the application of law and the resolution of disputes. At the time of writing (March 2025), the objective of creating a marriage act to regulate Muslim marriages had not yet been achieved.

[32] Legal pluralism may also find expression in the federal dispersing of powers and functions whereby the legal system of a federal state may be different to the legal system of a national state. The federal state may, for example, adhere to and give effect to a traditional non-state legal system of which it is not the author. Note, for example, how in Indonesia and Malaysia, within some provinces and states respectively, traditional laws and customs are consistently adhered to in alignment with the authority of the local monarchy. However, these same rules do not apply at the national level. (Ikhwan and Aidulsyah 2020) The regional rules and laws applied in the provinces/states are a mixture of state law, non-state customs and religious practices. In Indonesia the following has been said about pluralism and asymmetry: 'Asymmetric decentralization is a special method given to certain provinces in Indonesia amidst the diversity of cultures, customs and specialties of certain regions.' (Sejati and Kartono 2024, 1)

[33] Note, for example, the special status of Aceh within Indonesia, and Bangsamoro in the Philippines. (De Villiers 2016b) Additionally, observe how the European Court of Human Rights has embraced an approach known as the 'margin of appreciation' to accommodate diverging perspectives among signatory states to the European Convention on Human Rights. This approach allows states maximum autonomy for each state to decide how it recognises and operationalises the universal provisions of the Convention. In the Handyside case the ECtHR acknowledged that when there is significantly more pluralism involved within a particular state, that state ought to be granted a margin of appreciation in how it applies the Convention. (Handyside case 1976) Richardson points out that many of the signatory European parties have refused to give effect to the judgments of the ECtHR since they are of the view that these judgments do not adequately reflect the unique circumstances of the specific nation. (Richardson 2019, 306) As a result, the ECtHR is under pressure to 'more fully recognise the legal pluralism that exists with the many diverse nations'. (Richardson 2019, 307) Sottiaux cautions, however, that the margin of appreciation may have contributed to inconsistency within the ECtHR about matters of dogma, giving rise to a failure on the part of the court to 'provide practical and predictable standards' to protect fundamental rights, such as in the area of freedom of expression and hate speech (see Chapter 5). (Sottiaux 2023, 1211) Breuer, meanwhile, speaks about the 'principled resistance' in some European jurisdictions to ECtHR judgments. (Breuer 2019, 5) It must be noted that the concept of the 'margin of appreciation' is widely used by the ECtHR to allow for state-based diversity in all areas of law, not only in the field of human rights.

in relation to areas such as personal and family disputes, inheritance, minor criminal offences, intra-community commerce, alternative dispute resolution[34] and land use.

The principle of individual and community self-determination associated with legal pluralism reflects the concepts of limited government and subsidiarity where local communities, boards, clubs, institutions and organisations are regarded as best suited to make decisions about local and community issues in accordance with their own customs, traditions and circumstances. Essentially, the community, regardless of its structure, is best placed to make its own laws and enforce them. (Seinecke 2018, 24) A matter that requires state regulation moves up to a higher level of authority only when it cannot be effectively regulated at the community level. (Delcamp 1994)

There is unfortunately a potential dark side to legal pluralism. Within a non-state legal system the predominant view of those 'in control' of a community may exhibit a lack of tolerance, refusal to accommodate different views, failure to respect intra-community diversity, lack of accountability, or failure to adhere to democratic principles towards individuals or minorities within the community.[35] The decision-making processes of non-state legal systems are often not consistent with contemporary democratic norms of representation, accountability and transparency. Despotism and personal fiefdoms may therefore easily find shelter in a community under the veil of legal pluralism.

For legal pluralism to serve individual rights and freedoms it must be attenuated by liberal democratic values and principles as well as be subject to

[34] Note, for example, how in the United Kingdom the informal dispute resolution mechanism adopted by the Kurdish community (called the Kurdish Peace Committee) has, after initial scepticism from public authorities, become recognised in practice and even funded by the public authorities, particularly the police, for enabling good governance and community liaison to be pursued. (Tas 2013) This development highlights how scepticism towards plurality can evolve into recognition and even embracing of plurality. Tas also points out that the pluralism approach pursued by the Turkish community is comparable to the informal, non-territorial arrangements of the *millets* in the Ottoman empire. (Tas 2016)

[35] Note in this regard how in Australia community organisations, be they religious, cultural or indigenous, may become incorporated but even so they remain subject to judicial oversight. Discrimination or unfair treatment within an association can therefore be referred by a disgruntled person for judicial review. The associations function autonomously, but they are nevertheless accountable. Many cultural, language and religious communities in Australia incorporate in this manner (see, for example, the Incorporations Act 2015 in the state of Western Australia).

judicial oversight.[36] This explains why the South African Constitution recognises customary law but within the context of sovereignty of the Constitution and judicial oversight. The risk of legal pluralism giving rise to undemocratic practices calls for some form of mitigation and oversight. Praet, for example, expresses concern that within the European context Sharia law often operates in a manner inconsistent with fundamental rights, particularly those pertaining to equal treatment of women, and that state authorities not only tolerate such undemocratic practices, but endorse them 'under the guise' of informal community arbitration institutions. (Praet 2018, 47)[37] Sharia is a 'comprehensive legal frame work' that affects the personal and public life of Muslims. (Husain, Ayoub and Hassmann 2024, 2)[38] Dogmatically Sharia views itself as the sovereign legal system.

Ultimately, there is a risk that in some circumstances legal pluralism with its roots in historic practices and beliefs may seek to justify practices that 'clearly border on illegality'. (Praet 2018, 48) Conversely, a situation may arise, particularly in emerging democracies, where state law institutions, including the judiciary, are so corrupt, ineffective, inaccessible and illegitimate that the public prefers to resort to non-state law courts and arbitration bodies to resolve their disputes because of the efficiency they offer. This is exemplified in Afghanistan, where the constitutionally created judicial system suffers from low credibility and legitimacy, whereas informal systems arising from Sharia provide the most consistent service. (Tamanaha 2021, 85) The *shuras* and *jirgas* in Afghanistan are generally community-based, quick to convene and accessible to community members, and solve issues through the application of known rules and customs. Despite facing criticism, the public legitimacy accorded to these religious forums, particularly in rural areas, generally outweighs the legitimacy of constitutionally created bodies of justice.

---

[36] This principle is clearly illustrated in the Gaum case, where the court did not involve itself with the teachings or dogma of the church when it declared discrimination against same-sex couples in the rite of marriage as unconstitutional. (Gaum case 2019)

[37] Note, for example, the analysis in the South African case of the Women's Legal Trust, where the court acknowledged how the lack of recognition of Muslim marriages infringes on the dignity of women and highlighted the vulnerability of women and children when Muslim marriages dissolve. (Women's Legal Centre Trust case 2018, para 136)

[38] Although legal pluralism may be beneficial in its reflection and tolerance of diversity, 'it necessitates careful attention to the rights and freedoms of all individuals, especially those who may face marginalization or disadvantage in specific legal systems'. (Husain, Ayoub, and Hassmann 2024, 9)

In short, legal pluralism is tolerated as a reality within many liberal democracies, but only to the extent that non-state laws do not conflict with state laws or the constitution.

2.8 INTERACTION BETWEEN STATE LAW AND NON-STATE LAW

The complexity that arises from pluralist legal systems is not necessarily rooted in its social existence, but rather in the interaction between state law and non-state law. Legal systems often cannot be neatly compartmentalised into distinct enclaves, as they inherently aim to regulate rights and interests within the same subject field. An individual may traverse both systems, living under state law and also under a community-based system of non-state law, custom and tradition.[39] For example, the non-state legal system's treatment of women, resolution of criminal disputes, allocation of rights to land, restrictions on freedom of expression, rules of inheritance or accountability and transparency may, at worst, be inconsistent with state law or, at best, differ from state law.[40] Sometimes the

[39] For example, observe how in Australia legislation has been enacted in different states to accommodate the traditional rights of Aboriginal people, particularly concerning fishing and hunting. These laws exempt Aboriginal people from certain restrictions that apply to the rest of the population in these activities. As an illustration, in the state of Western Australia the Fish Resources Management Act 1994 (WA) exempts Aboriginal people from the requirement to hold a recreational fishing licence in accordance with the *continuing* Aboriginal tradition, provided that the fish are caught for personal and/or family purposes and not for commercial use. (Fish Resources Act 1994, s 6) Customary fishing is defined as fishing by an *Aboriginal person* that is in accordance with *continuing Aboriginal customary law and the tradition* of the area being fished, and is for the purpose of satisfying personal, domestic, ceremonial, educational or non-commercial communal needs. While the intention of the legislation is to accommodate, and even codify, the scope of legal pluralism by elevating a non-state rule to state law, the practical application may give rise to challenges since a person must prove they are Aboriginal and that the manner of fishing is consistent with ongoing Aboriginal tradition. When considering such a defence by an Aboriginal person the courts must therefore be satisfied of evidence of ongoing customary practices and proclaim whether the assertion by the defendant is accepted. This statutory arrangement reflects the common-law position, where it has been held that an Aboriginal person who had caught and kept two undersized crocodiles did so in accordance with traditional law and custom. (Yanner case 1999) This recognition of legal pluralism is not without controversy, as critics argue that using race or indigeneity as a basis to differentiate between the rights and obligations of individuals under state law can turn legal pluralism into the legalised face of discrimination and inequality.

[40] Husain et al observe as follows: 'Legal pluralism presents substantial human rights dilemmas, especially in situations where religion or customary rules coexist with secular legal systems. An urgent issue is the violation of women's rights, as legal pluralism can lead to discriminatory behaviors and unequal treatment within the legal system. Within numerous jurisdictions regulated by Islamic law, women may encounter limitations on their entitlements to divorce, inheritance,

source and exact nature of the non-state legal system may not be clear because of a lack of codification, different or competing interpretations of non-state law, reinforcement of domination through interpretation and perpetuation of previous (correct or incorrect) interpretations. The concept of non-state law as a 'living' legal system or 'living law' (Ehrlich 1913) that is not codified reflects, on the one hand, the reality of continual change and adaption of non-state legal systems. This approach has also been endorsed by the Constitutional Court of South Africa with reference to customary law being regarded as 'living'. (Bhe case 2005)[41] On the other hand, for courts to ascertain the applicable norms under non-state law for a dispute can be extraordinarily challenging and complex, as well as prone to error, disagreements in interpretation and lack of consistent adherence (Chapter 10).[42]

Adding to the complexity, an individual may seek relief in the state law system for an alleged breach of their rights under the non-state law community system.[43] This then raises the question of the extent, if any, to which the national

---

and child custody, along with constraints on their movement and engagement in public affairs.' (Husain, Ayoub, and Hassmann 2024, 10)

[41] Note, for example, the Shomang case, where the court had to strike a balance between the ownership of property under common law and the ownership of property under customary law. The court emphasised that customary law must be understood with reference to customary law and not by reference to another legal system. (Shomang case 2022, para 57) This includes taking account of the 'fluidity' of customary law (para 60). The way that common law views ownership of property does not necessarily correlate with the customary holding of property (para 73). Property law must therefore develop in a manner consistent with the recognition of customary law (para 77). The house which was the subject of the proceeding was therefore declared a 'family house' rather than a house belonging to an individual (para 81).

[42] Ehrlich's theory of living law allows for a distinction between 'rules of decision' and 'rules of conduct', with the former based on legal positivism where the law is declared by a competent authority, while the latter derives from custom. (Ehrlich 1936, 11) Ehrlich equates legal norms to customary norms since a person conducts themselves in compliance with laws and norms according to the social relationships in which the person finds themselves within a community. A *legal* norm, therefore, does not necessarily differ in substance from a *social* norm. (Ehrlich 1936, 63) Pursuant to this proposition, a law enacted by parliament and a custom adhered to by a community, treated as if it were a law, share a similar status.

[43] For example, an individual may endure a form of corporal punishment within the non-state law system for a crime, even though the corporal punishment may constitute assault under the criminal code of the state law. In Australia, a sanction such as spearing or another type of physical punishment, imposed by an Aboriginal community for a misdemeanour committed by a member of the community that may ordinarily constitute assault, is often applied in rural areas and is given *de facto* recognition by the police. (Australian Law Reform Commission 1986, paras 499–503) The challenge that arises from the state law system recognising non-state law forms of punishment or initiation practices is how to respond if a person who has been punished or initiated in this way

state law legal system recognises the existence of the plurality of non-state legal systems in general and, more specifically, how it gives effect to the rules of the non-state system when disputes are litigated under state law. While informal legal pluralism may be noted, tolerated, treated with common sense and even encouraged as a way to deepen democracy and maximise individual autonomy, when a conflict between a non-state law and a state law appears, such as in the area of criminal or family law, the inevitability of establishing a superior right, law or obligation becomes obvious. (Bhe case 2005)

While tolerating a plurality of legal systems may in one sense signify the maturity of a liberal democratic system, in another sense clashes between these systems inevitably lead to the acknowledgment of the importance of a hierarchy of laws. This is evidenced by the South African Constitution, which elevates customary law to the same status of other laws, but it also reiterates that the Constitution is supreme.[44] Munby J expresses it as follows:

> It is important to realise that reliance upon religious belief, however conscientious the belief and however ancient and respectable the religion, *can never of itself immunise the believer from the reach of secular law.* An invocation of religious belief does not necessarily provide a defence to what is otherwise a valid claim. Some cultural beliefs and practices are simply treated by law as being beyond the pale. (emphasis added) (R case 2008)

---

complains that they have been assaulted by Aboriginal elders. If the state organs disregard the complaint, it implies condoning unauthorised violence against a person. Note, for example, the deaths and serious injury caused by initiation practices in South Africa. (Meel 2010) During the winter of 2024 around 14 boys died in the Eastern Cape province because of initiation practices having gone wrong. (Dorfling 2024a) During the summer of 2024/5 around 28 young men died in the same province in initiation practices. (Dorfling 2024b) It is reasonable to suggest that if around 60 young men died in six months as part of any religious or cultural ritual, there would be public outrage and prosecutions. On the other hand, if the state prosecutes, it may undermine the traditional system of laws. Provision is sometimes made in parts of Australia for Aboriginal elders to form part of the judicial proceedings to make inputs into appropriate sentencing for young offenders. In a similar vein, a woman who has entered into a customary or religious union under Islamic law may seek relief from state law if she does not receive the same benefits or protection that exist in civil law for a married or *de facto* married couple. (Rautenbach 2021a)

[44] Placing customary law on equal footing with other legal systems may on the one hand be a simple exercise in legal prescription, but on the other hand it does not necessarily change cultural and customary practices within communities. For example, striking a balance between male and female regarding access to and control of land in Africa remains problematic and often gives rise to females being discriminated against, suffering greater poverty than men, and being socially locked into arrangements that may not be in their best interests. (Mubecua and Nojiyza 2022) The removing of such inequalities may in turn signify the gradual erosion of customary law as a distinct legal system since under the Constitution a person cannot be treated unequally at law for the mere reason of adhering to a custom or tradition.

2.9 LEGAL PLURALISM AND MINORITY RIGHTS

The realms of legal pluralism and the protection of minority rights may overlap. Generally, legal pluralism tends to emphasise a distinct *legal system*, while minority protection emphasises institutional design to facilitate *political participatory rights* even if the community does not have a separate legal system. Such a categorisation is not watertight, however, since some cultural communities, e.g. the European Roma, may seek political participatory arrangements and acknowledgement of their non-state law. (Nafstad 2018) While not identical, legal pluralism and the protection of minority rights share common ground in some respects. Both are founded on individual rights, which only find practical application when exercised in association with others from the same community. Both rely on a unique community identity that is sought to be recognised and protected by the community. Both represent pluralism and diversity. Both assert a form of collective rights.[45]

Arguably, there is a closer causal link between legal pluralism and the recognition of religions and indigenous laws, since religious and indigenous rights often stem from an ancient legal system with norms, rules and customs that continue to be adhered to, despite being subject to adjustment and modernisation.[46] It is

[45] As I explain below, international law does not recognise collective rights by ethnocultural communities as if the community is a legal entity. But, as McCorquodale points out, in practice there is both an acknowledgement and application 'of groups having rights distinct from the rights of individuals'. (McCorquodale 2022, 284) This reflects the opinion of Kymlicka, who views identity rights not as collective 'group' rights, but as rights that are excised collectively by individuals. He summarises this position as follows: '[M]ost [group rights] are not about the primacy of communities over individuals. Rather, they are based on the idea that justice between groups requires that the members of different groups are accorded different rights.' (Kymlicka 1995, 47) This is reflected in the Fosen case, in which it was held that the individual right to culture is directly linked to the collective rights of a community to exercise their rights in unison. (Fosen case 2021)

[46] Note, for example, the Australian judgment in the Yorta Yorta case, in which it was held that Aboriginal people must meet the following thresholds to prove their ongoing traditional connection to traditional land: Aboriginal people must for the purposes of native title land rights (a) prove that they continue to function as a 'society' of traditional owners, (b) pursuant to their ancestral laws and culture; and (c) culture and cultural practices are not frozen in time and therefore customs and practices can be adjusted to suit contemporary circumstances. (Yorta Yorta (HCA) case 2002) Ahren also observes that for indigenous people to fall within the scope of protection by UNDRIP they must demonstrate having '*established societies* in their traditional lands with at least *key institutions* intact'. (Ahren 2023, 175) In the Awas Tingni and Sawhoyamaxa cases the link between institutions and traditional lands was also highlighted. (Awas Tingni case 2001; Sawhoyamaxa Community case 2006, para 118)

generally not overly difficult to prove the existence of an indigenous system of law and ongoing adherence to its rules and customs.[47] Religious minorities, such as Muslims, Jews and Orthodox Christians, may have established rules and customs in areas such as family and personal law, to which followers may adhere. Minority protection does not rely principally on the recognition of a distinct legal system, but rather on the protection of cultural identity and the risk of being politically marginalised.

Newman expresses the view that 'increased instabilities' arising from the relationship between the state and religion are becoming more apparent and that this has 'complicated' the rights of minorities. (Newman 2023, 156) These complications are, however, nothing new. In many respects they have existed since the formation of the state. Nonetheless, contemporary efforts to recognise individual rights, minority rights and indigenous rights have highlighted how far we are yet to travel to reach equilibrium.

Since cultural and linguistic minorities do not necessarily rely on ancient legal systems to justify their demand as a society for special protection and collective political rights, they may feel threatened, persecuted and marginalised because of their unique culture, language or traditions. As a result ethnocultural communities may advocate for specific design measures to safeguard their identity, language and culture – not necessarily recognition of a separate legal system. Language and cultural minorities may accept the state law in its entirety, but they may also seek special *political* participatory rights in the formulation of state laws. Meanwhile, indigenous and religious communities may seek recognition of their non-state law systems, but without necessarily demanding special political participatory rights.[48] Religious minorities often straddle the realms of state law and

[47] For example, observe how in the Alexkor case in South Africa it was found that the indigenous community continued to exercise rights to land collectively and hence they retained the right to use the land in accordance with their traditional laws and customs. They could, therefore, be compensated for the diminution of title and use as a result of mining. (Alexkor case 2004) The court noted that those customs of the Richtersveld community were transferred from one generation to another through oral tradition and practices. The challenge for courts, however, lies in determining with certainty what those pre-colonial traditional laws and customs were. Cultural laws are living and adaptable, often vague, usually uncodified, subject to various interpretations and typically male-dominated. This complexity may reinforce existing power imbalances rather than promote the equality demanded by contemporary international and national state law. Establishing a causal link between current customs and pre-settlement traditional customs can therefore be a complex task.

[48] Note, for example, how this proposition was on display in the South African constitution-drafting process. The Afrikaners, who do not have a community non-state legal system as a

non-state law. Cultural minorities, such as the Roma in Europe, may also adhere to their own laws. (Nafstad 2018)[49] As discussed in more detail in Chapter 8, religious groups may challenge the state's authority for sovereignty, or they may operate in the private sphere in obedience to state law, albeit that religious edicts are also obeyed.

Legal pluralism is evidently a net that can be cast very wide, as it displays many dimensions.

In the context of this book the commonality between the recognition of minority rights and the existence of legal pluralism lies in their shared objective: both aim to coexist with the majority within the same territory and under the same state law legal system. In broad terms legal pluralism surpasses the scope of the minority rights discourse. Legal pluralism entails the acknowledgment and presence of non-state legal systems, including traditional, religious or customary norms, that function as laws for individuals associated with a specific community. In contrast minority rights and protection typically aim to secure collective *political participatory rights* and *autonomy* within the institutional framework of governance, particularly within the scope of public law. (UN Declaration on Minorities 1992; European Framework Convention 1998; Lund Recommendations 1999; Ljubljana Guidelines 2012)

Ethnocultural minority groups seeking special protection may not necessarily share a non-state legal system, typically adhering instead to their own unique customary rules and practices.[50] The uniqueness of cultural customs does not,

---

distinct society and who subscribe to state laws, sought special political participatory rights as a racial and linguistic minority. Meanwhile, the Jewish community, which does have religious non-state laws, did not seek special collective political participatory rights as a minority. There is no predictive model or rationale in comparative constitutional law whereby a threshold is defined when an ethnocultural minority or indigenous community may demand or qualify for special collective political participatory rights. (De Villiers 2022g) The answer, as discussed in chapter 4, is dictated by political reality and societal events, and most often by the ability of the minority to cause instability if it is not suitably accommodated.

[49] Nafstad observes: 'Roma culture and traditional ways of life can in some areas be difficult to reconcile with other national legislation and human rights law. Tensions between Roma rights as a national minority on one side and other legislation and normative expectations on the other might arise. The practice of the non-state Roma law is one example of this. In addition, there could be tensions between minority rights as a group right and individual rights for persons belonging to the group. Women's and children's rights are examples of this.' (Nafstad 2018, 102)

[50] Note, for example, the Afrikaans-speaking community in South Africa, which shares a common language, but few or no other common customs, traditions or laws that apply to all of the Afrikaans community. (De Villiers 2022a) The Afrikaans community in its own composition

however, equate to non-state *law*, since ordinary cultural or religious customs and practices do not meet the criteria of legal rules. While ethnocultural minority protection proposals can be regarded as part of a broader theme of legal pluralism, not all communities that subscribe and adhere to customary laws and practices within the realm of legal pluralism demand collective recognition or protection as minorities in the institutional design of the state.

It is notable that in its Certification judgment (Chapter 3), the Constitutional Court of South Africa repeatedly referred to the 'diversity' of culture, religious and language communities, but did not suggest that those communities function within the context of legal pluralism with non-state legal systems and procedures that ought to be separately accommodated in the constitutional design. (Certification case 1996, paras 179, 205, 210)[51] Furthermore, the Constitutional Court was cautious not to endorse legal pluralism as if implying the existence of competing or equal legal orders within the same national territory. The Constitutional Court commented as follows regarding the recognition of customary law and traditional forms of government: 'a *degree of cultural pluralism* with legal and cultural, *but not* necessarily *governmental, consequences*'. (emphasis added) (Certification case 1996, para 195) The court hereby drew a fine distinction: pluralism exists as a societal reality, but pluralism is not to be construed as a basis for separate political collective rights.

As is shown in Chapter 4, international law favours an approach to the protection of minority rights whereby the individual rights of the persons who belong to minorities are protected, rather than collective rights of the community.[52] As a

---

exhibits characteristics of a plural society, encompassing Afrikaans-speakers with diverse affiliations to different faiths and religions, social classes, regions, localities, histories, cultural practices, races and political persuasions. Therefore the self-determination sought by some members of the Afrikaans community, during and after the negotiation process, was not related to them pursuing their own ancient legal and customary system. Instead, it was oriented towards seeking political participatory rights, a measure of self-government and autonomy, and state funding for mother-tongue education. Critically, however, they also relied on a race-based self-identification approach which was and remains inconsistent with international law. The racial predisposition of some within the Afrikaans community in their attempt to distinguish between Afrikaner and Afrikaans-speaking (e.g. Afrikaner Declaration) continues to sabotage the case of Afrikaans.

[51] The Constitution recognises the status of traditional leaders and customary law. (Constitution of South Africa 1996, secs 211, 212)

[52] Although there are state-based examples where courts have given effect to individual rights by reference to the importance that the right can only be effectively exercised in community with others, (e.g. Fosen case 2021) the essence of the right remains individual and not collective as if exercised by a legal entity. As I explain below, international law does not recognise collective

result an ethnocultural minority lacks a legal *persona* or any collective rights in international law, although courts have recognised that indigenous communities at common law may possess a legal identity in addition to the identity of their individual members. (De Villiers 2023f, 40) The same reasoning does not apply (so far) in international law in respect of ethnocultural minorities. The individual rights emphasis of international law tends to favour legal pluralism by focusing on the rights of the individual to associate with a community of their choice. However, this approach typically does not grant the community itself, as a legal entity, the exercise of political rights. Nonetheless, *realpolitik* sometimes demands the formal recognition and protection of minority rights on a collective basis. This can be achieved through special arrangements such as decentralisation, institutional design, reserved seats, quotas, coalitions, special funding or community-directed policy measures. Topidi reminds us that 'the war in Ukraine constitutes a brutal reminder of the significant challenges in ethnocultural minority protection standards and policies on our continent'. (Topidi 2025, 3)

In short, it can be inferred that the protection of ethnocultural minorities may fall within the general description of legal pluralism. However, not all instances of legal pluralism imply a demand for or the existence of collective political participatory rights.

2.10 LIMITS TO LEGAL PLURALISM

The dilemma posed by the recognition and application of legal pluralism is obvious: while the right to freedom of association enables individuals to function within communities sharing the same religion, traditions, culture or customs, the intriguing question arises about how the state law system responds to activities deriving from the customs, rules and practices of a community that do not align or correspond with state law.[53] On the one hand, the state law system may impose

rights by ethnocultural communities as if the community is a legal entity. But, as McCorquodale points out, in practice 'there is both an acknowledgement and application of groups having rights distinct from the rights of individuals'. (McCorquodale 2022, 284) This reflects the opinion of Kymlicka, who views identity rights not as collective 'group' rights, but as rights that are exercised collectively by individuals. He summarises this position as follows: '[M]ost [group rights] are not about the primacy of communities over individuals. Rather, they are based on the idea that justice between groups requires that the members of different groups are accorded different rights.' (Kymlicka 1995, 47)

[53] It is important to note it is not the 'idea' or teaching that is tested for constitutional compliance, but rather 'actions' arising from the idea. For example, courts would not be drawn

its own rules on the entire population regardless of any informal legal pluralism. On the other hand, the state law system may accommodate, apply, recognise and give effect to non-state legal pluralism to the extent that it is not inconsistent with state law, or even allow an inconsistency to prevail. It is ultimately for the courts to declare the limits of legal pluralism, and thereby determine the rules of engagement and coexistence between state law and non-state law. The courts must consider constitutional provisions, the purpose of the constitution, the public interest, common law, customary law, the reasonableness of the non-state law, and the principle of proportionality to determine whether a non-state law is upheld, enforced, given effect, noted or restricted. As Sachs observed: 'Court decisions help to create the basic value system of society and establish the character of our constitutional democracy. And every detail matters. . . . God is in the detail. One cannot be precise and accurate enough.' (Sachs 2009, 148)

While legal pluralism is often associated with liberal democracies and the expression of fundamental rights and freedoms, there is also a fault line along which legal pluralism may erode the very freedoms and tolerance sought to be protected by a liberal democratic system.[54] In the most extreme outcome legal pluralism may cause the state law system to be challenged or even rejected, giving rise to conflict, violence, civil disobedience or even secession.

Divergent forces are exhibited in the interaction between state law uniformity and non-state law pluralism: on the one hand, universal human rights norms encourage and even demand greater uniformity, while, on the other, legal pluralism, as an expression of fundamental rights, demands greater localised diversity. It is ironic that in contemporary literature and legal practice both the internationalisation of human rights and the localisation of non-state laws, as expressed in legal pluralism, are encouraged and applauded. However, these

---

into the constitutionality of religious dogma, but if the dogma gives rise to actions that offend the Constitution, courts may intervene. (Freedom of religion case 2019)

[54] Macioce expresses the concern that multiculturalism and, by extension, legal pluralism, may pose a threat to the fabric of society by undermining social cohesion and eroding an individual's sense of belonging to the entire political system within a national territory. (Macioce 2016, 1) While Kymlicka contends that equality also includes the recognition of diversity (Kymlicka 1995), Macioce expresses concern that, at some point, the recognition of diversity may threaten social integration, social harmony and social acceptance. (Macioce 2016, 4) Gunther, meanwhile, poses the proposition that legal pluralism is a 'symptom of the deterioration, of a step backwards behind the achievements of modernity' since the universality of basic rights seems to be challenged by legal pluralism, particularly when non-state law may be inconsistent with those universal rights and freedoms. (Gunther 2020, 87)

two approaches may lead to inconsistencies, whereby universal rights take on a colonial effect by submerging local identities and customs, while legal pluralism in its most extreme form may threaten the existence of the national legal system and even the sovereignty of the national state. Legal pluralism has the potential to legitimise discrimination and segregation, as different non-state norms may be applied to different segments of the population. Legal pluralism may give rise to a sanitised version of apartheid where, under the veil of individual self-determination, individuals are locked into silos of inequality – particularly women and children, but also young men dying in initiation ceremonies without the protections offered to other young men of their age. In the pursuit of accommodating plurality there is a risk that the universality of international human rights norms and standards may be compromised.

The former Chair of the UK's Commission on Equality and Human Rights, Trevor Phillips, has cautioned that while the accommodation of pluralism is an essential characteristic of democracy, one should be careful not to sleepwalk into a form of segregation under the veil of legal pluralism whereby 'we are becoming strangers to each other and leaving communities to be marooned outside the mainstream'. (Phillips 2005) In its extreme, legal pluralism may condone communities living in legal silos regardless of them sharing the same territorial space.[55] This was a major concern of opponents of an Aboriginal Voice in Australia, who argued that the Voice could racialise social policies and turn into a form of administrative apartheid. (De Villiers 2024c)

A balance should therefore be struck between the national (and international) norms and standards applicable to all individuals and the acceptance of non-state legal pluralism, whereby the richness of the traditional laws and customs of ethnocultural, religious and indigenous communities can be maintained by those who prefer to adhere to them. Kymlicka is arguably correct when he proposes that the acceptance of pluralism or multiculturalism may strengthen liberal democratic institutions by 'encouraging and enabling immigrants to participate more comfortably and more effectively' in democratic institutions of governance (Kymlicka 2008, 165). However, it is essential to caution that legal pluralism

[55] Note, for example, the observation of Bottoni in respect of Ethiopia where, in theory, parties can consent to Sharia being applied to their dispute, but in reality 'women are frequently pressed or coerced by their own family and community to resort to it, or may do so out of lack of knowledge of their own rights or for economic reasons'. In fact, in some instances the civil courts have even overruled efforts by women for civil law rather than Sharia to apply. (Bottoni 2023, 202–3)

may become an impenetrable realm within which individuals of a community become trapped and subject to unfair and unreasonable community practices, without being able to enjoy the fruits of the rights and freedoms promised by democracy and international law.[56] Al-Nuaimi cautions that in Muslim communities there may be many disagreements about dogma and differences of levels of adherence to religious prescriptions, but because of societal pressure and circumstances from within and outside the Muslim community, Muslim are 'obligated to pay for these differences and conflicts which are irrelevant and unrelated to them. . . .' (Al-Nuaimi 2024, 35) It is therefore erroneously assumed that Muslims as a community of believers subscribe to the same non-state laws and that their actions are motivated by the same religious edicts.

In this respect Epple summarises the challenges experienced by Ethiopia in the interaction between state law and non-state law as follows:

> However, in practice, the multiplicity of the often opposing and competing norms of the different legal forums poses a challenge to both legal practitioners and justice seekers. As will be shown in this volume, certain gaps in the law have left the system *open to abuse and exploitation for personal advantage.* There are also examples of power

[56] The debate about multiculturalism and what it implies in the context of legal pluralism has been particularly evident in recent times in European liberal democracies, where the homogeneity of the state, particularly regarding the principle of a single uniform legal system, has come under pressure because of increases in migration into Europe. In contrast, in young and emerging democracies the notion of multiculturalism and legal pluralism is a 'normal' condition under which the constitutions of those nations function. Countries such as South Africa, India, Nigeria, Ethiopia, Indonesia, Malaysia and Brazil have numerous non-state legal systems, formal and informal, that must be accommodated, accepted, endured and harmonised. The following objective in Ethiopia as described by Epple might as well apply to any of those countries mentioned: '[R]especting religious and cultural diversity, ensuring the implementation of state law throughout its territorial domain, and committing itself to international standards of human rights through the ratification of global conventions and agreements'. (Epple and Assefa 2020, 11) The view that 'the law' emanates from a single source is arguably a misrepresentation of most legal systems of the world. (Hooker 1975, 6) Also note how in Indonesia the Rejang Tribe of Rejang Lebong Regency continues to apply their customary laws, called *Kelpeak Ukum Adat Ngen Ca'o Kutei Jang*, in villages, including by local magistrates. 'They [village magistrates] help resolve conflicts and disputes peacefully and tactfully, often through mediation and negotiation, allowing both parties to reach a satisfactory solution.' (Dahwal and Fernando 2024, 2) The application of customary law and Islamic law requires careful navigation. Even in Europe, where the debate on legal pluralism is currently most prominent, the proposition of 'one law for all' inadequately acknowledges the longstanding existence of informal legal pluralism. (Cumper 2014, 35) In the United Kingdom, for example, various non-state 'minority legal orders' have existed for some time. The question arises as to the relevance these orders hold for the public administration of the nation. (Cumper 2014, 55)

> being accumulated by individuals who hold prominent positions in more than one legal system, and in some places offenders are being sanctioned more than once for the same wrongdoing. The criminalization of certain cultural practices that contradict the state law and international human rights – labelled as 'harmful traditional practices' – has caused disappointment among local communities and occasionally led to avoidance of and resistance to the state law. At the same time, state institutions have remained difficult to access, especially in rural areas, not only because police stations and courts do not exist everywhere and often lack staff and equipment where they do, but also because local acceptance is still low. *In addition, in some places pressure is put on individuals to not take their cases outside the community.* (emphasis added) (Epple and Assefa 2020, 12)

Non-state legal systems may lack public accountability, transparency, respect for human rights, options for judicial review and popular checks and balances – basic principles that support the liberal democratic state. Simultaneously, however, they may enjoy public support within the community, accessibility, tradition and enhanced legitimacy that surpasses state law arrangements.

2.11 BALANCING STATE LAW AND NON-STATE LAW PLURALISM

Striking a balance between state law conformity and non-state law diversity is generally best achieved by considering factual circumstances rather than adhering to dogma or rigid prescription. Many customs and practices exist outside the realm of state law, and whether those can be accommodated is often a challenging question. For example, in the Refah Partisi case brought before the European Court of Human Rights (ECtHR) the court emphasised that pluralism is not only a consequence of a free and democratic order, but also a requirement for the existence of such an order.[57] Pluralism as a sociological reality contributes to

---

[57] The court declared, controversially, that Sharia principles as a legal system are not compatible with democratic norms and fundamental rights, and that the decision by Turkey to dissolve a political party that promoted Sharia law in Turkey, which is a secular state, was consistent with the European Convention on Human Rights. While this judgment has garnered both praise and criticism, it is noteworthy that the court's reliance on evidence was primarily centred on general statements made by the political party. The evidence did not specifically address any proposed plans, programmes or actions to be undertaken by the banned party. The judgment raises the question of whether the mere presence of an idea that threatens to encroach upon fundamental rights is sufficient for a party to be banned or whether there should be some concrete action, plan, incitement or deed before a court can determine that an actual encroachment has occurred. In the Molla Sali case the ECtHR adopted a seemingly more nuanced approached, allowing states to accept that parties to an inheritance dispute within their jurisdiction could seek resolution

the deepening of individual freedom, personal self-determination and personal autonomy. Legal pluralism can embody the principle of subsidiarity, wherein individuals assume responsibility to the greatest possible extent for their own lives, culture, traditions and affairs. Nonetheless, legal pluralism may also open the door to discrimination, unequal treatment, and non-compliance with human rights standards.

Legal pluralism is a general, undefined concept not to be romanticised. The right of the individual to self-determination can be practically expressed through the freedom of association within the context of legal pluralism. However, constraining an individual's rights because of adherence to the rigid rules of a community contradicts the principle of subsidiarity. In the Refah Partisi case the court observed as follows: 'The court considers that there can be no democracy without pluralism. . . .The pluralism indissociable from a democratic society, which has been dearly won over the centuries, depends on it.' (Refah Partisi case 2003, para 90) Yet in the same case Kolver J expressed the following caution: 'Admittedly, this pluralism, which impinges mainly on an individual's private and family life, is limited by the requirements of the general interest. However, it is, of course, more difficult in practice to find a compromise between the interests of the communities concerned and civil society as a whole than to reject the very idea of such a compromise from the outset.' (Refah Partisi case 2003)

Macklem has suggested that legal pluralism, pursuant to the European Convention (and potentially also in a generic context in other countries), must comply with three essential requirements: first, individuals must retain the freedom to *choose* whether they wish to be bound by the norms, customs or values of the community with which they associate; secondly, the scope of rule-making within such a community must be limited in range and effect, as it cannot *compete with* or replace the national constitutional allocation of powers and functions; and

---

of the matter under Sharia law. (Tsevas 2023) However, the court emphasised that the parties cannot be compelled to accept religious law. (Molla Sali case 2020) Richardson describes the potential impact of this judgment as 'immense' since it may be viewed as 'another example of the court recognising *legal* pluralism in the contemporary [European] world'. (Richardson 2019, 311) Farzan comments that the message of the Molla Sali case to the public 'is that political Islam and outright expression of Islamic religious identity are considered a threat to democracy and secularism; however, under religious peace, Islam can be protected. These factors and messaging have led to inconsistency in jurisprudence and abstract mechanisms that lack foreseeability.' Furthermore, 'the court had a lenient attitude toward legal pluralism in the Molla Sali case by allowing opting out of the minority legal order (Mufti jurisdiction) optional, provided it is informed'. (Farzan 2023, 52)

thirdly, the role of the state as the nation's *sole guarantor* of individual civil and political rights must be respected. (Macklem 2006, 498) These principles arising from legal pluralism are, according to Macklem, rooted in the civil and political rights of individuals, and do not amount to collective minority or community rights or some form of legal autonomy for a community.

The acknowledgement of legal pluralism is therefore not to be seen as justification for collective indigenous or minority rights, neither as justification to weaken or erode fundamental human rights. Within the diversity of pluralism certain national minimum standards of protection and conduct must apply to all individuals.

2.12 LEGAL PLURALISM AND THE DRAFTING OF THE SOUTH AFRICAN CONSTITUTION

The drafting process of the South African Constitution had to navigate the seemingly divergent forces of prioritising national unity and acknowledging sociological and legal pluralism – both practically and legal. The principal concern that captured the attention of the negotiators was the institutional response to the diversity of the population. The desire for national unity, common patriotism, protection of universal human rights and compliance with universal norms and standards potentially contrasted with the practical reality of ethnocultural diversity, pluralism, recognition of minority and indigenous rights, and the presence of non-state laws and customs.[58] These divergent priorities impacted the content of conflicts and compromises between the parties throughout the negotiation process. While at the overarching level the conflict was between apartheid and majoritarianism, at the negotiating table the predominant question was how to accommodate the practical ethnographic and indigenous diversity of South Africa within the context of a liberal democracy based on majoritarian principles. (Henrard 2002) Striking a balance between national unity and the

[58] In reality South African society had already, regardless of apartheid, exhibited at a social level the values of common patriotism and respects for ethnocultural and indigenous diversity. However, the question was how to give legal effect to this plurality in the design of the institutions of the new democracy. No political party could seriously suggest a strict mono-legal system for South Africa, where only one set of legal norms enacted by the national parliament would govern the entire society at all levels and in all possible respects. Such a legal fiction would have been untenable, especially considering the historical existence of customary and religious law practices.

accommodation of diversity was arguably *the* most influential factor on the policy positions adopted by the respective parties.

The emergence of a justiciable entrenched constitution that set out governmental powers and functions, the nature and scope of fundamental rights, the powers and functions of provincial and local authorities, the recognition of customary law and traditional institutions, the acknowledgment of individual identity rights, the potential for collective rights, and the establishment of an independent judiciary may, in retrospect, appear as an obvious outcome of the negotiations. However, at the time of the adoption of the Constitutional Principles (see Chapter 3), it represented a significant breakthrough where common ground was found. It was agreed that the new legal *grundnorm* would be the Constitution and legal supremacy, rather than parliamentary sovereignty. The Constitution was envisioned to transform South African society, moving it from its discriminatory past towards a future characterised by equality and non-discrimination while recognising diversity. The Constitution was established as the supreme law of the land against which the validity of all state law and non-state law would be assessed.[59]

The apartheid history of South Africa made it unpalatable to formally accommodate collective minority rights, but at the same time democratisation did not change the plural nature of the country, with its multitude of ethnocultural communities, religious groups, indigenous people and customary systems. South Africa is, by its nature, a legally, socially, religiously, culturally plural state with many subcommunities practising and adhering, to varying degrees, to their own non-state laws and customs within certain subject areas. (Rautenbach 2021b)

For negotiators the question revolved around whether the institutional design of the Constitution should reflect the pluralistic nature of society and, if so, how institutions and the Bill of Rights should be designed to accommodate and reflect the social and legal plurality.

On the one hand, it can be asserted that the legal order of South Africa already comprises both state laws and non-state laws, with instances where the dominance of state law is challenged at a community level by non-state law. On the other hand, it can be argued that the Constitution reflects an already existing plural social and legal order where the law is composed of multiple

[59] Note, for example, how the courts in South Africa have relied on the inherent meaning of Ubuntu as a tool of interpretation, as a source of rights and as a mechanism for the transformation of society. (chapter 6) (De Villiers 2022c)

elements. (Sani 2020, 98) These two approaches to law and society overlap and are not necessarily mutually exclusive. Overall, although the Constitutional Assembly did not engage in philosophical discourse about the nature and origin of laws, the Constitution endorses a position where the dominance of state law is qualified by the provisions of the Bill of Rights. State courts may acknowledge and accommodate the relevance of non-state legal rules and customary norms through fundamental rights, provided that these non-state laws align with the provisions of the Bill of Rights. As elaborated on later, the courts have in several respects interpreted the Constitution in a manner that accommodates legal and sociological plurality and allows for non-state law arrangements to continue. Notably in this respect courts have utilised the customary norm of Ubuntu to enrich common law and expand the interpretation of rights outlined in the Constitution. (Chapter 6)[60]

The pursuit of 'nation-building' through a written constitution had to reconcile with the plural nature of South African society, encompassing diverse populations and legal systems. This endeavour carried the risk, as described by Griffiths (1986, 7), of introducing a 'formidable layer of complexity' to the legal system. For instance, although the Constitutional Court acknowledged in the Certification case that traditional customary courts need not be explicitly recognised in the Constitution, such courts may be recognised in legislation enacted pursuant to the Constitution. The underlying theme of the constitution-drafting process was that a new legal order should be founded on the principle of constitutionalism. In this context the Constitution serves as the embodiment of these norms. Meanwhile, the plurality, both legal and social, of South Africa, as expressed by individuals through free association, should be accepted.[61]

---

[60] The recognition of the equality of legal systems under the Constitution is, in effect, a double-edged sword since, on the one hand, the equal status of non-state legal systems is recognised and hence the status of customary law is enhanced, but on the other hand the Constitution may give rise to the possibility that core aspects of the non-state legal systems may be declared unconstitutional or be adjusted to comply with the Constitution, thereby eroding the uniqueness of the customary system.

[61] The Constitutional Court, in the Certification case (Chapter 3), was cautious not to endorse legal pluralism as a term as if there were competing or equal legal orders within the same national territory. The Constitutional Court commented as follows regarding the recognition of customary law and traditional forms of government: 'a *degree of cultural pluralism* with legal and cultural, but *not necessarily governmental, consequences*'. (emphasis added) (Certification case 1996, para 195) This statement emphasised that pluralism is not to be used as a basis to design separate political participatory institutions.

While the richness of the country's population was metaphorically described as a 'rainbow' by Bishop Desmond Tutu, it proved challenging to accommodate the complexity of its diversity and pluralism through the newly created institutions, particularly within the context of a singular system of human rights protection. The plurality of the population simultaneously presented a threat to and a foundation for deepening democracy. In the run-up to the negotiations Albie Sachs, for example, cautioned as follows about the interaction between religious non-state legal pluralism and national civil and political rights: 'Differences of religion should not in any way be allowed to form the basis of differences of civil, political and legal rights.' (Sachs 1992, 85) Many international case studies highlight the risk of ethnocultural and indigenous diversity becoming vehicles for political mobilisation and group nationalism. The challenge was therefore to recognise and embrace pluralism, but without diversity translating into political forces or separate political participatory rights.

Ultimately, the predominant position arising from the constitution-drafting process was that the recognition of plurality (the term 'legal pluralism' did not appear in the Constitutional Principles and no reference was made to the term in the Certification cases) had to be assessed within the context of a democratic system of government, as expressed by the Constitution. The validity of all laws, state laws, customary law and non-state laws is to be tested against the Constitution. This also solidified the secular basis of jurisprudence, wherein the values by which actions are assessed are enshrined in the Constitution rather than in a religious code, indigenous customs or other dogma.

The literature arising from the study of legal pluralism highlights a 'deep analytical problem' with the meaning of the term. (Sani 2020, 101) The freedoms granted, and limits imposed, by democracy impact the nature and extent of legal pluralism. As Osman puts it: the complexities arising from legal pluralism in South Africa are 'palpable'. (Osman 2019, 98) As described by Ehrlich (1936, 493), the reality of multiple legal systems in South Africa is a typical example that the state is not always the exclusive source of laws. Other sources of law, rooted in religion, customs and traditions, may be adhered to, even if the state disapproves of them.[62]

[62] Osman cautions that non-state law should not be idealised or romanticised, since customary and religious law and practices often reaffirm existing power relationships, enhance intra-community inequality and retain marginalised persons within their pre-allocated position of weakness. (Osman 2019, 101) Even if customary law has been codified or recorded, those records often reflect the position of dominance versus subjugation and hence cannot necessarily

The interaction between state law and non-state laws seeks to strike a balance between the universality of certain legal principles and the recognition of pluralism and diversity. In short, pursuant to the Constitution legal pluralism cannot be used as a justification to encroach on fundamental rights and freedoms, and it cannot be used as a basis to undermine national unity. Recognition of legal pluralism is intended to enhance and expand individual liberty, empower individual autonomy and encourage freedom of association. It is also intended, however, to acknowledge that, pursuant to the principle of subsidiarity, certain disputes may only be resolved by the application of a higher state law. This new philosophy enshrined in and reflected by the Constitution requires that courts depart from their traditional literalism-cum-intentionalism approach to interpretation. Instead, a purposive approach should be adopted, wherein the deeper values embedded into the Constitution are identified and applied. (Alexkor case 2004) This approach facilitates societal transformation, applies the true effect of constitutionalism and the rule of law, and allows non-state legal systems to operate, provided they do not conflict with the Constitution.[63]

Legal pluralism is therefore deeply embedded in the thoughts of the Constitution, even if the term does not appear in the Constitution.

In this regard, the underlying consensus in the constitution-drafting process aligned with the opinion expressed by Justices Ress and Rozakis of the ECtHR in the Refah Partisi case. In that case the limits that can be imposed on freedom of association were considered, as well as to the importance of proportionality in restricting any fundamental right:

> It is difficult to give an exhaustive list of the rules of democracy, apart from the basic ones. It is without doubt correct to say that parties that aim at the destruction of democracy cannot enjoy protection against even such drastic measures as dissolution. But whether the failure to respect this or that rule of democracy justifies dissolution or whether a less drastic measure is the only appropriate and adequate one is again a question that has to be judged with regard to the principle of proportionality. (Refah Partisi case 2003)[64]

---

be sustained by state law as arising from the Constitution. The concept of living law as applied to indigenous customary law seeks to reflect the dynamic nature of customary law rather than its codified status, including how customary law adjusts to the new standards set by the Constitution. (Bhe case 2005)

[63] The orthodox approach to constitutional interpretation was seen as 'too restrictive and legalistic' and not suitable to accommodate and reflect the 'changing social dynamics' of South Africa. (Nortje case 1995, 471)

[64] It is important to note, however, that any restriction on a fundamental right, on the basis that it may cause harm to democratic norms and standards, ought not to be resolved in the

2.13 IN SUMMARY

The topic of legal pluralism is relatively new to scientific study and, at the same time, a well-trodden path for heterogeneous communities. Legal pluralism existed long before state or international legal uniformity. Non-state laws predate the establishment of the modern state and in many instances they persist at a social level despite the advent of the modern state and the uniformity it seeks. The following are the essential principles to be drawn from this chapter:

First, legal pluralism is a relatively recent scientific concept with varied applications, yet its definition remains vague and ambiguous. In practice legal pluralism has existed since the formation of the first communities, predating the modern state. Nonetheless, only recently have social scientists attempted to define the concept, to explore it, to develop a thesis for its consistent application and to find more predictable and reliable ways to harmonise different legal systems within the same territorial space.

Secondly, legal pluralism aims to describe an existing social condition where more than one legal system operates within the same territorial jurisdiction. However, these legal systems are not equal in terms of their source, scope, enforcement or jurisdiction. In this chapter I referred to the principal, or dominant, legal system as state law since it derives its authority from the constitution, sovereignty of parliament and common law. State law applies to the entire population and is enforced by the organs of state. I have denoted other legal systems as non-state law because their legal character emanates from longstanding culture, custom, habits, practices, beliefs and tradition. These non-state legal systems apply principally to individuals rather than territory (although there may be tribal areas where customary law principally applies), adherence to them is generally voluntary, they are formed through freedom of association, and

abstract but considering the facts of the dispute. When this general principle is applied to laws, practices and customs arising from legal pluralism a restriction, if any, imposed must not only be proportional to the potential threat or harm, but must also be established within the facts of a specific situation. In this regard the judgment of the ECtHR in the Refah Partisi case is open to criticism since the question of whether a political party should be dissolved was answered with a 'low standard of proof' applied. (McGoldrick 2009, 609) As political parties are such an essential element of a free and open democratic society, the banning of a party should arguably require a very high threshold and a high level of tolerance, particularly since there were not specific plans in place to harm the public interest. A restriction on a fundamental right is inevitably contextual, as illustrated by the interaction between freedom of expression and the varying limits imposed by different jurisdictions on purported hate speech. (De Villiers 2022e; Chapter 5)

enforcement primarily occurs through community traditions and customs rather than by state organs.

Thirdly, while state law applies to all persons within a territorially defined space (such as a country, region or local government), non-state law applies primarily to persons and not to territory. A person cannot therefore opt out of state law (unless they relocate), but can opt out of non-state law (for example by disassociating with the community concerned or refusing to comply with its rules). However, disassociating from a religious or indigenous customary community may be much more challenging in practice than it appears in theory.

Fourthly, legal pluralism can deepen democracy, enhance individual rights and freedoms and promote the principles of subsidiarity and self-determination. It is within the space of their community that an individual may feel most at home, fulfilled and acknowledged. However, if taken to its extreme, legal pluralism can also undermine national unity, erode social integration, weaken community cohesion, challenge the legitimacy of state law, encroach on individual rights and even cause violence or the breakup of the state. A balance is sought between the simplicity of state law and the recognition of diversity in the form of non-state law. That said, caution should be exercised to ensure that the universality of rights does not negate social plurality and the importance and value of non-state law and practices.

Fifthly, courts do not create legal pluralism; legal pluralism inherently exists within the social fabric as a fact. However, courts may determine whether a non-state legal system is recognised, what those non-state rules are, the relevance of non-state law to a proceeding, the relevance of non-state law in dispute resolution, its enforcement or implementation, and its consistency with the Constitution.

Sixthly, a threshold question arising from legal pluralism is what constitutes 'law'. This chapter does not purport to answer this question. Not all customs, practices, habits and beliefs of a community can be elevated to the status of 'law'.[65] For simplicity, I refer to non-state law in the context of a rule of conduct, whether written or unwritten, that impacts the rights and interests of those *who*

[65] Badejogbin suggests that recognition of non-state customary law by state law 'bestows on it [customary law] the status of state law'. (Badejogbin 2022, 254) This statement is open to challenge as is shown in chapter 10 since the mere fact that courts recognise an indigenous custom does not make the state the author of that custom. The principle of a separate legal system remains intact; it may evolve if aspects of it are recognised by courts. On the other hand, the way the courts have used Ubuntu has arguably shifted its ownership from the community to the state. But such a binary application of non-state law versus state law is in itself subject to criticism.

accept it as law. These rules are treated by an ethnocultural, religious or indigenous community as if possessing legal power, and they are capable of being enforced, either formally or informally, by the community from which they originate through means other than state sanction.

Seventhly, the following four principles are essential to harmonise legal pluralism in the judicial system in the context of state law and non-state law: (a) the individual must elect whether or not they submit to the authority of the non-state laws in general and the specific non-state legal norm of relevance to the dispute; (b) the non-state law must be consistent with the Constitution; (c) courts, ultimately, determine the validity and relevance of non-state law; and (d) the enforcement of law remains an exclusive function of state organs.

CHAPTER 3

CONSTITUTION DRAFTING AND CERTIFICATION

As we are liberated from our own fear, our presence automatically liberates others.

– Nelson Mandela, Inaugural Speech, 1994

3.1 INTRODUCTION

South Africa's constitution-drafting process did not originate from a grand design. It developed by trial and error, deadlock and breakthrough, and ultimately culminated in give and take in a compromise. The political forces involved had divergent objectives. On the one hand, the liberation parties, such as the ANC, PAC and SA Communist Party, sought a one-person-one vote election of a constitutional assembly to negotiate and draft a new constitution based solely on majoritarian principles. In contrast, parties such as the National Party, Progressive Federal Party, Inkatha Freedom Party, Conservative Party and other smaller parties sought assurances and guarantees that the rights of minorities – political, racial, indigenous and cultural – would be protected against outright majority rule. One side sought security in numbers, while the other side pursued security through an elite settlement and constitutionalism. As it turned out, these approaches proved neither achievable nor sustainable.

Both sides had merit to their arguments, finding substantial support in the literature of the time. For instance, social scientist Donald Horowitz theorised that in heterogeneous societies, cross-party alliances and freely formed coalitions between political parties should be developed informally based on a common identity and shared policies, rather than by relying on ethnic vetoes and quotas. In response, Lijphart argued that, in deeply divided societies, elections tend to become ethnic or racial referenda, resulting in the establishment of a permanent majority and permanent minorities. He proposed various forms of *formal* minority protection arrangements based on mandated cooperation between elites, such as a government of national unity, mutual vetoes, community autonomy (territorial and non-territorial) and minority quotas, pursuant to the concept of what he termed 'consociational democracy'. (Horowitz 1993; Lijphart 1969; Horowitz 1990; Lijphart 1977; Horowitz 1991)

Their respective approaches and offspring theories regarding the most effective means of addressing institutional design in deeply plural societies continue to stimulate debate in constitution drafting. Ironically, both schools of thought have found some application and justification of their respective theories in South Africa when analysing different phases of the post-1993 democratisation process. In a previous publication I pointed out that upon reflecting on the successes and failures of institutional designs in aspiring democracies since the 1990s it seems that the art of institutional design remains highly unpredictable regardless of the advances that have been made in political theory to better understand and manage political conflict. Theoretical expositions and comparisons eloquently explain in hindsight why certain models and approaches failed or succeeded. However, when looking forward the ability to predict which institutional designs will work or not work in a specific situation and what will be sustainable remains elusive and speculative. (De Villiers 2022g)[1] Bernauer and Vatter critically comment on Lijphart, but they also note the 'global trend towards democratic backsliding' (Bernauer and Vatter 2024, 425) which in turn highlights the complexity of constitutional design.

The constitutional transition in South Africa drew, to some extent, on the thoughts of both the Horowitz and Lijphart schools. On the one hand, the foundation of the first democratic election under the interim 1993 Constitution was a system of universal franchise, non-discrimination and equality in the Bill of Rights. (Steytler 2024a) On the other hand, explicit mechanisms to protect the rights of minorities were incorporated into the same Constitution. (Steytler 2024a) These mechanisms included a government of national unity for a transitional period, limited vetoes, proportional representation in the electoral

[1] Many variables may affect the democratisation process of a country, such as leadership, history, population composition, economic stability, social dynamics and land distribution, to name a few. Note, for example, the ongoing challenges experienced in democratisation efforts in central and eastern Europe, the Russian Federation, the Middle East, South America and parts of Africa such as Ethiopia, Sudan, South Sudan and Somalia.

system with no minimum threshold for a party to be elected, decentralisation to local and provincial governments,[2] recognition of the rights of tribal communities, recognition of the right of cultural communities to self-determination and to establish cultural councils (De Villiers 2014a), as well as cultural, linguistic and educational individual rights.[3] This was reflective of the 'liberal argument that modern states should be active contributors to pluralistic public spaces and defenders of cultural differences'. (Topidi 2024, 397)

Particularly relevant to this chapter are the Constitutional Principles that bound the Constitutional Assembly elected pursuant to the 1993 Constitution (also referred to as the interim constitution, given its intended lifespan of only three years). The Constitutional Principles became the embodiment of compromise and settlement. Sachs J described the role of the Constitutional Principles as follows:

> There is a lot of detail in the principles because this was our modality for making everybody feel comfortable with the proceedings and ensuring that no one felt the constitution was a result of the triumph of one section of society over another. (Sachs 1999, 673)

The focus of this chapter is on the unique process through which South Africa transitioned from apartheid to the enactment of the interim constitution of 1993, the conduct of the first democratic election in 1994, the adoption of the final constitution in 1996 and the final certification of the Constitution in 1997. This transitional process provides the background to the content of this book because

---

[2] One of the criteria for the demarcation of the provinces was linguistic and cultural residential patterns of the population. While the objective was not to create ethnic regions, the practical effect of historic and residential patterns is that most of the large language communities form a majority, or at least a substantial minority, within a specific province. (De Villiers 2008) South Africa cannot, however, be described as an ethnic federation, unlike Ethiopia, where regional demarcation was principally motivated by ethnic considerations, or Nigeria, where state creation to accommodate minorities based on an 'own' state has, since independence, led to an increase in the number of states from 3 to 36. Note also the efforts in northern Canada, Belgium, Italy, Spain and the Russian Federation to accommodate indigenous self-determination by way of territorial autonomy. (Wilson and Fondahl 2024)

[3] Powell comments that, although the idea of power-sharing as reflected in group autonomy and consociation 'had airtime during the constitutional changes', it never 'had the traction its proponents wanted'. (Powell 2024, 57) I explain below how the main proponent of power-sharing, the Afrikaners through the National Party, could not agree internally about what proposal for power-sharing to advance, since the right wing under the leadership of Constand Viljoen rejected any form of power-sharing and promoted an own *Volkstaat*, while the centre under the leadership of FW de Klerk confused a racially-based arrangement with cultural protection.

so much of the transition was influenced by the theme of how to respond to ethnocultural and indigenous diversity. The process was remarkable, given that it was designed and agreed upon hastily, had no international precedent and it remains unique in its design, short time frame and successful implementation.[4] Critics may say that 'the nuts-and-bolts legal rafting and technical expertise that crafted the present constitutional text and jurisprudence was largely dominated by an influential coterie of left-liberal human rights lawyers hailing mainly from the English-speaking law schools with strong leanings to Euro-American schools of legal thought', (Modiri 2024, 93), but in my experience and recollection the process was more inclusive and open than many critics today would acknowledge.

The aspect of the transition especially pertinent to this book is the adoption of 34 Constitutional Principles that were included in the 1993 Constitution, and with which the 1996 Constitution had to comply.[5] The Constitutional Court had the responsibility to certify that the 1996 Constitution met the standards set by those Constitutional Principles. (De Villiers 1994b) This is what I have referred to as the Great Settlement. The Constitutional Principles turned out to be 'significant in reassuring parties' that their interests would be accommodated, paving the way for a peaceful transition between the elite-based interim constitution of 1993 and the democratically drafted 1996 Constitution. (Maharaj 2008, 26)

Klug described the process whereby the Constitutional Principles served as a bridge and guarantee between the interim and final constitutions as a 'legal revolution'. (Klug 2010, 8) In its Certification case, the Constitution Court observed that 'judicial "certification" of a constitution is unprecedented . . .'. (Certification case 1996, para 1) Woolman describes the adoption of the Constitutional Principles as 'the most critical concession' by both sides of the negotiating process. (Woolman and Swanepoel 2013, 2–37)

The three-step transitional process is arguably *the* most important contribution the South African democratisation process has made to the international theory and practice of democratisation and transitional politics. (De Villiers 2021b)

The Constitutional Principles were effectively a political and legal guarantee that an elected constitutional assembly would be bound by essential democratic power-sharing checks and balances and power-distribution principles. The impact

---

[4] For a succinct overview of the process that led to the adoption of the 1993 Constitution, see Eloff, who played a leading role in facilitating the day-to-day management and coordination of the negotiation process. (Eloff 1994)

[5] The Constitutional Principles are included at the end of this chapter for convenience.

of unbridled majority rule within the Constitutional Assembly was therefore, in effect, attenuated by the limits outlined in the Constitutional Principles. (Kemp 2023, 169) Another important rationale for the Constitutional Principles was to 'keep the parties in the process' by showing them that their concerns or interests were being acknowledged. (Klug 2008, 184)[6]

Considering the above, it is appropriate that a chapter of a book that deals with an overview of judicial outcomes of litigation concerning ethnocultural and indigenous plurality is dedicated to the three-step transitional process, the principles underlying it and the certification of the Constitution by the Constitutional Court. At the time of drafting, there was no comparable case study to adopt and no roadmap to follow. Up until the publication of this book no other transition had taken the same route. It was a homegrown approach, standing as a unique inspiration and potential guide for other aspiring democracies dealing with the complexities of transition and the interaction between different political entities and communities.

In essence, the legal transition process from apartheid to democracy unfolded in three phases. The *first phase* involved negotiation of an interim constitution by unelected leaders representing political parties and political movements across the political spectrum (often referred to as the CODESA process). Some leaders had been elected, but only through the racially-based 1983 Constitution, some had been elected through apartheid-based homeland systems and some represented political and liberation movements. The collective leadership reflected a diverse mix of political parties and political movements, with no party having had its popular mandate tested. Accommodating these divergent interests and untested support was crucial in a transition where many tipping points could easily have derailed the process.

Each participating party held a potential veto, but in practice an approach of 'sufficient consensus' prevailed.[7] This meant that at least the main parties had to agree on an outcome – an undefined, informal arrangement of firsts among equals. (Horowitz 2021, 98) The first phase entailed negotiations of an interim constitution (later also known as the 1993 Constitution) under which the first democratic election would take place. The interim constitution was passed

[6] I can attest from own experience and observation at the time how parties were citing various parts of the Constitutional Principles to motivate to their supporters how their interests were being accommodated.

[7] Note that in the agreement to establish a government of national unity after the 2024 general election a similar phrase had been adopted for decision-making within the GNU.

into law on 2 December 1993 by the apartheid Parliament. (Constitution 1993) The first popular democratic election took place on 27 April 1994 pursuant to the 1993 Constitution. This concluded the first phase of the transition from an apartheid Parliament to a democratically elected Parliament.

The *second phase* of the transition commenced immediately after the first democratic election. The bicameral democratically elected Parliament had a dual function – to legislate as a sovereign national Parliament[8] *and* to be constituted as the Constitutional Assembly to draft a final constitution. This dual function – as both Parliament and constitutional assembly – presented unique challenges and, in turn, had an impact on the functioning of the government of national unity under the 1993 Constitution. On the one hand, parties were competing publicly for power and popularity in the legislative and executive process. On the other hand, the same parties had to cooperate and find common ground behind the scenes to draft a final Constitution.[9] The final Constitution had to comply with the Constitutional Principles that were enshrined in the 1993 Constitution. The second phase concluded when the Constitutional Assembly adopted the new Constitution on 11 October 1996.

The *third phase* commenced when the Constitutional Court had to certify that the 1996 Constitution complied with the Constitutional Principles enshrined in the 1993 Constitution. These two Constitutions, 1993 and 1996, were therefore

[8] Provision was also made for elected assemblies with guaranteed constitutional powers for the nine provinces. Part of the consensus reached between the parties was that a decentralised (not called federal, but nevertheless complying with federal elements) system would be created, whereby the Constitution would protect provincial and local governments, with guaranteed powers and functions under the supervision of the Constitutional Court. Since South Africa did not have any historic provinces that could be utilised for the purposes of decentralisation, a demarcation commission, on which I served as a technical expert, was established. Its role was to hear public submissions and propose the demarcation of provincial boundaries. Nine provinces were proposed and those boundaries have essentially remained unchanged. (De Villiers 2008; De Villiers 2012a; De Villiers 1993) Note Inman, who contends that 'democratic federalism' in South Africa, and the distributive effects via the provinces, played an essential role in the peaceful transition to democracy. (Inman and Rubinfeld 2013, 36)

[9] The complexities arising from simultaneous co-government *and* negotiating a constitution took their toll by undermining the partnership between the coalition partners and, in particular, eroding the personal relationship between Mr Mandela and Mr De Klerk. This ultimately led to the withdrawal of the National Party from the government of national unity. Ironically, the National Party's withdrawal left that party in a much weaker position politically, and it soon disbanded. The post-2024 arrangements for government of unity at national, provincial and local levels are likely to experience similar stress fractures, with parties constantly weighing up the pros and cons of working together versus running public campaigns against each other.

linked by the umbilical cord of the 34 Constitutional Principles. On 4 December 1996 the Constitutional Court certified that the 1996 Constitution complied with the Constitutional Principles set out in the 1993 Constitution. (Constitution of South Africa 1996) President Mandela promulgated the 1996 Constitution on 18 December 1996 and it took effect on 4 February 1997.[10] With this act, the legal transition process from apartheid to democracy had been completed.[11]

The three-step transitional process saw the leaders of political parties and movements across a wide political and social spectrum negotiate the 1993 Constitution, pursuant to which the first democratic election took place in 1994. These leaders had not been elected by the general population, but it was accepted that they collectively had adequate legitimacy and credibility among the respective constituents to negotiate an interim Constitution. The Constitutional Principles formulated by these unelected leaders were intended to act as a check on the powers of the elected Constitutional Assembly and to offer guarantees to minority and indigenous interests. The Constitutional Principles aimed to ensure that a final Constitution would adhere to essential principles of representative and responsible government, and to guarantee the decentralisation of powers and functions, protection of individual and minority rights, independence of the judiciary, recognition of customary law and traditional leaders, and supremacy of the law – all of which are hallmarks of constitutionalism and the rule of law. In the words of Klug, the Constitutional Court, through its certification process, 'civilized' the potential for conflict. (Klug 2008, 191) At the practical level of negotiations the Constitutional Principles served as a yardstick for parties to assess their own positions and evaluate proposals from the other side. Consequently, the Constitutional Principles directly influenced the style and content of the negotiations for the final Constitution by removing, or at least reducing and mitigating, the sharp edges and pushing the parties towards compromise.

Returning to the propositions made by Lijphart and Horowitz: the consociational process leading to the 1993 Constitution incorporated elements of segmental, community representation, accommodation of minority parties and

---

[10] The first text of the final Constitution was approved by the Constitutional Assembly on 8 May 1996. On 6 September 1996 the Constitutional Court held that not all the Constitutional Principles had been complied with in the first constitutional draft, and thus referred some aspects back to the Constitutional Assembly for further consideration. (Certification case 1996) The Constitutional Assembly approved further amendments and a second draft, leading to the final certification of the Constitution on 4 February 1997. (Certification Amended text case 1997)

[11] It is acknowledged that the socio-economic transformation process will take much longer to accomplish.

interests, autonomy for provinces, cultural and customary rights, and informal vetoes. Simultaneously, it laid the groundwork for the Horowitz propositions of informal rather than formal accommodation of minority interests through cooperation, coalition, proportional representation and exploration of mutual interests. (Lijphart 1998; Horowitz 2021, 100) In reality, however, coalition-forming has not come easy for South Africans.[12] The outcomes of all elections since 1994, including 2024, indicate that race and ethnicity remain prime motivators to predict and explain voting patterns. The hope that elections post-1994 would soon become issues-based rather than *de facto* racial and ethnic referenda remains unfulfilled.

The following essential principles, adopted in the 1993 Constitution, are particularly relevant to the subject of this book, which deals with the recognition of cultural and indigenous rights:

Constitutional Principle II

Everyone shall enjoy all universally accepted fundamental rights, freedoms and civil liberties, which shall be provided for and protected by entrenched and justiciable provisions in the Constitution, which shall be drafted after having given due consideration to inter alia the fundamental rights contained in Chapter 3 of this Constitution.

Constitutional Principle XI

The diversity of language and culture shall be acknowledged and protected, and conditions for their promotion shall be encouraged.

Constitutional Principle XII

Collective rights of self-determination in forming, joining and maintaining organs of civil society, including linguistic, cultural and religious associations, shall, on the basis of non-discrimination and free association, be recognised and protected.

Constitutional Principle XIII

The institution, status and role of traditional leadership, according to indigenous law, shall be recognised and protected in the Constitution. Indigenous law, like common law, shall be recognised and applied by the courts, subject to the fundamental rights contained in the Constitution and to legislation dealing specifically therewith.

---

[12] The 2024 general election introduced a new era whereby the 30-year one-party dominance at the national level was replaced with multi-party governance with national and provincial coalitions. Many who had been dreaming about the day when the ANC would itself become a minority party may, however, better understand the curse 'may you get what you wish for', since coalition government can be very unstable. The leadership and statesmanship required for coalition government to be effective and enduring post-2024 would have to match the leadership that gave rise to the 1996 Constitution.

Constitutional Principle XXXIV

1. This Schedule and the recognition therein of the right of the South African people as a whole to self-determination, shall not be construed as precluding, within the framework of the said right, constitutional provision for a notion of the right to self-determination by any community sharing a common cultural and language heritage, whether in a territorial entity within the Republic or in any other recognised way.
2. The Constitution may give expression to any particular form of self-determination provided there is substantial proven support within the community concerned for such a form of self-determination.
3. If a territorial entity referred to in paragraph 1 is established in terms of this Constitution before the new constitutional text is adopted, the new Constitution shall entrench the continuation of such territorial entity, including its structures, powers and functions.

The following section provides an overview of the process that led to the adoption of the Constitutional Principles in general, with a specific focus on the elements of the principles related to minority, indigenous and identity rights.[13]

3.2 PROCESS LEADING TO THE ADOPTION OF THE CONSTITUTIONAL PRINCIPLES

The process of political normalisation and transition started formally on 2 February 1990 with the announcement of the unbanning of liberation movements and the release of political prisoners. The transitional process included setting up several interim executive structures that coordinated day-to-day policy between the then government and the liberation movements until such time that a democratic government had been elected. (Heunis 1994) The formal process of structured multiparty negotiations commenced on 20 December 1991 with the Convention for a Democratic South Africa (CODESA), in which around 20 political parties, movements and organisations participated. The CODESA process adopted a joint accord to negotiate a constitution and engage in other interim and transitional arrangements. In May 1992 the CODESA process became gridlocked and ground to a halt owing to disagreements about issues such as power-sharing, federalism, minority protection and other essential

[13] In this book, I use the term 'identity rights' to refer to those fundamental human rights that relate particularly to the unique cultural, religious, linguistic and customary rights of individuals, such as the right to culture, language, religion, script and customary law.

elements of a future constitution. In April 1993 the negotiations resumed with the establishment of the Multi-Party Negotiation Forum (MPNF).[14]

The MPNF comprised the following informal[15] institutional arrangements: a *Plenary Session*, in which all the participating organisations, political parties and political movements had a seat. In theory all the participants enjoyed equal status, with each holding a potential veto. In practice, however, it was accepted that, at least, the agreement of the National Party/government and ANC was required for a decision. Nonetheless, in certain aspects the approval of the other parties was also deemed essential, such as for the powers and functions of provinces, the potential Volkstaat (Norval 1998) and the recognition of traditional leaders. This was informally referred to as the principle of 'sufficient consensus'.[16] The *Negotiating Council*, the principal working body, played a crucial role in disseminating the reports and recommendations made by the respective working groups. The *Planning Committee* consisted of key negotiators, who did not, however, necessarily represent all the parties and movements. The Planning Committee played an operational role in keeping the negotiations moving forward, identifying and resolving issues, and making recommendations to the Negotiating Council. *Technical Committees*, seven in total, comprised technical experts and were tasked with making recommendations on the technical aspects of the constitutional arrangements. The rationale behind the Technical Committees was to involve individuals from academia and practice with high levels of skills and knowledge in these quasi-negotiations without their necessarily representing a firm political conviction. The Technical Committees were designed to prevent and resolve conflicts by fostering common ground on the technical aspects of the Constitution to be settled. In addition to the Technical Committees, two specialist bodies were established: the Commission on the Demarcation of Provinces[17] and the Commission on National Symbols.

---

[14] For a collection of material and documents that formed part of the transitional process, see the UNESCO collection. (UNESCO collection 2012)

[15] These arrangements were 'informal' in the sense that there was no statute or international protocol to give effect to them. The process worked by mutual agreement, rather than by statutory obligation or international oversight.

[16] As explained above, 'sufficient consensus' was an undefined term. The level of actual consent required depended on the specific issue for which agreement was sought. Van Wyk describes it in the following way: 'Although it is fair to say that sufficient consensus was not readily declared, if either of the large parties, the ANC or government [NP], objected to a resolution, it was not a hard-and-fast rule.' (Van Wyk 1994, 141)

[17] I was a technical advisor to the Commission on the Demarcation of Provinces and assisted with the drafting of the recommendations that were ultimately accepted by the Negotiating

The remarkable aspect that underpinned these respective committees was the commitment of the political parties in general, and the experts in particular, to develop common ground, secure consensus and accommodate diverse interests. (Eloff 1994, 17) The procedures followed by the committees were informal, flexible, non-legalistic and generally non-dogmatic, marked by an underlying attitude that failure could not be contemplated.[18] In their operations the committees also relied on and utilised international expertise in comparative constitutional models and techniques for conflict resolution. Regardless of the differing positions held by the respective parties, the process was supported by a deep commitment to keep things going forward.

On 2 July 1993 the Negotiating Council accepted a package of Constitutional Principles to be included in the interim constitution, with which the permanent constitution would have to comply. This represented a significant breakthrough in the negotiations, solidifying the transition from an interim to a final Constitution. It provided certainty to the minority parties *and* liberation parties alike that a Constitution could be drafted by a popularly elected constitutional assembly within the framework of essential, broadly agreed to Constitutional Principles.

Ultimately 34 Constitutional Principles were adopted. These pertained to the sovereignty of the state, principles of equality and non-discrimination, a Bill of Rights, a three-tier government, the decentralisation of powers and functions, collective rights to self-determination, the recognition of customary law and traditional leaders, the separation of powers, criteria for the allocation of powers and functions to provincial and local governments,

---

Council and the Plenary Session for the demarcation of provinces. Those demarcations have essentially remain unchanged, which is remarkable if compared with some other countries where regional/provincial boundary demarcations have been highly political and even conflictual. (Commission on Demarcation 1993) Notable in this regard is Nigeria, which moved relatively quickly from three regions to 36 states and a capital territory. Furthermore, it is worth noting the instability and violence that have arisen in Ethiopia, Indonesia and South Sudan in relation to federal boundaries. In India there are ongoing demands for the creation of additional states. Germany also went through a complex and highly politically charged process of adjusting *Länder* (state) boundaries after its unification. (Leonardy 2003) The South African provincial boundaries, except for a few provincial border towns, have been widely accepted.

[18] Many serious political events threatened the negotiation process, such as the assassination of SACP leader Chris Hani, ongoing township violence, the state of emergency, the withdrawal of COSAG (an alliance of political parties and movements) from the negotiation process, the risk of right-wing violence, and the internal constituency pressure experienced by each of the negotiating parties. At more than one stage the entire process 'hung in the balance' and could easily have been derailed. (Eloff 1994, 19)

the establishment of independent institutions of oversight, the organisation of the civil service, the right to self-determination of cultural communities, and the supremacy of the Constitutional Court (see the annexure to this chapter for the Constitutional Principles).[19]

These adopted Principles embodied a wide-spectrum compromise and served a dual purpose: first, they facilitated the buy-in of minority parties to endorse an elected constitutional assembly by assuring them that the assembly's actions would align with the fundamental Principles; at the same time, the Principles reassured the liberation parties that the majority within the Constitutional Assembly would possess the latitude to draft the finer details of a future constitution, while exercising its discretion within the limits set by the Principles. The critical element of the compromise was the requirement for the Constitutional Court to certify that the final Constitution complied with the Constitutional Principles enshrined in the interim Constitution. The role and function of the Constitutional Principles arose spontaneously, with none of the parties having proposed such an arrangement in their initial negotiation positions. (De Villiers 1994b, 37)[20]

In its Certification judgment the Constitutional Court summarised the positions of the opposing sides as follows:

> The government and other minority groups were prepared to relinquish power to the majority but were determined to have a hand in drawing the framework for the future governance of the country. The liberation movements on the opposition side were equally adamant that only democratically elected representatives of the people could legitimately engage in forging a constitution: neither they, and certainly not the government of the day, had any claim to the requisite mandate from the electorate. (Certification case 1996, para 12)

---

[19] It is noted that self-determination is not a term of art and hence its meaning adapts, evolves and changes. Jones speaks about the changing nature of self-determination as 'irksome' but also a 'great strength' since the ambiguity allows for development. (Jones 2024, 18)

[20] The suggestion has been made that the ANC had, in the Harare Declaration, initiated the concept of the Constitutional Principles. (Harare Declaration 1989) However, such a proposition is not supported by proper analysis. Although the Harare Declaration identified important principles of a democratic government, these were used in a generic sense, akin to a political manifesto. Most importantly, the Declaration was not used in the context of serving as a legal *nexus* and assurance between the interim and final Constitutions. The nuanced nature of the Constitutional Principles, including their specific details and the subsequent certification process by the Constitutional Court, arose spontaneously and played a pivotal role in bridging this gap. Van Wyk also observes that the negotiation process had an open-ended beginning, with none of the parties submitting a draft constitution that could be used as a point of departure for negotiation. Instead, the certification process developed organically without a master plan. (Van Wyk 1994, 157)

The process leading to the adoption and drafting of the Constitutional Principles involved difficulties in distinguishing 'principles' (to be included in the Constitutional Principles) from 'details' (to be left to the discretion of the Constitutional Assembly). Differentiating between what could be termed a *principle*, serving as the foundation for a future constitution, and what constituted a *detail* of specific arrangements to give effect to the principle, proved challenging for the technical advisors and political negotiators participating in the process. In practice it soon became apparent that what certain parties considered a principle, like constitutionally protected provincial governments with a list of guaranteed powers, was a matter of detail to other parties.[21] The liberation parties were concerned that a greater level of detail included in the Constitutional Principles would limit the scope and discretion of the Constitutional Assembly to draft a final Constitution. In contrast, the minority parties worried that, without adequate detail in the Constitutional Principles, the majority party in the Constitutional Assembly would have carte blanche when drafting the final Constitution. The fear, animosity and distrust the parties displayed toward each other were reflected in the intensity of the debate about the level of detail to be included in the Constitutional Principles.

The phrase 'headline negotiations' aptly described this situation where parties seemingly agreed in public on the essential elements for the future constitution. However, whenever details were discussed, it became apparent that any private agreement on a constitutional principle was wafer-thin in the public arena. The

[21] While the ANC, for example, was willing to consent to some form of decentralised regional government as a principle, some other parties sought greater certainty about the actual list of provincial powers. Those parties advocated for not only constitutionalising provincial government but also outlining its powers and functions in the Constitutional Principles, following a federal model as a principle. The ANC model favoured a decentralised, unitary state approach, whereas some of the other parties favoured an explicit federal approach. They proposed setting out the actual powers and functions of provinces in the Constitutional Principles. An ad hoc technical team, on which I served, attempted to specify particular powers and functions for the to-be-created provinces. However, since this proved impracticable we settled on drafting essential principles, which were later included in the Constitutional Principles (XVI–XXIV). Those principles outlined what we believed were appropriate to establish constitutionally protected second-tier government without explicitly labelling it federal or decentralised unitary. I held the opinion then, and continue to do so, that those principles established what could be called a federal state. (De Villiers 1995) Elazar, who at the time was arguably internationally the most eminent scholar in the theory and practice of federalism and who had visited South Africa during the initial negotiation process, concurred that the Constitutional Principles and the 1993 Constitution complied with federal characteristics. (Elazar 1994, 36)

public disagreements that arose about the content of the Constitutional Principles threatened to undermine the good faith and trust that privately exited between the parties. On the one hand, this re-energised the minorities to seek even more detailed Constitutional Principles. On the other hand, the liberation parties were motivated anew to pursue very vague principles, fearing being hamstrung in the Constitutional Assembly by too much detail in the Constitutional Principles.

Extensive efforts were made at a technical level to bridge the gap between principle and detail. For instance, the disagreements about the future nature of provincial government led to a report about greater detail of provincial powers and functions compiled by a group of technical experts in March 1993. This report outlined a future framework for provincial and local government and served as the basis for multiparty consensus on the principles and the broad framework of provincial and local government.[22]

The adoption of the Constitutional Principles was a major reassurance and compromise for both sides of the negotiation table. One side accepted that the final Constitution would be drafted by a majority in the Constitutional Assembly, while the other side accepted that the scope of the Constitutional Assembly would be restricted by the Constitutional Principles. Both sides acknowledged that, while the Constitutional Assembly would be bound by the Constitutional Principles, those Principles would lose their efficacy immediately upon the enactment of the 1996 Constitution. Therefore, the Constitutional Principles would not limit any future Parliament from amending the Constitution.[23]

---

[22] The report, entitled 'Regions in South Africa', led to one of the major breakthroughs in the negotiations, as it enabled the pro-federal parties, such as the Inkatha Freedom Party, National Party and the Progressive Federal Party, to endorse the process. It also made movements such as the ANC feel comfortable with the principle and some detail of provincial government without the word 'federal' being used. (Expert Report Provinces 1993) I participated, under the facilitation of Clive Menell and Frederick Van Zyl Slabbert, in a two-month roadshow, which included a presentation to President Mandela and his constitutional advisors, to explain the report to key political, business and financial stakeholders to secure their backing for a constitutionally entrenched system of provincial and local government.

[23] There was some theoretical debate at the time of the enactment of the Constitution whether any future amendments to it would also have to comply with the Constitutional Principles. While this question is interesting from a theoretical perspective, it is moot since there is nothing in the 1996 Constitution or the debates in the Constitutional Assembly to suggest that any future amendments to the Constitution would have to comply with the Constitutional Principles. The 1996 Constitution can be amended pursuant to its own provisions, with no further reference to the Constitutional Principles of the 1993 Constitution. (Constitution of South Africa 1996, s 74)

Particularly relevant for the purposes of this book is how the Constitutional Principles were to deal with the pluralism of South Africa and how ethnocultural realities of the country could or should be reflected in institutional design. Examples include the recognition of customary law vis-à-vis the provision of the Bill of Rights, collective rights for cultural and linguistic minority groups, the protection of individual rights related to culture, language and identity, and the question of whether the state should fund communities to maintain, protect and promote their unique languages, cultures and traditions.

Considering the apartheid background of South Africa, in which racial and ethnic identity had been used as the basis for extensive discriminatory laws and practices, the recognition of any form of right – be it individual or collective – within the context of race, language or cultural rights for communities and members of communities was unpalatable. However, minority parties, particularly those from within the Afrikaans community[24] but also from within

The Constitutional Principles had served their purpose and are now historic. (Rautenbach and Malherbe 2004, 31)

[24] There was fierce debate within the Afrikaans community about the most appropriate way to protect their interests. On the one hand, under the leadership of FW de Klerk, a power-sharing approach was adopted, envisioning that through formal and informal alliances a one-party dominant system could be prevented. On the other hand, on the right of the spectrum under the leadership of Constand Viljoen, the emphasis was placed on a territorial solution called a Volkstaat where Afrikaners could govern themselves. The Volkstaat idea implied that the area would essentially withdraw from the rest of South Africa and, as a result, the right-wing made minimal contributions to the wider constitutional debate about minority or cultural rights. The Volkstaat idea never materialised, save for an informal territorial arrangement called Orania in the Northern Cape province, where around 4 000 people reside. (De Villiers 2014a, 50) Mokwena refers to Orania as a 'micronation'. (Mokwena 2024, 2) The informal power-sharing model likewise failed to materialise, although now, after some 30 years, the dominance of the ANC is waning and coalition governments at all levels are becoming reality. The question could be posed whether the 1993 government of national unity should have been retained for longer (even if by way of informal arrangements). However, the political climate between the ANC and NP, as well as the personal relationship between Mandela and De Klerk, had become so toxic that the NP withdrew before the initial term of the government of national unity had been completed. As an observer, I found it ironic that, at the time of the NP's withdrawal from the government of national unity, while it was advocating the Lijphart principle of elite cooperation, in practice, the NP had come to believe (mistakenly) that it could, in the future, become the majority party. The NP felt, however, that the government of national unity with the ANC had shackled it, preventing it from reaching its 'full potential' in the electorate. The withdrawal of the NP from the government of national unity was therefore, from the perspective of some within the NP, deemed a necessity for the party to challenge the ANC at the ballot box and potentially become a majority party in the future. Ironically, this decision enhanced a majoritarian rather than the consociational approach. This tactic proved to be a fatal miscalculation, leading to the

the ranks of traditional leaders, felt that the very existence and survival of their cultural identities, legal pluralism and indigenous customs were potentially under threat. The working group dealing with the Bill of Rights thus had to grapple with these issues.

The recognition of customary law was a subject of intense debate, revolving around the challenge of reconciling it with a contemporary Bill of Rights. (Du Plessis 1994, 98) Concerns were raised that certain customs and practices within customary law, such as access to and management of tribal land, rights of minors and women, and the administration of criminal justice might be inconsistent with fundamental rights.[25] In a broader context the question was whether a sustainable separate indigenous legal order could exist, where the rights of certain individuals depended on whether they fell within the jurisdiction of a customary or constitutional system. While the reality of a customary system was accepted, the question revolved around the extent to which such a non-state legal system would operate, if at all, solely within the context of people's private lives or become part of the formal legal order of the country.[26]

---

disbandment of the NP shortly after its withdrawal from the government of national unity. The hope of the NP to use the GNU to win a next election is mirrored some three decades later in a statement by ANC Secretary General Fikile Mbalula, who said the post-2024 GNU is only a 'tactical decision' for the ANC to return to majority at the next election. (Delport 2024, 2) This highlights that neither the NP in 1996 nor the ANC in 2024 saw the respective GNUs as a requirement for stability *regardless* of the political support those parties receive. My impression in the late 1990s was that both President Mandela and President Mbeki had an openness to continue a GNU even if not mandated by the Constitution, but putting together a joint policy platform for GNU at the time would have been challenging.

[25] Note, for example, the Bhe case, in which the court struck down the indigenous rule of primogeniture. (Bhe case 2005) The concern about non-state laws being in breach of the Bill of Rights not only related to customary law. There was also concern that some of the religious practices of certain communities may be in breach of the fundamental rights of the Constitution. In this regard Sachs (prior to his appointment as a Justice of the Constitutional Court) made the following observation about the application of Sharia to individuals of the Islamic faith: 'The sovereignty of sharia in matters of faith cannot be questioned. It is quite clear that on questions of religious organizations, attendance at mosque, marriage ceremonies and burial rites, the Constitution will not intervene. Yet there might be other areas where, for example, Muslim women might wish to seek the aid of the courts, just as non-Muslim women do, to protect themselves against unjust behaviour by husbands, fathers or sons who might be abusive.' (Sachs 1990, 90) This topic is discussed in greater detail in Chapter 8.

[26] This debate about the recognition of customary law resonates in some respects with the debate about the recognition of customs and practices of non-indigenous cultural communities. Cultural and linguistic identity rights attach to the individual, not to a group as a collective entity, and the exercise of those rights is by way of individual remedy, even if the rights can sometimes

The concept of legal pluralism was not explicitly used in the negotiations, but the underlying theme of how to accommodate both state law and non-state customary law within the same governmental system had a consistent presence in the negotiations. Constitutional Principle XIII outlined as follows the institution, status and role of traditional leadership, as well as the application of indigenous law by the courts – it is noteworthy that traditional laws and customs are subservient to the constitutional Bill of Rights:

> **Constitutional Principle XIII**
>
> The institution, status and role of traditional leadership, according to indigenous law, shall be recognised and protected in the Constitution. Indigenous law, like common law, shall be recognised and applied by the courts, ***subject to*** the fundamental rights contained in the Constitution and to legislation dealing specifically therewith. (emphasis added)

The demand for recognition of a form of collective rights for cultural and linguistic communities within the domain of public law became a serious hurdle in the finalisation of the 1993 Constitution. While the National Party/government had primarily sought a form of power-sharing arrangement, the right-wing Afrikaner Volksfront movement pursued territorial self-determination through a homeland or Volkstaat for Afrikaners. In a last-minute effort to secure the support of the right-wing Afrikaners for the 1983 Constitution and owing to concerns about the risk of violence, including a potential military coup by current and former soldiers, the National Party government and the ANC entered into an Accord with the Freedom Front on 23 April 1994, just a few days before the first non-racial general election was scheduled to take place. The Accord provided that an Afrikaner homeland, as well as all other 'possible forms of Afrikaner self-determination', would be the subject of further research and negotiation after the

---

only be realised as a form of class action in association with others of the same community. This approach is consistent with the interpretation that has been given to art 27 of the International Covenant on Civil and Political Rights. (ICCPR Comment Minorities 1994) While there is greater acceptance under international law of the *collective* right to self-determination for indigenous people based on their pre-settlement sovereignty, pursuant to the Universal Declaration of the Rights of Indigenous People (UNDRIP) (UNDRIP 2007), practically the legal systems and norms that regulate the lives of indigenous people and cultural minorities typically operate within the private realm or non-state law, rather than being integrated into public (state) law. (Chapter 2) As I explain below, international law does not recognise collective rights by ethnocultural communities as if the community is a distinct legal entity. But, as McCorquodale points out, in practice, there is both an acknowledgement and application of groups having rights distinct from the rights of individuals. (McCorquodale 2022, 284)

election.[27] It was anticipated that international mediation may also be required in those negotiations. Constitutional Principle XXXIV provided as follows:

Constitutional Principle XXXIV

1. This Schedule and the recognition therein of the right of the South African people as a whole to self-determination, shall not be construed as precluding, within the framework of the said right, constitutional provision for a notion of the right to self-determination by any community sharing a common cultural and language heritage, whether in a territorial entity within the Republic or in any other recognised way.
2. The Constitution may give expression to any particular form of self-determination provided there is substantial proven support within the community concerned for such a form of self-determination.
3. If a territorial entity referred to in paragraph 1 is established in terms of this Constitution before the new constitutional text is adopted, the new Constitution shall entrench the continuation of such territorial entity, including its structures, powers and functions.

As far as collective rights are concerned, the Bill of Rights in the 1993 Constitution and the Constitutional Principles emphasised the individuality of identity rights. Rights can be exercised in association with other persons, but the bearer of the right is the individual and not the community to which the individual may belong. While this is consistent with the interpretation given to art 27 of the ICCPR,[28] there were strong propositions from within the Afrikaans community who believed that some form of collective right for Afrikaner self-determination

[27] This was arguably one of the biggest capitulations of negotiations where on the eve of the 1994 election the only concession Constand Viljoen could draw was an undertaking that research would be conducted into his political proposal.

[28] In the Fosen case the Supreme Court of Norway ruled that the construction of a windfarm violated the rights of the indigenous Sámi to enjoy their culture pursuant to art 27 of the ICCPR. The windfarm constituted a 'significant adverse effect' on their cultural rights to practise reindeer herding. (Fosen case 2021) The interesting aspect of the judgment for purposes of this book is that the rights of the community collectively were upheld pursuant to an individual rights to enjoy culture. This highlights how the seeming divide between an individual right and a collective right can be overcome within the context of art 27 of the ICCPR. The collective exercise of an individual right does not, however, translate into political rights of self-determination on a collective basis. This reflects the opinion of Kymlicka, who views identity rights not as collective 'group' rights, but as rights that are exercised collectively by individuals. He summarises this position as follows: '[M]ost [group rights] are not about the primacy of communities over individuals. Rather, they are based on the idea that justice between groups requires that the members of different groups are accorded different rights.' (Kymlicka 1995, 47)

should be included as a constitutional principle.[29] They were, however, not able to produce a concrete or detailed proposal that reflected their political desire.[30]

The following Constitutional Principles relating to cultural and linguistic rights were duly included in the 1993 Constitution:

> **Constitutional Principle II**
>
> Everyone shall enjoy all universally accepted fundamental rights, freedoms and civil liberties, which shall be provided for and protected by entrenched and justiciable provisions in the Constitution, which shall be drafted after having given due consideration to inter alia the fundamental rights contained in Chapter 3 of this Constitution.
>
> **Constitutional Principle III**
>
> The Constitution shall prohibit racial, gender and all other forms of discrimination and shall promote racial and gender equality and national unity.
>
> **Constitutional Principle XI**
>
> The diversity of language and culture shall be acknowledged and protected, and conditions for their promotion shall be encouraged.

---

29 While it is accepted in contemporary literature and jurisprudence that art 27 of the ICCPR is the mainstay of international law for the protection of minorities, it must be noted that, under the League of Nations, efforts had already been made to protect the rights of minorities collectively, even though this was not regarded as a universal principle, but rather applicable to specific problem areas. (Chapter 4) It is also noteworthy that contemporary international law recognises the collective rights of indigenous people *in addition* to the individual rights of persons belonging to an indigenous community. This prompts the following question: Why, as a matter of principle, does an indigenous community have a collective right under ILO 169 and UNDRIP, while a similar right is not accorded to an ethnocultural community? (De Villiers 2023f, 20) The answer is usually found in the pre-existing sovereign systems of indigenous people, which generally do not apply to ethnocultural minorities.

30 Numerous issues of relevance to community self-determination – such as the role of race and the Christian faith in defining the community, the definition of the Afrikaans community, representation of the community, the nature of self-determination (territorial or non-territorial) and the specific collective rights sought in public law – lacked agreement within the Afrikaans community, and still do. Note, for example, how the Afrikaner Declaration of 2024 relies on the term 'Afrikaner' rather than on the Afrikaans language community, and thereby (again) seeking to define the Afrikaner along racial lines rather than inclusively on the basis of language. (Afrikaner Declaration 2024) In respect of the minority protection provisions of the Constitution, Henrard observed as follows: 'The current minority rights standards [in the 1996 Constitution] are indeed rather weak in that they include many escape clauses, leaving too much discretion to the state; avoid the recognition of clear positive state obligations regarding minorities; and do not substantially acknowledge and protect the essential group dimension of the minority phenomenon.' (Henrard 2002, 16) However, Henrard's criticism did not adequately acknowledge that, despite theoretical room for improvement to the minority rights provisions in the 1996 Constitution, the Constitution as drafted arguably met the standards of international law at the time. (Chapter 4)

> **Constitutional Principle XII**
>
> Collective rights of self-determination in forming, joining and maintaining organs of civil society, including linguistic, cultural and religious associations, shall, on the basis of non-discrimination and free association, be recognised and protected.

An initial set of Constitutional Principles was adopted by the Negotiating Council on 2 July 1993, with the addition of further Principles on 17 November 1993 and in March and April 1994.

Legally, the effect of the Constitutional Principles was set out as follows in the 1993 Constitution: the Constitution that follows the 1993 Constitution shall comply with the Constitutional Principles enshrined in the 1993 Constitution; (Constitution 1993 1993, s 71(1)) the Constitutional Principles are annexed to the 1993 Constitution; (Constitution 1993 1993, Sched 4) the Constitutional Court shall certify that the Constitution complies with the Constitutional Principles; (Constitution 1993 1993, s 72(2)) any proposed constitutional provision that is the subject of negotiation may be referred to the Constitutional Court for a declaratory order on whether it complies with the relevant Constitutional Principles; (Constitution 1993 1993, s 71(4)) any provincial constitution would also have to be certified as in compliance with the Constitutional Principles; (Constitution 1993 1993, s 160(3))[31] the final ruling of the Constitutional Court is binding and cannot be the subject of any litigation or proceeding before another court. (Constitution 1993 1993, s 71(3))

In an assessment of the Constitutional Principles shortly after their adoption, I described them as follows:

> The application of the Constitutional Principles will be one of the greatest challenges that future legislatures, the Constitutional Assembly, and the courts will have to contend with.

[31] To date, only two efforts have been made to enact a provincial constitution, with both drafts arising from provinces where a party other than the ANC held the majority. In the Western Cape the effort was successful and the provincial constitution was certified by the Constitutional Court (Western Cape Constitution 1997), whereas in KwaZulu-Natal the Constitutional Court declined to certify the draft constitution. (KwaZulu/Natal Certification 1996) KwaZulu-Natal has not made another attempt to enact a constitution and no other province has pursued a constitution of its own. Time will tell if provincial constitution-drafting may become more relevant as the political power of the ANC within provinces declines. For example, in some provinces different forms of *governments of provincial unity* (GPU) may be considered as an institutional mandate to provide some stability, rather than relying on ad hoc coalition agreements that have proven to be elusive and unstable at the local government level. Given the crisis in various areas of public service delivery, the potential for political stability and the pooling of resources and expertise, a constitutionally protected government of provincial unity may become an attractive option.

> The South African principles were born of the general suspicion, fear, and distrust the different parties had of one another, and in particular the suspicion and fear of minority parties in respect of the anticipated majority party. *The Constitutional Principles are accordingly underpinned by different interpretations and intentions.* Some of the parties see them as an indispensable 'insurance policy' and 'guarantee', while others regard them as a forced compromise that, in the medium and long term, can have a curtailing and inhibiting impact on the popular will. (emphasis added) (De Villiers 1994b, 46)

In the following section the certification of the 1996 Constitution is considered in general, with a specific focus on its provisions pertaining to safeguarding the rights of cultural, linguistic, religious and indigenous communities.

3.3 CERTIFICATION OF THE 1996 CONSTITUTION

On 4 December 1996 the Constitutional Court certified that the 1996 Constitution complied with the Constitutional Principles enshrined in the 1993 Constitution. (Constitution of South Africa 1996) The 1996 Constitution duly took effect on 4 February 1997.[32]

In the reasoning of the Constitutional Court the following parts of the judgment are particularly relevant to this book:

Solemn pact

The Constitutional Court acknowledged that the Constitutional Principles constituted a 'solemn pact' among the negotiating parties. The pact facilitated the breakthrough that was so needed in the negotiations. (Certification case 1996, para 15) Those Principles were 'crucial' to the process of certification. The function of the court was to certify the entirety of the constitutional text, but not to reformulate, to second guess deals done or to 'improve' it. However, at the same time the court had a broader function than 'merely checking off each individual provision' of the constitution against the Constitutional Principles. (Certification case 1996, para 17)

---

[32] The first text of the final Constitution was approved by the Constitutional Assembly on 8 May 1996. On 6 September 1996 the Constitutional Court held that not all the Constitutional Principles had been complied with in the first constitutional draft. (Certification case 1996) The court did observe, however, that the clauses of non-compliance did not present a 'significant obstacle' to the overall certification. (Certification case 1996, paras 481–482) On 11 October 1996 the Constitutional Assembly approved further amendments and a second draft to address the shortcomings identified by the Constitutional Court, thereby leading to the certification of the Constitution on 4 December 1996 and its proclamation on 4 February 1997. (Certification Amended text case 1997)

Mandate of the Constitutional Court

The Constitutional Court emphasised that in its certification mandate it exercised a judicial function rather than a political one. (Certification case 1996, para 27)[33] The certification process could therefore not be used to re-argue a political position, revisit a preferred constitutional option that had not gained support during the negotiation process, or insert a clause into the new Constitution that had been included in the 1993 Constitution.[34] The court stressed that its assessment was not based on the provisions of the 1993 Constitution in general, but only on the Constitutional Principles included in the 1993 Constitution. The court reiterated that the political choices about appropriate constitutional institutions had been made by the Constitutional Assembly and the role of the court was to certify that those political choices complied with the Constitutional Principles.[35] The court was not to improve the text or cast political judgment on the appropriateness of the solemn pact. The court described the Constitution as a 'monumental achievement'. (Certification case 1996, para 31) The initial refusal of the Constitutional Court to certify the constitution was 'without precedent' and demonstrated the court's authority to independently scrutinise the text.[36]

[33] Implementing this was challenging, as the certification process, unlike a conventional legal dispute, involved value judgments and discretion regarding an appropriate constitutional model in its entirety in relation to a Constitutional Principle. Choices made about institutional arrangements are more susceptible to political preference, discretion and give and take than legal arguments in ordinary litigation.

[34] The Constitutional Court recognised the inherently political nature of adopting a constitution, acknowledging that the final text had involved compromise and negotiation. One could therefore not read any specific clause in isolation since its formulation may reflect a compromise that had been reached regarding another section. In this way the Constitutional Assembly had overwhelmingly adopted the constitutional text. The court was not to be used as an academic forum to argue whether certain sections could be better formulated or whether certain provisions could be strengthened, expanded or enhanced. Critics may highlight (then and now) how specific clauses could be better or differently formulated, but the court had to adopt a holistic approach.

[35] As discussed in chapter 6, there was ironically no objection raised in either the Constitutional Assembly or the Constitutional Court about the exclusion of the concept of Ubuntu from the 1996 Constitution. Although Ubuntu had appeared in the 1993 Constitution, it made no appearance in the 1996 Constitution.

[36] Woolman and Swanepoel note, in their interpretation of the respective clauses, that 'despite its initial claims that its judgment was purely legal and in no way political, the Constitutional Court did adopt interpretations of the next text [second draft of the constitution] that clearly reflected a preferred political reading of the new text'. (Woolman and Swanepoel 2013, para 2.42)

Principles of interpretation

The court had to determine at the outset what principles of interpretation would apply to give effect to the Constitutional Principles. The court emphasised that the Constitutional Principles had to be interpreted conducive to the objectives of a new democratic constitution, but cautioned against an overly technical approach. Furthermore, the court stressed the need for a holistic interpretation of the Constitutional Principles, considering them as integral parts of a larger framework. This approach aimed to assess the draft constitution in its entirety rather than scrutinising individual clauses disjunctively.[37] As such, the new constitution had to comply in all respects with all the Constitutional Principles.[38] Any interpretation of any Constitutional Principle which might impede the realisation of this objective had to be avoided. The court thus embraced a purposive approach, rather than employing a technical, black-letter, or restrictive interpretation, explaining it as follows:

> The Constitutional Principles must be applied purposively and teleologically to give expression to the commitment 'to create a new order' based on 'a sovereign and democratic constitutional state' in which 'all citizens' are 'able to enjoy and exercise their fundamental rights and freedoms'. (Certification case 1996, para 34)

Structural and specific compliance

The court explained that in the discharge of its duties it first had to be satisfied that the new Constitution complied with the Constitutional Principles overall,

---

[37] The reason for this approach is that in the negotiation process parties may have reached agreement on the wording of a specific clause based on another clause being formulated in a certain way. It would be inconsistent with the process of give and take for the court to solely weigh the merit of individual clauses without taking account of the entirety of the text. Retrospective criticism of the Constitution in general or specific clauses in particular often ignores the reality in which each clause was drafted, which critics often suggesting what they would have preferred, not what could have been agreed. The following are a few examples of constitutional provisions on which there was give and take: constitutional entrenchment of provincial government; protection of property rights; inclusion of the right to mother-tongue education; the inclusion of a right to self-determination of communities; and the recognition of official languages.

[38] At the conclusion of its first Certification case the court found that only a few clauses of the proposed Constitution did not comply in all respects with the Constitutional Principles. The entire constitutional text was remitted to the Constitutional Assembly to make the necessary adjustments and resubmit it for reconsideration and certification, duly leading to the certification of the final text. (Certification Amended text case 1997) In its reassessment the court adopted the reasons for judgment in the first certification and refused to entertain any re-arguing of clauses that had already been accepted.

in terms of the general structure, checks and balances, and other constitutional guarantees. Additionally, the specific provisions of the new constitution had to be weighed against the specific provisions of the Constitutional Principles. (Certification case 1996, paras 44–46)

Specific provisions

The Constitutional Court explained that, although the 1993 Constitution contained a Bill of Rights, the final Constitution did not have to contain exactly the same rights, provided that the general ambit of rights as stated in Constitutional Principle II had been met.[39] The Constitutional Assembly could therefore expand, reduce or reformulate the scope of rights provided for in the 1993 Constitution on condition that the standard set by the relevant Constitutional Principle was fulfilled. The court noted the following about the general characterisation of the Bill of Rights:

> It should be emphasised that in general the Bill of Rights drafted by the Constitutional Assembly is as extensive as any to be found in any national constitution. (Certification case 1996, para 52)

Education in language of choice

Similar to debates in international law and various domestic jurisdictions, an important topic of relevance during negotiations concerned the protection of cultural and linguistic communities in general, and more specifically the right to (a) receive education in one's language of choice and (b) receive state support for such education. (Chapter 9) This is particularly significant since few communities can financially sustain private education in their native language.[40]

---

[39] Constitutional Principle II: 'Everyone shall enjoy all universally accepted fundamental rights, freedoms and civil liberties, which shall be provided for and protected by entrenched and justiciable provisions in the Constitution, which shall be drafted after having given due consideration to inter alia the fundamental rights contained in Chapter 3 of this Constitution.' This Constitutional Principle highlighted the challenge of separating principle from detail.

[40] In Chapter 9 reference is made to the debate about state support for cultural and linguistic communities pursuant to provisions of international law. It is important to note that while international law does not mandate state-financed education in one's language of choice, it does envisage that individuals who choose to finance their own education in their mother tongue should have the option to do so.

The 1993 Constitution protected the rights to use language and practise culture in the realms of both private and public education,[41] but was silent about state funding to realise such rights. (Dlamini 1994) Section 29 of the 1996 Constitution contained more elaborate provisions regarding education, but also stopped short of guaranteeing the right to state-funded education in one's language of choice in any circumstance.[42] Curiously, there were no objections from the Afrikaans community to the Constitutional Court against the absence of a right to state-funded, single-medium mother-tongue education.[43]

The Constitutional Court found that s 29 complied with Constitutional Principle II, and that the regulatory power of the state over private education does not erode the fundamental right of communities to establish private educational facilities. (Certification case 1996, para 81) While the right to education in one's language of choice is recognised, there is no constitutional obligation for the state to fund, or otherwise contribute to, the realisation of the right in any

[41] Section 31 Language and culture: 'Every person shall have the right to use the language and to participate in the cultural life of his or her choice.' Section 32 Education: 'Every person shall have the right – (a) to basic education and to equal access to educational institutions; (b) to instruction in the language of his or her choice where this is reasonably practicable; and (c) to establish, where practicable, educational institutions based on a common culture, language or religion, provided that there shall be no discrimination on the ground of race.'

[42] Section 29 Education. '(1) Everyone has the right – (a) to a basic education, including adult basic education; and (b) to further education, which the state, through reasonable measures, must make progressively available and accessible. (2) Everyone has the right to receive education in the official language or languages of their choice in *public* educational institutions where that education is *reasonably practicable*. In order to ensure the effective access to, and implementation of, this right, the state must consider all reasonable educational alternatives, including single medium institutions, taking into account – (a) equity; (b) practicability; and (c) the need to redress the results of past racially discriminatory laws and practices. (3) Everyone has the right to establish and maintain, at their own expense, independent educational institutions that – (a) do not discriminate on the basis of race; (b) are registered with the state; and (c) maintain standards that are not inferior to standards at comparable public educational institutions. (4) Subsection (3) does not preclude state subsidies for independent educational institutions.' Section 30 Language and culture. 'Everyone has the right to use the language and to participate in the cultural life of their choice, but no one exercising these rights may do so in a manner inconsistent with any provision of the Bill of Rights.' (emphasis added)

[43] This can be explained for at least three reasons: first, the inclusion of the right to mother-tongue education was seen as a major breakthrough; secondly, the Afrikaans community was so focused on political participatory rights that individual rights within the bills of rights did not attract major attention; and, finally, there was a tacit understanding that in the exercise of its powers government would not discriminate in funding allocation against Afrikaans-medium teaching in public schools.

circumstance. State funding of language teaching in any of the official languages in public schools depends on considerations such as practicality, affordability, equity and redress of discrimination.[44]

Absence of rights to marriage and family

Objections were received against the constitutional draft on the basis that the Bill of Rights did not include specific provisions about the right to family and marriage. The basis of these objections was that: several international instruments and constitutions refer to these rights; these rights are essential in a heterogenous society such as South Africa;[45] and the norms underlying these rights are widely endorsed in South Africa. The Constitutional Court rejected these submissions on the grounds that Constitutional Principle II does not mandate the inclusion of these rights, the comparative approach adopted by nations and regional instruments with regard to family and marriage is neither consistent nor universal, and the generality of the protections in the Bill of Rights is adequate for the purposes of future development and interpretation. (Certification case 1996, para 100)

Recognition of traditional leadership

In ss 211 and 212 the Constitution recognises and protects the institution of traditional leadership.[46] Nonetheless, objections were raised in the Constitutional

---

[44] These are not unreasonable conditions to qualify state support of mother-tongue education and are consistent with the interpretation given to art 27 of the ICCPR. (Chapter 9) While the educational merit of mother-tongue education, particularly at the primary level, is widely recognised internationally, the obligation for the state to fund the realisation of mother-tongue education is not a universal legal norm. While 'the right to learn one's mother tongue is an absolute condition sine qua non for the survival' of cultural and linguistic minorities, there is *no universal right for public funding* of language, culture or religious educational facilities. (emphasis added) (Hofmann, Malloy, and Rein 2018a, 19) Even if mother-tongue education is financed by the state, it is suggested by Roter that funds should be allocated on the basis of *needs* rather than *equality*, whereby minorities that suffer greater marginalisation would duly receive greater funding. (Roter 2018, 135) This proposal opens the risk of minorities as groups being treated differently on the basis of their needs and ability to self-fund, which in turn is open to criticism.

[45] Note, for example, how since 1993 the courts, Parliament and the public have been struggling to deal with the complexity of co-habitation arrangements that exist pursuant to several non-state, religious and customary codes. (Rautenbach 2021a) At the time of writing (March 2025), the objective of creating a Marriage Act to regulate Muslim marriages had not yet been achieved.

[46] Section 211 Recognition. '(1) The institution, status and role of traditional leadership, according to customary law, are recognised, subject to the Constitution. (2) A traditional authority

Court that these provisions were not compliant with the Constitutional Principles since they did not adequately acknowledge the role of traditional authorities and leaders *in government.* (Certification case 1996, para 189) The objectors in effect sought to expand the constitutional role of traditional leadership as a fourth level of government.[47] The Constitutional Court rejected the submissions and said that its 'role is limited to ensuring that the institution, status and role of traditional leadership are recognised and protected in the Constitution, and that it is satisfied that the objective had been achieved.' (Certification case 1996, para 193)

Recognition of traditional courts and customary law

Submissions were made to the Constitutional Court that the failure of the Constitution to explicitly recognise traditional courts amounted to a breach of Constitutional Principle XIII. The Constitutional Court rejected the complaint and stated that the power outlined in s 166[48] for Parliament to establish courts by statute, in due course, was broad enough to also include traditional or tribal courts. (Certification case 1996, para 199) Additionally, the court also noted that s 211(1) of the Constitution recognises customary law,[49] but that application thereof is subject to the protections in the Bill of Rights. (Chapter 10) The court

---

that observes a system of customary law may function subject to any applicable legislation and customs, which includes amendments to, or repeal of, that legislation or those customs. (3) The courts must apply customary law when that law is applicable, subject to the Constitution and any legislation that specifically deals with customary law.' Section 212 Role of traditional leaders. '(1) National legislation may provide for a role for traditional leadership as an institution at the local level on matters affecting local communities. (2) To deal with matters relating to traditional leadership, the role of traditional leaders, customary law and the customs of communities observing a system of customary law – *(a)* national or provincial legislation may provide for the establishment of houses of traditional leaders; and *(b)* national legislation may establish a council of traditional leaders.'

[47] Constitutional Principle XIII: 'The institution, status and role of traditional leadership, according to indigenous law, shall be recognised and protected in the Constitution. Indigenous law, like common law, shall be recognised and applied by the courts, subject to the fundamental rights contained in the Constitution and to legislation dealing specifically therewith.'

[48] Section 166 Judicial system. 'The courts are – *(a)* the Constitutional Court; *(b)* the Supreme Court of Appeal; *(c)* the High Court of South Africa, and any high court of appeal that may be established by an Act of Parliament to hear appeals from any court of a status similar to the High Court of South Africa; *(d)* the Magistrates' Courts; and *(e)* any other court established or recognised in terms of an Act of Parliament, including any court of a status similar to either the High Court of South Africa or the Magistrates' Courts.'

[49] Section 211(1): 'The institution, status and role of traditional leadership, according to customary law, are recognised, subject to the Constitution.'

did not deal at any length with the complexity of legal pluralism since the opinion prevailed that the Constitution would establish a normative standard whereby all state laws and non-state laws and customs could be adjudicated. Customary law and traditional courts were, therefore, not in parallel to the Constitution, but subject to it.

Recognition of language and cultural rights

In a multilingual country such as South Africa the treatment of language and cultural rights in a constitution and in practice is a sensitive matter. While some communities may view language and cultural rights as belonging to the informal civil sphere, the Afrikaans-speaking community, in particular, insisted that their cultural and linguistic rights should be recognised in both the public and private spheres and receive state funding support.[50] This position of the Afrikaans community intersected with its demands for some form of political power-sharing, on the one hand, and a separate Volkstaat, on the other. Put simply, there was no agreed position within the Afrikaans-speaking community during the negotiations (or since) about the most appropriate way for Afrikaans cultural and language rights to be protected. (De Villiers 2022a)[51] The following constitutional principles dealt primarily with language and cultural rights:

---

[50] Notably, the demands by the Afrikaans community for collective rights and state support were not reflected during the negotiations in proposals adopted by other language and cultural communities. The lack of a shared position between languages communities on state funding of education in one's language of choice weakened the ability of those in the Afrikaans community seeking such support to propagate their case. The absence of support from other (black) language communities for the position adopted by some of the Afrikaans negotiators furthermore reaffirmed the perception that 'race' was being substituted with 'culture' as a mechanism to shore up the Afrikaners' position of privilege. It should, however, also be acknowledged that the languages of many of the black communities are spoken at a regional and local level (and often taught in primary schools), and in many instances their traditional customs and practices are given effect in traditional areas. It is therefore explainable that they did not necessarily place a similar premium on the formal protection of ethnocultural rights as did the Afrikaans community.

[51] There were, and remain, within the Afrikaans-speaking community deep cleavages along the lines of race, religion, region, class and political persuasion that make it practically impossible to reach a common position on the rights of this community. (De Villiers 2021a) The divisions were (again) apparent in the wake of the 2024 Afrikaner Declaration, on which prominent leaders from the Afrikaans-speaking Coloured community expressed concern at being excluded based on their race or religion. As an advisor to and observer of the negotiation processes between 1990 and 1996, it was apparent to me how the representatives of the Afrikaans community weakened their negotiating position through a lack of internal cooperation and consultation, along with distrust of one another. There was little attempt to develop a middle ground *within* the Afrikaans

Constitutional Principle XI

The diversity of language and culture shall be acknowledged and protected, and conditions for their promotion shall be encouraged.

Constitutional Principle XII

Collective rights of self-determination in forming, joining and maintaining organs of civil society, including linguistic, cultural and religious associations, shall, on the basis of non-discrimination and free association, be recognised and protected.

Constitutional Principle XXXIV

1. This Schedule and the recognition therein of the right of the South African people as a whole to self-determination, shall not be construed as precluding, within the framework of the said right, constitutional provision for a notion of the right to self-determination by any community sharing a common cultural and language heritage, whether in a territorial entity within the Republic or in any other recognised way.
2. The Constitution may give expression to any particular form of self-determination provided there is substantial proven support within the community concerned for such a form of self-determination.
3. If a territorial entity referred to in paragraph 1 is established in terms of this Constitution before the new constitutional text is adopted, the new Constitution shall entrench the continuation of such territorial entity, including its structures, powers and functions.

The following observations can be made about language rights in the Constitutional Principles: While under the pre-democracy regime there were, in essence, two official languages in South Africa, namely Afrikaans and English,

community, with the extremes of the community falling into the trap of a zero-sum game between power-sharing and Volkstaat (homeland). As a result, at the time of publication the Afrikaans community continues to argue and assign blame for what they perceive as relatively weak language and cultural rights, as well as poor political participatory rights in the 1993 and 1996 Constitutions. On proper analysis they primarily have themselves to blame for not being able to agree on a common position to put forward during the negotiations. For example, while at one stage there was a willingness among the ANC negotiators to entertain a form of cultural council for Afrikaners, the idea was rejected by the National Party since that party sought a race-based, power-sharing outcome, while the right wing also rejected it because they sought a race-based, Afrikaner Volkstaat. The failure of Constand Viljoen to extract concessions of substance on the eve of the 1994 election, other than an undertaking to look into the idea of a Volkstaat, was arguably one of the greatest capitulations in the negotiation process. The leverage that Viljoen and De Klerk jointly had in the days leading to the first election to maximise their support for a peaceful election remained underutilised because of the internal rifts within the Afrikaner community.

the 1996 Constitution provides for the recognition of 11 languages (in 2023 sign language was added).[52] Constitutional Principle XI dealt with languages, but only in general terms.[53] The Constitutional Court emphasised that this Constitutional Principle addressed the *recognition* of languages, rather than the *status* of a language. The status of each language was a matter to be determined by the Constitutional Assembly through subsequent legislation and policies. (Certification case 1996, para 211)[54] The court went on to comment, specifically in relation to the Afrikaans language, that the Constitutional Principle concerning official languages did not diminish the status of Afrikaans as an official language. Furthermore, it stated that the elevation of other languages to the status of official language does not reduce Afrikaans to a *legally* weaker position.

In regard to cultural rights, the Constitution contains a prohibition of discrimination on the grounds of culture, (s 9(3)) the right to use language and participate in culture, (s 30)[55] the right to enjoy and express rights collectively with other members of the community, (s 31)[56] the possible establishment of a

[52] Section 6 refers to the 11 official national languages, adding that one or more of those languages may be used for the purposes of official business within a province. (Constitution of South Africa 1996, s 3)

[53] Constitutional Principle XI: 'The diversity of language and culture shall be acknowledged and protected, and conditions for their promotion shall be encouraged.'

[54] While this legal reasoning of the Constitutional Court is correct, in practice the status of Afrikaans as an official national language has indisputably diminished. This can, however, also be explained in light of political events, the demography of the country, the common use of English as the most spoken second language, as well as the use of English as the common language for government and commerce. Many parents, including Afrikaans speakers, are 'voting with their feet' by enrolling children in English schools and tertiary institutions for reasons of commerce and international opportunities, while nevertheless maintaining their Afrikaans home language and practising their culture, music and traditions. (Chapter 9) Afrikaans-speaking private educational institutions, as well as various forms of community services that can be regarded as a form of functional autonomy, are widespread, but these are inevitably dependent on the financial means of the users since they do not receive government grants. (De Villiers 2023c, 330)

[55] Section 30: 'Everyone has the right to use the language and to participate in the cultural life of their choice, but no one exercising these rights may do so in a manner inconsistent with any provision of the Bill of Rights.'

[56] Section 31: '(1) Persons belonging to a cultural, religious or linguistic community may not be denied the right, with other members of that community – *(a)* to enjoy their culture, practise their religion and use their language; and *(b)* to form, join and maintain cultural, religious and linguistic associations and other organs of civil society. (2) The rights in subsection (1) may not be exercised in a manner inconsistent with any provision of the Bill of Rights.'

cultural council by a cultural community, (s 185(1)*(c)*)[57] and the right to self-determination of a cultural community (s 235).[58] The Constitutional Court found that the Constitutional Principles did not mandate the establishment of a Volkstaat for Afrikaans speakers (Certification case 1996, para 215)[59] and that the various provisions of the Constitution that recognise cultural and language rights complied with the relevant Constitutional Principles. The court furthermore concluded that the proposition that those clauses failed to comply with the Constitutional Principles because they were framed in the Constitution only as permissible (negative rights) rather than mandatory (positive rights) had no substance. (Certification case 1996, para 220)

Right to self-determination

The Constitution provides for the right to self-determination, but the Constitutional Court has emphasised that this right relates to the self-organisation of cultural communities (s 235) and not to the secession of a territorial part of South Africa.[60] The right to community self-determination, if it ever becomes operational, must also be exercised within the unity of South Africa. (Certification case 1996, para 218) The right to self-determination is essentially promissory and subject to legislation yet to be enacted, and not obligatory. The Constitution does not offer a definition of self-determination and, as is also evident in

---

[57] Section 185: '(1) The primary objects of the Commission for the Promotion and Protection of the Rights of Cultural, Religious and Linguistic Communities are – . . . *(c)* to recommend the establishment or recognition, in accordance with national legislation, of a cultural or other council or councils for a community or communities in South Africa.' While Henrard says the symbolical importance of this Commission 'cannot be overemphasised' (Henrard 2002, 146), it is glaring that in 30 years the Commission has not conducted a study, invited public submissions or made any recommendations about the possible establishment of cultural councils.

[58] Section 235: 'The right of the South African people as a whole to self-determination, as manifested in this Constitution, does not preclude, within the framework of this right, recognition of the notion of the right of self-determination of any community sharing a common cultural and language heritage, within a territorial entity in the Republic or in any other way, determined by national legislation.'

[59] It must also be noted that only a very small percentage of Afrikaans speakers supported a separate Afrikaans state or region. Although an informal Volkstaat, called Orania, has been developing in the Northern Cape, it has a population of only around 4 000, constituting a minute fraction of the Afrikaans-speaking community. Mokwena refers to Orania as a 'micronation'. (Mokwena 2024, 2)

[60] Note the background explanation of Van der Westhuizen, who had first-hand experience of the birthing process of s 235 of the Constitution. (Van der Westhuizen 2023)

international law, the term 'self-determination' is widely used and abused to range from individual rights and liberties to secession by states. (Alfredsson 2019) At the time of publication no legislation had been introduced pursuant to s 185 of the Constitution and no community had demanded self-determination pursuant to s 235 of the Constitution. This begs the question whether it is too early or too late to operationalise these rights. (De Villiers 2014a)

Recognition of traditional authorities

The Constitutional Principles provided for the recognition of traditional authorities.[61] The Constitution recognises the role of traditional authorities and the functions of traditional leaders, provided that these institutions function subject to the provisions of the national Constitution. Sections 211 and 212 provide as follows:

> **211. Recognition** (1) The institution, status and role of traditional leadership, according to customary law, are recognised, subject to the Constitution. (2) A traditional authority that observes a system of customary law may function subject to any applicable legislation and customs, which includes amendments to, or repeal of, that legislation or those customs. (3) The courts must apply customary law when that law is applicable, subject to the Constitution and any legislation that specifically deals with customary law.
>
> **212. Role of traditional leaders** (1) National legislation may provide for a role for traditional leadership as an institution at local level on matters affecting local communities. (2) To deal with matters relating to traditional leadership, the role of traditional leaders, customary law and the customs of communities observing a system of customary law – *(a)* national or provincial legislation may provide for the establishment of houses of traditional leaders; and *(b)* national legislation may establish a council of traditional leaders.

The Constitutional Court was satisfied that the scope for traditional authorities to exist is consistent with the Constitutional Principles and the provision that those authorities function pursuant to the Constitution and any applicable legislation does not derogate from the Constitutional Principles. (Certification case 1996, para 406)

---

[61] Constitutional Principle XIII: 'The institution, status and role of traditional leadership, according to indigenous law, shall be recognised and protected in the Constitution. Indigenous law, like common law, shall be recognised and applied by the courts, subject to the fundamental rights contained in the Constitution and to legislation dealing specifically therewith.'

3.4 COMMENTARY IN CONCLUSION ON THE TRANSITIONAL PROCESS

In the context of this book, which concerns the recognition of plurality in law and cultural, linguistic, religious and indigenous rights in the 1996 Constitution, the following conclusions can be drawn about the transition process and its outcomes:

Homegrown settlement

The 1990–1996 transition process in South Africa was distinctive in many respects. This chapter has underscored two aspects of its uniqueness: the utilisation of constitutional principles to connect the interim and final Constitutions and the Constitutional Court's role to certify that the 1996 Constitution adhered to the Constitutional Principles outlined in the 1993 Constitution. The accommodation of ethnocultural identity rights, the right of the majority to draw up a final constitution, the primacy of the rule of law and the principles of constitutional supremacy were accepted as fundamental points of departure. This creative arrangement provided all the main political groupings with a rational foundation to endorse the transition, preventing any attempts to undermine or derail the process. Each side found enough positive elements to favour participation and to secure a settlement rather than abstention or opposition.

The legal transition from apartheid to democracy thus took place in three steps: initially, the unelected leaders of political parties and movements negotiated the 1993 Constitution, which enshrined the essential Constitutional Principles for the final Constitution; next, the Parliament, democratically elected pursuant to the 1993 Constitution, also constituted as the Constitutional Assembly, drafted a final Constitution; and, finally, the final Constitution took effect after being certified by the Constitutional Court as compliant with the Constitutional Principles. This process was unprecedented.

The 1993 and 1996 Constitutions and transitional arrangements contained elements of the theories of Lijphart and Horowitz, but most importantly the practical effect given to those propositions were negotiated by South Africans. The homegrown nature of this process ensured widespread ownership of the 1996 Constitution, contributing to a non-violent first election in 1994 and subsequent peaceful elections. It is not surprising that, owing to its legitimacy, the Constitution has endured for three decades, while several other constitutions have faltered during the same period.

Community rights rather than minority rights

Two key issues had to be addressed by the negotiators in their efforts to give effect to minority and indigenous rights: (a) the principle of recognising minorities in light of South Africa's apartheid history in which race and identity had been used to such devastating effect to disenfranchise and discriminate; and (b) the definition of the terms 'minority', 'indigenous', and 'tribal'.[62]

The outcomes of the debates were relatively simple: the term 'community' was preferred to the term 'minority', and the rights attributed to a community were protected through the individual members of the community, rather than as collective rights for a community as if it were a legal entity (which it is not). The terms 'community', 'indigenous', 'traditional' and 'tribal' are not defined in the Constitution.[63] While the rejection of the term 'minority' circumvented the challenges experienced in international law to define the term, the use of 'community' gives rise to the same definitional questions as faced by 'minority', except that it does not explicitly rely on a numerical element. (Chapter 4)[64] I would suggest that 'community' refers to four essential requirements: first, the numerical status of a community as a minority; secondly, the non-dominant status of the community; thirdly, the sharing by individuals within the community of common language, religious and cultural characteristics; and, fourthly, a sense of solidarity within the community to preserve their identity collectively. (De Villiers 2020c, 837) Notably, community is not defined by race but by voluntarily acquired cultural, linguistic and religious characteristics.

[62] It was acknowledged that the term 'minority' had little value since it is vague, flexible, dynamic and non-legal. (Chapter 4) It has been said that there is 'nothing normative in the notion of a minority; it is just a residual category in respect to the idea of majority rule' and that it was a 'naïve dream' to try to define it, and even more to attach collective rights to it. (Fortman 2011, 285) See Chapter 4 for a discussion about the inability of international law to define terms such as 'minority' and 'indigenous', with the preferred option being for states to give content to the terms in their domestic arrangements.

[63] This is consistent with international law where these terms are not defined in instruments such as ILO 169 or UNDRIP. Instead, states are entrusted to determine, within their domestic context, the appropriate definition, description or naming of a particular community the subject of special collective rights. Note, for example, the 13 nationalities listed in the constitution of Hungary that are entitled to elect nationality self-governments. (De Villiers 2012b; European Framework Convention 1998; Hungary Nationalities Act 2012)

[64] The use of the term 'community' in South Africa is akin to the use of the term 'nationality', 'peoples', or 'national minority' in the European context.

The outcomes of the negotiation and certification process are reflected in two *potentially* powerful sections (ss 185(1)*(c)* and 235) that have proved to be consistent with Constitutional Principle 34 and that provide the groundwork for the possible self-determination and autonomy of communities. There is, however, no legal obligation in the 1996 Constitution for Parliament to give effect to s 185(1)*(c)* or s 235. In fact, since 1996 Parliament has been silent about the possible operationalisation of these provisions. (Geldenhuys 2020)[65] The sections, on the one hand, cannot be deemed irrelevant as they acknowledge a community's right to self-determination, though the specifics must be addressed through legislation. On the other hand, no community has asserted demands or presented a comprehensive proposal for the exercise of collective rights pursuant to s 185(1)*(c)* or s 235.

Several questions persist regarding ss 185(1)*(c)* and 235, such as: What constitutes a community? How does a community attain legal personhood? How is a community's stance on self-determination ascertained? How is community membership determined? Can subcommunities within a principal community seek recognition? What powers and functions can be conferred upon a community? And what level of internal community support is requisite for recognition in the context of self-determination? These questions remain unanswered at the time of publication since no community in South Africa has attempted to leverage these sections and Parliament has yet to enact legislation to operationalise them. (De Villiers 2022a)

In summary, elucidating the meaning of 'community' in s 235 of the Constitution can be facilitated by considering the following points: (a) akin to 'minority,' there exists no legally binding definition in international law for 'community,' thus presenting similar definitional challenges; (b) the concepts of 'minority' and 'indigenous' are not terms of art and their meanings must be deduced in the specific context of the country where employed – the same principle applies to 'community'; (c) individuals, as the right-bearers, do not automatically render the minority community a legal subject with collective rights, unless specific statutory arrangements recognise a corporate status, such

---

[65] Geldenhuys observes as follows: 'Afrikaners are worried about their language and culture but, unlike most European minorities, they also have profound concerns about the consequences of state weakness. Poor governance threatens not only standards of living but also the physical safety of South Africans.' (Geldenhuys 2020, 107) Notably, he does not refer to the Afrikaans-speaking community in general, thus reinforcing the racial element of using Afrikaner as a description.

as a cultural council, reserved seats,[66] a legal corporation for the community[67] or pursuant to customary law; and (d) the typical fundamental rights of individuals to be exercised within a community relate to the enjoyment of language, religious and cultural rights. These rights attain their full realisation through individual interactions, underscoring the principle that it is the individual, not the community, who bears these rights, but notably courts can take note that the identity rights only come to true fruition when exercised by an individual in community with other individuals.

Principle versus detail

During the negotiations it proved challenging to distinguish between the *principle* of community rights and the *detail* of community rights. This is not surprising, given that international law and municipal constitutional law are rarely detailed in their support for the collective protection of community rights or indigenous rights.[68] Clauses designed to safeguard community and indigenous rights are frequently framed in a general, somewhat vague and promissory manner, lacking

---

[66] See how in New Zealand seats have been reserved for the Māori, including a separate voters roll. (De Villiers 2023e, 218)

[67] In Australia the federal parliament has enacted legislation to enable any Aboriginal community or a subgroup of an Aboriginal community to register a legal entity, called an Aboriginal Corporation, whereby the community becomes incorporated and manages their affairs collectively through the legal entity. (CATSI Act 2006) At the time of publication around 4 000 Aboriginal corporations had been registered in Australia. In Hungary each of the 13 nationalities recognised in the constitution may establish an elected cultural council with legal personality to tend to the affairs of the community within the sphere of public law. (Dobos 2016) Other examples of legal entities are those of the Russian Federation, Serbia, Kosovo and Estonia, where statutory arrangements exist for nationalities/minorities to register a corporate entity to act on their behalf and to promote their cultural interests. (Panzano 2018; Filippova and Filippov 2015; Osipov 2015) Malloy contends that non-territorial arrangements 'should be distinguished from civil society and social movements, which are based on universal access. They could perhaps be described as a "layer" of the political organization of society since they coexist within state institutions of similar functions. . . . However, as new types of NTA of a formal as well as an informal nature emerge, it is important to monitor how governments recognize these. If they go without receiving recognition and accommodation in law and politics, there is a potential risk that beneficiaries will feel their claims are neglected. This could result in internal social unrest. For this reason, it is imperative that more knowledge is gathered in this area of ethnocultural studies.' (Malloy 2022, 61)

[68] The same can be said about individual rights, where the actual nature, content and scope of a right is ascertained from time to time by courts. See, for example, how the right to freedom of expressions vis-à-vis the combating of hate speech is addressed in different ways by jurisdictions. (Chapter 5; De Villiers 2022e)

specificity.[69] This poses a challenge for ethnocultural communities and indigenous peoples, who may feel that the lack of detail will inevitably imply a lack of adequate protection and recognition. These concerns were notably highlighted in the debates surrounding education and the right to receive education in one's language of choice.

While the Afrikaans community insisted that the right to *mother-tongue* education should be supported by a guarantee of state funding, the other parties were concerned about the financial and practical implications of such an arrangement in a country that has 11 official languages, not to mention other dialects and unofficial spoken languages. A compromise was reached wherein the Constitution would acknowledge the right to public funding for language-of-choice education, contingent upon its practical feasibility. (Chapter 9) Additionally, the right to establish private self-funded educational institutions eligible for state grants was also recognised. While this compromise exceeds international law and practice, the implication of relying on self-funding for education is that millions of children receive their education in a second (or third) language, typically English, in state schools – a form of English 'imperialism'. (Woldeyes 2023) In contrast, only the affluent can afford education in their language of choice within a private setting. Consequently, the wealthy have the means to ensure their children receive education in a language of choice, often resulting in enhanced educational outcomes, particularly in early learning and transfer of culture.[70] Meanwhile, the less privileged are primarily educated in English, a

---

[69] Note, for example, how the term 'self-determination' is widely used in indigenous and minority rights debates at international forums without any agreement of its definition or practical application. (Xanathaki 2022) The seemingly positive progress that has been made in international law often leaves indigenous people and minorities disillusioned since it is so challenging to transform municipal systems to adhere in practice with the promises of international law. (De Villiers 2023f, 105)

[70] Note how the reading skills of primary school children at year 4 level in South Africa are falling below the established standard. One contributing factor is the practice of educating children in a language that differs from their home language. (Spaull 2023) UNESCO has also emphasised that mother-tongue teaching for children is essential to improve literacy standards. (UNESCO mother tongue 2022) The national government has pledged to enhance support for mother-tongue education, particularly at the primary level. However, it is evident that the importance of state-supported mother-tongue education was not accorded sufficient attention and acknowledgment during the constitution-drafting process. (Chapter 9) It also appears when reflecting on jurisprudence (Chapter 9) that the South African courts have been attentive of equality and non-discrimination but without giving due consideration to the importance of mother-tongue education in the context of a cultural right and an individual right to self-determination.

language that is not their home or mother tongue, potentially leading to a less effective transfer of language and culture.[71]

While substantial time was devoted to negotiations on the theoretical and practical feasibility of collective rights, it is important to note that ultimately the rights of communities are primarily delineated through the individual rights of their members, complemented by the right to freedom of association. This approach is consistent with the stance adopted by s 27 of the ICCPR.[72] While some in the Afrikaans community retrospectively criticise this outcome, it is essential to acknowledge that 'community' is not a legal term; it lacks definition as a term of art and is inherently a sociological concept. Consequently, its definition is naturally broad, inclusive and vague. Although it is feasible to refer to the Afrikaans-speaking 'community' from a sociological standpoint, translating this concept into a legal definition where the entire Afrikaans community is recognised as a legal entity with collective rights is not practically or legally tenable.[73] While jurisprudence has acknowledged the collective nature of certain

---

[71] Malloy points out that the mere assertion (within the context of the FCNM) by a state that limited financial or other resources render it incapable of adopting measures to facilitate the use of minority languages at a local level for the purposes of communication and administration constitutes a breach of international law. (Malloy 2018, 219) I am not aware of jurisprudence to support this proposition.

[72] There is a group right dimension in s 38 of the Constitution since it enables any individual to bring a proceeding on behalf of a group, class or association of persons. The right-bearer remains, however, the individual even if that the person can demonstrate that the nature of the grievance derives from the person's association with a specific community. This is not unique to South Africa. Note, for example, how the African Commission has found that the failure to perform consultation on land access affected the property rights of the entire community. (Endorois Welfare Council case 2003; Sing'Oei 2013) Section 38 of the Constitution provides as follows: 'Enforcement of rights: Anyone listed in this section has the right to approach a competent court, alleging that a right in the Bill of Rights has been infringed or threatened, and the court may grant appropriate relief, including a declaration of rights. The persons who may approach a court are – (a) anyone acting in their own interest; (b) anyone acting on behalf of another person who cannot act in their own name; (c) anyone acting as a member of, or in the interest of, a group or class of persons; (d) anyone acting in the public interest; and (e) an association acting in the interest of its members.'

[73] It is worth noting that some major language communities are indirectly accommodated by way of the demarcation of provinces and local governments, as well as the authority vested in a province to adopt one or more official languages for its jurisdiction. This means that at least eight of the nine provinces have a dominant language in addition to English, while in Gauteng there are multiple language communities. (Census 2011; De Villiers 2021b, 60) Each of the 11 main language groupings therefore has a province where its language is spoken in addition to English. The Constitutional Court has noted that clear majorities in South Africa are not easily discernible

indigenous communities (De Villiers 2023e, 33–41), it is important to note that a cultural community typically lacks the attributes of a 'society' with its own legal norms and traditions associated with pre-settlement land, as commonly observed in the case of indigenous peoples.[74]

Promise, but no duty to act

Sections 185 and 235 of the 1996 Constitution, addressing the potential self-determination rights of communities including the possible establishment of a cultural council for a community, have not been accorded any legal or policy effect. This prompts the question of whether there should have been some form of obligation or a specified timeframe outlined in the Constitutional Principles, or within the Constitution itself, mandating Parliament to develop procedures or enact legislation to give effect to these purported rights.

In its current form the promissory elements of the two self-determination clauses are strong, but the practical effect is non-existent.[75] The establishment of a cultural council for a language or cultural community is not without complexity, but a few countries have endeavoured to grant some form of personal or non-territorial self-management to communities.[76] Topidi expresses the view

unless determined by race. However, if language is considered as the determining factor, there exist only minorities. (Gauteng Education Bill case 1996, para 81)

[74] Consider, for instance, the Yorta Yorta judgment from the High Court of Australia, wherein it was emphasised that for the recognition of indigenous native title rights and interests an indigenous community must demonstrate its continued functioning as a 'society' adhering to the traditional laws and customs of their ancestors. (Yorta Yorta (HCA) case 2002) Such a requirement distinguishes indigenous people from ethnocultural minorities. While both groups may possess unique customs and traditions, ethnocultural minorities do not constitute a 'society' with pre-existing sovereignty, their own legal system and connection to ancestral lands. Some ethnocultural communities, for example the Roma, may also lay claim for their legal system to be recognised. (Nafstad 2018)

[75] In the absence of statutory provisions to implement ss 185 and 235, communities like the Afrikaans-speaking community have through private initiatives evolved a kind of informal functional autonomy. NGOs within the Afrikaans community have established legal entities that provide services such as education, vocational training and tertiary education, basic municipal services and cultural activities to both community members and other communities. Through this process the arrangements have become so well organised that, in certain aspects, they exhibit elements akin to a parallel state at the local level. (De Villiers 2023c, 436)

[76] See, for example, the community/nationality councils for some form of collective self-government and self-administration in Hungary, Estonia, Slovakia, Serbia, the Russian Federation and Brussels. (De Villiers 2022c; Malloy and Salat 2021; Hungary Nationalities Act 2012, s 1(3))

that the contemporary state 'may require rerouting to more dialogical forms of cooperation between the state and cultural minority groups in order to enhance the possibilities for the latter to shape their cultural destinies'. (Topidi 2024, 415)

A compelling argument can be advanced for the Commission for the Promotion and Protection of the Rights of Cultural, Religious, and Linguistic Communities, established by the Constitution (Constitution of South Africa 1996, s 184), to be mandated to investigate and report on the feasibility and practicality of establishing cultural councils for cultural and language communities, as envisioned in s 185(1)*(c)* of the 1996 Constitution.[77] The Commission might, for example, invite public submissions and, if necessary, formulate enabling legislation outlining benchmarks for a community to register a cultural council. This is clearly an aspect of the constitutional settlement that has not been given legal, policy or practical effect.

Protection of identity rights without state support

The protection of identity rights, encompassing cultural, linguistic, educational, traditional, religious and customary rights, resonates universally, but only to the extent that these rights are attached to the individual. Pursuant to the freedom of association, individuals may exercise these rights with others from the same community. Furthermore, these rights are primarily exercised within the context of civil law. This implies that these rights do not extend to any special collective rights and privileges in public law, such as self-government or autonomy, unless explicitly provided for by legislation. The realisation of these rights, however, largely hinges on the private resources available to individuals. Consistent with international law, the South African state is not legally obliged to fund the realisation of mother-tongue education or the exercise of cultural, religious, or indigenous rights.

The predicament posed by self-funding is that minority languages and cultures may be endangered, because public funding might either be unavailable or the government might decline to support the funding of these rights. It is, however,

[77] '(1) The primary objectives of the Commission for the Promotion and Protection of the Rights of Cultural, Religious and Linguistic Communities are . . . *(c)* to recommend the establishment or recognition, in accordance with national legislation, of a cultural or other council or councils for a community or communities in South Africa.' Note, for example, how in Hungary the nationalities that qualify for the establishment of nationality councils are explicitly named, rather than relying on the nationalities concerned to identify themselves.

important to consider that public resources are scarce and must inevitably be allocated to achieve the most beneficial outcomes. This may result in minorities and their members being treated equally under the law while, in substance, experiencing inequality. This stems from the fact that some may have the means to self-fund and promote their cultural and language interests, while others may lack the necessary resources.

Consideration of international law

A notable aspect of the 1996 Constitution, not mandated by the Constitutional Principles, is the recognition of the potential utility of international law and foreign state constitutional law jurisprudence in interpreting the Bill of Rights. (Chapter 4; Constitution of South Africa 1996, ss 39(1), 231, 232, 233)[78] These sections essentially stipulate that courts *must* consider international law when interpreting South African law for consistency, *may* take into account foreign state constitutional jurisprudence, and must recognise the binding nature of international agreements approved by Parliament.[79]

The Constitutional Court in 2011 declared succinctly as follows: '[There is] no escape from the manifest constitutional injunction to integrate, in a way the Constitution permits, international law obligations into our domestic law.' (Glenister case 2011, para 202) This interpretation guide may assist courts in considering developments in both international and municipal law concerning the rights of minorities and indigenous peoples.[80] The following caution expressed by Coutsoudis and Du Plessis can, however, be endorsed:

---

[78] Authorisation for courts to consider international law is not the sole domain of the South African Constitution. For example, in s 94 of the Constitution of the Netherlands the courts are granted judicial review powers to test the constitutionality of the laws of the Netherlands with reference to international law. In Botswana treaties may be relied on to interpret domestic legislation. (Constitution of Botswana, s 4) The courts of Botswana regularly cite foreign case law, notably from the ECtHR. (Dinokopila and Kgoboge 2021, 343) The reference by the 1996 Constitution of South Africa to the power of the courts to consider municipal jurisprudence of other states as well as jurisprudence arising from international law was, at the time of the drafting of the Constitution, exceptional.

[79] Constitution of South Africa 1996, s 39. Section 39(1) provides as follows: '(1) When interpreting the Bill of Rights, a court, tribunal or forum – *(a)* must promote the values that underlie an open and democratic society based on human dignity, equality and freedom; *(b)* must consider international law; and *(c)* may consider foreign law.'

[80] See, for example, the extensive references to international and foreign law in the first judgment of the Constitutional Court when it abolished the death penalty, and also more recently the reference to international law to ascertain the consultation standards and practices

> In general, there are at least two broad, and interrelated, dangers that one must seek to avoid, in order to adroitly incorporate international law into our law as envisaged by the Constitution. First there is the danger of *jurisprudential cherry-picking.* That is the danger of selecting, on a piece-meal basis, only those international law principles that support the case the court or a practitioner wishes to make, rather than taking account, on a holistic basis, of all the relevant international law, and setting any specific principles that appear, at first, favourable to the approach that one wishes to take, within its broader international law context. The second danger is failing to appreciate the subtle manner that *international law operates in distinctly different ways to domestic law.* Thus, for instance, a domestic lawyer might erroneously approach an international agreement on the basis that it should be understood and interpreted as something akin to a piece of domestic legislation, when in reality within the often consensual setting of international law, it may be more akin (broadly) to a private agreement between equal parties. (emphasis added) (Coutsoudis and Du Plessis 2020, 188)

Summary of community and indigenous rights in the 1996 Constitution

The 1996 Constitution embodies a negotiated outcome and does not claim to represent the ideal international standards or practices.[81] The Constitution is a

---

that ought to be adhered to when consulting with indigenous people about their traditional lands. (Makwanyane case 1995; Baleni case 2019) There is often reference in South African jurisprudence to the jurisprudence of other countries as well as to regional instruments such as the European Convention on Human Rights. (Chapter 4) This approach reflects what had been stated by the Constitutional Court of Germany, namely that international human rights treaties should be offered as an 'interpretative aid' to the court when declaring the scope and ambit of rights under the Basic Law. (BVerfGE 74 case 1987) Note in the Batwa case of Uganda, in which the Constitutional Court sought to draw a distinction between 'interpretation' of a legal text, on the one hand, and 'reading in', on the other. The court reasoned that the former involved having regard to the 'plain and ordinary meaning of the words used in the provision', and that once this exercise was complete the court's interpretative function was complete. The court emphasised that it 'may make reference' to international law in 'explicating the import of a constitutional provision', but it could not 'rely on international law to "read words" into a constitutional provision'. (Batwa case 2021, para 17; Paterson 2022)

81 When comparing the 1996 Constitution against international norms regarding the rights of minorities, the question naturally arises which norms are indeed 'universal'. In chapters 4 and 9 this question is considered, but it should be noted that international law does not mandate collective political or autonomy rights of minorities. Instead, it primarily protects the rights of individuals while encouraging – but not mandating – public funding for minority languages and cultures. Furthermore, it leaves practical measures to the discretion of sovereign states to operationalise. Within the European context, two useful discussion papers have been published about practical measures to promote and enhance the rights of minorities, particularly in regard to effective political participation. However, these do not have any legal standing and are merely useful sources of reference. (Lund Recommendations 1999; Ljubljana Guidelines 2012)

negotiated document, not an academic proposition. Nevertheless, the process leading to its formulation benefited from the contributions of some of the world's foremost legal minds in the field of minority rights. While the text of the Constitution could be critiqued by suggesting the insertion, deletion or reformulation of specific clauses, a negotiated outcome inevitably carries the DNA and the weight of compromise. A negotiated outcome represents what parties *were able to* agree to, not what they *aspired* to. It reflects *consensus*, not *demands*.

In the context of this book the Constitution could have stronger minority and indigenous protections, but it also could have weaker protections. There is no constitution that contains the perfect mix of ethnocultural and indigenous protections.

In many respects the criticisms expressed in contemporary society against the Constitution should be directed at government and Parliament for the *management* of the Constitution, rather than questioning the inherent merit of the constitutional settlement. The Constitution's management and implementation have faced challenges because of one-party dominance, resulting in issues such as corruption, state capture (Zondo 2022), the deployment of political cadres and supporters, and non-meritorious appointments and promotions, as well as numerous other shortcomings that have contributed to socio-economic malaise. However, these concerns reflect on the actions of the leaders operating under the Constitution rather than the normative value of the Constitution. One can agree with Davis and Klare in their observation that the blame for 'failure' of socio-economic transformation is 'squarely on the politics and policies of ANC governments in power over three decades'. (Davis and Klare 2024)

The Constitution generally complies with contemporary constitutional theory and practice as well as provisions of international law regarding the rights of cultural and linguistic communities and indigenous people.[82]

---

[82] This statement does not imply that the Constitution is beyond criticism when it comes to the protection of the rights of minorities and indigenous people. It merely signifies that the Constitution complies with the Constitutional Principles, that the mechanisms and protections provided for in the Constitution are consistent with international norms and practice, and that the rights are subject to practicality and funding. As Henrard pointed out in an earlier assessment of the minority protection arrangements of the Constitution, the *actual* scope of protections enjoyed by communities is also dependent on various non-constitutional factors, such as funding, policies, community demands, practical considerations and the 'volatile' nature of the society and complexities of transition. (Henrard 2002, 268)

The following are the essential rights of direct relevance to cultural, language and indigenous communities which are recognised under the Constitution:

- individual identity rights related to the freedom of association, practice of religion and culture, and use of language are recognised (Constitution of South Africa 1996, ss 15; 16; 17; 18; 29; 30; and 31);
- the right to state-funded mother-tongue education (in any of the official languages) is recognised (Constitution of South Africa 1996, ss 29; 30; and 31);
- the right to privately funded education facilities is recognised (Constitution of South Africa 1996, ss 29; 30; and 31);
- potential collective rights related to the establishment of a cultural council and self-determination on a territorial or non-territorial basis are recognised (Constitution of South Africa 1996, ss 185; 235);
- customary law is recognised, subject to the provisions of the Bill of Rights (Constitution of South Africa 1996, s 39);
- the institutions of traditional authorities are recognised (Constitution of South Africa 1996, ss 211, 212); and
- the demarcation of the provinces takes account of linguistic, cultural and tribal settlement patterns.

Schedule 4 of the Interim Constitution, 1983

CONSTITUTIONAL PRINCIPLES

I The Constitution of South Africa shall provide for the establishment of one sovereign state, a common South African citizenship and a democratic system of government committed to achieving equality between men and women and people of all races.

II Everyone shall enjoy all universally accepted fundamental rights, freedoms and civil liberties, which shall be provided for and protected by entrenched and justiciable provisions in the Constitution, which shall be drafted after having given due consideration to inter alia the fundamental rights contained in Chapter 3 of this Constitution.

III The Constitution shall prohibit racial, gender and all other forms of discrimination and shall promote racial and gender equality and national unity.

IV The Constitution shall be the supreme law of the land. It shall be binding on all organs of state at all levels of government.

V The legal system shall ensure the equality of all before the law and an equitable legal process. Equality before the law includes laws, programmes or activities that have as their object the amelioration of the conditions of the disadvantaged, including those disadvantaged on the grounds of race, colour or gender.

VI There shall be a separation of powers between the legislature, executive and judiciary, with appropriate checks and balances to ensure accountability, responsiveness and openness.

VII The judiciary shall be appropriately qualified, independent and impartial and shall have the power and jurisdiction to safeguard and enforce the Constitution and all fundamental rights.

VIII There shall be representative government embracing multi-party democracy, regular elections, universal adult suffrage, a common voters' roll, and, in general, proportional representation.

IX Provision shall be made for freedom of information so that there can be open and accountable administration at all levels of government.

X Formal legislative procedures shall be adhered to by legislative organs at all levels of government.

XI The diversity of language and culture shall be acknowledged and protected, and conditions for their promotion shall be encouraged.

XII Collective rights of self-determination in forming, joining and maintaining organs of civil society, including linguistic, cultural and religious associations, shall, on the basis of non-discrimination and free association, be recognised and protected.

XIII The institution, status and role of traditional leadership, according to indigenous law, shall be recognised and protected in the Constitution. Indigenous law, like common law, shall be recognised and applied by the courts, subject to the fundamental rights contained in the Constitution and to legislation dealing specifically therewith.

XIV Provision shall be made for participation of minority political parties in the legislative process in a manner consistent with democracy.

XV Amendments to the Constitution shall require special procedures involving special majorities.

XVI Government shall be structured at national, provincial and local levels.

XVII At each level of government there shall be democratic representation. This principle shall not derogate from the provisions of Principle XIII.

XVIII The powers, boundaries and functions of the national government and provincial governments shall be defined in the Constitution. Amendments to the Constitution which alter the powers, boundaries, functions or institutions of provinces shall in addition to any other procedures specified in the Constitution for constitutional amendments, require the approval of a special majority of the legislatures of the provinces, alternatively, if there is such a chamber, a two-thirds majority of a chamber of Parliament composed of provincial representatives, and if the amendment concerns specific provinces only, the approval of the legislatures of such provinces will also be needed. Provision shall be made for obtaining the views of a provincial legislature concerning all constitutional amendments regarding its powers, boundaries and functions.

XIX The powers and functions at the national and provincial levels of government shall include exclusive and concurrent powers as well as the power to perform functions for other levels of government on an agency or delegation basis.

XX Each level of government shall have appropriate and adequate legislative and executive powers and functions that will enable each level to function effectively. The allocation of powers between different levels of government shall be made on a basis which is conducive to financial viability at each level of government and to effective public administration, and which recognises the need for and promotes national unity and legitimate provincial autonomy and acknowledges cultural diversity.

XXI The following criteria shall be applied in the allocation of powers to the national government and the provincial governments:

1. The level at which decisions can be taken most effectively in respect of the quality and rendering of services, shall be the level responsible and accountable for the quality and the rendering of the services, and such level shall accordingly be empowered by the Constitution to do so.
2. Where it is necessary for the maintenance of essential national standards, for the establishment of minimum standards required for the rendering of services, the maintenance of economic unity, the maintenance of national security or the prevention of unreasonable action taken by one province which is prejudicial to the interests of another province or the country as a whole, the Constitution shall empower the national government to intervene through legislation or such other steps as may be defined in the Constitution.
3. Where there is necessity for South Africa to speak with one voice, or to act as a single entity – in particular in relation to other states-powers should be allocated to the national government.
4. Where uniformity across the nation is required for a particular function, the legislative power over that function should be allocated predominantly, if not wholly, to the national government.
5. The determination of national economic policies, and the power to promote interprovincial commerce and to protect the common market in respect of the mobility of goods, services, capital and labour, should be allocated to the national government.
6. Provincial governments shall have powers, either exclusively or concurrently with the national government, inter alia –
   (a) for the purposes of provincial planning and development and the rendering of services; and

(b) in respect of aspects of government dealing with specific socio-economic and cultural needs and the general well-being of the inhabitants of the province.

7. Where mutual co-operation is essential or desirable or where it is required to guarantee equality of opportunity or access to a government service, the powers should be allocated concurrently to the national government and the provincial governments.

8. The Constitution shall specify how powers which are not specifically allocated in the Constitution to the national government or to a provincial government, shall be dealt with as necessary ancillary powers pertaining to the powers and functions allocated either to the national government or provincial governments.

XXII The national government shall not exercise its powers (exclusive or concurrent) so as to encroach upon the geographical, functional or institutional integrity of the provinces.

XXIII In the event of a dispute concerning the legislative powers allocated by the Constitution concurrently to the national government and provincial governments which cannot be resolved by a court on a construction of the Constitution, precedence shall be given to the legislative powers of the national government.

XXIV A framework for local government powers, functions and structures shall be set out in the Constitution. The comprehensive powers, functions and other features of local government shall be set out in parliamentary statutes or in provincial legislation or in both.

XXV The national government and provincial governments shall have fiscal powers and functions which will be defined in the Constitution. The framework for local government referred to in Principle XXIV shall make provision for appropriate fiscal powers and functions for different categories of local government.

XXVI Each level of government shall have a constitutional right to an equitable share of revenue collected nationally so as to ensure that provinces and local governments are able to provide basic services and execute the functions allocated to them.

XXVII A Financial and Fiscal Commission, in which each province shall be represented, shall recommend equitable fiscal and financial allocations to the provincial and local governments from revenue collected nationally, after taking into account the national interest, economic disparities between the provinces as well as the population and developmental needs, administrative responsibilities and other legitimate interests of each of the provinces.

XXVIII Notwithstanding the provisions of Principle XII, the right of employers and employees to join and form employer organisations and trade unions and to engage in collective bargaining shall be recognised and protected. Provision shall be made that every person shall have the right to fair labour practices.

XXIX The independence and impartiality of a Public Service Commission, a Reserve Bank, an Auditor-General and a Public Protector shall be provided for and safeguarded by the Constitution in the interests of the maintenance of effective public finance and administration and a high standard of professional ethics in the public service.

XXX 1. There shall be an efficient, non-partisan, career-orientated public service broadly representative of the South African community, functioning on a basis of fairness and which shall serve all members or the public in an unbiased and impartial manner, and shall, in the exercise of its powers and in compliance with its duties, loyally execute the lawful policies of the government of the day in the performance of its administrative functions. The structures and functioning of the public service, as well as the terms and conditions of service of its members, shall be regulated by law.

2. Every member of the public service shall be entitled to a fair pension.

XXXI Every member of the security forces (police, military and intelligence), and the security forces as a whole, shall be required to perform their functions and exercise their powers in the national interest and shall be prohibited from furthering or prejudicing party-political interest.

XXXII The Constitution shall provide that until April 30, 1999 the national executive shall be composed and shall function substantially in the manner provided for in Chapter 6 of this Constitution.

XXXIII The Constitution shall provide that, unless Parliament is dissolved on account of its passing a vote of no-confidence in the Cabinet, no national election shall be held before April 30, 1999.

XXXIV 1. This Schedule and the recognition therein of the right of the South African people as a whole to self-determination, shall not be construed as precluding, within the framework of the said right, constitutional provision for a notion of the right to self-determination by any community sharing a common cultural and language heritage, whether in a territorial entity within the Republic or in any other recognised way.

2. The Constitution may give expression to any particular form of self-determination provided there is substantial proven support within the community concerned for such a form of self-determination.

3. If a territorial entity referred to in paragraph 1 is established in terms of this Constitution before the new constitutional text is adopted, the new Constitution shall entrench the continuation of such territorial entity, including its structures, powers and functions.

CHAPTER 4

BENCHMARKS IN INTERNATIONAL LAW FOR THE PROTECTION OF IDENTITY RIGHTS

Where, after all, do universal human rights begin? In small places, close to home – so close and so small that they cannot be seen on any maps of the world. . . . Unless these rights have meaning there, they have little meaning anywhere. Without concerned citizen action to uphold them close to home, we shall look in vain for progress in the larger world.

– Eleanor Roosevelt

4.1 INTRODUCTION

The constitution-drafting process of South Africa was in general profoundly influenced by developments in international law and experiences within municipal law of other liberal democratic states.[1] In particular the negotiators were keenly aware of the balance that had to be struck between majoritarian principles of a one-person one-vote election, on the one hand, and the safeguarding of individual, minority and indigenous rights, on the other.[2] While the concept of legal pluralism did not explicitly emerge during negotiations, there was a weighty awareness that the rich diversity of South Africa – encompassing social, cultural, indigenous and religious dimensions – needed to be accommodated in some way to foster national unity and uphold individual freedom.

The early 1990s witnessed numerous democratisation efforts across the globe, the majority of which, if not all, incorporated elements of minority accommodation, including indigenous populations.[3] Literature at the time was

[1] While one should exercise caution in associating specific influences of municipal law from other states with the South African constitution-drafting process, my personal observations were that the experiences of the following countries were particularly relevant to assist in certain aspects of the negotiations: Bill of Rights (Canada, Germany, India, USA); decentralisation, federalism, intergovernmental relations (Germany, Canada, India); electoral system (several countries with various forms of proportional representation); demarcation of provinces (India, Nigeria, Germany); fiscal and financial commission (Australia, Germany); indigenous rights (various African and Asian arrangements); community rights (Belgium, Canada); government of national unity (Switzerland, Belgium); asymmetry in provincial power allocation (Spain, Italy, Canada); bicameralism (Germany).

[2] The apartheid background of South Africa significantly complicated negotiations concerning the design of institutions aimed at ethnocultural and indigenous protection. Nonetheless, there was an acute awareness that, given the diversity of the South African population, both direct and indirect measures were imperative to reflect and accommodate this population plurality – referred to by Bishop Desmond Tutu as the 'rainbow nation'. The provisions of the Bill of Rights, especially those pertaining to identity rights, recognition of 11 official languages, demarcation of provinces with an acknowledgment of linguistic patterns, decentralisation to provincial and local governments, recognition of traditional leaders, elevating the status of customary law, proportional representation without a minimum threshold, and clauses anticipating a form of community self-determination, all represented institutional responses aimed at accommodating the societal plurality. (Chapter 3; De Villiers 2022a; De Villiers 2012a; De Villiers 2017; Henrard 2002; Strydom 1997; Barrie 2000)

[3] While the South African negotiations were under way the relevance of minority protection, or absence thereof, was particularly under debate in the post-Soviet Union states in central and eastern Europe. (Coakley 2017; Poleshchuk 2015; Filippova and Filippov 2015) Ironically, many of the liberation leaders in South Africa had, over the years, received training and various other forms of support from the then Soviet Union. During the negotiations it became evident that

saturated with minority-accommodation theories, propositions and experiences. In South Africa the 1990–1996 constitution-drafting process, the 1993 Constitution, the Constitutional Principles and the 1996 Constitution shared a common thread – the challenge to democratise through liberal democratic principles with majority rule at the core, while concurrently to accommodate individual, minority and indigenous rights.[4]

It is therefore appropriate, in this 30-year review of certain landmark South African judgments addressing identity rights and plurality within the context of international law, to provide a brief overview of key developments in international law related to identity rights. The objective in doing so is to identify themes that may hold relevance to South Africa and the judgments discussed in the ensuing chapters.

A notably pertinent aspect of the 1996 Constitution, not explicitly mandated by the Constitutional Principles, is the consideration of international law and the jurisprudence of municipal constitutional law from other countries to assist with interpreting the South African Constitution as a whole, with a specific emphasis on the Bill of Rights. (Constitution of South Africa 1996, ss 39, 231, 232, 233) These provisions sought to cement South African jurisprudence into the family

---

the central and eastern European states that were formerly part of the Soviet Union, including the Russian Federation, had become particularly proactive since the 1990s to develop policies, mechanisms and institutional arrangements for the protection of minorities. Even today, the eastern and central parts of Europe continue to serve as a 'laboratory' for testing and assessing institutional arrangements for minority protection. (Palermo and Constantin 2021, 179) Baranyai highlights how minority-based political parties in central and eastern Europe have been promoting language and cultural interests. (Baranyai 2024)

[4] This chapter does not consider the developments in international law concerning the rights of indigenous people, as, during the negotiations for the South African constitution, UNDRIP had yet to be adopted. Nevertheless, there was a general agreement among the negotiators that traditional leaders and customary law should be accommodated. The interests of traditional leaders during the negotiations were principally advocated by CONTRALESA (Congress of Traditional Leaders of South Africa), the Inkatha Freedom Party and several homeland governments. The topic of indigenous rights was therefore not as contentious as that of minority rights. Since the 1990s UNDRIP has served as an important instrument to guide and assist with policy-making, and encourages advocacy for indigenous rights, even though it is not legally enforceable. In recent years legislation has been enacted in South Africa to better protect the rights of, among others, traditional leaders and the Khoisan. (Pieterse-Robertson 2019) Despite this, the Khoisan Act was declared unconstitutional because of the inadequate public consultation that preceded its formulation. (Chapter 7) Parliament has been given three years to rectify its shortcomings. (De Villiers 2023b, 48; Khoisan Act appeal 2023) At the time of writing (March 2025), a new Khoisan Act had not yet been adopted by Parliament.

of international law and adherence to universal democratic principles, giving guidance to universal democratic, human rights, minority rights and indigenous rights.[5] Section 39(1) of the Constitution outlines the following regarding the interpretation of the Bill of Rights:

> (1) When interpreting the Bill of Rights, a court, tribunal or forum
>
> *(a)* must promote the values that underlie an open and democratic society based on human dignity, equality and freedom;
>
> *(b)* must consider international law; and
>
> *(c)* may consider foreign law.

These sections determine in essence that: international law *must* be considered by the courts when interpreting South African law in order to ensure consistency between domestic law and international law; state constitutional jurisprudence of other nations *may* be considered as a tool to assist with interpretation, but it does not constitute a binding precedent;[6] and international treaties which have been approved by Parliament are binding. This interpretation guide is intended to assist the courts when considering developments in international and municipal law concerning the rights of individuals, minorities and indigenous people.[7]

---

[5] While the notion of 'universal rights' rolls easily off the tongue, in practice the universality is not always simple to apply in the context of legal pluralism, which is characterised by diversity of local norms, laws, customs and cultures. (Chapter 2) An emphasis on universal rights may therefore, ironically, reduce the scope of individual identity rights and liberties because of the emphasis on universal consistency and uniformity. The understanding and application of rights such as freedom of expression, association, religion and culture in domestic settings may vary based on the customs, practices and traditions of the local populace. See, for example, Chapter 6 in the discussion about Ubuntu, how a customary concept has become a vehicle for bringing international human rights norms into South African jurisprudence. Some may be concerned that Ubuntu is being misused as a Trojan horse to introduce foreign concepts into customary law at the cost of tradition.

[6] Note, for example, how South African courts have, in the recognition of native title, drawn from the Mabo judgment of Australia. (Alexkor case 2004; Barrie 2018) The Constitutional Court in 2011 declared succinctly as follows about the utility to consider international jurisprudence: There is 'no escape from the manifest constitutional injunction to integrate, in a way the Constitution permits, international law obligations into our domestic law'. (Glenister case 2011, para 202)

[7] See, for example, the extensive references to international and comparative municipal law in the first judgment of the Constitutional Court, in which the court abolished the death penalty. Additionally, more recently there has been an emphasis on referencing international law to ascertain the consultation standards and practices that should be followed when consulting with indigenous people about activities that may affect their traditional lands. (Makwanyane case 1995; Baleni case 2019) There are often, as Ndulo highlights, references in South African

International law has experienced fluctuations in its stance regarding the recognition and protection of minority rights. Some of the earliest treaties between European states dealt with the protection of specific vulnerable minorities, with particular consideration to their religious rights. Historically the protection of minority rights was not constitutionally relevant outside the European sphere. The recognition and protection of minority rights was a major concern (principally within the European theatre) of the League of Nations. After the Second World War the United Nations initially sought to redirect the debate from collective minority 'rights' to solely the protection of individual rights. Practical realities, however, demanded a re-think, and since the 1960s various initiatives have been taken in international law under the auspices of the United Nations, as well as other international and regional agencies, to protect and promote more effectively the rights of minorities, including political participatory collective rights in pluralistic settings.[8]

---

jurisprudence to the jurisprudence of other countries as well as to regional instruments such as the European Convention on Human Rights. (Ndulo 2021) Note below my concern and criticism that insights from foreign law are not sought consistently, when sought it is often applied selectively, and the weight attributed to foreign jurisprudence is not clear. There is a risk of case law hunting, whereby judges find judgments that suit a particular outcome, rather than using foreign judgments to assist with an outcome.

[8] As explained later, the awareness of the importance of minority protection as a politically desired outcome should not be construed as minorities under international law enjoying collective group rights. International law does not support collective rights for minorities as if they are distinct legal entities separate from individuals. The legal entity that is the bearer of identity rights is the individual. Awareness of minority rights must therefore be understood within the context of bills of rights, whereby the right of individuals to practise their culture and speak their language *in association* with other members of the same minority is recognised. To the extent that specific *political participatory rights* are granted to minorities in the institutional design of the state, for example through quotas, guaranteed seats in the legislature, vetoes over certain policy areas, participation in a government of national unity and cultural self-government on a territorial or non-territorial basis, those arrangements do not derive from justiciable rights in international law, but are rather designed for the specific circumstances of a specific state. (Hannum 2023) See, for example, the non-binding guidelines that have been developed in Europe to encourage institutional arrangements that better accommodate political participation by ethnocultural minorities. (Lund Recommendations 1999; Ljubljana Guidelines 2012) Although international law emphasises the rights of the individual as the cornerstone in protecting minorities, these should be considered a minimum threshold. States are encouraged to go beyond this threshold and establish expanded institutional and policy arrangements for the protection of minorities. Close examination of international institutional arrangements is striking in revealing how many states have adopted some form of protection of minorities, even if only indirectly by way of design of the electoral system or decentralisation to regional and local governments. (Dinstein and Tabory 2023)

As complex and controversial as the topic of minority rights may be, there is a realisation in international organisations and within states, especially in emerging democracies, that the failure to successfully accommodate the rights of minorities can often be directly linked to civil and social unrest, sometimes escalating to violence and, in some instances, demands for secession.[9] The protection of minority rights, vague as it may be, remains at the top of the agenda of democratisation and stabilisation efforts internationally. Topidi reminds us that 'the war in Ukraine constitutes a brutal reminder of the significant challenges in ethno-cultural minority protection standards and policies on our continent'. (Topidi 2025, 3)

Regardless of efforts to individualise minority rights, political reality and democratisation have kept the collective protection of minority rights on the agenda of international organisations, including the UN. For example, in December 2022, at the close of a two-day summit conducted by the United Nations under the auspices of the Human Rights Committee, Special Rapporteur on Minority Issues Fernand de Varennes made the following concluding observation:

> [N]ot enough is being done at the international level: minorities are the last major group at the United Nations with *no specific mechanism* or initiative to strengthen the discussion and protection of their human rights such as a permanent forum or a voluntary fund. Many recommendations clearly show this needs to be addressed as a matter of urgency. . . .The most emphatic recommendation not only coming out of this forum but from all regional forums was about the *need for a legally binding treaty on minority rights with an associated oversight mechanism* which would guide both states and non-state actors. It was widely regarded as the best possible way forward for all major stakeholders since it would provide the opportunity to channel minority activism, diplomacy and expertise into a systematic, long-term conversation about

---

[9] During the negotiations to design the South African Constitution, many well-established liberal democracies were also grappling with demands for greater accommodation and recognition of ethnocultural minorities. Examples included Belgium (process of federalisation of the regions on the basis of language and community self-government in Brussels); Australia (recognition of indigenous people); Finland, Denmark and Norway (recognition of Sámi people); New Zealand (adjustment of the electoral system to better accommodate the Māori); Canada (new Bill of Rights, indigenous rights and demands for autonomy and secession by Quebec); United Kingdom (decentralisation demands of Scotland, Wales and Northern Ireland); Spain (decentralisation and asymmetry between regions); Hungary (introduction of nationality councils); Estonia (re-introduction of cultural councils); Italy (special arrangements in South Tyrol); Ukraine (protection of nationality rights); Nigeria (demarcation of additional states and introduction of the 'federal' principle for informal power-sharing); Ethiopia (accommodation of nationalities); and efforts at the supranational level in Europe to develop more effective regional minority protection standards.

> ways to respond to the world's many changes and challenges, including the impact of social media and the rise of hate speech and incitement to violence (emphasis added). (de Varennes 2022a)

Given the overemphasis that had been placed in the immediate post-Second World War period on individual rights as the sole basis for the protection of minorities, it was no surprise when Francesco Capotorti, Special Rapporteur of the Sub-Commission on the Prevention of Discrimination and Protection of Minorities of the United Nations, made the following observation in his groundbreaking report on the protection of minorities in 1979:

> For quite a long time after the end of the Second World War, it was thought – and stated in writing – that the question of the international protection of minorities was no longer topical. During the past few years however, *that view has proved to be mistaken* (emphasis added). (Capotorti 1979, iii)

The sentiment of Capotorti was echoed by the Venice Commission, when in 1994, at the time of the South African negotiations, it observed that since the 1970s the recognition and protection of minority rights had become a priority within the European sphere:

> It was an *urgent choice*: violent ethnic conflicts were beginning to rise up in several places on the new European map. (emphasis added) (Venice Commission 1994, 2)

In 2021 Special Rapporteur de Varennes made the following observation about the contemporary relevance of the protection of minorities and the risks faced by communities who feel excluded, discriminated against or marginalised:

> [I]t is important to highlight and illustrate the direct connection between the denial of the human rights of minorities and so many of the world's growing number of conflicts. This connection is sometimes obstructed behind the more general terms of 'exclusion', 'group-based grievances' and 'inequalities'. In their joint report, the United Nations and the World Bank assert, for example, that 'many of today's violent conflicts relate to group-based grievances arising from inequality, exclusion, and feelings of injustice' and that 'it is when an aggrieved group assigns blame to others or to the state for its perceived economic, political, or social exclusion that its grievances may become politicized and risk tipping into violence'. (UN–World Bank 2018, 109) In making that assertion, they are actually pointing the finger at situations that most likely involve legislation, policies or practices that unreasonably or unjustifiably have a negative impact on national or ethnic, religious and linguistic minorities, and that therefore presumably risk violating one of the fundamental pillars of the global human rights regime – the right to equality without discrimination in international law. (emphasis added) (de Varennes 2021 para 43)

In the next section a brief overview traces the development of minority protection arrangements in international law. It begins with ad hoc arrangements within states prior to the League of Nations, followed by a shift to attempt to establish universal norms by the League of Nations among states, then progresses to the individualisation of minority rights by the United Nations, and finally the narrative leads to the gradual acceptance by international organisations, such as the United Nations, that special institutional arrangements may be necessary for minorities, either through individual identity rights or special collective political participatory arrangements in institutional design. (De Villiers 2022g)

4.2 INTERNATIONAL LAW – FROM 'ADHOCRACY' TO INDIVIDUALISM, AND ON TO THE (LIMITED) RECOGNITION OF MINORITY RIGHTS

4.2.1 Minority rights prior to the League of Nations

The recognition and protection of the rights of minorities is a topic that has attracted attention for many centuries, gaining prominence since the beginning of the twentieth century.

One of the most notable earlier arrangements for minority self-government was enacted during the Ottoman empire (c AD 13–1923), when the millet system was used to grant to communities, principally religious (Greek Orthodox, Armenian and Jews) but also ethnic (the Kurds also had a millet (Tas 2013, 168)), a form of self-government that could, within the highly centralised empire, arrange their community affairs consistent with their traditions, customs and beliefs. (Barkey and Gavrilis 2017) The communities did not live separately in a territorial sense, instead intermingling with the rest of the population while maintaining their own institutional and autonomy arrangements for aspects of their faith and traditions. (Tamanaha 2021, 37) In contemporary terms this amounted to a form of non-state law pluralism. (Chapter 2) These communities not only self-governed according to their own beliefs and customs, but also raised taxes from their community and provided social services such as education, family law, dispute resolution, medical treatment and elderly care to their community. (Cakal 2020) The Christian Orthodox Church, for example, was for all practical purposes transformed into a quasi-political governing institution that represented the interests of the Greek faithful on a local community and household basis. As the Ottoman empire declined, approximately 18 self-governing millets were in operation. These millets functioned with what is now described as 'non-territorial' jurisdiction, addressing the needs of their members regardless of their intermingled living arrangements with other communities. (De Villiers 2022a, 44)

Another noteworthy example of an early instrument of minority protection in Europe was the Edict of Nantes, signed on 30 April 1598, which recognised the rights of the Protestant minority in Catholic-dominated France. (Sutherland 1987) Meanwhile, the 1648 Treaty of Westphalia, comprising the Treaty of Münster (24 October 1648) and the Treaty of Osnabrück (15 May 1648), which brought an end to the Thirty Years War fought over religion, was particularly aimed at the protection of religious (Christian) minorities. (Reus-Smit 2013) The Treaty of Westphalia has been described as the first 'World Charter' for a world order based on the independence of states, non-intervention in the domestic affairs of states and legal equality between states. Although this categorisation may not be entirely accurate, the treaty was indeed groundbreaking in seeking an international order whereby states respected each other's sovereignty while simultaneously safeguarding the rights of religious minorities. The Treaty of Westphalia has also been described as the 'traditional birth date of the Euro-Christian type of international law'. (Pascale and Tonolo 2022, 2)

One of the first international instruments to formally recognise the rights of minorities was the Polish Minority Treaty (1919).[10] This provided that minorities, most notably Jewish communities residing in Poland, had the right to establish, manage and control, at their own expense, charitable, religious and social institutions, schools and other educational establishments, with the

[10] 28 June 1919. (Fink 1998) Fourteen countries (Albania, Austria, Bulgaria, Czechoslovakia, Estonia, Greece, Hungary, Iraq, Latvia, Lithuania, Poland, Romania, Turkey and Yugoslavia) adopted similar treaties aimed at protecting minorities within their national boundaries. These were ad hoc arrangements, primarily due to concerns about the disruptive potential of minority demands not being accommodated, and arising from the insistence of kin-states whose citizens were residing in other countries. The role of kin-states to promote the interests of members of their community residing in other countries remains relevant in contemporary society. (Hofmann, Malloy, and Rein 2018a, 21) As is evident in European history, the activism of a kin-state may increase the risk of conflict (the most notable contemporary example is the invasion of Ukraine by Russia). On the other hand, a minority without a kin-state (such as the Roma in Europe) may find that its interests are not adequately advocated or taken seriously. There are also many other instances where the foreign policy of states is influenced by the plight of their cultural citizens in other countries. An example of this is the relationship between Turkey and Greece in reference to the status of Cyprus, and Turkey and the ethnic Turks living in North Macedonia. (Gözübenli 2023) Also note how in some instance states grant nationality to their cultural citizens who live in another state. (Erez and Banai 2024)

right to use their own language and to exercise their religion freely therein.[11] Notable in the Polish Treaty was a proviso stipulating that in localities where a 'considerable proportion' of the population consisted of a minority, an 'equitable share' of public funds should be allocated for their education (Minority Treaty 1919, art 9). Several other European-based treaties aimed at protecting the rights of minorities were also concluded around the same time.[12]

The general approach prevalent in the European context before the League of Nations could be characterised as a form of 'adhocracy' whereby special arrangements were enacted on a needs basis to relieve pressure points. During this period no regional or universal interstate norms or standards for the recognition or protection of minorities existed. Instead, limited arrangements were made within states at the sole discretion of governments, typically in response to potential or actual trouble spots involving minority populations.[13]

4.2.2 Minority rights under the League of Nations

The League of Nations was established in 1919 with the objectives of maintaining and promoting international peace.[14] The League of Nations witnessed the establishment of new territorial arrangements, particularly in Europe and parts of the Middle East, where populations in many states were diverse in language,

[11] Article 8: 'Polish nationals who belong to racial, religious or linguistic minorities shall enjoy the same treatment and security in law and in fact as other Polish nationals. In particular, they shall have an equal right to establish, manage and control, at their own expense, charitable, religious and social institutions, schools and other educational establishments, with the right to use their own language and to exercise their religion freely therein.'

[12] Refer, for example, to the treaties between the Allied and Associated Powers involving Poland (28 June 1919), Serbia, Slovenia and Croatia (10 September 1919), and Greece (10 August 1920).

[13] Note, for example, the proposals made by Bauer and Renner to accommodate nationalities in the Austro-Hungarian empire. (De Villiers 2016a) These proposals were not implemented in the empire (owing to the outbreak of the First World War, which saw the dissolution of the empire), but the ideas remain at the forefront of contemporary literature and discussions about community self-government and power-sharing where an own territorial basis is not suitable or where a combination of territorial and non-territorial arrangements are required. (Nimni 2007; Andeva et al 2023)

[14] Article 22 of the Covenant of the League of Nations made reference to religious and other communities within certain parts of the world, but there was no universal commitment to protect the rights of minorities. The so-called Minority Treaty that arose from the Treaty of Versailles sought to address the situation of minorities in particular countries but did not establish binding international norms.

religion and culture. Many ethnocultural communities had been split into two or more national territories and found themselves within newly created states or on the 'wrong' side of newly drawn international borders.[15] Extensive arrangements were practically implemented to recognise population diversity, driven by the concern that overlooking plurality might lead to new instability within the broader European context. (Roucek 1929) This fear stemmed from the potential for kin-states to interfere in the domestic affairs of another state to protect the interests of their members. At that stage there was little concern about minorities (or indigenous people) in other parts of the world (besides in parts of the Middle East such as Iraq and Turkey).

It was, however, acknowledged that each minority could not be endowed with its own nation-state and therefore arrangements had to be made to protect minority groups within the states in which they resided. The principal mechanisms to achieve this were decentralisation to areas where minorities resided and country-specific self-management and power-sharing arrangements. (Rosting 1923, Scheu 2020) The minority arrangements primarily focused on the individual right to practise culture, language and religion, as well as the freedom to speak their own language. The emphasis was on individual identity rights rather than the design of institutions for collective self-government, autonomy or power-sharing. (Åkermark 1927) Furthermore, the recognition of minorities was often prompted by the insistence of a kin-state, which may have had concerns about the security and safety of its cultural citizens residing in another state.[16] At the time the typical rights of minorities sought to be protected by international law included equality and non-discrimination, the right to practise their language, culture and religion, an informal obligation on states to support minority institutions when the concentration of people or the size of the group justified it,[17] recognition of the customs and practices of minorities

---

[15] Consider, for instance, the extensive efforts under the European umbrella to foster greater harmony, cooperation and integration among communities that are divided by international borders. (De Villiers 2009; Medeiros 2018; Bober 2019)

[16] Note how in light of the ongoing Ukraine–Russian conflict, the status of Russians in other parts of Europe has given rise to security concerns in the context of minority rights. (Csergő, Kallas, and Kiss 2025)

[17] Refer, for example, to art 9 of the Polish Minority Treaty, which provided as follows: 'Poland will provide in the public educational system in towns and districts in which a considerable proportion of Polish nationals of other than Polish speech are residents adequate facilities for ensuring that in the primary schools the instruction shall be given to the children of such Polish nationals through the medium of their own language.'

in the public sphere – particularly at the local level – and decentralisation and autonomy for regional and local areas. In exceptional cases, like Estonia, the special rights included some autonomy for cultural groups on a non-territorial basis. (Ermacora 1983; De Villiers 1989; Tark 2022)[18]

The challenge to define what is meant by 'minority' had already presented itself at this stage. As Nagy and Vizi put it: 'The lack of a definition of the term "minority" has haunted the international community for quite a long time, and despite all the efforts made, there is still no universally accepted definition of the minority concept.' (Nagy and Vizi 2024, 2) Who constitutes a minority, how is the collectively of a group of individuals defined, and who acts on behalf of a community of people without it being incorporated into a legal entity? The Permanent Court of International Justice, created by the League of Nations in 1922, attempted to give content to the concept of 'minority' by suggesting that the term refers to a group of persons living in a given country or locality, having a race, religion, language and traditions of their own and who are united by this identity in a sentiment of solidarity, with a view to preserving their traditions, maintaining their form of worship, ensuring the instruction and upbringing of their children in accordance with the spirit and traditions of their race, and rendering mutual assistance to each other. (PCIJ-Greco-Bulgarian case 1930, para 17)

International law, as applied to the European context, essentially acknowledged that an adequate system for minority protection would rely on two fundamental principles: first, it would require non-discrimination and equal protection for members of the relevant minority; and, secondly, in certain cases, it would involve the recognition of special minority rights, the content of which would

[18] In regard to non-territorial arrangements, Estonia, in the period between the world wars, was arguably *the* most prominent example of a nation providing protection of community autonomy *without* using territory as a basis for decentralisation. (De Villiers 2012c) While the Estonian system of minority protection was hailed at the time as an example of how minorities who live intermingled with the rest of the population could be granted a form of personal or non-territorial autonomy, the system was abolished at the advent of the Second World War when Estonia was invaded by Russia. Efforts since the 1990s by Estonia to reintroduce cultural councils for minority communities have had only very limited success. (Poleshchuk 2015; Smith 2023, 76) In Chapter 2 it was noted that legal pluralism implies an own non-state *legal* system. The ethnocultural minorities in Estonia were primarily concerned about their right to effective political participation in matters affecting their culture, religious customs and identity, rather than an own non-state legal system to replace the state legal system, albeit that the Jewish community's self-determination also had a religious component. (Salat 2023, 10)

be determined on a state-by-state basis.[19] In the Albania case the court declared that the right of the minority must be assessed as follows:

> If the object and effect of the second sentence of the paragraph is to ensure that Albanian nationals belonging to racial, linguistic or religious minorities shall in fact enjoy the same treatment as other Albanian nationals, it is clear that the expression 'equal right' must be construed on the assumption that the right stipulated must always be accorded to the members of the minority. The idea embodied in the expression 'equal right' is that the right thus conferred on the members of the minority cannot in any case be inferior to the corresponding right of other Albanian nationals. *In other words, the members of the minority must always enjoy the right stipulated in the Declaration, and, in addition, any more extensive rights which the State may accord to other nationals.* The right provided by the Declaration is in fact the minimum necessary to guarantee effective and genuine equality as between the majority and the minority; but if the members of the majority should be granted a right more extensive than that which is provided, the principle of equality of treatment would come into play and would require that the more extensive right should also be granted to the members of the minority. (emphasis added) (Albania case 1935 para 70)[20]

Although the League of Nations attempted to secure the rights of minority communities more effectively, it must be noted that at the time the plight of minorities (and indigenous people) in large parts of the world, such as Africa, Asia and South America, was not its immediate concern. The same standards of recognition of plurality being applied to the European sphere was not accorded to minorities in the colonies of European states. The League of Nations nevertheless represented the first attempt to develop general 'universal' norms aimed at preventing and resolving conflicts that arise from disgruntled ethnocultural minorities, even though those arrangements were primarily applicable to some European states.

---

[19] In the Albania case the court found that the right to establish and manage their own schools is 'indispensable in enabling the minority to enjoy the same treatment as the majority, not only in law but also in fact'. (Albania case 1935 para 67) The court did not, however, mandate state funding for such community schools. (Albania case 1935 para 79) This recognition highlights the crucial role of mother-tongue teaching to promote cultural identity, a theme that continues to challenge South Africa. (Chapter 9)

[20] As far as the *funding* of educational facilities is concerned, the court declared as follows: 'Albanian nationals belonging to racial, linguistic or religious minorities have the right to maintain, manage and control *at their own expense*, or to establish in the future, charitable, religious and social institutions, schools and other educational establishments, with the right to use their own language and to exercise their religion freely therein.' (emphasis added) (Albania case 1935 para 79) As shown in Chapter 9, international law remains supportive of mother-tongue education as a sound policy measure, but not as a legal entitlement to be funded by the state.

4.2.3 Minority rights under the United Nations

Following the Second World War and its associated atrocities, where the identification of individuals belonging to certain minorities was exploited for persecution and genocide rather than protection, the international focus shifted away from collective minority rights. Attention was redirected to safeguard individual rights as the sole means to protect the rights of individuals belonging to minority groups. It was thought, overly optimistically in hindsight, that the rights of all individuals, including those that belong to minority groups, could best be protected through a bill of rights which protects the rights of individuals to equality, non-discrimination, freedom of association, religion and so forth. (Capotorti 1979) There was a belief that no additional mechanisms, institutional designs or special categories of rights for the purposes of political participation or self-determination were required to protect minorities collectively as communities. (Korkeakivi 2018)

The Preamble to the Charter of the United Nations thus speaks of 'faith in fundamental human rights, the dignity and worth of the human person, and the equal rights of men and women'. The Universal Declaration of Human Rights 1948 seeks to establish a 'common standard of achievement for all peoples and all nations', despite making no mention of minority protection or minority rights (or indigenous rights).[21] Although the Universal Declaration is not a treaty, it has set a universal standard and its provisions have arguably become part of customary international law. (Petane case 1988)[22]

[21] The approach towards the rights of indigenous people has evolved since their collective rights became the subject of recognition pursuant to ILO 169 and UNDRIP. The collective rights of indigenous people, such as self-determination and autonomy, are recognised *in addition* to their rights as individuals to equality and non-discrimination. (De Villiers 2023f, 64) The reasoning in international law behind the proposition that indigenous people also have collective rights is based on the recognition that: indigenous people had systems of government and sovereignty *prior* to colonisation or settlement; those rights were exercised over traditional territories; and those ancient rights may be recognised in contemporary law if the indigenous community continues to function as a society. (De Villiers 2023e, 31; Yorta Yorta (HCA) case 2002) The distinction between minority rights and indigenous rights within international law is not, however, without controversy, and it should be noted that UNDRIP is not legally binding, meaning the collective rights of indigenous people recognised therein are at best aspirational. (De Villiers 2023b, 52)

[22] The court acknowledged at (58G–J) that, while the 'abstract statements' included in the Universal Declaration may be regarded as rules of customary international law, this has not prevented states from committing atrocities against their domestic populations with seeming impunity. The limitations of international law and lack of effective enforceability are inevitably affected by the willingness of states to adhere to those norms.

No special mechanisms for the protection of minority rights in the context of institutional design were therefore catered for by the United Nations in the immediate post-Second World War period. In the words of Kunz in 1954, the accepted approach in the immediate post-Second World War period was as follows: '[T]he well-dressed international lawyer wears "human rights" as the new fashion, while prior to World War II the fashion was "minority rights"'. (Kunz 1954, 282)

Since the 1960s there has been an evolution in international opinion regarding minority protection. In contemporary international and constitutional law, as well as in political science, there is now a greater awareness of the importance of protecting ethnocultural minorities and the merit in developing institutional arrangements and political processes that facilitate their effective participation in public affairs. This is because the inadequate recognition and protection of minority rights often result in permanent marginalisation and the absence of minority voices in policy-making, leading in turn to discrimination and potential political instability. The topic of minority protection has therefore, for all practical purposes as a result of political instability, forced its way back onto the agenda of international law and democratisation efforts. While the legal subject eligible for protection remains the individual, greater regard is being given to the identity rights claimed by minorities in functional areas such as culture, language, education and religion. International law seeks to protect individual rights in the context of those rights being exercised in community with others, but without granting a legal identity to the community. In addition, there is greater pragmatism within states about incorporating special arrangements into institutional design and policy procedures to accommodate the political participatory rights of specific minorities. This includes mechanisms such as power-sharing, guaranteed representation, vetoes, advisory bodies and self-government. In this regard, Hilpold observes as follows:

> Over the last years, it has, however, become clear that minority protection is no longer an issue only for specialists and of secondary importance as it has been viewed at the UN level for many years. . . . Minority rights protection has been identified as a major factor for securing peace and stability. (Hilpold 2007, 204)[23]

[23] The United Nations recognises that the outcome and stability of democratisation efforts often hinge on the ability of the rights of ethnocultural minorities to be peacefully accommodated. (UNHRC 2022; UNHRC 2010)

The adoption of the International Covenant on Civil and Political Rights (ICCPR) (ICCPR 1966) and the International Covenant on Economic, Social and Cultural Rights (ICESCR) (ICESCR 1966) in 1966, and their coming into force in 1976, represented a major step towards the recognition of identity rights that relate to culture, language, religion and self-determination. Of special relevance to this book is art 27 of the ICCPR, which provides as follows:

> In those states in which ethnic, religious or linguistic minorities exist, persons belonging to such minorities shall not be denied the right, in community with other members of their group, to enjoy their own culture, to profess and practice their own religion, or to use their own language.

Article 27 is *the* principal international standard for the recognition and protection of the rights of persons belonging to minorities. (Taylor 2020)[24] Although this article is an important milestone in the recognition and development of minority rights, it leaves unresolved many questions. These include the definition of a minority, whether the rights are exercised by individuals or by a community as a collective entity,[25] whether there is a duty on the state to take positive action to assist members of a minority group to enjoy their rights or whether the state should merely refrain from interfering with minorities exercising their rights, and whether art 27 provides the basis for institutional development that may assist minorities – for example, by providing different forms of political participation via autonomy, self-determination and power-sharing. (Tomuschat 1983)

Most importantly, art 27 does not provide a normative framework, objective standard or universal criteria for the protection of *political participatory* and self-determination rights of minorities. The article establishes important principles regarding the rights of individuals, but lacks substance in setting out how, if at all,

[24] It is said that art 27 marked a 'new era' for the protection of minorities (Taylor 2020, 787) and that 'the promotion and protection of the rights of persons belonging to national or ethnic, religious and linguistic minorities contribute to political and social stability and peace, and enrich the cultural diversity and heritage of society as a whole in the States in which such persons live'. (UN Resolution 2004)

[25] It is widely accepted that art 27 *does not* accord a collective right to minorities as groups. As Taylor summarises: 'Article 27 rights belong to the individual, like all rights in Part III of the Covenant, in spite of there being a collective dimension to art 27 because they are enjoyed in community with the other members of their group.' (Taylor 2020, 789) In this respect note the Fosen case, in which it was held that the right of an individual is protected against the backdrop of the cultural association of the person with other persons from the same community and hence the concern of an indigenous person could be taken as representative of a community. Thereby the individual and collective dimensions of art 27 were highlighted. (Fosen case 2021)

those principles translate into practice for the purposes of power-sharing, self-determination, autonomy or other collective political participatory rights. As a result the international yardstick by which states are expected to respond to minorities remains vague and subject to domestic discretion. (Yupsanis 2013)[26]

For the purposes of this chapter the following principles were relevant during the constitution-drafting process of South Africa in terms of the practical implementation of art 27 of the ICCPR:[27] first, the article relates to the recognition and protection of individual rights, and not to the collective rights of a minority; secondly, the rights exercised pursuant to art 27 can form the basis of a class action by individuals working together, but the primary right-bearer who must enforce the right remains the individual;[28] thirdly, the term 'minority' is not defined in international law and hence it is left to states to ascertain whether there

[26] Yupsanis concludes that despite art 27 being lauded as a 'hard law' protection of the rights of minorities and a '*grundnorm*' for minority protection, on plain reading it does not offer such a level of certainty owing to the ambiguity it leaves and the absence of clearly articulated and enforceable universal norms. (Yupsanis 2013, 360)

[27] In the few years preceding the constitution-drafting process in South Africa, Cloete and De Villiers published their respective PhDs, in which essential principles for the protection of minorities based on international law and practice were identified and recommendations were made for South Africa. (Cloete 1981; De Villiers 1989) They emphasised that any sustainable minority protection arrangement under a future South African Constitution would have to be *non-racial* and based on voluntary association. This universal standard posed a challenge to the desire of the Afrikaans community to be accorded special participatory rights. At the time of writing of this book, disagreements remain within the broader Afrikaans-speaking community (whites, blacks and coloured) about what special measures, if any, are suitable to protect and promote the interests of the Afrikaans language and culture. These disagreement are evidenced by the mixed response from within the Afrikaans-speaking community to the release of the Afrikaner Declaration in April 2024 (Afrikaner Declaration 2024). The racial element underlying the Declaration suggests that there remains within the Afrikaans-speaking community strong disagreement about the relevancy of race to define themselves. No other ethnocultural community in South Africa has demanded collective rights, except perhaps the Khoisan, but they do so under the banner of indigenous people. (De Villiers 2023b, 47)

[28] Note in this respect the Fosen case, in which the Supreme Court of Norway ruled that the construction of a windfarm violated the rights of the indigenous Sámi to collectively enjoy their culture pursuant to art 27 of the ICCPR. The windfarm constituted a 'significant adverse effect' on their cultural rights to practise reindeer herding. (Fosen case 2021) The interesting aspect of the judgment for purposes of this chapter is that the rights of the community collectively were upheld pursuant to an individual rights to enjoy culture. This highlights how the divide between an individual right and a collective right can be overcome. The court emphasised that art 27 ICCPR 'must be viewed in context with art 108 of the Constitution [of Norway], which imposes a duty on the state authorities "to create conditions enabling the Sámi people to preserve and develop its language, culture and way of life"'. (Fosen case 2021, para 99; Ravna 2022)

are communities within the state that merit the protection accorded by art 27; fourthly, the article does not grant collective rights to political participation of self-government, self-determination, autonomy or power-sharing; and, fifthly, the article does not impose a positive duty on the state to support, financially or otherwise, individuals who belong to minorities to exercise their individual rights, or to financially or otherwise support the associations, schools and clubs established by minorities.[29]

The UN Declaration on the Rights of Persons belonging to National or Ethnic, Religious and Linguistic Minorities (UN Declaration on Minorities 1992)[30] seeks to expand the intended operation of art 27 of the ICCPR by requiring that states take positive action to assist minorities. (Phillips 2015) While not legally enforceable, the adoption of the Declaration highlights how the protection of minorities has gained credibility and prominence since the establishment of the UN.

The Declaration attempts to set a new standard for the protection of minorities, such as in the way it recognises the rights of minorities to 'participation'[31] and 'mother-tongue education'.[32] Although the Minorities Declaration (similar to UNDRIP) does not have the status of an international treaty and therefore cannot be regarded as binding in international law, the Declaration's recognition of the positive role that the state should play to assist minorities is a major step forward

[29] Dlamini observes that art 27 does not provide for a right to education and, to the extent that education may be read into the article, it does not place an obligation on the state to fund this education. (Dlamini 1994, 578) Although art 26 of the Universal Declaration does recognise the right to education, it does not make mention of education in language of choice or state funding of mother-tongue education. Article 13 of the ICESCR also recognises the right to education, but it does not recognise a right to state-funded education in language of choice. The same applies to art 17 of the African Charter on Human and Peoples' Rights. Note the Belgian Linguistic case, in which the European Court of Human Rights held that the right to education does not imply a right to state-funded mother-tongue education since there is no positive obligation on the state to fund specific language schools for minorities. (Chapter 9; Belgian Linguistic case 1968)

[30] Adopted unanimously by the General Assembly of the United Nations on 18 December, 1992. Although the Declaration was inspired by art 29 of the ICCPR, it is not a treaty under international law and therefore, similarly to UNDRIP, it is not legally binding.

[31] UN Declaration on Minorities 1992, art 2(3): Participation: 'Persons belonging to minorities have the right to participate freely in decisions on the national and, where appropriate, regional level, concerning the minority to which they belong or the regions in which they live, and in a manner not incompatible with national legislation.'

[32] UN Declaration on Minorities 1993, art 4(3): Education: 'States should take appropriate measures so that, wherever possible, persons belonging to minorities have adequate opportunities to learn their mother tongue or to have instruction in their mother tongue.'

to develop a more secure political and moral basis for protecting minorities. (Barten 2015)

In the field of education, for example, the Declaration seeks to place an obligation on states to 'take appropriate measures in the field of education in order to encourage knowledge of the history, traditions, language and culture of the minorities existing within their territory'. (UN Declaration on Minorities 1992, art 4(5)) The underlying question remains, namely which minorities 'deserve' special measures since it is legally, practically, administratively and financially impossible to accord special protection to all ethnocultural minorities. (Magazzini 2024, 1829)[33]

4.2.4 Regional instruments: European Convention on National Minorities

The most important contemporary regional instruments designed for the protection of minorities are the European-wide European Charter for Regional or Minority Languages (European Charter for Languages 1992) and the Framework Convention for the Protection of National Minorities (FCNM) (European Framework Convention 1998). (Hofmann, Malloy, and Rein 2018b)

The FCNM is so far the first and only legally-binding charter solely designed for the protection of minority rights within international law, although its scope is limited to the European region.[34] (Weller 2005) It is exclusively dedicated to the rights of minorities, acknowledging in its Preamble that, within the context of Europe, 'the protection of national minorities is essential to stability, democratic security and peace'. (Hofmann, Malloy, and Rein 2018a) Regardless of the priority given to the protection of minority rights, a 'fundamental problem'

[33] This challenge to determine when a minority is entitled to special measures is highlighted in the discussions in South Africa on the status of the Afrikaans language. While some contend that Afrikaans is entitled to special measures and protection, such as state funding in single-medium schools, others respond by saying such measures amount to ongoing discrimination and the shoring up of the privileged position that Afrikaans gained under apartheid. The persistence by some within the Afrikaans community that race forms an essential element to define their community (e.g. Afrikaner Declaration 2024) undermines the very protections sought under international law.

[34] At the time of publication 39 countries and Kosovo had ratified the FCNM. Note that the European Union and its member states are not bound to the FCNM pursuant to the European Union's founding treaties. The FCNM is a separate treaty to which individual states in the European Union may choose to become signatories. As a distinct treaty it has also been signed by states that are not members of the European Union.

remains the lack of definition of minority. (Chronowski and Nagy 2024, 3) The ECtHR has observed that 'in the area under consideration [identification of a minority group] it may be difficult to frame laws with a high degree of precision. It may well even be undesirable to formulate rigid rules.' (Gorzelik case 2004, para 69) In the Sidiropoulos case the ECtHR observe that the identification and presence of a minority is an 'historical fact' of each country. (Sidiropoulos case 1998, para 41)

The FCNM contains general principles to which practical content must be given by the respective member states through their constitutional, political and policy arrangements. (Explanatory Report on FCNM 1995, para 11) The FCNM does not define what constitutes a national minority, instead leaving it to the states to determine which communities within their population ought to be treated as a national minority for purposes of the FCNM. (Explanatory Report on FCNM 1995, para 12) It prescribes general principles, but is silent on the specific methods for implementing these principles within states.[35] The enforceability of the FCNM is based on consensual political processes and advocacy, rather than litigation.[36]

[35] The FCNM is not enforceable through litigation, but rather through political mechanisms, reporting and advocacy. The Committee of Ministers of the Council of Europe and the Advisory Committee are involved in monitoring the implementation of and adherence to the FCNM. The Advisory Committee is responsible for ensuring that the standards of the Convention are applied by member states. The Advisory Committee comprises 18 experts appointed by the Committee of Ministers under the FCNM. States are required to submit a report containing comprehensive information on legislative and other measures taken to comply with the principles of the Framework Convention within one year of becoming a party to the FCNM. Further reports must be made on a periodic basis, or whenever requested by the Committee of Ministers. If a state fails to submit a report, the Committee of Ministers can authorise the Advisory Committee to start the monitoring process nevertheless. The Advisory Committee examines reports prepared by states and typically carries out country visits to hear submissions and conduct interviews. The Advisory Committee adopts an Opinion, which is given to a state for comment. A final report is then prepared and made public, containing findings, observations and recommendations. Follow-up meetings may be arranged to discuss the implementation of specific recommendations. The process is essentially consensual rather than litigious. Although at the outset the ACFC was originally seen as a weak arrangement without effective sanction powers, 'in reality, the ACFC has turned the tide and become an effective watchdog in Europe. Together with the European human rights regime, spearheaded by the European Court of Human Rights (ECtHR), the ACFC has created a niche for national minority rights protection that is requiring European governments to react and act. The ACFC has contributed considerably to the forming of this normative force.' (Malloy and Caruso 2013, 12)

[36] The lack of consistency in minority protection among states within the European context has been critically referred to as 'double standards'. (Henrard 2010)

Although the FCNM is limited in its application to states within the European domain, some of its principles may be relevant to other parts of the world where the protection of minority rights provides challenges to institutional design and policy processes.

In the context of the negotiation process in South Africa the *principles* underlying the FCNM were taken into account in expert meetings and workshops.[37] Among the FCNM's important principles, relevant for the purposes of this book, are the following: art 1 determines that the rights of minorities form an integral part of the international protection of human rights. (Hofmann 2018) According to the FCNM, 'no collective rights of minorities are envisaged', which means that in order to exercise the rights provided for in the Convention, individual members of a minority must act in their individual capacity and not as a collective entity. (Explanatory Report on FCNM 1995, para 31) This is consistent with the approach adopted by art 27 of the ICCPR. The rights under the FCNM can be collectively exercised when individuals jointly initiate proceedings, but this does not imply that the right itself is held by the community as a legal person; (Explanatory Report on FCNM 1995, para 37) Article 3 recognises the rights of individuals to choose to belong to a minority and to be treated as being part of a minority group. Self-identification is therefore acknowledged and members of a minority group may exercise their rights individually or collectively with other members of their community;[38] art 4 recognises the principles of non-discrimination and equality, asserting that no person may be disadvantaged for reasons of belonging to a minority group; art 5 refers to the essential elements of minority identity as 'religion, language, traditions and cultural heritage',

[37] The FCNM had not been adopted at the time of the South African negotiations, but the European efforts to codify a framework for minority protection through minimum norms informed the South African debate.

[38] The principle of freedom of association is not simple in its application to the membership of minority groups. The FCNM accepts there is a subjective and an objective element involved to determine membership of a community. Note the following examples of how disputes in various countries have arisen regarding purported membership of a community: in Finland the Sámi Parliament wishes to be able to assess the registration of Sámi voters and reject persons who do not meet certain criteria; in Australia there has been extensive litigation about who is an Aboriginal person and furthermore who belongs to a native title group; in New Zealand the self-declaration of a person as being Māori can be legally challenged; and in Hungary the initial elections for the nationality councils became discredited owing to non-nationality persons voting in nationality elections. (De Villiers 2021b) Free association with a community should therefore not be regarded as arbitrary and solely at the election of the individual, since 'individual choice shall be linked to some objective criteria'. (Marsal and Palermo 2018, 94)

while art 5(1) places an obligation on the states to promote conditions in which minorities can maintain their culture, language, traditions and religion; and arts 10, 11 and 14 acknowledge that minorities inhabiting specific areas may be entitled to enhanced rights such as various forms of territorial autonomy.

The FCNM does not mention non-territorial rights or non-territorial forms of autonomy. (Malloy and Salat 2021) The emphasis of the FCNM is principally on the cultural, linguistic and religious rights of nationalities as exercised by individuals, rather than on a form of legal pluralism whereby separate collective legal systems exist within the same national territory. The provisions of the FCNM apply to minorities wherever they live, whether concentrated in a specific geographical area or dispersed across a territory.[39] Article 10 recognises the right of minorities to use their language in private and in public, in particular when interacting with public authorities such as the judicial system. Article 13(2) recognises the right of minorities to establish educational institutions, but it does not place an obligation on the states to support or finance such institutions. (Explanatory Report on FCNM 1995, para 73) Article 15 requires states to create conditions for the effective participation of minorities in public affairs, particularly regarding matters that affect their identity.[40] This provision relates not only to various forms of autonomy that may be granted to minorities, but also to provide them with the opportunity to participate in the legislative and executive processes of government.[41]

---

[39] Malloy points out that the ACFC has consistently held that a requirement by a member state that a minority group represents half or more of a local population for its language to receive special status at the local level is incompatible with art 10(2) of the FCNM. Malloy notes that thresholds of as low as 10–20% have been declared compatible with this provision. (Malloy 2018, 213) No similar arrangement exists in South Africa, even though the language of education in public schools often reflects the language of the local community. (Chapter 9) Residential living patterns in South Africa are often so intermingled that there is no clear majority language at a community level. This often gives rise to the challenge for school boards to determine the language of education of public schools.

[40] Article 15 provides as follows: 'The Parties shall create the conditions necessary for the *effective participation* of persons belonging to national minorities in cultural, social and economic life and in public affairs, in particular those affecting them.' This may, in practice, give rise to power-sharing arrangements as well as territorial and non-territorial forms of autonomy, without constituting a justiciable right.

[41] The Explanatory Report which accompanied the Convention refers to the following measures as examples of steps that can be taken to give effect to art 15: consultation when states are contemplating legislative or administrative measures that affect minorities; involving minorities in the preparation, implementation and assessment of development plans; effective participation

In the European context, where the codification of minority rights is actively pursued and arguably the most advanced of any region in the world,[42] a detailed outline of practical mechanisms that may facilitate the protection of minorities through political participatory rights is included in the 1999 Lund Report entitled 'Lund Recommendations on the Effective Participation of National Minorities in Public Life' (Lund Recommendations 1999), as well as in the 2012 Ljubljana Guidelines on Integration of Diverse Societies. (Ljubljana Guidelines 2012) These recommendations serve as pragmatic guidelines intended to assist parties, not only in Europe but also in other countries, in the design of institutions and formulation of policies to accommodate minority rights. The recommendations do not have any legal status in international law.

Weller, following an assessment of the developments in international law to develop uniform standards for the protection of minorities, concluded as follows:

> One may therefore note that full and effective participation of national minorities in public life has been *established itself as a right* in international documents concerning the protection of national minorities. (emphasis added) (Weller 2007, 56)[43]

In addition to the instruments referred to above, several other standards aimed at protecting the rights of minorities and persons belonging to minorities have been adopted under the auspices of the United Nations.[44] While these international instruments are not legally enforceable, they nevertheless demonstrate the growing awareness on the part of the international community of the rights of minority groups and indigenous people. In addition to the UN-inspired

in decision-making processes and elected bodies at the national and local levels; and decentralised or local forms of government. (Explanatory Report on FCNM 1995, para 80)

[42] Palermo and Constantin suggest that the central, eastern and south-eastern parts of Europe are 'perhaps the most advanced laboratory for minority rights in general'. (Palermo and Constantin 2021, 179)

[43] Weller identified the following consultative and participatory mechanisms: co-decision making; consultation; coordination; and self-governance. The exercise of the right to participation, however, is not achievable through normal avenues of litigation and judicial remedy. Political effect can be given to rights to participation, but legal effect can only be given to the individual rights of persons belonging to minorities, not to the collective rights of minorities as if a corporate entity.

[44] These include the following: International Convention on the Elimination of all forms of Racial Discrimination (adopted by the UN in 1965 and entered into force in 1969); Convention on the Elimination of Discrimination against Women (adopted in 1979 and entered into force in 1981); Declaration on the Elimination of All Forms of Intolerance and Discrimination Based on Religion or Belief (adopted in 1981); ILO 1969 (adopted in 1989 and entered into force in 1991); and UNDRIP (resolution passed in 2007).

norms various regional human rights instruments have also been adopted in the Americas, Europe and Africa.[45]

4.2.5 Summary of minority protection in international law

In summary, a dichotomy persists between universal standards safeguarding minority rights through individual rights, and the demands of marginalised and threatened minorities seeking recognition and collective protection of their rights to effective political participation in matters that affect them as a community. This is not equated with legal pluralism since ethnocultural communities often do not adhere to an own legal system, but rather focus on a specific cultural, language or customary identity. This is because members of a minority community may feel excluded, discriminated against or disempowered because of their membership of a *community*. Their sense of exclusion is therefore felt collectively. The emphasis in international law on the protection of minorities by way of individual rights may therefore be legally sound and valuable as a minimum norm, but the sole focus on the rights of the individual is practically inadequate or ineffective in many circumstances. Although international law does not provide a benchmark about when special institutional arrangements for effective political participation should be made for minorities, it is accepted that political and social realities demand that some minorities require special protection, recognition or assistance to facilitate political participation as well as educational and other support.

The unresolved predicament of lack of a threshold when a minority is granted some form of collective participatory rights is highlighted in a report by a group of experts who advise the United Nations, in which they observe that 'many United Nations member states lack effective and genuinely comprehensive legal frameworks for the prevention of discrimination and promotion of equality'. (UN Experts 2022) States are generally concerned that any recognition of collective rights may cause balkanisation of the population into ethnic enclaves, but on the other hand a disgruntled minority may bring instability that could threaten the entire state. Pragmatism seems to be principal guide, rather than universality of norms.

[45] These include the following: European Convention for the Protection of Human Rights and Fundamental Freedoms (adopted by the Council of Europe in 1950 and entered into force in 1953); European Social Charter (adopted in 1961 and entered into force in 1965); American Convention on Human Rights (adopted in 1969 and entered into force in 1978); and African Charter on Human and Peoples' Rights (adopted in 1981 and entered into force in 1986).

The precarious position of some, although not all, ethnocultural communities in South Africa was described as follows in the Kill the Boer case of 2011:

> Minorities have no legislative or executive powers and are compelled to approach the court to protect their rights. They are particularly at risk due to the expense involved in such approaches. The fact that they are minorities and experience such difficulties frequently results in them being driven to protect their identity by invoking and enforcing within their group, customs, practices and conventions which are believed to be appropriate. In addition, they are fragile in that they are readily assumed by the mass and lose their identity. (Kill the Boer case 2011, para 36)

Regardless of the criticism by the UN Experts of the lack of universal norms for the protection of minorities, there does not seem to be an appetite in the international community to adopt a legally binding treaty whereby the rights of minorities are protected collectively as a universal standard. As is the case with UNDRIP, international organisations recognise that special provisions may be needed for ethnocultural minorities, but the only justiciable universal norm that can be agreed on is that the individual rights – and not collective rights – of persons belonging to minorities should be protected.[46] The 'homogeneity' approach adopted by international law emphasises a bill of rights as the sole instrument for the protection of minorities, as opposed to the 'pluralism' approach that encourages additional mechanisms, in particular collective rights, for protection of minorities. (Ahmed 2011, 3) While special collective political rights of minorities are not uncommon, they are restricted to the states in which the special measures apply and have not been elevated to a universal standard.

Those who advocate for some form of collective *justiciable* right of minorities in international law have not been able to address three fundamental areas of question obstructing the recognition of such a collective right: first, who is the bearer of the collective right and, if it is a community of individuals, how is the legal entity defined and from where does it derive its corporate status? Secondly, what is the legal object, meaning what is the nature of the right that is collectively exercised by the community as a legal entity? And, thirdly, what is the remedy sought by the minority that is capable of enforcement by a court?[47]

[46] Note that while UNDRIP is not legally enforceable, it is regarded as important soft-law (being unenforceable) which can provide guidance and assistance in the relevant field. (Isa 2021)

[47] These questions not only challenge the minority rights debate but also the indigenous rights debate. (De Villiers 2023e, 61)

For the purposes of this review of jurisprudence in South Africa dealing with rights pertaining to diversity and to contextualise the negotiation of the Constitution of 1996, the following benchmarks may be identified from international law:

- First, it is recognised in international law and by international organisations that the protection of the rights of minorities is an essential requirement for peace, stability and democratisation.
- Secondly, the protection of minorities in the context of individual rights, as well as in the context of political participatory rights in international law, is based, as a point of departure, on the rights of the individual. More particularly, these rights include rights to equal treatment, non-discrimination, freedom of association and the rights to practise religion and culture, and use language.
- Thirdly, international law does not recognise collective legally enforceable rights of minorities as if a community of persons constitutes a distinct legal entity. However, international law does not preclude states from enacting special institutional and policy arrangements that, in particular circumstances, accommodate minorities collectively, particularly concerning political participatory arrangements.
- Fourthly, international law acknowledges that special policy measures and institutional arrangements should, in appropriate circumstances, be adopted by states to facilitate effective political participation of minorities. This may involve specifically designed electoral systems, power-sharing, self-government, decentralisation, special vetos, autonomy and advisory bodies, particularly in matters that affect the communities in question.
- Fifthly, the definition of 'minority' is not settled in international law. Each state may determine or name, within the context of its own circumstances, the minorities, if any, to which special measures apply.
- Sixthly, while states are obligated to create a framework within which minorities can exercise their rights, there is no legal obligation on states to support or fund the activities of minorities or the institutions established by them.

In the next section we reflect on the authorisation in the Constitution of South Africa for international law and foreign municipal law to be considered when disputes are judicially resolved. This authorisation has assisted the courts to reflect international norms and jurisprudence when giving content to the South African Bill of Rights.

4.3 RELEVANCE OF INTERNATIONAL AND FOREIGN LAW TO SOUTH AFRICAN JURISPRUDENCE

The Constitution of South Africa authorises courts to consider international law and jurisprudence of state constitutional law when the Bill of Rights is interpreted. (Constitution of South Africa 1996, ss 39, 231, 232, 233) These sections of the Constitution provide, in essence, that: (a) international law *must* be considered[48] by the courts when interpreting South African law to ensure consistency between international law and jurisprudence in South Africa; (b) foreign municipal jurisprudence *may* be considered in order to take into account the practical application of legal norms in different municipal settings; and (c) international agreements that have been approved by Parliament are binding.[49]

Several questions emerge from this constitutional authority, with the following four of particular relevance for the purposes of this book: *Why* should foreign municipal jurisprudence be considered? *When* should foreign municipal jurisprudence be considered? In *what context* should foreign municipal jurisprudence be considered? What *weight* should be given to foreign municipal jurisprudence and, if there is a difference between states in the application of a legal principle, which approach should be afforded greater weight?

When selecting and weighting foreign municipal jurisprudence precedents there is an obvious risk that judges use foreign law selectively to support their own biases or preferred outcomes. In doing so, judges can potentially rely on case law that suits their predisposition, even if the judgment may not be compatible with the context, legal traditions and background of South Africa. It is practically impossible to undertake a complete international overview of all potentially relevant municipal jurisprudence in every case where foreign law considered the same subject-matter. The citation of international jurisprudence can, arguably, at best be discretionary, selective, rudimentary, cursory and

---

[48] The word 'consider' in its ordinary meaning implies a non-binding, serious or careful consideration of a legal principle or judgment in international and foreign law. In the case of international law, consideration 'must' take place, whereas in foreign domestic law, consideration 'may' take place. The weight of foreign law can at best be persuasive, but more likely it is treated as informative and may assist with the purposive interpretation of the Constitution. International law must be considered, but is not necessarily binding unless South Africa has entered into a treaty.

[49] Constitution of South Africa 1996, s 39. Section 39(1) provides as follows: '(1) When interpreting the Bill of Rights, a court, tribunal, or forum – *(a) must* promote the values that underlie an open and democratic society based on human dignity, equality and freedom; *(b) must* consider international law; and *(c) may* consider foreign law. (emphasis added)

possibly influenced by actual or apprehended bias.[50] While there may be benefits to reflect on developments in international law and foreign law, the following caution expressed by Coutsoudis and Du Plessis can be endorsed:

> In general, there are at least two broad, and interrelated, dangers that one must seek to avoid, in order to adroitly incorporate international law into our law as envisaged by the Constitution. First there is the danger of *jurisprudential cherry-picking.* That is the danger of selecting, on a piece-meal basis, only those international law principles that support the case the court or a practitioner wishes to make, rather than taking account, on a holistic basis, of all the relevant international law, and setting any specific principles that appear, at first, favourable to the approach that one wishes to take, within its broader international law context. The second danger is *failing to appreciate* the subtle manner that international law operates in distinctly different ways to domestic law. Thus, for instance, a domestic lawyer might erroneously approach an international agreement on the basis that it should be understood and interpreted as something akin to a piece of domestic legislation, when in reality within the often consensual setting of international law, it may be more akin (broadly) to a private agreement between equal parties. (emphasis added) (Coutsoudis and Du Plessis 2020, 188)

International law, as expressed by way of treaties or customary international law, is binding and must be given consideration by courts. In contrast, comparative municipal law may be considered, but it carries no weight other than to inform. In addition to there being no obligation to consider international municipal jurisprudence, even when it is considered it is not binding. This interpretation guide may assist courts to consider developments in international and municipal law regarding the rights of minorities and indigenous people.[51] It is, however, remarkable that, despite the many examples of South Africa courts considering foreign law, courts have been slow to consider case law dealing with the rights of ethnocultural minorities. Note, for example, how courts in India have responded

[50] Note in this regard the concern expressed by Maron against the 'selective and biased application of law according to the ideological key' of judges and that judicial 'arbitrariness' can cause a 'blatant distortion' of the standards of adjudication. (Maron 2023, 48)

[51] See, for example, the extensive references to international law in the judgment of the Constitutional Court when it abolished the death penalty and, more recently, the references to international law to ascertain the consultation standards and practices that should be followed when consulting with indigenous people about their traditional lands. (Makwanyane case 1995; Baleni case 2019; Alexkor case 2004) There is often reference in South African jurisprudence to judgments of other countries as well as to judgments arising from regional instruments such as the European Convention on Human Rights. But notably those foreign judgments often cite jurisprudence that is consistent with the preferred outcome – hence adding to the perception that foreign judgments are predominantly used to justify a particular outcome.

to the right to mother-tongue education, a topic one would have thought could at least be considered by courts in South Africa. (Chapter 9)

It was not unexpected that these provisions were included in the Constitution, since in the lead-up to its formulation much emphasis had been placed on comparative constitutional law and jurisprudence in the field of human rights.[52] Because of South Africa's many years of political isolation, the South African negotiators were keen to incorporate universal human rights norms and standards, especially by using them to inform the interpretation of the Bill of Rights. This approach was not without criticism since some held the view that international jurisprudence is biased towards Western liberal perspectives of fundamental rights and do not adequately respect African values and customary law. In this respect the use of Ubuntu has assisted to bring an African element to judicial thinking. (Chapter 6) Note in this respect the observation made by Marin and others regarding the use of and reliance on foreign law by the Constitutional Court of Chile. They are of the view that citations have been rather one sided by Chile citing European law, without a give and take where comparative law considers a wider range of constitutional interpretations. (Marin, Inatani, and Infantino 2021, 195)

The attention paid to comparative law by the Constitutional Court of South Africa has, in turn, contributed to international scholarly debate about the appropriateness and application of international law to domestic settings. (Ackermann 2005; Ginsburg 2012) In a world where vast amounts of information can be accessed via the internet and discourse related to jurisprudence is easily obtainable through a variety of specialised search engines, justices regularly convene at international conferences and workshops, engage in scholarly debate and contribute to publications, legal practitioners study and become qualified in different jurisdictions, and comparative studies are arguably more advanced than ever, the opportunities to consider jurisprudence arising from various diverse jurisdictions being practically overwhelming.

---

[52] The principle of comparative law being cited in judgments was not in itself a new experience for South African courts, since consideration had traditionally been given in civil and commercial law in South African courts to jurisprudential developments in other jurisdictions, in particular the United Kingdom and other common-law jurisdictions. During the apartheid years many South African legal practitioners had practised in other common-law jurisdictions and even served on the judiciaries of other countries. (Rautenbach 2016) Ackerman J expresses the view that, because of the 'comparative ethos in South Arica', the courts would have considered foreign law even if the power to do so had not existed under the Constitution. (Ackermann 2005, 500)

Caution must be exercised, however, when engaging in jurisprudential case-hunting, as comparative analysis for the purposes of a scientific work is not to be equated with the use of foreign law to resolve a legal dispute where the rights and interests of parties are affected in a participatory democratic order. Comparative research is burdened by the limitations of comparing countries, and such a burden lies even more heavily on a court that declares law. The following observation made by Viellechner about the use of and reliance on comparative jurisprudence by the Constitutional Court of Germany may apply equally to South Africa:

> The approach appears random and arbitrary and there is general inconsistency if and when international jurisprudence is cited; the context in which it must be understood; and how representative it should be of the spectrum of international courts. (Viellechner 2020, 198)

Chaskalson P puts the approach adopted by the South African courts under the guidance of the Constitutional Court as follows:

> In dealing with comparative law, we must bear in mind that we are required to *construe* the South African Constitution, and not an international instrument or the constitution of some foreign country, and that this has to be done with due regard to our legal system, our history and circumstances, and the structure and language of our own Constitution. We can derive *assistance* from public international law and foreign case law, but we are in no way bound to follow it. (emphasis added) (Makwanyane case 1995, para 34)

While one can agree with Chaskalson P, the practical application of the thesis remains challenging since reference to foreign law can so easily be abused, taken out of context or used to justify a pre-existing bias. Even if 'assistance' is gained from foreign law, the question arises: if there are different approaches in foreign law to the application of a legal principle, why should precedence be given to an approach adopted by one state vis-à-vis the approach of another state?[53] This

[53] Note, for example, the consideration, or rather lack thereof, of international comparative jurisprudence by the Equality Court of South Africa in the Old Flag case (Old Flag case 2019), as well as the scant reference to international jurisprudence in the Old Flag appeal case (Old Flag appeal case 2023, paras 52–55). These two judgments, which would arguably have benefited from reflecting on the challenges faced in international law and municipal law to respond to hate speech and limitations on the right to freedom of expression, highlight questions such as: when is international case law considered; which case law is considered; what is the weight attached to foreign case law? As argued in Chapter 5, the interaction between freedom of expression and the limitations on it arising from hate speech presented an ideal opportunity for both courts to reflect on international jurisprudence and the challenges faced by many jurisdictions to delineate

highlights the risk of judges using (or even abusing) or ignoring comparative law to suit a particular outcome.[54] An overview of judgments in which foreign case law is cited also shows how the foreign jurisdictions relied upon are not necessarily representative of all the democracies of the world. This in turn raises the question: on what basis are judgments of selected countries included or excluded from judicial consideration?

The questions of why, when and how to use comparative law in domestic settings remain largely unresolved at a normative level. This is exemplified by the Baleni case, in which Basson J cited international jurisprudence and literature to ostensibly demonstrate what the contemporary requirements are in international law for consulting with indigenous people when their traditional lands are accessed. (Baleni case 2019, paras 78–82) While these references may have been useful in a scientific paper, not much turned on those citations because the statute under which the dispute was determined in South Africa gave very explicit rights to the indigenous community to be consulted and to give or withhold consent.[55] The international citations considered by Basson added little, if any, value to the outcome of the dispute. In fact, the statement by Justice Basson, that 'granting

reasonable restrictions on free speech without imposing too onerous a burden on the freedom of expression. As I pointed out in an earlier critique of the Old Flag case, hate speech is universally ascertained by courts with reference to a specific incident, whereas the appropriate forum to effectively ban the display of a symbol is Parliament. In these two cases a broad approach, arguably not supported by comparative international or municipal case law, was adopted by declaring the display of a symbol into perpetuity as hate speech. (De Villiers 2022d) The scope of this restriction arguably placed an undue and unjustified burden on the freedom of expression.

[54] Note, for example, how the Indian Supreme Court went to great lengths, in contrast to the South African courts in the Kill the Boer and Old Flag cases, to consider and reflect on international jurisprudence to delineate the contours of hate speech. (Amish Devgan case 2020, paras 19–29)

[55] Barrie is of the opinion that the Baleni judgment has 'far reaching implications' for the South African land reform process because of the standard of consent required pursuant to international law. (Barrie 2024a, 900) My proposition is that Judge Basson erred by stating that international law requires free, prior and informed consent as is understood by *actual consent*, not striving towards consent. The conclusion drawn by Barrie is therefore also challenged, including his assertion that FPIC 'has evolved into a norm of customary international law'. (Barrie 2024a, 906) FPIC is in an evolution process that may or may not ultimately become a norm of customary international law, but its use, consistency and clarity are thus far inadequate to be declared a binding legal norm in international law. Barrie seems to agree with my observation when he states as follows: 'Measured against the requirements necessary for customary international law, FPIC is moving inexorably towards meeting such demands' albeit that the standard of legal norm has not been reached. (Barrie 2024b, 219) On proper analysis, the Baleni judgment ultimately turned on the statute under which it was brought, not on the provisions of international law.

special protection to these communities by requiring consent as opposed to mere consultation *is in accordance with international law*' (emphasis added) (Baleni case 2019, para 78), is open to challenge since there is no binding treaty in international law that mandates the consent of indigenous people when their interests in land are affected. (De Villiers 2023h, 80) While Basson relied on international law to support her finding in South Africa, she failed to acknowledge the limitations of international law when it comes to consultation rights of indigenous people.

It therefore comes as no surprise that Kriegler J cautioned that the reliance on foreign precedent 'requires circumspection' and 'careful management'. (Sanderson case 1998, para 26) Cases in point are the Old Flag (original and appeal judgments) and Kill the Boer judgments (original and appeal), in which no or little regard was given to the way international and foreign law have struggled with the notion of hate speech and to what extent, if any, freedom of expression ought to be curtailed. These were ideal factual scenarios to undertake an overview of foreign jurisprudence in order to assist the courts in their deliberation to determine: the parameters of hate speech; whether it is confined to the specific incident; and proportionality when restricting free speech. (De Villiers 2022d) Notable in this regard is how in the Kill the Boer appeal case (Kill the Boer appeal case 2024) no consideration takes place of international law or foreign law, while in my view comparative jurisdictions could have assisted the court, or at least could have been relied on by the court in support of its findings.

The following questions remain largely unanswered when one reflects on the use of foreign law by the courts: Why would a judge cite foreign law? When should foreign law be cited? What is the purpose of citing foreign law? How representative should the cases cited be of the vast scope of international case law? What weight ought to be given to foreign judgments? If parties to litigation cite a foreign judgment in their submissions, are courts expected to respond to the relevancy of it in the South African context?

The application and integration of foreign law into a domestic jurisdiction should be approached with a fair degree of caution and even scepticism.[56] The

[56] Justice Antonin Scalia of the US Supreme Court suggested that reliance on and reference to foreign law may be more appropriate when a constitution is newly drafted, rather than interpreting an existing constitution. (Jackson 2013, 17) There is some logic to this proposition since the interpretation of a constitution is inevitably imbued with domestic standards of interpretation, laws, policies and facts. Therefore caution should be applied when importing or relying on a foreign judgment in a specific dispute. A judgment is not to be approached in the same manner as a scientific article in comparative law, where a scientist is at liberty to identify, at their own

most eloquent of judgments in one country may prove to be inappropriate in another country. Judgments are not scientific papers. Judgments make findings of fact and application of the law. While higher principles of law or universal values may be suitable to apply across jurisdictions,[57] it is essential to consider that, despite the generality of human rights principles, there are likely underlying differences between legal systems in their respective histories, values and norms.[58]

Inter-judicial dialogue, whereby courts and tribunals of state and international organisations take note of and even cite each other's judgments, has contributed to international norm setting. However, reliance on foreign law has the potential to threaten the domestic plurality of legal and customary systems by purporting that there are international norms that are not accommodating to local, non-state legal

discretion, the case studies to be analysed. Judgments deal with rights and interests within a particular legal and social setting, while scientific works often seek to draw lessons or identify trends against the background of scientific discourse, as opposed to dispute resolution. At the same time, however, reference by South African scientists to international jurisprudence can provide useful context, comparisons and even lessons without courts necessarily being bound by it. In this regard note, for example, how the concept of *Bundestreue* in Germany, which implies federal comity and cooperative federalism, was used in the South African constitution-drafting process to codify cooperative intergovernmental relations and to structure Chapter 3 of the Constitution dealing with Cooperative Government. (De Villiers 2022c) Moreover, jurisprudence from the German Constitutional Court has been used in a scientific context to propose how the duty to cooperate can be applied to the dispute involving ESKOM, South Africa's electricity utility company. (De Villiers 2019)

[57] Note, for example, how Justice Langa of the Constitutional Court of South Africa explained the utility of reflecting on comparative jurisprudence when discussing how the topic of corporal punishment ought to be approached. While the facts of the dispute before the South African Court were unique to that setting, the legal principle by which the dispute was resolved derived benefit from comparative analysis. He said: 'While our ultimate definition of these concepts must necessarily reflect our own experience and contemporary circumstances as the South African community, there is no disputing that *valuable insights* may be gained from the manner in which the concepts are dealt with in public international law as well as in foreign case law.' (emphasis added) (Williams case 1995, para 23)

[58] Note, for example, the different approaches adopted by states, and even within states, to the question of to what extent, if any, the right to freedom of expression can be curtailed to protect individuals against hate speech. While at first glance one might currently assert that freedom of expression is a universal right, the question of whether the right could be subject to reasonable restrictions depends on the constitutional values, history and traditions of the nation in which a specific factual situation arises. (De Villiers 2022e) Note, for example, how in Germany the display of Nazi insignia, such as the swastika, is banned by the Criminal Code, whereas no similar general restrictions apply in the USA or United Kingdom. In Australia, meanwhile, the display of some Nazi insignia and symbols had only recently (2024) been banned following events in Israel and Gaza.

pluralism. In other words, the richness offered by diversity *within* states can be eroded by the blandness of universality *imposed* onto a state. There has been some noteworthy criticism expressed in this regard in Europe against certain judgments of the ECtHR, to the extent that some countries have refused to give effect to these judgments, since they feel that the judgments do not adequately reflect or accommodate the specific circumstances of the country. (Murauskas 2023)[59] Such refusals shed light on the tension that exists between developing universal norms and allowing legal pluralism, diversity and subsidiarity within states.[60]

In light of South Africa's apartheid history the Constitutional Court has emphasised that when interpreting the Constitution 'its relevant provisions must therefore be interpreted so as to give effect to the purposes sought to be advanced by their enactment', namely the promotion of equality and non-discrimination and the eradication of past injustices. (Du Plessis case 1996, para 127) This approach highlights how the interpretation of text may be influenced by the context of the domestic setting and the objectives of a statute. In South Africa, where an emphasis has been placed on the 'transformative' nature of the Constitution, the meaning of words may be construed differently within a purposive context than in another context. (Kibet and Fombad 2017; De Villiers 2023a)

In this respect it is notable how the seminal judgment of Mabo in Australia, in which indigenous native title was first recognised in a common-law jurisdiction, has reverberated in various countries with different legal traditions. (Barrie 2021) Nonetheless, it is rare for a single judgment to have such a marked impact on the jurisprudence of other states as in the case of Mabo.

The US Supreme Court was the first to embark on what is today known as judicial review based on constitutionalism, but there are nowadays many courts with constitutional-testing powers across the world. It is assumed, when new constitutions are designed, that the principle of constitutional sovereignty rather than parliamentary sovereignty would prevail.[61] It is also inevitable that justices will

---

[59] Note, for example, the refusal of the Parliament of Switzerland to give effect to a judgment of the ECtHR ordering that country to take action regarding climate change. The Parliament denied that it was ignoring the judgment and said that it already had an adequate climate change policy in place. (Foulkes 2024)

[60] Gutan observes that many of the so-called 'landmark' judgments of the ECtHR have arisen from disputes within the 'peripheral EU member states' where there has been 'democracy backsliding' since the 1990s. This trend is particularly noticeable where states have intervened with the independence of the local judiciary. (Gutan 2024, 30)

[61] Breyer estimates that in as many as 20% of the US Supreme Court's judgments, comparative law is taken into account. (Breyer 2018) This is a surprisingly high figure given that, in contrast

exchange views, take note of each other's judgments and learn from one another – even if only out of curiosity.[62] Although there has often been consideration of international jurisprudence in South African judgments,[63] especially in the years after the enactment of the Constitution,[64] the introduction of foreign law has also been criticised, given that comparative judgments may be miscontextualised, misused, stem from different legal traditions, be Eurocentric, invite manipulation or be set in different social, political and historic circumstances.[65] For example,

---

to the South African Constitution, the US Constitution does not specifically mention a power or obligation to consider foreign or comparative law. In the case of Chile it is calculated that of 721 judgments analysed, 246 cited references to foreign case law. (Marin, Inatani, and Infantino 2021, 187)

[62] For example, one significant, though not exclusive, forum where justices from over 70 courts (including South Africa's) with constitutional review powers convene periodically is the World Conference on Constitutional Justice, organised under the auspices of the Venice Commission. Justices from a wide range of countries come together to discuss common issues under consideration and exchange approaches to constitutional interpretation, comparative jurisprudence and trends in constitutional law. The Conference acknowledges the relationship between constitutional justice and peace, and reaffirms the primacy of the protection of human rights for the sake of conflict resolution and sustained peace. (WCCJ, n.d.)

[63] It is estimated that between 1995 and 2011 the Constitutional Court of South Africa cited international jurisprudence in around 54% of its judgments. (Rautenbach 2016) This trend of citing foreign case law, which is unlikely to be continued at the same scope and intensity as in the phase immediately after the enactment of the Constitution, may be partly explained by the historic comparative constitutional emphasis in the legal tradition of South Africa, as well as by efforts after 1993 to promote human rights practices in South Africa in a manner that conforms with international precedents. Foster observes that, although foreign law is often cited in South African courts, in many instances the courts have resisted its application, as the foreign law may not be applicable to South Africa in the specific dispute in question. (Foster 2011, 80)

[64] It has been observed that the reliance on and reference to foreign law in the period immediately after the enactment of the new Constitution was much more frequent than in more recent times. This may be attributable to various reasons, such as: the court developing its own confidence and jurisprudence; staff becoming less interested in foreign law or less capable in foreign languages; the declining availability of foreign-trained judges; foreign-trained judges associates in the period after the enactment of the Constitution inadvertently seeking to promote the jurisprudence of their country of origin; political and judicial resistance to foreign or colonial jurisprudence; a lack of comparative law training for justices; the passing of the old guard; or an emphasis on finding local solutions to local disputes.

[65] See, for example, the analysis by Foster in which he refers to the prosecution against the former State President of South Africa, Mr Zuma. Foster mentions how the Acting National Director of Public Prosecutions, Moketedi Mpshe, decided to withdraw charges against Zuma based on references to English jurisprudence – without noting that the very judgments being relied upon had been set aside on appeal. The cases Mpshe sought to rely upon were not only substantively different from the matters being considered in South Africa, but also inconsistent with South African precedent. Foster concludes as follows: 'As a result, there is limited evidence

in the Fose case, Krieger J challenged the use of comparative case law when referring to jurisdictions such as the USA, United Kingdom, Canada, Tobago, Ireland and New Zealand. He commented as follows:

> In my respectful view, it is neither necessary nor prudent to range as wide as does Ackermann J in his judgment. I decline to engage in a debate about the merits or otherwise of remedies devised by jurisdictions whose common law relating to remedies for civil wrongs bears no resemblance to ours and whose constitutional provisions have but a passing similarity to our section 7(4)*(a)* [of the interim constitution]. (emphasis added) (Fose case 1997, para 90)[66]

The impact of international jurisprudence on South African case law arising from the new constitution was evident from the judgment in the Makwanyane case, in which extensive reference was made to international jurisprudential developments.[67] In this case the Constitutional Court elaborated on the cautious approach that should be adopted when foreign law is cited:

> Although we are told . . . that we 'may' have regard to foreign case law, it is important to appreciate that this will not necessarily offer a safe guide to the interpretation of Chapter 3 of our Constitution. This . . . is implicit in the injunction given to the courts . . ., which in permissible terms allows the courts to 'have regard to' such law. *There is no injunction to do more than this.* . . . In dealing with comparative law, we must bear in mind that we are required to construe the South African Constitution, and not an international instrument or the constitution of some foreign country, and that this has to be done with due regard to our legal system, our history and circumstances, and the structure and language of our own Constitution. We can derive assistance from public international law and foreign case law, but *we are in no way bound to follow it.* (emphasis added) (Makwanyane case 1995, paras 37–39)

---

from South Africa for those who fear that consideration of foreign law will lead judges to derogate from the constitutional text and compromise national values.' (Foster 2011, 80)

[66] Note in this respect also criticism expressed about citations of the Constitutional Court of Chile (in about one-third of its judgments) to foreign law. It is said by Marin and others that an analysis of citations 'displays an uncomfortable double standard' since the court does not explicitly accept the precedent value of foreign judgments nor has the court established a method for the use of foreign judgments. (Marin, Inatani, and Infantino 2021, 188) The concern is expressed that selective citations of case law, particularly originating from the ECtHR and Spain, may reflect a form of 'subservience' and Eurocentric approach. (Marin, Inatani, and Infantino 2021, 190)

[67] The comparative approach to the resolution of municipal disputes applies not only to South African courts. Note, for example, how in Australia the concept of native title was 'discovered' by the High Court after extensive reference to international law developments in the area of recognition of indigenous land rights. (Mabo case (2) 1992)

South African jurisprudence has also, in turn, enriched international law. Both international law, in general, and the municipal jurisprudence of other countries have benefited from jurisprudential developments in South Africa. For example, the Constitutional Court's approach to social and economic rights in the Grootboom case (Grootboom case 2000) has been acknowledged for its influence on the drafting of art 8(4) of the Optional Protocol to the International Covenant on Economic, Social and Cultural Rights (Porter 2009). Similarly, the recognition of native title in the Richtersveld case (Alexkor case 2004) has been cited in other judgments in southern Africa. Furthermore, the Supreme Court of Canada referenced the Makwanyane judgment when considering whether a person should be extradited to a country where the death penalty may be imposed. (Burns case 2015)

South African jurisprudence has therefore benefited from *and* contributed to international jurisprudence. (Goldstone 2008) Justice Goldstone, for example, observes the important influence of Canadian jurisprudence, in particular, on the thinking of the Constitutional Court in the years after its conception. He goes so far as to say that 'South Africa has good reason to *feel indebted* to Canada for the advances we have made on the often-difficult road from oppression to freedom and democracy'. (emphasis added) (Goldstone 2008, 33)

There are indeed risks and benefits for courts in citing international and foreign law. (Foster 2011, 79) Courts may play a transformative role in society, drawing inspiration and guidance from international jurisprudence (Gargarella, Domingo, and Roux 2006). However, there is also a risk that courts may exceed their mandate, eroding their legitimacy by encroaching on the separation of powers, and promoting their own view of what society ought to look like by consideration of and reference to foreign law. Most of all, justices may use foreign and international case law selectively for domestic 'strategic use'. (Benvenisti 2008) While this chapter does not delve deeply into the debate about the utility of referencing or relying on comparative law within the South African judicial system, it is noteworthy that the extent of the Constitutional Court's citations of foreign law has decreased over the years. Foster explains as follows: 'As the court developed its jurisprudence, it became unnecessary to cite foreign law for propositions now firmly established in South African jurisprudence.' (Foster 2011, 90) Rautenbach observes as follows: 'Despite criticisms raised against the South African judiciary for citing numerous foreign precedents without a clear basis, it is clear that foreign precedents have contributed to the development of post-apartheid constitutional law by filling the gaps as "they are revealed", especially in the area of constitutional interpretation and the development of human rights jurisprudence.' (Rautenbach 2020, 125) This statement is, however, rather bland since, in at least three areas covered in this book, the courts had not been enriched by consideration of foreign law as it could have been, namely the interaction between hate speech and freedom of expression; the nature of consultation rights of indigenous people under international law; and the nuances adopted by courts regarding the importance of mother-tongue education.

The reason, timing, method and significance (why, when, how and weight) of incorporating foreign law into domestic settings continue to be topics of debate in South Africa. There is little doubt that in the formative years of the Constitutional Court the constitutional jurisprudence of the young democratic South Africa benefited greatly from using, referencing and relying upon foreign law. This can be attributed to various factors, such as: the absence of relevant jurisprudence in South Africa; the legal tradition of comparative law in the country; the Constitutional Court's aspiration to be part of the global democratic community; the reluctance of judges to assert the law without some form of external validation; the initial availability of associates with foreign legal training to assist the Constitutional Court judges with research and writing; the utility of academic citation where judgments become in effect scientific contributions; the citation of judgments for their mere availability; and a desire for international insights.

While this chapter does not claim to provide definitive guidance on the use of foreign law, it suggests that the following principles may serve as a helpful guide when international law and foreign municipal law are considered in the context of ethnocultural and indigenous rights:

(i) *Why consider foreign law* Considering foreign law can be justified by the universality of recognition of a legal norm and efforts to promote consistency when interpreting legal instruments. Referencing foreign law is grounded in the principle that individuals should universally be entitled to the same minimum human rights protection, regardless of their place of residence. A thorough consideration of foreign law may therefore assist in some instances, but only if it is a *bona fide* effort to consider the richness of foreign law and not merely to cite selected case law or use consideration under the pretext of justifying a specific outcome.

(ii) *When to consider foreign law* Consideration of foreign law may be appropriate when a dispute involves a right of which the content has been the subject of international jurisprudence, and where the circumstances in which the dispute arises are comparable to those in the cited judgment. If legal systems and the social circumstances in which they operate are incompatible, caution should be displayed before relying on foreign case law to justify a domestic outcome.

(iii) *How to use foreign law* Foreign law should be used as a reference to inform, inspire and give purpose to the Constitution, rather than as a precedent to bind. Care should be taken to also reflect disagreements between countries in their applications of rights. Citations of judgments and consideration thereof should not be selective, favouring only those that support a specific finding in the South African situation.

(iv) *What weight to attach to foreign law* Foreign law can, at best, be treated as a supplementary and informative source, and not as a precedent.

4.4 FROM 'MINORITY' TO 'COMMUNITY' – HOW TO DEFINE THOSE WHO MAY REQUIRE SPECIAL MEASURES

For many decades international and municipal constitutional law and literature have been attempting to secure a universal definition for the concept of 'minority' that would satisfy all the practical circumstances in which the definition could be applied. The futility of trying to define the term is nowhere better illustrated than in the following response given by the first European High Commissioner on National Minorities, Max van der Stoel, to a question on what, in his view, constitutes a minority: 'I know a minority when I see one.' (Van der Stoel 1993)

Capotorti proposed the following working definition for 'minority', but it has not been endorsed in any legal instrument and remains the subject of refinement, clarification and debate in literature:

> A group which is numerically inferior to the rest of the population of a State and in a non-dominant position, whose members possess ethnic, religious or linguistic characteristics which differ from the rest of the population and who, if only implicitly, maintain a sense of solidarity, directed towards preserving their culture, traditions, religion and language. (Capotorti 1979, para 568)

In the midst of the South African constitutional drafting the Venice Commission observed: 'There is no generally accepted definition of the concept of a "minority"'. (Venice Commission 1994, 33) Despite multiple efforts in international law, settling on a definition of 'minority' has seemingly become more, rather than less, problematic. It is now accepted that the preferred approach in international law is not to define 'minority'. Instead, it is left to domestic law to clarify when minorities receive special rights, to identify those minorities, and to determine the content, if any, of special protection or measures.[68]

International law is primarily concerned with ensuring that all individuals belonging to a minority are treated equally, without discrimination and pursuant to instruments of international law such as the ICCPR and ICESCR. Once the threshold of minority protection through individual rights is reached, states may, through institutional design or policies, enhance the collective rights of minorities, particularly in terms of their political participation, subject to the ongoing equal treatment of individuals.

The negotiators of the South African Constitution were challenged by two seemingly contradicting trends in international law during the early 1990s: on the one hand, a greater awareness of the importance in international law to protect the rights of minorities (both individually and collectively). On the other hand, an inability of international law to define, with any degree of clarity, who qualifies as a minority and what collective rights, if any, are held by a minority. International law faced a complex challenge to respond to the South African context, where the white numerical minority had been the dominant political and economic force. Similar challenges were evident in other parts of the world

---

[68] A similar debate has characterised the protection of the rights of indigenous people, with international law not being able to settle a definition of 'indigenous people'. (De Villiers 2023f) It is therefore left to individual countries to determine whether there are any indigenous people in their territory and, if so, whether any special measures are adopted for their benefit. This often leaves indigenous people in a state of uncertainty, as the state in which they find themselves may not recognise them as being indigenous. Note, for example, the debate in South Africa over whether the Khoisan are the *only* 'true' indigenous people of the subcontinent, or whether all African tribes should be regarded as indigenous, even if they arrived in parts of southern Africa later in time than the Khoisan. (Veracini and Verbuyst 2020) Also note for how the UN Committee on the Elimination of Racial Discrimination has attempted to side-step the issue of who is indigenous in Botswana by referring to 'ethnic' communities rather than indigenous people. For example, when making recommendations to allow indigenous Khoisan people from a certain area to return to their ancestral lands, the Committee says as follows: 'The Committee urges the State party to fully implement the High Court's decision in Roy Sesana and others v. Attorney General, by allowing *all ethnic groups originating from the Central Kalahari Game Reserve* to return and settle there unconditionally. The Committee also recommends that the State party provide them with effective access to basic social services and enable them to resume their traditional activities without hindrance.' (Mackay 2022, 29) While the issue of the protection of ethnocultural minority rights has attracted substantial international debate around the importance of a numerical element, the protection of indigenous rights refers to neither the numerical size of the community nor its dominant or non-dominant status. (O'Sullivan 2022)

where ethnic minorities also wielded dominant influence within a country. International law was therefore guarded about placing too much weight on the numerical aspect of the concept of 'minority', despite the numerical element the word implies. In short, the reliance in South Africa during negotiations by the white minority on minority protections in international law to retain or buffer their position of dominance or privilege under a democratic constitution was unfathomable to the liberation parties in the South African negotiations as well as the international community.

International law therefore adopted a pragmatic approach whereby 'minority' is taken to imply 'non-dominant', rather than to refer to a numerical size.[69]

At the time the Constitution was drafted, the progress made in international law towards the development of universal standards for the protection of minority rights had run into a maze of practical questions for those tasked with implementing international law within a municipal setting. Seven of those questions are briefly discussed below:

4.4.1 Does size matter?

Does the phrase 'minority' refer to a numerical entity? Usually reference to 'minority' can, on plain reading, be expected to imply the numerical size of a group vis-à-vis the rest of the population. However, it is accepted in international law that 'minority' principally refers to an ethnocultural community that is in a *non-dominant position.* (De Villiers 2012b)[70] Practically this means that a minority

[69] In the South African constitutional negotiations during the 1990s the Afrikaans community was the only ethnocultural community that sought special rights and protection for minorities. Their negotiation position was weakened, however, by four critical limitations: first, their Afrikaner representatives could not internally agree on a definition of the Afrikaans or Afrikaner community and those divisions continue to divide them; secondly, the perception existed that the Afrikaans community sought to use cultural minority protection measures to safeguard and sustain their historic position of being *racially* privileged; thirdly, none of the other ethnocultural communities joined forces with the Afrikaans community to seek special recognition of minorities; and, fourthly, the Afrikaans negotiators pursued, on the one hand, a race-based power-sharing arrangement for the *white* community, while simultaneously seeking cultural rights for the *Afrikaans* community. The credibility of those seeking certain special measures for the Afrikaans community was therefore seriously eroded by the mixture of racial and cultural protections sought.

[70] Note that, although the phrase indigenous people is not defined in international law, it is a positive description of a community that does not depend on their status as dominant or non-dominant, majority or minority. In practice, indigenous people, with the exception of a few cases, are in a minority. However, the question can be raised in the context of South Africa whether

may be in a numerical majority but in a non-dominant position (the word 'dominant' also gives rise to additional definitional challenges). For example, the whites in apartheid-era South Africa were a numerical minority and yet could not be regarded by international law as a 'minority' for the purposes of special rights under international instruments, given that they were in a politically and economically dominant position vis-à-vis the black population.[71]

The phrase 'minority' is, to some extent, falling into disuse within municipal law because other terms that do not refer to a numerical element are preferred in legal instruments. These include 'national minority', 'community', 'nationality', and 'people', while, in some cases, the specific naming of a community is preferred in domestic settings.[72]

4.4.2 When are special rights or arrangements for minorities justified?

International law is inconsistent in its response to the questions whether, when and how the presence of ethnocultural diversity should be reflected in the design of institutions. At the level of legal principle, international law emphasises the rights of individuals, with no explicit recognition of collective rights for minorities.

---

black communities are regarded as 'indigenous', and hence entitled to the protections on offer by international law, or only the Khoisan as the original occupants of the southern parts of Africa. The South African courts have not been drawn into this discourse; for example, in the Baleni case the occupiers of the land were regarded as indigenous or tribal based on their historic status within homelands. (Baleni case 2019; Mogale case 2023, para 43)

[71] The situation of a numerical minority dominating a numerical majority was not unique to South Africa at the time of the negotiations. Other examples included the dominant role of the Ibo in Nigeria, the ruling classes in India, the Amharic in Ethiopia and the Sunni in Iraq. The question, in theory if not in practice, may arise whether the Afrikaans community now, after 30 years of democracy, qualifies as a non-dominant 'minority' in international law.

[72] This is particularly the case in some eastern and central European states where the definition and identification of minorities highlight theoretical and practical challenges in the minority discourse. Note, for example, how in Hungary the 13 nationalities for whom special arrangements are made by way of nationality councils are explicitly mentioned in a schedule to the Constitution, namely: Bulgarian, Greek, Croatian, Polish, German, Armenian, Roma, Romanian, Ruthenian, Serbian, Slovak, Slovene and Ukrainian. (Hungary Nationalities Act 2012, s 1(3)) Minorities in Estonia and Slovenia are self-responsible for their electoral lists, whereas in Croatia and Serbia the state is responsible for managing electoral lists. Caution must, however, be exercised about persons who proclaim to be members of a minority when in fact they are not. In the case of Hungary, for example, it has been observed that 'group membership could be inflated by fraud and by people who presumably or obviously do not belong to the community, a phenomenon commonly referred as ethno-business or ethnocorruption'. (Beretka and Dobos 2023, 147)

There is no case law under international law, nor any acknowledgement by expert committees, that entitles ethnocultural minorities to a collective right to autonomy, self-determination, power-sharing or self-governance. Constitutions should, however, strive to increase public acceptance and hence popular legitimacy, and in those efforts attending to the rights and interests of minorities to effective political participation also become relevant. (Fruhstorfer and Hudson 2022, 104) Put simply: if minorities are involved in the drafting of a constitution, they are more likely to accept the rulings made pursuant to that constitution. This may explain why the South African Constitution had such longevity, since the drafting processes, influenced by the Constitutional Principles, were so inclusive.

At the practical level several international agencies, most notably the United Nations, promote political minority accommodation techniques in conflict situations based on coalition government, minority vetoes, consultation rights, decentralisation and federalism, self-government, advisory bodies and power-sharing. While the approach in international law to the protection of minority rights is arguably at an 'impasse', (Kymlicka 2008, 112) the reality of institutional design demands that solutions to minority and indigenous political participation are found within states. However, this inevitably gives rise to ambiguity and a lack of consistency at a supranational level. Weber observes that 'national constitutional protection of minorities has remarkably increased in the decades after World War II, not only in Europe but also in Asia, Africa, and especially Latin America'. (Weber 2024, 491)

The ambiguity in international law regarding minority protection is exacerbated by the fact that hard treaty law emphasises the primacy of individual rights, while soft law and policy measures call for different forms of group protection, and day-to-day practices in conflict situations allow for and encourage pragmatic solutions to accommodate minorities, including special autonomous regions (e.g. Bangsamoro in the Philippines, Aceh in Indonesia, South Tyrol in Italy, Basque country in Spain) and secession (such as in Kosovo and South Sudan).

At the normative level there is wide acknowledgment that the ethnic diversity of a population is potentially a relevant factor in the design of institutions. However, disagreement arises whether institutions should be designed based on ethnic composition or whether institutional design should merely be mindful of ethnic composition without making ethnicity a cornerstone of institutions. (Chapter 2)

The increased awareness of legal pluralism is also a relevant consideration in the context of institutional design, as this concept seeks to acknowledge, empower and give effect to non-state laws without necessarily attributing political participatory rights to the communities that adhere to those non-state laws.

Case studies provide support for both approaches, suggesting that specifically ethnoculturally designed institutions may be particularly relevant for short-term transitional and conflict resolution situations. Nevertheless, none of the major schools of thought on institutional design has been able to develop a normative framework for institutional design that could be implemented with any degree of certainty to all situations where heterogenous populations are present. Ultimately, the success of institutional design depends not only on the constitutional and policy ingredients that have crystalised internationally, but also on the willingness, capacity and ability of a population and its leaders to find common ground, build trust and display a culture of accommodation. The design of institutions in response to population diversity is often a shot in the dark. There is no certainty that a specific institutional arrangement for minority accommodation will be effective in a particular setting, even if the arrangement has proven itself to be successful in another circumstance. Any comparative analogy is therefore subject to reality testing because institutional design is so context-specific. What works in one circumstance may not work in another, and what fails in one circumstance may be successful in another.

4.4.3 Are all minorities treated equally?

Are all minority groups in a country entitled to the same rights and protection, or are there special rights accorded to minorities that have been resident in a country for a substantial period compared to those that may have arrived in a country more recently? The response to this question is not definitive. In principle, all individuals are treated equally, but in practice some minorities attract collective participatory rights, while others do not. This is not based on any legal principle, but on the demands of history, reality and pragmatism.[73]

In this respect, a question has arisen in international law whether minorities that have recently arrived through contemporary migration are expected to assimilate with the majority of the population, while historical minorities, who have long been resident in a country, may advocate for some additional rights as a distinct community. (Kymlicka 1989)[74] The same question applies to members

[73] Note, for example, how in Canada special language and cultural rights in education are accorded to the English and French communities, but not to indigenous or other immigrant communities. (Chapter 9)

[74] The essence of the 'old' versus 'new' minorities discourse is along the lines that old minorities generally seek to ensure their survival as distinct historical societies with a long

of indigenous groups that are migrating to South Africa and whether their customary law ought to be treated similarly in South Africa to the customary law of South African indigenous people.

The debate regarding the accommodation of historic minorities within states other than their own state of origin has been, and continues to be, particularly relevant in the European region. Additionally, with new patterns of migration many new minority communities have become settled in host countries, further complicating the discourse. (Medda-Windischer, Boutler, and Malloy 2020) The recently arrived communities, which are often identified by race or religion (particularly Islam), are often expected, in practice if not in law, to assimilate with the dominant society. In contrast, greater tolerance is generally displayed towards historic minorities seeking to retain and develop their own unique identity, extending even to them state support in these endeavours.[75]

International law seeks to ensure equal treatment for all members of society, regardless of their community's historical association with a country. However, in Europe as an example, municipal law in conflict situations tends to provide special policy treatment or assistance to minorities enjoying a long association

association in their host country, whereas new minorities are formed by recent immigration and their goal is presumed to be to integrate with the recipient nation's culture pursuant to an approach of multiculturalism. (Modood 2007) The old versus new minority debate is rejected by international law because all individuals are entitled to equal protection under art 27 of the ICCRP, and individuals belonging to minorities are protected against forced assimilation with the dominant community. (Roter 2018, 145) Nonetheless, it must be noted that the individualisation expressed in art 27 does not remove the demand for some form of special political participatory arrangements from some minorities, particularly those who have had a long history in a country. Several European states initially sought to restrict the application of the European Convention for the Protection of National Minorities to old minorities with a long-standing relationship with the host nation in which they reside. It is, however, now accepted that the European Convention for the Protection of National Minorities in general, as well as art 27 of the ICCPR, apply equally to all members of minorities. Despite this, in practice special arrangements are occasionally made for minorities who enjoy a long-standing relationship with their host nation, even though such an approach is based on domestic pragmatism rather than accordance with an international norm, as in the case of South Tyrol, Macedonia, Serbia, Hungary, Kosovo, Estonia and Germany. (Salat et al 2014; Malloy, Osipov, and Vizi 2015; Andeva et al 2023) Some concern has been expressed that, by widening the scope of minority protection, the protection on offer to 'traditional minorities' may be 'watered down'. (Nagy and Vizi 2024, 24) The discourse about legal pluralism, particularly of a religious nature, in Europe is ongoing and is arguably most visible in the continued practice of non-state Sharia law by recent immigrant communities to Europe. (Chapter 8)

[75] Castellino identifies the following six options that face minorities, whether 'old' or 'new': assimilation; integration; fusion; pluralism; segregation; and ethno-development. (Castellino 1999, 406)

with a country. This may include measures such as establishing advisory bodies and providing decentralisation to regions and local governments, cultural autonomy and special representation.[76]

4.4.4 Minority at a national, regional or local level?

Is a minority determined based on its national, regional or local status? A group may be a national minority, but within a specific geographical area it might be a majority (or dominant). (Craig 2016) For example, the English national majority in Canada are a minority in the province of Quebec. Does this mean that the English minority in Quebec are entitled to special protection, like the French minority in the rest of Canada are entitled to protection at a national level?[77] This issue remains unresolved in international law, but the opinion is widely held that a minority is defined by reference to the *national* status of a community and not its regional or local status.[78] The Minority Rights Group has made the following observation about the numerous efforts to develop an appropriate definition for 'minority':

---

[76] In this respect the status of the Afrikaans community is noteworthy. While it is not disputed that Afrikaans speakers have been in South Africa for several centuries, there are two issues pertinent to this chapter that complicate their status: first, there is no agreed definition of the Afrikaans community (with some seeking to introduce a racial and Christian element into the definition, whereas others insist that the sole criterion should be speaking the Afrikaans language); and, secondly, although Afrikaans as a language is regarded as 'indigenous', Afrikaans speakers are not regarded as an indigenous people of South Africa. (Walker 2021)

[77] The Human Rights Committee has expressed the opinion that a minority for the purposes of art 27 must be a truly 'national' minority and not a local or regional minority. The English speakers living in Quebec are therefore not regarded as a 'minority' for the purposes of this article. (Korkeakivi 2018, 34)

[78] In South Africa there is no ethnic or language majority at a national level, even though, in racial terms, black people comprise a majority. The most widely spoken indigenous home languages are isiZulu, isiXhosa and Afrikaans, but no ethnic group constitutes more than around 25% of the population. (Census 2022 2023) While one of the criteria used in the demarcation of the provinces was language distribution (De Villiers 2012a), most of the major language communities have a province wherein their language is the predominant, or at least a major spoken, language. No province is unilingual. The diverse, or rainbow-like, nature of the population extends to provincial and even local areas. In South Africa it is common to observe that, within the context of local areas, greater attention is given to minority interests. This is evident in practices such as the naming of towns, streets and public signage. However, there is no formal policy that specifically authorises or mandates localised recognition of cultural symbols. This highlights what Korkeakivi refers to as the discretionary, and perhaps ambiguous, way in which universal norms operate in practice. (Korkeakivi 2018, 31) Malloy points out that the ACFC has consistently held that a requirement by a member state that a minority group represent half or more of a local population for its language to receive special status at the local level is incompatible with art 10(2)

> Thus, the definitions [of minority] will differ from state to state and the defining process *within* the state will differ according to specific circumstances, usually relating to the state's *perception* of the political power of groups under discussion. Even the definitions upheld by international organisations are subject to similar forces and will change over time, leading to further redefinition. (emphasis added) (Minority Rights Group 1994, 8)

Since individuals are principally the bearers of protection under s 27 of the ICCPR, the rights to equal protection and non-discrimination accorded would apply wherever members of the minority reside. However, if some form of collective participatory arrangement is made for a particular community, it is usually more likely to apply at a local and regional level, rather than nationally.

4.4.5 Identification as a member of a minority

A system of minority protection whereby some form of collective rights are recognised, can only be workable if there is an effective way of identifying the members of the minority. If that is not possible, minority protection arrangements can be easily abused. This raises the question: is a 'minority' and its members defined by way of subjective considerations (self-definition), through objective criteria (external definition), or by way of acceptance of a person (by the community)? Whatever option is supported, the result is complex and potentially controversial in its practical operation. (De Villiers 2021b) Weber suggests as follows: '[T]he essential element [of group identification] must remain the possibility of autonomy and self-identification of individuals to define their minority or "people" as a collective community, and to declare their adherence openly and without any coercion.' (Weber 2024, 492)

Caution has been expressed that 'group membership could be inflated by fraud and by people who do not belong to the community, a phenomenon commonly referred as "ethno-business or ethnocorruption"'. (Beretka and Dobos 2023, 147)[79] If the test of membership is purely subjective, in other words a person can

of the FCNM. Malloy notes that thresholds of as low as 10–20% have been declared compatible with this provision. (Malloy 2018, 213) Such a standard has not been adopted in South Africa, but it may provide a way forward in the ongoing debate about mother-tongue education. (Chapter 9)

[79] Note in this regard the debates about membership of a group in South Africa and Australia. In South Africa various policies have been enacted to give preference to previously disadvantaged persons, who are generally regarded as black. However, it is not simple to define in practice who those persons are. In Australia special programmes exist for the benefit of Aboriginal people and, similarly to South Africa, controversy often arises whether a person is indeed Aboriginal or merely claiming to be Aboriginal to receive beneficial treatment. (Chapter 10) The efforts to address

self-identify with a minority without their choice being challenged, a minority may become affected by imposters who are not *bona fide* members of the group.[80] Note in this respect the 2024 judgment in Australia, where the claim of a non-Aboriginal person to be accepted by the Aboriginal community as being one of them was rejected on the basis that he was not born into the community and hence could not claim Aboriginal ancestry. (Kapeli case 2024) The court found that there was 'no support for Mr Kapeli's contention that an Aboriginal Australian, in this constitutional context, can include a person who has no Aboriginal ancestry but has been adopted under the traditional law and custom of an Aboriginal clan, group or community'. (Kapeli case 2024, para 232)

If the test is purely objective, by some form of group definition, the following questions arise: Who determines the definition? Who ascertains whether an individual meets the objective requirements? How does one prevent intragroup discrimination against *bona fide* individuals who claim to be part of the group, but whose claim is denied because of internal disputation?[81]

If the test is based on group acceptance, questions emerge about who makes decisions on behalf of the group and how to prevent the exclusion of individuals who objectively meet the criteria but are excluded from participation by those who control the group for various reasons.[82]

The emphasis in international law is on personal self-identification based on free association. However, there are examples where municipal law allows scope for communities to have some control of their membership, pursuant to their

---

historic marginalisation highlight how legal principle can become the victim of pragmatism, for example while so much effort goes into the principle of the non-racial characteristics of the South African Constitution, race remains practically a highly relevant factor for the extension of beneficial programmes solely directed at black people.

[80] Notable in this regard was a phenomenon in Hungary during elections for the ethnic nationality councils in the 1990s. Individuals who were not *bona fide* members of a nationality participated as candidates in these elections. These were often referred to as 'ethno-businesses', as the individuals concerned had the expectation of receiving benefits that were exclusively available to the specific nationality or were acting otherwise in support of the nationality. (Carstocea 2011)

[81] Note, for example, the early efforts to define the Māori in New Zealand and Aboriginal people in Australia, and how historically 'objective' tests turned out to be racist and discriminatory. (De Villiers 2023e)

[82] Observe, for example, the jurisprudence arising from Australia about the application of the test of aboriginality (Gibbs case 1995), as well as the efforts by the Sámi Parliament in Finland to be the sole arbiter of the Sámi electoral role for the Sámi Parliament. (Stepien, Petretei, and Koivurova 2015) The relationship between the Sámi Parliament and the Supreme Administrative Court in respect to registration as a Sámi voter remained unresolved at the time of writing.

right to self-determination, enabling them to determine who may attend their institutions or participate in their activities.[83] Added thereto, municipal law may require biological linkage to a group other than mere association or acceptance. (Kapeli case 2024, para 232)

4.4.6 Incorporation of a minority

In the absence of a legal entity, minorities cannot exercise rights as a group other than by some class action whereby multiple persons act in their individual capacity to promote a broader interest. Since a minority is not a legal entity in civil, common or international law, the question arises whether a legal mechanism can be created to incorporate a minority, thereby giving the group the status of a legal person or corporate entity.[84] While members of ethnocultural communities may, pursuant to the right of freedom of association, become incorporated in the form of clubs, associations or religious bodies in accordance with domestic legislation, a few countries have created a statutory framework whereby minorities can become incorporated for the purposes of a form of collective (political) self-determination in public law. Australia, for example, has adopted a unique approach for the incorporation of Aboriginal people should they wish to adopt a corporate identity as a community. (CATSI Act: Register 2020) While minorities are not regarded as indigenous people, the legal mechanism whereby Aboriginal people can become incorporated may be of relevance to other ethnocultural minorities. Aboriginal persons in Australia may register a corporation to manage and promote their interests pursuant to the Corporations (Aboriginal and Torres Strait Islander) Act 2006 (CATSI Act; Bartlett 2020).

---

[83] Note, for example, the special arrangements in Schleswig-Holstein, South Tyrol and Brussels, where community facilities, such as schools and elderly care homes, are unilingual, but any person may attend/reside provided they can speak or use the language of the institution. (De Villiers 2017; Van Crombrugge 2017; Malloy 2020)

[84] Marsal and Palermo refer to the debate about the corporate identity of minorities as 'sterile'. (Marsal and Palermo 2018, 107) In my view, this is an unfortunate and unhelpful characterisation of the debate about how a community that is not territorially defined can achieve the legal status to protect and promote their interests. The worlds of science and literature continue to be challenged in their exploration of a normative standard and practice to address the plight of minorities that do not have their own territorial space. (Andeva et al 2023) The possibility of dispersed minorities becoming incorporated into a legal entity should not be discounted. The practical, legal, symbolical, spiritual and political benefits for a community that wishes to become incorporated should also not be underestimated. This is illustrated in Australia, where around 4 000 Aboriginal family groupings have, for various reasons, become incorporated under the Aboriginal Corporations Act. (De Villiers 2022h, 117–21)

The CATSI Act aims to address the need for simple, easy-to-run corporate legal structures for Aboriginal communities. (CATSI Act 2006) Special grants for training are available for Aboriginal people to establish and manage these corporations. Non-Aboriginal persons cannot register a corporation under the CATSI Act. An Aboriginal corporation enables the community to take legal actions, enter into contracts, receive grants and perform all the other functions open to a legal person. (CATSI Act 2006, s 96) These corporations represent a form of localised, community-based, non-territorial self-determination for Aboriginal people that is unparalleled in comparative indigenous experiences. (De Villiers 2023g, 390)[85] The corporations do not exercise political rights but, in doing their 'self-determination' of some sort, they nevertheless engage in a form of political expression. (De Villiers 2024b)

The absence of a legal identity for an ethnocultural community without its own territorial space is therefore not an insurmountable challenge. However, the community may require some form of enabling legislation to register a corporate entity capable of acting on its behalf, advocating, administering programmes and performing functions.[86]

Sections 185 and 235 of the South African Constitution reflect the possibility of non-territorial cultural arrangements for ethnocultural communities by way of some form of statutory incorporation. No legislation or policy measure has been adopted to give effect to this promise. (De Villiers 2022a)

---

[85] Note, for example, the enabling legislation in the Russian Federation, by which national minorities can become incorporated to promote their own cultural and linguistic interests, pursuant to the Federal Law on National-Cultural Autonomy of 1996. The autonomy so achieved is principally symbolic and non-political, but this does not detract from the fact that hundreds of ethnocultural and religious communities in Russia have become incorporated, albeit on the understanding that the autonomy arrangements are used for cultural and not political activities. In doing so they have established legal entities that can act on their behalf in the conduct of their cultural, religious and linguistic affairs. (Filippova and Filippov 2015; Smith 2016)

[86] Note, for example, how in Australia the Noongar Corporation has become akin to a fourth level of government in terms of its consultative and self-management activities on behalf of Aboriginal people. (De Villiers 2022b) Notable is also the Ngurrajuta Agreement in the Northern Territory of Australia, which envisages expanding of Aboriginal community control in a ten-year plan for projects that support training and pathways, housing development and management, community safety, family services and education which will be based on each community's priorities, needs and aspirations. (Ngurrajuta Local Decision Making Agreement 2024) The Ngurrajuta region identified six priority areas to be the focus of the Agreement, e.g. housing, municipal services, employment, educational attendance, welfare delivery and economic development. The principle of self-determination for Aboriginal communities underpins the Agreement. (Ngurrajuta Local Decision Making Agreement 2024, para 2.2)

4.4.7 Community rather than minority

In the constitution-drafting process in South Africa the decision was made to use the term 'community' because of the inability to define 'minority' under international law as well as the political toxicity surrounding the racial minority debate in the country. The term 'community', which is considered numerically neutral, is used to describe those who share a common language and culture. While the Bill of Rights recognises the diversity of rights of individuals to practise their language, culture and religion, two special sections were adopted to reflect the potential of collective rights of language and cultural communities. (Constitution of South Africa 1996, ss 185; 235) Both ss 185 and 235, acknowledge, in theory at least, a collective aspect of community rights.

Section 185 envisages that the Commission for the Promotion and Protection of the Rights of Cultural, Religious and Linguistic Communities may recommend the establishment of a cultural council for a cultural or linguistic community.[87] The Commission has not, however, acted on this mandate. The Commission has also not undertaken any public education or research regarding the options, if any, or suitability or demand related to the formation of cultural councils. Furthermore, it has yet to make any legislative proposals concerning the creation of a statutory framework for cultural councils.

Meanwhile, s 235 recognises the right to self-determination of any community that shares a common cultural and language heritage.[88] The manner and form for exercising the right to self-determination is to be set out by enabling legislation.

Sections 185 and 235 require a joint reading, given that the Commission created in s 185 may, through its recommendations, give effect to a statutory framework anticipated by s 235. Parliament has not yet enacted legislation to

---

[87] Section 185: '(1) The primary objects of the Commission for the Promotion and Protection of the Rights of Cultural, Religious and Linguistic Communities are – (a) to promote respect for the rights of cultural, religious and linguistic communities; (b) to promote and develop peace, friendship, humanity, tolerance and national unity among cultural, religious and linguistic communities, on the basis of equality, non-discrimination and free association; and (c) to recommend the establishment or recognition, in accordance with national legislation, of a cultural or other council or councils for a community or communities in South Africa.'

[88] Section 235: 'The right of the South African people as a whole to self-determination, as manifested in this Constitution, does not preclude, within the framework of this right, recognition of the notion of the right of self-determination of any community sharing a common cultural and language heritage, within a territorial entity in the Republic or in any other way, determined by national legislation.'

give effect to the constitutional promise of s 235. (De Villiers 2022a)[89] In light of the current socio-political circumstances in South Africa, the question inevitably arises as to whether it is too late or too early for the mandate foreshadowed in ss 185 and 235 to be enlivened. (De Villiers 2014a) There does not seem to be any political appetite for legislation to give effect to cultural councils and self-determination, which means, at least for the time being, initiatives of self-determination and informal functional autonomy are likely to be of a private nature rather than pursuant to legislation.

4.5 BENCHMARKS FOR MINORITY AND INDIGENOUS RIGHTS IN INTERNATIONAL LAW AT THE TIME WHEN THE CONSTITUTION WAS NEGOTIATED

The following benchmarks in international law for the protection of ethnocultural and indigenous communities prevailed when the South African Constitution was negotiated:[90]

First, the principal focus for the protection of minorities and indigenous people centred on individual rights, with the point of departure being equal treatment of all individuals and non-discrimination against individuals by reason of their ethnocultural or indigenous background, and therewith recognition of identity rights related to language, culture, religions, traditions and customs.

Secondly, the equality provision notwithstanding, in specific circumstances institutional design and political processes within states were encouraged to provide enhanced protection for and participation by marginalised ethnocultural minorities and indigenous people by way of special institutional arrangements. Those included power-sharing, territorial and non-territorial autonomy, guaranteed seats, minority vetoes and advisory bodies. The collective arrangements, as evidenced in the transitional government of unity in South Africa, for example, can be either ad hoc or more permanent, but are not enforceable as universal rights in international

[89] Despite the efforts of the negotiators of the South African Constitution to avoid the thorny issues associated with defining 'minority,' similar challenges (unfortunately) persist when attempting to define 'community': How is a community defined? Who is eligible to be regarded as a community? What collective rights can a community exercise? What are the potential powers and functions of a community or a cultural council? Is there an obligation on the state to support a cultural council or whatever self-determination arises from ss 185 and 235? It is therefore not surprising that no steps have been taken to enliven these provisions. (De Villiers 2021a)

[90] Those benchmarks remain current at time of writing.

law. In short, legal effect to ethnocultural and indigenous rights in international law is given by way of the rights of the individual as a universal norm, while political participatory rights of minorities and indigenous people may be given by way of institutional design on a pragmatic case-by-case basis.

Thirdly, the protection of individual rights of members of ethnocultural minorities and indigenous people foreshadows that for some rights to have any practical effect, the effective exercise of those rights necessitates collaboration with other members of the same community. Although there is a potential class action element embodied in these identity rights, the nature of the rights remains individual.

Fourthly, the term 'minority' remains undefined in international law (similar to the term 'indigenous people'). It is within the purview of individual states to determine, through their municipal law, how to appropriately characterise, define or identify a minority that is to benefit from special measures. States may choose to use the term 'minority' or opt for alternatives such as nationality, people, community or the naming of the specific community that is the subject of the special arrangements.

Fifthly, international law places an obligation on the state to protect and respect the rights of individuals belonging to minorities and indigenous people to associate, practise and enjoy their culture, traditions, religion, customs and language. There is no legal obligation in international law for the recognition of collective rights whereby the community is regarded as a separate legal entity that has collective rights of self-government or power-sharing distinct from those of its individual members.

Sixthly, there is no universal, justiciable obligation on states to support or fund minorities or indigenous people, or to assist them with the enjoyment and protection of their culture, traditions, education, religion and languages by taking positive actions in their favour. States may, within their domestic law and available resources, enact programmes and budget allocations to support minorities and indigenous people, particularly when their members are concentrated in certain localised areas. Assistance of minorities is encouraged by non-binding international standards, but support is not mandated by international law. The state is, however, legally obligated to adopt and facilitate policies to create an environment within which individuals that belong to minorities and indigenous people can freely enjoy their identity rights.

Seventhly, while the collective rights-based approach to minority and indigenous rights remains poorly developed in international law, there is an increasing awareness in the institutional design of constitutions, particularly for conflict-prone or post-conflict states that seek to democratise, that the rights of minorities and indigenous people ought to be given serious and special consideration on a transitional or permanent basis through mechanisms such as the electoral system, power-sharing, vetoes, decentralisation, autonomy arrangements, advisory bodies and symbolic recognition. International practice acknowledges that a marginalised minority or indigenous community may derail or frustrate democratisation efforts. Special political and institutional measures may therefore be required on a case-by-case basis to facilitate the effective participation of a minority or indigenous community in public affairs.

Eighthly, the rising interest in legal pluralism coincides with the ongoing discourse about the protection of minority and indigenous rights. Legal pluralism tends to place an emphasis on accommodating the separate *legal* systems of minorities and indigenous people. Meanwhile, the minority protection debates tend to focus on measures aimed at ensuring effective *political participation* by those communities. In both instances, however, the underlying motivation is that the modern state, with its uniform institutions and majoritarian basis, may not adequately accommodate or be reflective of the diversity of the population. With this in mind, special measures may be required to ensure that non-dominant communities, whether ethnocultural or indigenous, are accorded adequate protection and recognition to maintain and sustain their unique identity, customs, practices and non-state laws.

Ninthly, during the constitution-drafting process there was (and remains) in South Africa (and beyond) an ambivalence about how to approach legal pluralism in general, and the protection of the rights of ethnocultural communities in particular, from a legal-philosophical point of view. There was disagreement on whether ethnocultural diversity and pluralism should be embraced, celebrated, resisted or merely tolerated. There were two main schools of thought at a scientific and political level about the relevance of ethnocultural and indigenous diversity to the design of the constitution: those who viewed ethnocultural and indigenous diversity as irrelevant to constitutional design, a nuisance, a hindrance and something to be resisted; and those who viewed the recognition and accommodation of ethnocultural and indigenous diversity in its various forms as an expansion of rights that can deepen democracy, enhance popular legitimacy and recognise personal self-determination at all levels.

The debate is ongoing.

CHAPTER 5

HATE SPEECH VERSUS SPEECH THAT WE HATE: STRIKING A BALANCE BETWEEN FREEDOM OF EXPRESSION AND PROTECTION AGAINST HATE IN A PLURAL SOCIETY – THE OLD FLAG AND KILL THE BOER CASES

If freedom of speech is taken away, then dumb and silent we may be led, like sheep to the slaughter.

– George Washington

5.1 INTRODUCTION

Hate speech, or speech that we hate. The two are easy to confuse. The former must be restricted, the latter tolerated. Democratic societies are built on the foundation of free speech, but at the same time human dignity demands that the freedom to speak may sometimes be restricted in the interest of the public good. Speech that propagates hate undermines the fabric of society. It erodes human dignity. It attacks the very foundation of the freedoms of equality, non-discrimination, respect and tolerance, on which a democracy is built. It may threaten the very conditions required for plurality to thrive.

Freedom of expression, however, is a foundational right with wide boundaries that should not readily be contracted. Limits placed on the freedom of speech can become a slippery slope, leading to the stifling of public opinion, abuse by majorities of their powers, labelling of persons who hold a certain view, adopting an expanding meaning of hate and suppression of dissenting views. Therefore the scope of a hate speech prohibition must be 'narrowly drawn so it extends only to extreme speech'. (Moon 2022, 26) Within the content of the ECtHR it has been emphasised that any restriction on freedom of expression is to be narrowly interpreted and the necessity of a restriction must be 'convincingly established' in addition to the restriction being lawful and pursuing a legitimate aim. (Boulais, Marinkovic, and Palomares 2023, 730)

There is a particular risk that illiberal governments and biased judges may utilise and rely on purported hate speech to silence, curb or ban speech that they dislike. What is generally referred to as political correctness may also hold as hate speech that deviates from a particular norm. What is socially regarded as hate speech is not necessarily legal hate speech. As acknowledged by the then United Nations Special Rapporteur on Minorities, Prof de Varennes, 'the freedoms of opinion and expression should be viewed as a default starting point with only very strictly constructed restrictions'. (de Varennes 2021, 5) This reflects the caution expressed by the ECtHR that 'the role of the authorities in such circumstances is not to remove the cause of tension by eliminating pluralism [of opinion], but to ensure that the competing groups tolerate each other'. (Hamidović case 2018, para 127)[1]

Democracy demands tolerance towards different views, including radical views. It insists on public debate being able to absorb, deflect or ignore dislikeable speech, on providing space for opinions perceived to be radical and on showing lenience for speech that we hate.[2] It is the art of tolerance that distinguishes democracies, not the ability to censure.

[1] In this case the complainant had been expelled from court because he had refused to remove a skullcap. According to De Gaetano, this highlights how 'issues of secularism can get out of hand and endanger human rights'. (De Gaetano 2024, 150)

[2] With reference to hate speech judgments handed down by the ECtHR, Alkiviadou expresses concern that freedom of expression is in a 'state of severe recession', given that the concept of hate speech is constantly widening to include speech that ordinarily ought not be treated as 'hate'

The rights to practise, protect and promote cultural identity, particularly in plural societies, logically also include the rights to display signs, speak one's own language, sing songs of choice, use unique scripts, recognise historic events, acknowledge place names, practise customs and commemorate important days. (Shaheed 2010) In the context of this book it is accepted in international and municipal law that the right to speech includes the right to enjoy, practise and celebrate culture, symbols,[3] traditions and non-state laws and customs.[4]

Democracies consist of a plurality of views and opinions. In fact, respect for pluralism of peoples, cultures, customs, practices and opinions is an essential requirement for liberal democracy. Speech and political activities that seek to undermine the values of tolerance cannot claim protection under democratic constitutions. (Refah Partisi case 2003) While we may hate certain things that are said, these things do not necessarily meet the criteria for hate speech, as noted by the US Supreme Court:

> Speech that demeans on the basis of race, ethnicity, gender, religion, age, disability, or any other similar ground is hateful; but the proudest boast of our free speech jurisprudence is that we protect the freedom to express 'the thought that we hate'. (Schwimmer case 1929, para 625)

Nonetheless, the proliferation of hate speech internationally and the challenge this presents to liberal democracies are of concern to contemporary governments

speech, such as speech that causes offence or may be disliked. (Alkiviadou 2022, 2193) Sottiaux also notes that the ECtHR has been inconsistent in its approach to hate speech, to the extent that the court 'today fails to provide practicable and predictable standards to govern public and private responses to hate speech'. (Sottiaux 2023, 1211) As argued below, the same can be said about inconsistencies related to freedom of expression and hate speech in South African jurisprudence, as illustrated in the Old Flag and Kill the Boer cases.

[3] Note, for example, how memes so widely in use in social media can also constitute hate speech. (Martinez-Sanz and Durantez-Stolle 2024)

[4] The European Framework Convention for the Protection of National Minorities provides, for example, in art 5 that states shall promote conditions for minorities to maintain and develop their culture and to preserve the essential elements of their identity, namely their religion, language, traditions and cultural heritage. Article 7 protects the rights of expression, thought, conscience and religion. Article 8 protects the right to establish associations and institutions that promote the identity of the nationality. Article 10 recognises the right to use a minority language in private and public. Article 14 recognises the right to display signs, inscriptions and other information in public, including local and street names in areas where members of the minority live in concentration. Article 12, meanwhile, places an obligation on states to foster knowledge in the education system of the culture, history, language and religion of minorities. (European Framework Convention 1998)

and courts. Freedom of expression ought not be weaponised to demean others and reduce their humanity. Of concern too is the physical and psychological impact hate speech has on vulnerable people, the exposure to greater physical and psychological harm it causes for marginalised communities, and the increased risk of violence it creates. (Wilson 2021)

Striking a balance between the limits of freedom of expression and the utterance of hate speech is challenging.[5] Important to note is that what may be socially regarded as hate speech ought not necessarily be regarded in law as hate speech. (Brown and Sinclair 2023, 329)[6] Wherever the line is drawn, it is inevitably going to be skewed and riddled with large inconsistencies. As Agbor observes: '[O]ne would think that prosecuting hate speech is a well-settled issue in international criminal law. Recent developments in the jurisprudence thereon indicate to us that we are still very far from resolving this legal maze, especially with complicated scenarios evolving from additional conduct that modifies an individual's scope of criminal responsibility.' (Agbor 2024, ix)

Freedom of expression is at the core of any free and democratic society. Restrictions on such a fundamental freedom can easily slip into the realm of censorship, with a dominant majority determining what speech is deemed reasonable and what constitutes hate – thereby using judicial and police powers to curb speech not acceptable to the majority.

---

[5] Note, for example, how within the ECtHR two schools of thought have predominated regarding the test to be applied for hate speech. The one school adopts what has been described as a 'bad tendency' test whereby the trend of speech is ascertained, while the other espouses what can be described as an 'incitement' test which focuses on the actual harm or potential of harm. The former refers to the *potential* for speech to be harmful, while the latter considers the *actual impact* caused and risk posed by speech. Since there is no consistency in the standards imposed by these tests, the jurisprudence of the ECtHR in this regard has been described as legally uncertain, arbitrary and weakened by what has been labelled double standards. (Sottiaux 2023, 1195) As is shown later in this chapter, the application of these respective tests may have led to different outcomes in the Kill the Boer cases and the Old Flag cases, thereby highlighting the risk of arbitrariness and inconsistency in South African jurisprudence.

[6] Brown and Sinclair emphasise as follows: 'We suggest that whether a given law can be plausibly counted as a hate speech law depends on not simply what type of words or behaviour are prohibited or regulated by it but also certain legal-technical qualities of the law as well as the legislative purpose or function of the law.' (Brown and Sinclair 2023, 336) This highlights, correctly in my view, the locality and circumstance of speech within the context of it being uttered, rather than a general categorisation of speech in the abstract (e.g. the display of a flag) as hate speech.

Whatever limitation is placed on freedom of expression, it must be limited and proportionate to the speech in question and the objective sought to be achieved by any restriction. This is because, in the words of the Canadian Supreme Court, the link between freedom of expression and the political process is 'perhaps *the* linchpin' of a free and democratic society. Freedom of expression encompasses the right to say and publish things that may cause offence, be objectionable, hurtful or derogatory, or lack sensitivity. (Herz and Molnar 2012) It is through education and informed debate that dislikeable speech is opposed, not by way of censorship.[7]

The ECtHR has developed in its case law the 'autonomous concept' of whether an interference with freedom of expression is 'proportionate to the legitimate aim pursued', which is determined having regard to all the circumstances of the case using criteria established in the court's case law and with the assistance of various principles and interpretation tools. (Freedom of Expression ECtHR 2022, para 88) While as a principle this standard is acceptable, it is in the application that the discretion of judges often gives rise to what seem to be contradictory outcomes.

How should we then distinguish between hate speech and speech that we hate? To quote Shakespeare's *Hamlet*, 'that is the question'.

The threat posed by hate speech to stability, human rights and democratic peace and order was articulated recently by the Secretary-General of the United Nations, Antonio Guterres, in the following manner:

> Public discourse is being weaponised for political gain with incendiary rhetoric that stigmatises and dehumanises minorities, migrants, refugees, women and any so called 'other'. . . . Hate speech is a menace to democratic values, social stability and peace. As a matter of principle, the United Nations must confront hate speech at every turn. Silence can signal indifference to bigotry and intolerance, even as a situation escalates and the vulnerable become victims. . . . *Addressing hate speech does not mean limiting or prohibiting freedom of speech*. . . . By enhancing global resilience against this global phenomenon [of hate speech], we can strengthen the bonds of society and build a better world for all. (emphasis added) (UN Strategy Hate Speech 2019)

In recent years there has been a lively public discussion in South Africa about the practical application of the hate speech test. If ever there was a factual situation that has tested the theory and practice of the hate speech test, it has been the so-

[7] This is, ironically, illustrated by the fact that the old flag has since 1993 fallen into disuse and is rarely seen in public, not because of government prescription but rather the increased popularity of the new flag and the inclusion it represents. Put simply, before the Old Flag cases the actual display of the old flag had, through popular disuse, diminished.

called Old Flag cases (Old Flag case 2019; Old Flag appeal case 2023) [8] and Kill the Boer cases (Kill the Boer case 2011; Kill the Boer case 2022; Kill the Boer appeal case 2024).[9]

These cases encapsulate and embody the complexity of South Africa's history, encompassing the narratives of the oppressor and the liberated, the diverse perspectives of individuals, the interplay between remembering the past and seeking reconciliation, the definition and application of hate speech, the perceptions of observers, the intention of the speaker, the dynamic between subjective and objective evaluations of speech, the standard of proof for hate speech, the various interpretations of speech, the literal and figurative meanings of speech, and the potential value to consider international jurisprudence and Ubuntu.

The cases also highlight the principle that hate speech is local, circumstantial and time-bound. It has been observed that regardless of multiple efforts to define hate speech, there is no agreement yet among European countries on a definition of hate speech, albeit there is a common commitment in principle to curb and criminalise hate speech. (Stajnko and Siter 2023) One can attempt to develop

---

[8] Although in the Old Flag case no verbal utterances of hate or racism were made, the court (correctly) found that the display of a symbol such as a flag constitutes 'speech'. The finding that the display of a symbol is 'speech' is consistent with international law, as speech is interpreted broadly to encompass not only actual speech but also songs, chants, signs or symbols. For example, conduct such as the burning of a flag, the wearing of black armbands or other such protest actions can be regarded as a form of speech. (Barendt 2005, 78). In the USA it has been held that the burning of the flag is protected by free speech. (Texas case 1989). In the Qwelane case the Constitutional Court of South Africa emphasised that protective legislation should be given an expansive and purposive meaning, as the aim is to protect members of the public against hate speech. (Qwelane case 2021, para 115)

[9] The Afrikaans word 'boer' literally means 'farmer'. When sung, the word 'boer' can denote Afrikaners, white people, farmers (most of whom are Afrikaners) or members of the former apartheid government. According to Diko, this was one of many liberation chants that were sung during apartheid, but it is seen in contemporary circumstances by the 'global village' as 'promoting violence'. (Diko 2024, 4, 10) Since the chant is often heard in the context of land issues, it is arguably not unreasonable for farmers to feel they are being targeted by the words as one of the possible meanings of the chant. In the Kill the Boer appeal the court emphasised that the word 'ibhunu' should not be taken out of context to merely refer to white farmers, but should be read in the context of the song as part of the liberation struggle. (Kill the Boer appeal case 2024, para 91) While this is correct as one potential meaning, international comparative law suggests that *all* possible meanings of speech should be dissected for possible hate speech, not only the predominant meaning. If *any* of the meanings constitute hate speech, the speech is not protected by freedom of expression. It is not, as the court in the Kill the Boer case seems to suggest, a predominant meaning test. *All* meanings must be ascertained for the reasonable person to make an assessment.

universal definitions or benchmarks for hate speech, but in the application of universal norms the local circumstances, history, conditions, context and events surrounding the speech determine whether it meets the threshold of hate or whether it should be tolerated pursuant to freedom of expression.

Two judgments of the ECtHR can be used to illustrate the inconsistency applying what appear to be universal norms for the declaration of hate speech: in the Féret case the court found that '*ridicule or slandering* of specific groups of the population can be sufficient' to establish hate speech (Féret case 2009, paras 70–71), while in the Savva Terentyev case the test applied was whether the offending speech is 'likely to provide *imminent unlawful actions*' and a '*real risk* of physical violence'. (Savva Terentyev case 2009, para 77)[10] The use of words such as 'ridicule' and 'imminent unlawful actions' to meet the threshold of hate speech highlights the risk that the definition of hate speech is being expanded to include other forms of dislikeable or objectionable speech. It is perhaps not surprising that the ECtHR has struggled to achieve consistency in its approach to the categorisation of hate speech. (Martínez-Torrón 2024, 162)

The high regard in which freedom of expression is held in liberal democracies means that whenever an allegation is made of hate speech the starting point is the protection of freedom of expression, with the burden resting on the aggrieved person to prove that the alleged objectionable speech is disproportionate to freedom of expression, constitutes hate speech and merits the granting of a proportionate restriction or remedy.[11] This is because it is universally accepted in liberal democracies that the exercise of the right to free speech 'without fear or unlawful interference is central to living in an open and fair society; one in which people can access justice and enjoy their human rights'. (Amnesty International 2020)

The universal principles laying the contours of hate speech may be relatively simple to express generally, but putting those principles into practice is not simple. The complexities involved were evidenced in the Old Flag and Kill the Boer cases.

---

[10] In this case the speaker called for members of the police to be burned and murdered, but the ECtHR found that, within the context of public criticism of the police, the speech was protected and thus did not constitute hate speech.

[11] The difficulty to prove hate speech explains why some countries have opted to ban, regulate or restrict specific symbols and insignia pursuant to a criminal code rather than to rely on the common-law understanding of hate speech. The requirement for proof is thereby simplified since the state only needs to rely on evidence of the banned speech being uttered without having to prove it constituted hate speech. The burden then shifts to the speaker to raise a defence for purportedly breaching a statute. (Martínez-Torrón 2024)

In the Old Flag cases (original and appeal) the courts held that the display of the old republican flag of South Africa (the official flag of the South African state between 1928 and 1994) at a public march in protest about the high levels of crime constituted hate speech. The courts thus ordered that any future exhibition of the old flag, except for scientific, journalistic or educational purposes, would *ipso facto* be considered hate speech, regardless of the circumstances surrounding its display.[12] The display of the old flag, including for private or cultural use, was effectively banned.[13] An appeal against the judgment was dismissed and there was no further appeal to the Constitutional Court.

In the Kill the Boer cases two opposing outcomes were handed down by the courts in response to the chant. At first it was held in 2011 that the chant 'Kill the Boer, Kill the Farmer' constituted hate speech. The court declared that the chant was no longer suitable in a democratic South Africa. However, in a subsequent 2022 judgment and on appeal in 2024, it was found in another case involving the chant that the chant, when considered within its historical context rather than according to its literal meaning, did not meet the threshold for hate speech. The court declared that the singing of the chant was protected by freedom of expression. The Constitutional Court on 27 March 2025 refused leave to appeal the judgment.

It is not surprising that these judgments have sparked debates, both locally and internationally, regarding the definition of hate speech and the method to assess hate speech, as well as both the retrospective and prospective impact of a declaration of hate speech. The judgments also impacted on the limits of plurality,

[12] The court declared as follows: '[I]t is declared that subject to the proviso in s 12 of the Equality Act, any display of the old flag constitutes: (a) hate speech in terms of Section 10(1) of the Equality Act; (b) unfair discrimination on the basis of race in terms of Section 7 of the Equality Act; and (c) harassment in terms of Section 11 of the Equality Act.' (Old Flag case 2019, para 205(2)) Note that a new Act, the Prevention and Combating of Hate Crimes and Hate Speech Act 2023 took effect in May 2024 (Hate Speech Act 2023). The cases discussed in this chapter were determined under the Equality Act, but the issues remain relevant in South Africa and internationally. The Hate Speech Act specifically includes the display of a symbol as speech. It furthermore determines that speech constitutes hate speech when it is 'motivated by that person's prejudice or intolerance towards the victim of the crime in question' because of any of a range of characteristics. Certain speech is protected, for example speech in artistic creativity, scientific inquiry, reporting and commentary, and religious belief. (s 4(2))

[13] Ironically, the Communist flag, a symbol internationally associated with substantial and consistent human rights transgressions and human rights abuses, and emblematic of undemocratic and totalitarian governance, is neither prohibited nor is its display regarded as hate speech in South Africa. Moreover, the display of the Communist flag, or other insignia associated with communism, is not subject to the same restrictions as those that apply to the old flag.

as in both cases those who displayed the symbol (or sang the chant) drew upon its heritage and symbolism within a diverse cultural and political context.

In this chapter I assess those judgments, considering selected international jurisprudence and focusing specifically on the following questions:

- what is the definition of hate speech?
- what is the test for hate speech – subjective or objective?
- what is the effect of a declaration of hate speech?

5.2 PLURAL SOCIETIES: A POTENTIAL TESTING GROUND FOR FREE EXPRESSION AND HATE SPEECH

The history of plural societies is frequently marked by painful events, such as colonisation, occupation, migration, displacement, slavery, discrimination, oppression, skirmishes, violence and war. The formation of the modern state is rarely, if ever, a logical and peaceful process. Pluralism has a history, whether it is ancient or rooted in contemporary events such as immigration, arrivals of refugees, wars or changes to state borders. By its nature pluralism embodies the celebration of historic dates and events, adherence to customs and practices, display and singing of symbols and songs, teaching of varied histories and honouring of varied monuments, obeying or suppressing of non-state laws, and retaining, endearing or even encouraging of inter-community biases and prejudices.

Herein lies the problem: the display of symbols or adherence to non-state law, steeped in history and tradition, may be dear to one community, but offensive, or even perceived to be hateful, to another community, or vice versa. The very speech treasured by one may be perceived as hate speech by another. Take, for example, the annual Orange Marches in Northern Ireland – a celebration for one community (Protestants) and a potentially hateful commemoration for the other community (Catholics), and the Jerusalem Day march in Israel when Jews celebrate the recapture of East Jerusalem in 1967. Another illustration is religious orders that consider those who do not share their faith as condemned, often regarding non-believers as of lesser status than those deemed true believers. Also relevant is how museums and places of cultural historic importance in South Africa such as *Bloedrivier* are responded to within the democratic milieu. (Ngobese 2023) For many Jews the statement 'from the river to the sea' signifies a threat of genocide, although to Palestinians it may signify self-determination. Put simply: What to one is a celebration or commemoration pursuant to the right to free speech may to the other constitute an expression of hate speech.

Speech often comes with a package that reflects history, political events, social circumstances and perceptions. Steuer observes as follows:

> Evaluating the contextual characteristics of speech requires the awareness of historical, sociological, political, and even psychological factors, which goes beyond the usual capacities of public institutions, often with limited resources for specialised staff. (Steuer 2024, 217)

Against this backdrop, a flag that was once the lawful symbol of a sovereign state can transform into a perceived symbol of hate, and a chant once motivated by the cause of liberation can morph into a perceived chant of hate. It all depends on timing, perspective and circumstance. Hate speech, like love, is factual and personal in nature.

The question emerges about whose perspective determines whether speech constitutes hate: the speaker, the recipient, the onlooker, the affected community or society in general? There is a risk that, in an effort not to cause hurt, almost any form of objectionable, dislikeable or offensive speech may be classified as hate speech and thus restricted. A declaration of hate speech then potentially becomes a tool of censorship and repression, enabling Parliament, the executive or the courts to misuse and abuse their powers by unjustifiably curtailing free expression and stifling speech, including displays of symbols. This, in turn, may enforce majority hegemony.[14]

A defence of speech that is hateful should not be construed as defending hate speech. (De Villiers 2022d, 249) Dislikeable speech is meritorious of defence, without condoning the speech. Taib et al suggest that speech that 'promotes prejudices' or 'can cause harm' in deeply divided societies should be regarded as hate speech. (Taib, Sama, and Yusof 2024, 141) On the other hand, defending freedom of expression is the defence of a fundamental right without which democracies cannot properly function.[15] In a democratic society where the

---

[14] The non-binding Council of Europe Ljubljana Guidelines explain as follows: 'The display of symbols related to identity by private persons in public falls under freedom of expression *and should not be prohibited* unless there are legitimate and clearly defined legal grounds for doing so. These grounds should, in any case, be interpreted *narrowly* and any prohibition must be proportional to the legitimate aims.' (emphasis added) (Ljubljana Guidelines 2012, 64)

[15] Gelber speaks about the 'fragility of freedom of speech', given that governments are so prone to use their majority in Parliament to suppress freedom of expression. (Gelber 2012, 176) Brown also cautions that the term 'hate speech' has become so widely used that it potentially runs the risk of turning into a catch-all with divergent meanings of dislikeable, offensive or objectionable speech gravitating towards a categorisation of 'hate'. (Brown 2017, 422) Such a

exchange of opinions is centred on freedom of expression the threshold to define hate speech should be set high. Ideally, it is society through its norms and conduct that should reject and isolate hate speech in its response to the speech, rather than relying on the courts to do so. Public dismay, criticism, disgust and rejection should be the response to those who propagate offensive speech. Only the most extreme speech should be formally declared hate speech by courts. (Schweppe and Walsh 2008, 72) This explains the relatively low number of successful prosecutions under common law for hate speech, even though the display of certain symbols may be regulated or even prohibited under criminal statutes.[16] Enarsson explains how the absence of a definition of hate speech in European law complicates the ability of service providers and enforcers to regulate content of speech. (Enarsson 2024, 391)

Furthermore, societal values change.[17] What constitutes hate speech today may in the future not be regarded as such, and vice versa.[18] Hate speech is typically

---

wide categorisation of speech runs the risk of conflating social descriptions of hate speech with legal categorisation of hate speech, thereby reducing freedom of expression.

[16] Prosecution becomes simpler when specific speech or the display of a symbol has been banned by a statute. In such cases the state need only prove that the speech occurred in breach of an Act or Regulation, while the speaker must rebut the charge with some form of justification. To prove hate speech under common law is more onerous since the complainant carries the burden of proof that the speech complies with the hate test, while the presumption is that speech is lawful in a free and democratic system. Nemeiksis also points out how challenging it is to prove hate speech under criminal law. (Nemeiksis 2024, 205)

[17] Note, for example, how the old flag has also been the subject of a chequered history. The incorporation of the Union Jack into the design of the old flag in the 1920s was fiercely resisted by some Afrikaners as, in the aftermath of the Anglo-Boer War, this British symbol was detested and seen as a 'blood stain' on the proposed flag. In contemporary language the display of the Union Jack in the 1920s would arguably have been considered hate speech by some in the Afrikaner community, especially those for whom the atrocities committed by the English in the war, including concentration camps and a scorched earth policy, were still vivid. However, as time progressed the design of the old flag came to be accepted as reflective of the complex history of South Africa, and the controversy surrounding the Union Jack's inclusion into the old flag dissipated. In fact, over time the presence of the Union Jack became a topic of education rather than controversy. This is consistent with the refusal of the Supreme Court of India to declare an offensive film hate speech since the court held the view that the showing of the film would lead to discussion and debate about the past, thereby educating the public and deepening democracy. (FA Picture case 2005)

[18] Note, for example, that in the Hagan case in Australia, which involved the naming of a stadium grandstand the E S 'Nigger' Brown Stand – a nickname of a celebrated player – the CERD observed that cultural values change and a word that may have once been used to celebrate a player has, with the flow of time, become hurtful and discriminatory. (Hagan case 2003, para 7.3) This is regardless of the Federal Court of Australia having declared in 2000 that the naming

based on situations and circumstances. Take, for example, the changing attitudes about the public display of the Confederate flag in the USA (Updegrove, Cooper, and Dmello 2021). As an historic symbol the Confederate flag once represented the lawful authority of the day, but over time it has become associated with white supremacy and a defence of slavery. In contemporary American society the display of the flag is diminishing and is largely associated with racism and right-wing extremism. However, its display is not considered hate speech under US jurisprudence and it has not been banned by statute or regulation.[19]

Courts are reluctant to declare utterances hate speech without regard to the specific circumstances in which the speech was uttered.[20] This is because speech in the abstract can hardly be characterised as 'hate' without considering the statutory regime, context and circumstance. Courts focus on the event, specific circumstances and an objective assessment of the speech within the context in which it was used. A declaration of hate speech therefore usually applies to speech at a specific occasion, rather than a general restriction on the speech into the future. Judgments declaring speech to be hate speech are principally

---

of the same stadium stand *did not* meet the threshold for racism. (Hagan case 2000) The court declared as follows: 'The circumstances of the word's use also include the fact that it appears in a sign as an integral part of the name of a person who is clearly being honoured by having his name publicly applied to the stand. That is, the word "Nigger" is used in the context of giving public recognition to the achievements of a particular person associated with the Athletic Oval and the sporting activities carried on there.' (Hagan case 2003, para 26)

[19] The preferred approach adopted in the USA is that objectionable and hateful symbols tend to fall into disuse through societal pressure, public rejection or irrelevancy, rather than by some form of prohibition. (Rosenfeld 2003, 1538) This approach, in which freedom of expression is regarded as essentially sacrosanct, contrasts with many other liberal democracies where freedom of expression may be easier to restrict in the interest of combating hate speech. The various approaches to offensive insignia are perhaps best illustrated by interjurisdictional differences regarding Nazi symbols. While these symbols are banned or restricted in some countries (e.g. Germany, Austria, Australia), they are not restricted in the USA, where their mere display does not necessarily constitute hate speech. Note also, for example, that in Australia there was no general ban against Nazi insignia until 2024, when legislation was enacted during the Israeli–Gaza war, even though some of the country's federal states had previously banned the public display of the Nazi salute, pursuant to the Criminal Code of the particular state. However, prior to the banning of those symbols courts had not declared that the public display of the symbols automatically constituted hate speech under common law. Note the country studies in Heinze about efforts by states to restrict hate speech within the context of fostering free speech and equality rights. (Heinze 2024)

[20] Note, for example, the M'Bala case, in which the ECtHR found that a gathering that started as a comedy show had midway changed character and became a political meeting and in such capacity the speech sought to be protected was an abuse of rights and therefore not protected speech. (M'Bala case 2015)

retrospective rather than prospective. Parliament or the executive are the appropriate authorities to ban, restrict or prohibit certain forms of speech prospectively, while courts weigh freedom of expression and purported hate speech within a specific factual matrix retrospectively. (De Villiers 2022e) Applying a finding of hate speech prospectively is likely to be disproportionate and wades into the field of other organs of government. Furthermore, any restriction on speech must consider other rights of the individual, for example rights to culture, identity, self-determination, information and religion. (Boulais, Marinkovic, and Palomares 2023, 794) Sultan and others caution, after a comparison of regulation of hate speech in Pakistan and the United Kingdom, that there may be a disk of 'disproportionate limitation on freedom of speech' in an effort to protect the public against dislikeable speech. (Sultan, Akhtar, and Imran 2024, 38)

Additionally, it is important to consider that sovereign states differ in their approach to hate speech. For instance, speech that may be regarded as hate speech in one jurisdiction, such as Germany, is granted constitutional protection in the USA. In Germany, for example, the 'value of personal honour' and dignity may limit the scope of free speech, (BVerfGE 7 198) while the same limitation may not apply to speech in the USA. The Supreme Court of India has also accepted that speech attacking the dignity of a person may be considered hate speech, although this leaves the door open to ascertain when 'dignity' is affected. Khanna J of the Supreme Court of India has defined the essence of dignity by referring to the loss thereof as follows: 'Loss of dignity and self-worth of the targeted group members contributes to *disharmony* amongst groups, and erodes tolerance and *open-mindedness* which are a must for a multi-cultural society committed to the idea of equality. It affects an individual as a member of a group'. (emphasis added) (Amish Devgan case 2020) Critics of the Amish Devgan case caution that relying on feelings of injury, the dignity of a person or disharmony in society may open the door to improper restrictions on free speech and that 'it will not be long before this definition will be used against individuals speaking against the government'. (Rao 2020, 25) Laroia commented that, 'despite the court's pragmatic distinction between free expression and hateful speech, the idea of what is and is not acceptable continues to be too broad to be applied universally. True, defining hate speech too narrowly might lead to overly tight limits on freedom of expression. . . .' (Laroia 2022, 80) The Constitutional Court of South Africa also declared that feeling 'hurt' is not an adequate benchmark for a finding of hate speech. (Qwelane case 2021)[21]

[21] For a critical assessment of the judgment, see Winks. (Winks 2023)

The absence of consistent jurisprudence internationally in response to complaints about hate speech highlights the challenge for South African courts to 'consider', pursuant to s 39 of the Constitution, the approaches adopted regarding hate speech in international law and foreign law. (Chapter 4) The different views expressed by municipal courts internationally concerning freedom of expression, and any limitations thereto, are strongly influenced by the history, traditions, social situation, politics and legal framework of a particular country.[22] It is therefore not surprising that what constitutes hate speech in one jurisdiction is not necessarily considered hate speech in another.[23]

As a general principle, the approach adopted by the Canadian Supreme Court to the definition of hate speech can be endorsed. This approach involves the application of three principles when interpreting prohibitions on hate speech: first, the prohibition must be applied *objectively*; secondly, hatred must be interpreted as being restricted to *extreme manifestations* of harmful speech; and, thirdly, courts must focus on the effect of the *expression* at issue, rather than the nature of the ideas expressed. (Saskatchewan case 2013)

At law a complaint about hate speech is determined objectively, according to a reasonable-person-type assessment. While it may seem simple, how does one objectively determine the feelings of a person or a community that feels

---

[22] To illustrate this point, the display of South Africa's old flag in another country, such as the United Kingdom or the USA, is unlikely to be declared hate speech, since the circumstances of the country in which the symbol is displayed would determine the objective message conveyed by the flag. On the other hand, an offensive word in South Africa has influenced the naming of a street in Australia where the word 'kaffir' was used in reference to a tree but, because of the offensive nature of the word in South Africa, the name was removed from the Australian street. (Fenner 2024)

[23] In Australia, for example, it has been found that the word 'nigger' does not always constitute racism. In the context of the historic naming of a stadium grandstand as the E S 'Nigger' Brown Stand, the word 'nigger' was, in fact, used as a nickname in honour of a celebrated player. (Hagan case 2000). In a similar vein, in some countries that were subjugated by Communism the display of the Communist flag, regardless of how hateful and offensive it is to those who suffered under it, is not considered adequate reason to curtail freedom of expression. (Vajnai case 2008) Meanwhile, in Germany the display of the Communist flag is restricted pursuant to the Criminal Code, as it represents an unconstitutional organisation. The decision of Germany in 1957 to ban the Communist Party was upheld by the European Commission of Human Rights on the basis of the aims of the Party to destroy 'many of the rights or freedoms' enshrined in the Convention, including the right to freedom of expression. (Communist Party case 1957) It must be noted that the Parliament of South Africa has neither opted to ban the old flag or the Communist flag, nor to impose any restrictions on the display of either of those flags.

offended by speech?[24] This is different to the reasonable person test in torts or delict, where a general community standard about the appropriateness of conduct may be relatively simple to ascertain.[25] What type of evidence is required and how does one ascertain whether an individual who perceives speech as hateful is representative of the objectively assessed perception of the community of which the individual is part? How does a fictional reasonable person understand hate when certain speech is uttered?[26] To what extent, if any, can judges rely on their own knowledge and assessment of speech, even if there is not adequate evidence before them to support such judicial knowledge?[27] Or is the objective assessment, in reality, a test exercised in fiction whereby judges revert to the

[24] Note, for example, the political chant that has received so much attention during the invasion of Gaza – 'From the river to the sea'. This is seen by some as a hateful chant implying the eradication of the state of Israel, while to other it is seen as a chant confirming that a political solution must be found to the entire area. Its meanings range from genocidal to democratic. It illustrates how challenging it can be to ascertain the objective meaning of speech. The chant has not been declared by any country or court as hate speech.

[25] Note, for example, how in Switzerland the court considered the detail of speech, the circumstance in which it was made and the previous record of the speaker to declare that the denial of the Holocaust was discriminatory in that context. (SUI-2024-1-001 2024) This suggests a highly subjective and personalised test rather than a remote and objective test.

[26] It may be simple to identify hate speech in extreme cases, as in the Qwelane case, where hate speech was directed at a person for their gender. (Qwelane case 2021) However, it becomes more challenging when speech is capable of multiple meanings or interpretations or where the application of hate speech is not obvious and the presumption of freedom of expression is strong. Note, for example, the Savva Terentyev case, in which the ECtHR dismissed a complaint that speech calling for police to be 'killed' and burned in 'Auschwitz ovens' constituted hate speech. The court reasoned that police, in the exercise of their duties, may expect extreme criticism of this nature and hence the speech did not meet the threshold test for hate speech. (Savva Terentyev case 2009) This reasoning would mean that the same chant directed at a different audience may be held to constitute hate speech, but the police are expected to absorb such chant in the exercise of their duties.

[27] Note, for example, that in the cases under discussion the courts accepted in the Old Flag case the evidence of one witness about the emotions he felt when he heard that the old flag had been displayed. In contrast, in the Kill the Boer case of 2022 and on appeal in 2024 the court did not accept the evidence of witnesses who spoke about their fears and angst upon hearing the chant and their personal experiences of violent farm crime. Furthermore, in the 2011 Kill the Boer case the court adopted a flexible approach to the admission of evidence, including hearsay evidence, while in the 2022 Kill the Boer case and on appeal in 2024 the court rejected expert evidence about farm murders because of technical considerations. In the Kill the Boer appeal the court accepted the evidence of an expert about the meaning of liberation songs, but was not swayed by the symbolic use of a firearm despite evidence of two witnesses who had personally experienced farm attacks and the high incidence of farm-related crime and violence in South Africa. (Kill the Boer appeal case 2024, paras 68–69) This treatment of evidence contrasts with

so-called reasonable person test to give legitimacy and credibility to their own views? (De Villiers 2022e, 207)[28] The reasonable person test is seen by some as Eurocentric and foreign to African thought and tradition. (Khanyile, Iyer, and Matadi 2024) Notable in this regard is the caution expressed by Majiedt J in the Qwelane case:

> [W]hen plugging in an abstract reasonable person test in order to construe the meaning of alleged hate speech, courts ought to be mindful of our diverse and dynamic society and not inadvertently reify prejudices. (Qwelane case 2021, para 100)[29]

Viewing purported hate speech at arm's length may make it easy to dismiss a person who perceives speech as hateful as being oversensitive and thin-skinned. However, when standing in the shoes of this person, hatefulness may be real and palpable. In this regard it is worth noting the caution expressed by the ECtHR, namely that '[hurt] feelings, however understandable, cannot alone set the limits of freedom of expression'. (Refah Partisi case 2003, para 57) This gives rise to a dilemma – if speech is viewed subjectively from the perspective of the person complaining about it, given their potential personal sensitivities and lack of tolerance, one may conclude too easily that the speech is indeed hateful.[30] In contrast, when viewed objectively there's a risk of the assessment of the speech being so remote and dispassionate from the feelings of the person complaining about the alleged hate speech that one may lose sight of the hateful nature of some

the Old Flag case, in which the court found that the mere display of the old flag was adequate evidence of hate speech.

[28] The question inevitably also arises whether the personal background of judges may influence the way they perceive speech on behalf of the fictional 'reasonable person' – note, for example, that in the 2011 Kill the Boer case the justice was white, while in the 2022 Kill the Boer case the justice was black. On appeal in 2024 the majority of justices were black. Could the race or cultural background of the respective judges have impacted on their assessment of evidence? Ironically, the white judge cited Ubuntu in declaring the chant as hate speech, while the black judge made no mention of Ubuntu in finding that the chant did not constitute hate speech, neither did the court of appeal cite the relevance or lack of relevance of Ubuntu. (Chapter 6) One will never know whether race or cultural background were relevant factors that influenced the outcome of the judgments. However, supposedly relying on an objective test through the eyes of a reasonable person may serve as a cloak under which judicial bias, assumptions and personal views could be expressed with credibility and judicial authority.

[29] Notably, the court did not cite Ubuntu in its reasoning for persons to be treated equally and with respect and dignity. As discussed below, this illustrates the unpredictability of use of Ubuntu in judicial reasoning.

[30] The Constitutional Court of South Africa has, for example, declared that the use of the word 'hurt' as a requirement for hate speech is too vague and lacks the clarity required for a finding of hate speech. (Qwelane case 2021)

speech in the circumstances of the aggrieved community. Furthermore, when applying the objective test the question arises whether it entails the objective opinion of the broad society or merely the opinion of the community targeted by the alleged hate speech. This is exemplified by the cases under discussion in this chapter – can a non-black person truly grasp objectively what the display of the old flag means to black people? Conversely, can a non-white person, or someone other than a farmer, genuinely comprehend the fear of a white person when the chant 'Kill the Boer' is sung? In these two cases the reasonable person test was applied by both judges, but only one judge declared the old flag to constitute hate speech.

In both Old Flag and Kill the Boer judgments the court stated that it had applied the objective reasonable person test. Inherent in this situation is the risk that the emotions felt by one community may be treated differently to the emotions felt by another. In light of this risk the US Supreme Court has cautioned courts *not* to adopt a position of favouritism where the sensitivities of one group are given preference over those of another. (RAV case 1992) In Bosnia and Herzegovina caution was expressed that the penalties imposed for criticising state symbols may be so severe and disproportionate that it would have a chilling effect on freedom of expression. (BIH-2024-1-001 2024)

The challenge faced by courts to establish, based on the evidence before them, what an objective assessment of speech implies for a hate speech complaint is highlighted by the Old Flag and Kill the Boer cases.

In short, in few areas of law are the boundaries of what is considered reasonable and proportionate so difficult to determine as in the intersection between freedom of expression and hate speech. This challenge is particularly pronounced in plural societies, where communities with diverse cultural, religious, indigenous and customary backgrounds may express opinions about each other, or celebrate events, or display symbols, or adhere to practices and customs that may cause offence or indignation and, in the worst cases, result in the occurrence of hate speech. In this regard the Supreme Court of India aptly noted how challenging it is to 'confine the prohibition [against hate speech] to some manageable standard'. (Amish Devgan case 2020, para 16)

5.3 SPEECH IN CONTEXT

In the context of this book it is essential to note that what constitutes hate speech is inevitably determined by factors such as place, time, history, perception, population composition and circumstance. Unless a Parliament or executive authority bans or restricts a specific form of speech, the role of a court is to ascertain whether, in a particular setting, the speech complained about constitutes hate speech. Courts do not make general declarations about the appropriateness of speech; instead, they assess and weigh its suitability while considering the specific circumstances when the speech was uttered.[31] In the case of the display of Nazi insignia, for example, Germany's Criminal Code prohibits the display of the swastika. This contrasts with some other European countries, such as the United Kingdom and France, where there is no outright ban on any Nazi insignia, although the display of the swastika may be restricted or even, in specific circumstances, considered hate speech by a court. In France it has also been held that even controversial speech such as Holocaust denial must be assessed in the context in which it takes place. (Faurisson case 1996)

The context of speech is particularly relevant in deeply divided societies with high levels of ethnocultural plurality and a poorly developed common identity, where one person's freedom of expression may be perceived by another as hate speech.[32] It is essential for young and emerging democracies that free speech is tolerated rather than supressed. This may explain why Parliament in South Africa has not opted to ban or restrict flags and symbols, such as the old flag or the Communist flag.

To illustrate the importance of context of speech note by way of summary the different reasoning provided in the two cases involving the Kill the Boer chant. In the 2011 Kill the Boer case the court found that the significance of speech may change, such that something formerly considered hate speech can become acceptable and vice versa. The categorisation of speech as 'hate' is therefore dynamic and circumstantial. In the context of South Africa the court explained as follows in the 2011 Kill the Boer case:

---

[31] Note, for example, the Taqiyev case, in which the ECtHR held that offensive speech did not meet the requirement for hate speech since it contributed to the discussion about the role of religion in society. The court noted that the domestic court erred by drawing a conclusion 'without assessing the author's intention' and that the context of the speech was such that it could have contributed to 'openly discussing matters relating to religion'. (Tagiyev case 2020, paras 48–49) The court clearly had regard for the subjective circumstances and context of the speech – an approach that I argue below was not adopted in the Old Flag cases, yet relied on in the Kill the Boer (2022 and 2024) cases.

[32] Added to the different meanings attached to speech, the world of fake news often intersects with hate speech to the detriment of minority communities. While fake news is not in itself hate speech, the harmful effects of fake news can in appropriate circumstances be regarded as hate speech. (Topidi 2023, 150)

> [T]he enemy has become the friend, the brother. . . . It must never be forgotten that in the spirit of *Ubuntu* this new approach to each other must be fostered. (Kill the Boer case 2011, para 108)

The court declared that the chant constituted hate speech. In contrast, in the 2022 Kill the Boer case the court rejected the complaint that the chant constituted hate speech. The court explained that the chant should not be taken literally and, instead, should be seen in the context of the history of the liberation struggle. The court viewed the chant principally through the eyes of those who sang it as a liberation song. Ironically, both these judgments cited international law, the history of South Africa and the importance of an objective test to assess speech – and yet the two justices came to diametrically opposing judgments about the same chant. On appeal the court did not cite foreign law nor refer to the relevance of Ubuntu, but also declared that the aggrieved speech should not be taken literally. (Kill the Boer appeal case 2024, para 91) 'So much for the objective assessment test and for considering international law,' one might cynically observe.

Hate speech is, of course, not limited to inter-ethnic utterances. It can also be directed at individuals based on their social and personal circumstances, such as their social status or gender. (Qwelane case 2021)[33] While its effects can be wide-ranging, hate speech eludes precise definition. What is certain, however, is that it presents as an extreme form of speech that seeks to dehumanise and marginalise a person or a community.[34]

[33] Note the Lenis case, in which the ECtHR held that the speech uttered by a church leader against civil unions for same sex couples *was not protected* because of the hateful nature of the speech, which was inconsistent with the values of the European Convention, and that the applicant could not 'benefit' from the protections under the Convention for free speech. (Lenis case 2023, para 57) Furthermore, the ECtHR also relied on the principle of pluralism to explain its judgment that a ban on the 'promotion of homosexuality or non-traditional sexual relations' among minors was *incompatible* with the 'notions of equality, pluralism and tolerance inherent in a democratic society'. (Macatė case 2023, para 202) These judgments highlight the highly discretionary nature of how justices may depict speech.

[34] Notably, the court in the Qwelane case did not cite Ubuntu in its reasoning for persons to be treated equally and with respect and dignity. This illustrates the unpredictability of use of Ubuntu in judicial reasoning since one would have thought the inherent values of Ubuntu would find application in a case with such a factual matrix.

The Supreme Court of Canada has described the effect of hate speech in the following way:

> Using expression that exposes the group to hatred, hate speech seeks to delegitimise group members in the eyes of the majority, reducing their social standing and acceptance within society. *Hate speech therefore rises beyond causing distress to individual group members.* It can have a societal impact. Hate speech lays the groundwork for later, broad attacks on vulnerable groups that can range from discrimination, to ostracism, segregation, deportation, violence and, in the most extreme cases, to genocide. Hate speech also impacts on a protected group's ability to respond to the substantive ideas under debate, thereby placing a *serious barrier to their full participation in our democracy.* (emphasis added) (Saskatchewan case 2013)

To sum up, a determination of what constitutes hate speech is shaped by various factors. These include the historical context of a country or community, the timing of the speech as it may evolve in 'hate status' over time, the specific circumstances in which it is uttered (such as political events, social media, the privacy of one's home, political rallies or scientific and educational forums), the speaker's intention, the various meanings of speech and the varied perceptions of those at whom the speech is directed.[35] With regard to the latter, it is important to note that individuals from the same community may not uniformly exhibit the same sensitivity when exposed to the same speech, thus highlighting how challenging it can be to assess a person's claim of hate speech.

Although hate speech is frequently directed at ethnocultural minorities or indigenous people who may already politically marginalised, this is not always the case. Hate speech can also be directed at a member of the majority in a population, a dominant community or solely to an individual. All of this adds to the complexity of defining hate speech. Nonetheless, ethnocultural minorities or indigenous people may be more vulnerable to hate speech, particularly in young and emerging democracies, because they may not have the institutional or political means to combat it, or to have speech declared a criminal act through legislation. In the 2011 Kill the Boer case, the court observed as follows about the vulnerable status of minorities:

> It must not, however, be forgotten that minority groups are particularly vulnerable. It is precisely the individuals who are members of such minorities who are vulnerable to discriminatory treatment and who in a very special sense must look at the Bill of Rights for protection. The court has a clear duty to come to the assistance of such affected people. (Kill the Boer case 2011, para 35)

---

[35] Note, for example, the Lilliendahl case, in which the ECtHR accorded protection to a person's speech because it was uttered by a member of the general public 'not expressing himself from a prominent platform likely to reach a wide audience'. (Lilliendahl case 2020, para 39)

The majority have the power to criminalise hate speech directed at them, to ban symbols and insignia that offend them or to appoint the judges who preside over hate speech complaints. In contrast, the principal recourse of an individual who is the subject of hate speech is to rely on courts to make a finding under common law or statutory law to the effect that the speech in question constitutes hate speech. The reality, however, is that justices are appointed by the majority and they may bring their perceptions and biases into court with them. This often leaves the minority or individual not only exposed to hate speech, but potentially without effective legal remedy to challenge it. Assessing speech fairly may not always be within the capacity of a judge. In this respect Steuer observes as follows:

> Evaluating the contextual characteristics of speech requires the awareness of historical, sociological, political, and even psychological factors, which goes beyond the usual capacities of public institutions, often with limited resources for specialised staff. (Steuer 2024, 217)[36]

In order to give greater guidance on what is meant by hate speech the United Nations, through the office of the Secretary General, has suggested the following working definition for it:

> The term hate speech is understood as any kind of communication in speech, writing or behaviour, that attacks or uses pejorative or discriminatory language with reference to a person or a group on the basis of who they are, in other words, based on their religion, ethnicity, nationality, race, colour, descent, gender or other identity factor. (UN Strategy Hate Speech 2019, 2)

5.4 THE OLD FLAG AND KILL THE BOER CASES

To elaborate on the interaction between freedom of expression and hate speech in an international context, four judgments are discussed in this chapter. The factual backgrounds to these judgments are summarised below.

[36] Later Steuer acknowledges that experts themselves may be tainted by their view of events and in some instances may be nothing but 'hired guns' (Steuer 2024, 223), thus highlighting the challenge to neutrally and dispassionately viewing speech that to one community may seem hate speech and to another community a mere freedom of expression.

5.4.1 Old Flag cases (original and appeal)

In the Old Flag case the Equality Court of South Africa declared that the 'gratuitous'[37] display of the former flag of South Africa on 30 October 2017 by a person participating in a public demonstration against the high levels of crime in South Africa, most notably farm-related murders and assaults, constituted hate speech against black people. The court concluded that the flag's display was not protected by the constitutional right to freedom of expression. (Old Flag case 2019)[38]

The old flag refers to the flag that served as the official national flag of South Africa from 1928 to 1994. With the dawn of democracy in the country in 1994 South Africa adopted a new flag to represent the new democratic Constitution. The old flag has not been banned by Parliament, however, and there has not been any restrictive executive regulation concerning its display. This notwithstanding, the court not only declared the display of the old flag on the day of the protest as hate speech, but also ruled that any future display of it at any time would be considered hate speech, except for journalistic, educational or scientific purposes.

As previously mentioned, the old flag was displayed in the context of a public protest in response to the high levels of crime in South Africa. There is no dispute that South Africa has witnessed a substantial increase in crime and lawlessness. The country has been characterised, for example, as ranking 19 in the world for levels of organised crime (Delport 2022). In 2023 it was reported that the murder rate had reached its highest point in 20 years, with around 75 people murdered per day. (Bruce 2023) It is against this backdrop that a series of public marches took place on 30 October 2017. The marches, coordinated by an Afrikaans-speaking non-governmental organisation called AfriForum, were attended by people from all racial groups. During the protests the old flag was displayed by some of the participants. (BBC Old Flag 2017) It was, however, accepted that the display of the old flag was not orchestrated by the event organisers, the display of the old flag was isolated to a few people and the protests did not take place under the banner of the old flag. Furthermore, it was never

---

[37] The court did not define 'gratuitous' but, according to the *Macquarie Concise Dictionary*, it means 'without good reason, cause or justification'.

[38] The court declared as follows: '[I]t is determined that the display of the old national flag of South Africa, introduced on 31 May 1928, and used throughout apartheid until it was abolished on 27 April 27 1994 ("the Old Flag"), at the "Black Monday" demonstrations on 30 October 2017 constituted: *(a)* hate speech, in terms of section 10(1) of the Equality Act. . . .' (Old Flag case 2019, para 205 1)

asserted that the protestors, including those who displayed the old flag, rejected the existing constitutional order or the new flag, neither did they promote or threaten violence. Additionally, no racist or hate slogans were alleged to have been uttered by any of the individuals displaying the old flag. According to all accounts, the marches were a peaceful protest against crime. It was solely the display of the old flag that caused offence.

The Chief Executive of the Nelson Mandela Foundation, Mr Sello Hatang, filed an affidavit with the Equality Court in which he explained his feelings, as a black person, about the display of the old flag during the march, despite him not witnessing the march. He said:

> 14. [T]he old flag represents nothing other than the inhumane system of racial segregation and subjugation that governed South Africa before 27 April 1994. . . .
> 15. To *hear* that the old flag has been displayed gratuitously in 2017, more than a generation after apartheid had been abolished, reminded me that some South Africans still see me and other blacks as 'other', and would deny us the opportunity just to be human. (emphasis added) (Old Flag case 2019, para 23)

The Nelson Mandela Foundation sought a declaration from the Equality Court that *any* display of the old flag (not just the display on the particular day) that does not serve a genuine journalistic, academic or artistic purpose in the public interest *ipso facto* constitutes hate speech against black people pursuant to s 10 of the Promotion of Equality and Prevention of Unfair Discrimination Act 4 of 2000. (Equality Act 2000, s 10)[39] The court found in favour of the applicant and declared the 'gratuitous' display of the old flag on the day of the march, *and* into the future, hate speech – effectively banning the display of the old flag at any public or private cultural, sporting or political event.

The judgment was appealed. On 21 April 2023 the Supreme Court of Appeal dismissed the appeal and declared that 'any gratuitous public display of the old flag' constitutes hate speech as intended by s 10(1) of the Equality Act. (Old Flag appeal case 2023, para 75) The court found that the display of the old flag was tantamount to celebrating racism, legitimising white supremacy, glorifying apartheid and intimidating onlookers. (Old Flag appeal case 2023, paras 49, 53)

[39] In the meantime the Constitutional Court had declared parts of the Act that referred to 'hurt' as a requirement for hate speech to be unconstitutional (Qwelane case 2021). However, relevant to this chapter, the legality of the Act was not challenged and the principle of restricting freedom of speech to protect persons against hate speech, as per the amended s 10 of the Equality Act, was also not challenged.

In its reasoning the court issued the following declarations on the three questions central to this chapter.

- *What is the definition of hate speech?* The court emphasised that hate speech is the 'antithesis' of democracy, it is 'destructive' to democracy and it undermines the 'substantive equality' that the Constitution seeks to promote and achieve. (Old Flag appeal case 2023, para 30; Qwelane case 2021, para 130) The court stated that human dignity 'informs the interpretation of all other rights'. (Old Flag appeal case 2023, para 32) The statutory prohibition of hate speech stipulates that no person may publish, propagate, advocate or communicate words that could reasonably be construed as a *clear intention* to be harmful or to incite harm and to promote or propagate hatred.[40] The court declared that the display of the old flag met the requirements to be a form of communication or advocacy (Old Flag appeal case 2023, para 38), adding that the 'message conveyed' by its public display is 'plainly one based on race – apartheid and white supremacy.' (Old Flag appeal case 2023, para 39)[41] The court then went on to explain why, in light of the apartheid history of South Africa, the old flag is such a powerful symbol and so emblematic of racism and hate.
- *What is the test for hate speech – subjective or objective?* The court confirmed that the test to ascertain hate speech is objective, namely whether a 'reasonable person, in the circumstances surrounding the expression, would reasonably construe the words or conduct as demonstrating an intention to be harmful, incite harm or propagate hatred'. (Old Flag appeal case 2023, para 42) It is the effect of the speech, as opposed to the intent of the speaker, that is considered. The court emphasised that 'incitement to harm' or 'promotion or propagation of hatred' are 'key elements of hate speech since freedom of

[40] Section 10(1) of the Equality Act determined as follows: 'Subject to the proviso in s 12, no person may publish, propagate, advocate or communicate words that are based on one or more of the prohibited grounds, against any person, that could reasonably be construed to demonstrate *a clear intention* to be harmful or to incite harm and to promote or propagate hatred.'

[41] Note the approach adopted by the ECtHR in the Fáber case, in which it was held that the mere display of a symbol that could cause offence to a group was *not adequate* for the display to be restricted. The court took account of the conduct of the person displaying the flag and noted that he did not behave violently or abusively. The court emphasised that 'the expressive nature of the display of an object depends on the circumstances of the situation'. (Fáber case 2012, para 52) The mere display of the flag, unless it was banned by legislation, could not be construed as hate speech. If the flag had been banned, as is the case with Nazi insignia in Germany, the display may not be protected against criminal prosecution. (Nix case 2018)

expression requires tolerance of speech that shocks and offends'. (Old Flag appeal case 2023, para 44)[42] There is no requirement for actual violence or harm to have been caused.[43]

- *What is the effect of a declaration of hate speech?* The court ruled that it had the power to issue the declaration that the display constituted hate speech retrospectively on the day of the old flag's display *and* prospectively into the future, as the Equality Act empowers it to 'make any appropriate order in the circumstances'. (Equality Act, s 21) The court said that its declaration did not amount to the banning of the old flag, as the flag may still be displayed for artistic, academic and journalistic purposes. (Old Flag appeal case 2023, para 57) The court stated that, as far as the private display of the old flag is concerned, it is a 'case for another day' to ascertain whether a display in private would offend the order of the court. (Old Flag appeal case 2023, para 73)[44] The court emphasised that it had a 'direct interest' in regulating hate speech, given the harm it may cause to individuals and communities. (Old Flag appeal case 2023, para 29; Islamic Convention case 2002, para 33)

5.4.2 Kill the Boer (Kill the Farmer) cases

The two Kill the Boer cases resulted in divergent outcomes; the 2011 judgment declared that the chant constituted hate speech, whereas the 2022 judgment declared that the chant did not constitute hate speech and this judgment was upheld on appeal. The Constitutional Court refused leave for the 2022 judgment to be appealed.

---

[42] In the Qwelane case the court emphasised that the hate speech prohibition in South Africa must be seen against the 'constitutional object of healing the injustices of the past', and in the context of 'curtailing speech which is part and parcel of the system of subordination of vulnerable and marginalised groups'. (Qwelane case 2021, para 86) In the Erkizia Almandoz case the ECtHR found that speech at a Basque separatist gathering in Spain that did not propagate violence or terrorism was protected. (Erkizia Almandoz case 2021) The ECtHR has in many decisions emphasised that the objective test includes a reasonable person taking into account the circumstances and intent of the person uttering the speech.

[43] Note that in the 2022 Kill the Boer case discussed below the court went to some length to reason that, in the absence of evidence of *actual* violence against farmers, the chant did not constitute hate speech. In contrast, no such test of violence or threat of violence was applied in the Old Flag case and yet the display of the old flag was found to be hate speech.

[44] Note in the Qwelane case the opinion was held that private communications should not fall within the scope of the Equality Act 'because that would be incongruent with the very purpose of regulating hate speech – that public hateful expression undermines the target group's dignity, social standing and assurance against exclusion, hostility, discrimination and violence'. (Qwelane case 2021, para 118)

In the 2011 case the complainant, AfriForum, sought a declaration from the Equality Court that a chant in public sung by the respondent, leader of the Economic Freedom Fighters (EFF), Mr Julius Malema, constituted hate speech pursuant to the then s 10 of the Equality Act. Mr Malema did not deny that he had publicly chanted 'Kill/Kiss the Boer; Kill/Kiss the Farmer' and that the media had reported it to the broader public. (Kill the Boer case 2011, paras 67–77) Although Mr Malema defended the chant as a liberation chant and part of South Africa's history (Kill the Boer case 2011, para 54), the court declared that the words are 'derogatory, dehumanising and hurtful'. (Kill the Boer case 2011, para 107)[45] The court found that the chant constituted hate speech and there was no justification for it to be sung in the new democracy, adding that while historically the chant was fit for the liberation struggle, 'the enemy has become the friend' under the new Constitution. (Kill the Boer case 2011, para 108) The court cited the 'spirit of Ubuntu',[46] which means the characterisation of the chant had effectively changed from a call for liberation to becoming a hateful chant. The court thus declared the chant to be hate speech. Mr Malema was ordered to comply with the provisions of the Equality Act by not singing the chant at any public or private event. (Kill the Boer case 2011, Orders) In contrast to the Old Flag judgments, the orders in the 2011 Kill the Boer case were directed at the parties to the hearing, rather than at the public in general.

In the 2022 case the complainant, AfriForum, again sought a declaration from the Equality Court to the effect that the chant sung by the respondent, the Economic Freedom Fighters (EFF), constituted hate speech pursuant to s 10 of the Equality Act. The EFF did not dispute that its members frequently sing the chant 'Kill/Kiss the Boer; Kill/Kiss the Farmer' in public, occasionally accompanying it with a gesture mimicking a rifle. AfriForum contended that the chant constituted hate speech, as it 'advocates hatred on the grounds of race and ethnicity, and constitutes an incitement to cause harm'. (Kill the Boer case 2022, para 3) AfriForum also relied on the 2011 judgment of the Equality Court, which had declared that the chant constituted hate speech. (Kill the Boer case 2011)[47]

---

[45] The court also found that substituting the word 'kill' with the word 'kiss' made no material difference to the content of the speech. The intention of the chant was deemed clear, and when sung in that manner it had 'exactly the opposite' effect of what one would associate with the word 'kiss'. (Kill the Boer case 2011, para 101)

[46] See Chapter 6 for a discussion of Ubuntu and its application in jurisprudence.

[47] The 2011 judgment was appealed, but the parties reached a mediated agreement for the appeal to be discontinued and for the orders as mediated to be made. (Kill the Boer case 2022,

AfriForum argued, in essence, that the chant incites violence, represents a form of hate speech and potentially correlates with the increase in violence against farmers and their workers. According to AfriForum, in 2019 there had been 552 farm attacks and 57 murders in South Africa. (AfriForum Research Institute 2020, 3) AfriForum contended that the chant contributed to a political climate in which white persons are portrayed as the 'source of evil', depicting farmers as criminals who exploit workers and 'romanticising' violence against farmers. (Kill the Boer case 2022, para 37) In response the EFF stated that its movement was formed to promote the economic emancipation of black people and, in doing so, it supports, inter alia, the expropriation of land without compensation. The EFF argued that the song should not be taken literally, but should instead be assessed in light of the oppressive apartheid system, the effects of which continue to manifest in visible socio-economic inequality. The word 'Boers', the EFF contended, refers to the system of oppression under apartheid and the associated ongoing inequality, rather than to a specific community. (Kill the Boer case 2022, paras 69–71) The Equality Court dismissed the complaint and found that the chant did not constitute hate speech.

In the 2011 and 2022 reasonings concerning the Kill the Boer chant the respective courts found as follows regarding the three questions focused on in this chapter:

- *What is the definition of hate speech?* In both proceedings the courts, having referred to international law (but no in-depth consideration of foreign case law) and the background to the constitution-drafting process, adopted the definition of hate speech as set out in s 10 of the Equality Act. The courts acknowledged that a tension exists between freedom of expression and hate speech, particularly in the context of political participation. (Kill the Boer case 2011, paras 31–33; Kill the Boer case 2022, paras 89–91, 112; Kill the Boer appeal case 2024, para 53) Surprisingly, little reference was made to jurisprudence arising from international law and comparative foreign law in the cases. Both justices accepted that hate speech is not restricted to words, acknowledging that it can also involve a sign or symbol that conveys a message, given that the protection against hate speech must be interpreted broadly to safeguard vulnerable individuals and communities.

paras 5–6) On appeal the court did not get drawn into whether Mr Malema had breached the mediated agreement, but the court accepted that the fresh complaint against the chant could proceed. (Kill the Boer appeal case 2024, para 49)

Both justices also accepted that the individual complaining about the speech need not have been present when the speech in question was uttered. The potential benefit that may have been gained to 'consider' international and foreign case law remained untapped.[48]

- *What is the test for hate speech – subjective or objective?* Both proceedings accepted that the test to be applied is objective, namely what a reasonable listener having the common knowledge and skill attributed to an ordinary member of society would conclude when hearing and seeing the chanting. (Kill the Boer case 2011, para 109; Kill the Boer case 2022, para 92) The justices also noted that speech may have different meanings and that it is not the intention of the person uttering the speech that is to be ascertained. (Kill the Boer case 2022, para 92; Khumalo case 2019, para 58) In the 2011 case the court said that each meaning of speech must be considered and the perception of the reasonable listener 'in each portion of society' must be considered to ascertain the appropriate meaning. (Kill the Boer case 2011, para 109 8.) In the 2022 case the court stated that the complainants 'have failed to show that the lyrics in the song could reasonably be construed to demonstrate a clear intention to harm or incite to harm and propagate hatred'. (Kill the Boer case 2022, para 101) Notably in the Kill the Boer appeal the court adopted a predominant approach to assess the speech, with little consideration of the other possible meanings of the speech. Ultimately the court of appeal was satisfied that a reasonable person would only consider the chant in the context of a liberation chant, and not in any other context. (Kill the Boer appeal case 2024, para 95) In the 2011 case the court accepted that the lyrics, even if not meant to be taken literally, could be reasonably so interpreted and thus constituted hate speech, whereas in 2022 the court found that the lyrics ought not to be interpreted literally and thus the chant did not constitute hate speech. (Kill the Boer case 2022, paras 106, 109, 111) In the 2024 appeal the court found that the reasonable person would assess the chant in the context of it representing a political objective (Kill the Boer appeal case 2024, para 102) albeit that the same tolerance was not displayed by the court in the waving of the old flag at a public demonstration against crime.

[48] The lack of consideration of foreign case law highlights the relevance of the questions put in Chapter 4, namely when do judges consider foreign case law? What is the weight attached to foreign case law? Which countries are considered? Is there a risk of foreign case law being cited to give credibility to an outcome already reached in the mind of the judge?

- *What is the effect of a declaration of hate speech?* In both judgments, the justices emphasised that the scope of their powers under the Equality Act was extensive, thus allowing them to make orders to address the speech that was the subject of the complaint. (Kill the Boer case 2011, para 110) In the 2011 judgment the orders were specifically addressed to the first and second respondents, restraining them from singing the chant 'at any public or private meeting'. (Kill the Boer case 2011, para Order 2) In the 2022 case, the complaint was dismissed (but it should be noted that in the Old Flag case, orders were made not only against the parties to the proceeding, but against the general public). The court, in essence, found as follows: the test to be applied is objective, 'requiring a reasonable person test'; the objective test includes taking into account the mindset of a reasonable listener having regard to the historical context of the speech; offensive or controversial statements do not equate to hate speech; the lyrics of the chant cannot reasonably be construed to incite hatred; the chant should not be taken in its literal meaning; there was inadequate evidence to link violence on farms to the chant; and curtailing the singing of the chant would place an undue restriction on freedom of expression since it falls within the scope of 'political contestations'. (Kill the Boer case 2022, paras 92, 97, 107, 112) In the Kill the Boer appeal in 2024 the court also declared, correctly, that it is the speech at a particular event by a particular person that is considered, not the speech in a general context. (Kill the Boer appeal case 2024, paras 79–80)

The judgments illustrate the discretion judges have to evaluate speech, the risk of different standards being applied to purported hate speech, the possibility that the background of a judge may impact on the way the court views speech, the haphazard and unpredictable way in which international and foreign case law is relied upon or ignored depending on the discretion of the court, and the inconsistent use of Ubuntu as an implied term of the Constitution.

5.5 REFLECTING ON THE OLD FLAG AND KILL THE BOER CASES IN LIGHT OF INTERNATIONAL AND FOREIGN LAW

The four judgments discussed in this chapter embody and reflect the challenges, in South Africa and beyond, to determine the limitations of free speech and setting the contours of hate speech. These judgments reflect the myriad complexities inherent in hate speech complaints, including aspects such as: the meaning of hate speech; applicable tests; potential multiple meanings of speech; weightings of these meanings; the speaker's intention; required evidence; relevance of the literal and figurative meaning of speech; potential role of judicial bias and backgrounds of judges; appropriateness of the 'consideration' of international law and foreign law, as authorised by the Constitution; retrospective or prospective nature of a declaration of hate speech; whether a declaration is limited to the parties to the proceeding or can extend to the general public; scope of the court's powers; and the meaning of applying proportionality to any limitation on free speech.

In this section the four judgments are assessed by considering international jurisprudence, with particular attention to the following aforementioned questions that may have relevance in international legal contexts:

(i) What is the definition of hate speech?

(ii) What is the test for hate speech – subjective or objective?

(iii) What is the effect of a declaration of hate speech?

5.5.1 What is the definition of hate speech?

The judgments relied on the statutory test for hate speech, as found in s 10 of the (then) Equality Act. Hate speech is notoriously difficult to delineate by way of a common-law or universal definition, particularly considering the presumption in international and constitutional law in favour of freedom of expression. Several instruments of international law – both hard and soft law – refer to the primacy of freedom of expression in a free and democratic society, such as: art 19 Universal Declaration of Human Rights; art 19 International Covenant on Civil and Political Rights; art 5 International Convention on the Elimination of all Forms of Racial Discrimination; art 11 European Charter of Fundamental Rights; art 13 American Convention on Human Rights; art 9 African Charter of Human and Peoples' Rights; art 32 Arab Charter on Human Rights; and art 10 European Convention for the Protection of Human Rights and Fundamental Freedoms. In addition to these international instruments an explicit or implied protection of the right to freedom of expression is associated with modern democratic constitutions and constitutionalism.[49]

[49] Note, for example, how in Australia, where there is no justiciable bill of rights in the Constitution, the High Court has held that a limited right of freedom of political communication is implied in the Constitution as a necessary requirement for a representative democratic government. (Australian Capital Television case 1992)

There is neither an agreed international law definition of hate speech, nor a closed list of words, signs or symbols that constitutes hate speech. (Topidi 2019b, 32) It is accepted, however, that 'speech' is not limited to actual words being uttered. Instead, it can also consist of a sign, symbol, flag, emblem, gesture, meme, emoji or any other means by which a message can be conveyed. It is also accepted that speech can have different meanings, of which only one may be perceived as hate speech. A complaint about purported hate speech must consider *all* the possible meanings of the speech, not only the predominant meaning.

International law and statutes enacted by states usually deal with hate speech by way of generality. Courts must ascertain whether, in a particular context, freedom of expression should be curtailed. Although the meaning of the term 'hate speech' is to be ascertained objectively in a factual situation, international jurisprudence emphasises that using the term 'hate' to categorise speech in a legal sense is reserved for extreme circumstances. (Schweppe and Walsh 2008, 72) The reasonable person is therefore presumed to understand the importance of freedom of expression in a democratic society. Brown makes a pertinent point in the following:

> Given that hate speech laws provoke such strong moral reactions, on the part of defenders and critics alike, and given that legal meanings will themselves draw on a range of deeper values and principles about which people reasonably disagree, it is no surprise that there remains such divergence over how to define the very term that stands at the epicentre of the disagreement. (Brown 2017, 422)

The difficulty in determining hate speech in a practical setting and the relatively low number of successful prosecutions of hate speech under common law have led Brown to observe that 'there are many instances of hate speech where this putative connection is not merely weak but non-existent'. (Brown 2017, 466) In simple terms, prosecuting a case becomes more straightforward when dealing with the display of a statutory *banned* symbol or expression, as opposed to proving that an expression in a specific context constitutes hate speech.[50]

International experiences in dealing with freedom of expression vis-à-vis hate speech make for fascinating, albeit confusing, analysis. An overview of

---

[50] Note, for example, how in the Williamson case the ECtHR held that although a person had expressed Holocaust denial outside of Germany, he did so knowing the statements would be available in Germany and hence he breached the German Criminal Code (which criminalised Holocaust denial). (Williamson case 2019) In the Pastörs case the ECtHR held that the intentionally spread of falsehoods to defame Jews was not protected by freedom of expression and that the conviction was 'necessary in a democratic society'. (Pastörs case 2019)

judgments shows the lack of consistency not only *among* nations, but also *within* nations when it comes to determining what speech constitutes hate speech. (Topidi 2019b) For example, it is noticeable how the ECtHR has, within the context of the European Convention of Human Rights, been inconsistent in its approach to hate speech. (Enarsson 2024) The ECtHR sometimes relies on a relatively low threshold based on the 'ridicule or slandering of groups' (Féret case 2009, paras 70–71), while, at other times, such as in the Savva Terentyev case, it has applied a higher threshold based on the 'likelihood' for speech to provoke actions. (Savva Terentyev case 2009, para 77)[51] However, an important principle identified in the Faurisson case is that any power to place restrictions on freedom of expression '*must not* be interpreted as licence to prohibit unpopular speech, or speech which some sections of the population find offensive'. (Faurisson case 1996, para 8) An individual's or community's sensitivity to speech should therefore not be used as a pretext to censor speech for potentially being hateful.

Tolerating speech, even when it is hurtful, dislikeable, and offensive, may contribute to the growing maturity of public debate. In this regard, the Supreme Court of India has ruled that showing a film which may be offensive or perceived as hate speech by some in the community could help elucidate hurtful aspects of the past. In turn, the debate arising from the film may contribute to explaining why past actions should not be repeated, thereby deepening democratic discourse and public education in India.[52] The court declared as follows:

> On the contrary, stability in society can only be promoted by introspection into social reality, however grim it be. Ours, we believe, is a mature democracy. *The view of the censor*

---

[51] In the Savva Terentyev case a blog that called for police to be 'burned' in order to 'cleanse society' by using 'an oven like Auschwitz' was found by the ECtHR *not to* constitute hate speech. (Savva Terentyev case 2009, para 13) In contrast, speech that vilified LGBT+ counselling in schools as a 'sexual deviation' was found to constitute hate speech. (Lilliendahl case 2020, para 5) The court found that the comments in the Lilliendahl case were 'severely hurtful', while the incitement to kill police officers was protected speech as police may be reasonably expected to be publicly criticised in the discharge of their duties.

[52] In India, for example, it has been stated that the right to free expression contributes to society's ability to reflect on its past and present social reality. In the FA Picture case the court found that, although a section of society may perceive a film or image as hate speech, the public debate caused by such a display may contribute to discourse about the wrongs committed under the symbol and those discussions could, in turn, deepen and strengthen democracy. (FA Picture case 2005, para 13) German critics of legislative intervention to ban the display of Nazi symbols in that country have cautioned that such regulation 'creates a useful template for autocratic countries to use to censor political opponents and other members of marginalised groups'. (Delcker 2020)

> *does no credit to the maturity of a democratic society by making an assumption that people would be led to disharmony by a free and open display of a cinematographic theme.* The certifying authority and the Tribunal were palpably in error in rejecting the film on the ground that it had characters which bear a resemblance to real life personalities. The constitutional protection under art 19(1)(a) that a film maker enjoys is not conditioned on the premise that he must depict something which is not true to life. The choice is entirely his. Those who hold important positions must have shoulders which are broad enough to accept with grace a critique of themselves, and critical appraisal is the cornerstone of democracy and the power of the film as a medium of expression lies in its ability to contribute to that appraisal. (emphasis added) (FA Picture case 2005, para 13)

A democracy is built on the pillar of free and robust speech that may sometimes cause offence. Although hate speech often has a suggestion of violence or it may sometimes seek to normalise or encourage violence, evidence of actual violence or a threat of violence is not a requirement for hate speech to be proven. (Qwelane case 2021, para 181)[53] The International Criminal Tribunal for Rwanda has declared that hate speech does not necessarily require an incitement to violence as the nature of the speech in itself can meet the threshold of 'hate'. (Nahimana case 2007)

While generally speech itself may be adequate to be considered hate speech without any actions or threats arising from it, there are several judgments (some cited below) in which courts have sought evidence of *some* level of threat or incitement to violence as a prerequisite for a declaration of hate speech. For example, in the Zana case the ECtHR considered, in addition to the intention of the speaker and the circumstances of the speech, the *actual threat* of violence. (Zana case 1997, para 61)

It is notable how the reasonings by the courts in the Kill the Boer and Old Flag cases differ about the relevance of a threat or encouragement of violence. In the 2022 Kill the Boer case the court emphasised that the chant should not be taken literally, rejecting the evidence of fear and angst felt and expressed by people upon hearing it. The court went to some length to criticise and reject expert evidence presented about farm violence, on the basis that a causal link between the chant and farm violence could not be established. This contrasts with the Old Flag cases, where the courts underscored that there was *no need*

---

[53] In the Féret case the ECtHR correctly noted that actual violence or incitement to violence is not a requirement for hate speech. However, the court then went on to speak about the 'irresponsible use of freedom of expression' (Féret case 2009, para 73), raising concerns that the bar for proving hate speech is being lowered since irresponsible speech is a net cast very wide. (Alkiviadou 2022, 2201)

for any threat of violence to exist for speech to be regarded as hate speech. The courts in the Old Flag cases accepted evidence that the mere sighting of the old flag can evoke memories and feelings of hate. The contrast in the approaches adopted by the courts is clear: in the 2022 Kill the Boer case the court made considerable efforts to discount the potential causal link between the chant and farm crimes, including murders, while in the Old Flag case the court accepted that the display of the old flag constituted hate speech despite being exhibited by an unidentified individual at a multiracial, peaceful public protest against crime with no threats of violence or other statements of racism.[54]

Hate speech is influenced by time and circumstance, implying that speech may lose its classification as hate speech over time or, alternatively, come to be regarded as hate speech under new circumstances. This principle was well elucidated in the 2011 Kill the Boer case through the analogy used by the presiding judge that the 'enemies have become brothers' through the process of democratisation and nation-building in South Africa. A chant that was once suitable in the liberation struggle against an apartheid government can now be construed as hate speech. The same argument, however, was rejected by the court in the later Kill the Boer case regarding the same chant. In a similar vein, the flag that served as the official national flag of South Africa under which Nazi Germany was defeated, and later was the flag under which the United Nations Charter was drafted, has, according to the court, evolved into a symbol of hate. The nuance of speech changing its meaning is nothing new. In the Australian judgment of the Catch the Fire case French J explained that what constitutes offensive speech in one circumstance may not constitute offensive speech in another, even if the same symbol is shown or the same words are uttered. (Catch the Fire case 2006) What is observable in these two South African judgments, however, is how two judges relying on the same principles came to diametrically opposed conclusions.

It is important to bear in mind that as circumstances evolve the perceived offence caused by speech may change. The Old Flag cases highlight the challenge involved in determining the evolving meaning of a symbol and assigning weight to its potentially offensive nature, considering both its historical context and the present circumstances.[55]

---

[54] The manner in which the courts dealt with lay and expert evidence in these cases highlights the following observation by Steuer in regard to extreme forms of speech: '[A] neat distinction between facts and value judgments is impossible to make.' (Steuer 2023, 162)

[55] Note that in the Hotz case the court found that the words 'sKILL ALL WHITES' printed on a shirt could only be interpreted as hate speech since it had no secondary meaning or other context. (Hotz case 2017)

Given the various characteristics of speech, including defamatory, dislikeable, objectionable, discriminatory, hurtful and offensive elements, it is not simple to identify when speech meets the standard of hate speech. None of these descriptive terms can be captured precisely by definition and they are not terms of art. Owing to definitional vagueness and judicial discretion, there is a risk that speech which may otherwise be regarded as offensive is held to be hate speech through a gradual process of preverbal bracket creep, thereby unjustifiably restricting free speech. What may be socially regarded as hate speech does not necessarily meet the legal threshold of hate speech. While there is consensus that hate speech represents the most extreme form of speech, justices may differ regarding the definition and application of what constitutes extreme.

The caution expressed above is highlighted in the Old Flag and Kill the Boer cases, where the waving of the formerly official flag of South Africa was characterised by the court as constituting hate speech, despite being displayed at a public rally against crime, while a chant calling for the killing of farmers, sometimes accompanied by the display of actual or symbolic rifles, was characterised as not constituting hate speech.

It is noticeable how in the one case the court went to some length to explain that the symbolic effect of the old flag is relevant to establish hate speech, while in the other case the court dismissed the complaint about the symbolic meaning of the chant to white persons, asserting that it should be seen as symbolic from the perspective of the liberation struggle and not be taken literally. The court on appeal in 2024 adopted the same reasoning about the figurative nature of the chant. Both courts in the Kill the Boer cases arguably failed to credit that only one of the meanings of a speech may be regarded as hate speech. This raises the concern that the perception of one community may be treated differently to the perceptions of another community. In light of this risk the US Supreme Court has cautioned the courts *not* to adopt a position of favouritism where the sensitivities of one group are given preference over those of another. (RAV case 1992) The US Supreme Court has also noted that courts must examine the 'content, form, and context' of the perceived offensive speech. In doing so they have to evaluate all the circumstances of the speech, 'including what was said, where it was said, and how it was said'. (Snyder case 2011)

In Canada the Supreme Court described the test to ascertain hate speech as follows:

> The repugnancy of the ideas being expressed is not sufficient to justify restricting the expression, and whether or not the author of the expression intended to incite hatred or discriminatory treatment is irrelevant. The key is to determine the likely effect of the expression on its audience. (Saskatchewan case 2013)

The context of speech is important, even if the subjective intention of the person expressing the speech is not a determinative consideration. This principle is, in its application, as argued below, not as simple as it may seem.

In comparative jurisprudence the courts often spend substantial time ascertaining what happened in a specific circumstance, why certain speech was uttered and what the rationale of the speech was. Courts also consider the different potential meanings of speech. This approach is often adopted in instances where, for example, Nazi insignia are displayed or Holocaust denial occurs. Speech occurring at a public rally where the Holocaust is denied may be regarded in a different light to speech emanating from an intellectual exchange where questions are raised about specific aspects of the topic.

In the Old Flag case the individuals who displayed the flag were never identified, while the organisation that convened the marches said that it had not arranged for the display of the old flag, an assertion accepted by the court. Furthermore, there were no findings of fact that the march had been racist, a celebration of apartheid, inciting violence or a rejection of the prevailing democratic order. Furthermore, no persons who had seen the march lodged an objection. On all accounts the march was a *bona fide* protest against high levels of crime affecting all of society. In the Kill the Boer case, on the other hand, the person who sang the chant was identified as a senior political figure and explained that its singing in public aimed to promote the radical expropriation of land without compensation. The court accepted Malema's explanation for the chant, despite the complainants' assertion that to them the chant constituted hate, fear and a threat to violence. They added that the chant instilled angst and encouraged aggression and thus it should be assessed in the context of the country's proliferation of farm murders in the most horrific of circumstances. The court on appeal placed substantial weight on the political profile of Malema and the EFF being a 'leftist-aligned party'. (Kill the Boer appeal case 2024, para 96) An argument can be made that the very fact of Malema being a political leader and using a public platform to call for the killing of boers can, in one interpretation as reasonably and objectively viewed, constitute hate speech. Arguably, a higher burden of responsibility for speech may apply to Malema than to an unidentified person waving a flag during a public protest.

The importance of context of speech was recognised by the UNHRC in France when it declared that, in the context of the 'conditions of present-day France, Holocaust denial may constitute a form of incitement to antisemitism', albeit that in another circumstance, time or place the same denial may be judged otherwise. (Faurisson case 1996) In the Faurisson case, concerning the denial by a person of the Holocaust, the UNHRC found that the intention of the person who expresses the denial is indeed a relevant consideration, but that in this particular case the denial did constitute hate speech. (Faurisson case 1996, para 10.50) The UNHRC considered the context in which the Holocaust denial occurred, as well as the intention of the person making the statement. This included assessing whether the statement was made in the context of a scientific discourse.

The ECtHR in the Handyside case emphasised that, arising from the demands of pluralism, any condition imposed on freedom of expression must be proportionate to be legitimate aim pursued. (Handyside case 1976, para 49) The Constitutional Court of Germany has also noted that the question whether speech ought to be prohibited must be assessed considering the circumstances of each case. (BVerfGE 7 198 case) This approach was also reflected in the Perinçek case in Switzerland, in which the court took detailed account of the context in which potentially hateful speech had occurred. (Perinçek case 2015)

Jurisprudence arising from the ECtHR consistently shows that the court carefully considers the specific circumstances in which purported hate speech took place to assess the speech and, if it was hate speech, to make a finding regarding the specific incident. (Freedom of Expression ECtHR 2022)

This raises the question: What evidence is relied upon when a complaint is received that speech is hateful?

In the Old Flag and Kill the Boer cases there was little evidence in the form of perceptions of laypersons or opinions of experts. To a judge not trained in or exposed to South Africa the evidence heard in the two cases would likely be inadequate to sustain the respective findings. These cases highlight the importance of substantial evidence – from laypersons and, if necessary, experts – being heard before freedom of expression is curtailed based on a complaint of hate speech. In the absence of adequate evidence there is a risk that judges rely on their own understandings, recollections, undisclosed biases or personal experiences to assess speech.[56]

[56] Note in this regard the concern expressed by Maron against the 'selective and biased application of law according to the ideological key' of judges and that judicial 'arbitrariness' can

The Supreme Court of India in the Amish Devgan case also observed that evidence of the context and content of the speech is important to determine whether it amounts to hate speech.[57] 'Content' is more related to the expression, language and message which, in the case of hate speech, is typically aimed at vilifying, demeaning and inciting psychosocial hatred or physical violence against the targeted group. Meanwhile, 'context' involves certain key variables, namely 'who' and 'what' is involved, 'where' the case arises and the 'occasion, time and under what circumstances' it occurs. (Amish Devgan case 2020) The court went on to say consideration must also be given to the position and status of the person making the statement. For example, the statement of an ordinary individual at a private event may not be met with the same scrutiny as a statement made by a public figure at a public rally. (Amish Devgan case 2020, para 52) A similar approach has been adopted by the ECtHR: a statement in the privacy of the home is not treated the same as a statement from a public platform, and a statement made by a comedian is not treated the same as a political statement at the same event. (M'Bala case 2015)

This raises a question regarding the four South African judgments under discussion: Should different weight be accorded to an unidentified private person displaying the old flag at a public rally against crime than that accorded to the leader of a political party chanting 'Kill the Boer' at a public rally about the expropriation of land? International case law suggests that the conduct of a private person displaying the flag at a public rally against crime may be given lessor weight to a political leader displaying a replica firearm against the background of crime and farm violence while chanting for boers to be killed.

It was accepted in the Old Flag and Kill the Boer judgments that a flag and a chant may have multiple meanings. The courts, however, adopted different approaches in their assessment of the meanings of the speech. In the Kill the Boer case the first court (2011) stated that each meaning of the chant had to be explored

cause a 'blatant distortion' of the standards of adjudication. (Maron 2023, 48) In the Kill the Boer appeal the evidence of expert Prof Gunner was accepted about the historical meaning of the chant, but that historical meaning was never in dispute. It is accepted that the chant is a liberation song, but the proposition is, as was held in Kill the Boer 2011, that the chant also has other meanings and that as a chant of perceived hate it is no longer suitable in a democratic South Africa.

[57] Note how the court went to great lengths, in contrast to the South African courts in the Kill the Boer and Old Flag cases, to consider and reflect on international jurisprudence to delineate the contours of hate speech. (Amish Devgan case 2020, paras 19–29)

and if *any* of its possible meanings constituted hate speech, then the chant itself did constitute hate speech, whereas the later court (2022) said the chant should not be taken in its literal meaning, in effect discounting the perceived hate that the speech may portray to communities other than the majority. Even if the court in 2022 took into account multiple meanings of the chant, it opted to accept the majority view of its being a chant of liberation. Meanwhile, in the Old Flag case the court declared that the *predominant* meaning of the old flag is one of hate. However, it left unexplained from whose perspective and on what basis 'predominance' is established (considering there was little evidence before the court), as well as what impact the restriction might have on the ability of communities to display and enjoy a cultural and historic symbol. In the Kill the Boer appeal the court did not give weight to the other possible meanings of the chant and concentrated only on the liberation background of the chant.

Does this mean, in effect, that the sensitivities of the majority in the Old Flag and Kill the Boer cases are accorded greater weight by the court than those of minorities?

Furthermore, in the 2022 Kill the Boer case and the 2024 appeal the courts relied on a lack of adequate evidence linking the chant, which encourages the killing of boers, to actual violence against farmers and their workers. The courts concluded that the song did not meet the threshold of hate speech. The court in 2022 found that there was inadequate evidence to show that the aggrieving chant contributed to *actual* violence, including the murders of farmers. (Kill the Boer case 2022, para 101) In the 2024 appeal the court emphasised that 'context [of speech] is everything'. (Kill the Boer appeal case 2024, para 94) But that nuance was not displayed in the Old Flag case. If, however, one adopts the reasoning of the UN Special Rapporteur for Minorities, who described hate speech as 'dehumanising language' that 'normalises violence' against a minority (de Varennes 2021, 8), it seems as if a compelling case can be made that a chant calling upon people to kill (white) farmers does meet the threshold of hate speech, even if that chant may have been appropriate as part of the pre-democracy liberation struggle. Also note that the Act did not require evidence of actual violence, with a threat of violence being adequate for a declaration of hate speech. An argument can be made that the chant, sung in public, accompanied by the figurative display of a rifle, would in international case law be adequate for a declaration of hate speech. In the Qwelane case the Constitutional Court considered the complaints lodged against the speech, which allegedly targeted the sexuality of individuals, as well as the evidence presented in court concerning the effects of the speech.

(Qwelane case 2021, para 6) The court accepted the presence of hate speech even in the absence of evidence that violence or threats of violence had arisen from the speech. (Qwelane case 2021, para 187)

Ultimately, hate speech gives rise to a restriction of freedom of expression, provided that the limitation on the speech is reasonable and proportionate. The approaches adopted by the courts in the two Kill the Boer cases differ fundamentally. In the 2011 Kill the Boer case the symbolism of the chant to one portion of the community was adequate for it to be held as hate speech, whereas in the 2022 Kill the Boer case and its 2024 appeal the context, history and symbolism of the chant were considered and accepted in its defence regardless of a section of the community perceiving it as hate speech. Meanwhile, in the Old Flag case the mere display of a symbol at a public rally against crime was regarded as hate speech.

Comparative jurisprudence suggests that a wide net is cast to evaluate all evidence before speech is restricted. This includes considerations such as the background to the speech (or symbol), the circumstances in which the speech is made, the content of the speech, the forum where the speech is made, the profile or status of the speaker, the speaker's intention, the audience, the perceptions of individuals exposed to the speech and any other relevant factors. The reason for considering all these factors is that courts should be slow to restrict freedom of expression. It is only when a court is satisfied that speech exceeds the boundaries of reasonableness, and the speech is duly declared hate speech as the most extreme form of speech, and that no other option is available, that freedom of expression should be restricted. Furthermore, if a restriction of freedom of expression is deemed appropriate, the restriction should be proportionate and limited to the specific event which forms the subject of the complaint.

In Chapter 4 the power of South African courts to 'consider' international law and foreign comparative jurisprudence, pursuant to s 39 of the Constitution, is discussed. It is noticeable how, in the four cases focused on this chapter, the courts did not use that power to inform themselves about the full potential of developments in foreign law about hate speech. In the 2011 Kill the Boer and Old Flag cases some scant references were made to international law, but not to foreign judgments dealing with the application of hate speech and freedom of expression. The courts could have utilised the guidelines and lack of consistency that have characterised international and comparative municipal case law more effectively when dealing with complaints of hate speech. Each of the questions under consideration in this chapter has given rise to a vast number of judgments internationally. The courts in each of the four cases could have benefited from greater reflection on international jurisprudence. Note in contrast to the South African courts how the Supreme Court of India went to great lengths in the Amish Devgan case to consider and reflect on international jurisprudence (although the Constitution of India does not contain an empowering section similar to the South African Constitution) to delineate the contours of hate speech. (Amish Devgan case 2020, paras 19–29)

The lack of consideration of international law and foreign law in these cases underscores the questions raised in Chapter 4: When does a court choose to exercise its power to consider foreign judgments? Which countries are selected for consideration and comparison? What weight is attached to the judgments of different countries? What role does the predisposition of a judge play when foreign case law is selected or ignored? These questions remain unanswered.

In summary, the principles derived from international law to safeguard individuals against hate speech can be outlined as follows: first, the right to freedom of expression is a foundational right in a free and democratic society; secondly, any restriction placed on the right must be proportionate and confined to extreme forms of speech; thirdly, speech encompasses not only spoken words but also symbols, insignia and publications; fourthly, there exists no universal definition of hate speech, but it pertains to the most extreme forms of speech; and, fifthly, while states are encouraged to enact legislation prohibiting hate speech, a finding of hate speech is based on an objective assessment of the speech in question and is contingent on the specific circumstances surrounding the aggrieving speech.

5.5.2 What is the test for hate speech – subjective or objective?

The test to determine whether speech constitutes hate speech comprises an objective assessment which considers the perception of a reasonable person observing the speech, rather than relying on the subjective intention of the speaker or the sensitivity of a single onlooker. (Old Flag appeal case 2023, para 42; Kill the Boer appeal case 2024, para 102)[58] The objective test does not imply that no regard is given to the context of the speech or the intention of

[58] Winks is critical of s 10 of the Equality Act since it is not made clear if the test for liability – 'could reasonably be construed to demonstrate a clear intention' – was meant to be 'objective, or some sort of objective–subjective hybrid test'. (Winks 2023, 70)

the speaker. Instead, all evidence must be examined from the perspective of a reasonable person, including the intention of the speaker and the circumstances of the speech as well as an understanding of the importance of freedom of speech in a democratic society.[59] The court seeks to determine the perception of a fictional reasonable onlooker who is adequately informed about the issue and the circumstances of the speech, based on all the evidence presented. The judge must refrain from relying on personal understanding of history, experiences or other biases when assessing speech, and the evaluation must be evidence-driven. Even a foreign judge lacking knowledge of a country or the speech's circumstances should be able to determine, based on the evidence, whether speech meets the threshold of hate speech. If the evidence is not adequate, the judge cannot use personal understanding to supplement or interpret evidence through the eyes of a reasonable person or to supplement evidence in a manner that reflects personal bias or understanding. If the evidence does not support a finding of hate speech, the reasonable person would prioritise freedom of expression.

While this general standard for judicial conduct may seem clear, it is in the practical application of the test that gremlins hide, as exemplified by the inconsistency in the approaches adopted by the ECtHR regarding the threshold for hate speech. Should it be a 'tendency' test, indicating a certain trend, or mere risk of violence exhibited by the speech? Or should it be an 'incitement' test, suggesting some form of threatened or actual violence or hatred towards the target? (Sottiaux 2023, 1195)

The application of the objective test is therefore more complex than it may initially seem, considering that some members of a *targeted community* may objectively view certain speech differently to members of the *rest of society*.[60]

---

[59] Note, for example, in the Belkacem case the ECtHR found that the incitement of violence and hatred against non-Muslims was, regardless of the intent of the speaker, hate speech and thus not protected by freedom of expression. Although the applicant said he merely expressed his personal opinions, the ECtHR found that the content had sought to stir up hatred against non-Muslims and was incompatible with the objectives of the European Convention of tolerance, social peace and non-discrimination. (Belkacem case 2017) With particular reference to Belkacem's remarks concerning Sharia, the court reiterated that it had ruled previously that the fact of defending Sharia while calling for violence to establish it as state law could be regarded as hate speech and that each Contracting State of the Convention was entitled to oppose political movements based on religious fundamentalism, for instance a movement that aimed to establish a political regime based on Sharia. (Refah Partisi case 2003, paras 123–124)

[60] Consider, for example, the research findings of Munzert et al, illustrating how respondents in the USA and Germany differ in their assessments of what constitutes hate speech, as well as the unpredictable nature of their responses regarding the same speech. (Munzert et al 2020)

There may even be within the targeted community differences of sensitivity in response to the speech. It was acknowledged in the 2011 Kill the Boer case, as well as in the Old Flag case, that speech may have different meanings and that different sections of the community may view speech differently. While it has been suggested that the reasonable person test in hate speech proceedings is akin to the test of a reasonable person in tort or delict, this is not necessarily a simple avenue. In tort or delict the general community standard of conduct is indeed appropriate, while with hate speech the experience or perception by an individual or a minority community is at issue, particularly when the speech in question, for purposes of this book, affects their culture, traditions, customs and symbols. This raises the question of whether the opinion of an objective informed person must arise from that *reasonable* person being part of the community at whom the speech is directed or if the reasonable person should be considered as part of the broader society. Whichever way, it may be challenging for a court, other than in the case of obviously hateful speech, to ascertain how a reasonable person would perceive speech. This may be why the ECtHR in the Zana case opted for an approach consistent with jurisprudence from the USA where some form of *incitement* to violence, not actual violence, could be identified within the context of the speech. (Zana case 1997)

The Supreme Court of India has also emphasised that the courts must apply the hate speech prohibition cautiously and objectively. The question the courts must ask is whether a reasonable person, aware of the context and circumstances, would view the expression as exposing the protected group to hatred. (Pravasi Bhalai Sangathan case 2014) In Norway the Supreme Court has formulated the objective test as being the average reader's or listener's 'natural perception of the statement made from the context . . .'. (HR-2020 case 2020, para 29) The average person's perception of the aggrieving speech is therefore essential. (Duy 2020, 242)

Their analysis of public reactions to speech reveals no clarity about when speech is regarded as hate speech by members of the public. Most importantly, they recommend that speech not be assessed in abstract but only by way of 'concrete examples' – and, even then, persons will tend to categorise the speech differently. These research findings serve as an example of how challenging, unreliable and potentially unscientific it can be for a judge to declare with confidence what a reasonable person would conclude when exposed to purported hate speech.

However, as highlighted in the Féret case, there is a risk that the benchmark of what constitutes hate speech may be relaxed to include speech 'incompatible with a serene social climate' that 'could undermine confidence in democratic institutions'. (Féret case 2009, para 73) By using such categorisation bracket creep may cause the prohibitions against speech to expand. Courts have acknowledged the relevance of considering the context in which the speech occurs (Qwelane case 2021, para 20), but in the cases under discussion the assessment by the judges of those circumstances gave rise to potential bias. The Constitutional Court of South Africa has emphasised that the hate speech must be 'reasonably construed' and cannot be based on an inference or assumption made by the targeted individual or group. (Qwelane case 2021, para 96) The ECtHR has stressed that 'freedom of expression . . . is applicable not only to "information" or "ideas" that are favourably received or regarded as inoffensive or as a matter of indifference, but also to those that offend, shock or disturb the state or any sector of the population'. (Handyside case 1976) The reasonable person test must assume that this high principle is understood by the fictional person.

The Supreme Court of Canada reasoned in the Saskatchewan case that the harmful effect of hate speech must be evidenced in the level of 'detestation' and 'vilification' of the target group. The court was cautious to draw a distinction between the emotional reactions of the target group in response to the speech vis-à-vis the way a reasonable person would assess the speech. The response of the targeted community was a relevant consideration, but not adequate for a finding of hate speech, because the objective test seeks to determine how people 'external to the group' view the speech. (Saskatchewan case 2013, para 82)

The test of objectivity therefore implies objectivity within the nation or circumstances where the speech is expressed, not objectivity from the perspective of universal norms. It is a test in situ and not a test in the abstract. This is a reasonable proposition as speech taken out of context is unlikely to be categorised as breaching the limits of freedom of expression.

The foregoing highlights that hate speech is not only determined by the jurisdiction (country) where the speech is expressed, but also by the context and the time in history in which it is used. In India, for example, it has been stated that the right to free expression contributes to society being able to reflect on its past and present social reality, to enter into discussions and to educate the public. Speech must therefore be used to grow and develop maturity in public discourse, even if the speech is challenging to sensitivities of a particular community or audience. In the FA Picture case the court found that, although a section of

Indian society may perceive a film or image as hate speech (FA Picture International case 2005, para 13), the public debate caused by such a display may contribute to discourse about the wrongs committed under the symbol and those discussions could, in turn, deepen and strengthen democracy.

In South Africa the Supreme Court of Appeal in the Old Flag case accepted as fact that public displays of the old flag had declined (similarly to the display of the Confederate flag in the USA) since 1993 because of evolving community attitudes and acceptance of the new flag.[61] This trend is consistent with what emerged in the Rosenfeld case that in the USA displays of Nazi and Ku Klux Klan symbols have become isolated as a result of increasing popular irrelevancy of those symbols and the rejection of those symbols stemming from informed debate based on freedom of speech, rather than due to legislative or judicial intervention. (Rosenfeld 2003, 1538)

With this in mind, the question arises whether the restrictions imposed on the display of the old flag were proportionate to the infringement of the right to free speech.

While the test for hate speech is objective, it remains fictional in nature because what is considered reasonable and proportionate is highly discretionary. Additionally, not all persons may display the same sensitivity to public speech. Some justices have therefore been looking for an *actual* threat or act of violence, or a high propensity or risk of potential violence, before declaring speech to be hate speech since it is so easy to gravitate towards offensive speech being regarded as hate speech.

---

[61] The court also noted that AfriForum did not arrange for the old flag to be displayed during the march and that the organisation actively discourages its members from displaying this flag. (Old Flag appeal case 2023, para 39) In the 2019 Old Flag case the court also acknowledged that AfriForum 'frowns upon' and discourages the display of the old flag. (Old Flag case 2019, para 203) In contrast, in the Kill the Boer case of 2022 and its appeal in 2024 the evidence showed that the chant is often sung in public with encouragement and regularly in situations of potential political conflict, outside courts, during litigation or as part of statements being made by political leaders. It is arguable that a reasonable person would conclude that the chant in those circumstances constitute hate speech as one of its potential meanings. The court found, however, that in effect there is only one discernible and reasonable observation that could be made, namely that the song is not to be treated literally. (Kill the Boer appeal case 2024, para 103) The court in effect adopted a predominant test that coincides with the interests of the majority and overrules other possible meanings of the chant.

The risk of freedom of expression being limited in an arbitrary and inconsistent manner is illustrated by the following observation made by the ECtHR in the Féret case:

> The court reiterates that inciting to hatred does not necessarily entail a call for an act of violence, or other criminal acts. Attacks on persons committed by *insulting*, holding up to *ridicule* or *slandering* specific groups of the population can be sufficient for the authorities to favour combating racist speech in the face of freedom of expression exercised in an irresponsible manner. (emphasis added) (Féret case 2009, paras 70–71)

ECtHR jurisprudence seems to adopt two divergent approaches to the likelihood of possible or actual violence arising from speech. In the Sanchez case the court asserted that a threat of violence, or actual violence, is not required. (Sanchez case 2015, para 88) In contrast, in the Zana case the court took into consideration the actual threat of violence, intention of the speaker and circumstances of the speech. (Zana case 1997, para 61) This illustrates the risks of both the arbitrary curtailing of free speech and judicial censorship under the veil of protection against hate speech.

The four South African judgments highlight the inconsistencies in the normative standards used when ascertaining hate speech. In the Old Flag judgments the courts were primarily swayed by the symbolic meaning of the old flag and the hurtful memories it evokes. However, the judges gave little, if any, consideration to the actual circumstances of the march and the intention of the person displaying the old flag, nor that it was a legitimate public march against high levels of crime attended by persons from all races. Meanwhile, in the 2022 Kill the Boer judgment and its 2024 appeal the courts went to some length to justify that the chant should not be taken literally, that it had been sung in the context of a political protest and that the singer had not intended to encourage fear, violence or hatred. These four cases showcase the broad discretion given to the courts, thereby raising the risk of inconsistency and personal bias prevailing.

It is not surprising that in the Vejdeland case, European Court Justices Spielman and Nussberger cautioned that the test applied by the majority for hate speech, namely 'statements that are unwarrantably offensive to others', is too vague. (Vejdeland case 2012, paras 4–5) In the Perinçek case, meanwhile, the ECtHR undertook an in-depth assessment of the speech and the context in which it was made before concluding that it was protected – hence emphasising the contextual circumstances of speech and its possible effects. (Perinçek case 2015, para 280) In the USA, where freedom of expression under the First Amendment is seen as sacrosanct,[62] the Supreme Court has declared that speech constituting a 'true threat', such as the burning of a cross in front of the home of an African American, is hate speech. (Virginia case 2003) In the RB case the ECtHR also found that the failure to prosecute when a person was clearly the subject of 'intention of intimidation' was an error on the part of the authorities. (RB case 2016, para 76)

When assessing the potential impact of speech, a substantial body of cases have required at least 'potential harm', threats of violence, incitement to violence or actual violence, which, in effect, may raise the threshold for successful hate speech prosecution.

As recently stated by the Supreme Court of India, 'when statements are made with the objective and intent to cause public disorder or to demean the dignity of the targeted groups' they should be regarded as hate speech. (Amish Devgan case 2020) Any categorisation of speech as hate speech should be reserved to 'cover only the most intense form of dislike'. (Keegstra case 1990, para 122) The Constitutional Court of Germany has cautioned that, although the glorification of Nazi ideology may be declared a criminal act, it does not justify a general ban on the dissemination of radical right-wing, or indeed National Socialist, ideas. The court emphasised that there must be proportionality between the fundamental right and the restriction that is being placed on it. (BVerfGE Case No 1 BvR 2150/08) This should be read with the caution expressed by Justice Pavli in the Bayar and Gürbüz case – that hate speech complaints should have greater regard to the context of the speech and the probability of harmful consequences. (Bayar and Gürbüz case 2012, paras 14–16) In the Vejdeland case, meanwhile, Justice Zupančič expressed concern that the majority may be overstating the importance of what had been said. (Vejdeland case 2012, para 12) In the Sokolovskiy case the ECtHR held that the restriction on the speech of a blogger who was critical of religious beliefs was excessive and disproportionate since inadequate evidence existed about the speech causing hatred or risk of violence. (Sokolovskiy case 2024)

The challenge of applying the test of an objective, fictional person is highlighted by the South African cases under discussion.

[62] The First Amendment guarantees as follows: 'Congress shall make no law respecting an establishment of religion or prohibiting the free exercise thereof; or abridging the freedom of speech, or the press; or the right of the people peaceably to assemble, and to petition the Government for a redress of grievances.'

While each of the justices in the four South African cases subscribed to the reasonable person test, the outcomes of their assessments of the fictional person's perceptions differed. The realisation that a declaration of hate speech may indeed, in some instances, be very subjective and dependent on individual perspectives of judges is likely to leave readers with a feeling of unease. In the 2011 Kill the Boer case the court concluded that the reasonable person would view the chant as hate speech, while in the 2022 and 2024 Kill the Boer cases the courts concluded the opposite. In the Old Flag case the court found that the predominant message conveyed by the old flag was one of racial hatred, while in the Kill the Boer cases the courts explained why the chant should not be taken literally, why it is part of South Africa's history and why the reasonable person would not perceive it as hate speech. The court declared that the old flag, objectively, has only one predominant meaning and this represented hate speech. In contrast, in the Kill the Boer cases the courts rejected evidence from individuals who spoke about the hurt, fear and anxiety they felt upon hearing the chant. The courts instead accepted the defence that it is a pre-democracy liberation chant, the words of which should not be interpreted literally in the current democratic order. In the Old Flag case, meanwhile, the court adopted the position that the old flag has a predominant meaning and this meaning takes precedence over any secondary interpretations.

The reasonings of the courts in these four cases raise questions about the relevance of context when speech is uttered. While an objective assessment of speech may seem to imply a dispassionate context-free approach, it is important to recognise that context and intention are relevant considerations, and so is the understanding of judges and their biases regarding the historic circumstances.

In the Zana case the ECtHR stressed that speech must be protected unless 'it incites to violence' (Zana case 1997, para 61), while the US Supreme Court held in the Brandenburg case that freedom of expression is not protected when speech 'is directed to inciting or producing imminent lawless action and is likely to incite or produce such action'. (Brandenburg case 1969, para 447) This would suggest a consideration not only of the content of the speech, but also of other relevant circumstances related to it, including the intention of the speaker and the potential consequences of the speech. (Sürek (No. 1) case 1999, para 62)

These cases also highlight the complexities involved in ascertaining, through the eyes of the so-called reasonable person, whether speech meets the hate threshold. In extreme cases of hatred it may be simple to formulate an assessment based on the common good through the eyes of a reasonable person.

However, when it comes to contentious circumstances the risk of judicial bias increases, particularly in a country such as South Africa, where justices come from completely different backgrounds. Differing contextual factors may render the same speech protected by free speech and barred by hate speech. In the Gül case, for example, the ECtHR found that in the absence of a 'clear and imminent danger' the speech should be protected. (Gül case 2000, para 42) Meanwhile, in the Savva Terentyev case the ECtHR ruled that 'unless it is likely to provoke imminent unlawful actions' and poses 'a real risk of physical violence', freedom of expression should prevail. (Savva Terentyev case 2009, para 77) In the Terminiello case the US Supreme Court said that freedom of expression is protected against censorship or punishment, unless shown likely to produce a 'clear and present danger of a serious substantive evil that rises far above public inconvenience, annoyance, or unrest'. (Terminiello case 1949) In the Matal case the Supreme Court declared that even profane speech is protected under the Constitution.[63] (Matal case 2017) In the Maria Alekhina case the speech was protected as the Russian authorities had failed to examine whether the speech could have led to harm. (Maria Alekhina case 2018, para 226)

If this test as expressed by the ECtHR and the US courts had been applied to the four South African cases under discussion, the outcomes would arguably have been different. The observation by Justice Sajo in the Féret case is of note:

> Content regulation and content-based restrictions on speech are based on the assumption that certain expressions go 'against the spirit' of the Convention. But 'spirits' do not offer clear standards and are open to abuse. Humans, including judges, are inclined to label positions with which they disagree as palpably unacceptable and therefore beyond the realm of protected expression. *However, it is precisely where we face ideas that we abhor or despise that we have to be most careful in our judgment, as our personal convictions can influence our ideas about what is actually dangerous.* (emphasis added) (Féret case 2009, para 52)

5.5.3 What is the effect of a declaration of hate speech?

The final question to consider concerns the effect of a declaration of speech as hate speech. Does the declaration apply to the specific speech with reference to the day, the person who expressed it and circumstances giving rise to the complaint? Or can a declaration of hate speech also apply to restrict any similar

[63] In this case a music group wanted to register a trademark which was declared to be too derogatory and offensive to Asian people to be protected. The Supreme Court overruled the refusal and said that different viewpoints are protected even if they are deemed to be offensive.

future speech? In other words, is the effect of a declaration limited to (a) the speaker or does it apply to the general public, and (b) is the declaration *retrospective* by reference to a past event or *prospective* by reference to potential future events?

The Kill the Boer and Old Flag cases exhibit inconsistencies in response to this question. In the 2011 Kill the Boer case the court declared the chant to be hate speech and ordered the *respondents* to the proceeding not to sing it 'at any public or private meeting held by or conducted *by them*'. (emphasis added) (Kill the Boer case 2011, para Order 2) In the 2019 Old Flag case the court declared the display of the old flag to be hate speech, ordering that '*any* display of the old flag constitutes hate speech in terms of Section 10(1) of the Equality Act'. (emphasis added) (Old Flag case 2019, para Order 2) The 2011 Kill the Boer order was directed prospectively but limited to the respondents in the proceeding, whereas the 2019 Old Flag case order was also prospective but extended beyond the immediate parties to include all members of the public (the bearer of the old flag was never identified). In effect, it suggested a ban on the display of the old flag. In the Kill the Boer appeal of 2024 the court correctly emphasised that the chant must be assessed in its context, the event and who uttered it. (Kill the Boer appeal case 2024, paras 91, 94)

Comparative jurisprudence favours that a declaration of hate speech applies retrospectively to a certain incident and to the person who spoke. In other words, the effect of the finding is principally circumstantial to the actual speech that was the subject of the complaint and it does not regulate any future speech of the same nature. Furthermore, the finding is not directed at the public, who were not party to the proceeding. The reason for this approach is that parliaments may ban or restrict certain forms of speech prospectively pursuant to a criminal code, while courts are limited in their jurisdiction to a specific event and a particular circumstance.

International theory and jurisprudence suggest that, unless Parliament bans certain speech or insignia, a declaration of hate speech should be directed at the *specific incident* and the *person* against whom the complaint is made. It is not a test to be applied in the abstract or by general declaration of the meaning or impact of speech. The court plays a crucial role as the ultimate protector of the basic rights and freedoms in a democratic society, as articulated by the Supreme Court of India:

> The role of the court is to protect fundamental rights limited by lawful restrictions and not to protect restrictions and make the rights residual privileges. (Kaushal Kishor case 2023, para 33)

The general restriction imposed by the court in the 2019 Old Flag case arguably exceeded what was reasonable and proportional to the offence caused by the display of the old flag, especially considering the other meanings attributed to it, the rarity of its public display and the fact that the order was not made against the individual who displayed it. This assessment is confirmed by the court in the Kill the Boer appeal when it says that the procedure was not about an 'outright ban' of the chant, but rather an assessment of the chant on the day. (Kill the Boer appeal case 2024, para 80)

The Constitutional Court of Germany has formulated the importance of proportionality as follows:

> This setting of boundaries must also be followed by a review of proportionality. The more concretely and directly a legal interest is placed in danger by an expression of opinion, the less stringent are the requirements when it comes to an encroachment; the more indirect and distant the threatening violations of legal interests remain, the greater are the requirements to be made. *Accordingly, encroachments on freedom of opinion are more to be accepted when they are restricted to the forms and circumstances of an expression of opinion in the outside world.* The more, by contrast, they ultimately result in a content-related suppression of the opinion itself, the higher are the requirements as to the concrete threat of a danger to legal interests. (emphasis added) (BVerfGE 2150/08 case, para 52)

The ECtHR has developed in its case law the 'autonomous concept' of whether an interference is 'proportionate to the legitimate aim pursued', which is determined having regard to all the circumstances of the case using criteria established in the court's case law and with the assistance of various principles and interpretation tools. (Freedom of Expression ECtHR 2022, para 88) Importantly, arising from this standard is the principle that a restriction of speech must be the 'least restrictive' measure to be adopted. (Freedom of Expression ECtHR 2022, para 96) Importantly, a 'blanket measure' that may deprive a category of persons from their rights may be disproportionate. (Boulais, Marinkovic, and Palomares 2023, 84)

5.6 CONCLUSION

Several indicia can be identified arising from the approaches in international law and comparative constitutional law to the interaction between freedom of expression and hate speech. Among all forms of objectionable speech, hate speech as the most extreme speech also requires the most stringent threshold to satisfy. Even if hate speech is defined by legislation, the practical circumstances of the speech will determine whether speech meets the threshold of hate speech.

There is a risk of bracket creep in the application of the hate speech test, where the boundaries of acceptable expression become so fluid that over time substantial parts of objectionable or offensive speech drift into what is regarded as hate speech. In the words of the US Supreme Court, there exists a fundamental principle that 'government may not punish or suppress speech based on disapproval of the ideas or perspectives the speech conveys'. (Matal case 2017)

The test to be applied for hate speech is objective from the perspective of the reasonably informed onlooker, rather than subjective from the mind of the speaker or the person exposed to the speech – although the circumstances of the speech and intention of the speaker are relevant factors to be considered by the reasonable person. If freedom of expression is to be curbed, its curtailment should be proportionate, retrospective and narrow rather than broad. Determining whether speech qualifies as hate speech depends on the circumstances. Speech that may be hate speech in one circumstance may not be hate speech in another. That is why courts declare hate speech by reference to an event rather than in general or in the abstract.

It has been emphasised that establishing the perception of a reasonable person is a fictional and potentially highly unreliable exercise, especially in deeply divided societies where judges might introduce their biases and subjective views of history and socio-political events into the purported opinion of the reasonable person. All relevant evidence should be considered by a court in the light of the fundamental importance of freedom of expression to a free and open democratic society. If evidence is not adequate to declare speech hate speech, a judge may not supplement the evidence with their own understandings of the topic, history or circumstance.

The Old Flag and Kill the Boer judgments as well as foreign case law cited in this chapter highlight the complexity involved to apply an objective assessment of the reasonableness of speech. This is particularly true in a deeply divided society, where the history of the respective communities, as well as their perceptions of history, are multidimensional, nuanced and complex. In both the cases the courts preferred a predominant assessment with lesser regard to other meanings of the offending speech. In India the Supreme Court has stressed the right to engage in certain forms of contentious speech, arguing that such expression can aid the public to reflect on the past. However, the approach taken regarding the Old Flag and the Kill the Boer chant seems to place a higher value on the experiences, fears and perceptions of one community over another. The caution expressed by the minority (Judges Sajo, Zagrebelsky and Tsotsoria) in the Féret case can equally be applied to South Africa:

> Humans, including judges, are inclined to label positions with which they disagree as palpably unacceptable and therefore beyond the realm of protected expression. However, it is precisely where we face ideas that we abhor or despise that we have to be careful in our judgment, as our personal convictions can influence our ideas about what is actually dangerous. (Féret case 2009)

Ultimately, the judgments referred to in the course of this chapter underscore the inherent complexities to determine hate speech. They bring attention to the challenge of weighing the different histories of peoples and communities, the difficulty of distinguishing between literal and figurative interpretations of speech, and the intricacies arising from the so-called objective test. Regarding the last point, it is shown that in a deeply divided and plural society the application of a reasonable person test may not be as straightforward in practice as theory seems to suggest and the background of judges may impact on the way speech is assessed.

The lack of consistency evident in comparative jurisprudence reaffirms the argument that the declaration of speech as hate speech and its consequent curtailment on freedom of expression should be: reserved for the most extreme forms of speech; proportionate to the speech in question, taking into consideration where and when it was expressed and by whom; and only directed at the specific incident concerned as opposed to imposing a broad restriction on speech.

CHAPTER 6

IMPACT OF UBUNTU ON SOUTH AFRICAN JURISPRUDENCE: FROM A SOURCE OF RIGHTS TO A CUSTOMARY WAY TO EXPLAIN COMPLEX JUDGMENTS

There is a Zulu proverb called Ubuntu that says: 'I am a person through other people. My humanity is tied to yours.'

– Archbishop Desmond Tutu

6.1 INTRODUCTION

'Ubuntu' – a word that resonates with many meanings. It has a warmth, closeness and comfort to it. It carries a significance that transcends different cultures and finds widespread usage in many languages. It conveys a sense of romanticism, serving as a foundational concept, a useful band-aid covering many wounds, and a religious and cultural *grundnorm*.

Philosophically, Ubuntu embodies pluralism and non-state customary law since its meaning is not codified, yet it has legal normative content. Its application is found in African culture, religion and tradition, its meaning is dynamic and its value is reflected in its practical application. Ideologically, it implies equality, fairness, Africanism and even anti-colonialism. In a religious sense it reflects love, caring and neighbourliness. Socially, it implies kindness and sharing, particularly in the context of individual vis-à-vis community. Economically it is said to imply 'caring, inclusiveness, and egalitarian redistribution'. (Davis and Klare 2024) Spiritually, it refers to the place of the individual in society and the importance of community in sustaining us. In legal philosophy and in its practical application Ubuntu has become the symbol word of constitutional transformation in South Africa. (De Villiers 2023a, 132) In the Beadica case it was said that Ubuntu encompasses the values of 'fairness, reasonableness and justice'. (Beadica case 2020, para 72)

The word has been given a raft of legal, social, psychological, spiritual and cultural meanings and applications. It can be used (and abused) in many circumstances. Kayange elevates Ubuntu to a quasi-ideology with an 'ism' by stating: '*Ubuntuism* is a theory of human nature in sub-Saharan Africa, where in most cases, philosophers claim that relations with others determine the essence of being a person.' (Kayange 2023, vii) While the virtue of Ubuntu as a spiritual concept is widely acknowledged in Africa, its application as a legal norm is predominantly associated with South Africa. Dladla is critical of the South African application of Ubuntu and suggests the time is not yet arrived for real Ubuntu. (Dladla 2025, 159) He proposes that real Ubuntu can only be achieved when the current constitutional hierarchy is 'overturned' and Ubuntu is placed at the 'zenith of the legal and political order' through parliamentary sovereignty rather than the current constitutional order. (Dladla 2025, 182)

Ubuntu has, in many respects, evolved into a mega-norm with practically no boundaries, as it seeks to represent 'humaneness, social justice and fairness'. (Makwanyane case 1995, para 236) Radebe and Phooko describe Ubuntu as 'a way of life of the African people which is underpinned by certain components that make up its substantive content, and which permeates every aspect of their everyday existence and interactions with each other and the world at large'. (Radebe and Phooko 2017, 240)[1] Ubuntu has, in a way, become a soul word in South African jurisprudence, in a similar way (albeit to a lesser extent) that *Bundestreue* (federal partnership)[2] and *Pancasila*[3] have become soul words in the constitutional traditions of Germany and Indonesia respectively. (De Villiers 2022c)

[1] Radebe and Phooko offer the following meanings of Ubuntu to place it in an African context: my child is your child; the child belongs to the community; obligation of family members towards each other; communitarianism in contrast to individualism; people first in service delivery; the one hand washes the other; community-centric; spiritual focus on the now, rather than the afterlife; generosity; shared ownership; importance of land to identity. (Radebe and Phooko 2017, 240–5)

[2] *Bundestreue* refers to the federal trust, partnership or comity that describes the relationship in the Federal Republic of Germany between the federal government and the *Länder* (federal states), as well as the relationships among the *Länder* themselves. (De Villiers 1994a) The term specifically applies to the conduct of intergovernmental relations, and in its modern context it embodies what is known as 'cooperative federalism'. (Burgess 2012) Although the word *Bundestreue* does not appear in the Basic Law (constitution) of Germany, the Constitutional Court has based many of its judgments on it as being *an implied term* of the Basic Law that originates from German constitutional history. The implied term requires respect, cooperation and consultation between the different levels of government. (De Villiers 2022c; BVerfGE 1 56) Chapter 3 of the Constitution of South Africa, which deals with cooperative government, is in effect a codification of *Bundestreue*. The main negotiating parties in South Africa were, in the early 1990s, so impressed by the philosophy and practice of cooperative government in German federalism that they wanted to dedicate an entire chapter of the Constitution to the importance of cooperative government. (De Villiers and Sindane 2011) Chapter 3 of the Constitution was at the time of its drafting the most detailed constitutional framework in the world for the conduct of intergovernmental relations.

[3] *Pancasila* has been referred to as the 'source of all laws'. (Prasetyo 2016, 103) The five essential principles of *Pancasila*, as found in the Preamble to the Constitution of Indonesia, are: belief in one and only God; just and fair humanity; unity of Indonesia, democracy; and social justice. (Black 2024) Pesurnay says the following about *Pancasila*: '*Pancasila* must be understood through *causalis* theory. The material realisation of *Pancasila can be seen in the habits, culture, and religion* of Indonesia. Habit in the wider sense refers to the political dimensions of statehood, and the social and economic realms that are stored in the common memory of Indonesian society and also within the group. . . . The flexible dimension of *Pancasila* refers to the necessity for it to be able to adapt to the social processes of Indonesian society. Not only does *Pancasila* direct social change according to the hopes and aspirations of citizens, but this adaptation requires the continued involvement of the wider society in evaluating and interpreting the ideology's meaning according to the needs of the current historical period. It is in this sense that *Pancasila* can be considered an "open" ideology, one whose underlying spirit doesn't change but can be developed creatively and dynamically to remain relevant in the face of social transformations in the life processes of Indonesian society. . . .' (Pesurnay 2018, 162, 165)

The wide application and popularity of Ubuntu has, however, also been criticised on grounds that the term is being abused by Western capital and neo-liberal proponents. (Mwipikeni 2018) According to sceptics, Ubuntu has become colonised, its African component has been weakened and its effect has been usurped by liberal individualistic values. The word has, according to some critics, effectively become a Trojan horse whereby foreign values are disguised by using an African customary term and value system.[4] On the other hand, some view Ubuntu as 'the overarching philosophy of Black people in Africa' (Mugumbate 2024, 1123), which raises the question whether it can be applied in a non-racial manner. If Ujomu is correct that Ubuntu 'is defined by a set of human values central among which are reciprocity, the common good, peaceful relations, an emphasis on human dignity and the value of human life, as well as consensus, tolerance, and mutual respect' (Ujomu 2024), then those are surely not solely the exclusive ownership of African thought.

There is to some extent an ideological battle to claim the proprietary rights to Ubuntu, namely who ascertains the meaning of the term, when it can be used, how it can be adjusted and whether its interpretation is the sole domain of those from whose culture (race?) the term originates. Kayange even suggests that Ubuntu must undergo a form of 'purification' for its justice virtue to be applied. He says: 'All this means that for justice to be ubuntu virtue, it must undergo this purification, where the elements of ubuntu self-regarding virtues, other regarding virtues, practical reason, wellbeing, etc, are the absolute test (the human nature-based test as per the above assumption that it is good and tends towards this good).' (Kayange 2023, 108)

The Constitutional Court has, in its efforts to popularise Ubuntu, also contributed to it becoming an overly shared concept, thereby possibly weakening its fundamental meaning within the African customary-law context. The courts have been inconsistent in their application of Ubuntu, sometimes lauding its interpretive value, but then at other times not citing it at all and not explaining why it is not being cited. Furthermore, the use of the word by the Constitutional Court in complex disputes is often not well explained by judges. Frequently, Ubuntu is inadequately justified with reference to its established meaning in African custom.

[4] Coleman suggests that Ubuntu can be used to inform through African values the relevant law applicable to international contracts. (Coleman 2024)

As discussed below, Ubuntu is sometimes cited in judgments without clear justification or sufficient evidence of how a particular meaning arising from African customary law can be attributed to it in the factual context of a specific dispute not related to customary law. It appears as if judges rely on Ubuntu within the notion of judicial knowledge, but, if so, it may be an error in law since it is not a term the meaning or the application of which is settled. Furthermore, judges are not consistent about when Ubuntu ought to be cited; for example, as shown in Chapter 5, in the 2011 Kill the Boer case the judge relied on Ubuntu to declare the chant hate speech, while in the 2022 Kill the Boer case no mention was made of Ubuntu and there was no explanation why Ubuntu had not been cited, and yet the judge concluded that the chant was not hate speech. The same applies to the 2024 Kill the Boer appeal case, in which no mention is made of the relevance of Ubuntu. (Kill the Boer appeal case 2024)

In a similar vein to Germany, where the word *Bundestreue* is not mentioned in the Basic Law, the word Ubuntu does not appear in the 1996 Constitution. Ironically, Ubuntu appeared in the interim 1993 Constitution, but neither was it included in the Constitutional Principles (Chapter 3) nor does it appear in the final 1996 Constitution. No mention was made of the term in the Certification judgments, and no reason was given in the debates conducted by the Constitutional Assembly leading to the creation of the Constitution for the exclusion of Ubuntu from the constitutional text. The term simply disappeared, perhaps erroneously, from the formal legal instruments for reasons that remain unexplained. And yet it has under the 1996 Constitution become a term used often to explain judgments, identify rights and responsibilities, interpret statutes and determine appropriate remedies. The rationale for the ongoing reliance on Ubuntu is perhaps best explained by Mokgoro, when she said that the principle of reconciliation and reconstruction goes beyond the truth and reconciliation process. (Cornell and Mavangua 2012, 25) However, Cornell and Mavangua acknowledge that 'there has, inevitably, been confusion as to what the precise role of Ubuntu is now that it has lost its literal status on the face of the document that is the final Constitution'. (Cornell and Mavangua 2012, 30)

While *Bundestreue* in Germany has found application solely in the field of public law, traces of Ubuntu in South Africa can be found much more extensively, such as in judgments dealing with human rights, criminal law, contractual law, immigration law, hate speech, employment law and other aspects of jurisprudence. While in the first judgment of the Constitutional Court under the 1993 Constitution (in which Ubuntu was mentioned in the postamble)[5], there was detailed reliance on the humanity and dignity that underpin Ubuntu as a rationale for abolishing the death penalty (Makwanyane case 1995), after the enactment of the 1996 Constitution the courts continued to cite Ubuntu, but without explaining why the term could be relied on despite not appearing in the text of the 1996 Constitution.

The best explanation for the ongoing use of Ubuntu may be that it is an *implied* term[6] of the Constitution that derives its meaning from customary law. (Chapter 10) However, none of the judgments post-1996 has offered an in-depth philosophical or legal justification for the use of the term other than citing the Makwanyane case. Curiously, Ubuntu is a word widely used in *social* contexts in southern Africa and in large parts of Africa, but it has not had the jurisprudential impact in other states in Africa that it has had in South Africa. This does raise the question whether the meanings attributed to Ubuntu in South African jurisprudence are indeed implied in the Constitution, arise from customary law and supported by expert evidence, or judge-created.

The use of Ubuntu, for the purposes of this chapter, is unique for two reasons: first, although the word appears in the culture of many African countries, it is only in South Africa that it has become a legal-philosophical term relied on extensively by courts; and, secondly, its application has become widespread in jurisprudence, but without any real scrutiny whether the application is justified based on the inherent meaning of the term or is merely a rationale whereby judges can give credibility to their bias behind an Ubuntu-shaped veil.

In this chapter we reflect on the use of Ubuntu in three different contexts: first, as a *source* of rights; secondly, as an instrument of statutory *interpretation*; and, thirdly, as an *aide-memoire* whereby judges can explain their judgments to laypeople. It is shown that Ubuntu is in effect used by the courts as an open-ended customary-law term to inform common law in a manner which now applies to

[5] There was only scant reference to Ubuntu in the 1993 Constitution, in the postamble under the heading National Unity and Reconciliation: 'These can now be addressed on the basis that there is a need for understanding but not for vengeance, a need for reparation but not for retaliation, *a need for ubuntu* but not for victimisation.' Ubuntu was not defined by the 1993 Constitution.

[6] Implied terms are, in general, words or provisions that do not appear explicitly in a contract, but which are assumed by a court to have been implied by the parties to constitute part of the contract. (Wilmot-Smith 2023) Note, for example, how in Australia the High Court has held that the principle of freedom of political speech is implied in the Constitution even if there is no explicit reference to it. (Australian Capital Television case 1992)

all aspects of society, serving as a foundation to facilitate transformation of South African society from apartheid to a free and democratic state. Judges of various courts have relied on and applied Ubuntu in divergent contexts, albeit principally to interpret rights and duties, as well as to balance competing interests. In doing so the courts have imparted a strong African identity to judgments, using the term not only to legitimise the Constitution but also to justify its application to a specific dispute and develop a homegrown jurisprudence.

However, in doing so, as also discussed in this chapter, there is a risk of Ubuntu being used as a term of discretionary self-justification by judges to potentially lend credibility and legitimacy to their own personal biases by referring to Ubuntu as if it is a term of which the meaning is clear. Chapter 5, for example, elaborates on how the 2011 Kill the Boer case was presided over by a judge who relied on Ubuntu to explain why the chant in question constituted hate speech (Kill the Boer case 2011, para 108), whereas in the 2022 Kill the Boer case and the 2024 Kill the Boer appeal case, different judges found no reason to cite Ubuntu at all, nor to explain why Ubuntu did not apply to the dispute. These judgments highlight the potential for the highly arbitrary and selective use of Ubuntu. Even if, as Radebe and Phooko suggest (Radebe and Phooko 2017), Ubuntu should not have been applied to the 2011 case, the court in the 2022 judgment and in the 2024 appeal could have been expected to at least refer to Ubuntu and explain why it was not applicable to the Kill the Boer chant. Ignoring the potential applicability of Ubuntu raises the risk that courts may selectively cite Ubuntu, introducing an element of arbitrariness that could undermine the legal certainty purportedly associated with the term.

The potentially selective use of Ubuntu prompts questions such as: Is the term indeed implied in the Constitution as a basis to infuse common law and, if so, by what reasoning? When is an implied term relied upon in judgments and is its use discretionary? What meaning and effect are given to an implied term such as Ubuntu, and on the basis of what evidence can an ever-expanding meaning be attributed to the term? And, how can inter-court consistency be ensured in the application and meaning of an implied, undefined term such as Ubuntu?

6.2 UBUNTU IN ITS ORIGIN

The word 'Ubuntu' is often relied upon in South Africa's legal, social, political, economic and constitutional discourse to reflect the fundamental equality of individuals and their interrelatedness and dependence upon one another, as well as their interactions with and responsibility to the community. Ubuntu, in its customary context, has a reciprocal nature, signifying a relationship between the individual and the community, as well as the community and the individual. One cannot exist without the other. Each part makes the joint parts complete.

In South Africa the origin of Ubuntu is associated particularly with the Xhosa and Zulu languages, and it reflects and combines essential human virtues, compassion and humanity. (Ubuntu Lexico 2020) The word has, however, become part of lingua franca, not only in Africa but also abroad. Literally translated, the word seeks to reflect the belief that 'a person is a person because of what the members of the community have done for him'. (Netshitomboni 1998, 5) Application of the word is also found in the local languages and customs of other countries such as Zimbabwe, Botswana, Malawi, Uganda, and Tanzania. (Mugumbate and Nyanguru 2013, 85) Underlying Ubuntu is also the notion that 'individual rights and duties to the collective were intimately intertwined, and that without duties, no individual rights would have meaning'. (Kelly 2023, 113) Ubuntu is widely regarded as a word that resonates socially, linguistically and culturally with peoples in large parts of sub-Saharan Africa in some way or another. (Hailey 2008) Some even liken the meaning of Ubuntu to general African humanism and a continental philosophy. (Amin 2021) Sachs describes Ubuntu as a 'profound and all-encompassing social philosophy'. (Sachs 2012, 326) In the Greater Tzaneen Municipality case the court observed that the common law can be decolonised through the application of Ubuntu with the emphasis on 'harmonious relationships and co-operation with others'. (Greater Tzaneen Municipality case 2024, para 38)

In its application in jurisprudence in Africa, Ubuntu has been most often cited in South African jurisprudence.[7] Under law, Ubuntu is often used by the courts in South Africa as if it is a term of art rather than an undefined customary concept. Therefore in this chapter, when reference is made to Ubuntu in the context of court proceedings, it is referred to as a 'term', rather than a 'word', 'phrase', or a 'concept'.

Ubuntu is not constrained by definition. It is described by its inherent values and its cultural and customary understanding, rather than by the narrowness of definition. Thus applying Ubuntu to legal proceedings is not simple, as it was not in its origin intended to be a legal term. Sometimes it appears as though justices cite the term arbitrarily and in different contexts. It is perhaps best described as

[7] Roberts suggests that wider use could be made on Ubuntu in sentencing in Tanzania. (Roberts 2023)

a term that represents an expression of a living culture that adapts and adjusts as time passes. (Chapters 3 and 10)

It is therefore fitting that Ubuntu is considered in the context of legal pluralism and the recognition and application of non-state law. Ubuntu is arguably unique in its status as a customary non-state law concept that has been elevated by courts to become a state law constitutional and customary norm.[8] The caution expressed by Maujib that an 'evolutive interpretation' of customary law may give rise to outcomes that are contrary to the intent and consent of parties (Mujib 2023, 73) may also be applied to the uncritical use of Ubuntu to provide a rationale to justify a specific outcome.

The following values seem to be embedded in Ubuntu: humanity, gentleness, hospitality, empathy, deep kindness, friendliness, generosity, vulnerability. (Mangena 2020) In a legal context Mokgoro viewed Ubuntu as a 'legal principle' of which the content is flexible and open to ongoing change and adjustment. (Mokgoro 2011, 2) In its essence the word refers in customary law to the importance of community and the role of the individuals therein to serve and support each other.[9] Ubuntu is also a quasi-religious term, perhaps akin to the biblical understandings of love, compassion, caring and good neighbourliness. It has been referred to as an 'ancient African code of ethics that emphasizes the importance of hospitality, generosity, respect for all members of the community, and embraces the view that we all belong to one human family'. (Ramcharan et al

[8] Although in Indonesia the term *Pancasila* also carries symbolic and practical meanings (Isra and Faiz 2024), the term is not so readily relied on by courts as the case has been with Ubuntu in South Africa.

[9] The application of Ubuntu is not limited to political and constitutional rights. It spans the field of all human interaction. See, for example, Tsotetsi, who applies Ubuntu to the field of postgraduate supervision. (Tsotetsi and Omodan 2020) Dumisa seeks answers in Ubuntu to combat the corruption which afflicts South Africa. (Dumisa and Amao 2015) Samuel explores Ubuntu and the philosophy of selflessness. (Samuel 2023) Naude calls on Ubuntu to provide better business ethics. (Naude 2019) Omodan looks at Ubuntu as a tool for conflict management in universities. (Omodan 2022) Jedege and Stoffels liken Ubuntu to various fundamental rights, such as the right to protection, association, freedom of expression, and a clean environment. (Jegede and Stoffels 2022, 305) Ogunde applies Ubuntu to the empowerment of communities through consultation and involvement. (Ogunde 2019) Ndeunyema proposes that Ubuntu implies access to water to communities. (Ndeunyema 2021) Tshoose expands on the use of Ubuntu to facilitate access to social security. (Tshoose 2023) Emelianenko applies Ubuntu to South Africa's foreign policy. (Emelianenko 2022) The term has even lent itself to the name of a well-known computer software program to signify interconnectedness. (Ubuntu Software n.d.) Kotze et al rely on the 'care and humility' of Ubuntu to propose indigenous environmental protection and care. (Kotze, Adelman, and Dube 2023, 13)

2023, 45) Since Ubuntu does not have a set expression or definition, judges have used judicial discretion to apply Ubuntu in the broadest of circumstances, ranging from the importance of simply 'being' because others exist, to conflict resolution, reconciliation, restorative justice, sentencing, recognition of customary law, autonomy and self-determination of the individual, fair employment practices and equality in commercial bargaining. The variety of ways in which Ubuntu is applied can in part be explained by the impossibility of distinguishing between law, religion and custom in the context of African customary law.

In some respects Ubuntu, with its emphasis on community in general and tribe in particular, signifies a form of collective responsibility which resonates with a group right and collective approach, as found in theories concerning the protection of minority rights.[10] In this sense it can be argued that Ubuntu stands in contrast with liberal democratic values espousing the sovereignty of individual rights, since Ubuntu captures the collective nature of society in general, and community in particular. However, to suggest that the essence of Ubuntu boils down to community rights versus individual rights would be an oversimplification of the richness of the concept. (Tom 2018) There is, however, the possibility, as critics have pointed out, that the community element of Ubuntu has been usurped by individualism.

In essence Ubuntu reflects the principle that a person's 'humanity is dependent on the appreciation, preservation and affirmation of another person's humanity'. (Eze 2008, 107) Such an interpretation of Ubuntu is not inconsistent with liberal democratic values, whereby fundamental rights and freedoms must be exercised in a manner that respects and upholds the rights of others. International and foreign law acknowledge that the scope of fundamental rights may be limited within the context of the rights of others. As previously mentioned, (Chapter 5) courts in Germany and India, for example, have relied on the concept of 'dignity' (which is also an undefined community value) to limit the scope of freedom of expression in order to protect certain individuals against hate speech. Unlike Western concepts of law, however, Ubuntu jurisprudence is not determined by the typology of laws such as contract law, defamation law, delict, and so forth. It is determined, rather, by its 'appetite to find the truth and its consideration of

---

[10] Note, for example, the MEC for Education case, in which the court explained that Ubuntu reiterates that 'dignity and identity are inseparably linked to one's sense of self-worth' as defined by 'one's identity'. The court then went on to say that 'cultural identity is one of the most important parts of one's identity precisely because it flows from belonging to a community and not from personal choice or achievement'. (MEC for Education case 2007, para 53)

the humanity of the parties to a case' (Kamga 2018, 847) and is to be applied to all spheres of law.

The risk in applying Ubuntu, like any other undefined customary concept, to resolve legal disputes in *all* spheres of law is obvious. There is inevitably a peril that a socio-cultural living concept that evolved in the hearts and spirit of a particular community, like any other religious or customary value, is being applied within a legal context to society at large. For example, imagine the discrepancies that would arise if the courts were to apply the biblical concept of 'love' to adjudicate secular disputes. If ever there is a risk of subjective dogmatic interpretation, it occurs when customary or religiously ambiguous concepts, such as Ubuntu or love, are used to resolve contemporary secular disputes. Ubuntu as a value system is not necessarily unique since similar principles are found in other cultures, traditions and religions (Ramcharan et al 2023, 45), but the active manner in which the courts have sought to use Ubuntu as a tool to expand human right protection in South Africa is unique.

In the literature the moral obligation of justices under the Constitution to give effect to its underlying objectives has been described as 'transformative constitutionalism'. (Himonga, Taylor, and Pope 2013, 373) The two clauses of the Constitution that principally inform its transformative objectives are s 39(2)[11] and s 8(3)*(a)*,[12] both of which contain 'peremptory or commanding language'. (Mlambo 2022, 597) According to s 39(2), courts 'must' promote the spirit, purpose, and objects of the Bill of Rights. According to s 8(3)*(a)*, when giving effect to a right in the Bill of Rights, judges 'must' develop the common law and fill gaps in legislation to give effect to the rights enshrined in the Constitution. Letseka suggests that Ubuntu represents the 'constitutional values of non-racialism, non-sexism, non-discrimination, and respect for freedom, human rights and dignity'. (Letseka 2012, 47) Letseka also suggests, in a somewhat Lockean idyllic state-of-nature assessment, that in communities where Ubuntu is subscribed to, persons 'embrace ubuntu by a commitment to treating others with a sense of botho or ubuntu, which entails treating them with justice and fairness'. (Letseka 2000, 149) This almost reverent view of Ubuntu highlights

---

[11] Section 39(2): 'When interpreting any legislation, and when developing the common law or customary law, every court, tribunal or forum must promote the spirit, purport and objects of the Bill of Rights.'

[12] Section 8(3)*(a)*: 'When applying a provision of the Bill of Rights to a natural or juristic person in terms of subsection (2), a court – *(a)* in order to give effect to a right in the Bill, must apply or, if necessary, develop the common law to the extent that legislation does not give effect to that right.'

the aspirational value of the concept, but also serves as an example of how, as a legal term, it can become many things to many people. (De Villiers 2023a, 133)

The undefined nature of Ubuntu makes it appealing, on the one hand, as a tool for educating and encouraging tolerance and civil human behaviour. On the other hand, it lacks the clarity and clarity typically associated with a legal term. The vagueness of the term in a legal context lends itself to many applications and interpretations, mostly highly discretionary, yet it is this broad generality that also holds the potential to undermine the certainty and clarity required of a legal term. See, for example, the very general meaning of Ubuntu as proposed by Mugumbate and Nyanguru: 'Ubuntu echoes the *African* thought of *acceptable ideas and deeds*.' (emphasis added) (Mugumbate and Nyanguru 2013, 82) This underscores the undefinable breadth and scope of the term and raises the questions: what is African 'thought' and who would determine what is an 'acceptable idea and deed'?

It is evident how easily Ubuntu can become an ideological tool that is used to restrict, rather than to expand, fundamental individual freedoms and liberty under the veil of some 'common good' or 'Africanism'. Although Letseka asserts that the essential significance of Ubuntu is 'fundamentally a matter of reverence of human life' (Letseka 2000, 57), many philosophies and religions, as well as international human rights instruments, have expressions or terms that require a respect for life and dignity – and these are not cited by the courts or used to infuse common law or transform societies. The justification why Ubuntu, rather than any other customary or religious term or value, is given such a dominant status in the context of constitutional transformation remains to be explored and explained by the courts. There has been no in-depth explanation why a term that left was out of the 1996 Constitution became so important in jurisprudence.[13]

It should furthermore be taken into account that Ubuntu carries an applicable customary-law meaning that may hold greater significance for certain sections of South African society than it does for others. Elevating Ubuntu to a generic legal term with general application in dispute resolution outside customary law inevitably raises the risk of it being relied on without adequate justification, cited out of context, employed selectively or utilised without the required evidentiary base in a particular dispute. Given that Ubuntu is inherently linked to African

[13] Note, for example, how in English law, substantial explanations have been given when and why a term can be implied in a contract. (Austen-Baker 2023) It is not unreasonable to expect a similar explanation from the highest courts about the status of Ubuntu as an implied term of the Constitution.

customary law and religion, it may be superficial to suggest it should be applied to give content and effect to liberal democratic individual rights as enshrined in the Constitution or be used outside the context of customary law to resolve disputes. Historically Ubuntu found its meaning in a socio-cultural-lingual context and in non-state law. Had the Constitution referred to Ubuntu as a constitutional founding term, it would have been elevated for general application. However, the fact that the concept appears to be implied prompts debate about its status, weight, applicability, and meaning.

The widespread traction Ubuntu has gained in judicial reasoning since the enactment of the 1993 Constitution, however, is not entirely surprising, given that it embodies values that are at face value universal in nature and flexible enough to be applied in various contexts. It also gives an African feeling to the Constitution, which otherwise reads like any Western liberal democratic treatise. There is of course the risk of the legal romanticising of Ubuntu, attributing meanings to it that stretch, or even exceed, its customary boundaries, especially when applying it to resolve legal disputes outside the customary context. While applying Ubuntu in the context of good relationships, decency and caring may be suitable in the humanities and social sciences, its undefined nature in the legal sciences diminishes its capacity to serve as a clear legal norm.

Enslin, for instance, illustrates the uncertainty of Ubuntu's meaning when used in public education. He does concede, however, that Ubuntu has a truly 'African' meaning that may align more closely with the perspectives of African communities than it does with foreign imposed legal concepts. (Enslin and Horsthemke 2004) This then raises the question about who is an 'African'. Letseka seems to suggest that African people are defined by their race and not by their residence when he states: 'It is my view that at the heart of the debates on Ubuntu is how people, in this case the African peoples, perceive Ubuntu as a worldview that embodies their notions of morality and personhood.' (Letseka 2000, 54) If Letseka is correct, the challenge remains whether Ubuntu can indeed be a 'shared moral compass' to *all* who live in South Africa, including those who do not share African laws and religion, as proposed by Morrow. (Morrow 2007, 6)

It is understandable, in this regard, why Oyowe cautions as follows:

> All this leads me to suggest that an ***ubuntu ethic is not entirely suitable for grounding public morality***. Perhaps for more industrialised and globalised societies, in which the liberal ideals of freedom and human rights are of paramount importance in shaping public morality, an ubuntu ethic can only play a much more restricted role than it did in pre-industrialised African societies. (emphasis added) (Oyowe 2013, 124)

Mangena warns that Ubuntu is no 'panacea to the socio-political problems affecting the continent of Africa, especially the southern part of the continent'. (Mangena 2020)[14] This is evident, given the apparent lack of a spirit of Ubuntu as evidenced in the extraordinary levels of crime, violence and corruption in South Africa. The contrast between fact and legal customary concept could hardly be greater.

Critics argue that the contemporary jurisprudential use of the term 'Ubuntu', purporting to support individual equality as found in the liberal democratic principles of the Constitution, is unfounded, contending that the use of Ubuntu is a creation by justices rather than a concept informed by rigorous legal debate and scientific analysis. Liberal democratic values of equality and non-discrimination cannot necessarily be said to be shared by traditional African custom and customary law, and constitutional values ultimately trump indigenous laws and customs. (Bhe case 2005, Chapter 10) In fact, using Ubuntu as a vehicle to introduce universal liberal understandings of human rights into South African law may have the perverse effect of diminishing the uniqueness of customary law.

As discussed below, it is apparent that the wide-ranging contemporary meanings that have been attributed to Ubuntu by the judiciary have generally been neither objectively nor scientifically verified through expert evidence or legal lexicon. The legal basis of Ubuntu in essence is found by one court citing another, but with little in-depth judicial explanation of what the term means, why it has found its way into jurisprudence after it had been left out of the 1996 Constitution, or why a traditional concept can be applied to a specific contemporary, non-customary setting.

In response to this criticism proponents of the contemporary use of Ubuntu retort by saying its inherent values enable the term to be applied to modern settings, without its meaning being frozen in the past. This argument is not dissimilar to how the courts in Australia have acknowledged that the content of traditional native title rights and interests may have changed over time, but the element of traditional land ownership has not fallen away. (De Villiers 2022h, 112; Yorta Yorta (HCA) case 2002) In similar vein, Ubuntu may well trace its roots to African law and custom, but the South African courts have endeavoured

---

[14] Note in this respect the suggestion, somewhat romantic and idealistic, by Manthwa that Ubuntu must be 'allowed to form part of the mainstream law and can contribute to overcoming socio-economic challenges such as poverty and unemployment'. (Manthwa 2023, 667) This view of Ubuntu can, however, be equated to other values of governance such as love, compassion, fairness, equity and fairness. But the wider the ambit of the use of Ubuntu, the greater the difficulty to define it as a legal term.

to expand its application across the entire society to inform and infuse common law, while also broadening its relevance to disputes in a manner that permeates all aspects of society, thereby developing a homegrown jurisprudence. Such a creative and transformative approach is consistent with the Constitution and gives jurisprudence a unique South African fingerprint.

6.3 EVOLUTION OF UBUNTU FROM CUSTOMARY LAW TO COMMON LAW

The 1993 Constitution of South Africa contained, in its postamble, the following single reference to Ubuntu, without the term being defined:

> **National Unity and Reconciliation**
>
> This Constitution provides a historic bridge between the past of a deeply divided society characterised by strife, conflict, untold suffering and injustice, and a future founded on the recognition of human rights, democracy and peaceful co-existence and development opportunities for all South Africans, irrespective of colour, race, class, belief or sex. The pursuit of national unity, the well-being of all South African citizens and peace require reconciliation between the people of South Africa and the reconstruction of society.
>
> The adoption of this Constitution lays the secure foundation for the people of South Africa to transcend the divisions and strife of the past, which generated gross violations of human rights, the transgression of humanitarian principles in violent conflicts and a legacy of hatred, fear, guilt and revenge.
>
> These can now be addressed on the basis that there is a need for understanding but not for vengeance, a need for reparation but not for retaliation, *a need for ubuntu but not for victimisation.*
>
> ...
>
> With this Constitution and these commitments we, the people of South Africa, open a new chapter in the history of our country.

The use of Ubuntu in the 1993 Constitution is relevant to this chapter in five respects: first, Ubuntu does not appear in the Bill of Rights of the 1993 Constitution; secondly, Ubuntu is used only in the postamble within the context of National Unity and Reconciliation; thirdly, Ubuntu was not included in the Constitutional Principles as a fundamental value or an essential term to be inserted into the 1996 Constitution; fourthly, no objection was raised in submissions to the Constitutional Court as part of the certification process about the exclusion of Ubuntu from the constitutional text of the 1996 Constitution; and, fifthly, the potential judicial application and reliance on Ubuntu in both the

1993 and 1996 Constitutions was not foreshadowed by any of the committees that assisted with the drafting of the 1996 Constitution. In short, Ubuntu did not appear in the constitutional debates or the certification of the Constitution as an essential norm to be included into the Constitution. It is curious, considering the importance courts have been attaching to Ubuntu since 1996, that the term did not feature more prominently in the Constitutional Principles, the Certification judgments or the 1996 Constitution.

The term, as it appears in the 1993 Constitution, had specific relevance to the reconciliation and truth-telling process. Bishop Desmond Tutu, for example, relied on the spirit of Ubuntu to encourage forgiveness and reconciliation within the context of the Truth and Reconciliation Commission of South Africa. (Tutu 1999) Others, however, were critical of the use of Ubuntu in that context, as they saw it as a misuse of the term to justify a political process whereby the remnants of apartheid were dealt with in an unacceptable manner. The perceived success of the truth and reconciliation process was, according to critics, a 'false' Ubuntu. (Kamga 2018, 268) Kamga criticises the process of the Reconciliation Commission as 'a mere amnesty for the perpetrators of apartheid; it was not Ubuntu that insists on reparation'. (Kamga 2018, 629)

This criticism of the use of Ubuntu in the Truth and Reconciliation process illustrates the diverse interpretations of Ubuntu, as some assert it as a principle supportive of forgiving and restorative justice, while others argue that it inherently entails a demand for reparations.[15] While Ubuntu was therefore seen as a *grundnorm* for truth and reconciliation, there are divergent views on whether the actual reconciliation process was indeed reflective of Ubuntu, thus encapsulating the different meanings and values attached to the term.

As mentioned above, the 1996 Constitution contains no reference to Ubuntu. The Certification judgments (Chapter 3) made no reference to Ubuntu as a core value of the new democracy and there is no mention in the records of the Constitutional Assembly or submissions to the Constitutional Court that Ubuntu was intended to be used and relied on as a fundamental norm of the new constitutional dispensation, a tool for interpretation or a source of rights. It

[15] The interface between restorative justice and Ubuntu reflects the emphasis in indigenous courts of reconciliation and restoring social harmony. In this way social tensions are diffused and the 'prevailing community moral code is applied and upheld'. (Van Schalkwyk 2006, 69) Note, however, the caution expressed by Polavarapu, who says that it is 'unclear exactly how much of modern restorative justice practice can be found in historical, indigenous approaches around the world'. (Polavarapu 2023, 952)

remains a mystery why a term that underlies the application of the Constitution and is now said to be such a core principle of African thought and philosophy was completely ignored during the process of drafting the Constitution, particularly after it had appeared in the 1993 interim constitution.[16] Kamga contends that, in retrospect, it was an error not to have included Ubuntu in the Constitution. (Kamga 2018, 635)

The Constitution, however, provides that courts may, where appropriate, apply customary law to resolve disputes, thereby offering a legal avenue for using Ubuntu. This again raises the question why the term was not included as an integral part of the drafting process and why the highest court has not given an explanation why Ubuntu remains a foundational term regardless of it not appearing in the Constitution. (Constitution of South Africa 1996, s 211(3))[17]

Radebe and Phooko offer the following explanation about the reliance on Ubuntu under the Constitution:

> It can therefore be said that since the courts, especially the Constitutional Court, have recognised ubuntu as a constitutional value, the courts are taking heed of sections 39(3) and 211(3) of the Constitution, thereby giving life to the challenge in both sections 39(3) and 211(3), that firstly, the ***constitutional values*** expressly mentioned in the Constitution are not a closed list, second, that the courts are willing to apply ***components of African customary law***, such as ubuntu, so long as these are consonant with the Constitution. (emphasis added) (Radebe and Phooko 2017, 246)

Although Ubuntu is not a legal term that bestows specific rights or duties in customary law, one could argue that it underlies customary law as a fundamental norm and moral code. While not an explicit term in customary law, the courts have nevertheless accepted that Ubuntu is so linked to customary law that it does indeed constitute an implied legal norm underlying customary law. (Dalisile case 2018) The courts have therefore shown great awareness of customary-law principles and enabled some fusion between these principles, common-law

[16] Cornell and Mavangua speak of the 'revival' of Ubuntu: 'uBuntu has seen a revival in constitutional jurisprudence in the last several years. As will be confirmed, ubuntu never lapsed as an important value and ideal in the Magistrate Courts and even the Supreme Courts of South Africa.' (Cornell and Mavangua 2012, 1)

[17] Section 211 provides as follows: '(1) The institution, status and role of traditional leadership, according to customary law, are recognised, subject to the Constitution. (2) A traditional authority that observes a system of customary law may function subject to any applicable legislation and customs, which includes amendments to, or repeal of, that legislation or those customs. (3) The courts must apply customary law when that law is applicable, subject to the Constitution and any legislation that specifically deals with customary law.'

principles and constitutional obligations. (Ntlama 2019) A non-state customary-law principle has thereby become sanctioned for general application by the state through its judicial system. Ubuntu has effectively been elevated to state law status for application throughout the entire country, serving as a source of rights, a tool for interpretation and a means of organically growing common law. (Chapter 2)

The Constitutional Court in its first judgment (handed down pursuant to the 1993 Constitution in which the term 'Ubuntu' appeared) elevated Ubuntu from a customary concept to a legal term. (Makwanyane case 1995) This was to some extent surprising since, as pointed out above, the word 'Ubuntu' played no significant role in the 1993 constitution-drafting process or in the customary-law hearings prior to the enactment of the 1993 Constitution, and the term appeared in the 1993 Constitution only in the context of the Truth and Reconciliation process.

This use of Ubuntu resonates with the way the Constitutional Court of Germany incorporated *Bundestreue* into the constitutional lexicon of the new federal democracy after the Second World War. In the first judgment of the Constitutional Court of Germany in which *Bundestreue* was referred to, the word was simply applied by the court with no explanation why it was sought to be relied upon, what the origin and meaning of the word was, or why it had been elevated to a constitutional principle. The word was also absent during the debates leading to the drafting of the Basic Law of Germany, suggesting it had not been considered such a core principle of intergovernmental relations at the time of drafting as it was later made out to be. (De Villiers 2022c, 180) The Constitutional Court of Germany simply used and applied *Bundestreue* without any in-depth analysis or justification. Over the years legal and social scientists have attempted to dissect *Bundestreue* and give further content to it. Nonetheless, during this time the courts have consistently applied the term without providing an in-depth analysis of its origin or rationale. (Bauer 1992; Egli 2010; De Villiers 1994a; De Villiers 2019) The debate in Germany continues whether *Bundestreue* is to be approached as a source of rights or as a tool of interpretation. The same discourse applies to the use of Ubuntu.

The Constitutional Court of South Africa, more than any other court in southern Africa, has elevated Ubuntu to a legal term to legitimise the 1996 Constitution and the judgments arising from it. The Constitutional Court has, since its first judgment, also declared a link between international human rights concepts and the application of Ubuntu to the African continent. (Keevy 2009b, 20) In this sense Ubuntu may be a valuable reference point to 'deepen our disposition for compassion and caring'. At the same time it is essential to note that the values and virtues of sharing and caring are not unique to Ubuntu. (Nkondo 2007, 95) Although a definition of Ubuntu is not possible, the Constitutional Court has determined that the values it represents may inform the context within which constitutional norms are applied and disputes are resolved. (Mokgoro 1998; Cornell and Mavangua 2012)

It is especially regarding South Africa's Constitution, which has been described as not merely a black letter text but rather a breathing document with a soul that seeks to transform society (Gargarella, Domingo, and Roux 2006), that Ubuntu has provided a practical and philosophical basis to interpret the Constitution, enrich common law and transform society. (Klare 1998) It has been asserted that judges under the Constitution play a role akin to 'social engineers and social and legal philosophers' to promote the values enshrined in the Constitution. (Baloro case 1995, para 235) Although, strictly speaking, Ubuntu is not a legal norm in African customary law, the term nonetheless shapes the context within which customary law and human and community interaction are to be understood. (Himonga, Taylor, and Pope 2013) The value set represented by Ubuntu is therefore so inherently intertwined with customary law that, although not a legal term, Ubuntu forms a basis from which to derive meaning and content of rights in legal disputes. (Kamga 2018)

Since its first judgment the Constitutional Court has declared its role to pronounce justice and develop the Constitution through a value-oriented and purposive approach. This allows for the reliance on extratextual aids, such as Ubuntu in its customary-law context, to give meaning and effect to the provisions of the Constitution. (Makwanyane case 1995, paras 9–95) In doing so the court, in various contexts, has sought to promote the values enshrined in the Constitution. This includes encouraging an open and democratic society, protecting human dignity, advancing equality and freedom, safeguarding social and economic rights, and striving towards social justice. (Constitution of South Africa 1996, s 39) Langa J said the following about Ubuntu in the Makwanyane case:

> The concept [Ubuntu] is of some relevance to the values we need to uphold. It is a culture which places some emphasis on communality and on the interdependence of the members of a community. It recognises a person's status as a human being, entitled to unconditional respect, dignity, value and acceptance from the members of the community such person happens to be part of. It also entails the converse, however. The person has a corresponding duty to give the same respect, dignity, value and acceptance to each member of that community. More importantly, it regulates the exercise of rights by the emphasis it lays on sharing and co-responsibility and the mutual enjoyment of rights by all. (Makwanyane case 1995, para 224)

It is useful to note that the court has drawn a link between the constitutional values of equality, fairness and reasonableness and the customary principles inherent in Ubuntu. The courts seek to integrate these values and Ubuntu into its wider jurisprudence, rather than restricting the application of Ubuntu to customary-law disputes. Ubuntu serves therefore as a proverbial umbilical cord, linking customary with contemporary law as well as international law with constitutional law.

Keevy raises concerns about the purported synergy between Ubuntu and international human rights values, noting that the connection is weak and raises 'serious questions'. This is because the term may not inherently reflect or represent the values of the Constitution, considering the societal and structural inequalities in African law from which Ubuntu originates. (Keevy 2009b, 21) To support this proposition, Keevy points, for example, to the subservient status of women in customary law. He argues that the purported linkage of Ubuntu to international human rights norms, such as the ICCPR, is ill-founded.[18] As discussed below, the Constitutional Court has led the way to address inconsistencies between the Constitution and discrimination in customary law while at the same time retaining the inherent values represented by Ubuntu, but the sovereignty of the Constitution may over time render many customary laws invalid. (Chapter 10)

The reliance by courts on Ubuntu has faced criticism about the soundness of its legal basis. Scholarly perspectives on Ubuntu vary. Some view Ubuntu as an extratextual aid, justifiable only within the rules of statutory interpretation, whereas others see it as integral to customary law and inherently part of the South African legal system. There are others who argue that Ubuntu has evolved into part of the common law supporting the Constitution, requiring no specific justification for its use or application.

The debate is ongoing, particularly because of the discretionary and selective use of Ubuntu. Cockrell, for instance, criticises the reliance on Ubuntu and its purported linkage to African law as not having been subjected to 'a rigorous jurisprudence of substantive reasoning'. (Cockrell 1996, 11) Keevy is also

[18] Keevy's criticism about the use of Ubuntu as a purported inter-community constitutional norm is reflected in the following conclusion: 'Deconstruction of the Constitutional Court's definitions of Ubuntu has revealed the following: The court's translation of ubuntu as "humanness" is meaningless and does not convey the meaning or essence of the philosophy of ubuntu. There is no European word which describes the ancient collective African worldview. The court's definition of ubuntu as a "moral philosophy" is misleading as ubuntu is at best a form of religion.' (Keevy 2009a, 84)

concerned that Ubuntu is so inherently part of African customs and tradition that the concept cannot simply be transformed into a democratic, constitutional norm. (Keevy 2009a, 63)

The approach adopted by the Constitutional Court is essentially that although Ubuntu is originally part of customary law, it can also be applied and used as a source of law regarding non-customary disputes without having to resort to the rules of statutory interpretation.

This prompts the question whether a court is obligated to consider Ubuntu in every case, only when it appears relevant, or when it is significant to the subject of a pleading by one of the parties. Or is the relevance of or reliance on Ubuntu at the sole discretion of the presiding judge? Furthermore, can all judges equally cite Ubuntu or are judges with a racially African background more capable of applying Ubuntu based on their judicial notice and cultural knowledge? An overview of judgments suggests that judges are not necessarily consistent when referring to Ubuntu. It appears that the reliance on Ubuntu is highly discretionary and selective for any of the three usages discussed below in this chapter.[19]

Kroeze cautions that Ubuntu is being used so widely that the 'problem with this kind of "bloated" concept is that it tries to do too much. The concept simply collapses under the weight of expectations!' (Kroeze 2002, 260) There is also criticism that the 'courts have applied the legal concept of ubuntu uncritically, without reference to African sources to illustrate its meaning in different contexts, and without questioning its compatibility with the Bill of Rights'. (Himonga, Taylor, and Pope 2013, 424)

The first judgment of the Constitutional Court under the new democratic dispensation was to abolish capital punishment. (Makwanyane case 1995) In the judgment extensive reference was made to Ubuntu and the values represented by the term.[20] Madala J spoke about Ubuntu as a term that 'permeates' the

---

[19] There may be many reasons why the approaches of judges to the application of Ubuntu to develop common law differ. For example, the fact that not all judges share the same cultural background raises the question whether some judges are better placed to cite and rely on Ubuntu than other judges because of their ethnic origin. As Mlambo observes, a 'constraint is probably the diverse backgrounds from which current members of the bench are drawn'. (Mlambo 2022, 599) Manthwa also suggests that the reliance on Ubuntu by a justice familiar with the meaning thereof may give rise to different outcomes than in the case of someone who is not versed in Ubuntu. (Manthwa 2023, 665)

[20] As explained above, it is important to note that the Makwanyane judgment was handed down pursuant to the interim constitution of 1993, in which mention was made of Ubuntu in the

Constitution. (Makwanyane case 1995, para 237) Mokgoro J referred to Ubuntu as an instrument by which the Constitution should be interpreted, as it represents the underlying values of South African society. Mokgoro J made the following observations: 'Although South Africans have a history of deep divisions characterised by strife and conflict, one shared value and ideal that runs like a golden thread across cultural lines is the value of ubuntu – a notion now coming to be generally articulated in this country.' (Makwanyane case 1995, para 306) Mohamed J also spoke about the meaning of Ubuntu, describing it as follows:

> [T]he ethos of an instinctive capacity for and enjoyment of love towards our fellow men and women; the joy and the fulfilment involved in recognizing their innate humanity; the reciprocity this generates in interaction within the collective community; the richness of the creative emotions which it engenders and the moral energies which it releases both in the givers and the society which they serve and are served by. (Makwanyane case 1995, para 262)

Chaskalson P referred to the postamble and spoke about Ubuntu not justifying an 'eye for an eye'. (Makwanyane case 1995, para 131) He emphasised that Ubuntu requires criminals to be dealt with humanely in a manner that accords with the values underlying the concept. Madala J echoed this sentiment in his emphasis on the rehabilitation of criminals. (Makwanyane case 1995, para 242) Sachs J noted the importance of giving recognition to 'African law and legal thinking as a source of legal ideas, values and practice', thereby acknowledging Ubuntu as an implied constitutional principle. (Makwanyane case 1995, para 365) Finally, Mokgoro J likened the respect for dignity, as found in Ubuntu, to the principles of human respect and dignity found in the International Covenant on Civil and Political Rights. (Makwanyane case 1995, para 308)

According to the reasoning of the Constitutional Court, Ubuntu finds its origin in African customary law, yet the values it represents also possess a national and universal character. Kamga describes the utility of Ubuntu to the courts as follows: 'In its quest for social harmony, it becomes flexible and provides the necessary space needed by judges to reach their objective of ensuring that their judgment is responsive to a specific context at a particular time.' (Kamga 2018, 647)

The rationales of the respective justices in the Makwanyane case highlight three aspects of Ubuntu that are important for the purposes of this chapter: first, Ubuntu is seen as an underlying implied value in the Constitution that

---

postamble. Following this, the 1996 Constitution was enacted, in which no mention is made of Ubuntu albeit that courts continued to cite and develop the term.

originates from customary law, upon which the new constitutional and social order is based; secondly, the term eludes definition and it is therefore capable of being applied to different circumstances in all facets of criminal, civil and public policy[21] as an evolving term; and, thirdly, justices play a transformative role to interpret the Constitution within the context of a specific environment for the betterment of society, and Ubuntu may be a source of law from which to draw values and interpretation.

6.4 THE LEGAL FACES OF UBUNTU

This section reflects on the use of Ubuntu in three different contexts: first, as a *source* of rights; secondly, as an instrument of *interpretation*; and, thirdly, as an *aide-memoire* for judges to explain their reasoning to laypeople. These categories are not mutually exclusive, with several judgments falling within each of the categories. Notably, however, Ubuntu is often used without any in-depth exploration of its meaning or applicability to a particular factual matrix, and without expert or other evidence to justify its application to a specific dispute or the reason why it is not applicable. In the cases where Ubuntu has been cited it appears as if the judges:

- relied on their own understanding of what the term means
- without explaining why it is applicable in a particular circumstance
- with a lack of clarity when and why Ubuntu is cited
- with no justification or explanation why Ubuntu is not applicable to a specific dispute.[22]

[21] Caution should be employed when viewing public policy through the prism of Ubuntu, as Ubuntu is multifaceted and different persons may come to different conclusions when relying on the same term. As has been observed: 'Public policy is now informed by constitutional values and there are usually several ways to adjust an existing common-law rule or doctrine to satisfy the Constitution. However, although such different ways to develop the common law might be consistent with s 39(2), not all of them would necessarily be equally beneficial for the common law. Similarly, the "different ways" may not advance the objects of s 39(2) equally. It is a constitutionally ordained task of the courts to choose a developmental pathway that best advances the values of the Constitution in a manner that is less disruptive to the common-law fabric.' (Moleya 2023, 184)

[22] As discussed in Chapter 5, by way of example in the 2011 Kill the Boer case the court cited Ubuntu as rationale why the chant is no longer suitable and is regarded as hate speech, while in 2022 the court found, without any reference to Ubuntu, that the chant does not constitute hate

As shown in this section, Ubuntu, which has its origin in non-state customary law, has in effect been elevated to state law to modernise common law. In this capacity it is applied to a wide variety of disputes. Mlambo, for example, refers to principles of fairness, reasonableness, and justice and says that Ubuntu 'encompasses these values' and should inform public policy. (Mlambo 2022, 600) Justices of various courts have relied on and applied Ubuntu in divergent contexts, although principally to interpret rights and duties as well as to balance competing interests. In doing so these justices have imbued their judgments with a strong African identity, using Ubuntu not only to legitimise the Constitution but also to justify its application to a specific dispute within the context of fairness, transformation and equity. It must be emphasised that the justices in their use of Ubuntu do not necessarily distinguish between the suggested categories I use in this section. I have categorised these aspects merely to underscore the varied applications of the term 'Ubuntu' in different contexts, highlighting its flexibility in contributing to the development of South African law and explaining complex judgments to laypersons.

6.4.1 Ubuntu as a source of rights

Although not defined as a legal term, Ubuntu has been utilised as a source of rights that can be employed to resolve disputes, extending beyond fundamental rights to encompass civil and commercial litigation, as well as into public policy.

In the Makwanyane case, in which the Constitutional Court abolished the death penalty, Chaskalson P referred to Ubuntu as the basis of the right to life. In accordance with this, society does not kill perpetrators 'simply to get even with them', but to punish in accordance with the principles of humaneness that underlie Ubuntu. (Makwanyane case 1995, para 131) Langa J explained that violence and the taking of a life destroy Ubuntu and the court is called upon to restore the equilibrium that has been upset by murder. (Makwanyane case 1995, para 227) The right to life is fundamental to Ubuntu and hence the death penalty cannot be sustained. Madala J said that Ubuntu 'permeates the Constitution generally' and the Bill of Rights in particular. Ubuntu 'carries in it the ideas of humaneness, social justice, and fairness,' placing supreme emphasis on the life of a person. (Makwanyane case 1995, para 244) Ubuntu is a basis for maintaining law and order, but not for 'dehumanising and degrading the individual'.

speech. There was no explanation by the court in 2022 why Ubuntu was not applicable or why the court erred in 2011 when it cited Ubuntu.

(Makwanyane case 1995, para 250) Mokgoro J said that 'the concepts of life and dignity are two sides of the same coin. The concept of Ubuntu embodies both of them.' (Makwanyane case 1995, para 310) Sachs J observed that in traditional African law and custom the death penalty was not generally imposed for murder. (Makwanyane case 1995, para 381) According to Sachs, 'everyone, including the most abominable of human beings, has the right to life, and capital punishment is therefore unconstitutional'. (Makwanyane case 1995, para 392) Sachs J observed the importance of giving recognition to 'African law and legal thinking as a source of legal ideas, values and practice' and thereby acknowledged Ubuntu as an implied constitutional principle. (Makwanyane case 1995, para 365)[23]

In the Hoffmann case the question arose before the Constitutional Court whether it was reasonable to refuse a person a certain operational deployment on the basis that the person is an HIV/Aids sufferer. Ngcobo J cautioned against prejudice and the stereotyping of persons living with the illness. He emphasised that people with Aids must be treated compassionately and that 'we must show ubuntu towards them'. (Hoffmann case 2001) The court declared that HIV sufferers 'must not be condemned to "economic death" by the denial of equal opportunity in employment' and that research has shown that not all sufferers pose a risk to those with whom they come into contact. (Hoffmann case 2001, para 39)

This prompts the question of whether this interpretation of the Constitution required reliance on Ubuntu or if a similar outcome could have been reached by way of the reasonable and proportional application of rights to equality and non-discrimination. In this respect it is evident how Ubuntu is used not only as a source of rights, but also as an instrument for interpretation, as well as a mechanism for explaining the merit of complex issues to the public by reliance on a customary concept that is well known to them.

In the MEC for Education case the court relied on Ubuntu as a source of rights in responding to the rights of immigrants and foreigners. (MEC for Education

[23] Elevating Ubuntu to a constitutional value and a source for interpreting the Constitution has not been without criticism. Keevy, for example, is critical of the reference by Sachs to African values as if those values can automatically be presumed to embody the same principles espoused by the Constitution and international law. (Keevy 2009b, 25) Keevy refers to several examples where African laws and traditions purportedly represented in the term Ubuntu *do not* reflect the values of equality and freedom enshrined in the Constitution. (Keevy 2009, 34–51). Keevy criticises the 'utopian' meaning that has been accorded to Ubuntu and says that in law and fact Ubuntu 'represents an oppressive reality' towards women and other marginalised persons. (Keevy 2009, 41).

case 2007) The common element arising from Ubuntu, as described by Chief Justice Langa, was the importance that people exist and coexist. He added that in essence 'a person is a person through other people'. (MEC for Education case 2007, para 53) In this respect Ubuntu focuses on the dignity of other persons and a respect therefor. This sentiment was also echoed in the Union of Refugee Women case, in which the court acknowledged that the right of refugees to take up employment in South Africa was consistent with the hospitality and acceptance displayed towards foreigners within African custom. (Union of Refugee Women case 2007, para 145) It was emphasised that African tradition involves accommodating foreigners and caring for them, and that the courts may refer to those inherent Ubuntu values to ascertain the reasonableness of policy measures.

Sachs J, in the Port Elizabeth Municipality 2005 case, cited Ubuntu to explain the notion of restorative justice. Sachs J described Ubuntu as the 'underlying motif' of the Bill of Rights. (Port Elizabeth Municipality case 2005, para 37)[24] In the Dikoko case the court defined restorative justice with reference to the values that underpin Ubuntu as

[24] In the Port Elizabeth Municipality case the court had to consider the lawfulness of an eviction notice that impacted on many persons occupying a building. The court reasoned that persons are not isolated from one another and their rights require a balance within the context of community and humanity. Evicting people who unlawfully occupy a building may be consistent with a strict application of a contractual provision, but the values of Ubuntu require that account must also be taken of the interests of those persons and where they would be accommodated once evicted. Sachs J explained that the 'spirit of ubuntu, part of the deep cultural heritage of the majority of the population, suffuses the whole constitutional order. *It combines individual rights with a communitarian philosophy.* It is a unifying motif of the Bill of Rights, which is nothing if not a structured, institutionalised and operational declaration in our evolving new society of the need for human interdependence, respect and concern.' (emphasis added) (Port Elizabeth Municipality case 2005, para 37) The use of Ubuntu in this context can be equated to what in other foreign jurisdictions may be principles of proportionality or reasonableness. Note, however, the inconsistency in application of Ubuntu: in the Stay case, in which the court evicted students from a hostel, *no mention* was made or consideration given to Ubuntu. (Stay case 2023) The same applies to the Paradise Park case, in which the applicants unsuccessfully sought to be protected against an eviction order. No mention is made in the judgment of Ubuntu, its relevance or lack of relevance to the proceeding. (Paradise Park case 2023) In the Charnell Commando case the court highlighted that the reliance on Ubuntu enabled South Africa to develop a 'home-grown approach to socio-economic rights' and the 'deliberate dislocation of individuals and families' requires a 'strong burden of justification' to be sustained. (Charnell Commando case 2024, para 174) This again raises the question – who decides when Ubuntu is relied on as a source of rights in a particular dispute, and what weight is given to it? Equally important, if Ubuntu is not cited, should an explanation be given why it is not relied on?

> an approach to justice that aims to involve the child offender, the victim, the families concerned and community members to collectively identify and address harms, needs and obligations through accepting responsibility, making restitution, taking measures to prevent a recurrence of the incident and promoting reconciliation. (Dikoko case 2006, paras 114–15)

The link between restorative justice and Ubuntu was echoed in the Van Vuren case, in which Ubuntu was described as a 'foundational norm' of the Constitution. (Van Vuren case 2012, para 37)

In the Bhe case the prevalence of male primogeniture rule under customary law was declared unconstitutional, with the court explaining that the customary-law aspects of the South African community had long been neglected. (Chapter 10)[25] Nonetheless, the court referred to several aspects of customary law that have retained their relevance, such as consensus-seeking, respect for families and constructive communication. In this context the court referred to 'healthy communitarian traditions such as ubuntu', although the court did not rely on Ubuntu for the purposes of statutory interpretation in this case. (Bhe case 2005, para 45)

In the Centre for Child Law case it was emphasised that the principle of restorative justice, as it finds expression in Ubuntu, is of particular importance when the rights of children are affected by the criminal justice system. (Centre for Child Law case 2019, para 76) The court stated the following about the fundamental rights embedded in Ubuntu and restorative justice:

> When it comes to a child in the criminal justice system, a restorative justice approach is optimal for all three classes. However, a restorative justice approach is of particular importance when considering a child in conflict with the law. In this sense, a key justification for ongoing protection is to give effect to restorative justice. (Centre for Child Law case 2019, para 76)

Metz highlights how the internationally accepted concept of restorative justice has been given a domestic content in South Africa through the court's reliance on Ubuntu and the values it represents. (Metz 2019) This application of Ubuntu

[25] In customary law of succession the principle of primogeniture applies, meaning only a male who is related to the deceased estate qualifies as an intestate heir. Widows therefore do not qualify intestate to benefit from the estate of their husband. Malepe and Odeku are of the view that 'women and girls now have the right to inherit properties, and the jurisprudence of the South African courts has affirmed equal recognition for both male and female primogeniture'. (Malepe and Odeku 2023)

as a source of law demonstrates how the customary values of the concept are being developed and adjusted to contemporary circumstances. While critics may be sceptic about this dynamic use of Ubuntu, it is important to note that traditional fundamental rights, for example the right to life, have also undergone adjustments with the effect that freedoms, as defined today, differ to the way they, along with rights, were defined a century ago.

In the Occupiers of Erven case the court once again addressed a question of eviction and emphasised, by referring to Ubuntu, that contractual relationships demand a 'more expansive enquiry than simply determining rights of occupation', since the court must ascertain if it is 'just and equitable' to evict. (Occupiers of Erven case 2017, para 65) The court observed that the availability of alternative housing was a relevant factor to consider when reviewing an eviction notice. (Occupiers of Erven case 2017, para 81) The question is whether it is 'just' to evict in the particular circumstances. (Occupiers of Erven case 2017, para 65)[26] In the Fujitsu case the court reiterated that ubuntu plays 'a fundamental role in the application and development of the rules of contract law'. (Fujitsu case 2023, para 77) In the Charnell Commando case the court highlighted that the reliance on Ubuntu enabled South Africa to develop a 'home-grown approach to socio-economic rights' and the 'deliberate dislocation of individuals and families' requires a 'strong burden of justification' to be sustained. (Charnell Commando case 2024, para 174)

The application of Ubuntu as a source of rights to resolve contractual disputes was further seen in the National Union of Metalworkers case, when the court referred to good faith negotiations pursuant to the principles that underlie Ubuntu within the context of contractual law in order to 'infuse good faith into unequal contractual relationships'. The court declared as follows:

> This court's development of good faith and Ubuntu in contractual relationships is intended to infuse good faith into unequal contractual relationships, or *more equality into hierarchical relationships* precisely where the hierarchy leads to the exertion of unfair power over the subordinated party.... If the Ubuntu analogy were appropriately applied here, it would be in relation not to the subordinated employee but to the employer. (emphasis added) (National Union of Metalworkers case 2019, para 65)

[26] The reference to the 'justness' of an eviction order does not only arise from Ubuntu. The concepts of justness and reasonableness are also found in foreign jurisdictions to guide a court on whether an eviction order should be issued.

In the Everfresh case the court held that 'in the *development of the common law*, it is highly desirable and, in fact, necessary to infuse the law of contract with constitutional values, including values of ubuntu which inspire much of our constitutional compact'. (emphasis added) (Everfresh case 2012, para 71) By referring to the development of common law the court acknowledged that, like Ubuntu, common law is not static and can adjust to reflect changing circumstances and new societal values.[27] In the Makate case the court also linked Ubuntu to 'good faith' negotiations in contractual disputes. (Makate case 2016, para 14) The court accepted that Ubuntu can be used to 'infuse' what is meant by good faith negotiations. The court did not elaborate on this reasoning, nor did it explain it, other than by simply referring to the term 'Ubuntu' and assigning to it an inherent meaning which relates to good faith negotiation. It appears as if the court relied on Ubuntu as a general source of fairness or equity in giving meaning to a dynamic relationship. In the Liberty Group case, however, it was found that Ubuntu could not be relied upon to grant the relief sought in the contractual dispute in question. (Liberty Group case 2019, para 37) However, in the Azrapart case the court cautioned that Ubuntu could not be relied upon to infuse values into a contract that may invalidate the terms of the contract. (Azrapart case 2024, para 19)

In the 2011 Kill the Boer case the question arose as to whether a pre-democracy liberation chant 'Kill the Boer, Kill the Farmer' constituted hate speech within the context of a democratic South Africa. The case also addressed whether limits could be imposed on freedom of expression to protect individuals against hate speech. (Chapter 5) The court found that the chant may have had merit previously during the liberation struggle, but that those circumstances no longer apply under the new constitutional dispensation since 'the enemy has become the friend, the brother. . . . It must never be forgotten that in the *spirit of ubuntu* this new approach to each other must be fostered.' (emphasis added) (Kill the Boer case 2011, para 108) The use of such speech to call for the killing of farmers was therefore deemed inconsistent with the spirit of Ubuntu. The declaration of the chant as constituting hate speech thus warranted the restriction of the constitutional right to freedom of expression. In the Kill the

[27] Note, for example, how in the Mabo judgment in Australia it was declared in 1992 that native title is recognised by common law, thereby overturning more than a century of theory that Australia was regarded at common law as *terra nullius* at the time of settlement. (Mabo case (2) 1992) This highlights how common law is not static, but can adjust to new circumstances, legal developments, and policy initiatives.

Boer case of 2011 the court referred to Ubuntu as 'being an important *source of law* within the context of strained or broken relationships amongst individuals or communities, and as an aid for providing remedies which contribute towards more mutually acceptable remedies for the parties in such cases'. The court went on to summarise the main elements of Ubuntu as follows:

> Ubuntu is a concept which:
>
> 1. is to be contrasted with vengeance;
> 2. dictates that a high value be placed on the life of a human being;
> 3. is inextricably linked to the values of and which places a high premium on dignity, compassion, humaneness and respect for humanity of another;
> 4. dictates a shift from confrontation to mediation and conciliation;
> 5. dictates good attitudes and shared concern;
> 6. favours the re-establishment of harmony in the relationship between parties and that such harmony should restore the dignity of the plaintiff without ruining the defendant;
> 7. favours restorative rather than retributive justice;
> 8. operates in a direction favouring reconciliation rather than estrangement of disputants;
> 9. works towards sensitising a disputant or a defendant in litigation to the hurtful impact of his actions to the other party and towards changing such conduct rather than merely punishing the disputant;
> 10. promotes mutual understanding rather than punishment;
> 11. favours face-to-face encounters of disputants with a view to facilitating differences being resolved rather than conflict and victory for the most powerful;
> 12. favours civility and civilised dialogue premised on mutual tolerance. (Kill the Boer case 2011, para 18)

The potential discretionary and inconsistent manner of applying Ubuntu is, however, highlighted by the subsequent 2022 Kill the Boer case in which, based on similar facts and dealing with the same chant, it was found – *without* reference to Ubuntu – that the chant *does not* constitute hate speech. (Chapter 5; Kill the Boer case 2022) In the 2022 case the court did not cite Ubuntu or explain why it did not apply. Radebe and Phooko express the view that the reliance of the court in 2011 on Ubuntu to restrict the chant was based on an 'erroneous understanding' of the term. (Radebe and Phooko 2017, 247)

The differing approaches adopted by the two courts regarding this controversial chant underline the challenges involved in relying on Ubuntu as a source of rights that underpins the Constitution. This is because it is not clear *when* Ubuntu should be relied upon as a source of rights, *what evidence* is required to sustain a particular meaning being attributed to Ubuntu, and *what weight* is to be given to a right or value that is said to arise from Ubuntu.

There seems to be a risk that a judge may use, even abuse, or ignore Ubuntu to justify or give credibility to a particular outcome. The following was observed by Davis and Le Roux concerning the relevance of the backgrounds of the judges in the Makwanyane case. The same may apply to the two Kill the Boer judgments:

> The judgment was influenced by the personal and cultural backgrounds and experiences of the judges, by acceptance of traditionally African concepts, such as Ubuntu, and by the court's recognition that this judgment would describe and set the course for the new South African constitutional democracy. (Davis and Le Roux 2019, 189)

Does this imply that some judges may cite Ubuntu with greater credibility because of their cultural or racial background, albeit that Ubuntu arguably does not fall within the scope of judicial notice? And, if not, how would a judge who does not share the customary values of Ubuntu apply the term without some form of expert evidence to show that it can be applied to a specific case?

In the Reddell case, which aimed to determine whether the constitutional right to dignity is reserved for natural persons or extends to juristic persons, the court observed that Ubuntu is a 'core foundation of the constitutional right to dignity'. (Reddell case 2022, para 58) It was held that, while the reputation of a corporation can be protected under law, a corporation does not have 'dignity' as understood with reference to natural persons. (Reddell case 2022, para 150)

In the Centre for Child Law and Home Affairs case the court declared that s 10 of the Births and Deaths Registration Act 51 of 1992 was unconstitutional because it discriminated against the father of a child born out of wedlock by denying him access to the child. With reference to Ubuntu, the court stated as follows:

> The application of the right to dignity embraces and stands alongside the value of ubuntu. A basic application of the principle of ubuntu shows that, in the operation of section 10, the unmarried father and his child are not only deprived of their dignity, but also of ubuntu. Undoubtedly, section 10 is an injury to an unmarried father's dignity, and perpetuates the societal stigma attached to unmarried couples and their children. It deems his bond with his child as less worthy, merely on account of his marital status. Furthermore, in doing so, it demeans this particular class of individuals (unmarried fathers and their children). For all these reasons, the impugned provision is clearly inconsistent with our fundamental constitutional right to human dignity, and the value of ubuntu which that right embraces. (Centre for Child Law and Home Affairs case 2022, para 67)

In the Damons case Pillay AJ observed the 'evolution' of Ubuntu since 1993 and emphasised that it should be applied with 'vigour' to prevent unfair discrimination and welfarist responses to people with disabilities. (Damons case 2022, para 85) Ubuntu must therefore be added to the 'raft of employment equity and disability laws'. (Damons case 2022, para 84)[28]

The cases cited above illustrate how the courts view Ubuntu as a source of rights that permeates society in general and the Constitution in particular. However, it is also noticeable that the courts rarely explain in detail how they arrive at the conclusion that an element of Ubuntu applies to a specific set of facts, instead resorting to general statements. There is often a lack of clarity regarding the evidence considered by the court to reach a conclusion that Ubuntu applies, whether the judge relied on personal knowledge and understanding of Ubuntu, and when and why Ubuntu were to be applied or not applied.

The highly discretionary manner in which Ubuntu is applied, coupled with the lack of a clear definition for it, highlights the risk associated with a term which has a primarily non-legal customary meaning being used as a legal term and a source of rights in a non-cultural context.[29]

Overall an argument can be made that each of the judgments touched on could have been rationalised without reference to Ubuntu by relying instead on established legal principles such as proportionality, equity, fairness and reasonableness. In response to this criticism it can be argued that the value system within Ubuntu provided a basis for these judgments, reflecting South African customary law and contemporary values; the meaning given to Ubuntu is consistent with the principles of equity, fairness and proportionality in foreign and international law; moreover, it is to be welcomed that a non-state law

[28] See the criticism by Laubscher of the majority judgment, in which she stated that the majority relied too much on the 'letter of the law' and did not adequately reflect on the 'indigenous value of ubuntu' as a rationale to find the policy, or absence of a policy, discriminatory. (Laubscher 2023, 318)

[29] Note, for example, how in the Everfresh case, the court sought guidance in Ubuntu to resolve a dispute concerning eviction. (Everfresh case 2012) This contrasts with the Stay case, in which the court evicted students from a hostel with *no mention* or consideration of Ubuntu. (Stay case 2023) The same applies to the Paradise Park case in which the applicants unsuccessfully sought to be protected against an eviction order. No mention is made in the judgment of Ubuntu, its relevance or lack of relevance to the proceeding. (Paradise Park case 2023) This again raises the questions – who decides when Ubuntu is relied on as a source of rights in a particular dispute, what weight is given to it, or why Ubuntu is not relevant?

customary concept can form the basis of a homegrown jurisprudence based on values that South Africans can relate to.[30]

6.4.2 Ubuntu as a tool for statutory interpretation

There has been some debate in the literature whether Ubuntu is best utilised as a source of rights or as a tool for statutory interpretation.[31] The courts have not been drawn into this discourse. Reference to Ubuntu in judgments must generally be assessed within the context that it is used, without the judges explaining whether it is a term of law, an instrument for interpretation or an aide-memoire to explain certain complex judgments – or all of the foregoing. As discussed above, even in those instances where Ubuntu is cited as a 'source' of law courts have not unpacked the term with sufficient clarity about the detail of the rights it is said to espouse. On analysis it appears that judgments predominantly use Ubuntu as a tool to *interpret* constitutional and statutory provisions and to determine the scope of laws and regulations.

Mokgoro J referred to the values underlying Ubuntu as essential for '*interpreting* the Bill of Fundamental Rights and Freedoms'. (emphasis added) (Makwanyane case 1995, para 306) She furthermore likened the respect for dignity as found in Ubuntu to the principles of human respect and dignity found in the International Covenant on Civil and Political Rights. (Makwanyane case 1995, para 308) The South African courts may therefore, pursuant to s 39 of the Constitution as previously discussed (Chapter 3 and 4), consider foreign judgments and international law to give practical meaning to Ubuntu. Just as the meaning of the word 'dignity' must be ascertained by the court according to the circumstances of a case, the meaning of Ubuntu is similarly not set in stone. Instead it is determined in the context of the set of facts giving rise to the dispute before the court.

The fact that 'dignity', like Ubuntu, is not a defined term poses a challenge. It is worth reiterating here the previously quoted words of Khanna J of the Supreme Court of India, who defined dignity in terms of its loss: 'Loss of dignity and self-worth of the targeted group members contributes to disharmony amongst groups, erodes tolerance and open-mindedness which are a must for a multi-

[30] Mokgoro spoke about the potential that 'ubuntu will enhance the legitimacy of jurisprudence'. (Mokgoro 2012, 336)

[31] As discussed above, this is similar to the discourse about the application of *Bundestreue* in Germany.

cultural society committed to the idea of equality. It affects an individual as a member of a group.' (Amish Devgan case 2020) The broad-brush reliance on dignity includes the use of several vague and non-legal terms. Critics of the Amish Devgan judgment understandably caution that relying on feelings of injury to the dignity of a person or disharmony in society may open the door to unjustified restrictions on fundamental rights. (Rao 2020, 25) The same risk may arise from the use of Ubuntu in a non-customary setting.

In the Investigating Directorate case it was emphasised that, since the Constitution of South Africa is regarded as 'transformative', with the objective of creating a new and just legal, political and socio-economic order, it should be interpreted in a manner that promotes those objectives. (Investigating Directorate case 2001, para 22) Although the court did not refer to Ubuntu in the judgment, the transformative purposes of the Constitution, as mandated by the Bill of Rights and infused by Ubuntu, were recognised. The Nkosi case emphasised that the interpretation given to the Constitution should take into account the unique circumstances of South Africa and seek to facilitate the transformation of the country into a fairer and more equitable society. (Nkosi case 2008)

In the Mhlungu case Sachs J explained that the Constitutional Court should not constrain itself with the 'inflexible rules' of constitutional interpretation.[32] The court should instead grant itself space to take into account the origins of the Constitution, its spirit and style, the inner logic it possesses, the place it occupies in the 'evolution of our country', and its existence 'as part of the global development of constitutionalism and human rights'. (Mhlungu case 1995, para 127) It is particularly in the protection of their fundamental rights that individuals may find that a strict application of legal text and traditional rules of interpretation may cause their rights to be diminished.[33] The court rejected a legalistic approach to statutory interpretation and declared that 'such a result would be inconsistent with the international culture of constitutional jurisprudence which has developed to give to constitutional interpretation a

[32] Sachs J did not, however, acknowledge that the rationale for the purported inflexibility of rules of statutory interpretation is grounded in the need for certainty, persistency and predictability to prevent or curtail unbridled judicial discretion. Without those rules judges would be able to come to contrary and highly discretionary findings on the admissibility and weight of evidence, something that undermines trust in the judicial system.

[33] This reasoning adopted by Sachs J is not dissimilar to the way in which the Supreme Court of India has approached the non-justiciable Directive Principles of State Policy, by utilising those objectives to give dynamic content to fundamental rights and even to restrict the scope of fundamental rights. (De Villiers 2023a, 123–7; De Villiers 1992)

purposive and generous focus'. (Mhlungu case 1995, para 8)[34] Ubuntu therefore opens the door to expand a purposive approach to interpretation within the context of the South African circumstances.

The courts have generally adopted a value-orientated and purposive approach to constitutional interpretation rather than a restrictive one. (Nyamakazi case 1992, para 39) In this context Ubuntu provides an implied reference point to give effect to fundamental rights as the values reflected by the term (if not the term itself) are widely shared across many communities in South Africa. Judges may, in order to fulfil the transformative obligations expected of the courts, rely on extratextual aids to assist in the interpretation of the Constitution and the discharge of their functions for the betterment of South Africa. (Netshitomboni 1998, 1) It is accepted that judges are not only declarers of law but also agents of transformation and therefore they may use Ubuntu as an interpretive and contextual tool to resolve disputes to achieve transformative objectives.[35]

It is, however, within their context as agents of transformation that members of the judiciary have in recent times come under pressure and criticism for not being active enough to effect transformation in South Africa. Courts have been criticised for adopting a narrow approach to statutory interpretation in which they give effect to the letter of the law and thereby protect vested interests. Critics say the transformative role of the courts has fallen by the wayside. Aziz talks of a 'juristocracy' that impedes the socio-economic development of the poor masses. (Aziz 2023)[36] On the other hand, in fairness to the judiciary it must

---

[34] It is worth noting that many courts, including those in common-law jurisdictions, function within the context of the 'principle of legality', which implies that legislation is interpreted in a manner that does not abrogate fundamental rights and freedoms unless the legislation contains clear words with that effect or if it is necessary by implication. (Coco case 1994) This principle arises from the effect of democratic representative government. In the Zheng case the High Court of Australia explained the principle as follows: '[J]udicial findings as to legislative intention are an expression of the constitutional relationship between the arms of government with respect to the making, interpretation and application of laws . . . the preferred construction by the court of the statute in question is reached by the application of rules of interpretation accepted by all arms of government in the system of representative democracy.' (Zheng case 2009, para 28)

[35] Note, for example, how in Germany the Constitutional Court has used the undefined term '*Bundestreue*' to develop basic principles of cooperative federalism. (De Villiers 2022c)

[36] Judge President of the Gauteng Division of the High Court Dunstan Mlambo summarised in 2023 the criticism against the courts as follows: 'Currently there are themes that seek to suggest that our Constitution has been a failure in that it has not resulted in better living conditions for the poor masses; *there are themes that suggest that judges and courts have become a juristocracy that impedes the socioeconomic development of the poor masses*; and there are yet other themes that suggest

be noted that the dogma behind the separation of powers is enshrined in the Constitution and there are limits to what courts can achieve in terms of day-to-day socio-economic issues that affect South Africa.

In the Mayelane case the Constitutional Court reiterated the value of Ubuntu as an interpretive tool. The court referred to the rich tradition and inheritance of customary law with its ability to adjust and reflect community values. The court described customary law as 'nurturing of healthy communitarian traditions like ubuntu', but without the concept being elevated to a constitutional principle or legal norm. (Mayelane case 2013, para 24)

In the City of Tshwane case, in which the changing of place names was challenged, the court declared, with reference to Ubuntu, that 'all *peace* and *reconciliation-loving* South Africans whose *world-view* is inspired by our constitutional vision must embrace the *African philosophy* of "Ubuntu."' (emphasis added) (City of Tshwane case 2016, para 11) The court accepted that, as part of the transformation of society, names of streets, towns and places would change to reflect the new circumstances of South Africa. This statement highlights, on the one hand, the extent to which Ubuntu has become common property in South Africa – to be applied to a wide range of disputes. On the other hand, it also demonstrates the risk that the meaning of Ubuntu has become so generalised that it no longer refers to its African roots but has instead become a repository within which many interpretations can be found. By accepting that name changes of streets had been conducted in a proper manner, the court made reference to a so-called 'ubuntu world-view' (City of Tshwane 2016, para 137) without much consideration of how such a world-view is judicially linked to the inherent meaning of Ubuntu. The reliance on a 'world-view' meaning of Ubuntu also raises the spectre of the term becoming imbued with an ideological imposition, where a one-dimensional and majoritarian world-view is assumed or, even worse, a particular view is imposed. The question also arises whether the endorsement of the new place names could not have been achieved by means other than by

---

that courts and judges, unelected as they are, have become too powerful and must be reined in and that South Africa could do better under a parliamentary supremacy framework. Propagating these themes are predominantly political party members, members of parliament, and members of the executive in the different spheres of government who openly decry the power of judges and courts. We should also factor the role of the media in all this. I cannot stand here and deny that there are fault lines on a number of fronts in this country, be it service delivery or worrying levels of corruption especially in state departments and state entities. . . . This must give us all cause to reflect on *why our constitutional project is failing.*' (emphasis added) (Mlambo 2022, 602)

referring to Ubuntu. Arguably, Ubuntu was not needed for the justification of the judgment, given that the constitutional responsibility for naming streets, towns and cities is a lawful power allocated to a sphere of government. Thus the decisions made by the relevant sphere of government should, pursuant to democratic principles, prevail.

Ubuntu was also used as an explanatory tool to convey the reasoning of the court in the Sigcau case. In this case the court highlighted the importance of customary law and reflected that a 'flexible and fluid approach to interpretation that is alive to the changing traditions of the particular people who practise the specific custom must be favoured over one that views customary law as fixed'. (Sigcau case 2018, para 73)

In the Beadica case the court reiterated the importance of considering the values underlying Ubuntu in the realm of public policy. The court declared that 'public policy takes into consideration the necessity to do simple justice between individuals and is informed by the concept of ubuntu'. (Beadica case 2020, para 201; Du Plessis 2022) The court referred to the 'constitutional value of Ubuntu' that provides a 'transformative basis in the adjudicative process' when deciding whether to set aside an unfair contractual term or unfair enforcement. (Beadica case 2020, para 206; Thompson 2020)

In a judgment where the lockdown arrangements arising from the COVID-19 pandemic were at issue, the court relied on the character of Ubuntu to uphold the restrictions. In the Mohamed case the court observed that 'having regard to the context in which the Lockdown Regulations have been imposed, it is important that the value and ideals of Ubuntu be considered'. (Mohammed case 2020, para 63) The court went on to say that 'in South Africa right now, every citizen is called upon to make sacrifices to their fundamental rights entrenched in the Constitution. They are called upon to do so in the name of "the greater good", the spirit of "ubuntu", and they are called upon to do so in ways that impact on their livelihoods, their way of life and their economic security and freedom. Every citizen of this country needs to play his/her part in stemming the tide of what can only be regarded as an insidious and relentless pandemic.' (Mohammed case 2020, para 75)[37]

[37] Note criticism by Singh and Tembo that the limitations imposed of fundamental rights were disproportionate and in some instances 'lacked rationality and proportionality'. (Singh and Tembo 2022, 166)

It is questionable, again, whether there was any need for the court to rely on Ubuntu to justify the above ruling, given that so many other countries had upheld COVID-type restrictions pursuant to established legal principles, such as public interest.[38] However, in this case Ubuntu arguably proved useful to interpret and explain the rationale behind the lockdowns in a manner that South Africans were able to understand. While the judgment could have stood without citing Ubuntu, there was no legal error since Ubuntu was used in an explanatory sense rather than as a distinct principle of law.

The relevance of Ubuntu as an instrument for interpretation should be evaluated against the background of the purposive approach to statutory interpretation and the objective for the Constitution to transform society. In the Economic Freedom Fighters case the court spoke about an 'ubuntu-inspired order' under the new Constitution. (Economic Freedom Fighters case 2020, para 4) Ubuntu therefore seemingly grants to courts the discretion to interpret rights and interests with a sense of equity, fairness, reasonability, humanity, community and responsibility, free from the constraints of traditional rules of statutory interpretation. In doing so a more comprehensive consideration can be given to the circumstances in which South Africa finds itself, taking into account its historical background, inequalities, plurality and need for transformation. Notably, however, while the rules of interpretation have developed over centuries to give certainty and predictability to the interpretation of statutes, using Ubuntu to facilitate greater flexibility in those aged interpretation rules may instead give rise to inconsistency and unchecked exercise of discretions, considering that the concept as a legal term is poorly defined and the discretionary powers under which it is exercised are broad.

6.4.3 Ubuntu as an aide-memoire

Perhaps the most consistent theme found in Ubuntu judgments is the utilisation of the term to elucidate the rationale adopted by a court in its reasoning. Ubuntu seems to be the go-to word used to summarise, in a nutshell, the reasoning or logic of the court, at times without providing a clear explanation why the term is pertinent or applicable to a specific dispute. It is a term, despite being undefined, to which ordinary persons can relate. The value system that underlies Ubuntu speaks to the general community in a similar way in which terms such as equity, fairness, proportionality, dignity and reasonability may be used in

[38] Note, for example, the Falconer case in Australia, where the obligation for police officers to be immunised against COVID-19 was upheld. (Falconer case 2024)

foreign jurisdictions to explain complex judgments. However, there is also a presumption embedded in the use of Ubuntu that all persons have a similar or consistent understanding of it – which is not necessarily the case. Ubuntu is at times employed as a kind of band-aid, serving the purpose of healing by way of explanation, yet without a substantive exploration of its suitability. In some respects the ownership of Ubuntu has shifted, from custodianship in customary law to the judges of courts, where an interpretation has been given to it within and outside the realm of customary law.[39]

While Ubuntu has been likened to the common-law version of equity, (Bennett 2011) it is important to note that, in English law, equity in a legal sense, rather than in a popular use of the word, has a relatively restricted application within the common-law framework. Equity only intervenes when no other common-law remedies are available and it is confined to specific types of disputes, such as wills and matters of family law. (Bryan and Vann 2012) The likening of Ubuntu to equity is therefore more in a social context of fairness than to the legal application of equity. Kamga views Ubuntu as broader in scope than equity since 'unlike Western law, which finds its source in equity, ubuntu jurisprudence goes beyond equity and is based on local reality for the sake of preserving harmony, social justice and dignity'. (Kamga 2018, 648) In South African jurisprudence Ubuntu's application in disputes takes on a much more generalised approach that the common-law approach to equity, with Ubuntu extending across all spheres of law despite its inconsistent application in practice by the courts.

Mokgoro J characterised Ubuntu as 'one shared value and ideal that runs like a golden thread across cultural lines'. When applied to define rights or explain judgments to the public, there is a common understanding of its intended purpose. (Makwanyane case, 1995, para 306) In South Africa Ubuntu has become synonymous with democratisation, pluralism and constitutional transformation. Ubuntu forms part of the 'rainbow' heritage of South Africa (Makwanyane case, 1995, para 307), reflecting both the pluralism of the country and the unity of all its citizens. Despite its non-state law customary origin, the term has become part of state law as a source of rights and an instrument of interpretation. Consequently, the term is used for norm-setting and education by reminding people of their place in society, their relationship with the community and the interplay between individuals and the community.

[39] While this elevated status of Ubuntu from a customary term to a constitutional term elevates it to state law, is open to scientific discourse, but it highlights the limitation of the state law versus non-state law classification.

Sachs J explains that when interpreting the Constitution factors such as the context in which it was drafted, the history of South Africa and insights from external sources can all be considered for making judgments. In this regard, considering all the information that may assist with interpretation is 'entirely consistent' with the 'constitutionally acknowledged principle of ubuntu'. (Makwanyane case 1995, para 374) The court should therefore not be restricted by the traditional rules of interpretation.

Mohamed J speaks to the meaning of Ubuntu, adding that it expresses 'the ethos of an instinctive capacity for and enjoyment of love towards our fellow men and women; the joy and the fulfilment involved in recognizing their innate humanity; the reciprocity this generates in interaction within the collective community; the richness of the creative emotions which it engenders and the moral energies which it releases both in the givers and the society which they serve and are served by'. (Makwanyane case 1995, para 262)

Ubuntu has also been used to describe the interrelatedness of individuals and the interdependence of individual and community. Its use aims to strike a balance between the rights of the individual, the interests of other individuals and the interests of the community. Each aspect is interdependent and cannot exist in isolation from the others. In the MEC for Education case the essence of Ubuntu was described as follows:

> The notion that 'we are not islands unto ourselves' is central to the understanding of the individual in African thought. It is often expressed in the phrase umuntu ngumuntu ngabantu, which emphasises 'communality and the interdependence of the members of a community' and that every individual is an extension of others. (MEC for Education case 2007, para 53)

Sachs J has used Ubuntu to explain the principles of restorative justice (Dikoko case 2006, para 86), emphasising that restorative justice, as found inherently in Ubuntu, reflects 'reparative rather than purely punitive principles'. (Dikoko case 2006, para 114) Seeking to establish a link between Ubuntu and restorative justice, Sachs J reasoned as follows:

> Ubuntu/botho is highly consonant with rapidly evolving international notions of restorative justice. Deeply rooted in our society, it links up with world-wide striving to develop restorative systems of justice based on reparative rather than purely punitive principles. The key elements of restorative justice have been identified as encounter, reparation, reintegration and participation. Encounter (dialogue) enables the victims and offenders to talk about the hurt caused and how the parties are to get on in future. Reparation focuses on repairing the harm that has been done rather than on doling out punishment. (Dikoko case 2006, para 114)

This perspective on sentencing is not unique to Ubuntu, but reference to Ubuntu does provide a common-person mechanism for the court to explain the rationale for its judgments in a manner that reflects local customs, beliefs and understanding. Sachs furthermore has linked Ubuntu to the Roman-Dutch law concept of '*amende honorable*' (public apology or reparation) (Mukheibir 2022)[40] and said that, although the principles arise from two different legal cultures, both promote a form of restorative resolution of disputes whereby in effect harmony in the community is also repaired.

In the Barkhuizen case the court explained that all aspects of public policy must be viewed with Ubuntu in mind: 'Public policy is informed by the concept of ubuntu.' (Barkhuizen case 2007, para 51) Du Plessis, meanwhile, explains that the courts have, through the use of Ubuntu, been able to develop an equitable remedy where unfair terms of a contract can be set aside. (Du Plessis 2022)

The values of dignity, equality and restorative justice are, of course, not solely within the domain of Ubuntu, yet the courts have used Ubuntu as an explanatory framework to link those universal concepts to African values and understanding. While this approach might invite criticism, it also highlights, for the purposes of this chapter, how the judiciary can identify a community socio-cultural value as a source of rights for interpreting, explaining or justifying a particular interpretation of constitutional text. This process serves to legitimise a particular outcome.

In the AB case the court referred to the fundamental human right of personal autonomy in the context of a dispute about reproduction and surrogacy rights. The court stressed that the 'repeated endorsement of ubuntu underscores' the principle that 'autonomy is a necessary, but socially embedded, part of the value of freedom'. (AB case 2017, para 51) In this regard the respect for individual decision-making is related to the international principle of individual self-determination, as found in the ICCPR. It is worth noting that, by relying on Ubuntu, the court attempted to find a way to explain the rationale behind its judgment, setting out the discretion that is inherent to such a dispute and asserting that the customary values of Ubuntu may be relied upon in exercising that discretion.

In the Mahlangu case the court referred to Ubuntu to explain why domestic workers should not be excluded from the definition of 'worker' for the purposes

[40] In regard to the applicability of Ubuntu to *amende honorable*, Mukheibir says: 'One could only hope that ubuntu does not degenerate into an over-utilised cliché which is seldom practised, and that true regard will be had to the spirit thereof. . . .' (Mukheibir 2022, 589)

of the protection of their rights pursuant to the Compensation for Occupational Injuries and Diseases Act 130 of 1993. The court declared s 1xix*(d)*(v) of the Act to be unconstitutional and, in explaining its reasons, it observed the following about Ubuntu:

> In considering those who are most vulnerable or most in need, a court should take cognisance of those who fall at the intersection of compounded vulnerabilities due to intersecting oppression based on race, sex, gender, class and other grounds. To allow this form of state-sanctioned inequity goes against the values of our newly constituted society, namely human dignity, the achievement of equality and ***ubuntu***. To exclude this category of individuals from the social security scheme established by COIDA is manifestly unreasonable. (Mahlangu case 2020, para 65)

In the King case the court had to consider whether a clause in a will that discriminated against unknown descendants was unconstitutional. The freedom of testation and the right to equal treatment had to be balanced. (King case 2021) The court made extensive reference to Ubuntu as a basis for an egalitarian society (King case 2021, para 202) and a society of equality. (King case 2021, para 204) It cited Ubuntu as a 'constitutionally integrated norm' (King case 2021, para 237), and mentioned its 'transformative power' (King case 2021, para 241), concluding that the testamentary clause was discriminatory since 'in the context of freedom of testation, ubuntu means that the Constitution places a high premium on establishing a compassionate society which does not discard the humanity of any of its members. [Therefore], the right to dispose of one's property upon one's death must be balanced against the discriminatory effect it may have by precluding members of society from an adequate share in the wealth and resources of the nation.' (King case 2021, para 243)

In this context Ubuntu embodies a dynamic interpretation that implies notions of fairness and reasonableness. The creative use of Ubuntu encapsulates a homegrown African jurisprudence in a world where Western jurisprudence is prevalent and dominant. (English 1996) In the Western world the works of various philosophers are relied upon to teach, explain and sustain modern constitutional concepts and traditions. The same arguably applies to Ubuntu, which reflects African values and attitudes, particularly as they relate to community, the individual and the interaction of the interests of the two.

Ubuntu is invoked to address the criticism of the South African Bill of Rights that it lacks an adequate African fingerprint. It is important to acknowledge too that, although Ubuntu cannot be neatly defined, neither can 'democracy', 'liberty', 'equity', justice', 'self-determination' or any of the terms that underpin liberal democratic theory and practice. In the same way that the meanings of these foundational terms in liberal democratic theory and practice have evolved over centuries, so too has the meaning of Ubuntu been subject to change. Words representing a value system often reveal their underlying characteristics when applied in practice. Similarly to how 'democracy' is not defined by reference to the myriad institutional arrangements associated with it, Ubuntu also possesses numerous practical facets. In this regard, for example, the recognition and protection of second-generation rights to health and housing can also be approached from an Ubuntu-informed perspective. (Himonga 2013)

The reliance on Ubuntu as an aide-memoire to explain the rationale behind judgments is a popular approach adopted by courts. Ubuntu, however, is not consistently used or relied upon, but courts often tend to use it as an explanatory tool rather than as a source for rights. By citing Ubuntu, judges call upon the community's deeper understanding and popularity of the term and hence seek to legitimise its reasoning and judgment.

6.5 CONCLUDING ASSESSMENT

This chapter has investigated the use of Ubuntu by the South African judiciary as an embedded customary term of law that can be relied upon when the Constitution is interpreted. The use of Ubuntu by courts to approach the Constitution as a living organism that reflects changing community values was highlighted. In a plural society like South Africa, where a balance between individual and community rights is sought, Ubuntu serves to inspire and guide the judiciary with the term's emphasis on respecting diversity, appreciating cultural differences, placing the individual within the community and fostering the promotion and survival of unique identities.

The South African reliance on the term 'Ubuntu' underscores the unique interaction between the humanity of the individual, the customary use of non-state law, the recognition of non-state law by state law and the collectivism of the community. International law recognises that true freedom for individuals, and acknowledgement of their fundamental rights, is found within respect for their identity, culture and customs. The humanity of a person is often best displayed within the context of community. Giving effect to fundamental rights and freedoms should therefore not be blind to, or ignorant of, the composition of the population or the plurality of legal and customary systems in existence. Instead the legal system should embrace and accommodate such diversity, recognising that it provides individuals with the opportunity to fully realise their potential.

Ubuntu has become a widely used term in South Africa, arguably exceeding the traditional customary meaning of the word. In its application the courts have found a unique way to link the legalities of the Constitution with the soul of African values and traditions. Consequently the courts have used Ubuntu in various contexts such as fundamental rights, criminal law, law of contract and law of defamation. The universality of individual rights has in this way been given content and effect within the context of African customs and traditions. Therein lies the plurality of law. Particularly in countries characterised by deep societal divisions, courts can play a crucial role by recognising deeply ingrained norms of tolerance and accommodation of diversity and by setting the contours for interpreting constitutional rights and duties within the context of recognition of non-state law. Through the use of Ubuntu the legal pluralism of South Africa has been given further visibility, credibility and legitimacy.

In summary the following observations can be made about the impact of Ubuntu as a non-state law term on jurisprudence in South Africa:

6.5.1 Ubuntu remains undefined

Ubuntu does not appear in the Constitution and remains undefined as a term of law. Ubuntu is described rather than defined. Ubuntu was neither cited during the constitutional debates nor referred to in scholarly works or committee proceedings leading to the adoption of the Constitution. Ubuntu did not appear as an essential value-laden term in publications leading up to the constitution's drafting. The term was briefly referred to in the postamble of the interim constitution of 1993, but with reference also to reconciliation, and not as part of the Bill of Rights. In retrospect the exclusion of Ubuntu from the Constitution was an opportunity lost. All efforts by the courts to clarify the term for legal application have been descriptive of its character rather than definitive of its meaning. Ubuntu is in essence open-ended and dynamic in its interpretation and application. In summary Ubuntu implies basic principles of fairness and equity that regulate interactions between individuals and community, as well as those among individuals themselves.

6.5.2 Ubuntu originates from customary law and tradition

Ubuntu is a customary non-state concept based on relationships that underlie African law, religion and tradition, particularly in the context of southern Africa. While its meaning in African tradition is not primarily legal but rather relational

(African Congress for Transformation case 2024, para 156) it has been elevated by the Constitutional Court to a state law legal term that can imply a source of law, a mechanism for statutory interpretation or a useful way to explain the rationale of a judgment to the population. By relying on the term the courts have developed a homegrown jurisprudence. Ubuntu in many respects reflects the legal meaning of equality, equity, proportionality and fairness, as are prevalent in foreign and international jurisprudence. Those terms, frequently relied on in foreign legal systems, are equally as undefined as Ubuntu and yet they are regularly cited by courts in foreign jurisprudence to balance competing interests and to develop as societies change.

6.5.3 Ubuntu has multiple applications

Ubuntu is like a Swiss Army knife, a handy tool to use in many different situations. An overview of jurisprudence highlights how the term is applied to various disputes, often with an element of romanticism, without a precise exegesis of how a specific meaning within the context of the specific dispute is derived. The term is often approached as if it has a precise legal definition with a meaning that falls within judicial knowledge. The reality, however, is that there are few cases, if any, where expert evidence is heard to justify the specific meaning attached to the term. Courts generally cite each other without providing an in-depth explanation that attaches a particular meaning to the term. In general Ubuntu is relied on as a source of law, an instrument for statutory interpretation and an explanatory term. Ubuntu is not only applied to public law, but also to civil, commercial, family, customary, employment, criminal and contractual law. This demonstrates how Ubuntu has become an operative term in a wide range of judgments affecting various parts of South African society.

The risk of course is that Ubuntu, with its origins entrenched in African tradition, is now being employed to resolve disputes arising across a multicultural community such as South Africa. Not all communities may display an affinity or understanding of Ubuntu (Malan 2014) and even if different persons use the same word, their cultural understanding of the meaning of it may vary. On the other hand, many terms that originated from liberal democratic theory have gravitated into non-Western legal traditions. Although the term 'Ubuntu' is easy to use and has become integrated into other languages in South Africa, the set of cultural, religious and customary values it embodies may not represent all the communities that comprise the South African population.

The use of Ubuntu by the Constitutional Court has demonstrated how a non-state law term pertaining to a specific community may be elevated to a state law term pertaining to an entire population.

6.5.4 Utility of citing Ubuntu

Questions arise whether the outcome of Ubuntu-based judgments in South Africa would have been different had the courts not relied on Ubuntu. One could argue that achieving the same outcome, such as the abolition of capital punishment, upholding COVID-19 immunisation or the refusal to issue an eviction notice could have been accomplished without relying on Ubuntu as a source of law or as an interpretation mechanism. Reliance on internationally endorsed principles of equality and non-discrimination, proportionality, restorative justice, equity and reasonableness could arguably have produced the same results.

This may be correct, but the utility of Ubuntu lies in its legitimising impact, aiding courts to establish contours by which powers and functions are to be exercised in accordance with a term that resonates with 'South Africa'. Political realism, legal pragmatism and the transformative objectives of South Africa are served by the values represented by Ubuntu. Given that Ubuntu is principally used as an explanatory tool to provide the rationale behind a judgment, rather than constituting a legal right in itself, the application of the term has generally speaking gained acceptance and credibility. I would not be surprised if citations of Ubuntu will in time expand to other African countries as a reflection of African identity.

6.5.5 Ubuntu as an inspiration for transformation

Ubuntu has been used by the courts to transform a post-conflict society into one that is more democratic, just and equitable. South African notions of individual rights, humanity, community and fairness all bear the imprint of Ubuntu. It is, however, crucial to recognise the ambiguity surrounding the invocation and application of Ubuntu. This ambiguity poses the risk of Ubuntu becoming an ideological tool used to enforce a form of hegemony under the guise of being authentically African. In the same way that Ubuntu can reflect national reconciliation and nation-building, it can represent Africanism in an ideological sense that resists liberal democratic values.

The overview of case law highlights that it is not clear whether judges with a particular cultural Ubuntu background, black judges for example, have greater freedom and discretion to cite and interpret Ubuntu than judges who cannot first-hand speak about its inherent meaning, considering their different cultural background. If a non-black judge applies Ubuntu, are they restricted in citing previous applications of it? Or can they expand the application of the term without some form of expert evidence? The use of a customary non-state law term by persons who do not share the customs from which the term originates may be more complex than it seems at first glance. Ubuntu has indeed become a repository of many purported meanings and the very breadth of the meanings may erode the core customary relevance of the term.

6.5.6 Ubuntu is shared by many countries, but only judicially used by South Africa

Ubuntu is a customary word that resonates far beyond the borders of South Africa. However, the elevation of the concept to a widely used legal term is unique to South Africa.[41] The use of and reliance on the term in South African jurisprudence give it a jurisprudential base which may not, however, be consistent with its customary basis. It remains unexplained why other courts in Africa have not utilised the term so extensively, if indeed it bears all the meanings and hallmarks attributed to it in South African jurisprudence. It is also notable that Ubuntu offers accommodation to many interpretations by courts, often not entirely related to each other and sometimes not even related in substance to the cultural or historic origin of the word itself. Ubuntu has, in its use by the courts, become an overarching mega-norm. However, its enormously broad interpretation potentially weakens the ability for it to be defined as a legal term.

Nonetheless, Ubuntu arguably addresses the perceived lack of African identity attributed to the South African Constitution, which formed the subject of much criticism during the negotiations leading to its enactment. Under the guidance of the Constitutional Court the South African Constitution, enshrining universal human rights, norms and values, has been given a distinct character with its roots firmly based in the African context. Ubuntu's role to popularise the Constitution and to explain complex issues in lay language, in line with familiar customs and traditions, ought to be welcomed.

---

[41] This again is not dissimilar to the application of *Bundestreue*, in that several countries share the term, including Germany, Australia, Switzerland and Belgium. Only Germany, however, has elevated it to an implied constitutional term. (De Villiers 1994a)

6.5.7 Is Ubuntu somewhat idyllic?

The use of Ubuntu has become so widespread in South Africa that it may give rise to a romantic and poetic approach to dispute resolution which, in turn, may be marred by inconsistencies and unbridled judicial discretion. The very rigidity of the rules of interpretation so criticised by Sachs may be lacking in the arbitrary reliance on Ubuntu. The term furthermore opens the door to judicial creativity and interventionism. One cannot but observe some discrepancies that prevail when Ubuntu is applied (and not applied) in practice by the courts. The meanings ascribed to Ubuntu often emerge without expert evidence, relying instead on one judge citing another judge or judges offering their understanding of Ubuntu without explaining how they came to such knowledge.

It remains unclear whether Ubuntu is a foundation for pleading by parties or a basis for interpretation raised by judges. While Ubuntu may play a useful role to rationalise judgments, it prompts the question whether courts are obligated to cite Ubuntu or if reliance on Ubuntu is entirely discretionary. Where the rules of statutory interpretation may be old and perhaps uncompromising, Ubuntu brings a flexibility and unpredictability that may also lead to a lack of consistency and unbridled discretion.

Reference to and reliance on Ubuntu have imbued South African jurisprudence with a distinctly African character that enhances its legitimacy and popular understanding. As a legal term Ubuntu is vague. However, as a soulful concept underpinning the Constitution it represents the values and aspirations cherished by the broader community, such as fairness, neighbourliness, restoration and kindness, mutual dependence and reasonableness. As a term of law it lacks precision, but as a spiritual value it adds life and purpose to the Constitution. Ultimately, the use of the term 'Ubuntu' illustrates how a constitution can be interpreted in a customary manner by recognising non-state law to give effect to the societal values of the nation that the Constitution is intended to serve.

6.5.8 Ubuntu and liberal democratic values – are they the same?

The values promoted by Ubuntu may indeed contain universal elements, but, given its association with African customary value systems and religions, the use of the term may be alienating to certain segments of the community, especially if it is applied selectively and at the discretion of the courts. The suggestion that there is an Ubuntu way of thinking or an Ubuntu world-view may imply a level of uniformity that would raise concern to civil libertarians. On the other hand, Africanists have been concerned that an African customary concept is being colonised by applying it to non-African customary disputes and attributing meanings to it that derive from international law, thereby weakening the cultural and customary nature of the concept. The strong individualistic approach of international human rights norms may not show adequate tolerance to the community aspect of Ubuntu, while relying on Ubuntu to sustain international norms in South Africa may delink Ubuntu from its cultural and customary roots.

On balance, Ubuntu has been effectively used as a vehicle to bring into South African law universal concepts underlying dispute resolution and human rights protection and also to develop customary law in the process. Critics have noted that the concept of community or group solidarity arising from Ubuntu may be at odds with individualism as expressed by liberal democratic principles. In African customs and traditions there is often an emphasis on the subservient role of the individual to the community. This hierarchical relationship may erode fundamental individual rights and freedoms, particularly in regard to women, children and persons based on sexual orientation. But customary law is also dynamic and the relationships between individuals are subject to change. Historical gender inequality will not necessarily persist, in the same way that gender inequality in Western systems have been changing. Given that Ubuntu is a culturally informed concept lacking a precise definition, it could furthermore potentially be applied in situations to which it may not be appropriate. Finally, the meaning attributed to Ubuntu may be influenced by the cultural, customary, and ideological background or biases of the judge relying on the term.

6.5.9 Concluding remarks

The above citations of jurisprudence highlight four important aspects of Ubuntu for the purposes of this chapter:

First, Ubuntu is accepted as an implied norm of the Constitution that is derived from African customary law, but it is also treated as an interpretive tool, a source of law and an explanatory aid.

Secondly, the Constitutional Court, consistent with its transformative role, draws on Ubuntu according to a dynamic purposive interpretation rather than freezing its meaning within a particular customary milieu. This approach may be open to criticism, but the courts have been largely successful in combining international human rights norms with African values using Ubuntu in a contemporary African setting.

Thirdly, although many democratic nations have found a way to interpret their bills of rights within the context of their particular society, the manner in which the South African courts have used Ubuntu to give effect to the Bill of Rights and as a foundation for societal transformation imparts a distinctive character to the jurisprudence arising from this country.

Fourthly, the use of Ubuntu in dispute resolution is not inconsistent with the way foreign legal systems have developed concepts such as equity, fairness, proportionality and reasonableness. While the South African Constitution draws inspiration from Western liberal democratic values, the criticism often heard that the Constitution does not adequately reflect an African culture and identity is to some extent addressed by the use of Ubuntu. Ubuntu provides the Constitution with a soul, serving as a source of rights, a purposive instrument for interpretation and a mechanism for explaining judgments in a manner that resonates with the public. Thus Ubuntu lends credibility and legitimacy to judgments that otherwise would have to rely on foreign concepts and precedents.

Ubuntu is, in more than one respect, an example of contemporary legal pluralism whereby a non-state law principle applicable to one part of society is acknowledged and absorbed, becoming a principle of state law applicable across the entire society.

CHAPTER 7

RECOGNITION AND RESTORATION OF INDIGENOUS PEOPLES' RIGHTS TO LAND: FREE, PRIOR AND INFORMED CONSENT – THEORY AND PRACTICE

Take only what you need and leave the land as you found it.

– Arapahoe proverb

7.1 INTRODUCTION

The 'right' of local communities in general, and indigenous communities in particular, to be consulted when their interests in land and environment are affected is becoming synonymous with contemporary democratic practices. (Flemmer 2022) Local communities now, to an unprecedented degree, insist on being heard when legislation, government policies,[1] administrative actions and development plans directly impact their interests.[2] This raises the question whether consultation is a justiciable right or rather a demand or expectation in the guise of a right. Democratic governance is no longer seen as a narrow form of representative democracy where regular elections are the only mechanism by which the populace can express their views about government policies and keep governments accountable. Ongoing public participation is becoming an essential requirement to ensure the legitimacy of legislation, policies and administrative measures. This new awareness of accountability is evidenced in the way that individual rights have been interpreted to encompass meanings of consultation, self-determination, informed consent and good faith communications. (Endorois

[1] The question arises whether *executive policies* (e.g. entering into international treaties, foreign affairs, budget allocations and spending priorities, economic growth policies, response to climate change, defence policies), which are distinct from *administrative actions* and *legislative measures*, can also be the subject of judicial review. In the Law Society case Mogoeng CJ rejected the proposition that the executive is subject to the same public participatory obligations as the legislatures. He explained his reasoning as follows: 'Public participation in the law-making process is a requirement, specifically provided for in our Constitution, that must be met by our law-making institutions. But participatory democracy is not provided for in similar terms in relation to the exercise of presidential or executive power. . . . And there is no legal provision or principle that *even remotely* imposes an obligation on the executive to invite the public to participate in its decision-making processes as proposed.' (emphasis added) (Law Society case 2019, paras 86–88) Note, however, the propositions put forward by Ally and Murcott, who express the opinion that the executive should be held equally accountable pursuant to the principles of participatory democracy. (Ally and Murcott 2023) Note also the criticism expressed in Australia against the proposed Voice for Aboriginal people which, if it had passed the referendum in 2023, would have enabled the Voice to make 'representations' about anything that even remotely affected Aboriginal people to the 'executive government'. (Constitution Alteration Act 2023) There were concerns that all policies made by executive organs could by such a wide power become the subject of judicial review because of a representation made by the Voice having been rejected or not having been given adequate weight or attention by the executive organ. (De Villiers 2024c, 294–6)

[2] Note also how in Germany the notion of Citizen's Assemblies, as a form of direct democracy, is increasing in popularity. (Heidemann 2024) Also note in this respect the National Dialogue under way in South Africa to involve communities at all levels in discussions about essential policy issues. (Ramaphosa National Dialogue 2024)

Welfare Council case 2003; Sesana case 2006; Kichwa case 2012; Saugeen First Nation case 2017; Tipakalippa case 2022; Munkara case 2024; African Centre for Biodiversity case 2024)

The South African Constitution, arguably more than any of the other constitutions drafted during the 1990s, imposes the notions of public accountability and the public's right to participation on all organs of state. Two elements are reflected, namely representation and participation, with representation referring to elections and participation referring to ongoing involvement. In the South African Doctors for Life case the court emphasised that 'our constitutional democracy is not only representative but also contains participatory elements'. (emphasis added) (Doctors for Life case 2006, para 111)[3] Accountability of government is therefore given an expansive meaning, implying that not only elected parliamentarians but also those in the executive and in the civil service are continually held to account for their decisions and actions. There are elements of the traditional Swiss form of direct democracy identifiable, whereby communities – indigenous and non-indigenous – prefer to express their opinions directly to those in power by way of village-square meetings.

The South African legislative processes have become characterised by the extensive efforts to hear public submissions and to conduct public meetings in an effort to meet the constitutional demand for participation. The understanding of public involvement in the general process of government, through what has been described as 'participatory democracy', was put as follows in the Doctors for Life case:

> Participatory democracy is of special importance to those who are relatively disempowered in a country like ours where great disparities of wealth and influence exist. (Doctors for Life case 2006, para 115)

In the Khoisan appeal, nearly two decades after the Doctors for Life case, the court again observed as follows about the importance of public participation in the context of a participatory democracy and the rationale for declaring the Act unconstitutional:

[3] The public participation philosophy is also reflected in various policy documents adopted by the government since 1996, such as the Reconstruction and Development Programme, the Growth, Employment and Redistribution Strategy, the Accelerated and Shared Growth Initiative, the National Growth Path, and the National Development Plan. (Mukwevho 2022, 150–2) All these policies refer to the importance of public input and participation.

> Public participation is a crucial part of participatory democracy and the law-making process as it affords the public a *meaningful opportunity* to participate in the legislative process and strengthens the legitimacy of legislation in the eyes of the people. This court has set a standard for public participation facilitated by Parliament and the provincial legislatures. Parliament and the provincial legislatures have also set their own standards in the Public Participation Framework (Framework) and the Practical Guide for Members of Parliament and Provincial Legislatures (Practical Guide). (citations omitted and emphasis added) (Khoisan Act appeal 2023, para 33)[4]

The accountability of the legislative process is therefore not restricted to narrow parliamentary procedures and submissions to parliamentary committees, but also entails steps to facilitate public inputs and involvement, including public hearings and, if necessary, meetings outside the parliamentary facilities in various parts of the country. Few democracies, if any, place the equivalent of such a premium on taking Parliament to the people, rather than just to let the people come to Parliament. The increased accountability of Parliament and the importance of extra-parliamentary processes are growing exponentially in importance in contemporary democracies in general, and in South Africa in particular.

South Africa has a long history of extra-parliamentary processes such as strikes, protest actions and boycotts, particularly because of the exclusion of black people from democratic processes until 1994. It is, however, noticeable that despite – or perhaps because of – the dawn of democracy, extra-parliamentary processes in South Africa have retained and even increased their importance. This is perhaps partly due to distrust in government, rampant corruption, an active civil society, a free media, public desire to become involved in policy formulation and administration, the many failures of policy formulation and administration by government, the loss of elector-representative contact through the list-proportional system, and lawfare where the courts are so actively involved in adjudicating the appropriateness of legislative processes.[5]

---

[4] The word 'meaningful' resonates throughout South African and international jurisprudence. In this case the phrase 'meaningful opportunity' does not imply a veto, but rather consultation encompassing a style, process and substance that embodies sincerity, listening, responsiveness, accommodation, striving towards an agreed outcome and constructiveness. None of these requires a change in position. However, there is a fine line between maintaining firmness in negotiations and veering into bias, especially when a firm position may suggest a party approaching consultations with a closed mind. (Ka'a'Gee Tu First Nation case 2007; Tipakalippa case 2022; Barngarla case 2023; Saugeen First Nation case 2017)

[5] The list system of proportional representation, whereby the head office of the respective political parties controls the candidate list of who can be elected, has contributed to local

A democratic deficit has, in many respects, developed between elective processes and public engagement. Frustration at local levels therefore often spills out onto the streets and into courts, which form the *real* battleground of policy, rather than Parliament. The concept of lawfare seeks to encapsulate the increased turning to courts to determine the adequacy of consultation. (Davis and Le Roux 2019) A Justice of the High Court in Australia, Robert Beech-Jones, has cautioned that the increase in litigation is a symptom of distrust in political process and the same distrust may also spill over to the judiciary. (Shanahan 2024)

Since the 1990s, extra-parliamentary processes in South Africa have intensified in importance, frequency, subject-matter and scope. During apartheid these processes were principally aimed at resistance and protest against the entire apartheid government, whereas now they are much more sophisticated and community-based, encompassing a wide range of policy areas, legislation and other issues. The judiciary is often called upon to intervene about the adequacy of consultation, while the legality of parliamentary and administrative decision-making is constantly being challenged. In some respects, extra-parliamentary processes compete with Parliament as an alternative forum for legitimacy.[6] In essence, transparency and public participation have become keywords in day-to-day governance and policy implementation.

The legal sources of this newfound 'street accountability' are varied, generally involving a combination of an expansive interpretation of fundamental rights, specific consultative obligations arising from the Constitution and

communities often not knowing who represents them, or to whom they can turn at local level if their interests are affected. In other cases some NGOs such as the Afrikaans Afriforum, have directed their attention to the courts to achieve public accountability through lawfare since they feel politically marginalised or excluded for policy and legislative processes.

[6] In light of the theme of this book concerning the accommodation of ethnocultural plurality in South Africa, it is worth noting the 'functional autonomy' that has been developing from within the Afrikaans-speaking community in policy areas such as education, neighbourhood security, some municipal services and social-welfare programmes, as a result of what is perceived to be an inability of parliamentary and administrative processes to adequately address the needs and aspirations of the community, as well the decline in the quality of public services at a local level. (De Villiers 2023c) These extra-parliamentary activities by Afrikaans NGOs sometimes have the hallmark of 'government', in contrast to what would ordinarily be expected of a cultural club or an association. In some respects, the activities of an NGO such as AfriForum compete with, supplement and even substitute the services provided by governmental agencies, for example by them providing security services, community policing, maintenance of infrastructure, water, electricity and sanitation services, poverty relief, and other functions that ordinarily would be the responsibility of local governments.

statutes, consideration and implementation of international law and standards, incorporation of ever-evolving common law through concepts such as Ubuntu and acknowledgement of contemporary understandings of liberal democratic government.

While accountability and transparency beyond the sphere of parliamentary representation are accepted as a new normal, this does prompt the following questions, which will be discussed in this chapter: To what extent, if any, must indigenous people in South Africa be specifically consulted when their rights to and interests in their traditional lands are affected by legislation, government policies and administrative actions? Is consultation with indigenous people merely part of a new set of standards for *general* community consultation, or is indigenous consultation a *special* genus to be complied with?

In international law the concept of 'free, prior and informed consent' (FPIC) is often used to describe indigenous involvement in policy and administration that affects them, particularly regarding their rights to their traditional lands. (Barrie 2024b) The inclusion of a discussion on consultation with indigenous communities in this book is justified because indigenous people often maintain traditions and customs that predate the modern state. Consequently, within the context of legal pluralism, indigenous people often adhere to state law *and* non-state law.[7] Whenever the traditional lands of indigenous communities are affected, their customary rules and the state's constitutional rules may intersect. It is not only their customary proprietary rights to land that may be impacted. Their customs, traditions and storylines may also be affected by development on their traditional land.

The potential application of FPIC in the South African context raises several issues. In this chapter the following questions are addressed:

- What is the definition of indigenous people and, more importantly, does the categorisation of indigenous apply only to the Khoisan? (Pieterse-Robertson 2019) Or does it also apply to all other tribal communities residing on their traditional lands? Or does it apply to all black communities irrespective of whether they reside on their traditional lands or not?

[7] Note, for example, the Australian Forrest case, in which indigenous people cited their customary belief of a pre-ancestral snake and their obligation to adhere to it as a basis to oppose the development of weirs in a riverbed. (Forrest case 2023) Their objection was upheld under the relevant legislation that seeks to protect Aboriginal heritage. On appeal the judgment was remitted to the original tribunal because it was found that the tribunal had not adequately considered the public interest of the proposed development. (Forrest appeal case 2024).

- What, if any, consultation rights can indigenous people claim pursuant to the international understanding of FPIC and how do these rights compare to consultation rights under the South African Constitution and legislation?
- What are the practical requirements that satisfy the legal obligation to obtain FPIC from indigenous people?
- What are the consequences of FPIC not taking place or, if it does occur, the effect of an indigenous community withholding consent to a proposal?

In response to these questions this chapter reflects on recent developments in international law, as well as jurisprudence concerning FPIC arising from South Africa, Canada, Australia, South America and some southern African states.

It is shown that: there is no general definition in international law of indigenous people (Almanza and Salazar 2022); there is no specific standard in international law that mandates *by law* the specifics of consultation or FPIC with indigenous people, although some practical guidelines, demands and aspirations (not to be construed as rights) have been developed (De Villiers 2023b); FPIC does not imply a veto unless, pursuant to a specific statutory requirement, a veto or consent is mandated (World Bank 2016; Baleni case 2019); states are left to their own discretion to develop practical standards for indigenous consultation (UNDRIP 2007a); and projects can be delayed, disrupted or even derailed, or compensation claimed, if FPIC does not occur. (Timber Creek High Court appeal 2019)[8] In addition to consultative obligations on governments, private entities are also increasingly under scrutiny to comply with FPIC, with pressure coming from shareholders, public expectations, media, private bankers, the World Bank and the OECD. (Bornschlegl, Ocampo and Urrutia 2021; OECD Guidelines 2023) It is finally demonstrated that the 'consent' in FPIC in international law and practice is an objective, an idealistic expression, rather than a justiciable right.

[8] Also note, however, the risks faced by developers when they do consult but the outcome is rejected by a subgroup within the community. In the Munkara case the Federal Court of Australia rejected the evidence of the subgroup, but only after extensive delays and substantial costs for the developer. (Munkara case 2024) As is shown below, FPIC implies an effort to consult with subgroups but not a legal obligation to achieve their consent or involvement. International and municipal laws are cognisant that indigenous communities may also have internal differences of opinion and hence one cannot reasonably expect consensus by an entire community.

7.2 FPIC ARISING FROM THE SOUTH AFRICAN CONSTITUTION AND LEGISLATION

The statutory scheme in South Africa does not refer to the concept of free, prior and informed consent, regardless of South Africa being a signatory of UNDRIP. While principles of consultation and participatory government underlie the Constitution and several statutes and notable judgments, FPIC is not a legal term that has been adopted in South African lawmaking. South African courts may, however, pursuant to s 39(1) of the Constitution (Chapter 4), 'consider' international law and municipal law and jurisprudence – where the concept appears – in order to gain insight from its meaning and application, particularly in regard to the special consultation rights, if applicable, of indigenous people. (Baleni case 2019)

As demonstrated below, while international law does not provide a justiciable meaning of FPIC, courts in the Americas have referred to FPIC, and the notion of 'good faith consultation' with indigenous people is also known in some foreign jurisdictions such as Canada, New Zealand, Botswana, Kenya, Finland, Norway and Australia. However, even in those jurisdictions where good faith consultation with indigenous people is a normative requirement, the way good faith is given practical effect depends on the circumstances of each case. There is no international normative standard or checklist that can be used to prove conclusively whether good faith consultation has occurred. It depends rather on the facts of each dispute. (Sesana case 2006) This is exemplified by the ongoing efforts in Finland to clarify what exactly is meant by the obligation of government to 'negotiate' with the Sámi Parliament. (De Villiers 2023i, 141)[9] Meanwhile, in Australian native title proceedings the test for 'good faith' is applied to the *conduct* of the parties rather than the *merit* of their respective positions or the reasons for their disagreement. (WMC case 1999) The courts therefore do not focus on the acceptability of a proposal, but on the process by which it was put, discussed, modified and responded to.

General good practice guidelines on how to comply with FPIC have been developed internationally, but these do not constitute binding legal norms, as adhering to good faith consultation for compliance with FPIC ultimately depends on circumstance. (World Bank 2016)

---

[9] Finland has been attempting for some years to resolve in a politically and legally satisfactory manner what is meant by the negotiation obligations with the Sámi people. At the time of writing (March 2025) no final agreement had yet been reached.

Although there is no legislation in South Africa that purports to formally incorporate the principle of FPIC of indigenous people into domestic law, there are, however, several examples of legislation that mandate consultation with persons and communities affected by legislation and administrative actions.[10] These legislative standards, some of which are discussed below, are generally consistent with the understanding of FPIC in international law. In one instance, the case of the Interim Protection of Informal Land Rights Act, the South African legislation exceeds the FPIC standard, in that this Act grants an effective veto to a community whose land interests are affected. (Baleni case 2019)

The following are some of the most pertinent examples of statutes that mandate consultation with communities.

A *constitutional obligation* is placed on the National Assembly to facilitate public involvement in the legislative process. (Constitution of South Africa 1996, s 59)[11] A similar obligation is placed on the National Council of Provinces. (Constitution of South Africa 1996, s 72(1))[12] Provincial legislatures must also facilitate public involvement in the legislative process. (Constitution of South Africa 1996, s 118(1))[13] Local government has as one of its objectives the involvement of local communities. (Constitution of South Africa 1996, s 152(1))[14] The Constitution furthermore requires that the public administration of South Africa be conducted in a manner that encourages public participation. (Constitution of South Africa 1996, s 195(1))[15] The question whether the constitutional obligation has been

---

[10] Note, for example, the African Climate Alliance case in which the approval to open a new coal-fired power station was set aside because of inadequate consultation with the local community in general, and more specifically failure to consider the potential harmful impact on children now and in the future. (African Climate Alliance case 2024, para 25).

[11] '59. (1) The National Assembly must – (a) facilitate public involvement in the legislative and other processes of the Assembly and its committees; and (b) conduct its business in an open manner, and hold its sittings, and those of its committees, in public, but reasonable measures may be taken – (i) to regulate public access, including access of the media, to the Assembly and its committees; and (ii) to provide for the searching of any person and, where appropriate, the refusal of entry to, or the removal of, any person.'

[12] '72. (1) The National Council of Provinces must – (a) facilitate public involvement in the legislative and other processes of the Council and its committees. . . .'

[13] '118. (1) A provincial legislature must – (a) facilitate public involvement in the legislative and other processes of the legislature and its committees;'

[14] '152. (1) The objects of local government are – (a) to provide democratic and accountable government for local communities. . . .'

[15] '195. (1) Public administration must be governed by the democratic values and principles enshrined in the Constitution, including the following principles: . . . (e) People's needs must be responded to, and the public must be encouraged to participate in policy-making. . . .'

satisfied by an organ of government is justiciable. (Constitution of South Africa 1996, s 167(4)(e))[16] In the Khoisan appeal, the court emphasised the importance of public participation as follows:

> The importance of public participation in South Africa cannot be understated. Affected persons must be afforded the opportunity to *meaningfully participate* in the legislative process. Public participation acts as a safeguard to prevent the interests of the marginalised being ignored or misrepresented. The significance of public participation for the advancement of South Africa's democratic project is underscored by the colonial and apartheid governments' complete disregard of the views of the people in legislating their lives. (emphasis added) (Khoisan Act appeal 2023, para 3)[17]

The Constitution recognises the right to administrative justice and requires that the exercise of a public power which falls within the scope of administrative action must be procedurally fair. It also acknowledges that a person is entitled to written reasons to explain the rationale for an administrative action. (Constitution of South Africa 1996, s 33; Promotion of Administrative Justice Act 2000)[18]

---

[16] The justiciability of the adequacy of public participation does not relate to the *merit* of legislation, but rather to the *process* by which legislation came into being. This is consistent with the intention behind FPIC, because courts focus on the process of negotiation rather than the reason for or merits of disagreement. If a person therefore challenges an Act in South Africa, they may refer to the suitability of the legislation to demonstrate that the *legislative process* that had been followed did not comply with the constitutional or statutory obligation of public consultation. In this respect note, for example, how in the Khoisan appeal the applicant took issue with the process leading to the enactment of the statute and the lack of adequate public consultation, and how the inadequate consultation had given rise to legislation that was unsuitable to regulate the topic. (Khoisan Act appeal 2023, para 16) The court will, however, 'discourage opportunist reliance' on purported shortcomings in the legislative process as an excuse to challenge the validity of legislation. (Doctors for Life case 2006, para 216) Parliament therefore sets its own processes for public participation, whereas the courts determine whether those processes are 'reasonable', without expressing a view on the suitability or acceptability of legislation. (Khoisan Act appeal 2023, para 34) In the Doctors for Life case, the court usefully identified factors that would indicate whether the legislative and consultative process adopted by Parliament was reasonable. (Doctors for Life case 2006, paras 128–129)

[17] The use of the expression 'meaningfully participate' is not dissimilar to that of the expression 'reasonable opportunity to participate in decision-making' as used by the Federal Court of Australia in respect of consultation with indigenous people about what happens on their traditional lands. (Tipakalippa case 2022, para 104).

[18] '33. (1) Everyone has the right to administrative action that is lawful, reasonable and procedurally fair. (2) Everyone whose rights have been adversely affected by administrative action has the right to be given written reasons. (3) National legislation must be enacted to give effect to these rights, and must – (a) provide for the review of administrative action by a court or, where

The Local Government: Municipal Systems Act 32 of 2000 provides for consultation with local communities on municipal service agreements. (s 80(2)) Additionally, it emphasises the need for municipalities to 'develop a culture of municipal governance that complements formal representative government with a system of participatory governance'. (s 16(1)) Local community participation must be facilitated and encouraged in all aspects of local government. These provisions are intended to give effect to the Preamble of the Act, which explains that 'a fundamental aspect of the new local government system is the active engagement of communities in the affairs of municipalities of which they are an integral part, and in particular in planning, service delivery and performance management'. (Local Government: Municipal Systems Act 2000) Mukwevho refers to these provisions as 'another good example' of the principle of FPIC being applied to South African consultation processes. (Mukwevho 2022, 154) It is notable, however, that neither this Act nor FPIC mandates actual consent from an affected person or community. FPIC has nonetheless become a rallying-term for good faith consultation in general and not only directed at indigenous communities.

The Spatial Planning and Land Use Management Act 16 of 2013 provides for consultation with communities in matters such as: the adoption of land use schemes (s 24); timeframes for municipal planning (s 44); development applications (s 52(6)); making of regulations (s 54); and procedures for public consultation (Schedule 1) (Spatial Planning Act 2013). This Act highlights the importance of consultation with local communities in the conduct of planning affairs at local levels. Like the Local Government: Municipal Systems Act, this Act does not mandate actual consent from an affected person or community. Parties therefore can participate in consultation without ending up with an agreement.

The Interim Protection of Informal Land Rights Act 31 of 1996 deals with the acquisition of communal land. The Act provides that land *may not* be acquired without consent and, if held communally, only in compliance with custom and usage of the community. (s 2(1) and (2)) The process to be adopted when communal land is acquired is specified as follows:

> '[A] decision to dispose of any such right may *only* be taken by a majority of the holders of such rights present or represented at a meeting convened for the purpose of considering such disposal and of which they have been given sufficient notice, and in which they have bad a reasonable opportunity to participate.' (s 2(4)). As explained

---

appropriate, an independent and impartial tribunal; (b) impose a duty on the state to give effect to the rights in subsections (1) and (2); and (c) promote an efficient administration.'

> in greater detail below, actual consent is not required in international law under FPIC regardless of the word 'consent' being used. It is only when a statute specifically mandates consent, as in the case of the Interim Protection of Informal Land Rights Act, that *actual consent* of the land-owing community is required. (emphasis added) (Baleni case 2019, para 79)[19]

The standard for consultation established in the Interim Protection of Informal Land Rights Act reflects a significantly higher requirement than that sought by the general notion of FPIC, given that the Act requires consent while the international understanding of FPIC does not require consent. (De Villiers 2023h, 128) As Barrie puts it: 'Despite UNDRIP being a non-binding declaration, it is not without any standard-setting significance.' (Barrie 2024b, 200) UNDRIP refers to FPIC as an effort to achieve consent rather than an obligation to reach agreement. Although in Baleni it was suggested that FPIC means a veto in international law, such a statement is erroneous since FPIC in international law refers to the process and effort to reach agreement, not a right of veto.

The National Environmental Management Act 107 of 1998 aims to facilitate and encourage public participation in environmental governance. (National Environmental Act 1998 Preamble) The Act provides that decisions concerning the environment must be taken in consideration of the 'interests, needs and values of all interested and affected parties', including those with 'traditional knowledge', as well as with the objective of 'community well-being and empowerment.' (s 2(4)(g)–(h)) Several other pieces of legislation dealing with the environment and environmental impact assessments require similar obligations of community consultation. Most notable for this chapter is the Environmental Impact Assessment Regulations, 2014, which provide, in regs 39(1), 40 and 41, a useful standard comparable to the highest level of FPIC, as follows:

> If the proponent is not the owner or person in control of the land on which the activity is to be undertaken, the proponent must, before applying for an environmental authorisation in respect of such activity, obtain the *written consent* of the landowner or person in control of the land to undertake such activity on that land. (emphasis added) (reg 39(1))
>
> The public participation process contemplated in this regulation must provide access to *all information that reasonably has* or may have the potential to influence any decision with regard to an application . . . (emphasis added) (reg 40(2)).

---

[19] The Act acknowledges that a community may not be able reach internal consensus on its response to a proposal, and therefore mention is made of majority decision-making. This standard can also be achieved with reference to the traditional forms of decision-making of a community, which may not be based on an actual vote.

> The person conducting a public participation process must take into account any relevant guidelines applicable to public participation as contemplated in section 24J of the Act and must give notice to *all potential interested and affected parties* of an application or proposed application .... (emphasis added) (reg 41(2))

The Mineral and Petroleum Resources Development Act 28 of 2002 sets an objective for developers to 'contribute towards the socio-economic development of the areas in which they are operating'. (Preamble) Parties who have an interest in or who are affected by an application must be informed and given adequate opportunity to make submissions. (ss 10(b) and 24(4)(b)) The consent of interested parties is not required, but they must be given an opportunity to make inputs, albeit within a tight timeframe of 30 and 180 days respectively.[20] The statutory standard does not mandate consent or a veto, but it does require a timely sharing of information and consultation in an attempt to reach agreement. (Bengwenyama Minerals case 2011) In another context the court has emphasised that consultation implies that parties engage each other in a 'proactive and honest endeavour to find mutually acceptable solutions'. (Port Elizabeth Municipality case 2005, para 39) In the Baleni case the court declared that, while consent is not required pursuant to the Mineral Act, if the project affects an indigenous community, then their consent is required pursuant to the Interim Protection of Informal Land Rights Act (see discussion below). The standard for consultation set by the Mineral Act is consistent with good faith requirements under the Native Title regime in Australia (see discussion below). These good faith principles emphasise the importance of sharing information, doing so in a timely manner, declaring details for the life of the project, and attempting to reach agreement but without any obligation to do so. These principles are arguably as close as one could possibly get to codifying, by way of jurisprudence, an international standard for FPIC. (De Villiers 2023h, 104–5).

[20] The 180 days provided for in the Mineral and Petroleum Resources Act mirrors the six-month period in native title proceedings in Australia within which 'good faith' negotiation must occur when an activity such as mining is intended on traditionally held land. It is notable, however, that a vast administrative system under the Native Title Act 1993 and the National Native Title Tribunal exists in Australia to support and adjudicate on good faith negotiations. Aboriginal people can, within the constraints of the Native Title Act, object to the grant of a mining lease on the basis that good faith negotiations had not occurred. (Bartlett 2020, WMC case 1999) These objections are not often successful, but the objection process has empowered many Aboriginal communities to have a greater say about what happens on their traditional lands, while mining companies have, in many instances, developed advanced and far-reaching agreements with Aboriginal communities to ensure projects are not delayed through litigation. (O'Faircheallaigh 2021)

The Promotion of Administrative Justice Act 3 of 2000 sets out requirements for administrative decisions that require procedural fairness. This includes, but it not limited to, the right of an affected person to be given adequate notice of the intended measure and a reasonable opportunity to make representations to the decision-maker. (Promotion of Administrative Justice Act 2000, s 3) This right to procedurally fair administrative action avails itself to indigenous landowners whose interest in land is affected by a decision, for example the granting of a permit to access their land, to explore or to build infrastructure. In the Sustaining the Wild Coast case the court considered the consultation that had taken place with the local indigenous community about seismic blasts to be conducted on their land, and concluded that fair administrative procedures had not been followed. (Sustaining the Wild Coast case 2024)

These are a few examples of statutory provisions in South Africa that are directed at the empowerment of communities and individuals when their rights and interests are affected by legislative and administrative measures. While the concept of FPIC does not appear in the South African legislative lexicon, as elaborated on below, the elements of good faith consultation that make up FPIC are often reflected in South African legislation and jurisprudence. Few nations have included FPIC in domestic legislation, but many require good faith consultation when dealing with the rights and interests of indigenous people.

The framework within which consultation in South Africa must occur can, generally, be described with reference to the following benchmarks: (a) *information* about an intended event or action must be provided to those affected or with an interest; (b) the information must be provided in a *timely manner*; (c) the information must be detailed enough and understandable, for the entire project as well as rehabilitation, to enable those affected to obtain *advice*, including expert advice, and to formulate a *position* intra-community; (d) consultation must be *aimed* at reaching some form of agreement, without any legal mandate to reach actual agreement; (e) the position adopted by the community must be developed *freely*, without undue pressure or influence; and (f) both sides are under an obligation to conduct consultation in *good faith*.

7.3 THE SUBSTANCE OF FPIC IN SOUTH AFRICAN JURISPRUDENCE

Although the concept of FPIC is not a legal term in South Africa, reference has been made to it, for example in the Baleni case, and the phrase is often used in the literature. (Barrie 2024b) Additionally, statutory standards outlining consultation requirements bear similarities to the principles of FPIC. The following judgments are particularly relevant to this chapter:

In the Bengwenyama Minerals case (Bengwenyama Minerals case 2011) it was held that the consultation with a community affected by a proposal pursuant to the Mineral and Petroleum Resources Development Act 28 of 2002 must be *meaningful*, including making adequate information available to enable the community to make an informed decision about the application. The court highlighted that the scope and impact of a proposed project determines the nature and extent of consultation – a sliding scale approach, which reflects Canadian, Australian and Inter-American Court jurisprudence. (Saramaka case 2007) This is an approach consistent with international practice, namely that the greater the likely impact of a proposed development, the greater the expectation and duration of consultation. Ultimately, there is no fixed standard for consultation, as the specific circumstances of the community and the proposed development determine what consultation is adequate in a particular situation. The following principles of consultation identified by the court are relevant for the purposes of this chapter:

> [64] The purpose of the notification and subsequent consultation must thus be related to the impact that the granting of a prospecting right will have on the landowner or lawful occupier. The Community is the landowner of the farms at stake in this application and therefore I will restrict further discussion to the position of landowners.
>
> [65] One of the purposes of consultation with the landowner must surely be to see whether some *accommodation is possible* between the applicant for a prospecting right and the landowner insofar as the interference with the landowner's rights to use the property is concerned. . . . The Act's equivalent is consultation, the purpose of which should be to ascertain whether an accommodation of sorts can be reached in respect of the impact on the landowner's right to use his land. Of course the Act *does not impose agreement* on these issues as a requirement for granting the prospecting right, but that does not mean that consultation under the Act's provisions does not require engaging in good faith to attempt to reach accommodation in that regard. Failure to reach agreement at this early consultation stage might result in the holder of the prospecting right having to pay *compensation* to the landowner at a later stage. . . .
>
> [66] Another more general purpose of the consultation is to provide landowners or occupiers with the *necessary information* on everything that is to be done so that they can make an *informed decision* in relation to the representations to be made, whether to use the internal procedures if the application goes against them and whether to take the administrative action concerned on review. The consultation

> process and its result is an integral part of the *fairness process* because the decision cannot be fair if the administrator did not have full regard to precisely what happened during the consultation process in order to determine whether the consultation was sufficient to render the grant of the application procedurally fair.
>
> . . .
>
> [67] The consultation process required by section 16(4)(b) of the Act thus requires that the applicant must: (a) *inform* the landowner in writing that his application for prospecting rights on the owner's land has been accepted for consideration by the Regional Manager concerned; (b) inform the landowner *in sufficient detail* of what the prospecting operation will entail on the land, in order for the landowner to assess what impact the prospecting will have on the landowner's use of the land; (c) consult with the landowner with a *view to reach an agreement* to the satisfaction of both parties in regard to the impact of the proposed prospecting operation; and (d) submit the result of the consultation process to the Regional Manager within 30 days of receiving notification to consult. (emphasis added) (Bengwenyama Minerals case 2011, paras 64–67)

Several key elements arise from the Bengwenyama Minerals case to give practical content to FPIC:

- relevant information about a proposed project must be provided in time to the community;
- the information must be adequate with reference to the project's likely impact, duration, rehabilitation and scale, as well as any other relevant information;
- adequate time must be allowed for a community to obtain expert advice, and to consult and discuss within the community in order for a response to be formulated;
- the consultation with the community must be conducted in good faith, with an agreed outcome encouraged but not mandated; and
- the consultation is aimed at preventing litigation at a later stage, because a community may claim damages in the future if their interests had been adversely affected by a project as a result of consultation.

In the Maledu case the respondent sought an eviction order against an indigenous community. (Maledu case 2018) The respondent, who held mining rights over certain land, applied for an interdict to prevent the applicants from entering the land, bringing livestock onto the land, or erecting structures on the land. The applicants did not deny preventing the respondent from accessing the land in question. Instead, they asserted ownership of the land, emphasised the lack of consultation pursuant to the relevant legislation, and highlighted the absence of their consent for mining operations on the land to proceed. The applicants relied on the provisions of the Interim Protection of Informal Land Rights Act. (Maledu case 2018, para 16) While the court did not directly refer to international developments regarding FPIC, it acknowledged the essential principles underlying FPIC by stating the following: the legislature expressed 'serious concerns' about the rights and interests of landowners and lawful occupiers of land (para 78); some 'accommodation' needs to be sought between parties (para 79); adequate information is essential to enable landowners, including informal landowners and occupants, to make informed decisions (paras 80, 97); communities have a right to determine what happens on their land (para 95); and the impact of a mining lease would deprive the community of their rights (para 102). The court concluded that the mining lease could not be granted since the applicant community had refused the terms thereof (para 109). The reasoning of the court highlights the importance of the statutory regime under which the dispute emerged. The court found no reason to cite or consider international or foreign law, because the rights of the community to be consulted *and to consent* arose from the relevant statute. Therefore, there was no reliance on the concept of FPIC as understood in international law.

In the Baleni case (Baleni case 2019), the proceeding was brought by an indigenous community, the uMgungundlovu community, who opposed the grant of a mining lease in respect of their land. The principal ground for the objection was that they had not been properly consulted and had not given their consent for the grant to occur. (paras 24–25) The proponents of the development contended that the approval (consent) of a land occupier was not required, given that only consultation – and not consent – was mandated pursuant to the Minerals and Petroleum Resources Development Act. The court accepted that the concerns of the applicants were real and that the mining lease grant may seriously impact on their rights, stating: 'Their fears are not without merit. It is well documented that customary communities, such as the applicants, tend to suffer disproportionately from the impacts of mining activities as they are directly affected by the environmental pollution, airborne diseases, loss of their farmland and grazing land, forced displacement and the loss of community amongst other things.' (para 19) The court also acknowledged that there were, however, divisions within the community about the merit of the mining lease grant. (para 21)[21]

[21] For an in-depth discussion of the Maledu and Baleni cases see Massyn. (Massyn 2022) Massyn comes to the conclusion that the judgments left communities vulnerable and that their

Pertinent to the resolution of the Baleni dispute was the potential applicability of two statutes to the grant of the mining lease, each with different standards for community consent: the Minerals and Petroleum Resources Development Act refers to 'consultation' with a landowner, while the Interim Protection of Informal Land Rights Act refers to the 'consent' of a landowner.

The court acknowledged that international law 'plays an important role in interpreting statutes' (para 37), declaring that the grant of a mining lease does constitute a 'deprivation' under the Mining Act and that the activities arising from it may 'interfere substantially' with the agricultural activities of the community and its way of life. (paras 58–59) The court then explained the different focus of the Mining Act, which is concerned with the promotion of equitable access to mineral resources, and the Informal Land Rights Act, which seeks to protect communities that previously were victims of discrimination. (para 64) The Informal Land Rights Act aims to safeguard informal rights in land, including occupation and access, that are governed by tribal, customary or indigenous law. (para 71) The court went on to declare that 'consent' cannot be equated to 'consultation'; consent requires actual agreement, whereas consultation 'envisages a process of consensus seeking that may not necessarily result in an agreement.' (para 71) The two Acts therefore require different standards of consultation and serve different purposes. These can nonetheless be harmonised as the Informal Land Rights Act accords special protection only to traditional communities. (para 76)

The court then declared, in essence, that, pursuant to the Informal Lands Rights Act, the *consent* of the applicants had to be obtained for mining and, since such consent had not been provided, the approval of the mining lease was deemed invalid. (paras 84–85) The same standard of consultation rights, namely consent, *would not* be available to other communities, indigenous or tribal, who fall outside the scope of the Interim Protection of Informal Land Rights Act.

The court briefly referred to international law of relevance to the rights of indigenous people (paras 79–82), also noting, in passing, the international understanding of FPIC. (paras 79, 81, 82) Notably, the court did not engage in

---

ability to exert greater control about what happens on their land ought to be enhanced. (Massyn 2022, 105) In similar vein to concerns expressed about the operation of the Native Title Act in Australia, Massyn is of the view that, with the pre-eminence of mining, the rights of indigenous communities may suffer. In the case of Baleni it is argued by Massyn that the rights of customary owners and common-law owners are treated differently, with the former having the benefit of a veto while the latter communities only have consultation rights. (Massyn 2022, 108).

any in-depth analysis of foreign case law, other than to cite the Poma Poma case of Peru. (Poma Poma case 2009) While some authors (such as Mukwevho 2022, 159) suggest that the court not only relied on the concept of FPIC but actually endorsed FPIC in South African law, on close reading this is not an accurate analysis of the judgment.[22] The substance of the judgment, which demanded the consent of the indigenous community, was entirely based on the construction of the Informal Land Rights Act.

The status of FPIC in international law and its applicability to South Africa was, at best, raised *obiter* by Basson and most certainly not as a source of rights in South Africa, nor as a tool for statutory interpretation in this dispute. To suggest, as Mukwevho does, that the Baleni case 'cemented' the application of the FPIC principle within South African law (Mukwevho 2022, 160) is, with respect, an overreach. Barrie also suggests that the Baleni court was influenced by international law (Barrie 2024b, 216), but I would propose that on proper reading the right of the community to refuse consent was statute-based, not arising from common law, customary law or international law. Mensi acknowledges the importance of Baleni, but correctly notes that international law does not grant a veto to indigenous communities albeit that there is a duty to seek consent even if it is not achieved. (Mensi 2022, 394) As Meyer correctly observes: 'the continued invocation of the Baleni and Maledu judgments *is reliant* on the continued existence of the IPILRA [Informal Land Rights Act].' (Meyer 2020, 14)

In the Observatory Civic Association case the court issued an urgent interdict to prevent a development from progressing, regardless of concerns raised that the

---

[22] Barrie is of the opinion that the Baleni judgment has 'far reaching implications' for the South African land reform process because of the standard of consent required pursuant to international law. (Barrie 2024a, 900) My proposition is that Judge Basson erred by stating that international law requires free, prior and informed consent as is understood by actual consent. A preferred analysis of international law is that it requires striving towards consent. The conclusion drawn by Barrie is therefore also open to challenge, including the assertion that FPIC 'has evolved into a norm of customary international law'. (Barrie 2024a, 906) FPIC is in an evolution process that may or may not ultimately become a norm of customary international law, but its use, consistency and clarity is thus far inadequate to be declared a binding legal norm in international law. Barrie seems to agree with my observation that FPIC is not a justiciable right in international law when he states as follows: 'Measured against the requirements necessary for customary international law, FPIC is *moving inexorably* towards meeting such demands' albeit that the standard of legal norm has not been reached. (emphasis added) (Barrie 2024b, 219) I would challenge this statement since there is inadequate evidence of widely held state practice based on a belief its law in support of FPIC to adduce it is evolving into customary law. The Baleni judgment ultimately turned on the statute under which it was brought, and not on provisions of international law.

delay would cause loss of employment and other economic benefits. The court was concerned that, regardless of assurances being given by the developer of a project, adequate consultation with the local indigenous community had not occurred. (Observatory Civic Association case 2023) The court concluded as follows without citing FPIC but nevertheless reflecting the spirit of consultation:

> The fact that the applicants may have unduly delayed instituting urgent review proceedings did not detract from the relevant decision-makers' *duty to properly consult* with the First Nations peoples, and the duty of the courts to ensure that the rights of vulnerable indigenous groups were protected. This matter was urgent because, if not given an audience in the urgent court, the applicants and affected First Nations groups would be denied substantive redress in due course. There was no reason why an urgent review should not be heard after *proper consultation* with the affected First Nations peoples. Since the commencement of the construction works was irrelevant in the determination of the interdictory relief sought by the applicants, construction had to be halted pending a proper consultation process. (emphasis added) (Observatory Civic Association case 2023, 585)[23]

In the Sustaining the Wild Coast case the question arose whether the local indigenous community had been adequately consulted before a decision was made pursuant to the Minerals and Petroleum Resources Development Act for seismic testing to occur on their land. The court concluded that consultation had not been adequate. The court found:

> When administrative action materially and adversely affects the rights of any person, their right to procedural fairness is triggered. It can hardly be in dispute that Impact was required to meaningfully consult with the communities and individuals that would be affected by the seismic blasting. (Sustaining the Wild Coast case 2024, para 19)

The court identified the following practical steps as *indicia*, albeit not a closed list, of measures to ensure a process of consultation: adequate and timely notification, adequate detail to enable the community to assess the impact of the measure, using language and technical terms that are understandable to the community, speaking in a language that is known to the community, and placing notices in the media that are accessible and used by the community. (Sustaining the Wild Coast case 2024, paras 21–24) The court found that the consultation 'was more illusory than real, was thus manifestly inadequate'. (Sustaining the Wild Coast case 2024, para 24)

---

[23] The use of the phrase 'First Nations' is novel to South Africa since it is not clear who the community is that is being referred to and how they come to be described as first nations.

In short, it is one thing to say South African statutory law and jurisprudence are consistent with international understandings of FPIC, but it is quite another to suggest the Baleni case cemented an international understanding of FPIC, the meaning of which has not yet been clarified even in international hard or soft law, into South African law. Generally, courts do not distinguish in substance between FPIC and good faith consultation. Nonetheless, the Baleni, Bengwenyama Minerals, Maledu and Sustaining the Wild Coast judgments provide useful insights into the objectives and standards arising from specific legislation, as well as focusing the attention on the importance to distinguish between consent and consultation. While the word 'consent' is used in FPIC, its legal application, as discussed below, bears the hallmarks of consultation rather than actual consent.

7.4 THE SUBSTANCE OF FPIC IN INTERNATIONAL LAW

This section provides an overview of international legal efforts aimed at transitioning from theoretical discussions to the practical implementation of consultative rights for indigenous peoples. More specifically, it focuses on giving practical content to the legal meaning of FPIC. The examples presented, while not intended to be exhaustive, serve as an attempt to highlight the essential elements of consultation within the context of FPIC, as well as the universal norms that have developed in this regard, if indeed these norms can be regarded as 'universal' in the true sense of the word (perhaps a better approach is to talk about international *good practice*).[24] The focus lies specifically on the Indigenous and Tribal Peoples Convention, 1989 (No 169) (ILO 169 1989) and the United Nations Declaration on the Rights of Indigenous People (UNDRIP) (UNDRIP 2007) as the primary instruments in international law aimed at protecting the rights of indigenous people. Importantly, while the rights of indigenous people are principally associated with their traditional lands along with the customs and

[24] It is important to acknowledge that the jurisprudence resulting from consultations with indigenous peoples is limited to a few countries. Caution should thus be exercised before these judgments are purported to be 'universal' norms or deemed to form the basis of customary international law. Evidence in literature indicates a rush to declare the principles of FPIC to be universal legal norms, whereas, in fact, international and municipal law are still in their infancy when it comes to establishing the universality and content of the consultative rights of indigenous people. Some judgments are to be welcomed and can constitute useful precedents for purposes of 'consideration', but they are far short of reflecting customary international law or universal norms.

practices associated with these traditional lands, indigenous people also have the right to be consulted about polices that concern them directly or predominantly. (Erueti 2022) The importance of consultation about what happens on traditional lands was described as follows in the Awas Tingni case by the Inter-American Court of Human Rights:

> Land is not merely a matter of possession and production but a material and spiritual element, which they must fully enjoy . . . to preserve their cultural legacy and transmit it to future generations. (Awas Tingni case 2001, para 149)

7.4.1 Consultation pursuant to ILO 169

ILO 169 is the only legally binding instrument in international law that deals specifically with the rights of indigenous people.[25] South Africa is not a party to ILO 169. ILO 169 adopts a 'holistic' approach to a wide range of policy issues that affect indigenous people. Relevant for the purposes of this chapter, ILO 169 also specifically addresses the consultative rights of indigenous people. (Handbook ILO 2013, xi) It sets a minimum threshold for the protection of indigenous people in general, and for the consultative and participatory rights of indigenous people in particular. (Yupsanis 2011)

The underlying rationale for ILO 169 is that indigenous people retain an inherent sovereignty that had historically existed, and they are thus entitled as an ongoing society with own laws and customs to be accommodated, in accordance with their traditional laws and customs, about matters that impact on them, particularly concerning their traditional lands, customs and culture. (Kryazhkov and Garipov 2021, 1009) The limitations faced by ILO 169 are, however, of such a nature that Jiménez cautions that one should 'think twice before getting too enthusiastic' about its possible reach. (Jiménez 2022, 183)

---

[25] ILO 169 is an international treaty that becomes legally binding upon states through ratification. Beyond the ratifying countries, ILO 169 is also an international reference point which is often cited in the literature and used as a norm-setting standard by UN bodies, regional human rights bodies, literature, training materials, and occasionally national courts. ILO 169 has inspired numerous developments, safeguard policies and national legislative frameworks in municipal law. The decision to ratify ILO 169, like any other international treaty or convention, is a sovereign and voluntary decision of a state. (Handbook ILO 2013, 5) The binding nature of the treaty's provisions is likely the reason why so few countries have ratified ILO 169 (at the time of writing only 23 had done so). Larsen expresses the view that, 'despite relatively low ratification numbers, the relevance and global reach of the Convention has grown significantly not least through its incorporation in a wide range of complementary standards and jurisprudence.' (Larsen 2020, 94).

The concept of 'free, prior and informed consent' (as used in UNDRIP) is only used exceptionally in ILO 169, for example when relocation of an indigenous community occurs, and even then FPIC is not an absolute veto. (ILO 169 1989, art 16(2)) ILO 169 arguably seeks a similar outcome as FPIC by the generous use of the term 'consultation', albeit that in the literature it has been suggested that the 'consent' in FPIC carries more weight that 'consult' under ILO 169. I do not agree since, first, the 'consent' in UNDRIP is not interpreted as a legal veto; (Saugeen First Nation case 2017, paras 10–29) and, secondly, UNDRIP is not justiciable, while ILO 169 with its provision for consultation is at least justiciable to signatory parties. UNDRIP implies striving towards consensus, but on the other hand UNDRIP has no legal authority, while ILO 169 is a binding treaty.

Indigenous people in signatory countries cannot directly invoke ILO 169 before the ILO supervisory bodies or within their domestic setting, unless domestic legal arrangements specifically reference or incorporate ILO 169 within municipal law. ILO 169 can, however, be relied upon by ILO tripartite constituents to articulate the issues and concerns of indigenous people.[26] Domestic courts may also draw upon ILO 169 principles to guide or inspire them in giving content to domestic collective and individual consultation rights, particularly if the host nation of the court is a signatory to ILO 169.[27]

---

[26] Larsen describes the inability of indigenous people to directly litigate pursuant to ILO 169 as a serious hurdle in its operation which consequently frustrates the potential of ILO 169. (Larsen 2020) While this criticism is valid, it should also be noted that some municipal courts have nevertheless read into the existing constitutional and statutory text of their jurisdiction a legal obligation to consult with indigenous people akin to what is provided for by ILO 169. Even if ILO 169 is not explicitly cited in municipal jurisprudence, it fulfils at least an educative, interpretive and influencing role. ILO 169, in similar vein to UNDRIP, contributes to education, policy development, inspiration and development of common law. See, for example, how the court in Canada declared that 'the jurisprudence of this Court supports the view that the duty to consult and accommodate is part of a process . . . flowing from rights guaranteed by s 35(1) of the Constitution Act, 1982.' (Haida Nation case 2004, para 32) The Canadian court found no reason to revert to international law to substantiate the obligation to consult. However, it is not implausible that the court was influenced, or perhaps even inspired, by international law, similar to the inspiration the Australian High Court drew from international law in the Mabo judgments. (Mabo case (1) 1988); Mabo (2) 1992; Barrie 2021) There are several examples (see discussion below) in the Americas where ILO 169 has become incorporated into domestic law and where courts have relied on the principles espoused therein. (Doyle 2014; Tomaselli and Cittadino 2021)

[27] See, for example, how, although Canada initially regarded UNDRIP as having no legal effect in domestic Canadian law, in 2012 it adjusted its position by stating that Canadian courts could consult instruments of international law when interpreting the Canadian constitution and laws. (Canada case 2012) Courts and human rights bodies may therefore use the provisions of

The importance of consultation is a fundamental principle of ILO 169. The essence of the obligation to consult is found in art 6(1), which stipulates that governments must, 'in good faith',

> *consult* the peoples concerned, through appropriate procedures and in particular through their representative institutions, whenever consideration is being given to legislative or administrative measures which *may affect them directly.* (emphasis added) (ILO 169 1989, art 6(1))

In addition to the right to be consulted, ILO 169 also focuses on the right to participation, which is formulated in art 7 as follows:

> The peoples concerned shall have the right to decide their *own priorities* for the process of development as it affects their lives, beliefs, institutions and spiritual well-being and the lands they occupy or otherwise use, and to exercise control, to the extent possible, over their own economic, social and cultural development. In addition, they shall participate in the formulation, implementation and evaluation of plans and programmes for national and regional development which *may affect them directly.* (emphasis added) (ILO 169 1989, art 7)

The *right to participation* and the *right to be consulted* are two sides of a coin that can, in effect, be called a collective right of self-determination. Among the essential elements of self-determination are the ability to participate in decisions, to be consulted when interests are affected, to nominate negotiating representatives, and to make informed decisions. The duty to consult also implies the creation of institutions and processes whereby indigenous people can be consulted. (Handbook ILO 2013, 12) The procedural fairness of self-determination in general, and the right to consultation in particular, are confirmed in a handbook drafted by the United Nations, which states that:

ILO 169 and UNDRIP to inform and guide them when interpreting municipal law. In this respect, the Parliament of Canada is an example of one of a few countries that have enacted the United Nations Declaration on the Rights of Indigenous Peoples Act in which in the Preamble of the Act the UNDRIP is referred to as a 'source of law'. (Canada UNDRIP Act 2021, Preamble) UNDRIP is thereby declared in Canada as a 'universal international human rights instrument' with application in Canadian law and it is intended to 'provide a framework' to implement UNDRIP in Canadian law. (Canada UNDRIP Act 2021, art 4) Note in this regard Chapters 3 and 4, in which a discussion takes place about the power of courts in South Africa to 'consider' international law and foreign jurisprudence when resolving domestic disputes. (Constitution of South Africa 1996, ss 39(1), 231–233; Baleni case 2019, para 37)

> For an FPIC process to be effective and result in consent or lack of it, *the way* in which the process is conducted is paramount. (emphasis added) (Food and Agriculture UN 2016, 5)[28]

In the context of this book's theme, FPIC often represents the interface between state law and non-state law, where two systems meet and interact through a process of consultation.

The essential principles under ILO 169 that provide guidance for practical compliance with the duty to consult have crystallised to mean the following:

> Consultation under the Convention means: 1. Consultations must be formal, full and exercised in *good faith*; here must be a *genuine dialogue* between governments and indigenous and tribal peoples characterised by communication and understanding, *mutual respect*, good faith and the sincere wish to reach a common accord; 2. Appropriate *procedural mechanisms* have to be put in place at the national level and they have to be in a form appropriate to the circumstances; 3. Consultations have to be undertaken through indigenous and tribal peoples' *representative institutions* as regards legislative and administrative measures; 4. Consultations have to be undertaken with the *objective of reaching agreement* or consent to the proposed measures. Pro forma consultations or mere information will not meet the requirements of the Convention. At the same time, such consultations *do not imply a right to veto* nor is the result of the consultations necessarily the reaching of agreement or consent. (emphasis added) (CEACR 2011, 3)

The form and content of consultation procedures and mechanisms must essentially allow for the full expression of the viewpoints of the indigenous peoples concerned, in a timely manner, and based on their understanding of the issues involved, with account being taken of their spiritual beliefs.[29] In this way the indigenous peoples may be able to influence the outcome, and a consensus can be aspired to, and if possible achieved, enabling a policy or project to proceed in a manner that is acceptable to all parties. (CEACR 2011, 7)

---

[28] Note the UN practice manual that sets out, in a useful, practical guide, the recommended processes to seek and achieve consent pursuant to FPIC. (Food and Agriculture UN 2016)

[29] Note for example the Forrest case, in which the State Administrative Tribunal of Western Australia upheld an objection to a proposed construction of weirs in a river on the basis that the mythological sacred snake believed in by the local Aboriginal people may be disturbed and upset. Prichard J emphasised that the meaning of 'sacred' should not be confined by reference to concepts deriving from Christian religious usage or traditions. In construing an Act established to deal with Aboriginal culture, the word 'sacred' had to be understood to contemplate spiritual and mythological purposes consistent with the culture and traditions of the local indigenous people. (Forrest case 2023) On appeal the judgment was remitted to the original tribunal because it was found that the tribunal had not adequately considered the public interest of the proposed development. (Forrest appeal case 2024)

It must, however, be noted that 'there is no universally accepted definition of FPIC [or consultation]. Whatever the definition sought to be given to FPIC, the term *does not require unanimity* and the standards set by FPIC may be met even when individuals or groups within or among affected Indigenous Peoples explicitly disagree.' (emphasis added) (World Bank Environment and Social Framework 2016, 21) In other words, although the processes underlying FPIC are directed at *seeking* consensus, consensus is not mandated or legally required. Barrie puts it as follows: 'Measured against the requirements necessary for customary international law, FPIC is moving inexorably towards meeting such demands', albeit that the standard of legal norm has not been reached. (Barrie 2024b, 219)

Currently, it is possible that a government agency or a developer may comply with the requirement for good faith consultation pursuant to the principles underlying FPIC without an agreement being reached or conditions being imposed. In fact, access to land may be granted against the wishes of the indigenous community provided that FPIC processes have been adhered to. This highlights the imperfections of the FPIC processes, since participation by indigenous people may grant legitimacy to a project even if the project goes ahead against their wishes.

It is accepted in international law that the right to be consulted pursuant to ILO 169 does not imply the right of an indigenous community to veto a policy, bill or development. However, the consultation must be approached by the government or the proponent with a level of sincerity and an open mind *to attempt* to reach agreement, and thereby meet the requirements of good faith consultation.[30] At the same time, it is important to acknowledge that, under law, engaging in good faith consultation does not require a party to alter its negotiation stance (see, for example, Australian jurisprudence arising from good faith in native title proceedings, as discussed below). Put differently, good faith does not necessitate a shift in position by either party; rather, it entails an openness to consider divergent perspectives and reflect sincerely on them, as

[30] Note, for example, the Australian Barngarla case, in which the Federal Court found that, although extensive consultation had taken place with an Aboriginal community about the location of a nuclear waste storage facility, the facts supported a finding of 'apprehended bias' on the part of the government, as it had already made up its mind prior to the commencement of consultation about where nuclear waste should be stored. (Barngarla case 2023) This illustrates the distinction between standing firm in a position and being so biased that the outcome of a decision is already determined before consultation has begun.

well as a willingness to adjust a position based on thoughtful evaluation. Good faith consultation *may* in fact lead to a party changing its position, but this is not mandated. Furthermore, the requirements for good faith consultation apply to both sides of the negotiation table – the obligation to negotiate in good faith also rests on the indigenous party.[31]

The legal benchmarks for good faith negotiations can therefore be met without parties adjusting their respective position. This is highlighted in Australian jurisprudence where, as discussed below, the test for good faith negotiations pursuant to the native title regime is often met by governments and mining companies that comply by taking nominal *procedural* steps, but without changing their position or offering a substantive compromise. (Burnside 2009; Southalan and Fardin 2019) In light of this, I challenge the assertion made by an indigenous guide to self-determination, wherein indigenous peoples are advised that FPIC enables them to 'give or withhold consent to any activities that affect their lands, resources, and territories.' (Cultural Survival and First Peoples Worldwide, 2023, 1) This advice creates the unrealistic expectation of an ability to veto a proposed project, which is not generally provided for by ILO 169, UNDRIP or FPIC as a phrase or other provisions of international law. The withholding of consent does not imply a veto as if co-decision-making.

Free, prior and informed consent is therefore a moral claim or aspirational right, but not a justiciable right in international law. While consultation is a right under ILO 169, it does not entail a veto and legally only applies to signatory parties. Doyle acknowledges this 'interchangeable categorisation [of FPIC] as a right *or* a principle' (emphasis added), and says similar ambiguity applies to the term self-determination which is often presented as a right and as an aspiration. (Doyle 2014, 134)

It is important to acknowledge, however, that to an aggrieved indigenous community whose land is adversely affected by a development, there is a substantial difference between a right that can be legally enforced as a veto and a principle that may have important political imperatives but is unenforceable.

---

[31] Note, for example, the Munkara case in Australia, where the court found that evidence being relied upon to object to the laying of an undersea pipeline was not credible, that expert evidence supporting the objection was unreliable, and that coaching of witnesses may have occurred. (Munkara case 2024) The presiding judge described the expert evidence as 'so lacking integrity that no weight can be placed on [it]'. The court ultimately awarded A$9 million legal costs against the Environmental Defenders Office, who supported and financed the proceeding. (Rauso 2024; Munkara consent orders cost 2024)

Unfortunately, the literature and public statements often fail to distinguish between the justiciability of a right and the idealistic nature of a claim or a policy arising from FPIC. This overreach in the literature, where an aspiration is often presented as a judicially enforceable right, regularly causes despair among indigenous groups when they realise that within the context of their domestic situation their rights are weaker than had been assumed. (De Villiers 2023h, 81)

ILO 169 furthermore does not specify the nature of the consultative mechanisms or the procedures according to which they function. It does lay down, however, the general principle that whatever institutions are utilised for consultation, these institutions must reflect and accommodate the 'characteristics of the country, the specificities of the indigenous peoples and the subject and scope of the consultation'. (Handbook ILO 2013, 14) Therefore the consultative mechanisms must be tailor-made to fit the context of the country in question and the specific circumstances of the indigenous group involved.

The consultative mechanisms, whether temporary or permanent, must be developed through consultation with the indigenous people intended to be consulted, using relevant institutions that reflect indigenous laws and customs. This is an important step in the self-determination of a community. The task of setting up a process of consultation (so-called 'consultation about the process of consultation') is in itself an expression of self-determination, but it can also be a 'source of tension and negotiation'. (Larsen 2020, 98) Disagreements may arise about the process itself without discussion on matters of substance even having taken place.[32] These disagreements may extend to questions about who represents the community in negotiations, how decisions are made by the community, and what happens to minority views within the community.

---

[32] Observe, for example, Australia, where it has been held that, despite the failure of parties involved in negotiations pursuant to the Native Title Act to reach agreement within a specific time on the *terms* of the negotiation process, they can still nevertheless be deemed compliant with the duty to negotiate in good faith. Owing to disagreements in the FMG case about the process to be followed for substantive negotiations, the parties never got to the substance of the consultation. The court nevertheless found that the mining company had complied with good faith requirements. (FMG case 2009 para 29) Meanwhile, the refusal of an indigenous community to negotiate in good faith may be construed by a court as unreasonable conduct, and the community could potentially forgo the protections accorded by FPIC. This presents a potentially serious dilemma to indigenous communities: if they refuse to negotiate, a project may go ahead without them submitting inputs, extracting benefits for their community or imposing mitigations; whereas if they do negotiate, they may lend credibility to the approval process without having the means to prevent the project from proceeding or securing any benefits for their community.

The approaches adopted by signatory countries to enact ILO 169 into their municipal jurisdictions have been varied.[33] The reference to and reliance on ILO 169 by the Inter-American Court of Human Rights of the Americas have led Heinämäki and others to describe the Inter-American Court as *the* 'leading international judicial institution' in the field of indigenous rights, demonstrating how to integrate the principles of ILO 169 into domestic standards of consultation and indigenous protection. (Heinämäki, Allard and Kirchner 2017, 303)[34]

Similarly to the South African and Australian courts, the Inter-American Court of Human Rights places much emphasis on the *conduct* of parties in negotiations, rather than the legal entitlement of an indigenous community to veto a policy or measure.[35] Alva-Arevalo says that the discourse about actual consent or veto within the context of FPIC is 'a pointless discussion since veto power is not expressly recognised by any international instrument. The emphasis [of FPIC] is on the principle of good faith. . . .' (Alva-Arevalo 2021, 236)

The legitimacy of consultation is inevitably determined by whether the indigenous people whose views are sought to be canvassed endorse the consultative process and mechanism as credible and representative of their opinions. (Rombouts 2014) Although the principles underlying FPIC do not imply a veto

---

[33] For a useful analysis of compliance with ILO 169 in South America and several other countries, see the research report produced by Heinämäki and others from the office of the Prime Minister of Finland. (Heinämäki, Allard and Kirchner 2017, 308–491)

[34] Note, however, the observation made by the UN Committee on the Elimination of Discrimination about the failure of some states to comply with orders of the Inter-American Court: 'The Committee is concerned about the lack of the full implementation by the State party of the judgments of the Inter-American Court of Human Rights, specifically concerning the rights of indigenous and tribal peoples, in particular in the cases of Moiwana Community v. Suriname (2005), Saramaka People v. Suriname (2007) and Kaliña and Lokono peoples v. Suriname (2015) (arts. 2, 5 and 6).' (Mackay 2022, 49) The reluctance of states to adhere to international courts and tribunals is also evident in the case of the ECtHR.

[35] Doyle suggests that the right to FPIC implies 'that indigenous peoples have a *right to determine* if any projects that directly impact on them may, or may not, proceed and under what conditions'. (Doyle 2014, 146) This is an overreach, somewhat hyperbolic, and not consistent with nor reflective of the legal nature of the right to be consulted in international law pursuant to ILO 169 or UNDRIP. The statement also reflects the aspirational aspects of FPIC, and ignores its lack of justiciability. Doyle, in effect, concedes the validity of this criticism when she acknowledges that 'political will' is required to effectively operationalise FPIC. (Doyle 2014, 246) She concludes as follows: '[E]xperience [with FPIC] in contexts where consent is mandated by law, or commitments have been made to obtain it under voluntary standards, points to the limitations of the concept in practice and the challenges associated with operationalising it.' (Doyle 2014, 250) This observation from Doyle is consistent with that made by Southalan, that 'there is no universal agreement on exactly what FPIC entails'. (Southalan and Fardin 2019, 373)

for the indigenous community,[36] neither do they exempt the government or proponent of a development from good faith negotiations in an effort to achieve consent, including about the long-term effects of a proposal.[37] Consultation about a policy measure is not to be equated with a community merely being informed of a measure, or merely asked to express an opinion.[38] The government or development proponent must keep an open mind in heeding the concerns expressed by indigenous people. The opportunity granted to indigenous people must be meaningful. The proposal under discussion must also mitigate the impact made on the indigenous people, consider (but not necessarily reflect) any counter-proposals made by them, and make genuine efforts to accommodate any such proposals in good faith. For their part, indigenous people are expected to display similar good faith by taking into consideration the merit of the proposals put to them and the government's rationale for pursuing these options.

It has been suggested that the state has the duty to engage in a good faith attempt to 'obtain the actual consent' of the indigenous community concerned. (Heinämäki, Allard and Kirchner 2017, 457) This duty includes providing to indigenous people adequate information regarding the scope of a proposed development so they can make an informed decision about it. While 'actual consent' may be the ideal, international law does not mandate that agreement be

[36] In some exceptional circumstances, ILO 169 and UNDRIP foreshadow an explicit veto for indigenous people, such as when indigenous people are relocated from their traditional lands, their 'free and informed consent' is required. Article 16(2) of ILO 169 provides as follows: 'Where the relocation of these peoples is considered necessary as an exceptional measure, such relocation shall take place only with their free and informed consent.' But even in this context the right to veto is not absolute since policy or legislative measures may restrict it.

[37] Note the African Climate Alliance case in which the court was critical about the lack of consideration during consultation about the potential impacts of a coal-fired station on the long-term effect of children and the environment. (African Climate Alliance case 2024, para 25)

[38] See in this regard South Africa's Khoisan Act by which, in effect, the Khoisan community were to be *informed* of bills and may *comment* on them, but there was no obligation for government or Parliament to consult or negotiate in good faith. Furthermore, no prescribed time was granted for the Khoisan to be notified of a bill or policy measure, and there was no duty on Parliament to give proper weight to the advice received from the Khoisan. This cannot be regarded as meeting the standards of 'consultation' within the meaning of the term in international law, pursuant to ILO 169 or UNDRIP. The Constitutional Court in 2023 declared the Khoisan Act to be unconstitutional because of the lack of consultation leading up to its enactment. Parliament was granted three years to remedy the shortcomings. (Khoisan Act appeal 2023) The court did not comment on the merits of the consultation standards prescribed by the Act as its focus was on the inadequate legislative process followed to enact the statute. At the time of writing (March 2025), a new Khoisan Act had not yet been adopted by Parliament.

achieved, stipulating instead that serious consideration be given to the position put forward by the indigenous community. The ILO has commented as follows about the objective of reaching consent:

> The Committee considers that in the process of implementation of the law, all the representative organisations of peoples or communities should be able to participate and be consulted about legislative or administrative measures that may affect them directly, with the *objective of achieving agreement or consent.* The Committee points out, however, that art 6 does not stipulate that consent must be obtained in order for the consultations to be valid but it does require pursuit of the objective of achieving consent, which means setting in motion a process of dialogue and genuine exchange between the parties to be carried out in good faith. (emphasis added) (ILO Argentina 2008, para 81)

The practical meaning of good faith negotiations is therefore found in the specific circumstances of the consultation and cannot be encapsulated by a single set of criteria. Generally speaking, indigenous people must be provided with relevant and complete information about a proposed policy or project. Adequate time must be allowed for the indigenous leadership to consult internally with the community and consider the proposal. Support and resources may also have to be made available to the community to consult and obtain expert and legal advice.[39] There must also be acknowledgment that the extent of consultation may be more expansive, depending on the nature of the proposed measures to be undertaken. The ILO has summarised the obligation to consult in an effort to reach consent as follows:

> In keeping with paragraph 2 of art 6, consultation must take place in accordance with procedures that are appropriate to the circumstances, through the Indigenous peoples' representative institutions, in good faith and with the objective of achieving agreement or consent to the proposed measures. Appropriate procedures are those that create the conditions necessary to reach an agreement or consent concerning the proposed measures. This means that the expression 'appropriate procedures' must be understood in relation to the aims of the consultation. There is *no single model of appropriate procedures*, which should take into account national circumstances, the circumstances of the indigenous peoples concerned and the nature of the measures which are the object of the consultation process. (emphasis added) (ILO Brazil 2009, para 142)

[39] It is not unknown in land access negotiations in Australia that Aboriginal groups require a form of up-front payment from those seeking to access their lands to assist them with preparations for negotiations, or that proponents of a large development make available financial support for Aboriginal people to obtain expert assistance and advice in their negotiations.

The following essential principles about consultation, which are relevant to the questions under consideration in this chapter, have crystallised in the literature and jurisprudence arising from ILO 169:

First, ILO 169 offers no definition for who constitutes an indigenous people. Instead, it is left to individual states to determine, based on their historical circumstances, which, if any, community is regarded as indigenous.[40] While this may be very pragmatic, it creates much uncertainty and erodes the potential benefits to be derived from ILO 169. In practice, when applied to South Africa, it is not clear who the indigenous people of the country are – the Khoisan, African tribes who continue to live in a tribal manner on tribal lands, a sub-community of a tribal community, or all black communities (thereby rendering any special rights impractical because black people constitute a majority)?

Secondly, indigenous peoples have a right to be consulted about matters that impact directly or disproportionately on them, their identity, culture, traditions, customary laws, lands and their development. This right to consultation does not include consultation about other socio-economic policy considerations or legislation that may indirectly affect indigenous people as part of the general population. Such general socio-economic issues are dealt with by way of general democratic, political and legislative processes.

Thirdly, consultative mechanisms for indigenous people, whether ad hoc or permanent, must be designed in a manner that represents and reflects the wishes, traditions, rules and culture of the indigenous community. This implies the need for consultation on appropriate consultative mechanisms and processes. This includes determining who speaks on behalf of the community, how internal consultations with community leaders take place, authorisation for individuals to enter into agreements on behalf of the community, feedback mechanisms from representatives to the community, distribution of benefits arising from agreements within the community and resolution of disputes within

[40] Note for example how the UN Committee on the Elimination of Racial Discrimination has attempted to side-step the issue of who is indigenous (Khoisan) in Botswana by referring to 'ethnic' communities rather than indigenous people. For example, when making recommendations to allow indigenous people from a certain area to return to their ancestral lands, the Committee says as follows: 'The Committee urges the State party to fully implement the High Court's decision in Roy Sesana and others v. Attorney General, by allowing *all ethnic groups originating from the Central Kalahari Game Reserve* to return and settle there unconditionally. The Committee also recommends that the State party provide them with effective access to basic social services and enable them to resume their traditional activities without hindrance.' (Mackay 2022, 29)

the community. Representation and accountability *within* the community are important for purposes of accountability and transparency. It is important to note that absolute agreement within the community is not necessarily required, even in the establishment of consultation institutions.

Fourthly, consultation must take place in good faith, although this does not imply a legal veto, unless consensus is explicitly required by municipal law (as per statute in the Baleni case). Indigenous people, however, must be afforded the 'real possibility' to influence policies affecting their interests. Ideally, efforts should be made to reach agreement (Yupsanis 2011, 143), even though the term 'good faith' is not a term of art and circumstances determine whether, in a particular setting, good faith consultation did indeed take place.[41] Importantly, government does not abdicate its final approval power by requiring good faith consultation.

Fifthly, the nature of the consultation may be influenced by the gravity of the policy decision or impact of a proposed development on indigenous people, their lands and their culture. As a general principle, indigenous people must be provided with adequate time, information and resources to adopt an informed and free position.[42] The greater the impact of a proposed policy or development on the rights and interests of indigenous people, the more crucial it becomes for good faith negotiations to take place and the more important it is to reach an agreement, if possible, on the terms and conditions for the proposed policy

[41] In South Africa, Justice Basson has, for example, remarked as follows about the utility of international law as a source for interpreting statutes in South Africa: 'It is accepted that international law plays an important role in interpreting statues [in South Africa].' (Baleni case 2019, para 37) She then went on to say that the specific legislative scheme under which the dispute in the Baleni case was brought requires 'consent' from the local community, rather than mere consultation. She says this is consistent with international law, where in some circumstances a community has the right to refuse an activity on their land. (Baleni case 2019, para 78) These comments highlight the localised context of consultation and FPIC, since it deals with the specificity of a particular community and a proposed development, and is influenced by the particular statutory regime pursuant to which the development takes place. Although Basson seemed to suggest that consent is required in international law, the comment was made *obiter*.

[42] Note, for example, the Clyde River case in Canada, in which the court emphasised the importance of proper resourcing of indigenous people, the exchange of information and a demonstrated understanding of the position of the indigenous people. (Clyde River case 2017) O'Faircheallaigh cautions that indigenous people often do not receive full disclosure about the total impact of land-disturbing activities and that government should be obligated to fund and assist them to independently conduct impact assessments. (O'Faircheallaigh 2021, 75) Resource companies, on the other hand, often regard full disclosure as commercially sensitive, and a project sometimes develops its own momentum once mining starts. There is thus some uncertainty on both sides, with the effect that consultation may be an ongoing requirement.

measure or development. (Saramaka case 2007)[43] In some projects the scale of the operations may be of such a nature that ongoing consultation is required for the life of the venture.

These principles are not, however, regarded as hard law that can be judicially enforced under ILO 169 and on which indigenous people may rely to commence proceedings against their municipal governments. Instead, the principles represent important unenforceable soft law and serve as practical guidelines that may influence municipal policy and inform debate, as well as assist and inspire courts in their interpretation of duties arising from applicable legislation.[44] Consultation implies a commitment to a good faith process, and courts can consider these general principles to ascertain whether, in a particular circumstance, good faith consultation had occurred. (Ormaza 2017, 215) Municipal courts may, as in the Canadian Clyde River case, draw on general principles of good faith negotiations by importing them into domestic dealings with indigenous people. (Clyde River case 2017)

It is worth noting, however, the criticism expressed by Robinson towards Canadian courts when he argues that they are reluctant to give effect to FPIC unless explicitly authorised to do so by statute. (Robinson 2020) The same observation applies to South Africa, where courts have been careful to draw a distinction between consultation and consent based on the specific statute

[43] The court determined that in the event of a large-scale development or investment project which would have a major impact within Saramaka territory, the state has a duty not only to consult with the Saramaka People but also to obtain their free, prior and informed consent, according to their customs and traditions. They should also be allowed to effectively participate in the consultation process in accordance with their traditions and customs. (Saramaka case 2007, para 129) Clarity was, however, not given about the scope or definition of a large-scale project, or whether an effective veto is given to the community in the case of large projects. This is not dissimilar to the consultation requirements discussed below under the Australian Native Title Act 1993, where ground disturbance works require greater consultation than minor works. A sliding scale therefore applies to determine the nature and extent of consultation. (Pulver 2022, 121) The Sarama case remains one of the most relevant judgments to give content to the collective rights and right to consultation of indigenous people. (Carrasco 2019, 170) It is important also to note, however, that these legal victories do not always lead to social or policy change. In fact, according to Carrasco, the discrepancy between legal breakthroughs and social change is increasing. (Carrasco 2019, 177)

[44] Robinson says that the judiciary has demonstrated in the Canadian case of Ktunaxa (Ktunaxa case 2017) that 'Canadian law does not currently ensure that indigenous peoples enjoy UNDRIP rights concerning sacred sites, that it does not provide effective means to secure these rights, and that its provisions concerning rights limitations do not conform to UNDRIP requirements.' (Robinson 2020, 1643)

pursuant to which a dispute reaches the court. In the Americas, courts in countries such as Colombia, Peru and Belize have made use of international law to explain the rationale behind their judgments, although it should also be noted that many of those states have ratified ILO 169. In light of this, it is incumbent upon courts to consider judgments pursuant to ILO 169 and international developments pertaining to it. For example, in the judgment of the Maya Village of Conejo in Belize, the court observed that, although resolutions of the General Assembly of the United Nations are, generally, not binding on member states, states cannot disregard resolutions that set out parameters of general international law. (Maya Village case 2007, para 131) South African courts have not gone so far to derive rights from General Assembly resolutions, but by reference to UNDRIP a non-binding Declaration is considered.

Examples of the direct domestication of ILO 169 through municipal courts, however, are few and far between. ILO 169 (and UNDRIP) has changed international approaches to the right of self-determination of indigenous people, but municipal law and practice still lag behind the progress that has been made in international law. Furthermore, ILO 169 does not seek to endorse 'consent' as widely as UNDRIP. As observed by Pulver, ILO 169 'takes a less progressive stance' to consent. (Pulver 2022, 318)

Larsen, in summary, provides a sobering assessment of the implementation of consultation and FPIC pursuant to ILO 169:

> Implementation of Convention 169 reveals a contested field. On the one hand, three decades of implementation demonstrate the value of international frameworks in helping inform national discussions. On the other hand, legal re-negotiations from frontal attacks on collective rights to more subtle characterisations of indigenous rights as unrealistic reveal the risk of lowering the bar and ultimately perpetuating the very inequalities the Convention was set up to challenge. (Larsen 2020, 110)

7.4.2 FPIC pursuant to UNDRIP

The United Nations International Declaration on the Rights of Indigenous People (UNDRIP) is the most advanced and widely endorsed international instrument seeking to protect and promote the individual and collective rights and interests of indigenous people.[45] South Africa voted in support of UNDRIP.

[45] UNDRIP was adopted by the General Assembly of the United Nations on 13 September 2007. It was adopted with 143 countries voting in favour, 11 abstaining and four voting against. The countries that voted against UNDRIP are referred to as the CANZUS Alliance, being

UNDRIP is, in contrast to ILO 169, non-binding at law.[46] Countries are nevertheless expected to develop, promote and adjust domestic policies in a way consistent with the terms of UNDRIP since it constitutes important soft-law (unenforceable) standards.

UNDRIP was drafted through the standard-setting processes of the United Nations. Indigenous people participated in the lengthy (more than two decades) process. (McCreery 2012, 16) The scope and degree to which countries enact policies and practical measures to give effect to UNDRIP fall within the sovereignty of each country, as the circumstances of countries and the approach adopted regarding indigenous people within the respective countries are unique. (Macnab 2020)

UNDRIP does not seek to define the meaning of indigenous. In some countries, including South Africa, there may even be disagreements about who qualifies to be treated as indigenous.[47] This is particularly relevant in countries which have experienced various phases of population movements over centuries.[48] Adding to the complexity of giving special, collective rights to indigenous people is the

---

Canada, New Zealand, Australia and the USA. These four countries have since endorsed UNDRIP.

[46] UNDRIP has similar legal status to the UN Declaration on the Rights of Persons belonging to National or Ethnic, Religious and Linguistic Minorities. (Chapter 3)

[47] Note for example how the UN Committee on the Elimination of Racial Discrimination has attempted to side-step the issue of who is indigenous (Khoisan) in Botswana by referring to 'ethnic' communities rather than indigenous people. For example, when making recommendations to allow indigenous people from a certain area to return to their ancestral lands, the Committee says as follows: 'The Committee urges the State party to fully implement the High Court's decision in Roy Sesana and others v. Attorney General, by allowing *all ethnic groups originating from the Central Kalahari Game Reserve* to return and settle there unconditionally. The Committee also recommends that the State party provide them with effective access to basic social services and enable them to resume their traditional activities without hindrance.' (Mackay 2022, 29)

[48] In South Africa, for example, the Khoisan argue that they are the *sole* indigenous people of that country and that they were displaced from their traditional lands by the African tribes that arrived by way of southward migration. The Khoisan view the African tribes that moved south as settlers similar to how Europeans who arrived after the African tribes are seen as settlers. Secorun summarises the claims of the Khoisan as follows: 'The Khoisan were the first inhabitants of southern Africa and one of the earliest distinct groups of Homo sapiens, enduring centuries of gradual dispossession at the hands of every new wave of settlers, including the Bantu, whose descendants make up most of South Africa's black population today.' (Secorun 2018). However, according to Sapignoli and Hitchcock, the southern African countries of Botswana, Namibia and South Africa regard *all* (black) peoples of those countries as indigenous, and not just a specific historic community. (Sapignoli and Hitchcock 2013, 356) It is therefore not surprising that in South Africa the use of the words 'tribal' or 'traditional' is often preferred to 'indigenous'.

absence of an agreed definition in UNDRIP (and ILO 169) as to who constitutes indigenous people and what is meant by terms such as 'self-determination' and 'consultation'. (Kryazhkov and Garipov 2021, 1016)[49]

While the principles of UNDRIP are very important for encouraging conduct, from a legally enforceable perspective UNDRIP remains unclear about the definition of indigenous people, the legal interpretation of consultation and consent pursuant to FPIC, the legal understanding of self-determination and autonomy, and the criteria for referring policies and projects for consultation and FPIC. Self-determination has both an international and a domestic element to it, and the exact nature and scope of the domestic rights and obligations remain the subject of ongoing discussions. (Cassese 1995) Article 3 of UNDRIP acknowledges self-determination in a manner consistent with the recognition of the right to self-determination outlined in the International Covenant on Civil and Political Rights (ICCPR 1966) and the International Covenant on Economic, Social and Cultural Rights. (ICESCR 1966)[50] The problem is, of course, that pursuant to those instruments, the content, scope and enforceability of the right to self-determination are also not settled. Pursuant to the ICCPR the right to self-determination is seen as an individual right, while pursuant to UNDRIP self-determination is seen as an individual as well as a collective right.

It is not surprising that the lack of definitional clarity about terms such as 'indigenous', 'consultation', 'self-determination' and 'FPIC' has given rise to implementation shortcomings and frustration. On the positive side the judiciary

[49] In an analysis of the practical requirements for consultation with indigenous people it has been observed that 'the question of whom to consult is, at its core, the question of who counts as indigenous and which territories are considered to belong to Indigenous Peoples, which lands they traditionally own, use, and occupy'. (Bornschlegl, Ocampo and Urrutia 2021, 12) These questions are not always simple to resolve. Even in Australia, where there is no question about the indigeneity of the Aboriginal people, there are often competing and overlapping claims to land *between* the respective Aboriginal peoples about who speaks for a particular land area. Conflict may therefore arise *between* and *within* indigenous communities. This makes consultation and FPIC complex, as it may not always be clear with whom to consult on behalf of the affected community regarding a specific tract of land. Note, for example, the Munkara case, in which a subgroup of an Aboriginal community had objected to an approval that had been granted by the majority. The complaint was ultimately dismissed, but only after substantial delays and high costs. (Munkara case 2024)

[50] The term 'self-determination' in these instruments is used as an individual right, not as a collective right. Note, for example, how in Norway the court relied on the individual rights to culture in art 27 of the ICCPR to conclude that the disruption of reindeer herding affected the individual and the community to which the individual belonged. (Fosen case 2021)

of signatory countries may be informed by the content of UNDRIP and even use it as an interpretive and inspirational tool to give effect to domestic consultative rights within the context of practical circumstances, for example by developing domestic law in accordance with international understandings exhibited by UNDRIP. Private industries may also use the UNDRIP standards to develop self-regulating norms for their industry. (OECD Guidelines 2023) In practice, however, domestic courts have been reluctant to elevate the UNDRIP principles to binding law within municipal jurisprudence, unless authorised or mandated to do so by a domestic statute.[51]

The 'rights' referred to in UNDRIP can best be described as aspirational in character rather than judicially enforceable, since an indigenous group cannot, in municipal or international law, seek enforcement of an UNDRIP right by way of a specific remedy. Higgins states that FPIC pursuant to UNDRIP means that indigenous people must 'give their consent to initiatives that impact their lives.' (Higgins 2023, 203) This may be the ideal of UNDRIP, but it cannot be construed as a justiciable right.[52] Barrie is arguably correct in asserting that, as

[51] In this regard, it is noteworthy how the obligation for good faith negotiations has been interpreted by the courts in Australia. There is no indication that courts in Australia have adopted a different approach to the meaning of good faith after the country endorsed UNDRIP in 2009. The interpretation given by the courts to good faith in negotiations is determined by Australian jurisprudence, rather than by the non-binding provisions of UNDRIP. The effect of the Australian jurisprudence is, however, that good faith negotiation is given a narrow interpretation that focuses on the *process* instead of the substance of negotiation. Furthermore, it does not imply a veto for Aboriginal people whose land is affected. In the case of a specific legal entitlement to be consulted, the Federal Court has held that an indigenous community should have been consulted since their interests could be affected by the laying of a subsea pipeline. (Tipakalippa case 2022) The court observed that although there is no statutory definition of 'consult', the approach adopted by Australian courts is that the 'the underlying premise of the authorisation provisions is to give all group members a "reasonable opportunity" to participate in decision-making' (Tipakalippa case 2022, para 104). In this case it was held that the company seeking approval to lay the subsea pipeline had not provided satisfactory evidence of having consulted with all the subgroups of the indigenous community that could potentially be affected. In the 2023 Barngarla case the Federal Court of Australia found that although extensive consultation had taken place with the Aboriginal community about the location of a nuclear waste storage facility, the government suffered 'apprehended bias' as it had already made up its mind prior to the commencement of consultation and, hence, no good faith effort had been made to accommodate the concerns of the indigenous community. (Barngarla case 2023)

[52] Note the explanation by Pulver that the obligation to consult with indigenous people is regarded as a principle of international law and is undisputed, but that the statement in art 19 of UNDRIP that states must consult with indigenous people 'in order to obtain their consent' is a 'vague expression'. (Pulver 2022, 96) She concludes: '[T]he consultation process is deemed

promising as UNDRIP may be, its challenge lies in its implementation. (Barrie 2013) He also says that 'FPIC is a complex doctrine that includes a number of related aims and aspirations. It has room to evolve and its ongoing development will take time.' (Barrie 2024b, 224) Isa also observes that only 'some' local jurisdictions have sought to rely on UNDRIP to assist with the development of guidelines for consultation and FPIC. (Isa 2019, 16)

As a general principle, UNDRIP accepts that indigenous people are entitled to recognition of their traditional laws, customs and practices by sovereign states. It furthermore acknowledges that indigenous people are entitled to maintain, develop and promote institutional arrangements whereby their rights to self-determination, self-government and autonomy regarding their traditional laws, customs and practices are recognised. UNDRIP reflects the plurality of legal and customary systems within the same territory. If ever state law and non-state law interact, it is within the sphere of consultation rights.[53] It is further accepted by UNDRIP that consultation must occur with indigenous people whenever their interests and rights are affected by legislation, policies or developments that may impact their lands, culture, traditions, or development.

UNDRIP, like ILO 169, does not, however, require that *every* law, administrative action, policy measure or proposed development that may indirectly or remotely affect indigenous people become the subject of consultation. (Tomaselli 2017) Only those matters that impact directly or disproportionately on the traditional rights and interests of indigenous people should be the subject of consultation.[54] This implies a discretion on the part of government, or a

valid even in the absence of indigenous peoples' consent provided that certain requirements are met.' (Pulver 2022, 127)

[53] In this respect, the Parliament of Canada is an example of one of only a few countries that have enacted the United Nations Declaration on the Rights of Indigenous Peoples Act in which in the Preamble UNDRIP is referred to as a 'source of law'. (Canada UNDRIP Act 2021, Preamble) UNDRIP is thereby declared in Canada a 'universal international human rights instrument' with application in Canadian law and it is intended to 'provide a framework' to implement UNDRIP in Canadian law. (Canada UNDRIP Act 2021, art 4)

[54] Note, for example, the recommendation made in the Australian debate on a proposed Voice for indigenous people by the Final Report of the Indigenous Voice Co-Design Process that advice would be sought in 'matters of *national significance* to Aboriginal and Torres Strait Islander peoples relating to their social, spiritual and economic wellbeing.' (Calma-Langton Report 2021, 11) In the proposed constitutional amendment the word 'advice' was removed and replaced with the word 'representation', but the concern remained that *any* public policy, bill or administrative measure may become the subject of litigation because it may 'affect' Aboriginal people. (De Villiers 2024c, 293)

developer, to decide: in what circumstances a policy or development is likely to impact directly or disproportionately on the rights and interests of indigenous people; the scale of the potential impact; and whether, in light of the previous two considerations, specific consultation with the affected people is required.[55]

In regard to the right to be consulted, UNDRIP expresses the following principles that are relevant to this chapter:

> **The General Assembly,**
>
> *Encouraging* States to comply with and effectively implement all their obligations as they apply to indigenous peoples under international instruments, in particular those related to human rights, in consultation and cooperation with the peoples concerned
>
> . . .
>
> ***Solemnly proclaims . . .:***
>
> 15 2. States shall take effective measures, in consultation and cooperation with the indigenous peoples concerned, to combat prejudice and eliminate discrimination and to promote tolerance, understanding and good relations among indigenous peoples and all other segments of society.
>
> . . .
>
> 17 2. States shall, in consultation and cooperation with indigenous peoples, take specific measures to protect indigenous children from economic exploitation and from performing any work that is likely to be hazardous or to interfere with the child's education, or to be harmful to the child's health or physical, mental, spiritual, moral or social development, taking into account their special vulnerability and the importance of education for their empowerment.
>
> . . .
>
> 19 States shall consult and cooperate in good faith with the indigenous peoples concerned through their own representative institutions in order to obtain their free, prior and informed consent before adopting and implementing legislative or administrative measures that may affect them.
>
> . . .

[55] Note, for example, the position adopted by the Australian Heritage Council in its endeavours to include places of importance to Aboriginal people on the national heritage register. The Council set out to invite proposals from Aboriginal people and committed itself to a process of free, prior and informed consent. In its invitation, the Council stated the following: 'The council recognises that determining FPIC in practice will depend on the context of the particular case. In each case, the council will seek to determine questions such as from whom FPIC should be appropriately sought, at what stage of an assessment it should be sought, what form consent could take, and how to characterise FPIC in cases where there are disagreements.' (Heritage Council 2021) In stating this, the Council left no doubt that it ultimately held the discretion about the process and the inclusion of sites.

> 32 1. Indigenous peoples have the right to determine and develop priorities and strategies for the development or use of their lands or territories and other resources.
>
> 2. States shall consult and cooperate in good faith with the indigenous peoples concerned through their own representative institutions in order to obtain their free and informed consent prior to the approval of any project affecting their lands or territories and other resources, particularly in connection with the development, utilization or exploitation of mineral, water or other resources.
>
> . . .
>
> 36 2. States, in consultation and cooperation with indigenous peoples, shall take effective measures to facilitate the exercise and ensure the implementation of this right.
>
> . . .
>
> 38 States, in consultation and cooperation with indigenous peoples, shall take the appropriate measures, including legislative measures, to achieve the ends of this Declaration. (UNDRIP 2007b)

Article 38, in particular, places a general obligation on states to consult with indigenous people about the practical steps to be taken to give effect to UNDRIP. Such consultation includes: the right to self-determination (art 3); the right to autonomy (art 4); the right to maintain and strengthen their distinct political, legal, economic, social and cultural institutions (art 5); the collective right to live in freedom, peace and security as distinct peoples (art 7(2)); the right to uphold and practise cultural traditions (art 11); the right to establish and control their educational systems (art 14); the right to establish their own media in their own languages (art 16); and the right to participate in decision-making in matters which would affect their rights, through representatives chosen by themselves in accordance with their own procedures, as well as to maintain and develop their own indigenous decision-making institutions (art 18).

Arguably the most important article for the purposes of this chapter is art 19 of UNDRIP, which provides as follows about consultation rights of indigenous people:

> States shall consult and cooperate in *good faith* with the indigenous peoples concerned through their *own representative* institutions in order to obtain their *free, prior and informed consent* before adopting and implementing legislative or administrative measures that *may affect* them. (emphasis added)

The consultation rights outlined in art 19, when read in conjunction with the rights to self-determination and autonomy set out in art 3 and art 4 respectively, establish the principles upon which institutional and practical arrangements for consultation should be based. The consultative rights that arise from UNDRIP must therefore be assessed in the context of the right to self-determination of indigenous people, which is a foundational norm of UNDRIP. (Rombouts 2017) It is from their inherent right to self-determination that practical measures such as the right to FPIC arise.

UNDRIP seeks to acknowledge that the right to consult finds its origin in the sovereignty of indigenous people to govern themselves and make autonomous decisions.[56] It is therefore from the ancient right of indigenous people to make decisions about their laws, culture and traditional lands that their status as parties within the context of consultation must be approached. (Anaya 2004, 104–6) This implies that if an indigenous community has lost its connection to its land, fails to practise its traditions and beliefs, or no longer adheres to its traditions and customs, UNDRIP does not confer special rights of consultation associated with land to such a community.[57] Indigenous rights stem from the pre-colonial sovereign rights of indigenous people and hence the process of consultation must take account of the traditional laws, customs and practices of these people.

The reliance on an historic sovereignty is arguably *the* essential consideration that separates the rights of indigenous people from the rights of ethnocultural minorities. (Chapter 3) The origin of consultation with indigenous people is

[56] This proposition of UNDRIP cannot be accepted without circumspection as it is not always clear in contemporary law what such sovereignty meant traditionally, how rules were made, administered and enforced how overlapping and competing sovereignties interacted, and what the nature and extent of the rights of individuals were within such systems. Historic analysis is inevitably dependent on oral history, limited records and conflicting accounts of cultural customs. It is not unknown for contemporary power relationships within indigenous communities to influence accounts of historic practices. There is often some element of romanticism, and even revisionism, in historic analysis, whereby historians, anthropologists, lawyers and practitioners of other social sciences disciplines view ancient indigenous systems through contemporary perspectives. (De Villiers 2023g, 377) There is, however, the risk that evidence, including expert evidence, presented to a court may be skewed or unreliable, as was found in the case of Munkara in Australia, in which an opinion expressed by an expert about a mythical being was rejected for lack of a factual base to justify the opinion. (Munkara case 2024)

[57] The proposition is consistent with the common law of Australia, where in the Yorta Yorta case it was held that, for an Aboriginal community to prove native title, the community must show that: the indigenous community is related to the apical ancestors of the area; the indigenous community continues to function as a society; and the indigenous community continues to practise and adhere to its customs, even if those customs may have been adjusted and modernised. (Yorta Yorta (HCA) case 2002).

therefore causally linked to their traditional lands, laws and customs.[58] If not, the community is no different to any other ethnocultural community in society.

There remains, however, a 'wide margin' between the UNDRIP recognition of the right to self-determination and the practical effect to be given to consultation rights. (Cambou 2019, 50) The words '*in order* to obtain their free, prior and informed consent' in UNDRIP are not construed to imply a veto, nor a legal requirement that agreement *must* be reached.[59] Instead, these words signify that a *bona fide* effort must be made to reach agreement, rather than an enforceable requirement that mandates agreement. (Rombouts 2018, 7) It is therefore the *attempt* made by parties to reach agreement that is evaluated, rather than the outcome of the consultation.[60] Indigenous people must be given the opportunity to express their views, although this does not imply that their opinion is binding

---

[58] This is a principle that is not simple to apply. The question about what affects the lands, laws and customs of an indigenous community is usually answered in a restrictive sense by policy makers because they often seek to reduce the scope of consultation. Meanwhile, indigenous people often seek to expand the scope of consultation because they approach activities on their land in a holistic manner. There is frequently tension between indigenous people, who believe that a greater range of policy measures should be submitted to them for consultation, and governments, who feel that only a discrete range of policy measure that impact directly on the indigenous people should be submitted for consultation. Note, for example, the discourse in Australia surrounding the failed referendum of 2023 on the proposed Voice for Aboriginal people, through which Aboriginal people would have been able to make 'representations' about *any* policy or legislative measure, not only matters that directly or disproportionately affect their traditional lands, culture and customs. (Constitution Alteration Act 2023; De Villiers 2024c) Examples of policy areas on which advice would have had to be sought included life expectancy, education, youth imprisonment, housing, unemployment and other social policies. (Design Principles 2023) These wide powers of the proposed Voice were not reflected in the proposed powers of the Khoisan House, which did not envisage effective consultation at all. (De Villiers 2023h, 189).

[59] Macnab summarises the obligation arising from art 19 as follows: '[T]he emphasis is not on the consent or achieving the consent, it's in the *process of working towards* achieving consent. So, the idea is in a consultation context with Indigenous people, it should be the government's goal always to work to try and achieve consent with Indigenous people. *But it doesn't mean that if no consent is reached, nothing can go forward.*' (emphasis added) (Macnab 2020) This statement acknowledges that the sovereignty of government to grant approvals remains unaffected by the encouragement to reach FPIC.

[60] Note, for example, how in the Barngarla case the Federal Court of Australia found that, although extensive consultation took place with an Aboriginal community about the location of nuclear waste storage facility, the facts support a finding of 'apprehended bias' on the part of the government as it had already made up its mind about the location of the facility prior to the commencement of consultation. (Barngarla case 2023) The court did not consider the merit of the proposed location of the facility, but rather the inadequate consultation process that gave rise to the identification of the site.

on the decision-maker. (Tipakalippa case 2022) Because of the ambivalence of the legal obligation it is not surprising that the lofty principles espoused by UNDRIP are often 'neglected in practice'. (Mitchell et al 2021, 217)[61]

Each of the key words used in art 19 contains an inherent meaning that renders the article more substantial than it may seem at first reading. For example, 'free' implies unfettered, independent and unforced decision-making;[62] 'prior' implies adequate and advance notification of a policy, bill or development proposal to allow indigenous people an opportunity for internal debate and to seek expert advice;[63] 'informed' implies making available all relevant information about a project, its scope, impact, duration, cost and rehabilitation;[64] and 'consent'

---

[61] Mitchell observes, with reference to Canada (and the same could arguably be said of many, if not all, other countries inhabited by indigenous people), that there are consistent failures by the state and industry to appropriately consult with indigenous people; a failure to respect and adhere to indigenous norms; and a failure to implement in good faith the provisions of UNDRIP. (Mitchell et al 2021, 234).

[62] 'Free implies the absence of any manipulation, coercion or intimidation from any other groups, bodies and entities in the decision-making process of indigenous peoples. Any external influence that hinders self-determination in the process of decision-making and the outcome of their decision is a clear violation of this principle. Consent cannot be valid if it is taken from an authority or a group that is not recognised by the indigenous communities or not accountable to them. Further, the independence of their decision-making process and the outcome must be verifiable with the members of the indigenous communities.' (Maharjan, Carling and Sherpa 2012, 60)

[63] 'The informed consent must be sought first as a precondition before implementing any activity and project. It is an advanced authorisation from affected indigenous peoples' communities before the commencement of any activities or project. It shall respect the time requirements of indigenous peoples' consultation and the consensus processes defined by them. The prior consent requires a comprehensive procedure to ensure that indigenous peoples have sufficient time to understand, analyse and discuss the information they receive collectively. The element of prior also denotes respecting the duration of time for indigenous peoples to undertake their decision-making process according to their pace and circumstances. All parties requiring the consent of indigenous peoples must thereby engage them in good faith discussions to reach a mutual agreement on the timeline of the decision-making process.' (Maharjan, Carling and Sherpa 2012, 60)

[64] 'This is a core element of the FPIC decision-making process to reach or achieve a well-informed decision. It is thereby important not only to have access to information, but also to clearly understand the information provided to them. If necessary, information should be translated to the local language and put in a form and manner that is understood by the indigenous communities to facilitate better understanding. Further, indigenous community members must have a level of satisfaction on the level of information provided to them.' (Maharjan, Carling and Sherpa 2012, 61)

implies voluntary agreement in accordance with the decision-making processes of the community. (Rombouts 2014, 138–9)[65]

In addition to the obligation to consult arising pursuant to UNDRIP, there is also the democratic duty to consult, typically associated with respect for individual rights being impacted, such as the right to cultural integrity, equality and property. (Anaya 2010) This highlights how the consultation principles underlying UNDRIP (and ILO 169) have gravitated towards the general understanding and expansion of fundamental rights under the ICCPR, for example rights to culture and property. (Endorois Welfare Council case 2003; Fosen case 2021) What may initially have been primarily a collective right of indigenous people is finding its way into general human rights theory and practice.[66]

The Inter-American Commission has, for example, declared that the requirement for efforts to obtain consent is derived not only from the right to property and non-discrimination, but also from the right to life, cultural identity[67] and other essential human rights, in relation to the execution of development plans or investments that affect those rights. (Doyle 2014, 129) The principle that governments must consult with communities in general, and with individuals in particular, to the extent that their rights and interests are affected by a proposed policy, measure or bill, is therefore embedded in liberal democratic theory and practice and is not only related to, or limited to, ILO 169 or UNDRIP. This is exemplified by the ruling from the African Commission, pursuant to the African Charter of Human and Peoples' Rights, which stated that the failure of the state to properly consult with a tribal community about the management of their land effectively breached the individuals' right to property and development.

---

[65] 'It is a collective decision-making process of indigenous peoples that entails several steps. This may include a series of consultations as needed and it should allow enough time for indigenous communities to undertake their own internal deliberations prior to making their collective decision. The consultations shall allow community members, including women and youth, to express their views, raise their concerns, seek additional information, if needed, and seek clarifications on their questions and/or concerns.' (Maharjan, Carling and Sherpa 2012, 61)

[66] This approach reflects the Kichwa case, in which it was held that the right to a cultural identity is a fundamental and collective right of indigenous communities and must be respected in a multicultural, pluralistic and democratic society. (Kichwa case 2012, para 217)

[67] This approach was also reflected in the Norwegian Fosen case, in which it was held that the right of an indigenous person to the herding of reindeer is protected under art 27 of the ICCPR as an individual right to be exercised with other members of the Sámi community. (Fosen case 2021) This approach reflects the Kichwa case, in which it was held that the right to a cultural identity is a fundamental and collective right of indigenous communities and must be respected in a multicultural, pluralistic and democratic society. (Kichwa case 2012, para 217)

(Endorois Welfare Council case 2003) Indigenous groups may, on the one hand, welcome such an expansion of the scope of consultation to include individual rights, but they may also feel that it dilutes their collective rights as a community with special and sovereign interests over the land.

In response to the question of *when* an indigenous community should be consulted, UNDRIP does not give clear guidance, but Anaya proposes the following guideline:

> It [the duty to consult] applies whenever a state decision may affect indigenous peoples *in ways not felt by others in society*. Such a differentiated effect occurs when the interests or conditions of indigenous peoples that are particular to them are implicated in the decision, even when the decision may have a broader impact, as in the case of certain legislation. (emphasis added) (Anaya 2009, para 43)

This proposal by Anaya may seem logical, but it also gives rise to several questions. The most important one is: Who decides when a policy matter or a development adequately affects an indigenous community such that it must be consulted? And, can a process of environmental impact assessment that also involves the broader public be regarded as adequate consultation with indigenous people as a subset of the broader community? The unequal power relationship between governments and indigenous peoples is underscored by government's discretion to decide whether to refer a matter for consultation or not to do so, or to accept or not accept advice. This notwithstanding, indigenous people may, depending on statutory arrangements, seek review of an approval that had been given without adequate consultation.[68]

The challenge to settle the meaning of consultation is further complicated by the references also made by UNDRIP to different types of consultation processes that may precede agreement-seeking. Examples include 'in conjunction with' (arts 11(2), 12(2), 14(3) and 22(2) of UNDRIP), 'free, prior and informed consent' (art 10 of UNDRIP), 'in consultation and cooperation' (arts 15(2) and 17(2) of

[68] Note, for example, the Tipakalippa judgment in Australia, in which the relevant government department was found to have erred in the exercise of its discretion because it did not establish with adequate certainty that the proponent of a development had consulted with an indigenous community which could potentially be affected by the development. (Tipakalippa case 2022) Meanwhile, in the Barngarla judgment, it was held that the government had not approached the consultation with an open mind and hence suffered apprehended bias. (Barngarla case 2023) Also consider the Baleni case in South Africa, in which it was determined that the consent of the tribal community had to be obtained, not merely an engagement in consultation with them, pursuant to the relevant statute. (Baleni case 2019)

UNDRIP), 'consult and cooperate in good faith' (art 19 of UNDRIP), and 'the right to be actively involved' (art 23 of UNDRIP). Each of these obligations must be taken to require a different standard of consultation, otherwise the same wording would have been used.[69]

The following principles, relevant to this chapter, transpire from art 19 of UNDRIP to guide consultation in the context of FPIC:

First, consultation with indigenous people must be in good faith. Good faith applies to both parties, not just to those seeking access to land. Good faith is ascertained in the context of the consultation, the conduct of the parties, the exchanges of communications, the sharing of information, the time allowed for consultation and the conduct of meetings. The standards of good faith cannot be

[69] Note, for example, the Canadian judgment in the Mikisew Cree case, in which it was held that consultation had to occur in the policy and administrative phase, but not in the actual legislative phase. (Mikisew Cree case 2005) On close analysis the nuances of the judgment left open many unresolved questions. On proper construction one could contend that, depending on municipal law, bills before Parliament should also be subject to consultative processes. (Khoisan Act appeal 2023) However, it should be noted that the parliamentary process may become drawn out if amendments made in the parliamentary process must be resubmitted to the indigenous community for another round of consultation. For example, a bill may be substantially amended during the parliamentary committee process, and referring it back to community consultation at that stage could result in a circular process. This is because the committee may need to consider the outcomes of the new consultation, potentially leading to the resubmission of any subsequent substantial amendments for additional community feedback, and so on. Dunlap cautions that FPIC can become a 'bureaucratic trap' that potentially undermines the interests of indigenous people. (Dunlap 2018) He refers to a Mexican case study of FPIC and concludes as follows: 'Instead, the FPIC consultation in Juchitán all but mimicked all the negative features mentioned in the literature review and suffered a conflict of interest between state and corporate collaboration, violated cultural norms, provided inadequate information and also *served as a marketing platform to sell the idea* of the project rather than adequately address the issues raised by participants such as income transparency or social and environmental impacts. Consequently, the FPIC has *served to entrench state power* and reinforce existing political and economic asymmetry between different actors.' (emphasis added) (Dunlap 2018, 105) This observation is not dissimilar to concerns I have raised previously, namely that the FPIC process may grant a false legitimacy to a decision that goes against indigenous interests, given that indigenous people cannot veto a proposal and, yet, government can refer to the consultation process as proof that it did indeed consult the indigenous community. (De Villiers 2023h, 69) Note also the observation by Cambou that the Norwegian case of Fosen (Fosen case 2021) highlights that 'in the context of the green transition, consultation is assuredly considered a necessary instrument for guaranteeing human rights, but as the Fosen case illustrates, it is a *double-edged sword* that can either support Indigenous self-determination or legitimise green colonialism when it perpetuates decisions that deprive Indigenous communities from the benefits of their lands and livelihoods.' (Cambou 2024, 65)

objectively or definitively prescribed by way of fixed criteria, since the overall behaviour of the parties is relevant.

Secondly, the advice of indigenous people must be freely given based on relevant and complete information about a proposal that was provided to them in a timely manner to enable the community to discuss the proposal, seek expect advice and formulate a response in a culturally appropriate manner.

Thirdly, the advice of indigenous people is required about administrative and legislative measures and proposed developments that may affect their indigenous rights and interests directly or disproportionately, particularly about their traditional lands and waters.

Fourthly, the mechanisms or processes for consultation about a specific project can be ad hoc or of a permanent nature, provided that indigenous people are included in the design of such processes and institutions. A consultative mechanism must also address consultation *within* the indigenous community to ensure that intra-indigenous decision-making processes are credible and legitimate, and representative, responsible and accountable.

Fifthly, consultation and FPIC are not construed as mandating consent or granting a veto to an indigenous community, unless explicitly so determined by applicable legislation, as in the Baleni case.

Sixthly, indigenous people may, in accordance with their right to self-determination, decide on the most appropriate mechanism by which consultation is to occur, whether by way of an elected, appointed or hereditary body. Indigenous people may also adopt a negotiation protocol whereby they explain to third parties the consultation processes adopted by their community.[70]

---

[70] A concern often neglected in literature and jurisprudence concerning FPIC is that the body representing indigenous people must also be subject to some form of internal scrutiny to ensure that it is indeed representative of the community; that the negotiators consult with the community; that negotiators give feedback and seek instructions from the community; and that the body fairly distributes whatever benefits may be received because of negotiations. There is sometimes a rather romantic or even naïve assumption that indigenous negotiating bodies always do the right thing for their own constituents. Ubink and Pickering point out, in an assessment of case studies in South Africa, that negotiating bodies are sometimes used not as a mechanism for inclusion, but rather as an instrument for the *exclusion* of community views. (Ubink and Pickering 2020, 194) In the case studies considered by them numerous complaints were made by indigenous community members about a lack of internal consultation by those purporting to represent the community; that the community had not authorised agreements; and that only a small group of persons had benefited from the negotiations. (Ubink and Pickering 2020, 196) My experience is that one of the complaints most often heard from Aboriginal communities in Australia is that their negotiators either do not inform them adequately of what is being discussed or that benefits arising

Seventhly, government or a proponent of a development has a moral duty (albeit not a legal one), particularly so in the case of large-scale projects, to provide resources to indigenous people to enable them to effectively consult internally with their community, seek advice as well as expert and legal opinion, and participate in consultation.

Finally, if advice given by indigenous people is not accepted, the relevant government agency should, in the interests of good governance, transparency and accountability, provide the indigenous community with some explanation as to why their advice was not heeded. Consultation should ideally be holistic in nature, involving the provision of information about a project to the community, engaging in consultation and negotiation, receiving advice and recommendations from the community, considering the provided advice, making a decision and providing feedback to the community about the outcome of the process.

7.4.3 FPIC as understood by international agencies and expert bodies

The United Nations Human Rights Committee (UNHRC), the Committee on Economic, Social and Cultural Rights (CESCR) and the Committee on the Elimination of Racial Discrimination (CERD) have, over time, given useful expert guidance and opinions to the content of the rights of indigenous people with reference to consultation and FPIC. (Barrie 2024b; Heinämäki, Allard and Kirchner 2017, 308–491) These bodies, while not international courts, have played a leading role in providing practical content to the meaning of FPIC and its associated required consultation standards.[71] The advice and opinions

from negotiations are not distributed reasonably within the community. In Australia the registrar of Aboriginal Corporations, appointed pursuant to the CATSI Act, exercises some oversight over the functioning of the indigenous corporations. (CATSI Act 2006) This is, however, not without controversy, as it may be seen as impinging on the self-determination of the corporations. On the other hand, it does give disgruntled community members an independent avenue in which to issue complaints without having to resort to costly legal actions. (De Villiers 2022h, 185) In this regard, consider also the findings of Almanza and Salazar that the indigenous bodies analysed by them were often exclusionary, with leaders that stifled internal opposition and disagreement, and ultimately the process came to disempower the very community it was supposed to empower. (Almanza and Salazar 2022)

[71] Between 2008 and 2019 the CESCR handed down 41 Concluding Observations and three General Comments about FPIC affecting 32 states. Over the same period the HRC handed down 33 Concluding Observations involving 27 states, and the CERD issued 56 Concluding Observations to 36 states and 88 Early Warning Urgent Action communications to 28 states. (Doyle 2022, 109–11).

provided are not legally binding, so the weight attributed to them should be considered with caution. Nevertheless, they serve as useful indicia of FPIC.

The narrative of advice given by consultative bodies for indigenous people (and ethnocultural minorities)[72] does not always make for pleasant reading. If ever the dictum applies that the devil hides in the detail of constitutional and legal arrangements, it is applicable to the consultative processes underlying FPIC. The CERD was the first international human rights body that adopted the benchmark that free, prior and informed consent must be obtained from indigenous people when their rights and interests are affected. (CERD General Recommendation 1997)

The guidance of the UNHRC, CESCR and CERD does not constitute binding law on South African courts. The South African courts may, however, 'consider' the opinions of such specialist international bodies. (Chapters 3 and 4; Baleni case 2019) Such international opinions provide potential insight, not only to legislatures for the drafting of new laws but also to policy makers who design processes for consultation, as well as to courts that are called upon to resolve disputes about the appropriateness of consultation and FPIC in a domestic context. Expert comments may inform courts and give them insight into trends in international law, even though the courts are not bound by these comments and may not be able to formally integrate them into domestic law unless so authorised by statute.

The following guiding principles concerning consultation and FPIC have crystallised from the opinions of the UNHRC, CESCR and CERD:

Consultation regarding traditional lands

Indigenous people should be consulted about matters that could have an impact on their traditional lands, be it activities by government or by private entities. In the case of larger projects, the nature and extent of consultation should be more in-depth and elaborate. In the Clyde River case the court spoke about

---

[72] Although the term 'indigenous people' is used, the challenges that accompany consultation may also apply to instances where consultative mechanisms have been instituted for ethnocultural minorities. It is, however, acknowledged that the rights of indigenous people and those of ethnocultural minorities are the subject of different international law instruments. The rights of indigenous people are recognised principally by way of ILO 169 and UNDRIP, whereas there is no similar legally binding international treaty such as ILO 169 that so comprehensively recognises the collective rights of ethnocultural minorities, albeit that UNDRIP and the UN Declaration on the Rights of Minorities have similar legal status. (UN Declaration on Minorities 1992)

the need for 'deep consultation'. (Clyde River case 2017) The nature and extent of consultation can vary using the concept of a sliding scale, ranging from no impact on traditional lands (such as aerial photography, visual assessments of land) to serious impact on traditional lands (such as mining and deforesting). In commenting on Australia, the UNHRC stated the following:

> [I]n many areas native title rights and interests remain unresolved and . . . Native Title Amendments of 1998 in some respects limit the rights of indigenous persons and communities, in particular in the field of effective participation in all matters affecting land ownership and use, and affects their interests in native title lands, particularly pastoral lands. (HRC 2000, para 10)

In the Sámi mining case it was emphasised that human rights treaties are 'living instruments' and therefore their interpretation is influenced by evolving approaches to the rights of indigenous people. (Sámi mining case 2024, para 13) The right to practise culture pursuant to the ICCPR can therefore be read in the context of the reindeer herding of the community and their right to be consulted about activities that may impact on the expressions of their culture. (Sámi mining case 2024, para 14.1) The Committee observed as follows:

> The Committee further recalls that the communal dimension of Indigenous Peoples' cultural life, including traditional activities, is closely linked to their traditional lands, territories and resources, and is indispensable to their existence, well-being and full development. . . . The Committee observes that the protection of traditional lands, territories, and resources is also a prerequisite for the right to an adequate standard of living of Indigenous Peoples, as they are an important basis for their livelihoods (Sámi mining case 2024, para 14.2). . . . It follows that States parties must ensure the effective participation of Indigenous Peoples in decision-making processes that may affect their way of life, particularly their right to land, based on the principle of their free, prior and informed consent, so as not to endanger the very survival of the community and its members. . . . (Sámi mining case 2024, para 14.5)

Consultation as a fundamental human right

The right of indigenous people to be consulted finds it origin in the protection of fundamental individual rights and freedoms. A denial of consultation is, in effect, a breach of art 27 of the International Covenant on Civil and Political Rights (ICCPR). FPIC is therefore not only a collective right that can be exercised by an indigenous community, but has also found its way into the spectrum of fundamental human rights that may have application within domestic law. (Endorois Welfare Council case 2003) The right to consultation can be enforced individually, or in the context of a class action. (Fosen case 2021) The UNHRC commented as follows in an opinion affecting Canada:

> While all peoples have the right of self-determination and the right freely to determine their political status, pursue their economic, social and cultural development and dispose of their natural wealth and resources, as stipulated in article 1 of the Covenant, the question whether the Lubicon Lake Band constitutes a 'people' is not an issue for the Committee to address under the Optional Protocol to the Covenant. . . . These rights are set out in part III of the Covenant, articles 6 to 27, inclusive. There is, however, no objection to a *group of individuals*, who claim to be similarly affected, collectively to submit a communication about alleged breaches of their rights. (emphasis added) (RC Lubicon Lake Band 1984, para 32)

In the Sámi consultation case it was held that the failure to adequately consult with the Sámi about the potential impact of mining on their traditional lands and herding encroached on the rights of the children to cultural heritage, identity, livelihood and standard of living. Concern was expressed that interference with cultural traditions may have intergenerational impact on the individual and collective rights of the Sámi (Sámi consultation case 2024, para 9.2). The Committee observed as follows:

> The Committee considers that it is precisely because the State party is aware that transferring Sámi culture to Sámi children is 'becoming increasingly difficult', that it must be particularly cautious when regulating activities that *may endanger the continuity of their culture*. In the light of the above, the Committee considers that article 30 of the Convention enshrines the right of Indigenous children to enjoy their traditional territories and that any decision affecting them should be taken with their effective participation. (emphasis added) (Sámi consultation case 2024, paras 9.16–9.17)

Free, prior and informed consent (FPIC)

Indigenous people should be accorded consultation rights, consistent with the principle of free, prior and informed consent, about potential impacts on their traditional lands, customs and practices. The consultative processes may be ad hoc about a specific project or by way of permanent consultative bodies that meet regularly to consider applications for access to land. The UNHRC commented as follows about Chile:

> The Committee recommends that the State party should:
>
> (a) Speed up the process for amending the Constitution and include *recognition* of indigenous peoples;
>
> (b) Do everything in its power to establish a *council* of indigenous peoples in consultation with indigenous communities;

(c) Establish an *effective consultation* mechanism, in line with the principles set forth in article 27 of the Covenant, with a view to obtaining indigenous communities' free, prior and informed consent to decisions about projects that affect their rights and in particular, ensure that their free, prior and informed consent is obtained before any measures that might jeopardize, or substantially hinder, their culturally significant economic activities are taken;

(d) Intensify its efforts to guarantee the full enjoyment of the right of indigenous peoples to their *ancestral lands*. (emphasis added) (HRC 2014, para 10)

In the Poma Poma case the Committee emphasised the importance of the indigenous community's participation in the decision-making process. The participation:

> Must be *effective*, which requires not mere consultation but the free, prior and informed consent of the members of the community. In addition, the measures must respect the *principle of proportionality* so as to not endanger the very survival of the community and its members. (emphasis added) (Poma Poma case 2002)

In the Sámi mining case it was noted that there was inadequate consultation with the Sámi about the potential impact on their reindeer herding by the mining initiative. The Committee made the following observation:

> [T]hroughout the process, there was no independent assessment of the impact of the exploration activities on the reindeer herding, as a fundamental part of the Sámi culture and livelihood, their intergenerational transmission of the practice, and the right of the Sámi as Indigenous Peoples. The Committee is of the view that an adequate and effective process of free, prior and informed consent, when the rights of Indigenous Peoples may be affected by projects carried out in their traditional territories, must include not only the sharing of information and the reception of comments from the affected community, but also an *interactive and continuous dialogue* through Indigenous Peoples' own representative institutions, from the outset and through culturally appropriate procedures, respecting the right of Indigenous Peoples to influence the outcome of decision-making processes affecting them. (emphasis added) (Sámi mining case 2024, para 14.6)

Access to traditional lands

Indigenous people should be able to access their traditional lands and waters. To enable this objective these lands should be clearly and securely identified and demarcated. Indigenous people must be given the assurance that their rights to lands are properly defined, that they can exercise their traditional rights within the lands, and that they must be consulted about activities that may impact on their land. The CESCR observed the following regarding Brazil:

> The Committee recalls the recommendation made in its concluding observations on the State party's initial report in this regard and recommends that the State party expeditiously complete the process of *demarcation and allocation of indigenous land* in accordance with the Constitution and existing laws. (emphasis added) (CESCR 2009a)

Effective participation in decisions that affect indigenous people

Indigenous people should be consulted about matters that directly or disproportionately impact on them and their traditional lands, traditions and customs. This includes giving them timely information, an opportunity to seek expert advice and time for internal consultation, as well as showing respect for internal consultative processes. The CESCR observed the following regarding Cambodia:

> The Committee emphasises the need for carrying out environmental and social impact assessments and consultations with affected communities with regard to economic activities including mining and oil explorations, with a view to ensuring that these activities do not deprive the indigenous peoples of the full enjoyment of their rights to their ancestral lands and natural resources. (CESCR 2009b, para 16)

In the Sámi consultation case the complaint was heard from children who alleged their right to culture and self-determination had been infringed by the granting of a mining licence in their traditional lands. They said that the approval of mining impacted on their ability to learn and practise their traditional customs, particularly reindeer herding. (Sámi consultation case 2024) The Committee found that their right to effective participation through FPIC had been infringed:

> The Committee considers that if the granting of the permit on the authors' traditional territory occurred without seeking the free, prior and informed consent of their community, this fact may represent in itself, irrespective of future developments, a breach to the authors' rights under the Convention. Taking all the above-mentioned factors into account, the Committee concludes that the authors have victim status under article 5(1) of the Optional Protocol. (Sámi consultation case 2024, para 8.3)

Failure to consult implies discrimination

Failure to engage in consultation not only constitutes a breach of the duty to obtain FPIC pursuant to UNDRIP, but it can also be construed as a violation of the constitutional right of members of an indigenous people to equal treatment as individuals, as well as the right to be protected against discrimination. In a case involving the Sámi people of Sweden the UN Committee on the Elimination of Racial Discrimination ruled that the failure to consult with the local indigenous community about the impact of a mining project may constitute discriminatory conduct. The Committee observed a disregard for the territorial rights of the community and

> for their right to offer free, prior and informed consent whenever their rights may be affected by projects carried out in their traditional territories constitutes a form of discrimination as it results in nullifying or impairing the recognition, enjoyment or exercise by indigenous peoples, on an equal footing, of their rights to their ancestral territories, natural resources and, as a result, their identity. (Lars-Anders Ågren case 2013, para 6.7)

In the Sámi mining case it was accepted that FPIC does not require consent, but concluded nevertheless that 'the procedure provided in this case does not meet the standard of *effective participation* in accordance with the principle of free, prior and informed consent'. (emphasis added) (Sámi mining case 2024, para 14.6) The state had therefore failed to establish that prior to the grant of permits for mining it had adequately taken into account the impact on the traditional lands of the Sámi and their cultural rights, their right to self-determination, the right to adequate standard of living and their right to effective participation. (Sámi mining case 2024, para 14.8)

Legal mechanisms to resolve disputes

Indigenous people must have access to legal procedures and mechanisms which enable their rights in general, and in particular their rights to ancestral land, to be enforced and disputes to be resolved. These rights include respect for traditional decision-making processes and recognition of sovereign indigenous rights. The CESCR observed the following about Paraguay:

> The Committee is concerned that the State party still does not have a *legal mechanism* for ensuring that prior, free and informed consent is obtained from indigenous peoples in relation to decisions that may affect the exercise of their economic, social and cultural rights. The Committee also notes with concern that a significant number of indigenous peoples either still lack land or have not obtained *legal recognition* for their land and that, even when their lands have been registered, they may still be victims of forced eviction. In addition, the Committee is concerned about the fact that the State party has not yet legally recognised the right of indigenous peoples to dispose freely of their natural wealth and resources or put in place an effective mechanism to enable them to claim their ancestral lands (art 1). (emphasis added) (CESCR 2015, para 6)

Right to be consulted when traditional lands and livelihood are affected

Indigenous people have the right to be consulted when an activity affects their traditional lands and livelihood, with the prerogative to provide prior and informed consent before such an activity may proceed. The UNHRC has connected the right to self-determination arising from UNDRIP to art 27 of the ICCPR. This linkage underscores the right of an indigenous community to be consulted regarding events on their lands. This right includes the collective involvement of a community, encompassing the individual rights of community members, to be consulted on matters affecting their culture, identity and lands.[73] The UNHRC made the following observation about a complaint brought against the government of Paraguay:

> [I]t is of fundamental importance that measures that compromise or interfere with the economic activities of *cultural value* of an indigenous community have been subjected to the free, prior and informed consent of the members of the community, they must also respect the principle of proportionality, so that they do not endanger the very subsistence of the community. (emphasis added) (HRC 2021, para 8.7)

These findings expressed by the UNHRC, CESCR and CERD serve as a useful basis to review and inform domestic policies, processes and legislation, and to identify potential state-based shortcomings. The recommendations fall short of proposing specific normative or practical measures to be enacted within municipal settings, but the general importance of consultation with indigenous people within the context of FPIC about matters that impact on them, their lands and culture, is recognised. Domestic courts may also take note of these comments to be informed of developments in international law for the purposes of interpreting consultation rights in domestic settings. For example, in Colombia the Constitutional Court declared that merely sharing information with an indigenous community does not equate to effective consultation since

> the information or notification that is given to the indigenous community in connection with a project of exploration or exploitation of natural resources does not have the same value as consultation. It is necessary . . . that the community declares, through their authorised representatives their consent (Colombia Constitutional Court 1997).

---

[73] Note how in the Fosen case in Norway the court read within art 27 of the ICCPR the right of the Sámi to practise reindeering to be protected. (Fosen case 2021) This approach reflects the Kichwa case, in which it was held that the right to a cultural identity is a fundamental and collective right of indigenous communities and must be respected in a multicultural, pluralistic and democratic society. (Kichwa case 2012, para 217)

In Canada the court has emphasised that the adequacy of consultation is influenced by the nature, scope and potential impact of the proposed project. The greater the impact of the project on indigenous people and their land, the more extensive the consultation and the greater the effort to reach consent should be. (Delgamuukw case 1997; Wood and Rossiter 2022, 115–47) The nature and extent of the duty to consult therefore 'vary with circumstances'. (Haida Nation case 2004, para 39) In South Africa, Justice Basson remarked as follows about the utility of international law as a source for interpreting statutes in South Africa: 'It is accepted that international law plays an important role in interpreting statues [in South Africa].' (Baleni case 2019, para 37) She then went on to say that the specific legislative scheme under which the dispute in the Baleni case was brought required 'consent' from the local community, rather than mere consultation. She said this is consistent with international law where, in some circumstances, a community has the right to refuse an activity on their land. (Baleni case 2019, para 78)

In the literature, attempts have been made to distinguish between consultation and FPIC, but courts have not been so eager to distinguish between the two processes as if they are entirely different. Barelli refers to the flexibility of FPIC and says that it does not establish an absolute right but rather a *relational* right. The nature of FPIC therefore depends on the circumstances and relevant statutory regime,[74] but its practical application is determined by reading the obligations in conjunction with the right to self-determination and other pertinent rights under international law, with the focus on outcomes and self-determining choices of the peoples. (Barelli 2012, 23) It is not surprising that Reynolds remarks critically, in light of the variety of interpretations open to policy makers, that a 'fundamental feature of Aboriginal law [in Canada] is the ability of the federal and provincial governments to infringe constitutionally protected Aboriginal and treaty rights.' (Reynolds 2018, 108).

The judgments by the Inter-American Court of Human Rights in the Saramaka People case and Kichwa case (Saramaka case 2007; Kichwa case 2012) demonstrate that, in the case of large-scale projects, greater indigenous participation should be expected; benefits may be reasonably expected by the affected community to

---

[74] It is not only the statutory scheme that is relevant, but also compliance therewith. For instance, with regard to the Indonesian province of Papua, critics have argued that, despite the legislative requirement for actual consent from indigenous people, in practice this standard is not consistently applied, particularly in the management of forests considered ancestral lands by indigenous communities. (Soetjipto 2022, 141).

compensate them for damage or loss of use of their land; and consultation should include regular meetings, exchanges of proposals, good faith considerations of the other side's position and respect for the decision-making processes of the indigenous people. (Tomaselli and Cittadino 2021) Furthermore, consultation should be adaptable to the particular community and the project being proposed in a manner that is consistent with obligations arising from international law. (Kichwa case 2012, para 164)[75] These obligations also apply to private entities that seek to access the lands of indigenous people. (Kalina and Lokono case 2015)

In response to the question of who the holder of the right to FPIC is, the Inter-American Court declared that the right applies to communities that

> share similar characteristics with indigenous peoples, such as social, cultural and economic traditions different from other sections of the national community, identifying themselves with their ancestral territories and regulating themselves, at least partially, by their own norms, customs and traditions. (Saramaka case 2007, para 79)

Practical effect and useful guidance were provided in the Kichwa judgment about the meaning of FPIC. (Kichwa case 2012) In the Poma Poma case 'effective' participation in decision-making was declared to be an essential element of consultation. The Human Rights Committee held as follows:

> [T]he admissibility of measures which substantially compromise or interfere with the culturally significant economic activities of a minority or indigenous community depends on whether the members of the community in question have had the opportunity to participate in the decision-making process in relation to these measures and whether they will continue to benefit from their traditional economy. The Committee considers that participation in the decision-making process must be effective, which requires *not mere consultation but the free, prior and informed consent* of the members of the community. (emphasis added) (Poma Poma case 2002, paras 7.4; 7.6)

Doyle, after an overview of relevant international jurisprudence, concludes as follows:

> Taken together, this body of jurisprudence indicates that the requirement for consent constitutes the canopy for, and is a derivative of, a myriad of human rights, inter alia the right to self-determination and self-determined development, the right to property – including traditionally owned lands, territories and resources and associated customary laws – the right to practise traditional livelihoods, and collective dimensions of rights to health, food, life, housing, participation and cultural rights. (Doyle 2014, 130)

---

[75] In the Kichwa case it was held that the right to a cultural identity is a fundamental and collective right of indigenous communities and must be respected in a multicultural, pluralistic and democratic society. (Kichwa case 2012, para 217)

MacInnes and others caution, however, that regardless of the progress made at an international level in regard to norm-setting, at a practical level FPIC remains a challenging concept to operationalise:

> One of the major outstanding challenges with the FPIC standard, *remains its enforcement and compliance.* Evaluations of FPIC processes indicate the difficulties involved in actual implementation, especially in the absence of consensus among indigenous peoples (where some may favour cooperation with a company while others oppose). Similarly, challenges due to complex layers of legislation, unsettled land-tenure, low government capacity, lack of existing institution infrastructures and transparency regarding compensation make verification of compliance with the FPIC principles tough to determine. A concern is that companies and States alike are *turning FPIC into a formality no longer based on customary laws*, by manipulating processes and certifications without due verification of procedure in the community. (emphasis added) (MacInnes, Colchester and Whitmore 2017, 158)

Ultimately, the practical effect of meaningful consultation and practical measures to ensure free, prior and informed consent are to be worked out within domestic settings. The content of the right underlying FPIC is not a veto, but rather an objective to reach agreement. (Pulver 2022, 115) Victoria Tauli-Corpuz, special rapporteur for the United Nations on the rights of indigenous people, made the following observation after her fact-finding visit to the USA about the substance of FPIC:

> The goal of tribal consultation is not simply to check a box, or to merely give tribes a chance to be heard. Rather, the core objective is to provide federal decision makers with context, information and perspectives needed to support informed decisions that actually protect tribal interests. Treaty rights, the federal trust responsibility to tribes, environmental justice, and the principles enshrined in the Declaration all must be given life and meaning in federal decisions that impact tribes. Meaningful consultation has the potential to provide the solid foundation for such decisions, but federal agencies must be willing to recognise these principles and to work actively to put them into practice uniformly at the local, regional and national level. (emphasis added) (Tauli-Corpuz 2017)

In summary, although UNDRIP has elevated FPIC to the level of an obligation arising from an international instrument, the following is noted:

- UNDRIP is not a treaty; its provisions cannot be legally enforced;
- neither ILO 169 nor UNDRIP define FPIC;
- the 'consent' used in FPIC is aspirational and *not* a universal, justiciable right to veto;

- the procedures to give effect to FPIC under UNDRIP are essentially similar to the consultation procedures that give effect to ILO 169; and
- the right to be consulted arises not only pursuant to ILO 169 and UNDRIP, but also from an expansive interpretation of fundamental rights pursuant to art 27 of the ICCPR.

7.4.4 Judicial consideration of FPIC and consultation in municipal law

In this section a brief overview is provided of the meaning and interpretation given by a few selected municipal courts to the concepts of consultation and FPIC. It is demonstrated that the obligations arising from consultation and FPIC are, in substance, treated similarly. The emphasis lies on the engagement process, information sharing and an open mindset towards accommodating the views of others and giving them a reasonable opportunity to participate meaningfully. There is neither a common-law provision for a veto nor an obligation to reach an agreement – unless, as seen in the Baleni case, consent is mandated by the statute under which the consultation takes place. It is furthermore shown that consultation and FPIC are not necessarily collective rights that can only be claimed by a community. Instead, there is also a discernible trend to give individual rights, such as rights to equal treatment, non-discrimination, culture and property, an expanded meaning that in specific circumstances may include the right to consultation and FPIC. This is consistent with art 27 of the ICCPR. (Sámi mining case 2024; Sámi consultation case 2024; Fosen case 2021; Endorois Welfare Council case 2003). What started principally as a collective right claimed by indigenous people is evolving into a fundamental individual right that may be exercised by any individual belonging to a community, indigenous or otherwise. Indigenous people do, however, have a special standing in light of their traditions, connection to land and responsibility to look after ancestral lands.

The importance of FPIC has also been incorporated into agreements, conditions and standards set by international organisations such as the World Bank, the OECD and other international financiers for when developers interact with indigenous peoples and local, non-indigenous communities. (Tomaselli and Cittadino 2021; World Bank 2016; OECD Guidelines 2023)[76] It is, however,

[76] For example, the World Bank has endorsed the following statement as policy for its funding of projects, underscoring the interchangeable use of consultation and consent:

> Where Indigenous Peoples are present in, or have a collective attachment to, the proposed project area, the Bank will require the Borrower to undertake a process of *meaningful*

also acknowledged that there is often an 'implementation gap' that separates international norms from municipal practices. (Wright and Tomaselli 2019) Eichler suggests the following:

> International human rights law has established a sort of middle way conciliating the two positions: consent is understood as an objective to be reached in any prior consultation process affecting indigenous peoples in terms of its administrative, judicial or other measures; exceptions reserving consent to be legally binding are limited to forced relocation, the disposal of hazardous materials and military activities to be executed on indigenous peoples' territories. (Eichler 2019, 9)

The divergent understandings arising from the exact nature and obligations of the duty to consult and obtain FPIC are not easy to reconcile, often causing breakdowns in relationships *between* governments and indigenous people and even disputes *within* indigenous communities.[77] Examples of disagreements that may emerge within a community include issues related to the merit of a proposal, the response to a proposal, who speaks on behalf of a community, the acceptability of conditions, the designated negotiators, the appropriateness of consultation or compensation, and the distribution or sharing of benefits. There may also be

---

> *consultation* tailored to Indigenous Peoples. . . . In addition, the Bank recognises that Indigenous Peoples (or as they may be referred to in the national context) may be particularly vulnerable to the loss of, alienation from or exploitation of their land and access to natural and cultural resources. In recognition of this vulnerability, *the Bank will require the Borrower to obtain the Free, Prior and Informed Consent (FPIC) of the affected Indigenous Peoples*'. (emphasis added) (World Bank Environment and Social Framework 2016, 20-1)

[77] A potential conflict that may arise within an indigenous community is the perception that individuals serving in a consultative body or participating in a consultative process are 'sell-outs' or have been 'co-opted'. This arises because the consultation process may lend legitimacy to government policies or proposed developments, even though the consultative body lacks veto powers or effective participatory authority to ensure good faith consultation. Weller explains that the 'lack of powers' of consultative bodies is reflected in a 'softer process of consultation' (Weller 2007, 426), but this soft process may erode the credibility of those participating in the consultation process and bestow a false legitimacy on policies or developments that purportedly arose from consultation. For different perspectives of the interpretation of UNDRIP, see Hohmann and Weller. (Hohmann and Weller 2018) It is perhaps not surprising that criticism has been voiced regarding the use of FPIC as it does not give indigenous people a veto and it also potentially legitimises the actions of governments or developers. My experience, representing Aboriginal people in Australia in 'good faith' negotiations in the context of native title, has been that Aboriginal negotiators often have their hands tied: their community demands and expects a lot, but their actual bargaining position is weak as they must negotiate under very strict statutory and time limitations. This has the potential to erode the credibility and legitimacy of the indigenous negotiators, the consultation process itself and the credibility of the outcome.

disagreements within the community about who is to participate in negotiations, the role of women, elders and young people, and the manner in which benefits, if any, are extracted and are distributed within the community.[78] Further disagreement could extend to matters such as the definition of the indigenous community, the relevance of FPIC to other communities in society, or the inclusion of individuals within the community to be consulted. (Ezeani and Newman 2022) In some cases courts may be called upon to make determinations in such intra-indigenous disputes. (Ngadju case 2013, para 91; De Villiers 2021b)

The cause for divergent expectations of consultation within and with the indigenous community is simple: parliaments and governments are unlikely to fetter their sovereignty, while indigenous people are reluctant to serve in a body or participate in a process that is, in effect, little else than a 'toy telephone'. In such a scenario advice is given, consultations take place, but the advice is not accepted or taken seriously, or is even ignored. (De Villiers 2018b) The concepts of 'consultation' and 'consent' are notorious for being misapplied and misunderstood. The notion of FPIC seems to imply a veto through the use of the word 'consent', but proper legal construction and international advisory opinions do not support an actual veto.[79] In fact, 'the lack of conceptual clarity

---

[78] Note, for example, how within the context of the Sámi Parliaments, there have been concerns about the lack of influence and impact from women in their deliberations. (Kuokkanen 2011, 39) Engaging in FPIC with indigenous people can be challenging for third parties when there are internal divisions within the community. Questions may emerge such as who should be consulted, whether they are properly authorised, who should approve an agreement, whether there are community checks and balances in place, who can speak for a particular parcel of land, and who should be the recipients of any benefits that may arise from the agreement. In a recent dispute in Australia about the appropriateness of community consultation it is estimated that the cost of delays, due to a subgroup alleging that they had not been consulted, amounted to around A$1 million per day. The objection of the subgroup was ultimately dismissed with the judge making scathing comments about some of the lay evidence and expert evidence. (Munkara case 2024) A legal cost order of A$9 million was made against the objecting party.

[79] In the seminal case in Colombia of T-129/11 the question arose as to whether indigenous people had a veto if they disagreed with a proposal. (T-129/11 2011) The court did not expressly respond to the question and there is disagreement in literature about whether the court intended to recognise a veto or not. Herrera, who worked as a law clerk when the judgment was drafted, says that there was no explicit recognition of a veto, but rather that indigenous people could oppose a development on the basis of their right to self-determination. (Herrera 2019, 51) The court nevertheless emphasised that consultation with indigenous people should cover the entire lifespan of a project, including rehabilitation, or whatever happens in the long term. The question as to whether a veto exists is not answered by way of a formal power, but rather by way of assessment of the process that has been followed and whether it was fair and reasonable. It is therefore ultimately for the judiciary to declare, according to a specific set of facts, whether or not

surrounding the notion of Indigenous consent is rightly considered an obstacle to its institutionalisation.' (Papillon, Leclair and Leydet 2020, 224)

Furthermore, indigenous communities encompass a microcosm of opinions. Any suggestion that they act in absolute unison in all matters concerning access to their traditional lands is presumptuous and overly idealistic. It is inevitable that within an indigenous community minority opinions may exist and, ironically, the view of the majority may prevail even within the context of FPIC.[80] The pursuit of 'consent' between community and developer may end up causing division within the community. The UN Human Rights Committee acknowledged, in a dispute concerning the appropriateness of consultation between the government of New Zealand and the Māori about fishing rights, that internal disputation within an indigenous community may occur, but

> in such circumstances, where the right of individuals to enjoy their own culture is in conflict with the exercise of parallel rights by other members of the minority group, or of the minority as a whole, the Committee may consider whether the limitation in issue is in the interests of all members of the minority and whether there is reasonable and objective justification for its application to the individuals who claim to be adversely affected. (Mahuika case 2000, para 9.6)

The following are practical examples of the standards imposed in municipal law to give effect to the obligation to consult with indigenous people.

Inter-American Court of Human Rights

On the right to be consulted the Inter-American Court of Human Rights (IACrtHR) said the following in the Saramaka case:

> Indigenous and tribal peoples must be able to *significantly influence* the process and the decisions made in it, which includes the accommodation of their perspectives and concerns, for example, through provable and verifiable changes regarding the project objectives, parameters and design, as well as any concerns they may have about the acceptance of the project itself. (emphasis added) (Saramaka case 2007, para 134)

---

consultation has been adequate. This may be construed as a veto, but at law it is not considered a veto, as the focus is on process rather than substance.

[80] This raises the risk to those who are involved in consultation: what appears to be a final decision that a development may proceed may not in fact be a final decision since subgroups or individuals may challenge the process. (Munkara case 2024)

In the Kichwa case, the IACrtHR ruled that appropriate consultation in compliance with international standards must take place prior to the decision being made. This consultation should be conducted in good faith with the objective of reaching an agreement and should include the provision of adequate and accessible information about the proposed project. Additionally, the project and consultation must encompass social and environmental impact assessments, and the advice expressed by the community must derive from it being suitably informed. (Kichwa case 2012, paras 177–211)

In a 2018 judgment in the Xucuru case the IACrtHR emphasised that indigenous people are entitled to the protection of their rights to land, they have a right to be consulted about development that affects their lands, and they are entitled to a restoration of their rights in land. (Xucuru case 2018, para 117) Regardless of the positive measures emanating from the IACrtHR, many challenges remain, particularly since states do not always adhere to special measures or advisory recommendations, while indigenous people and their traditional lands remain the target of discriminatory actions. (Urrejola and Neira 2024, 266)

In a 2021 judgment the court held that the rights of the Maya people to protect and promote their culture were improperly constrained by limitations placed on the freedom of communication of their members by the manner in which the setting up of radio stations was regulated. (Maya Peoples case 2021) This dispute did not relate to traditional lands, but to the ability of community members to practise their culture without having access to radio. The judgment affirmed the rights of indigenous peoples to collective *and* individual freedom of expression, and the right to practise their culture without discrimination.[81]

India

In 2013 the Supreme Court of India found that consultation with a local indigenous community, the Dongria Kondh people, about the undertaking of

[81] The background to the dispute was that licences to operate radio frequencies were made available by way of public tender, rendering it difficult, if not impossible, for the Maya to secure such licences. The community emphasised that access to community radio is critical to the transmission of language and culture. The community explained how indigenous peoples rely on the medium of radio to inform and educate their communities, especially during the COVID-19 global health pandemic. Obstacles to radio frequency access translate into indirect discrimination against indigenous communities, perpetuated through apparently neutral legislation that *de facto* discriminates against indigenous peoples, as exemplified by Guatemala's general telecommunications law.

mining operations on their lands had not been adequate. The court found in the Orissa Mining case that a precondition for mining to proceed is approval by the indigenous community, as their collective rights and interests are directly impacted by the proposal. A detailed proposal had to be submitted to the representative body of the community, the Gram Sabha, for approval. (Orissa Mining case 2013, para 51) In this case, the court recognised that the community had a veto over the approval process, although the veto did not arise from international law but from local law (similar to the Baleni case in South Africa).

Canada

In the case of R v Sparrow the court considered the obligation to consult as a duty arising from s 35 of the Constitution of Canada, which mandates that 'existing aboriginal and treaty rights' are 'recognised and affirmed'. The court did not cite international law but relied on the recognition of indigenous rights in the Constitution, but the judgment was a 'significant departure' from previous decisions by recognising the dynamic nature of indigenous rights and not being frozen in time. (Borrows and Rotman 2023, 122) The court reasoned that 'aboriginal peoples, with their history of conservation consciousness and interdependence with natural resources, would surely be expected, at the least, to be informed regarding the determination of an appropriate scheme for the regulation of the fisheries', and that their opinion should be considered. (Sparrow case 1990) The phrase 'existing aboriginal rights' must also be interpreted flexibly to permit evolution. Significantly, the court declared as follows:

> The objective of this requirement is not to undermine Parliament's ability and responsibility with respect to creating and administering overall conservation and management plans regarding the salmon fishery. The objective is rather to guarantee that those plans treat aboriginal peoples in a way ensuring that their rights *are taken seriously*. (emphasis added) (Sparrow case 1990)

In the Haida Nation case the court held that the duty to consult means that, prior to a decision being made, there must be effective consultation with the affected indigenous people. (Haida Nation case 2004) The court declared as follows:

> The government's duty to consult with Aboriginal peoples and accommodate their interests is grounded in the principle of the honour of the Crown, which must be understood generously. While the asserted but unproven Aboriginal rights and title are insufficiently specific for the honour of the Crown to mandate that the Crown act as a fiduciary, the Crown, acting honourably, *cannot cavalierly run roughshod over Aboriginal interests* where claims affecting these interests are being seriously pursued

> in the process of treaty negotiation and proof. The duty to consult and accommodate is part of a process of *fair dealing and reconciliation* that begins with the assertion of sovereignty and continues beyond formal claims resolution. The foundation of the duty in the Crown's honour and the goal of reconciliation suggest that the duty arises when the Crown has knowledge, real or constructive, of the potential existence of the Aboriginal right or title and contemplates conduct that might adversely affect it. Consultation and accommodation before final claims resolution preserve the Aboriginal interest and are an essential corollary to the honourable process of reconciliation that s 35 of the Constitution Act, 1982 demands. (emphasis added) (Haida Nation case 2004)[82]

In response to the question of whether the duty to consult applies only to the state, or also to third parties seeking access to land, the court declared as follows:

> Third parties cannot be held liable for failing to discharge the Crown's duty to consult and accommodate. The honour of the Crown cannot be delegated, and the legal responsibility for consultation and accommodation rests with the Crown. This does not mean, however, that third parties can never be liable to Aboriginal peoples. (Haida Nation case 2004)

Importantly, the court emphasised that the duty to consult does not grant the ability to veto a development to the indigenous community, unless such a power is specifically so bestowed. (Haida Nation case 2004, para 48)

In the Rio Tinto Alcan case the court declared that the duty to consult arose from treaty; it is linked to the settlement of claims and reconciliation; and it has a prospective nature by looking at acts yet to take place and rights yet to be established. (Rio Tinto Alcan case 2010) The court declared as follows:

> The duty to consult arises when the Crown has knowledge, *real or constructive*, of the *potential* existence of the Aboriginal right or title and contemplates conduct that might adversely affect it. This test can be broken down into three elements. *First*, the Crown must have real or constructive knowledge of a potential Aboriginal claim or right. While the existence of a potential claim is essential, proof that the claim will succeed is not. *Second*, there must be Crown conduct or a Crown decision. In accordance with the generous, purposive approach that must be brought to the duty to consult, the required decision or conduct is not confined to government exercise of statutory powers or to decisions or conduct which have an immediate impact on lands and resources. The duty to consult extends to 'strategic, higher level decisions' that may have an impact on Aboriginal claims and rights. *Third*, there must be a possibility that the Crown conduct

[82] Note in this respect the right of Aboriginal people in Australia to negotiate after a native title claim has been accepted, but before the merit of their claim to land has been established. It can take many years for a claim to be fully investigated and litigated, but in the meantime the community attracts procedural rights under the Native Title Act. (De Villiers 2022h).

> may affect the Aboriginal claim or right. The claimant must show a causal relationship between the proposed government conduct or decision and a potential for adverse impacts on pending Aboriginal claims or rights. Past wrongs, speculative impacts and adverse effects on a First Nation's future negotiating position will not suffice. *Moreover, the duty to consult is confined to the adverse impacts flowing from the current government conduct or decision, not to larger adverse impacts of the project of which it is a part.* Where the resource has long since been altered and the present government conduct or decision does not have any further impact on the resource, the issue is not consultation, but negotiation about compensation. (emphasis added) (Rio Tinto Alcan case 2010)

Of importance is the court's emphasis that the consultation should focus on the immediate and localised impact of the project on indigenous rights and interests rather than assessing the overall merit of the project or its broader implications. Importantly, the duty only arises in the case of the existence of an Aboriginal land right and does not apply to consultation with indigenous people in general. Borrows and Rotman express the view that the judgment was a 'wasted opportunity' to provide greater clarity about the duty to consult. (Borrows and Rotman 2023, 472)

In the Saugeen First Nation case the court emphasised that consultation must be meaningful and the requirements for the obligations to be met must be set out in detail. (Saugeen First Nation case 2017, paras 10–29) Among the obligations is 'honourable negotiation' in vindication of indigenous rights and reconciliation. Furthermore, the duty of good faith is applicable to both parties and there is no obligation to reach an agreement, nor is there a prohibition against 'hard bargaining'. The duty to consult also extends to third parties, and funding may need to be provided to assist indigenous people in effectively participating in the consultation process.

In the case of larger projects the nature and extent of consultation should be more in-depth and elaborate. In the Clyde River case the court spoke about the need for 'deep consultation'. (Clyde River case 2017)

According to Borrows and Rotman, there remains 'considerable confusion' in Canada about the 'scope and content' of the duty to consult. (Borrows and Rotman 2023, 455) In contrast to South Africa, where the duty to consult arises principally from statute, in Canada the duty to consult finds it origin is a mixture of treaty obligations, the fiduciary obligations of the state towards indigenous people and the duty to consult.

New Zealand

In New Zealand complaints about lack of consultation have 'almost become a catch phrase which is consistently advanced as a ground on which to base an appeal'. (Land Air Water Association case 2001, para 443) The court went on to declare as follows about the substance of consultation:

> The essence of consultation is such that, at the end of the day, we can make an *informed decision*. That is, one that is sufficiently informed as to the relevant facts and law. . . . The method and degree of consultation, will depend on the facts of each particular case. In our view it matters little who facilitates or carries out the consultation. In some cases it may be the applicant. In other cases officers of the consent authority or a combination of both. The essential ingredient is that it is fair and enables the court to make an informed decision. The *underlying element of fairness* applies equally to the person required to consult and the person or body that is consulted. (emphasis added) (Land Air Water Association case 2001, paras 447–448)

In the Wellington International Airport case the courts emphasised that consultation must be in good faith, parties must act reasonably, an opportunity must be given for informed decisions to be made, information must be adequate for informed decisions, and an open mind must be held so a full consideration can be given to the opinions of the other side. (Wellington International Airport case 1991)

Indonesia

In the State Forest case in Indonesia a community of indigenous people objected to forests that traditionally had been known as customary forests being described in legislation as 'state' forests. (State Forest case 2012) The Constitutional Court granted the relief and removed the word 'state' from the relevant statute. The court cited the 1996 Rio Declaration on Environment and Development as an example of the importance placed by international law on the role of indigenous people to protect the environment. There is a duty on government to assist indigenous people in this function. The declassification of a customary forest without consultation and approval by the indigenous people is inconsistent with the Constitution of Indonesia. Although international instruments such as ILO 169 and UNDRIP are not legally binding in Indonesia, those international developments have had a 'major impact on the development of indigenous rights' in Indonesia. (Arizona and Cohen 2024, 189)

Norway

In the Fosen case the Supreme Court of Norway ruled that the construction of a windfarm violated the rights of the indigenous Sámi to enjoy their culture pursuant to art 27 of the ICCPR. The windfarm constituted a 'significant adverse effect' on their cultural rights to practise reindeer herding. (Fosen case 2021) The interesting aspect of the judgment for purposes of this chapter is that the rights of the community collectively were upheld pursuant to an individual rights to enjoy culture. This highlights how the seeming divide between an individual right and a collective right can be overcome. The court emphasised that art 27 of the ICCPR 'must be viewed in context with art 108 of the Constitution, which imposes a duty on the state authorities "to create conditions enabling the Sámi people to preserve and develop its language, culture and way of life"'. (Fosen case 2021, para 99) The court found that the Sámi is clearly a minority as intended by art 27 and that their reindeer husbandry is a form of protected cultural practice. This was a 'landmark' judgment with far-reaching legal and political implications. (Cambou 2024, 64) The court rejected the argument that art 27 only protects individual rights and not the rights of a community. The court declared:

> According to art 27, the protection applies to 'persons belonging to such minorities'. This wording in the first part of the provision indicates that the protection is enjoyed by the individuals in a minority group. However, the provision further states that the individuals have the right to enjoy their own culture, etc. 'in community with the other members of their group'. This element was added to clarify the collective nature of the provision. . . . *Article 27 protects the individual, but adds that the protection has certain collective features. . . .* Against this background, I find that art 27 at the outset protects individuals in a minority. However, the minorities' culture is practiced in community, which gives the protection a collective nature. (emphasis added) (Fosen case 2021, paras 104–106)

Australia – consultation in statute

In a 2022 judgment of the Federal Court of Australia the question arose concerning the entitlement of a traditional community to be consulted when an undersea pipeline was proposed to be laid in an area the community regards as its traditional waters. The court examined whether the concerns of the community, particularly regarding the potential impacts on its traditional fishing rights, had been adequately considered. The court held that the indigenous community, including subgroups, should have been consulted since its interests could be affected by the laying of the pipeline. (Tipakalippa case 2022) The court observed that, although there is no statutory definition of 'consult', the approach adopted by Australian courts is that 'the underlying premise of the authorisation provisions is to give all group members a "reasonable opportunity" to participate in decision-making. . . .' (Tipakalippa case 2022, para 104) In this case the company seeking approval to lay the undersea pipeline did not provide satisfactory evidence of having consulted with all the subgroups of the indigenous community that could potentially be affected. Notably, the court did not suggest that all the subgroups must be in agreement, rather that the proponent should demonstrate that consultation had been attempted.[83] While approval was ultimately granted for the project to proceed, the objection raised by a subgroup caused substantial delay but was ultimately dismissed, with the court being critical of some of the lay evidence and expert evidence sought to be relied on to prevent the project going ahead. (Munkara case 2024)

A 2023 judgment handed down by the Federal Court in the Barngarla case declared that, although extensive consultation had taken place with the Aboriginal community about the location of a nuclear waste storage facility, the facts supported a finding of 'apprehended bias' on the part of government since it had already made up its mind about the location of the site prior to the commencement of consultation. (Barngarla case 2023) The process that had taken place could better be described as information sharing rather than consultation. The court in this case did not consider the merit of the proposed location of the site, but rather the inadequate process that gave rise to the identification and acquisition of the proposed site.

Australia – statutory right to negotiate on native title, traditional lands

The Australian experiences gained to give practical and legal content to 'good faith' negotiations in the realm of native title offer useful insights into the questions

[83] In 2023 independent anthropologist Dr Brendan Corrigan reported that, after extensive consultation with affected indigenous people, no cultural heritage sites that may be impacted by the proposed pipeline could be identified. Despite the rejection of this finding by the local land council, the relevant regulating agency gave approval for the project to proceed based on the report's findings. After further consultation had occurred and approval given for the project to proceed a subgroup sought a stay on grounds that they had not been consulted. The expert evidence relied upon was criticised. The presiding judge described the expert evidence as 'so lacking integrity that no weight can be placed on them'. (Munkara case 2024) The court ultimately awarded A$9 million in legal costs against the Environmental Defenders Office, which supported and financed the proceeding. (Rauso 2024; Munkara consent orders cost 2024)

under consideration in this chapter. Despite the criticism it receives, Australia's native title regime is arguably the most advanced national statutory scheme when it comes to according indigenous people procedural rights and financial support with regard to development that may impact on their traditional lands. (De Villiers 2022h) In short, the scheme affords procedural rights to Aboriginal communities starting from the point when a native claim is registered (even if unproven) up to the point when the claim is successfully determined and an indigenous land use agreement concerning long-term native title rights takes effect. The Native Title Act grants Aboriginal people a 'right to negotiate' when their traditional lands may potentially be impacted by developments. (Native Title Act 1993, Subdivision P) Federal funding is made available to assist native title representative bodies to represent and assist indigenous communities in their negotiations with proponents of developments.

The right to negotiate is not purported to be a codification of the international standard of free, prior and informed consent (FPIC), but it 'has many provisions about Indigenous agreement and decision-making that have relevance for how FPIC may work in a domestic legal system'. (Southalan and Fardin 2019, 378) The notion of 'good faith' that underlies FPIC is also found in the normative standard underlying the right to negotiate.

The right to negotiate is, in essence, a statutory right available to those Aboriginal people who have a registered native title claim, or who have proven their native title rights over their ancestral land (called 'country'), to be consulted about developments (called 'future acts')[84] that are proposed to take place on the land. The right to negotiate allows for a relatively short period of a maximum of six months for parties to negotiate in good faith 'with a view to reaching an agreement' on the terms and conditions for the future act to proceed. (Native Title Act 1993, ss 25(2) and 31(1)(b))[85]

---

[84] A future act may, for example, include building of infrastructure, undertaking prospecting, exploration and mining, acquiring land for a public purpose, building roads, rails and ports, and acquiring land to develop new town sites. The greater the gravity of the impact of a future act, the greater the degree of good faith negotiation is required. For example, the issuing of a prospecting licence which does not involve any ground disturbance is likely to involve less negotiation than negotiations related to the issuing of a mining lease with the intent to do major ground disturbance works.

[85] The right to negotiate is intended to be a 'special provision' for the benefit of Aboriginal people, as foreshadowed in the International Convention on the Elimination of all Forms of Racial Discrimination and the Australian Racial Discrimination Act 1975 (International Convention on Discrimination 1965). Although the right to negotiate is not intended to formally incorporate

Although the right to negotiate grants procedural rights regarding notification of development proposals and an opportunity to negotiate conditions for access, it does not mandate consent by Aboriginal people.[86] There is no right of veto given to the indigenous community. If no agreement about a project proposal is reached, the proponent of the development may ask the National Native Title Tribunal to grant approval for the project to proceed, with or without conditions. (National Native Title Tribunal 2020) In practice a project is likely to proceed regardless of any objections raised by the traditional owners. In this way the negotiation table is skewed in favour of those seeking access to land, though it is not as one-sided as may seem the case at first glance.

The right to negotiate has, regardless of its shortcomings, enabled many Aboriginal communities to interact with government and developers to negotiate various types of benefits, as well as to establish corporate structures and processes, for their respective community. Examples of such benefits include: royalty payments from large-scale mining operations; heritage and sacred site protection agreements; consultative mechanisms; charitable funds for education and other beneficial purposes; joint management of nature reserves; administrative support for communities to run their own offices; acquisitions of parcels of land for use by a community; and employment, education and contracting opportunities on mine sites.[87] Smith correctly observes how Aboriginal people have made progress,

---

the FPIC contained in UNDRIP into Australian legislation, the principles found in the Native Title Act and the effect given to them by the Australian courts closely resemble developments in international law in respect of what is meant by good faith consultation.

86 Thousands of agreements have been entered into by Aboriginal people pursuant to the right to negotiate. Some of these agreements are limited to obligations to respect and protect important Aboriginal traditional and sacred sites, while others encompass substantial provisions for royalties, as well as employment and contracting opportunities. O'Faircheallaigh observes that, owing to the nature of the right to negotiate and the time restrictions it entails, both sides in a negotiation process tend to be under pressure to reach an agreement; the native title holders only have a short time frame in which to strike a deal under a statute that is skewed towards granting access to land, whereas the developer faces time constraints, as well as demands from financiers and shareholders to work with local communities. (O'Faircheallaigh 2016, 92) He observes: 'A number of agreements strongly favourable to Aboriginal interests have been negotiated pursuant to the Native Title Act, while some groups that lack even the minimal legal rights offered by the Native Title Act have also been able to secure favourable outcomes.' (O'Faircheallaigh 2016, 202)

87 One of the most extensive indigenous land use agreements concluded to date is between the State of Western Australia and the Noongar people, generally referred to as the Noongar Settlement. This agreement affects around 30 000 Noongar people and pertains to more than 200 000 km^2. The Noongar Settlement has been likened to a fourth level of government whereby the socio-cultural areas of the Noongar community are regulated. (De Villiers 2022a) Notable is

at a practical level, by experiencing a 'lived reality' through self-determination in aspects such as the recognition of their identity, entering into agreements, resolving conflicts with other communities and concluding commercial arrangements. (Smith 2019, 151) Larkin and Butler are, however, more sceptical of the native title negotiation processes. (Larkin and Butler 2019, 94)

A comprehensive analysis of the merits of the right to negotiate and the native title regime in Australia lies beyond the scope of this chapter. Nonetheless, it is arguable that, when compared to other systems in international and municipal law and practice dealing with the rights of indigenous people affected by land developments, the Australian system ranks favourably.

The right to negotiate is discharged by an Aboriginal community through their community-elected or -nominated representatives.[88] The appointment of these representatives requires internal consultation within the community, and the briefing of negotiators also necessitates interaction between the community and their representatives in a manner consistent with the traditions and culture of the specific community. An indigenous community may adopt a standard negotiation team process or negotiate on an ad hoc basis.[89] Approvals of

---

also the Ngurrajuta Agreement in the Northern Territory of Australia, which envisages expanding of Aboriginal community control in a ten-year plan for projects that support training and pathways, housing development and management, community safety, family services and education based on each community's priorities, needs and aspirations. (Ngurrajuta Local Decision Making Agreement 2024) The Ngurratjuta region identified six priority areas to be the focus of the Agreement, e.g. housing, municipal services, employment, educational attendance, welfare delivery and economic development. The principle of self-determination for Aboriginal communities underpins the Agreement. (Ngurrajuta Local Decision Making Agreement 2024, para 2.2)

[88] See, for example, ss 24DB; 30A and 56 of the Native Title Act 1993.

[89] In my experience representing Aboriginal people in the Goldfields of Western Australia in their negotiations with mining companies, many indigenous communities elect or nominate a negotiating team to represent them on an ongoing basis. The negotiating team often reflects diverse interests within the community, as may arise from different families, subgroups, gender and age groups. Having permanent members on a negotiating team contributes to a team's skills development, training and familiarity with topics. Some indigenous communities have even adopted their own negotiation protocols that apply to them as a community and are used to regulate their engagements with third parties. While non-legal and non-binding in nature, these community protocols have been considered by certain courts, with reference even made to their content in order to ascertain whether proper FPIC procedures had been followed by third parties in consultations with the indigenous community. This is exemplified by the reference made by the Supreme Court of Ontario in Canada to the failure of a developer to comply with the negotiating protocol of an indigenous community, prompting the court to issue an interim injunction. The court referred, in a 2006 case, to the following elements of the protocol: initial discussion with the Chief and Council; discussions with the community; consultation with individuals affected

negotiation outcomes must also follow a process that reflects the wishes of the community. (Southalan and Fardin 2019, 384)[90] These procedural rights of good faith negotiations ensure that Aboriginal rights and interests are protected from the moment a native title claim is registered, even if the merit of the claim has not yet been fully investigated. Once the Federal Court determines that native title does indeed exist over an area, enhanced consultation arrangements can be negotiated and registered in an Indigenous Land Use Agreement. (ILUA/Right to Negotiate 2020)[91] If, however, the claim is dismissed by the Federal Court, the community which lodged the claim forfeits all consultation and negotiation rights under the Native Title Act – the consultation rights under the Native Title Act effectively cease. However, communities retain whatever consultation rights may exist pursuant to common or statutory law.

The consultation rights arising from the Native Title Act right to negotiate are therefore limited in scope and only applicable to those Aboriginal communities with a native title *claim* or a successful native title *determination*.[92] The consultation

---

by the development; follow-up discussions with the community; a referendum; and approval in writing. (Planitex case 2006, para 20).

[90] In my experience in the Goldfields of Western Australia, communities often opt for a process of community meetings, whereby the community is informed of an application to access their land, instructions are given to the negotiating team, site visits are made by the families who speak for the particular part of country, the outcomes of negotiations are discussed with the community, potential agreements are discussed and approved or rejected, distribution policies are discussed, and certain persons are authorised to execute agreements. While these processes may lead to what some have called the corporatisation of indigenous communities, the oversight and transparency that arise from such a corporate process may prevent income, contracts, employment or other benefits flowing exclusively to a select few. See, for example, how in South Africa, in the case of the Bakgatla Traditional Authority, an internal audit found that only 1–5% of the proceeds acquired had been used for the benefit of the greater community (Claassens and Matlala 2014, 123). In a similar vein, the Khoisan Act (declared unconstitutional in 2023) empowered the leadership of a community to enter into agreements with other entities. (Khoisan Act 2019, s 24) However, critics were concerned that excessive trust was being placed in the leadership and that the internal accounting and transparency of Khoisan and other indigenous communities may be weak. (Ubink and Pickering 2020, 179)

[91] Gaffney observes critically that the native title agreement processes in Australia in general, and the ILUA process in particular, have been characterised by 'poor transparency', 'inadequate safeguards', 'lack of legal, political and economic capacity to effect change' and generally unable to extract the benefits to which they are entitled. (Gaffney 2021, 241–2) This criticism may have merit when the Australian system is assessed in isolation, but when compared to other indigenous land access arrangements internationally, the criticism is arguably not balanced or reasonable.

[92] In this regard, the right to negotiate has little relevance for Aboriginal persons residing in cities and towns as, according to law, the native title has been extinguished in those areas. The right to negotiate has consequently, in some instances, contributed to a schism among

rights should therefore not be construed as applying to all Aboriginal people in Australia, but the impact is nevertheless noticeable since more than 50% of Australia is covered by native title. (Native Title Map 2024) These rights are also project-specific to the extent that the intended project impacts on the native title of a specific community. Other general socio-economic policy issues that may be relevant to Aboriginal people do not fall within the right to negotiate. Thus the *obligations* arising from the right to negotiate exhibit elements of FPIC, but the *scope* of the items subject to consultation is limited.

Although the right to negotiate is an important step in terms of consultation with Aboriginal people, it must be noted that the parties around the negotiation table are not in a position of equality.[93] The reasons for this are as follows: first, the underlying assumption that approval for a development *ought* to be granted in the interest of Australia's socio-economic development; secondly, the maximum time limit of six months on negotiations; thirdly, the absence of veto power for the Aboriginal community; and, finally, the lack of judicial authority for courts to impose conditions requiring the payment of royalties or compensation to the community for any loss or diminution of their land rights.[94] The parties may, of

---

Aboriginal peoples, where those who reside in outback areas are often the primary beneficiaries of consultation rights, whereas those in urban areas often have no consultation rights or only indirect rights by way of family in rural areas. A similar situation may arise in South Africa, where communities subject to the Interim Protection of Informal Land Rights Act can veto a project, while other communities cannot veto a project that falls within the purview of the Mining Act. (Baleni case 2019) The experience in Australia is similar to the Sámi experiences in Finland, where a substantial number of Sámi reside outside of the Sámi homeland (estimated at 60%), thereby prompting the question whether the Sámi Parliament has any moral or other duty or right to advance the rights and interests of those Sámi outside the homeland. The Noongar Settlement in Australia seeks to address this urban–rural disparity by also granting, by means of the registered Indigenous Land Use Agreement, consultation and self-government rights to urbanised Noongar people where they reside in urbanised areas. (De Villiers 2022b, 157)

[93] Gaffney is critical of the unequal bargaining positions held by local Aboriginal communities and those seeking access to their land. He specifically observes that common-law safeguards which exist to protect parties in commercial arrangements are weakened by the Native Title Act. (Gaffney 2021, 241) Conversely, it must be recognised that the Australian native title regime arguably ranks, if compared internationally, high in terms of funding and approval processes when it comes to acknowledging and protecting the rights of indigenous people to be consulted about developments on their land. At common law the process to enforce consultation rights is complex and cumbersome, but under the Native Title Act the processes are relatively simple and more affordable than common-law litigation.

[94] The position of Aboriginal people is not, when compared to indigenous people subject to the Mining Act in South Africa, as weak as it may seem at first glance. Under the South African statutory regime there is also inequality between the proponent of a development and the

course, voluntarily agree on a compensation package, and this often happens in practice. If, however, agreement on the payment of a royalty is not reached, neither a court nor the Native Title Tribunal is able to impose financial compensation as a condition for the approval to be granted. (De Villiers 2022h, 127)[95]

In addition to these legal constraints, courts have adopted a rather narrow interpretation whereby good faith negotiations do not require a developer to 'make reasonable substantive offers or concessions to reach agreement'. (Strickland case 1998) A proponent of a development can therefore for all practical purposes comply with the *procedural gestures* of appearing to participate in negotiations, but without having any real substantive intent to consult, reach agreement or adjust their position. Ironically, this may be consistent with the letter of UNDRIP and ILO 169, since those international instruments do not mandate an agreement, but rather emphasise the cooperative style and conduct of consultation. It is also noteworthy that the obligation to negotiate not only applies to governments, but also to private entities.

While all parties are obliged to negotiate in good faith, the Native Title Act does not define what is meant by good faith negotiations. (Native Title Act 1993, s 31(1)) The Native Title Act does, however, declare that the negotiations must

---

indigenous people, but the statutory rights under the Native Title Act, as well as the procedures facilitated by the National Native Title Tribunal and the decisions it hands down about whether good faith negotiations have been complied with or not, give greater substantial and procedural rights to indigenous communities in Australia compared to tribal communities in South Africa.

[95] Despite the right to negotiate not giving Aboriginal people a veto over what happens on land, this right should nevertheless not be 'narrowly construed'. (FMG case 2009, para 18) It must, however, be borne in mind that, until a native title claim has been successful in the Federal Court, the rights claimed by Aboriginal people are only indicative of rights that could *potentially* be affected. (WMC case 1999) In addition, if native title has been validated by the Federal Court, then the traditional owners of the land may claim compensation for losses suffered by the impact of a development and the loss or diminution of their native title rights. The Native Title Act does not specify any criteria as to how compensation is to be determined (Native Title Act 1993 Division 5), although it does stipulate that the compensation must be provided on 'just terms'. (Native Title Act 1993, s 51(1)) For the first determination of compensation for loss or diminution of native title, see the Timber Creek judgment of the High Court. (Timber Creek High Court appeal 2019; De Villiers 2022c, 134) Owing to the potential risk of a compensation order in the future, many mining agreements have been concluded whereby, pursuant to the right to negotiate, a compensation arrangement is included in an agreement for final compensation in order to circumvent or mitigate the impact of future litigation. Note in this regard how in the Nordic countries there are also ongoing demands by the Sámi to be compensated for loss or diminution caused by developments on their ancestral and traditional lands. (Carstens 2016, 89) There is, however, no compensation arrangement yet in place in those countries for the Sámi, nor for tribal and indigenous communities in South Africa, comparable to Australia's native title regime.

be focused on the proposed future act for which approval is sought, and not on unrelated matters. (Native Title Act 1993, ss 30(3); 31(2)) Aboriginal people cannot place items on the negotiation agenda that are not directly related to the proposed development. If they insist on placing other items on the agenda, this may be considered to constitute a lack of good faith on their part. This potentially represents a serious limitation on the ability of Aboriginal people to raise wider cultural, heritage and social issues about the impact of a proposed development on the land which is the subject of native title. (Bartlett 2020, 615) In short, the right to negotiate cannot be used by Aboriginal people to promote a wider socio-economic or political agenda about their land, or a policy agenda for the region or the rest of the country.

The statutory period for good faith negotiations is limited to six months. (Native Title Act 1993, s 35) The parties may by mutual agreement take longer to negotiate, but after six months the proponent of a future act can request the National Native Title Tribunal to determine that good faith negotiations have been exhausted and that access to the land in question should be granted, even if no agreement has been reached or the parties have yet to engage in negotiations on the substance of the proposed project.[96]

Among the essential questions for the purposes of this chapter are: what is meant by 'good faith' negotiations in the context of the Australian right to negotiate? And what insight can be gained to give effect to the principles embedded in FPIC?

Since good faith is an 'integral part' of the protection of native title rights and the obligation to consult 'is not to be narrowly construed' (FMG case 2009, para 8), extensive litigation has occurred in Australia pursuant to the Native Title Act since 1993 to ascertain the contours of good faith negotiations.[97]

---

[96] Any party may terminate negotiations prior to the expiration of the six-month period if it becomes clear that the negotiation process is stalled. (Rita Dempster case 1999) This would generally work in favour of the proponent of a project since it means approval is likely to be granted for the proposed work to go ahead. It is, however, rare for companies to seek to declare a dispute before six months has passed. It is also noteworthy that if, after six months, the developer seeks approval and the native title community contends that negotiations were not conducted in good faith, further delays may ensue for the dispute to be heard by the Native Title Tribunal and for a determination to be made about the compliance or lack thereof with the good faith obligation. The six months can therefore extend to a year or more because of ongoing litigation, often placing pressure on the developer to enter into some form of an agreement with the indigenous community rather than risk litigation and delay.

[97] There is, in my assessment, no comparative domestic jurisdiction in international case studies where the rights to negotiation and consultation of indigenous communities have been so extensively litigated as under the native title regime in Australia.

The following are some of the essential elements of good faith negotiations that have been identified by the courts since the enactment of the Native Title Act.

First, the parties must demonstrate a genuine desire to reach agreement. This cannot be remotely ascertained by a set of fixed criteria. Instead, their efforts must be evaluated by considering their entire conduct during the negotiation process. A failure by parties to reach an agreement does not necessarily indicate an absence of good faith in the negotiations. The courts have accepted that parties can negotiate in good faith and yet not reach agreement. In a similar vein, parties may lose faith in each other, become frustrated or suffer a breakdown in their relationship without their conduct constituting a lack of good faith. (Marine Produce case 2018, para 66) If, however, a party is so committed to its own position that it does not engage the other party or show a willingness to listen to the position of the other party, this could indicate a lack of good faith.

Secondly, the overall behaviour and conduct of the parties must be assessed. This includes, for example, evaluating whether the parties were receptive to each other's positions, exhibited a willingness to adjust from their initial stance, and engaged in constructive dialogue. (ABC case 1995, para 421) The party claiming there had not been good faith negotiations bears the burden of proving this to be the case. (Strategic Minerals case 2003, 7)[98] Therefore, after the expiration of the six-month period, the proponent can seek approval for the development to proceed, placing the burden on the Aboriginal community to prove that negotiations had not been conducted in good faith. The mere absence of an agreement does not equate to proof of a lack of good faith. Rather, the onus lies with the party asserting that negotiations were not conducted in good faith to prove, by citing examples, why this was the case. This requirement generally works to the detriment of Aboriginal people because there is an assumption that negotiations were conducted in good faith unless otherwise proven.

Thirdly, the subjective attitude of the parties is relevant, but there is no objective test to determine what a 'reasonable' negotiator would offer, how a 'reasonable' negotiator would reply to an offer or what constitutes a 'reasonable'

---

[98] Note, for example, the Australian Barngarla case, in which the Federal Court found, in a dispute not limited to the good faith requirements of the Native Title Act, that although extensive consultation had taken place with an Aboriginal community about the location of a nuclear waste storage facility, the facts supported a finding of 'apprehended bias' on the part of the government, because it had already made up its mind prior to the commencement of consultation by acquiring land for the location of the facility. (Barngarla case 2023)

settlement. The reasonable person test does, however, find application in assessing the conduct of the parties. The inability of the parties to agree on the rules of negotiation does not necessarily imply an absence of good faith in negotiations. Even if the parties fail to reach agreement on preliminary issues, such as the conduct of the negotiations, rules for mediation or possible provision of financial or other support to the Aboriginal community to help it prepare for the negotiations, such that the main negotiations are yet to commence, the requirement for good faith negotiations may still be deemed to have been fulfilled. (FMG case 2009, para 29)

Fourthly, the parties must above all display 'an open mind, willingness to listen, and willingness to compromise, to reach an agreement . . .' (Brownley case 1999, para 25), but they may maintain a firm position without having to adjust their stance. The reasonableness or otherwise of the offers made by the respective parties is not an indicator of the presence or absence of good faith in negotiations. The courts do not consider the merit of the respective negotiation positions of the parties. The protection of consultation rights accorded to Aboriginal people is therefore principally procedural in nature and not about the substance of the proposal put to them. (Strickland case 1998, 9)

Fifthly, the willingness to reach an agreement does not equate to a legal obligation to change a negotiation stance or to adopt an approach considered more reasonable or beneficial. The Aboriginal party's lack of resources to effectively prepare for or participate in negotiations or the lack of capacity of the community's negotiators to assess the merit of a proposal about payment of royalties does not form a basis to find that good faith negotiations had not occurred. If, however, the Aboriginal party is not given adequate time to consider the nature or scope of the work involved, this may constitute a lack of good faith. (Daniel case 2002, para 146)

Sixthly, the right to negotiate requires that the parties must exchange proposals in oral and written communications and engage each other in a constructive and timely manner. The parties must demonstrate that they have made such proposals and responded to the proposals made by the other side, even if not reaching an agreement. (Walley case 1996, para 576)

In summary, although the right to negotiate does not grant a veto to Aboriginal people to prevent a proposed project on their traditional land from proceeding, it does protect important procedural rights, allowing the community some measure of control over their lands. The right to negotiate is not limited to a legal process, but also includes moral, public relations and social obligations.

The demands of shareholders, financiers and the public may also compel companies to negotiate reasonable terms to access land. The incurred costs resulting from delays and litigation, coupled with potential reputational damage to companies and negative publicity, encourage agreed outcomes or, at the very least, sincere consultation processes.

The increasing international stakeholder demand for good relationships with indigenous people, also referred to as 'social licence to operate' (Lehtonen and Kojo 2020), is sometimes more powerful and efficient than international soft law, because resources companies are often under direct pressure from shareholders and financiers to comply with FPIC and enter into negotiated agreements with local communities in general, and indigenous people in particular. This is exemplified by the World Bank's stipulation that indigenous consultation is an integral condition for funding (World Bank 2016) and the self-regulation imposed by the OECD to encourage agreed outcomes with indigenous people. (OECD Guidelines 2011 2011; Pulver 2022) In many respects the social, community and financial pressures imposed on companies to consult have become greater than the regulatory requirements of governments. (Kryazhkov and Garipov 2021, 1023) Gehman and others summarise the obligation to consult with indigenous people about what happens on their land as follows:

> [I]t is important to understand how the implications of social license to operate are evolving in the context of Indigenous engagement in regulatory processes and policy-making. On the one hand scholars have pointed out that First Nations are rightsholders who legally must be consulted. Thus, Indigenous communities already hold a legal status in regulatory and permitting processes that exists independent of concerns related to an organisation's social license to operate. Moreover, the concept of social license to operate has created new space for dialogue and potentially for shared decision-making among Indigenous communities, affected publics, and the Crown. (Gehman, Lefsrud, and Fast 2017, 310)

Kenya

The African Commission on Human and Peoples' Rights (ACHRP), which was established to oversee compliance with the African Charter on Human and Peoples' Rights, has also provided useful guidance about the obligation on states to consult with indigenous people when their interests are affected. The findings of the ACHRP are not binding, but they do provide useful insight and generally show consistency with the international precedents discussed above.

In the Endorois Welfare Council case in Kenya the ACHRP declared that the eviction of a traditional community from its land had not been preceded by adequate consultation. (Endorois Welfare Council case 2003) The community's eviction and relocation not only encroached upon its collective rights, but also on the rights of individuals, for example the right to property. (Sing'Oei 2013) The ACHRP acknowledged the importance of access by communities to their traditional lands to develop and maintain their culture and customs. The rights of the community included being consulted about their rights in property, as well as any limitations placed on the exercise of those rights. The ACHRP noted that, although there is no agreed international definition of indigenous people or peoples, it cannot be disputed that in giving effect to the rights outlined in the Charter there must be recognition of the 'linkages between peoples, their land, and culture and that such a group expresses its desire to be identified as a people or have the consciousness that they are a people'. (Endorois Welfare Council case 2003, para 151) The fact that the Endorois may have become modernised or may form part of a larger indigenous community does not detract from their rights as a community to be protected. (Endorois Welfare Council case 2003, paras 161–163) Importantly, the Endorois have a right to be consulted when their rights to their traditional lands are affected. (Endorois Welfare Council case 2003, para 268)

Botswana

In the Sesana case in Botswana a dispute arose from the removal of an indigenous community from their traditional lands to create a conservation area. (Sesana case 2006) The court emphasised that the burden to prove an absence of good faith consultation rests on the applicants. (Sesana case 2006, para 25) The applicants had a 'legitimate expectation' that they would be consulted before their rights were restricted by government action. (Sesana case 2006, para 28) The answer to the questions whether consultation had indeed taken place and whether the manner of the consultation met the standard of reasonableness depends on the specific facts of the case. While the applicants did not challenge the legal authority of government to terminate the provision of services to them where they resided, they did challenge the process of consultation. The court went into great depth about the manner in which consultation had occurred, the level of detail used to explain the steps involved, and the way in which those affected expressed their views, ultimately finding that the decision to remove the community from their land was unconstitutional. (Sesana case 2006, para 168)

7.5 CONCLUDING OBSERVATIONS ABOUT FPIC IN SOUTH AFRICAN AND INTERNATIONAL LAW

The following observations summarise the application of consultation obligations in the South African context against the backdrop of comparative international and municipal law.

7.5.1 Definitional issues

Neither the right to consultation nor the phrase 'free, prior and informed consent' (FPIC) is defined, prescribed or procedurally set out in detail in international law. While there is arguably an evolving duty in international customary law to consult with indigenous people, meeting the obligation depends on circumstances. The right to FPIC does not, regardless of the use of the word 'consent', imply a veto, unless specifically so determined by statute or treaty. The 'consent' contained in FPIC is at best to be understood as a sincere effort to reach agreement, but not a veto or co-decision-making.

The rights to consultation and FPIC are to be given practical content in each country depending on its circumstances, the nature and scale of the project in question, the rights and status of the indigenous people involved and the specific municipal legal arrangements. In this respect comparison of case law must be tempered by considering the legal regime pursuant to which a judgment was handed down.

In international law there are no legally prescribed pro forma requirements or conditions resembling a checklist that must be strictly followed to meet the criteria for good faith consultation or FPIC. Evaluating compliance with good faith consultation and FPIC typically involves assessing the overall *process, conduct and attitude* of the parties, rather than adhering to specific institutional or procedural tick-the-box requirements.

Good faith is a duty that rests on both parties. Importantly, the absence of a mutually acceptable agreement does not necessarily indicate a failure to strive towards or an absence of sincere effort to achieve FPIC. International and domestic laws and jurisprudence acknowledge that parties can engage in good faith negotiations and participate to achieve FPIC without necessarily arriving at an agreement. More specifically, the procedural requirements of FPIC can be satisfied without a mutually agreed outcome being reached. This spells some risk to indigenous people, since they may participate in FPIC processes and oppose a development, but approval may nevertheless be given for the development to go ahead. The participation by indigenous people may then render legitimacy to the project even if they opposed it. On the other hand, as has been shown in for example Australia, indigenous people may by their participation in consultation secure benefits from a project or reduce its impact even if it goes ahead.

South African jurisprudence provides in some respects greater clarity about consultation standards than is found in international law. The concept of FPIC, with its ambiguity about consent, has not found its way into South African statutory law. South African legislation is generally unequivocal about the nature of the duty to consult, specifying in legislation either the obligation to obtain consent or to engage in consultation. South African legislation also uses the respective phrases 'consult' and 'consent' in statutes. Reference is also made to the concepts '*in* consultation', to signify that consent is required, and '*after* consultation', to indicate good faith, taking into account the submissions made by the affected parties. (De Villiers 2023f, 123) These concepts are interpreted according to their plain English meaning. Consent is held to imply the ability to veto, while consultation aligns with international norms akin to good faith negotiation and conduct, but no right to veto.

7.5.2 Good faith – a standard to be met

Both consultation and FPIC must be conducted in good faith. This involves participating in consultations and negotiations with an open mind, providing sufficiently detailed information about the proposed project in a timely manner, demonstrating a willingness to compromise, responding to communications and sincerely considering the position adopted by the other party.

These obligations apply to all parties involved in the consultation, including the indigenous people. The indigenous party is expected, for example, to share any information it holds about the significance of the specific land in question, important sites that may be affected and mitigating steps that could be considered to limit damage to a site or interest in land. The entity seeking access must in turn provide information about the nature and scale of a project, environmental impact studies, rehabilitation of land and so forth. In short, good faith negotiation and FPIC entail obligations on both sides at the bargaining table, compelling them to keep an open mind, share information and demonstrate a willingness to compromise. Good faith negotiation does not, however, preclude a party from adopting a firm stance, engaging in robust negotiations or maintaining their position.

The content given to consult and consent in South Africa is principally determined by the relevant statute in municipal law. Although South African courts may consider international jurisprudence, disputes in South Africa about the adequacy of consultation are generally resolved based on South African law and statutes, with international jurisprudence either not cited or, if cited, only by way of *obiter* remarks. Although in the Baleni case mention was made of FPIC in the context of international law, this was also done *obiter* since the actual right to veto of the community arose from the relevant statute and not from any standard imposed through consideration of international law.

7.5.3 Indicia of consultation – no closed list

Consultation within the context of FPIC must occur in a manner whereby information about a policy, project or measure is timeously provided to the indigenous community and is supported by disclosure about the nature, extent, impact and duration of the development. If relevant, information must also be provided about the rehabilitation of the environment. As found in the Australian Barngarla case, consultation can be fatally flawed if the government is perceived to have suffered from apprehended bias by using consultation merely as information-sharing. If the proponent of a development adopts a predetermined position and uses the consultation process merely to inform a community about a measure, rather than to engage in good faith negotiation towards the search for a mutually agreed outcome, the good faith requirement is not met. Adopting a firm stance is not to be equated to displaying a closed mind.

Sharing information as part of the consultation process implies that certain commercially sensitive or culturally sensitive details may be considered confidential and not disclosed, or that specific information may be restricted to negotiators or legal representatives. The sharing of information is therefore subject to a consideration of the degree and reasonableness necessary to enable the indigenous community to make an informed decision and to participate effectively in consultation. Furthermore, if access to land is opposed by an indigenous community, they are obligated to explain the reason for their opposition to enable the developer to propose steps in mitigation.

Ideally, resources should be made available to facilitate internal consultation within the indigenous community, as well as to help the community access independent, expert and legal advice.[99]

---

[99] For example, there are many examples within the right to negotiate milieu in Australia where mining companies make available grants to assist the native title community with preparation for negotiations and to seek legal and other expert advice. In some instances

7.5.4 Who negotiates on behalf of a community?

The indigenous community is entitled to nominate the mechanism through which they want their leaders or elders to represent them in consultation. The representative forum may be based on hereditary considerations, nomination, election or a combination of mechanisms. The process of nominating negotiators is itself an extension of the right of self-determination for indigenous people and must be decided by them, rather than prescribed or elected by an external party. The indigenous community must, however, ensure that its own internal processes are transparent, representative and fair to the various segments of its community.

It is essential that third parties have confidence in the preferred negotiating mechanism of an indigenous community, including in the way the community deals with dissenting opinions in their midst and how a community makes decisions. It may erode the credibility of the consultation process if a community does not speak coherently through a unified negotiation process.[100]

Aboriginal negotiating teams in mining-intense areas require an up-front contribution to enable them to conduct their affairs. While there is no legal obligation to contribute to such a fund, in practice it has become standard in the case of large projects, as it often brings some level of stability and predictability to the consultation process. Enabling an indigenous community to seek expert advice is also an insurance that an agreement is not challenged at a later stage on the basis that indigenous people did not know what they were signing. Note, however, the criticism by Ubink and others in response to the payments made by mining companies in their dealings with communities. There is a risk that such payments may only benefit the negotiators, creating dependency between negotiators and mining company while keeping community participation to a minimum, with only negotiators understanding the relevant details. (Ubink and Pickering 2020, 193) In Australia Aboriginal people are also assisted in their negotiations by federally funded Native Title Representative Bodies. There are around 16 such bodies across Australia. These bodies have jurisdiction over a region and they represent and assist the local Aboriginal people within the region when someone seeks access to their traditional lands. The bodies can retain or engage experts to give independent advice to the communities in their dealings with third parties. I was employed as a lawyer by such an Aboriginal representative body for around six years and can attest from that experience the valuable contribution those organisations make to assist Aboriginal people in their good faith negotiations.

[100] Note for example in the Australian Tipakalippa case the approval to lay the undersea pipeline was overturned because of the failure to give subgroups a reasonable opportunity to be heard in the consultation process. However, in the case of Munkara the complaint of a subgroup that they had not been adequately consulted was dismissed. Although their complaint was dismissed, it came at substantial delay to the project, high cost and critical remarks of the lay and expert evidence sought to be relied on. (Munkara case 2024) The presiding judge described the expert evidence as 'so lacking integrity that no weight can be placed on them'. The court ultimately awarded A$9 million in legal costs against the Environmental Defenders Office, who supported and financed the proceeding. (Rauso 2024; Munkara consent orders cost 2024)

Dealing with various subgroups or factions may complicate FPIC, but an effort should at least be made by a proponent to create a reasonable opportunity for subgroups of the community to participate in the consultation process. That said, neither international law nor South African law mandates consultation with or agreement by all subgroups or with individuals in their personal capacity. If a community fails to participate in consultation as a cohesive unit or is splintered into feuding groups, it may collectively fall short of its obligation to engage in good faith consultation.

7.5.5 Scope of consultation

Unless otherwise specified, consultation is required, inter alia, about administrative, environmental and legislative measures that may affect indigenous people directly or disproportionately. It is particularly when indigenous peoples' interest in land is affected, but not limited thereto. Consultation is, however, not mandated for general socio-economic matters, public policies or legislation that also affect other communities and individuals.[101] In South African jurisprudence the obligation to consult with tribal communities or informal land occupiers arises from specific statutory and common-law entitlements related to their local rights and interests in land and does not relate to policy and governance issues of a general nature.

7.5.6 Compensation in absence of agreed access

In exceptional instances the failure to consult in good faith can lead to litigation, resulting in the possible setting aside of legislation, other administrative measures or approvals. Additionally, compensation may be awarded if an act had occurred or damage had been caused without good faith consultation having taken place. In practice, however, this is a rarity. The obligation to consult within FPIC is yet to become a legal norm of customary international law, but it can be regarded as a *de facto* standard of internationally recommended conduct.

---

[101] Notable in this respect is Australia's failure to approve, by way of referendum, in 2023 an Aboriginal advisory Voice that would have had the power to make representations to Parliament and the executive government on *any* aspect of public policy or legislation. (De Villiers 2024c, 294–6) Also of relevance are the ongoing efforts in Finland to clarify the nature and extent of the consultation rights of the Sámi Parliament. (De Villiers 2023b) At the time of writing (March 2025) no final agreement had yet been reached.

In South African jurisprudence and statutes a clear distinction is usually drawn between rights of consultation and consent. Since customary international law is derived from widespread practice accepted as law, it cannot be stated that the 'consent' in FPIC is universally acknowledged as a binding legal norm arising from international customary law.[102] A case can, however, be made that customary international law requires consultation, but consent is seen as an objective to be achieved rather than a veto. FPIC may have become a standard of *best practice*, but it is still too vague and inconsistently applied to be considered a binding legal norm pursuant to international customary law.

7.5.7 Consultation as an individual right

The right to be consulted does not only arise from UNDRIP and ILO 169; it originates also from fundamental individual rights pertaining to self-determination, human dignity, equality, non-discrimination, culture, property and a safe and secure environment, as embodied in the ICCPR and the ICESCR. While the processes associated with FPIC typically have a collective nature, an individual may also initiate action or demand consultation based on their individual rights and freedoms. This development is acknowledged in South African jurisprudence, where the principle of a 'participatory democracy' implies consultation when interests are affected, be they the interests of an individual or those of a community. Thus the legal obligation to consult is not limited to indigenous or tribal communities but extends rather to all communities and individuals when their interests are affected.

---

[102] Two important elements form the basis for international customary law: a general *practice* and its acceptance *as law*. (UN International Law Commission 2018, 123) The following commentary is important for the purposes of this chapter: 'Where the existence of a general practice accepted as law cannot be established, the conclusion will be that the alleged rule of customary international law does not exist.' (UN International Law Commission 2018, 125) Lenzerini holds that the 'main principles enshrined by the UNDRIP' have reached the status of customary international law. (Lenzerini 2022, 458) This statement is arguably an overreach. While the individual rights of persons belonging to indigenous communities are recognised and protected by international law, the collective rights of indigenous people, particularly the requirements of 'consent' as envisaged by UNDRIP, are of an aspirational character and cannot (yet) be regarded as sufficiently endorsed by widespread international legal practice to meet the threshold of a justiciable legal principle under customary international law. Barrie is of the opinion that international law is firmly on a course where FPIC would eventually be regarded as a principle of customary law. (Barrie 2024b, 220).

7.5.8 Response to questions

To address the four questions that were identified at the start of this chapter, the following can be concluded:

- *What is the definition of indigenous people and, more importantly, does the categorisation of 'indigenous' only apply to the Khoisan?* Or does it also apply to tribal communities residing on their traditional lands? Or does it apply to all black communities irrespective of whether they reside on their traditional lands or not? There is no agreed definition in international law of who constitutes 'indigenous people'. In South Africa, too, there is no agreed definition of who the real indigenous peoples of South Africa are. There is no consensus on how, if at all, indigenous people are to be distinguished from tribal or traditional communities. The cases cited in this chapter deal with communities under specific statutes and, hence, there has been no need for the courts in these cases to define or to distinguish between indigenous, tribal and customary.
- *What, if any, consultation rights can indigenous people claim pursuant to FPIC and how do these rights compare to consultation rights under the South African Constitution?* FPIC as understood in international law does not grant a justiciable right of veto or co-decision-making to indigenous communities. FPIC encompasses a consultative process that involves sincerity in seeking agreement, a willingness to compromise, an open-minded approach and respect for a party maintaining a firm position. FPIC focuses on processes and interactions, rather than the content of the positions adopted by the parties involved. South Africa reflects the standards of international law to ascertain whether consultation had been adequate by taking into account the *conduct* of the parties in all respects, and not the *merit* of their respective proposals.
- *What are the practical requirements that satisfy the legal obligation to obtain FPIC from indigenous people*? FPIC implies that indigenous people are to be consulted in good faith when an activity is likely to impact directly or disproportionately on their land or affect their traditions, customs or development. Information about an intended activity must be given to the community in a timely manner, allowing sufficient time for internal consultation and, if needed, for seeking external advice. Negotiations should be conducted in good faith with the aim of reaching an agreement even in the absence of a legal obligation to do so. A party may be deemed

to have complied with the requirements of FPIC even if, ultimately, an agreement is not reached. Sub-communities must also, as far as practicable, be given a reasonable opportunity to participate in consultation. However, it is accepted that a community may not necessarily have a unified agreed position such that minority opinions exist. Furthermore, if a party alleges that the consultation was not conducted in good faith, that party bears the onus of proving this assertion.

- *What are the consequences of FPIC not taking place or if it does occur but an indigenous community withholds consent to a proposal?* Failure to comply with FPIC may have legal, financial, practical and social consequences. Legal consequences may involve project delays owing to litigation, potential annulment of approvals and the possibility of communities seeking compensation in time to come for the diminution of their rights without having been compensated. Social consequences may manifest as public opposition to the project, shareholder disapproval or rejection, protests, financial concerns from investors, harm to the relationship with the local community concerned and reputational damage. Practical consequences might include protests against the project, damage to the developer's social reputation, potential forfeiture of benefits by the community and a questioning of the proponent's social licence to engage with other communities.

CHAPTER 8

RELIGIOUS RIGHTS: THE REAL TEST OF LEGAL PLURALISM IN LIBERAL DEMOCRACIES

When the elephants fight for superiority, the grass dies.

– African proverb

8.1 INTRODUCTION

If ever the interaction between legal pluralism and the liberal democratic secular state was being tested, it is in the field of religious rights.[1] This is because, of all the identities an individual may display, religious codes are most typical of what can be described as 'non-state law'. Religious codes are distinguishable from cultural or linguistic rules, practices and customs. While the latter are derived from intergenerational community practice, adherence and tradition, religious codes are derived from a higher being. They are superhuman, with their source being divine law. They achieve legality through prescription, not only through use. Failure to comply may have eternal consequences. As Bhuiyan and Black point out, even the origin of the word 'secular' is religious since it is derived from the Larin *saecularis* that was used to describe the religious clergy in medieval England and Europe who were not bound by the monastic order. (Bhuiyan and Black 2022, 5)

Religious codes predate the state and are not defined by nor restricted to state territorial jurisdiction. While religious codes principally affect the private sphere, in some respects religious codes also seek to cover the same social field occupied by state law, particularly in areas of personal, property, criminal and family law. Religious codes may even challenge the legality and legitimacy of the state and its laws. Religious codes often demand compliance as if they have the status of state law. The exclusivity of lawmaking by the state may therefore be substituted with concurrent, or even exclusive, lawmaking (to use terms associated with federalism theory), where both state law and religious law apply to a social field, or where religious law may assert that it exclusively occupies a certain social field.

[1] In this chapter I specifically discuss religion and pluralism in the liberal democratic secular state, rather than focusing on the challenges faced by countries where religious laws such as Sharia are regarded as state law or are endorsed and enforced as state law.

The individual may thus get caught between competing authorities – the divine and the secular – both of which have established legal norms and mandate obedience. When the elephants fight for superiority, the grass dies.

In this chapter we reflect on the jurisprudence of the European Court of Human Rights and courts in South Africa to identify principles that could offer guidance to respond to religious legal pluralism. Beginning with a brief overview of religious pluralism as a concept, the discussion moves on to examples of relevant case law by the ECtHR in its efforts to strike a balance between the regulatory authority of government and freedom of religion with examples involving face coverings. The focus then shifts to jurisprudence arising from the Constitutional Court of South Africa in dealing with religious pluralism in the context of transformative constitutionalism, specifically in its dealings with Muslim marriages. These two fields of social interaction present challenges to contemporary society. Both illustrate how the commands of religious law may conflict with the liberties of secular law.

State law and religious non-state law cite different authorities to justify and defend their sovereignty. Religious codes draw on a higher inspiration that existed before the birth of state law to validate compliance. Since religious codes existed before the modern state, the state, as it came into being, often utilised and relied on the imprimatur of these codes to formulate and defend its normative rules and legitimacy. The blessing by religion often legitimised the modern state.

The origin of state law, which is often found in a constitution, claims sovereignty as it purports to represent the will of the populace of a territorial space, regardless of their religious affiliations. However, in reality in many instances the modern state carries the blessing of the dominant religion in the state. Even if the state claims to be secular, a symbiosis often exists even within liberal democracies between the state and the dominant religion. This mutual dependency stems from the historical support provided by the religion in the creation of the state, duly reciprocated by the state's support, both direct and indirect, for the dominant religion. Regardless of the presence of a dominant religion, the notion of freedom of religion implies a plural state in which in some respects individuals may be conflicted between state and religious law. (Bhuiyan and Zoethout 2023, 6)

These two sources of law – secular and religious – are therefore forced to cohabitate in the same territorial sphere. This potentially creates challenges to individuals, governments, faith bodies and courts. Adding to this complexity there may also be other minority religions that similarly pursue their own non-state laws. Different religions may therefore compete for sovereignty against each other and against the state.

Civil courts adjudicate disputes under the constitution and state laws, but generally do not involve themselves in questions of dogma arising from the code of a particular religion. This separation between state court and religious dogma may seem simple in theory, but it can be complex in both legal and factual terms if the spheres of laws intersect.[2] In areas of intersection individuals may approach state courts to seek relief from the treatment they experience under religious non-state law, or to enforce rights that may arise from religious non-state law, or to defend an action that is in breach of state law but consistent with non-state law. Individuals may engage in forum shopping, selecting the court or religious tribunal that provides them with the most advantageous outcome in a dispute arising under their religious code.

Irrespective of efforts to clearly separate state law and religious non-state law, in reality they often overlap in some areas, compete and even demand compliance from the same individual on the same social topic.[3] The sanctions imposed by state and religious laws are different, but for the individual the burden of complying with two sets of laws can become unbearable, especially as achieving harmonisation between the two is sometimes impossible.

8.1.1 Different sources of authority

State law in liberal democracies claims supremacy over all other religious, traditional, customary and cultural laws and customs. This is evidenced in the Constitution of South Africa, which proclaims it as being the supreme law of the land. The principle of the rule of law deriving from constitutionalism together with the might of the state imply that the Constitution is the highest source of

[2] Büchler expresses concern that the 'pluralistic family-law structures [of Islam] pose a threat to social coherence and cohesion. Discourse on the degree of cultural autonomy in the realm of family law regularly centres on where the line is drawn in the dichotomy between the private and the public sphere. The duty of the state to guarantee human rights prohibits it from relinquishing its authority over any central area over which it legislates.' (Büchler 2016, 82)

[3] Note, for example, the Gaum case, in which the conferral of marriage blessings to same-sex couples in the Afrikaans Dutch Reformed Church (DRC) in South Africa became an issue. The court found, in short, that the constitutional rule of equality between individuals to marry trumps the church-rule to determine that marriage is solely between a man and a woman. (Gaum case 2019) The courts respect the freedom of religious organisation to *teach* their dogma, but the *practice* of the dogma may be inconsistent with state law.

law and forms the basis of law. This dogma dictates that, if an irreconcilable conflict arises between state law and religious non-state law, the former prevails. However, in exchange for accepting the supremacy of state law, religions have historically demanded the recognition of the right to freedom of religion, both individually and collectively. In liberal democracies there exists a historical trade-off where religious codes accept constitutional supremacy and, in turn, the constitution allows the existence of these religious codes, for faiths to self-organise, and the practice of individuals' faith.

The right to freedom of religion therefore has a counterpart – the religious code is subservient to the constitutional code. Therein lies the challenge: faced with conflicting authorities, individuals are compelled to navigate their lives through these competing laws and codes in deeply personal and intimate areas, such as marriage, property, divorce, raising children, penal code, testamentary disposition, freedom of expression and association, diet, medical treatment and more. A case in point: Muslim personal law has never been formally integrated into the South Africa legal system. (Mukaddam 2024, 141) Many of the day-to-day decisions that matter to individuals can become entangled in the overlap of state law and religious non-state law. While the universal right to freedom of religion seeks to recognise individual religious self-determination in a secular world, drawing tidy lines of demarcation between state law and religious non-state law is not always simple in practice. As Ferrari observes, the 'question of the veil' reflects on the attempts by states to 'domesticate religious transformations' within the context of established norms. (Ferrari 2022, 24)

While in this book I refer to state law as having a hierarchically superior order to non-state law because of the constitutional status of the former, religious codes may not necessarily accept such a subservient status for their codes.[4] As an example, lifting the sacredness of the Catholic confessional for the purposes of criminal proceedings would likely prove problematic. In fact, in some instances religious non-state law may challenge the validity of state law and might even seek to displace state law or encourage disobedience to state law, generally referred to in Christian dogma as civil disobedience, if an edict of state conflicts fundamentally with a dogma of faith.

[4] Note, for example, the refusal of Orthodox Jews in Israel to undergo military service. This is regardless of a court ruling that the 'distinction among persons designated for military service based on a religious worldview is discrimination without any relevant difference'. (Military Service case 2005, para 28) On 28 March 2024 the end of government subsidies to men who do not undertake military service was ordered.

Religious law, extending beyond its religious origins, can also symbolise political resistance to state law and may repudiate the legitimacy of the state. In the most extreme cases of religious non-state law, opposition and rejection of state law may lead to public resistance, civil disobedience, violence or even the creation of new regions or a new state where religious law seeks to become state law. Examples of this include efforts to establish an Islamic Caliphate in the Middle East and the unique arrangement concerning Sharia law in the Indonesian province of Aceh (De Villiers 2016b). To these religious codes it is the higher divine law that demands primary obedience, with state law being second in hierarchy. To them the state should ideally become one with the religion, thereby disregarding the separation of state and church that underpins liberal democracies. This would lead to state law and religious law merging into a unified system. (Black 2024)

8.1.2 Individuals in the crosshairs of dogma

The individual is often caught in the crosshairs of these competing dogmas. In such cases the individual bears the burden when some form of sanction is delivered by state law or religious non-state law for not abiding by their respective rules. This raises complex issues concerning the origin, role and legitimacy of 'the state', the meaning and source of 'law', the 'true' source of the power of government and the applicability and relevance of what are often perceived, arguably incorrectly, as 'universal' fundamental rights and freedoms.

The very universality of religious rights and freedoms may be questioned and challenged on the basis that they are foreign, Eurocentric, secular or colonial. One only needs to take a cursory glance at world events to realise how promissory and aspirational the notion of 'universal' individual rights is. Diala expresses the view that both globalisation and colonialism are supported by the underlying notion of dominant world powers seeking to extend their influence outside their own territorial space. Their efforts become 'self-replicating' and in the process local laws and customs are threatened. (Diala 2019, 11) In this context Diala claims that the supremacy of the South African Constitution 'exemplifies coloniality' since it seeks to impose Eurocentric values over customary values. (Diala 2019, 13) Harris raises a similar concern regarding indigenous rights in Australia, where the emphasis, according to her, is not on the sovereign rights of indigenous people, but rather on what is palatable to the Australian voters. This, according to her, is 'incompatible with human dignity'. (Harris 2024, vii) De Gaetano gives an overview of the ECtHR response to religious dress and concludes that there is no consistency in the practical applications of norms and that the rights of the individual ultimately depend on the state in which the individual finds themselves. (De Gaetano 2024, 142)

To make the plight of the individual more complex, while residence in a country automatically subjects the individual to state law because of territorial jurisdiction, the applicability of non-state law to a person depends on their association with a particular religious (or customary) community. Religious (and customary) communities organise themselves based on personality (non-territorial) rather than territoriality, which means a person may, in theory at least, opt in or out of the reach of religious non-state law. Regardless of this purported freedom of association, religious non-state law may be so dominant or controlling (even in a secular liberal democratic state) that it makes the individual's ability to opt out of its codes challenging or even practically impossible. This is particularly the case with immigrant communities, which may find themselves trapped and entangled in a closed religious community within their adopted country despite the freedoms promised under the constitutional law of the new state in which they now reside. The purported freedom of association of the individual to withdraw from a religious community may thus become encumbered by the dominance and control of the religious code. This is especially applicable to vulnerable groups, such as women and children, which may find themselves bound to a religious code through coercion and dominance, rather than by free will.

The individual is therefore presented with a choice – to obey state law or religious non-state law. The African proverb holds true – *when elephants fight, the grass dies.* The individual suffers in the clash of two powerful normative systems.

8.1.3 Dawn of post-secularism?

Although the complexity of the interaction between state law and religious non-state law is nothing new, this interaction is becoming increasingly relevant, particularly in the birthplace of secularism – Europe. In the past European democracies encountered legal pluralism principally through the imposition of their laws in overseas colonies. European laws superseded the laws and customs of their subjects in the newfound lands. Nowadays, however, people from those colonies are bringing their (religious and customary) pluralism to Europe, posing a challenge for the continent to formulate a judicial (and political) response.

Bottoni comments that there are 'few legal categories as ambiguous as secularism today'. (Bottoni 2022, 147) Recent international events, including mass migration,[5] the Arab Spring, the rise of Christian fundamentalism, the growth of Pentecostalism, a resurgence of interest in purported traditional values, increases in anti-Semitism, the prevalence of so-called culture wars, and an increase in religious nationalism raise questions about how, in the modern secular liberal democratic state, constitutionally inspired state law and religiously inspired non-state law can coexist. Europe has seen significant migration by Muslim immigrants, who in many instances form their own secluded communities within their new countries of residence, thereby challenging the notion of the secular state as they seemingly find comfort in the religious rules of their faith, especially at the personal level. Adhering to the moral codes of Islam is consistent with the principle of freedom of religion, but when those codes are inconsistent with European laws or, worse, when those codes reject civil law, pluralism becomes complex. The converse is that many Muslims in Europe live in fear and with a sense of rejection for being the subject of political and other negative publicity. Howard raises the concern that rather than motivating them to assimilate, negative policy and public sentiment may cause Muslim communities to retreat from mainstream society. (Howard 2022, 87)

The need for a sense of 'community', particularly for new immigrants, renders practically impossible the purported right to disassociate from one's own traditional religious community. However, in the event of a clash between state law and religious rules a hierarchy needs to be established. This issue often plays itself out in case law, where state law and religious non-state law seek to regulate the same social field.

It has been suggested that we may have entered, at least in some parts of the world, a 'post-secular' phase, where religious identity is becoming more, rather than less, relevant in social policy. The role of Christian communities in the election of Donald Trump in 2024 may be reflective of the cultural identity of faith. The power of secularism is said to be waning, and the interweaving of religious and cultural values is giving rise to what has been called a 'culture war' that aims for dominance rather than accommodation and plurality. (Appiah 2018, 195) Those who pursue what is regarded as a culture war say the

[5] Simion observes how the high levels of migration into Europe, especially in 2015, have challenged Europe at different levels, including the trust in European institutions, the security of Europe, and the ability of Europe to retain its identity while at the same time becoming the home of large communities from other countries. (Simion 2023, 210) The 2024 elections for the European Parliament, outcome of elections in Italy, France and Germany, highlighted the importance of migration and resultant pluralism as an unresolved but ever more challenging policy issue.

state should, even (or especially) in a liberal democracy, be an agent to defend and enforce essential elements of religious codes as state laws and 'protect' the (dominant religious) culture on which it is based.[6] Howard also observes that while attendance of Christian religious services may be in decline, the Christian faith and institutions continue to play an important role in European democracies, particularly in social and cultural life.[7] Closely linked to these developments is Euro-scepticism, where the plurality underlying the European experiment is challenged by national sovereignty. (Blokker 2024) The response of European institutions to legal pluralism must therefore bear the religious and cultural background of the continent in mind. (Howard 2024, 4) In this respect Bhuiyan and Black observe that what is religious is often conflated with culture (not only in Europe) since religion is 'not a societal silo, but saturates a nation's values, traditions, identity and governance'. (Bhuiyan and Black 2022, 5)[8]

Paradoxically, European democracies, which have contributed so much to the theory and practice of liberal democratic values and understanding, are being simultaneously challenged by the increase in religious pluralism and demands for a return to traditional Christian values or, if not to faith itself, then at least to a culture that is characterised by the normative underpinnings of Christianity. While many of the younger and emerging democracies in Africa, Asia and the

---

[6] Note, for example, Richard Dawkins describing himself as a 'cultural Christian' who may not subscribe to the dogma of Christianity but nevertheless draws from the Christian values and morals within a cultural rather than a religious context. ('Richard Dawkins: I'm a Cultural Christian' 2024) Notable in this regard is the observation by Oliva and Hall that many aspects of Western judicial precedent and norm-setting have originated from Christian thought and influence. Those principles have with the effluxion of time been adopted as so-called secular legal principles and hence form part of the secular legal culture, but their origins remain Christian with no one suggesting they should be discarded. (Oliva and Hall 2022, 141) Venizelos suggests that Europe is no longer to be characterised as 'Christian Europe' but rather 'Europe of liberal democracy', where fundamental values have replaced a central religion. (Venizelos 2024, 30)

[7] Note the empirical findings of Litina and Papastathis of attitudes of Christians in Europe towards Muslims. Some of the main findings are: there is no uniform pattern among European countries towards immigrants or Islamophobia; Christian attitudes do not substantially differ from secular attitudes; religious belief does not have a substantial impact on attitude towards immigrants; there is no discernible difference in Protestant and Catholic attitudes towards immigrants; circumstances within a country may be a greater determinant of attitudes towards immigrants. (Litina and Papastathis 2024, 271–2)

[8] Note, however, the 2022 report of the Open Society Justice Initiative on this topic, in which it concludes that the rationale for the restriction on headscarves and facial covering is often not motivated by concerns about security, safety or integration, but rather by 'anti-Muslim or anti-Islam sentiment and fear'. (OSJI Report 2022, 5)

Americas have been navigating their way through the pluralism associated with the interplay of state law and indigenous, cultural and religious non-state laws, European democracies have principally responded to religious pluralism by way of individual rights. It is only more recently where, in light of increased migration of particularly Muslims, that Europe has been challenged to respond more comprehensively to the interplay between state law and religious non-state law, where the latter competes in some social fields with the former.

8.1.4 South African contribution

Ironically, European democracies may gain insight from the way many of the countries to whom they have lectured over the years about democratisation have been dealing with the challenging issue of religious pluralism.[9] South Africa is one such example, having benefited greatly from the experiences of liberal democracies in the drafting of its constitution, but may now be able to offer insights into the understanding of cohabitation in legal pluralism.

South Africa has, from its earliest years of new settler arrival, grappled with the reality of religious pluralism. The management of religious pluralism in South Africa has often been influenced by the prevailing dominant political forces, yet the country has demonstrated remarkable religious tolerance at a social level regardless of its fractured political history. It is therefore not surprising that since the enactment of the new Constitution the approach to religious pluralism in South Africa has also been adjusted to reflect the values of constitutionalism.

8.2 RELIGIOUS PLURALISM – A BRIEF OVERVIEW

The principle of the separation of church (or any other relevant religious institution) and state rolls easily off the tongue, but it is complex to put into practice. While separation at an institutional level may be legally achievable, the separation of the values represented by religion from the policies enacted by the state may not be as easily accomplished. Religion is not confined to faith or the act of worship. Religious values permeate all aspects of life, including culture, customs, traditions, conduct, voting patterns, judgments, policies, politics and

[9] Note in this respect the observation made by Marin et al regarding the use of and reliance on foreign law by the Constitutional Court of Chile. They are of the view that citations have been rather one-sided with Chile citing European law without a give and take where comparative law considers a wider range of constitutional interpretations. (Marin, Inatani, and Infantino 2021, 195)

perceptions of rights and freedoms. Culture, in its broadest sense, often reflects aspects of religion, and cultural values in turn are often reflected in state laws. State laws and jurisprudence, even in purported secular states, often bear the imprint of religious values, even if only historically. (Oliva and Hall 2022, 141) Many of the state laws in liberal democracies, seen nowadays as secular, have their origins in the Christian faith.

While in European liberal democracies the normative importance of the separation of church and state is endorsed, the same norm does not necessarily apply to all countries that call themselves liberal democracies in other parts of the world. In fact, in many non-European democracies the interaction and even integration between state and faith is seen as a reality, if not an asset, rather than an encumbrance. Many non-European democracies have also, however, endorsed the notion of separation between state and religion, endeavouring to reduce the conflict potential that often accompanies inter-religious competition. (Bhuiyan and Black 2022, 11)

Constitutions are often described as 'secular' in a legal sense, but the practical application of the concept of separation of church and state varies. The purported separation ranges from being promissory to aspirational, from pragmatic to politically expedient.

8.2.1 Universality of religious rights?

The 'universality' of religious freedom rights and the separation of religious institutions and state are by birth primarily European concepts, developed out of the history of the region. (Ferrari 2020, 97) Exploring the rationale behind these principles necessitates reference to various historical events in Europe, including the Renaissance, the Reformation and the resulting religious wars and conflicts. European views on the secular state, the separation of church and state, religious freedom and humanism are intrinsically linked to historic events that had unfolded on the continent.

It is not surprising that An-Na'im's criticism of the assumption of what he calls a Eurocentric approach to the state and religion is indeed universal. (An-Na'im 2020, 173) The notion of secularism in liberal democracies is inherently linked to the fundamental rights and freedoms of the individual. In contrast, in many other parts of the world freedom is associated with faith, divine will and the importance of a religious or customary *community*. As discussed in Chapter 6, the origin of the term 'Ubuntu' specifically relates to the individual's subservient role to community. The proposition that the individual's rights are at the centre of freedom is not shared by all. For example, in Islam, as well as in the Orthodox Jewish and Christian faiths, individual freedom is both found within and circumscribed by the will of God. As put by Mukaddam: 'When women enter into marriages under Muslim Law only, they undergo significant transformation that curtails their independence. They become subjects of a fraternal pact that subjugates women.' (Mukaddam 2024, 145) The same may in some respects be said of Ubuntu, where the individual finds fulfilment within the community, but associated therewith may be a loss of personal freedom. As shown above, (Chapter 6) in African customary law Ubuntu has a religious component that reflects on the person as being subservient to the community to which they belong. Conversely, in liberal democratic theory individual freedom is rooted in the natural rights of a person in a world where God may or may not exist.

In many parts of the world plural religious arrangements are accepted as normal, with religious and state laws coexisting. This is evident, for instance, in countries such as Indonesia, Singapore, India, South Africa, Brazil and Malaysia. Few states, even in the European sphere, strive to achieve an absolute status of secularism. It is estimated that up to a third of the world's population lives under some form of personal law system, whereby non-state laws regulate aspects of their personal affairs. (Ahmed 2020, 415) In some Muslim majority states Sharia is considered the supreme law, holding authority not only over parliamentary laws but also over the will of the people. (March 2020, 69) Even in a liberal democracy such as Australia the prevalence of forced marriages under the sanction of Sharia has been so on the increase that it has been declared a crime. (Slavery and Trafficking Act 2013)

An-Na'im approaches Sharia with greater nuance, arguing that, while it is important at the social, political and personal level as a source of justice, it is not the sole basis of the legal system of any country, including those which claim to be Islamic states, such as Pakistan, Iran and Saudi Arabia. (An-Na'im 2020, 177) He nevertheless acknowledges that certain aspects of Sharia are 'fundamentally incompatible with the theory and practice of [democratic] constitutionalism'. (An-Na'im 2020, 181) This observation is not dissimilar to the conclusion of the ECtHR in the Refah Partisi case, when it was declared that Sharia as a *system of law* is incompatible with the European Convention on Human Rights. (Refah Partisi case 2003)

While the importance of the right to freedom of religion in liberal democracies is not necessarily challenged by legal pluralism, the manner of its application may differ. Perhaps the best example of state secularism is France, where the term *laïcité* reflects the idea of secularism underpinned by liberty, equality and tolerance. Under this secularist framework equality among all citizens is embraced as the common denominator for all individuals, regardless of any other characteristics or convictions they may possess. With this principle in mind France is 'spearheading the fight against new religious movements'. (Ferrari 2020, 104) This stands in contrast to the United Kingdom, where religious pluralism and its public expression of faith are viewed as practical realities, fundamental rights and even assets that enrich society, but it also gives rise to resistance. It therefore came as no surprise that the then Archbishop of Canterbury, Rowan Williams, in 2008 observed the following about the challenges arising from religious pluralism in the United Kingdom, as well as the necessity to address them:

> [T]he issues that arise around what level of public or legal recognition, if any, might be allowed to the legal provisions of a religious group, are not peculiar to Islam: while the law of the Church of England is the law of the land, its daily operation is in the hands of authorities to whom considerable independence is granted. . . . In conclusion, it seems that if we are to think intelligently about the relations between Islam and British law, we need a fair amount of 'deconstruction' of crude oppositions and mythologies, whether of the nature of *sharia* or the nature of the Enlightenment. But as I have hinted, I do not believe this can be done without some thinking also about the very nature of law. (Williams 2008)

The purist approach to separation of state and church adopted by France is not widely shared by liberal democracies. In both law and practice secularism is generally not regarded as an absolute principle. Secularism ought not be approached as a dogma, but rather as a value set whereby religion–state conflict is sought to be prevented or mitigated. Consider the following examples: In the United Kingdom, the head of state also serves as the head of the church. In the Western Thrace region of Greece, a special arrangement allows Sharia to apply to the Muslim community in tribunals overseen by a state-appointed Muslim mufti.[10]

[10] The background to the special arrangement in Thrace is that, upon the demise of the Ottoman empire, an agreement was reached between Greece and the Ottoman (later Turkish) government to the effect that, owing to the high concentration of Muslims in the Thrace region, Sharia could continue to apply in civil matters. Three Muslim muftis, appointed by the state of Greece, hear disputes in areas of family law. The decrees of the mufti can be enforced under Greek law. Criticism has been expressed at the muftis' lack of legal training as well as the lack of procedural requirements that would ordinarily apply to the secular court system. The concern, more particularly, is that the rights of female litigants to a fair proceeding may be prejudiced. (Tsavousoglou 2015) In the Molla Sali case the ECtHR declared that the application of Sharia law, contrary to the will of the testator (who wanted Greek law to apply), in an inheritance

In Germany public funds are allocated for the training of imams.[11] The United Kingdom permits civil law to give effect to arbitrations facilitated by Muslim Arbitration Tribunals. In the German state of Bavaria the Christian crucifix is displayed in public buildings. Hungary's constitution recognises the historical role played by Christianity in the nation. In Singapore the Sharia Court has jurisdiction over Muslims in specific areas such as marriage, divorce and personal family affairs, with concurrent jurisdiction shared with civil courts in certain fields such as maintenance, child custody and property disposition. In Malaysia civil courts lack jurisdiction over matters falling within the ambit of Sharia courts (Constitution of Malaysia 1957, art 121(1A)).[12] Germany's concept of 'optional civil law' creates space for Islamic marriage contracts. In the Netherlands Sharia law may be enforced if not inconsistent with Dutch law. In Australia state-funded religious and educational institutions managed by religious bodies play a crucial role in public social services. (Deagon 2023) In Indonesia the principle of

---

dispute constituted a violation of the European Convention on Human rights. (Molla Sali case 2020) Since then Greece has enacted legislation to clarify that Sharia only applies in the region in civil disputes if both parties to the dispute agree. The ECtHR accepted in essence that parties may elect to be bound by religious law, but this must be voluntary and not in contravention of fundamental rights. Topidi, however, raises the concern that 'consent' may be difficult to ascertain as some people, particularly women, may be subject to community control and domination that render any free consent theoretical rather than actual. (Topidi 2019a, 43) Note, for example, the analysis in the South African case of Women's Legal Trust, in which the court acknowledged how the lack of recognition of Muslim marriages infringes on the dignity of women, and adds to their vulnerability, as well as that of children, when such a marriage dissolves. (Women's Legal Centre Trust case 2018, para 136) The special arrangement in Thrace has the effect that Sharia within the region has gained the status of state law, while it has been generally held by the ECtHR that Sharia, as a legal system, is not compatible with the European Convention on Human Rights. (Refah Partisi case 2003)

[11] Note how in Belgium the court found efforts to restrict funding for religious organisations from abroad to be unconstitutional. The legislation was aimed at restricting funding that organisations associated with the Islamic faith could receive from abroad. The court emphasised that religious communities traditionally exist in the form of organised structures. Participation in the life of a religious community is an expression of religious conviction that enjoys the protection of freedom of religion. From the perspective of freedom of association, too, freedom of religion implies that the religious community can function peacefully without arbitrary interference from the authorities. The autonomy of religious communities is essential to pluralism in a democratic society and thus lies at the very heart of freedom of religion. The restriction sought to be imposed was vague and disproportionate to the objective sought to be achieved. (Restriction on funding case 2023)

[12] Jurisdictional disputes between civil courts and Sharia courts in Malaysia 'are far from being conclusively resolved', particularly in the areas of conversion of Muslims and custody disputes. (Neo 2020, 899)

Pancasila[13] is accepted as a fundamental norm for the state. Finally, in India many areas of personal endeavour are not regulated by law but left for non-state law to set the norms.

Legal pluralism, especially where state law and religious non-state law intersect, persists and thrives in many democracies.

8.2.2 Separation of church and state

It is worth recalling that the modern concept of the separation of church and state had its principal philosophical and historical origins in the mid- to late sixteenth-century Christian-based conflicts in Europe.[14] At the time the continent was torn apart by intra-religious conflicts within the Christian community, arising from the works of reformers who sought to challenge the authority and dogma of the Catholic Church. The Peace of Westphalia, which brought an end to the European wars, not only required respect between states, but also laid the basis for religious freedom of individuals within states.[15] Essentially, the path to peace involved agreement on the separation of church and state, and a commitment to respect the privacy of religious rights in municipal law.[16] In Western liberal

[13] *Pancasila* has been referred to as the 'source of all laws'. (Prasetyo 2016, 103) The five essential principles of *Pancasila*, as found in the Preamble to the Constitution of Indonesia, are: belief in the one and only God; just and fair humanity; unity of Indonesia; democracy; social justice. (Black 2024)

[14] Marko suggests that one should go beyond the Treaty of Westphalia to identify the roots of contemporary perspectives on the state and religion. He suggests that in what he calls the 'foundational area' of Islam there were commonalities with the 'Papal Revolution' in Europe since both Islamic scholars and Christian scholars had been influenced by translations of the works of Greek philosophers. (Marko 2022b, 177)

[15] Also note, as an example of an early instrument of minority protection, the Edict of Nantes, signed on 30 April 1598, recognising the rights of the Protestant minority in Catholic-dominated France. (Sutherland 1987) The 1648 Treaty of Westphalia (comprising the Treaty of Munster (24 October 1648) and the Treaty of Osnabruck (15 May 1648)), which brought an end to the Thirty Years' War between Catholics and Protestants, was particularly aimed at the protection of religious (Christian) minorities. (Reus-Smit 2013) The Treaty of Westphalia has been described as the first 'World Charter' for a world order based on the independence of states, non-intervention in the domestic affairs of states and legal equality between states. While this categorisation may not be entirely accurate, the treaty was indeed groundbreaking in seeking an order where states respected each other's sovereignty, while also protecting the rights of religious minorities within them. The Treaty of Westphalia has also been described as the 'traditional birth date of Euro-Christian-type international law'. (Pascale and Tonolo 2022, 2)

[16] Mancini expresses the concern that the current 'predicament' in international affairs is the 'undoing of Westphalia', by allowing religions to reapportion their international role and

democratic thought the Reformation and subsequent Enlightenment stand out as watershed events in the recognition of religious freedom and the separation of the state from the affairs of the church, and vice versa. The Enlightenment sought to confine religion principally to the private sphere, thereby removing it from the authority of the state. The modern liberal democratic state and its underlying democratic theory cannot be fully understood without acknowledging the historical context of the post-Reformation and Enlightenment eras from which it emerged.

Not all democracies, however, subscribe to European history or the liberal democratic dogma or norms espoused by European liberal democratic theorists. The purported universality of the rights arising from the European context may not necessarily practically resonate universally. In many parts of the world the norm rather than the exception is religious legal pluralism, whereby state law and religious law interact with, support and accommodate each other. While the assumption may have been that modernisation would usher in a world of democratic governance without religion, such a world has yet to materialise. In short, the 'neat dichotomy between private and public has proven unsustainable'. (Mancini 2020, 2)

Within the accommodation of religious pluralism hides the danger of conformity and domination. Individuals may become entrapped in a religious cocoon where freedom to disassociate is but an empty dream. A notable example is India, where, despite often being seen as a model for the accommodation of pluralism, non-state laws may apply to individuals who may not share or subscribe to the prevailing belief system. In fact, even renouncing the belief system in India does not necessarily ensure the laws of that system no longer apply to the individual. (Ahmed 2020, 419) Mukaddam observes that legal pluralism has become a 'political tool to serve political agendas' and that legal pluralism may give rise to impediments to full citizenship rights rather than a reflection of self-determination. (Mukaddam 2024, 142)

Many democracies acknowledge the constructive and destructive force of religious non-state laws. While secularism is often made out to be anti-religion, the truth about separation of state and religion is more nuanced. Secularism is often an attempt to minimise the instability that non-state law may bring to the broader society. In this context Bottoni observes that secularism ought not be

relevance. This, she says, is evident in the competition of religious world views, the claim by states of extraterritoriality of religion and religious conflicts and wars. (Mancini 2020, 13)

regarded as an end in itself, but rather as a method to respond to competing world views. Secularism is therefore not necessarily evidence of the democratic nature of the state, but rather a procedural arrangement to manage societal tension, particularly around religious rights. (Bottoni 2022, 168)

8.2.3 Universal right to freedom of religion

The principles of freedom of religion that mainly originated from the European experience and Western liberal democratic thought formed the basis of the Universal Declaration of Human Rights and other subsequent international and regional human rights instruments.[17] Over time, the right *to* religion has also come to imply freedom *of* religion. Nowadays, there are suggestions that a right to freedom of conscience should be invoked to reflect these spiritual values without specific reference to 'religion'. This notwithstanding, the right to religion is in some respects a 'first right' as it protects the most profound beliefs of the individual, and ultimately influences culture, policies and other values. (Domingo 2023, 420)

The application of the principle of separation of church and state, along with the right to religious freedom, varies across states. Newman proposes that the approach adopted by states can generally be divided into three categories: first, the *accommodation* of religion, where the state retains some link to religion and the services provided by religious bodies; secondly, the *separation* of church and state, where religion is a matter for private conscience while the state strives to be entirely secular; and, thirdly, a *hybrid* of the two, where the emphasis is on a secular state while incorporating numerous exceptions involving some interaction between the state and religion. (Newman 2023, 159–61)

These categories are subject to many permutations, as well as popular and judicial dynamics, because the situation of each polity is unique. It is important to note that religion and culture often overlap, and what some may view as a religious right may be seen by others as a cultural expression. This is exemplified by the judgment of the ECtHR in the Lautsi case, in which the *cultural*

[17] A notable exception is the Cairo Declaration on Human Rights in Islam, which does not recognise the principle of freedom of religion. (Cairo Declaration 1990) In a critical assessment of the Cairo Declaration Rapporteur Gutierrez of the Council of Europe's Committee on Legal Affairs and Human Rights observes that the Cairo Declaration 'fails to reconcile Islam with universal human rights, especially insofar as it considers Sharia law as its sole source of reference and does not recognise certain rights', notably the right to freedom of belief. (Gutierrez 2019)

preservation of the Christian faith in Italy was held to justify the ongoing display of the crucifix in classrooms. The court declared the following regarding the explanation provided by the government:

> The government, for their part, explained that the presence of crucifixes in state-school classrooms, being the result of Italy's *historical development*, a fact which gave it not only a religious connotation but also an identity-linked one, now corresponded to a ***tradition*** which they considered important to perpetuate. They added that, beyond its religious meaning, the crucifix symbolised the principles and values which formed the ***foundation of democracy*** and western civilisation, and that its presence in classrooms was justifiable on that account. (emphasis added) (Lautsi case 2011, para 67)

A similar approach was initially adopted in Germany, where the federal *Länder* could decide how to regulate the wearing of religious symbols and attire in public. Several *Länder* had enacted legislation to restrict the wearing of religious symbols by teachers, but in *Länder* such as Bavaria, Baden-Wurttemberg and North-Rhine Westphalia, Catholic nuns had been exempted from this restriction as their dress was regarded as cultural rather than religious. (Joppke 2013) In 2015, however, the Constitutional Court of Germany declared that the restrictions imposed on the wearing of headscarves were unconstitutional because the restrictions were disproportionate to the subject-matter sought to be regulated. (1 BvR 471/10 2015)

These examples highlight that even the non-religious may rely on religious values as part of their culture. In this sense a religious symbol such as a crucifix may also be regarded as a cultural symbol. ('Richard Dawkins: I'm a Cultural Christian' 2024) The same can however also be said of a headscarf: it may be an expression of faith, or it may also be compliance with a cultural norm of modesty.

8.2.4 State courts and religious tribunals

The interface of state law and religious non-state law is particularly visible at the level of law enforcement, where the authority of secular courts and religious tribunals may conflict. While in general areas of governance direct competition between religious law and state authority can be circumvented through skilful political manoeuvring, the resolution of disputes arising from two competing legal systems inevitably requires the application of state law *or* religious law. A nuanced approach is certainly not easy, if possible at all. Religious tribunals vary in nature: some derive their authority from the constitution or statute, some may be administratively tolerated, while others may rely on their very independence from the constitution to solidify their legitimacy. (Neo 2020, 891)

In fact, in some states the non-state judicial systems are of 'primary importance' to development agencies and democratisation. (Tamanaha 2015, 1)

Religious tribunals that apply religious laws predate the modern state by millennia. From the earliest formation of the state religious tribunals continued to exist alongside the state courts. This historical feature does not apply solely to the existence of religious tribunals. It also concerns indigenous and customary tribunals and community courts. Community justice forums, in their traditional sense, typically involve the community in the process and emphasise the restoration of community harmony. The rules of evidence are often flexible and informal, though procedural fairness may not always be accorded to vulnerable individuals. Nonetheless, such systems are often considered to have strong legitimacy, as they are rooted in the culture and tradition of the community. (Schuppert 2015, 190) Enforcement of traditional and religious judicial decisions in modern society is generally based on community and social pressure, exclusion and ostracisation, rather than an enforcement mechanism like those associated with state law. In liberal democracies this applies to Islamic tribunals as much as it does to Judaic and Christian tribunals.

The primary means of coercion employed by a religious body administering non-state law involves exclusion and other forms of community pressure. Some religious tribunal may seek enforcement through civil measures. This is exemplified by the operation of Sharia tribunals in the United Kingdom, where the Muslim Arbitration Tribunal (MAP) can have its decisions enforced by civil authorities. This stands in contrast to other informal Sharia tribunals in the United Kingdom which depend on the voluntary (and not so voluntary) submission of believers to their authority. Even in Europe, home of the nation-state and legal uniformity, it is increasingly accepted that non-state legal norms which are unique to a particular community may be applied by that community, provided that participation is voluntary and the codes do not breach any fundamental rights in state law.

As Wolfrum points out, the concept of a community being granted autonomy to govern itself in accordance with rules that do not apply to the rest of society is not a foreign principle to Europe. He cites the example of the Edict of Potsdam of 29 October 1685, which granted French immigrants 'far-reaching' autonomy within the context of what would nowadays be regarded as legal pluralism. (Wolfrum 2015, 216) Legal pluralism in Europe and other parts of the world should therefore be seen in its historic context and approached with pragmatism.

One of the earliest, best documented examples of how religious minorities were awarded autonomy to function collectively separate from the state are the arrangements in the Ottoman empire for religious groups to self-organise by way of non-territorial, community millets.[18] The millets had responsibility not only for religious affairs, but also to resolve disputes among the faithful. Additionally, the millets also had functions of civil government, taxation, dispute resolution and service delivery.

It is important not to overlook that the increasing role of secular courts in Europe evolved as the church's role as an arbiter of civil and criminal disputes diminished. The church's loss of public power and declining relevance, alongside the growing secularisation of states and population, are reflected in the limited role the church currently plays as an arbiter of secular disputes. Church tribunals have lost jurisdiction and relevance as their power has become confined to those who voluntarily subscribe to their authority within the private domain of family and personal law. Islamic tribunals have in many respects retained greater influence among its faithful, as Islamic law has not been subject to the same historical developments as has the Christian faith. However, even the scope of the application of Sharia depends on the state in which it exists and the willingness of individuals to submit to its authority since growing secularism also characterises the Muslim community.

Generally, the expansion of democratic governance and constitutionalism has reduced the influence and impact of all religious courts and tribunals. According

---

[18] The first prominent minority self-government arrangements were enacted during the Ottoman empire (c 13–1923), when the millet system was used to grant communities, principally religious (Greek Orthodox, Armenian and Jewish) but also ethnic (the Kurds also had a Millet (Tas 2013, 168)), a form of self-government whereby they could, within the highly centralised empire, arrange their community affairs consistent with their traditions, customs and beliefs. The communities did not live separately in a territorial sense. However, despite intermingling with the rest of the population they had their own institutional and autonomy arrangements for aspects of their faith and traditions. (Tamanaha 2021, 37) In contemporary terms, this amounted to a form of non-state law pluralism. (Chapter 2) These communities not only self-governed, but also raised taxes from within the community and provided social services such as education, family law, dispute resolution, medical treatment and elderly care to their community. (Cakal 2020) The Orthodox Church, for example, was for all practical purposes transformed into a quasi-political governing institution that represented the interests of the Greek faithful on a local community and household level. Upon the decline of the Ottoman empire around 18 self-governing millets were in operation. The millets had what is nowadays described as a 'non-territorial' jurisdiction that focused on the needs of their members, regardless of their coexistence with other people. (De Villiers 2022a, 44)

to Topidi, it appears (in Europe at least) that when parties can elect between secular and religious courts in areas such as personal law, the trend seems for them to opt for the 'rationality' of secular courts. (Topidi 2019a, 34) However, this proposition may be principally of relevance to liberal democratic case studies. In other parts of the world, notably in parts of Africa, Asia, the Middle East and South America, non-state judicial systems remain highly relevant and are often viewed as 'superior' and preferable to state systems because of the non-state system's accessibility, understanding of local culture and tradition, and speedy resolution of disputes. (Tamanaha 2015, 9)

Non-state legal dispute resolution should not, however, be assessed through rose-tinted glasses. These systems are not necessarily publicly accountable and they often tend to reinforce existing power imbalances and dogma that supports those power balances. The rules of procedural fairness and natural justice may not apply to them and the independence of their presiding officers may be compromised. Rules of evidence may be rudimentary. Nonetheless, disposing of the non-state systems is not simple, pragmatic or desirable. For example, as has been pointed out with reference to Pakistan, traditional *jirgas* tend to 'violate human rights', but banning them would conflict with centuries of tradition. (Röder and Shinwari 2015, 50) Similarly, customary justice systems have a wide influence in many parts of the world, with studies showing that people accept and make use of the authority wielded by the non-state bodies operating within them. (Aneme 2015, 96) For example, it has been said that the Ethiopian legal system comprises a complex web of laws and institutions that together perform all the functions of state. The same can be said of many democracies outside the European sphere.

In the European context different forms of *modus vivendi* have been secured between states and the two predominant branches of the Christian faith, Catholicism and Protestantism, through trial and error, war and peace, as well as policy changes and litigation. However, even this relationship is not static. The legal philosophical principle of the separation of church and state, along with the formulation of public policy within this evolving relationship, are subject to ongoing development within Europe, as well as in other liberal democracies.

8.2.5 Religious pluralism is not new

As observed, the current debate about religious legal pluralism is not new, although its relevance in Europe has been accentuated by recent large-scale migration events. While European democracies had been working for several centuries to settle the relationship between state and church, the scale of recent migration of Muslims has become a major social and political challenge for European democracies. The introduction of Sharia non-state law at a scale not previously encountered in Europe is testing the limits of religious freedom vis-à-vis the normative power of state law. Ferrari cautions that the right to religious freedom 'will be the source of increasingly significant conflicts in Europe'. (Ferrari 2020, 109)

As observed in Chapter 2, to subscribers of religious law the nature of their religious codes meets the requirements of binding state law. To them, their codes are not necessarily subservient to state law. This does not apply only to Islam. Jewish law requires that, while state law should be obeyed to the extent that it is consistent with Jewish law (*halakhah*), disputes should be taken to the rabbinical courts, the Beth Din, for resolution rather than to state courts. (Tamanaha 2021, 117) In the USA, for example, the resolution of intra-Jewish disputes can be recorded in accordance with secular dispute resolution rules, and then enforced by civil courts. (Rules Beth Din 2018) There are similar examples in the United Kingdom where, pursuant to local arbitration legislation recognising Muslim Arbitration Tribunals (MATs), parties to a dispute under Sharia can agree to be bound under civil courts.[19]

In many respects the interaction between Islam and liberal democratic thought, as well as with secular, liberal democratic government, is in its infancy. The Islamic faith is, of course, not new to liberal democratic theory or practice. However, the fundamental principle on which the normative systems of the two differ is that in liberal democracies the rule of law, often under a constitution, is supreme law, while Sharia dictates that the Qur'an constitutes supreme law not only in the religious domain but also the public sphere. To liberal democracies religious non-state law can exist and is tolerated within the limits of the constitution. On the other hand, in Islam Sharia is deemed the supreme law and obedience is exclusively commanded by the Qur'an. The ECtHR has declared in this context, where the two legal systems interact, that Sharia as a *legal system* is not compatible with the European Convention of Human Rights as a system of law, since it rejects the legal order upon which the Convention is based.

[19] MATs are not to be confused with informal Sharia religious councils that are also involved in dispute resolution and arbitration. The latter function informally and their decisions cannot be enforced by civil courts. MATs are required to take into account Sharia as well as the laws of England and Wales, and the rules by which they operate must be consistent with the rules for general arbitration in the United Kingdom. (MAT Procedure Rules 2015, para 10)

(Refah Partisi case 2003) Islam as a *religion*, however, is compatible with the Convention within the context of a plurality of faiths, religions and systems of belief.

While at a practical level Sharia coexists with constitutionalism in liberal democracies, the following question arises: what happens if an irreconcilable conflict occurs between a constitutional principle and an Islamic principle? It is in such a case that a hierarchy of laws must be established to ascertain which legal norm is binding in a specific situation. This is not dissimilar to the relationship between the Constitution of South Africa and customary law (Chapter 10), when the Constitution prevails in the event of an irreconcilable conflict. Since Sharia is directly derived from the Qur'an, it commands obedience in all aspects of the lives of its followers – in public law and private law. (Schacht 1983, 1) Mancini refers to several African countries, such as Burkina Faso, Mali, Senegal, Nigeria, Mozambique and Niger, where extremist Islamic groups advocate for state law to be based exclusively on Sharia. (Mancini 2020, 169) She observes that, although Sharia has not substituted civil law in any African country, 'most African countries – especially those with Muslim majorities – are still grappling with the challenges of religious diversity'. (Mancini 2020, 171)

Religious pluralism as a social phenomenon to be tolerated within the context of freedom of religion is not new to European liberal democracies, but working out a response to Sharia as a *potential competing legal system* presents ongoing challenges socially, politically and legally.

8.3 RELIGIOUS PLURALISM – A EUROPEAN CASE LAW PERSPECTIVE

European case law, particularly judgments that emanate from the European Court of Human Rights, serves as a useful case study of the dynamic interaction between constitutionalism and religious non-state law, illustrating the evolving state of the relationship. The ECtHR has taken more than 30 years to develop the concept of freedom of religion and the principle of religious pluralism (Pastor 2019, 13), yet in some respects it remains an 'uncomfortable topic' for the court. (Kiviorg 2014, 317) According to Joppke, the integration of Islam into Europe has been a relative success from a legal-institutional perspective. However, the presence of 'Islamophobia' persists at a social, policy and legal level in what seems to be an otherwise 'respectable' society. (Joppke 2020, 383) De Gaetano expresses the view that European democracies have in response to world events adopted a 'radical secularisation' particularly regarding clothing of Muslim women. (De Gaetano 2024, 144)

When public data along with social and political responses to Islam are assessed, it appears that the integration of Islam, particularly at a cultural level, lags behind the other parts of the Europeanisation experiment. This is perhaps not surprising given the sudden increase in the number of Muslims, the limited time for newcomers to be assimilated, cultural and religious differences, international political events, and the distinctive historical development of the state's relationship with Christianity in Europe over centuries. However, it appears that accommodation of Islam has in some cases been simplified, especially when religious exceptions, such as those in place for the Jewish faith, already exist. This is evident in specific areas such as the ritual killing of animals, male circumcision and non-state dispute resolution mechanisms.

8.3.1 Sharia and the European Convention on Human Rights

It is particularly in its response to the application of Sharia in social fields, which would otherwise be regulated by civil courts, that the ECtHR has been challenged. On the one hand, the ECtHR has found that Sharia *as a legal system* is not compatible with the European Convention on Human Rights. (Refah Partisi case 2003)[20] On the other hand, many European liberal democracies have, in their domestic law, made several adjustments over time to allow for greater accommodation of Sharia as a non-state law norm. For example, in some cases national courts have applied Sharia to family law disputes involving Muslims, exceptions have been granted for the ritual slaughter of animals, and in some countries there is greater tolerance for the public wearing of headscarves, facial coverings and other religious symbols. Additionally, in specific regions, such as Western Thrace in Greece, allowances have been made for the application of Sharia in civil disputes. Since 2008 the United Kingdom has officially recognised Muslim Arbitration Tribunals (MAT), enabling their decisions to be recorded and enforced by civil courts. In Germany, meanwhile, public funds are made available for the training of Muslim imams.

Nonetheless, the challenge for European secular liberal democracies is that the notion of fundamental human rights that exist *outside* of God, not *within* God, is 'entirely foreign to the Islamic tradition'. (Joppke 2020, 397) This is

[20] Note that the ECtHR approaches Sharia as a system of law different to the Islamic faith as a religion. According to the court, Sharia as a system of law is inconsistent with the European Convention since it challenges the legal authority of the Convention, while Islam as a system of faith is compatible with the religious pluralism of Europe.

because Islam is not only a religion in the context of a private belief system, but also a societal, legal and policy system that seeks to regulate all affairs of society. God is the source of law, the author of law and the ultimate adjudicator of law. In contrast, in liberal democratic thought God has become privatised and individualised, and exists principally in the private domain of the individual. The relationship between the Christian faith and European law is therefore different to the relationship between Sharia and European law. But, as has been shown in plural systems such as South Africa, the pathway is navigable.

These formal and informal accommodations of Sharia reflect the acknowledgement of legal pluralism. However, accommodation of religious plurality in Europe is generally based on the standard that national law is sovereign and, whatever religious laws or customs are practised, those may not breach fundamental human rights or other laws. There is thus a hierarchy of laws in which democratically endorsed laws are the highest authority.

This approach to religious pluralism is reflected in the Kokkinakis case, in which the ECtHR declared that 'freedom of thought, conscience and religion, which is safeguarded under art 9 of the Convention, is one of the foundations of a 'democratic society' within the meaning of the Convention. It is, *in its religious dimension*, one of the most vital elements that go to make up the identity of believers and their conception of life.' (emphasis added) (Kokkinakis case 1993, para 31) In regard to the concept of pluralism (read population diversity) of the *population* (not *legal* pluralism), the ECtHR regards diversity as 'indissociable from a democratic society'. (Kokkinakis case 1993, para 31) While the Refah Partisi case focused on the legal system of Sharia, the Kokkinakis case deals with Sharia as a system of faith.

The ECtHR has been somewhat ambivalent about the status to be accorded to Sharia as a non-state legal system. The Otto Preminger case cited the Kokkinakis case in holding that Islam as a faith is compatible with the Convention since freedom of religion is 'one of the most vital elements that go to make up the identity of believers and their conception of life'. (Otto Preminger case 1994, para 47) In contrast, in the Refah Partisi case the ECtHR found that the decision by the government of Turkey to ban a political party because it sought to promote the introduction of Sharia in Turkey (a secular state) was a lawful restriction. The ECtHR declared that Sharia may be 'prejudicial to the public order and the values of democracy' sought to be achieved under the Convention. (Refah Partisi case 2003, para 128) Essentially, the reasoning of the court was that a religious-based *legal* system that in effect challenges the central principles of the

European Convention cannot be consistent with the European Convention. The court stated that

> *it is difficult to declare one's respect for democracy and human rights while at the same time supporting a regime based on sharia,* which clearly diverges from Convention values, particularly with regard to its criminal law and criminal procedure, its rules on the legal status of women and the way it intervenes in all spheres of private and public live in accordance with religious precepts. (emphasis added) (Refah Partisi case 2003, para 123)

Criticism of the accommodation – whether formal or informal – of Sharia in the European context can be categorised into three main areas: first, there is concern about the unequal treatment of women (and other vulnerable individuals) by Sharia tribunals;[21] secondly, critics raise issues related to the lack of due process and rules of natural justice in the operation of Sharia tribunals; and, thirdly, there are concerns about the potential erosion of legal uniformity and consistency of European state law. Additionally, the interpretation of Sharia is not uniform and its application gives rise to national, regional and local inconsistencies. Aggrieved individuals could thus engage in 'forum shopping', where they select a Sharia tribunal or a civil court based on their expectations of the most favourable outcome. (Tamanaha 2021, 121)

A concern expressed by Gutierrez is that even if, in theory, individuals may opt out of Sharia, 'it is probable that a large number of cases concerning the position of Muslim women under Islamic law never come before the ordinary courts of the European Court of Human Rights because women are under enormous pressure from their families and their communities to comply with the demands of the informal religious courts'. (Gutierrez 2019, para 30) While plurality implies that persons can elect the religious identity, if any, to which they would like to subscribe, the concern is that individuals become entrapped within a religious identity from which they cannot practically withdraw.

8.3.2 Flexibility and margin of appreciation

Since there is no consistency between signatory states to the Convention in the manner they respond to religious and other diversity, the ECtHR has developed

---

[21] An-Na'im acknowledges that '*discrimination* on the grounds of sex and religion is *integral* to interpretations of Sharia accepted by the vast majority of Muslims today. This means it is not possible to expunge those discriminatory principles of Sharia and still claim to speak of the implementation of Sharia in an integrated, methodologically coherent normative system.' (emphasis added) (An-Na'im 2020, 181)

what is known as 'margin of appreciation' to allow member states some latitude to adopt different approaches about restrictions allowed on fundamental rights. The concept of margin of appreciation was relied on in the Handyside case in 1976, when the ECtHR accepted that a signatory state of the European Convention could place restrictions on a publication based on the mores of the state population, even if similar restrictions had not been imposed on the same book in other signatory states. (Handyside case 1976) The ECtHR declared that 'the domestic margin of appreciation thus goes hand-in-hand with European supervision'. (Handyside case 1976, para 49) Since the Handyside case the principle of margin of appreciation has been used widely under the Convention to allow states some discretion about limitations that are imposed on fundamental rights and to allow state-based exemptions in other areas of law.

In the Molla Sali case the ECtHR seemed to adopt a more flexible approach (compared to the Refah Partisi case) to the application of Sharia, by accepting that a different legal system, Sharia, could be applied to a particular region in Greece because of the unique circumstances of the state-based arrangement. (Molla Sali case 2020)[22] This appears to be consistent with the reasoning of the ECtHR in the Hasan and Chaush case, in which the court expressed respect for the right of a community to self-organise without state intervention, as 'the autonomous existence of religious communities is indispensable for pluralism in a democratic society'. (Hasan and Chaush case 2000, para 62)

Critically, however, Farzan notes that there has been inconsistency in the approach adopted by the ECtHR in its dealings with the Christian and Islamic faiths by exhibiting greater tolerance to Christianity, while enforcing secularism in the form of a separation of state and faith in regard to Islam:

> The principles of liberal democracy have undoubtedly impacted the court's judgments concerning Islam. Incompatibility of Sharia with the Convention system in the Refah Partisi case rested mainly upon the premise that Islamic rules and traditions conflict with notions of privacy, personal autonomy, neutrality, and equality – all which underlie the liberal democratic order in Europe. Among other factors, the fact that the Greek civil courts apply a secular approach to dispute resolution could have influenced the court decision in the Molla Sali case. It is also argued that the secularism has not influenced the court's judgments concerning the Christian majority and those dealing with Islam in the same manner. (Farzan 2023, 53)

[22] In this dispute, at issue was the validity of a will made under the Civil Code of Greece, and whether the Civil Code should prevail over the inheritance rules of Islam. In response to the proceeding the government of Greece enacted a provision that Sharia would apply only between consenting adults.

The ECtHR has recognised the right of religious communities to build places of worship, act as a legal person and receive donations (Bektashi Community case 2018), all of which is consistent with personal self-government. By allowing a religious body to self-organise, the state acts consistent with its obligation of non-interference and neutrality towards religion, without being obligated to assist the community. (Church of Scientology case 2007) The court has emphasised that the state's duty of 'neutrality and impartiality, as defined in the court's case law, is incompatible with any power on the State's part to assess the legitimacy of religious beliefs'. (Church of Scientology case 2007, para 72)

In the Church of Jesus Christ of Latter-day Saints case the ECtHR acknowledged the importance of a place of worship for faith communities, but also stated that, given the church's tax-exempt status, it was a reasonable demand that the services of the church be open to the public and, if not, the percentage of tax exemption could be reduced, thereby acknowledging a hierarchy of laws vis-à-vis religious codes. (Church of Jesus Christ of Latter-day Saints case 2014) The decision to ban a religious organisation for the doctrine it teaches its members was held to infringe the Convention on the basis that it rendered the religious community without a legal identity and it interfered with the private life of the believers. (Jehovah's Witnesses of Moscow case 2010, paras 103, 117) Yet, if believers withheld medical treatment from a child pursuant to their beliefs, it may constitute a criminal offence under state law.

While the ECtHR has been accommodating towards religious plurality in general, including Islam, within the private sphere it has been more critical of religious codes that may offend public mores (as defined by the majority). For example, many state-based restrictions on the wearing of religious insignia and clothing in public have been upheld by the ECtHR. The court has again relied on the concept of the 'margin of appreciation' to allow states to restrict conduct arising from religious beliefs in a manner that otherwise may be protected by fundamental rights. The margin of appreciation concept has in some respects become synonymous with inconsistency since the same human rights norm finds different application in various European states, albeit under the same judicial authority.

Marko correctly observes that in regard to the display of religious symbols in public there is no 'clear-cut line of legal argumentation' by the ECtHR or the European Court of Justice. (Marko 2022a, 5) Howard expresses the opinion that by upholding restrictions against facial covering the ECtHR in effect erodes the tolerance for diversity it seeks to promote. (Howard 2022, 90–1)

In order for the margin of appreciation to be upheld as a lawful restriction on a fundamental right the following benchmarks must be met: the limitation sought to be enforced must be prescribed by law; the restriction must pursue an enumerated public interest; and the restriction must be necessary in a democratic society. (Machnyikova 2005, 243)

The scope of the margin of appreciation is in each case subject to judicial review by the court, but the concept allows for asymmetrical restrictions in the respective member states based on the discretion of the particular state.[23] This is exemplified by the Dahlab case (Dahlab case 2001), where a teacher who had converted to Islam was directed by state authorities not to wear a headscarf while teaching.[24] This approach was consistent with the reasoning in the Karaduman case, in which the court upheld a refusal to allow a Muslim women to wear a facial covering at a graduation photo event since it had been known to her that the university was secular. (Karaduman case 1993) The ECtHR noted that the limitation on the fundamental rights of the teacher fell within the margin of appreciation. The ECtHR declared as follows:

> In those circumstances [teaching of young children], it cannot be denied outright that the wearing of a headscarf might have some kind of proselytising effect, seeing that it appears to be imposed on women by a precept which is laid down in the Koran and which, as the Federal Court noted, is hard to square with the principle of gender equality. *It therefore appears difficult to reconcile the wearing of an Islamic headscarf with the message of tolerance,* respect for others and, above all, equality and non-discrimination that all teachers in a democratic society must convey to their pupils. (emphasis added) (Dahlab case 2001, 13)

---

[23] It must, however, be noted that public morals and public policy are subject to change. Courts approach public policy and public morals not as questions of law, but rather as questions of fact. (Ryland case 1997, para 702) In the Ryland case the court held that the change of a constitution constitutes a new 'fact' that impacts on public policy and this includes the recognition of the plurality of the South African society. (Ryland case 1997, paras 707–709).

[24] One of the areas that is arguably most controversial in the public and policy milieu in Europe is the wearing of facial coverings arising from religious prescription vis-à-vis restrictions on facial covering. Several European states, for example France, Belgium, Austria, Denmark and Bulgaria, have imposed national restrictions on facial coverings in public. In addition several countries such as France, Denmark, Germany, Luxembourg, the Netherlands and Spain, have bans on headscarves or facial covering in specific settings. Added thereto, several municipal authorities have imposed bans or restrictions. The justification in general on the restriction of the right to wear clothing that reflects religion is found in the secular nature of the state and citizenship. For example, in the Ebrahimian case the ECtHR found that the refusal to extend the contract of a nurse was valid since she had insisted on wearing a facial covering while patients are entitled to receive treatment in the context of religious neutrality. (Ebrahimian case 2015) In the Leyla Sahin case the ECtHR upheld the refusal to allow a woman wearing facial covering to sit an exam since the secular basis of the Turkish state had to be respected. (Leyla Sahin case 2005, para 114)

Other notable examples where the concept of the margin of appreciation has been applied to uphold a restriction on a fundamental right imposed by a state are the Dogru, Dakir and Osmanoglu cases.

In the Dogru case the question revolved around whether a child participating in physical education classes could be compelled to remove her headscarf. The ECtHR noted that different practices concerning religious clothing exist across Europe, countries vary in their approach to the issue, and the court must allow a scope for such different approaches. (Dogru case 2009, para 63) The court declared that the restriction imposed on the student was reasonable, it sought to achieve a valid public objective, applied to all students and was not discriminatory.

The ECtHR has furthermore referred to the importance of a non-legal concept of 'living together' to justify restrictions against the public wearing of face covering, declaring that states are best placed to ascertain what regulatory powers should be applied to their population and what restrictions, if any, are to be imposed on the wearing of religious clothing and emblems in public. (SAS case 2014, para 122)[25]

In the Dakir case the ban on the wearing of face coverings in public was challenged. The court observed that a 'very wide' margin of appreciation should guide the court in its application of the Convention, as there is no agreement in Europe about restrictions of face coverings worn in public. (Dakir case 2017, para 59) However, the court expressed caution that the notion of 'living together' as a basis to restrict religious freedom is too wide and reflects a majoritarian undertone. (Dakir case 2017, para 5) Closely linked to the notion of living together is the justification of protecting a secular society, as was upheld in the Leyla Sahin case, where a university prohibition on headscarves for women and beards for men was upheld on the basis that secular values were sought to be protected as part of democratic values. (Leyla Sahin case 2005)[26]

[25] The ECtHR noted in the case that it was concerned about 'certain Islamophobic remarks' that had been made by some of the intervenors in the case, but as a court it is not to express a view about the desirability of legislation. (SAS case 2014, para 149) The court did not accept that the restriction was justified by public safety, but held that it was a legitimate aim to restrict the wearing of full facial covering for the protection of the rights of others. Two dissenting judges argued that the restriction allowed was in the abstract with inadequate evidence to support the finding. Note in this respect the finding of the UNHRC in the Yaker case that the concept 'living together' is not a fundamental right and thus could not be relied on to justify the restrictions imposed by France. (Yaker case 2018)

[26] In a dissenting opinion Baroness Tulkens reasoned that the protection of those values is a valid objective, the restrictions ought not be assessed in abstract but with reference to the

Restrictions on face coverings have been consistently upheld by the ECtHR as being justified in a democratic society and consistent with the margin of appreciation, whereby some degree of asymmetry between states regarding restrictions on fundamental rights should be accommodated. From the perspective of individuals who find themselves within different European countries but subject to the same Convention, their right to wear religious insignia or clothing may thus depend on the state in which they find themselves. While the margin of appreciation provides the court with a rationale for flexibility, it brings about uncertainty to the individual. A freedom in one state may be a criminal offence in another. It also renders a folly the concept of a 'universal' right, if such a right cannot even be consistently applied within the family of democracies of Europe.

In the Osmanoglu case the question arose whether the refusal to excuse students of the Islamic faith from participating in swimming classes was lawful. The ECtHR held that: the compulsory nature of swimming lessons had been well advertised to the parents of students; every act inspired by religion is not protected; the compulsory nature of the limitation is justified in a democratic society and serves a legitimate public interest; and the discretion of states to organise such practical measures must be respected. (Osmanoglu case 2017, paras 83–90)

The Court of Justice of the European Union (CJEU) has also adopted a restrictive approach to the wearing of headscarves at work by declaring that a receptionist who wore a headscarf while dealing with the public violated the neutrality policy of her employer. (Samira Achbita case 2017) The CJEU had handed down several judgments in which Muslim women had been affected by restrictions in the workplace on the wearing of headscarves. In the Belgium Headscarf case the restriction on the wearing of a headscarf in the workplace was upheld because of the 'neutral administrative environment' sought to be achieved by the employer. (Belgium Headscarf case 2023) These judgments were grounded in a prohibition by employers to the wearing of any religious, political or philosophical belief system at work. (Howard 2024, 3)[27]

There are also several notable examples where the ECtHR has had to balance the interest of the individual in the practice of their religion against communal interests. For example, in the Gatis Kovaļkovs case the court declared that the limits placed on the burning of incense in prison were reasonable as it is not

particular circumstance. Three questions then arise: Was the limitation appropriate to protect a legitimate interest? Was the restriction the least restrictive measure available? Was the restriction proportionate? (Leyla Sahin case 2005, Tulkens)

[27] For a discussion of these judgments of the CJEU, see Howard. (Howard 2024, 18–161)

'essential for manifesting a prisoner's religion', adding that the restriction was justified in light of the offence the smell may cause to other prisoners. (Gatis Kovaļkovs case 2012, para 68) In the Hamidovic case the court declared that the request of a prisoner to wear a skullcap was reasonable and should be protected, even though it is not justified by a religious duty but rather by religious custom. (Hamidović case 2018, para 30) In a similar vein, the ECtHR declared in the Jakóbski case that the dietary needs of a Buddhist prisoner, in the form of non-meat meals, were reasonable. (Jakóbski case 2011, para 54)

When it comes to the wearing of religious attire or insignia the ECtHR has acted pragmatically, albeit inconsistently, allowing itself to be guided by the specific circumstances surrounding a restriction in a particular country rather than laying down an overall European principle. (Pastor 2019, 25) For example, its approach to accept limitations on the wearing of facial coverings in public, based on the margin of appreciation which acknowledges state sovereignty, has been consistent. However, with regard to the wearing of religious attire in situations where civil servants and members of the public interact, the court has shown greater tolerance towards the latter. For instance, in a courtroom the wearing of a headscarf was permitted (Hamidović case 2018), whereas members of the civil service are not allowed to wear religious attire when dealing with the public. Notably, the Constitutional Court of Germany has adopted a more critical view of restrictions on the wearing of religious attire unless the restriction can be justified. (1 BvR 471/10 2015) The ECtHR has also determined that, in the private sector, prohibiting an individual from wearing the Christian cross encroached upon a complainant's rights even though there was no in-depth inquiry into the religious rationale for her wearing the cross, since it is known that the cross is often worn as a cultural expression or merely as a piece of jewellery with no religious connotation. (Eweida case 2013, paras 89, 94)[28]

De Gaetano expresses frustration at the state of European case law about the interaction between the right to religion and limitations imposed under the banner of good order, the rights of others, living together, security and margin of appreciation. He says:

> If one adds the concrete versus abstract analysis paradigm to the equation, it is perhaps no wonder that some of the aforementioned judgments leave one with a feeling that at

[28] Concerns have been raised about a shift from protecting religious liberty based on belief to safeguarding religious identity. In this paradigm religious manifestation is not necessarily required; rather, an association with a particular identity or culture is emphasised. (Sajo and Uitz 2020, 298)

> the end of the day the complainant at domestic level, and before the Strasbourg organs, was short-changed in the face of aggressive secular principles which find no proper anchorage in the European Convention on Human Rights. (De Gaetano 2024, 152)

This brief overview of case law arising from the ECtHR illustrates the complexity to give practical *consistent* content to normative principles of freedom of religion and any restrictions on the right to this freedom. The ECtHR has relied on the margin of appreciation to defend inconsistent practices and applications of law. (Henrard 2015) By doing so, the ECtHR has effectively acknowledged that the 'universality' of a fundamental right is often determined by local circumstances and political mores. In reality the 'generous margin of appreciation' hides what, in effect, are inconsistencies in the application of law. (Sajo and Uitz 2020, 288) While the ECtHR has consistently subscribed to the importance of plurality in general, and religious plurality in particular, in the specifics of case law the court has been criticised as being 'inconsistent and ambivalent'. (Pastor 2019, 32) The restrictions on wearing of religion-inspired clothing must clearly be balanced against the right to equal treatment, the right to religion, the right to culture, the right to self-determination and, added thereto, the proportional impact on persons who may face penalties or lose their employment, or who must withdraw from public. The wide discretion the ECtHR granted to states in the name of the margin of appreciation has meant that the universal nature of rights has been compromised within the European context when it comes to applying freedom of religion in practice. Some view this approach as either pro-Christian, or otherwise a dogmatic secularisation of Europe. (Sajo and Uitz 2020, 289) Howard is of the view that the restrictions are inconsistent with the statements of the ECtHR and the CJEA that diversity and pluralism are foundational principles of liberal democracies in Europe. (Howard 2024, 171)

8.3.3 Majority rule versus minority and individual rights

The margin of appreciation has in some respects become another term for majority rule, effectively contradicting the European drive for the accommodation of minority and individual rights. In defence of the principle of margin of appreciation it is now unknown for an allowance to be made in constitutions for a restriction of human rights in a manner that is reasonable in a free and democratic society. (e.g. s 36(1) Constitution of South Africa; art 1 of the Canadian Charter of Rights and Freedoms, 1982) The irony is that, while legal pluralism is generally understood in the context of the protection of diversity, under the banner of the margin of appreciation the role of the majority is affirmed, with the consequence that pluralism becomes 'rhetoric' which is 'blind to claims about the abuse of a majority position'. (Sajo and Uitz 2020, 294) It is therefore not surprising that Howard expresses the opinion that the restrictions on the wearing of religious clothing in public place works against minorities and discriminates against those who are already vulnerable. (Howard 2024, 177) While margin of appreciation may be a legitimate approach to accommodate some level of asymmetry between states, the question is whether the ECtHR has been adequately critical of the circumstances in which margin of appreciation is tolerated to justify a restriction of a fundamental right. For example, the courts have generally focused on the rationale presented by the state imposing the restriction, but with little or inadequate consideration of the need for the restriction, the proportionality thereof, the importance of pluralism and diversity, and the rationale for a neutrality policy in light of the multi-ethnic and multi-religious nature of the European population. In this regard the transformative role of the courts in South Africa is notable where in the areas of religious and customary rights the courts have accommodated diversity but have also laid down national norms to ensure equal treatment under the Constitution.

The margin of appreciation highlights the challenges states face to strike a balance between secularism, freedom of religion, separation church and faith, and the development of a common national identity based on a predominant civil culture, non-discrimination and equality. To many minorities the right to freedom of belief or religion is an essential element of their collective religious and cultural identity. This includes the right to publicly express their identity, be it through clothing, symbols, language or insignia. The ECtHR has thus far demonstrated a lack of consistency in dealing with religious rights as judgments seem to favour the majority opinion within states without a critical analysis whether the position of the majority meets the test of uniformity, proportionality and reasonability under the Convention. Both a consistent trend and an overarching methodology are absent, with judgments based primarily on the circumstances of each case and the majority position of the country from which the dispute arises. The acknowledgement by the ECtHR of the sanctity of pluralism is arguably undermined by its reliance on the margin of appreciation, whereby majority decisions are often upheld, arguably at the cost of individual and minority rights.

Four major forces possibly underlie the struggle of the ECtHR to develop a consistent approach to religious rights: first, the Christian heritage and tradition of the continent; secondly, the humanist and secular traditions and dogma originating from the continent; thirdly, efforts to protect minority rights within the framework of a democratic society; and, fourthly, the recognition of and respect for the sovereign state.

Some ambivalence remains about how to judicially respond to disputes involving the practical manifestation of Islam. On the one hand, there is a high degree of pragmatism in some states where the courts may consider Islamic laws and customs. In Germany the state even provides funding for the training of imams. In contrast, the Refah Partisi case declared Islam a system of law that is incompatible with the Convention, but stopped short of saying Islam as a religion is incompatible with the Convention. This was followed by the Gutierrez report of the Council of Europe, which stated that the Cairo Declaration is incompatible with the Convention. Nevertheless, in individual case law there has been a greater acceptance of the rules of Islam within the private sphere, despite lingering concerns that within the non-state nature of Islam and Sharia councils the rights of vulnerable individuals, in particular women, may be at risk. Topidi expresses the concern that Islam in Europe 'remains a riddle' and a 'dilemma of governance'. (Topidi 2019a, 49)

The overarching concern, applicable not only to Islam but also other religions, is that under the guise of religious freedom and freedom of association certain practices are accommodated that in other, non-religious, contexts may be regarded as incompatible with fundamental rights and freedoms. The freedom pursued under the protection of freedom of religion may then become a constraint on personal liberty. Religious and customary legal systems face the same question: why should an individual expect or experience different treatment merely for their religious or customary identity?

8.3.4 Observations about the ECtHR's approach to religious pluralism

The jurisprudential developments in the ECtHR in response to religious legal pluralism reflect the complexities involved in addressing, with clarity and consistency, the demands arising from the interaction of state law and non-state law. While social pluralism is on the one hand a strength of democracy, legal systems are challenged if the laws arising from plurality clash with state laws. Then a hierarchy of laws must be established, but in doing so pluralism may be constrained or even denied. Furthermore, these case law developments in the ECtHR highlight the shifting contours of majoritarianism vis-à-vis the protection of minority and individual rights. Striking a balance between majoritarianism and minority rights within the confines of a relatively homogenous nation state is not as challenging as finding an equilibrium between competing rights in the deeply pluralist arrangements evident nowadays in the combined European nations. Even within the European nation states, Appiah observes that 'as a rule, people do not live in monocultural, monoreligious, monolingual nation states, and they never have'. (Appiah 2018, 88) The challenge of religious plurality is therefore not only for the ECtHR but also for domestic courts.

Many democracies outside Europe, particularly democracies in the southern hemisphere, may perceive the European challenges to reconcile state law and religious non-state law with a touch of irony. This is because the struggles of these non-European democracies to establish and sustain democratic processes have often not been fully understood or appreciated by theorists and practitioners from relatively homogenous European liberal democracies. The complexities of democratisation in deeply plural societies are exacerbated by a range of socio-economic factors that challenge the legal principles and societal stability taken for granted by liberal democracies. In short, developing and sustaining a liberal democracy in a deeply pluralist society with an underdeveloped economy in which state law and non-state laws may seek to regulate the same social fields is exceedingly complex.

To elaborate on this further, the following observations can be made about the response of the ECtHR to religious legal pluralism.

The response to religious pluralism by the ECtHR cannot be assessed without considering the historical context of Europe. Factors such as the numerous religious conflicts in the continent, the role and influence of Christianity, the Reformation, the Treaty of Westphalia, the Enlightenment, the separation of church and state, the rise of secularism, and the contemporary challenges posed by the influx of large numbers of immigrants, particularly adherents to the Islamic faith, all contribute to shaping the European legal and political response. Historical experiences and the evolution of dogma underscore how the judgments of a court are inevitably influenced by the circumstances of a country and the philosophical framework within which the court operates. This also highlights the limitations of comparative law, given that the experiences of a country often determine the judicial response to the resolution of disputes. In many respects case law reflects municipal circumstance rather than universal principle.

Religious pluralism gives rise to challenges that are different to those posed by ethnocultural pluralism. Religious pluralism finds its origins in divine law rather than in constitutional instruments, tradition, custom or political agitation. Whereas constitutionalism emphasises the individuality of the person to self-decide, religious law limits the freedom of the individual self-determination because of divine prescription. In a religiously plural society the role of the court to resolve disputes may become complicated, as one party may invoke the supremacy of constitutionalism, while the other party may cite the divinity of religious law and godly rights. In its most radical format religious pluralism may even challenge the existence of the state, the constitution, fundamental human rights, the laws of the state and its democratic and judicial institutions.

While courts generally do not involve themselves in the dogma of religious disputes, it becomes inevitable to declare a hierarchy of laws when a dispute in which state law and religious law seek to govern the same social field is brought before a civil court. State courts in Europe and other liberal democratic dispensations often consider practical manifestations of Sharia in their adjudications, formally or informally. Examples of such concurrent areas are state and non-state laws pertaining to marriage, divorce, testamentary disposition, rights of children, rights of women and other personal areas. The question is to what extent, if at all, does a court take note of and accord recognition to a religious non-state law? Whatever the answer, there is a sting in the tail: if non-state law is recognised, the spectre of a competing legal system being endorsed by the court becomes reality; conversely, if only state law is acknowledged, serious injustices may befall those who are affected by and adhere voluntary to non-state laws pursuant to their right to freedom of religion.

The reasoning of the ECtHR highlights how what is purported to be a universality of fundamental human rights often lacks the practical content and legitimacy of 'universality'. While the term 'universal' rolls easily off the tongue when referring to a fundamental right, in practice there is often little of substantial universality of the right in question. By means of the margin of appreciation the ECtHR has allowed restrictions on fundamental rights based on majoritarianism within states, thereby potentially eroding the very concept of universality of a right. Although it is not strange for national courts to give different content to rights depending on the circumstances within which the courts function, the challenge for the ECtHR is to be a European court with consistent norms for its entire jurisdiction while simultaneously giving effect to state-based majoritarian preferences. Universal rights in this context are easily perceived as mere lip service.

The margin of appreciation developed by the ECtHR restricts, on the one hand, the development of truly universal norms within the jurisdiction of the court. On the other hand, it acknowledges that the same societal issue may be approached differently by the states that are signatories to the European Convention. Similarly to the way in which national courts rely on constitutional restrictions of human rights based on the democratic norms and standards of their respective nations, the ECtHR accommodates, through the margin of appreciation, a form of subsidiarity and asymmetry, allowing states to regulate their own affairs. This may, however, demonstrate the importance of majoritarianism at the expense of the protection of minority and individual rights. The principle of the margin of appreciation is, for example, evidenced in the regulations concerning the wearing of religious clothing and symbols in public spaces. While some signatories to the European Convention have sought to severely restrict, and even ban, such displays in public or public offices, other signatories have accepted these practices as part of individual diversity and freedom of choice. Individuals may feel burdened when they realise that they can wear or display their religious clothing of choice in one European state, while in another European state, subject to the same Convention, they may face prosecution for doing the same.

The ECtHR has, in its respect for the margin of appreciation (to placate national governments), not sufficiently acknowledged that the display of a religious emblem or the wearing of certain clothing by an individual does not necessarily imply that the individual subscribes to the dogma of the religion represented by the clothing. Furthermore, even if the individual subscribes to a particular religion, this does not mean that the individual necessarily poses any threat to the prevailing democratic or social system or supports a rejection of state laws by the wearing of certain clothing. The wearing of a symbol may furthermore be an expression of culture or modesty, rather than due to a religious belief. The proportionality sought to uphold a state-based restriction on a fundamental right vis-à-vis the threat posed by the wearing of certain emblems or clothing is arguably skewed in favour of the dominance of the state.

8.4 RELIGIOUS PLURALISM – A SOUTH AFRICAN OVERVIEW OF MUSLIM MARRIAGE RIGHTS AND THE LAW

8.4.1 Background

The wearing of religious clothing, insignia and symbols in public is, for all practical, social and legal purposes, not a confronting or socially complex issue in South Africa.[29] As observed by Vahed, 'while South Africa is beset by racial

[29] The courts have considered religious rights in areas such as burial and property rights, religious slaughter, religious noise and corporal punishment. (Van Coller 2022, 225–8)

problems, most South Africans respect the cultures and religious practices of their fellow citizens'. (Vahed 2022, 53) South Africans generally view European debates, particularly those around the restriction on the wearing of religious clothing and insignia in public, with a tinge of irony and amazement. Nonetheless, religious legal pluralism, especially in so far as it affects the rights of women and children, does present challenges to South Africa. This is particularly the case in the field of personal rights such as marriage and its subsequent implications, encompassing aspects such as rights at divorce, maintenance, child support, inheritance, property distribution and so on.

Arguably the most pertinent area within the religious legal pluralism debate (outside the context of African customary law) that has faced South African law is the legal effect to be given to Muslim marriages and, even more specifically, how the rights and interests of those in Muslim marriages, particularly women and children, can be protected under the Constitution. Muslim marriages are not recognised in South African law, but the persons involved in those marriages may have rights and interests that they seek to be protected pursuant to the Constitution. While the courts may not wish to become entangled in religious dogma concerning the role and status of women in accordance with Sharia law, the civil effect of a rule that arises from a Muslim marriage may be inconsistent with the Constitution.

Since the earliest times of the South African legal system, dating back to around 1658, when the first recorded Muslim migrants arrived, questions emerged about the legal status and effect of Muslim marriages. More specifically, concerns arose about the rights of persons married under Sharia law. Although South African law does not recognise Muslim marriages, proposals have been in place since the 1990s to codify Muslim marriage rules by way of legislation.[30]

[30] At the time of writing there had not yet been legislation enacted to regulate Muslim marriages. This is not due to a lack of effort. Since the enactment of the new Constitution efforts have been ongoing to enact such legislation, including the following: in 1996 the South African Law Reform Commission recommended that a project committee be tasked with investigating and making recommendations about the recognition of Muslim marriages. The committee issued a discussion paper in 2002, including a draft bill for the recognition of Muslim marriages. The draft bill was the subject of extensive public consultation and submissions. A further bill was published in 2011, but the process has not yet been concluded because of serious disagreements about 'complex theological and constitutional issues' (Women's Legal Centre Trust case 2018, para 22) In June 2024 the Constitutional Court granted an extension to June 2026 for legislation to be introduced. (Speaker of the National Assembly and Another case 2024) Clark and Van Heerden discuss the efforts to enact a single Marriage Act with reference to the draft Marriage Bill of 2022

At the time of writing (March 2025), the objective of creating a Marriage Act to regulate Muslim marriages had not yet been achieved.

One of the many challenges to be overcome to enact a Muslim Marriage Act is the lack of a single body that can speak for all Muslims on this topic. (Suleman 2023) In fact, there are strongly held views by some within the Muslim community that 'Islamic law cannot be intertwined with South African law'. (Suleman 2023, 30) This statement highlights the internal debate within the Muslim community where some view the Islamic faith as open to reformation and adjustment (perhaps similarly to the evolution of customary law, Chapter 10), while others approach Sharia as 'immutable'. (Vahed 2022, 45) This debate in South Africa reflects the disagreement in Europe within the Muslim community on the question of whether Sharia should remain a totally independent sovereign system of law, or whether it could be regulated, recognised, adjusted and accommodated by parliaments and courts. (Mukaddam 2024) Account should be taken that even if a Muslim Marriage Act is promulgated, a similarly situation to what happens with customary marriages (Chapter 10) may unfold where Muslims may elect to marry pursuant to Sharia and not pursuant to the Muslim Marriage Act.

As shown below, since the enactment of the new Constitution South African courts have made several attempts to incrementally expand the provisions of the Bill of Rights to include those that are married, or have been married, in accordance with Sharia. In some respects there seems to be a noticeable contrast between the South African Constitutional Court and the ECtHR in the latter's response to religious pluralism. While the Constitutional Court has interpreted constitutional protections more broadly to incrementally safeguard the rights of women and children in Muslim marriages in the absence of a Muslim Marriage Act, the ECtHR has sought, under the concept of the margin of appreciation, to narrowly construe the protections of the European Convention, thereby arguably limiting the scope of individual protection to accommodate majority decision-making.

Both the ECtHR and the Constitutional Court face a similar challenge – how to balance the provisions of state law, which purportedly reflects majority mores, with those of religious non-state law and the beliefs of a minority community, especially if there are disagreements *within* the religious community about

---

and the complexities associated therewith. (Clark and Van Heerden 2024) Ozoemena and others also reflect on the challenge to accommodate customary practices within the context of universal human rights in respect of a single Marriage Act. (Ozoemena, Wara, and Ramarumo 2024)

whether the religious rules should be codified at all. In the Women's Legal Centre Trust case it was observed that some of the rules that apply to women in Muslim marriages constitute a 'systematic violation of the rights of Muslim women'. (Women's Legal Centre Trust case 2018, para 123) The court asserted that the mere fact that Muslim marriages are not recognised in South African law cannot lead to the conclusion that women who have married according to Muslim law cannot be accorded protection under the Constitution. (Osman-Hyder 2022)

8.4.2 Culture and religion

South Africa's diverse population provides evidence of how rights to religion, culture, custom, language and identity are interwoven. Culture is clearly informed by religion and vice versa. Clear lines of demarcation do not exist. Culture and religion are simple words that seek to encapsulate the complexity of human existence. One thing is clear: for those who profess a faith, their religion often forms the core of their existence. One cannot simply 'opt out' of religion, especially if one is deeply integrated with a close-knit religious community. In addition to the religious commands of obedience, religious communities impose their own obligations, sanctions and pressures on those within them. Religious sanctions can be harsh – exclusion from their religious community can leave a person feeling isolated, vulnerable and without legal entitlements. Furthermore, individuals may find themselves caught up within the general framework of religious rules, such as those pertaining to marriage, without subscribing to all aspects of the dogma of their religion. This applies to individuals of all religions. The reality, however, is that religious communities are rarely homogenous in opinion, often holding diverse views about dogma and its practical application. It is not the place for courts to pronounce on such issues of faith-based disputation.

Generally, courts are, for good reason, reluctant to be drawn into 'religious entanglement', whereby they are called upon to resolve doctrinal issues of a specific religion. (Women's Legal Centre Trust case 2018, para 5) However, the reality is that when actions or consequences arising from doctrinal practice conflict with constitutional values, courts may inevitably be drawn into adjudicating the constitutionality of the doctrinal issues in question, as happened in the case of the Dutch Reformed Church (DRC) relating to same-sex marriages (Gaum case 2019)[31] and the Freedom of Religion case concerning the constitutionality of

[31] In the Gaum matter a decision taken and enacted by the General Synod of the DRC in November 2016 came under review. By way of background: Every Dutch Reformed congregation

corporal punishment of a child in a domestic setting. The Bill of Rights has horizontal application (s 8(2)), thus bringing conduct that may be regarded as private religious in nature within the purview of the Bill of Rights.

In the Freedom of Religion case it was held that freedom of religion and the justification of parental corporal punishment cannot be relied on as a basis to defend assault against a child. The court acknowledged that 'moderate and reasonable chastisement' finds its origin in religious and cultural practices. (Freedom of Religion case 2019, para 62) The court declared, however, that the constitutional protections available to the child override whatever religious or cultural principle is sought to be relied on in support of such punishment. The court furthermore reasoned that alternative non-violent mechanisms and options for discipline should be pursued if the best interests of the child are advanced. (Freedom of Religion case 2019, para 69) The court concluded that the common-law defence of reasonable and moderate chastisement is not a valid constitutional defence against a charge of assault. (Freedom of Religion case 2019, para 73) In essence, an individual who subscribes to a religious faith is not entitled to less protection under the Constitution than a person who is secular. Religion cannot be relied on to encroach on a right that otherwise would be inviolable.

In the Prince case, meanwhile, the court declared that a Rastafarian lawyer was not entitled to an exemption to use marijuana as part of his religious and cultural practices. (Prince case 2002) The court emphasised that the religious use

---

had to adhere to this decision, as the General Synod is the body which, in terms of art 42 of the *Kerkorde* (Church Order), is entrusted with the competency to determine the Church's communal identity in terms of the Bible, Creed, its Constitution, mission and policy. The 2016 decision's effect was to declare that a marriage in the DRC was between a man and a woman. The 2016 decision would have *reversed* the 2015 decision by which the Church recognised the equality of all people irrespective of their sexual orientation and gave recognition to the status of civil unions between persons of the same sex that are characterised by love and fidelity. The 2015 decision also permitted Ministers of the Church to solemnise such unions, but placed no positive duty on them to do so. This decision furthermore removed the celibacy requirement for persons that are gay or lesbian to be ordained as a minister or elder in the Church. Such persons could thus be ordained as ministers or elders in the Church. (Gaum case 2019, para 2) In 2016 the Church sought to return to the traditional approach whereby a marriage could only take place between a man and a woman. The court held that such a reversal would amount to discrimination under the Constitution, the 2016 resolution was not protected by the right to religion, and it could not be regarded as mere differentiation. (Gaum case 2019, para 68; 69) The court noted that, even within the Church as far as its dogma is concerned, there were differences of opinion on this topic. The court therefore declared that the decision taken by the Church in 2016 to seek to reverse the 2015 decision amounted to discrimination and did 'not accommodate diversity'. (Gaum case 2019, para 82) The 2016 decision was duly declared unlawful. (Gaum case 2019, para 96)

of cannabis cannot be equated to its use for medical reasons. (Prince case 2002, para 138) In the MEC for Education case the court held that an exemption ought to be made for a student to wear a nose ring as part of the student's religious and cultural customs. (MEC for Education case 2007) The court emphasised that its primary concern was to ascertain the reasonableness of wearing the nose ring, based on the student's beliefs.

8.4.3 Religious rules and constitutionalism

Religion-based rules can, in their practical effect, encroach on the civil and political rights of those who adhere to them. Religious dogma may not be consistent with the rights protected by the Constitution, giving rise to the concept of the separation of church (or any religious body) and state. Under this principle the state accepts that, within the private sphere, religions have the right to self-organise and their followers have the right to hold their private beliefs and to conduct their lives according to their own dogma. As explained above, state law and religious non-state law spheres generally coexist in liberal democracies, but when a conflict of norms arises which leads to conduct (a mere idea cannot be regulated) where a religious norm conflicts with a state norm, courts must declare which set of rules – state or non-state – applies to a particular situation. The reason for this is simple: religious dogma may tolerate, legitimise and even encourage practices that are not consistent with contemporary human rights standards. Religious doctrine may, for example, give spiritual blessing to discrimination, condone and defend inequality, seek to justify assault or domestic violence, condone underage sex, deny individual self-determination, and authorise bodily harm or corporal punishment.

Put simply, religions may condone certain conduct which in secular circumstances would be regarded as unlawful or discriminatory, and thus unconstitutional and unlawful.

While courts generally shy away from proclaiming on the dogma of a religious community, they cannot ignore the plight of individuals whose rights and interests are affected by their religion in a manner that would otherwise constitute discrimination and unequal treatment. In this way courts can inevitably be drawn into issues related to religious dogma, not to pronounce on the constitutionality of the religion, but rather to assess whether actions claimed to be justified by a religious belief are protected by the Constitution.

Importantly, just because an individual professes to a religion and its doctrine does not mean that the protections offered by the Constitution are not available to them.

8.4.4 Historical status of Muslim marriages in South African law

South Africa is a multi-religious society. While the majority of the community identifies in general as Christian, there are significant minority religions that coexist alongside the predominant faith. South Africa cannot be regarded as a secular state in the same sense as France seeks to be, but it could perhaps better be described as a 'religious neutral state'. (Henrico 2019) It is estimated that approximately 1.6% of the population identify as Muslim. (Census 2022 2023, 24) Despite its apartheid history, South Africa has, since its colonisation in 1652, displayed remarkable social tolerance towards religious diversity. (Mhango 2012) However, until recently, courts considered the values espoused by the Christian faith as the benchmark to define the boundaries of social relationships. Historically this has been particularly true when it related to issues surrounding the sanctity of the Christian view of marriage. For example, in a judgment of 1860 the following view of the beneficial nature of marriage under the Christian faith was expressed by the court in the Bronn case:

> By embracing marriage, polygamy and incest among them [Muslims] will be checked and discontinued; their wives will be placed under the protection of the law, and a step will thus be taken in the right direction to prepare them for the legitimate blessings accompanying the Christian marriage. (Bronn case 1860, para 321)

At law, until the mid-1990s the prevailing stance was that Muslim marriages and, consequently, the rights of women in such marriages were not recognised because these marriages were deemed 'repugnant to the moral principles' of Christianity. (Seedat case 1917, para 308) In the Ismail case the court reiterated that Muslim marriages were against the public morals of South Africa and that the system of monogamy formed the basis of South African law. The court declared that Muslim marriages were 'contrary to accepted customs and usages' and hence not consistent with the mores of South Africans. (Ismail case 1983, para 1026B) In essence the court observed that the notion of monogamous marriage was 'firmly entrenched' in South African society. (Ismail case 1983, para 1024) In the Johardien case of 1990 the court reiterated judicial precedents in refusing to recognise a Muslim marriage because of its polygynous nature. (Johardien case 1990)

These judgments highlight the complexity that faced the newly created Constitutional Court to respond to the reality of Muslim marriages in general and the question, in particular, of who is to be treated as a 'spouse' under the Constitution. (Jamneck 2014) The term 'spouse' could be interpreted restrictively, as defined by the relevant statute, or it could be read more broadly in its general meaning, reflecting a wider range of options beyond those arising from marriage.

The state's refusal to recognise Muslim marriages often led to unregulated situations for women and children in such marriages and meant that existing power relationships within those marriages were maintained and enforced. This left women potentially without legal recourse in case of relationship failure and children facing uncertainty about their legal status. The irony is that those most vulnerable within Muslim marriages were unable to seek protection under civil law.

The historical non-recognition of Muslim marriages and the unjust consequences of that non-recognition became unbearable under the new Constitution. The legal system, regardless of the absence of regulation concerning Muslim marriages, had to respond with greater empathy, fairness and justness to persons whose rights are affected by these marriages. This was imperative, given that marriage, in any form, is more than just a personal relationship; it is also of public significance (Dawood case 2000, para 31) and affects rights, interests and status. The courts, despite the lack of legislation in place to regulate Muslim marriages, began to demonstrate greater awareness of the parties in a Muslim marriage in the areas of civil law where general principles of law could be relied upon to protect their interests.

The enactment of the new Constitution introduced principles of constitutionalism, judicial oversight and protection of fundamental rights in a manner that had not existed under the previous dispensation, where the legal philosophy was based on parliamentary sovereignty. In contrast to courts merely giving effect to the will of Parliament, under the new Constitution courts have adopted a transformative character that enables them to actively contribute to the development of South Africa into a just and equitable society based on the rule of law, recognition of pluralism, development of law and accommodation of diversity. (De Villiers 2023a) In a relatively short space of time since the enactment of the new Constitution the judiciary has made 'commendable strides' to better assist women who are married under Muslim law, albeit in a piecemeal fashion. (Rautenbach 2021a, 87)

8.4.5 Expanding equality step by step

The Constitution recognises freedom of religion, belief and opinion, and it permits the enactment of legislation recognising 'marriages concluded under any tradition, or a system of religious, personal or family law; or systems of personal and family law under any tradition or adhered to by persons professing a particular religion'. (Constitution of South Africa 1996, s 15) In the absence of legislation to regulate Muslim marriages the courts have taken incremental steps to extend the protection of fundamental rights offered by the Constitution to those impacted by Muslim marriages.

The 1996 Constitution not only introduced new principles of law, most importantly the principle of constitutionalism, but it also involved a new generation of judges who were willing to use their powers to actively transform society. The courts accept the plurality of legal systems in South Africa, acknowledging that, as far as possible, religious and customary systems must be harmoniously interpreted with South African law. However, if a rule of non-state law is inconsistent with the Constitution, the latter must prevail. This happened, for example, in the Gaum case concerning same-sex marriages (Gaum case 2019); the Freedom of Religion case regarding the unconstitutionality of corporal punishment (Freedom of Religion case 2019); the Bhe case that declared the male primogeniture rule under customary law unconstitutional; as well as in the cases elaborated on below, which led to greater recognition of the rights of women in Muslim marriages.

The first judgment under the new Constitution to adopt a new approach to Muslim marriages was the Ryland case, in which the court gave effect to the contractual agreement of partners who had been in a Muslim marriage. (Ryland case 1997) The court accepted that public policy had changed since the Ismail case (1983), adding that, since the enactment of the new Constitution, the rules governing the functioning of society had evolved. The court observed that, while its previous dominant position had reflected the Christian faith, South Africa is a pluralist society in which the rights of all communities are protected by the Constitution. (Ryland case 1997, paras 704–709) The previous rejection of a contract entered pursuant to a Muslim marriage was therefore not followed, and a new standard was endorsed whereby such a contract was recognised and given effect. The judgment did not deal specifically with the recognition of a Muslim marriage, but instead addressed the contractual ability of the parties that arises from such a relationship. This newly found freedom under the Constitution for courts not only to interpret legislation but also to serve as agents of change, fairness and equity has effectively 'transformed' them from interpreters of law 'into law-makers'. (Rautenbach 2021a, 91)

In the Fraser case the court took a further step to protect the rights of those persons affected by Muslim marriages, by declaring as unconstitutional parts of the Child Care Act 74 of 1983 that discriminated against the rights of fathers of children born from Muslim marriages. (Fraser case 1997) The court explained that since Muslim marriages are not recognised under South African law, a child born from such a relationship was by law regarded as 'illegitimate' even if the relationship in question was monogamous. As a result of the child's status, the father would have no rights to make decisions regarding the potential adoption of the child. (Fraser case 1997, para 21) This arrangement thus discriminated against the father of the child.

In the Amod case the court noted that the *boni mores* of South Africa had changed since the enactment of the new Constitution and that 'tolerance, pluralism and religious freedom' constituted the 'new ethos'. (Amod case 1999, para 20) The court, without recognising Muslim marriages, declared that a duty of support between the parties arose from the relationship.

This new approach to determine the rights of persons in a Muslim marriage was given further impetus in the Daniels case. Two statutes, the Intestate Succession Act 81 of 1987 and the Maintenance of Surviving Spouses Act 27 of 1990, were declared unconstitutional, as both of them excluded a spouse involved in a Muslim marriage from being a beneficiary for the purposes of intestate succession. (Daniels case 2003) In the Constitutional Court it was declared that 'spouse' in its ordinary meaning includes those who are in a Muslim marriage. (Daniels case 2004, para 19) The court reasoned that there is no justification to treat a Muslim widow differently to women who had married under the Marriage Act. It was furthermore held in the Khan case that the duty of maintenance that arises under the Maintenance Act 99 of 1998 also applies to husbands in a Muslim marriage. (Khan case 2005)

The issue of the rights of multiple spouses in a Muslim marriage arose in the Hassam case. (Hassam case 2009) The court declared s 1 of the Intestate Succession Act unconstitutional, as it did not include an opportunity for more than one spouse to be a beneficiary of an estate under the relevant Act. The court was critical of the reasoning of earlier courts, stating that inadequate concern had been displayed for the hardships arising from the non-recognition of the rights of persons in a Muslim marriage. The court, through the words of Nkabine J, emphasised the following:

> I emphasise that the content of public policy must now be determined with reference to the founding values underlying our constitutional democracy, including human dignity and equality, in contrast to the rigidly exclusive approach that was based on the values and beliefs of a limited sector of society as evidenced by the remarks in Ismail. (Hassam case 2009, paras 25–26)

In the Moosa case the Constitutional Court continued the 'piecemeal basis to ameliorate the hardships faced by women and children in Muslim marriages', (Women's Legal Centre Trust case 2018, para 15) holding that the meaning of a 'surviving spouse' should in its ordinary sense include 'every husband and wife of a monogamous and polygamous Muslim marriage'. (Moosa case 2018, para 21)

In the MM case the court had to decide whether a so-called 'universal partnership' could exist between two persons in a Muslim marriage. (MM case 2019) A universal partnership refers to a relationship in which both partners contribute to the relationship in monetary or other terms; there is mutual benefit arising from the partnership; the object must be to make a profit; and the objectives must be legitimate. The parties had engaged in a dual marriage pursuant to a civil arrangement and a Muslim marriage. The civil marriage ended with divorce after about four years, and the Muslim marriage ended with *Talāq* (divorce) after about 26 years. The wife claimed a 50% interest in their joint estate, whereas the husband contended that Muslim law had to be applied, thereby excluding universal partnership. The court noted that the wife played an active part in the management of the joint estate, with specific reference to the shop they had run. After an assessment of the conduct of the parties during the period of their Muslim marriage the court concluded: a universal partnership did in fact exist; such a partnership could exist regardless of Muslim marriage law; and the woman was thus entitled to a 50% interest therein. (MM case 2019, para 70) The court was mindful not to engage in the question of whether Muslim law allows for a partnership of this nature, instead focusing on whether, under civil law, such a relationship had come into being and avoiding direct involvement in doctrinal issues concerning Islam. (MM case 2019, para 44)

In the Women's Legal Centre Trust case the court acknowledged that the non-regulation of Muslim marriages by law was to the detriment of the parties affected by such marriages, particularly women and children. (Women's Legal Centre Trust case 2018, para 125) It was acknowledged that parties in a Muslim marriage may also opt for registration of their marriage as a civil marriage, but for various reasons this may not occur. In any event the existence of an option for a civil marriage does not imply that a person had to opt for a civil marriage. (Women's Legal Centre Trust case 2018, para 134) A women may, for example, suffer a unilateral divorce by the husband through *Talāq*, with inadequate safeguards to protect her rights and interests and those of her children. She may revert to an Islamic body for protection of her interests, but these remedies do not have the same power or enforceability of civil remedies, which can only be granted by courts. (Women's Legal Centre Trust case 2018, para 137) The court concluded as follows:

> This all serves to indicate that there has been, and is, an ongoing infringement of the s 34 rights of persons in Muslim marriages, as well as the children thereof whose rights are stated in s 28 of the Constitution, to have any dispute that can be resolved by the application of law decided in a fair public hearing. (Women's Legal Centre Trust case 2018, para 140)

The court found that Parliament had breached its constitutional duty by not having enacted legislation to regulate Muslim marriages. (Women's Legal Centre Trust case 2018, para 252)

The judgment was referred to the Constitutional Court for confirmation of the order of constitutional invalidity of an Act of Parliament. (Women's Legal Centre Trust case 2022) The Constitutional Court confirmed that the Marriage Act 25 of 1961 and the Divorce Act 70 of 1979 were inconsistent with ss 9, 10, 28 and 34 of the Constitution 'in that they fail to recognise marriages solemnised in accordance with *Sharia* law [Muslim marriages] which have not been registered as civil marriages, as valid marriages for all purposes in South Africa, and to regulate the consequences of such recognition'; they fail to provide for a mechanism to safeguard the welfare of minor or dependent children born from Muslim marriages; and they fail to make provision for the forfeiture of the patrimonial benefits of a Muslim marriage when dissolved in a way similar to other marriages. (Women's Legal Centre Trust case 2022, para 86) The effects of the declaration were suspended for 24 months to enable the government and Parliament to remedy the shortcoming.[32]

In its reasoning the Constitutional Court observed that 'not recognising Muslim marriages as valid marriages sends a message that Muslim marriages are not worthy of legal recognition or protection. There is no justification for the continuing nonrecognition of Muslim marriages.' (Women's Legal Centre Trust case 2022, para 55) No cogent rationale exists for women in a Muslim marriage to be treated differently to women in any other marriage.

The court emphasised, however, that these findings on the effect of Muslim marriages do not test the constitutionality of Muslim law itself. (Women's Legal

[32] The judgment did not imply that Muslim marriages are recognised in South African law and that the non-recognition 'will continue to prove burdensome to Muslim women and children'. (Abduroaf and Moosa 2023) In June 2024 the Constitutional Court granted an extension to June 2026 for legislation to be introduced. (Speaker of the National Assembly and Another case 2024)

Centre Trust case 2022, para 60) Strictly speaking, the religious doctrine could remain the same, but the practical effect of that doctrine would have to be consistent with the Constitution. The question before the court did not pertain to the constitutionality of Muslim marriage, but rather to the consequences suffered by women who had been so married. The court was, however, concerned about the 'piecemeal' interventions to protect the rights of women under Muslim marriages and sought more comprehensive statutory reform. (Women's Legal Centre Trust case 2022, para 61)[33]

In the EB case the court had to deal with a complaint that arose that there was an unjustifiable differentiation, and indeed discrimination, because of the differentiation in entitlements after the death of a husband within a Muslim marriage. The court concluded that in both Muslim and customary marriages the rights of the surviving spouse must be protected in a manner consistent with those who survive a marriage under the Marriage Act. (EB case 2024, para 66) The court concluded: 'The conclusion I have reached thus far makes it unnecessary to spend time on the further grounds of discrimination alleged to exist in relation to other classes of marriage. All of them appear to me to boil down to the same indirect discrimination based on gender, because in all those other classes of marriage women have the benefit of the redistribution remedy whereas women in new ANC marriages are disproportionately prejudiced as against men by the absence of the same remedy.' (EB case 2024, para 144)

8.4.6 Observations about the approach adopted by South African courts to religious pluralism, as exemplified by disputes arising from Muslim marriages

South Africa is a pluralist society with a wide range of religions, faiths, customs, indigenous communities, cultural communities and language communities.

[33] At the time of writing (March 2025), no legislation to regulate Muslim marriages had been promulgated. Clark and Van Heerden have expressed the opinion that a single Marriage Act may not be suitable for the complexity of co-habitual arrangements in South Africa. They observe that Kenya is the only African country that has attempted to adopt a single Marriage Act (2014), but in their view, regardless of any statutory reform, 'Muslim family law and customary law would continue to be practised in South Africa regardless of non-recognition by the state'. (Clark and Van Heerden 2024, 482) Dyani-Mhango seems to suggest that the delay in enacting a Muslim Marriage Act is caused, in part at least, by the Christian background of South Africa. (Dyani-Mhango 2024) The reality is arguably more complex with disagreement also within the Muslim community about the appropriateness of state law regulating Muslim marriages.

The interaction between state law and non-state law has been part of the South African legal milieu since the first settlement of Europeans. Traditionally parliamentary sovereignty prevailed and associated therewith the predominance of the Christian values. The enactment of the Constitution introduced a new era of constitutionalism and pursuance of universal, secular values pertaining to equal treatment, dignity and non-discrimination. The primarily Christian values and supremacy of the Parliament that had dictated the first 300 years of jurisprudence were replaced in 1996 with the separation of state and religion, constitutional supremacy and judicial oversight.

In the discharge of their functions courts strive to avoid becoming entangled in or drawn into the constitutionality of religious dogma. Given that religions organise themselves internally pursuant to their doctrine, disputes about the interpretation of their beliefs are not for courts to resolve. It is, however, not unusual for courts to declare the law when a person, for whatever reason, relies on religious dogma as a justification for a specific action. The courts, when called upon, must determine whether certain conduct sought to be protected under freedom of religion is indeed protected by the Constitution or whether it offends the provisions of the Constitution.

There is a fine balance to assess the actions of a person belonging to a religious group without, in doing so, becoming involved in the constitutionality of the dogma or core teachings of the religion. In various disputes, such as the approach of a church to same-sex marriages, corporal punishment on children, slaughter of animals and the rights of individuals in Muslim marriages, South African courts have tested the constitutionality of the rules and practices of religions. They have done so without conducting an inquiry into the constitutionality of the dogma of the religion. Indeed, these judgments may assist religions to review their dogma, or at least their practices, in light of contemporary standards.

While religious groups may, collectively and individually and without state interference, adhere to their own non-state rules and prescriptions, it is when an action arising from a non-state law potentially offends the Constitution that the courts must proclaim on the constitutionality (and lawfulness) of the religious practice. This highlights the separation between religion and state, whereby the privacy of religion is respected, but within the civil sphere the values of equality, dignity and non-discrimination for all individuals as contained in the Constitution must prevail, regardless of their religious beliefs. The essence is that a person who professes a faith cannot expect to be treated differently or demand to be treated differently to a person who does not profess a faith, unless such a differentiation can be justified pursuant to constitutional criteria.

The right to religion does not grant to the believer a constitutional right to undertake an action that would in another circumstance be unconstitutional or unlawful. By the same token the Constitution provides safeguards for individuals irrespective of the religious context of the situation they may be involved in. For example, a female who lives as a spouse in a Muslim marriage cannot be held to have lesser protection of constitutional rights than a female who lives as a spouse in a civil relationship. When religious practice enters the civil arena it is treated in accordance with the civil standard as found in the Constitution. If a religious exemption is sought to be relied upon, such an exemption must be consistent with the exceptions arising from the Constitution.

8.5 THEMES ARISING FROM THE RESPONSES OF THE ECTHR AND SOUTH AFRICAN COURTS REGARDING RELIGIOUS PLURALISM

This chapter sought to provide a brief overview of the responses of the ECtHR and South African courts to the issue of religious pluralism, and to reflect on how state law and non-state law interact. While the right to freedom of religion has a broad scope, in this chapter I specifically focused on how the respective courts have reacted to two aspects emerging from interaction with Sharia: the public wearing of clothing and symbols that reflect the Islamic faith in the case of the ECtHR; and the treatment of individuals affected by Muslim marriages under South African law. These are just two areas among a wide range of issues that arise from the intersection of religious rights and state law.

The following themes have emerged from the chapter.

8.5.1 Separation of state and religion

South Africa and the European liberal democracies share a communality of responding to religious rights and the interaction between state law and religious non-state law. The dogma of separation of state and religion must be assessed within the context of the history and intellectual thought of Europe, while acknowledging that there is presently no agreement in European democracies about how this separation is to be given practical effect in all respects. In Europe, Christian religious identity, even under the guise of culture, remains an important consideration in political and social mobilisation. The growth of the right-wing in Europe and new forms of nationalism often display an element of religion and religious culture war. This is not so pronounced in South Africa, where religious identity is generally of a private nature; religion often provides a basis as a unifying function and a shared identity between persons from different racial or cultural backgrounds, and religious belief is generally not a politically relevant motivator.

The current challenges being experienced by Europe, especially with the arrival of large numbers of immigrants from countries where Sharia as a system of non-state law plays a key role in daily life, are testing the ability of the ECtHR to maintain a consistent balance between protecting and respecting universal human rights norms as enshrined in the European Convention on Human Rights, and to kneel to the prerogative of sovereign states to formulate policies, including to impose limits on religious rights, that suit their specific state-based circumstances. The ability of the ECtHR to recognise universal rights is constrained by the notion of margin of appreciation, which in effect curtails the scope of fundamental rights.

European jurisprudence has some way to go to successfully address the challenges associated with religious diversity in general, and particularly issues concerning Sharia non-state law and its interaction with state law. Legal plurality presents challenges to the ECtHR since the court presides over a variety of states and peoples in which in many respects there is no common or unified identity toward Europe as state or a polity. The institutional arrangements of Europe are based on voluntary participation of states in the absence of a binding European constitution. The ability of the ECtHR to deliver judgments that apply to all of Europe is thus limited by respect for national sovereignty of the respective states. The ECtHR is therefore involved in a balancing act where it seeks, on the one hand, to hand down judgments that set the standard for all of Europe, but, on the other, it must be cognisant that states may opt to pursue their own policies based on majoritarian rule. The ECtHR must therefore tolerate a degree of asymmetry.

The legal framework of the ECtHR contrasts with South Africa, where the Constitution applies to the entire country and the constitutional duty of courts is not only to respect and protect diversity, but also to ensure that actions motivated by religious belief comply with the Constitution. The courts are tasked with a twofold objective: first to accommodate pluralism, but, secondly, to ensure constitutionality prevails if there is an irreconcilable conflict between religious norm and the Constitution. Courts have been active to consider the constitutionality of religion-based conduct, for example in the areas of corporal punishment, same-sex marriage rights, customary law, slaughter of animals, and the rights of women and children in Muslim marriages. Although there has been no statutory restriction in South Africa on the wearing or display of religious clothing or emblems, I would be surprised if the courts upheld general restrictions on the wearing of religion-based clothing in public, as has been the case in the ECtHR.

While the authority of the ECtHR is weakened since it depends on the cooperation of the respective signatory states of the European Convention, the Constitution of South Africa is not subject to a similar constraint. The South African courts have arguably been more successful in responding to religious non-state law in its interaction with state law by setting national norms to be followed pursuant to the Constitution. But both the ECtHR and South Africa courts are limited in their accommodation of non-state religious laws: the ECtHR is limited by domestic majoritarianism, while the Constitution of South Africa is supreme when an irreconcilable conflict occurs between state law and non-state law.

8.5.2 Religion as a source of non-state law

The notion of the separation of church (religion) and state is conceptually closely linked to Europe and its historical development in its association with the Christian faith. The Christian faith is not only inextricably associated with European constitutional development, but it is an inextricable part of the European thinking as an extension of continental cultural values. While the concept of the separation of state and religion is generally accepted internationally as a foundational principle of democratic theory, its application differs even within European democracies. Note, for example, the variation from Hungary that 'recognise[s] the role of Christianity in preserving nationhood' (preamble to the Constitution) to the strict secularism aspired to by France. The divergent constitutional status accorded to religion in the constitutional arrangements across Europe is reflected in wide-ranging policies adopted by the respective countries in response to religious pluralism.

Religion continues to influence public policy generally throughout the world, and particularly in Europe. There are increasing examples in Europe of assimilation of religious values with cultural values, even finding common cause with nationalism in an extreme form. Non-Christians are known to defend so-called Christian values based on cultural grounds, rather than prescription to Christianity as a religion. Therefore individuals who are not necessarily Christian in faith may nevertheless rely on those values as part of their cultural expression and defence of the 'European identity'.

European states and South Africa are challenged by religion being a source of non-state law. While religion as a system of faith is accepted as an important part of individual and community self-determination, the laws that originate from religions may offend constitutional or majoritarian norms. In South Africa and Europe religion remains an importance source of non-state law and hence its influence on public policy remains clearly discernible.

The absence of an overarching European constitution and the lack of or a weak common European political identity present a challenge to the role of the ECtHR since signatory states may refuse to give effect to judgments of the ECtHR. The ECtHR has therefore sought to accommodate state diversity under the banner of margin of appreciation. In South Africa, in contrast to Europe, the Constitution performs a unifying function and judgments of the courts are respected and enforced across the entire nation. The role of the Constitutional Court in South Africa to transform society, accommodate pluralism and modernise religious and customary laws is in some respects advanced in comparison to that of the ECtHR.

The constitution-drafting process of South Africa set the standard for the courts to respect diversity, but also to ensure that constitutionalism prevails. The ECtHR is hampered since the signatories to the European Convention do not approach the Convention as the equivalent of a binding constitution and the margin of appreciation concept allows states scope to pursue domestic policies that may not be consistent with what the courts would ordinarily view as universal European human rights protection.

8.5.3 Courts and religious diversity

The ECtHR and the South African courts strive to navigate religion-based disputes, balancing the right to self-determination, self-organisation and the dogma of religions, while simultaneously ensuring that individuals do not receive either lesser or preferential constitutional protection merely because of their faith. While courts refrain from proclaiming on the constitutionality of religions and their dogma, courts cannot avoid making pronouncements if the dogma of a religion leads to an action that potentially offends constitutional rights.

The essential principle arising from jurisprudence in South Africa is that non-state law may exist pursuant to the unique doctrine of a religious group, provided that the dogma in question does not give rise to actions of inequality, discrimination or preferential treatment under state law. It is the action that may be caught up by judicial attention, not the dogma, belief or faith.

8.5.4 Majoritarianism and religious rights

The interaction between the democratic right of the majority to regulate or restrict certain practices and the right of a minority to engage in those very practices that are the subject of restriction based on their religious beliefs is demonstrated by the jurisprudence cited in this chapter. Religious rights are not absolute, but curbing those rights that are rooted in the word of a higher, godly being, carries the risk of exposing fault lines between state law and non-state law. A disregard for religious non-state law may give rise to violence, while the lack of legal uniformity and equal protection of rights under state law may undermine national unity and common identity. Through the concept of the margin of appreciation the ECtHR has adopted a flexible approach, based on respect for the regulatory regime of each state, to apply the right to religion in the respective signatory states. While this approach is pragmatic, it is open to criticism for eroding the concept of the universality of rights, since an individual right is not determined by the constitutional value in the European Convention, but by the majoritarianism in a particular state. This approach may be informed by *realpolitik*, but it can also be interpreted as a failure of the ECtHR to critically assess the restrictions on rights imposed by majority rule. In this respect the courts in South Africa have been relatively proactive to bring non-state law and acts arising from religious dogma into conformity with the Constitution to ensure national consistency, while the ECtHR has done much to accommodate state-based asymmetry, majority rule and national subsidiarity.

CHAPTER 9

EDUCATIONAL RIGHTS AND MOTHER-TONGUE TEACHING: THE CHALLENGE IN PLURAL SOCIETIES TO BALANCE ACCESSIBILITY, NON-DISCRIMINATION AND EQUALITY WHILE PROMOTING LANGUAGE IDENTITY

If you talk to a man in a language he understands, that goes to his head.
If you talk to him in his language, that goes to his heart.

– Nelson Mandela

9.1 INTRODUCTION

Mother-tongue education plays a crucial role in various ways in the life of children and how they become adults, for example fostering language development, preserving culture, helping to retain identity, facilitating intergenerational language and culture transfer, promoting social interaction, enhancing self-esteem and improving educational performance.[1] Mother-tongue education (also referred to as home-language education) is particularly important during a child's formative years in pre-primary and primary school. UNESCO has succinctly stated as follows:

> Research shows that education in the mother tongue is a key factor for inclusion and quality learning, and it also improves learning outcomes and academic performance. This is crucial, especially in primary school to avoid knowledge gaps and increase the speed of learning and comprehension. (emphasis added) (UNESCO mother tongue 2022)

Drawing from the rich linguistic landscape and legal pluralism of India, Nishanthi observes the following:

> Mother tongue is valuable due to several reasons. Mother tongue is vital in framing the thinking and emotions of people. Learning to speak in the mother tongue is very necessary for a child's comprehensive development. Being fluent in the mother tongue, which is also known as the native language, benefits the child in numerous ways. It associates him to his culture, ensures enhanced cognitive development, and supports in the learning of other languages. A child first comprehends what is around them through the language they hear their mother communicating in from before they are

[1] Although s 29 of the Constitution of South Africa refers to teaching in one of the *official* languages without explicitly using the term 'mother tongue', for the sake of consistency with international jurisprudence and literature, I use the term 'mother-tongue education' in this book in the context of the right to elect education in a particular language. Alternatively, the term 'home language' could be used, but to maintain consistency with internationally recognised terminology 'mother tongue' is preferred. The approach I adopt is consistent with that of UNESCO, which uses the term 'mother tongue' and defines it as the language(s) that one has learnt first; the language(s) one identifies with or is identified as a native speaker of by others; and the language(s) one knows best and the language(s) one uses most.

> born and throughout their lives. Many children across the developing world are learning very little in school, a reality that can be linked to teaching that is in a language they do not fully understand. It is a practice that leads to limited or non-existent learning and acquisition of knowledge and skills, alienating experiences, and high drop-out and repetition rates. To improve the quality of education, language policies need to take account of mother-tongue learning. Models of education which ignore the mother tongue in the early years can be unproductive, ineffective and have a negative effect on children's learning. Mother-tongue education at least in early years can enable teachers to teach, and learners to learn, more effectively. (emphasis added) (Nishanthi 2020)

These educational objectives identified by Nishanthi do not imply that the absence of mother-tongue education would lead to the diminishment of a spoken language or the collapse of the educational system because students are not taught in their language of choice. Countless examples from around the world demonstrate that languages and cultures can survive and endure even when children are not formally educated in their mother tongue.[2] In fact, some argue that education in another language may turn 'inward-looking communities outward', particularly in multilingual societies such as South Africa. (Woolman and Fleisch 2014, 137) However, the converse is also true: mother-tongue education, particularly during a child's formative years, yields distinct educational and social benefits, likely to lead to positive outcomes not only in education but also socially and economically. (Sodhi 2023) Furthermore, minority language facilities frequently play an instrumental role in the linguistic and cultural survival of a community. For example, minority language schools and facilities often serve as a foundation and space for community activities, sports, cultural events, service delivery

[2] The World Bank has observed the following about the lack of mother-tongue education in Asia and the negative implications for children from minority language communities: 'Many children in Southeast Asia are taught in languages that are not spoken in their immediate community. Research and data, where available, show that these children are over-represented among the out-of-school population. *There is an urgent need therefore to ensure that language of instruction issues receive adequate attention*. . . . Linguistic diversity is a characteristic of all Southeast Asian countries. Speakers of minority languages are far more likely to be excluded from the educational process than those belonging to the dominant groups. . . . *Mother tongue as a 'bridge' language* of instruction refers to situations in which an educational programme is organised so that mother-tongue speakers of non-dominant languages can build a culturally and linguistically appropriate educational foundation in their home language first, and subsequently learn additional languages. They thereby gain the potential to use all their languages for life-long learning.' (Kosonen and Young 2009, 14) The report concludes by outlining the following objective: 'The ultimate goal [in Asia, but the same can be said about South Africa] should be *strong forms of mother tongue-based multilingual education*, where the mother tongue is used as long as possible in as many ethnolinguistic minority/non-dominant languages as possible.' (emphasis added) (Kosonen and Young 2009, 192)

and recreation. The school in effect becomes the home away from home where children can develop in the comfort of their own language and culture.

9.1.1 Mother tongue and personal self-determination

Proficiency in speaking, reading and writing in one's mother tongue is essential for individuals to exercise their right to individual self-determination. (Henrard 2007) Chürr expresses the opinion that 'without mother-tongue education, every child's right to learn and to become a skilful adult, able to participate independently in society, is at risk'. (Chürr 2013, 275) In addition, when children are educated in their mother tongue the likelihood of that language being utilised in commerce, governance, politics, administration, science, media, literature, music, entertainment, advertising, research, public signage, place names and secondary and tertiary education significantly increases. These uses add to the self-esteem of the individuals who speak the language. Added thereto, education in mother tongue is not only associated with the right to culture, it is important for the socio-economic development of the person. (Henrard 2013, 7) The United Nations has expressed the following view of the interaction between cultural rights and development:

> Cultural rights are indispensable to sustainable development. Development will only be sustainable if it is shaped by the values of the people that it involves and the meaning that they ascribe to it, protects their resources and uses their heritage in all its dimensions – tangible, living and natural. A human rights approach with a strong consideration for cultural rights is both a framework for and a guarantee of success for any development agenda. (emphasis added) (Mackay 2022, 436)

In short, educating children in their mother tongue for as long as possible enhances their perception of self-worth, fosters a positive identity and reflects respect for plurality. While the seminal Brown v Board of Education case in the USA acknowledged education as the 'very foundation of good citizenship' (Brown case 1954, 493), the practical value of mother-tongue education for children's self-esteem and self-development is also crucially important. In Canada, for example, it has been shown that minority language schools facilities not only offer educational benefits but also serve as the basis for other community institutions, development of leadership and community activities. The facilities often function as a venue for community gatherings and activities and serve as a means of expressing cultural identity. (CSF case 2016, para 368)

9.1.2 Mother tongue and individual rights

Although there is no universal judicially enforceable 'right' to mother-tongue education, individual rights such as self-determination, equality, culture, association, identity, family, language, integrity, use of one's own name and script, and development arguably imply the elements of speaking, receiving instruction and being educated in one's mother tongue. Municipal courts, including those in South Africa, have correctly pointed out that there is no international legal norm obligating state-supported mother-tongue education. However, when considered alongside rights to culture, language and individual self-determination, a purposive approach to interpretation may lead governments and courts to prioritise the provision of mother-tongue education.[3] Courts can be expected to adopt an approach that facilitates mother-tongue education if possible, rather than to diminish it. In the aim to promote mother-tongue education discretions exercised by the state ought to encourage and expand rather than limit the right to mother-tongue teaching.[4] Saeed puts it bluntly: 'If children are taught in another language [than their mother tongue], they will suffer a lot.' (Saeed 2021, 38) In the Sami Chakma case in India the court observed as follows:

> It is undisputable that a child tends to learn new subjects best when taught in his mother tongue. Particularly, if the children come from a disadvantaged background, the efforts of learning a new subject in an alien language can seriously hamper his progress. (Samir Chakma case 2016)

[3] Froneman J, for example, explains as follows that he views the role of the court as encouraging and enhancing the multilingual nature of South African society: 'It may well be that it is better for the country to concentrate on the inclusiveness that English might bring as the sole language of instruction – but that is a choice that ought to be made by the public rather than this Court. From my perspective, *this Court's constitutional duty is instead to create space for other official languages*. That is what true unity in diversity entails.' (University of Free State case 2017, para 127)

[4] Note in this respect the Fosen case in Norway, where the court read the individual right to enjoy culture of a member of an indigenous community *in the context* of the right being exercised by the entire community to maintain their customs and identity. (Fosen case 2021) This approach reflects the Kichwa case, in which it was held that the right to a cultural identity is a fundamental and collective right of indigenous communities and must be respected in a multicultural, pluralistic and democratic society. (Kichwa case 2012, para 217) The South African courts have generally been reluctant to acknowledge the linkage between the right to culture and mother-tongue education.

The Dean of the Faculty of Humanities of the Nelson Mandela University of South Africa summarised the importance of mother-tongue teaching at all levels as follows:

> In the education context, when students are able to communicate in their mother tongue they are more likely to feel included in different communication acts of the university, and are also likely to participate fully in social, cultural and other aspects of university life. (Maseko 2023)

The challenge for minority languages in liberal democracies therefore does not lie in whether the freedom exists for their language to be spoken at home, in private, in public or at cultural meetings.[5] It is generally accepted that individuals may freely use their language of choice in social settings and associate with others who speak the same language. Rather, as elaborated on in this chapter, the question is whether education in the mother tongue should be considered an entitlement to be funded by the state, whether in public or private schools. This question arises because the reality is that, with the exception of wealthy individuals, few communities of minority-language speakers are likely to have access to the financial means to entirely self-fund education in their language of choice for all of those in the community who elect to be taught in the language.[6] Therefore if the opportunity for mother-tongue teaching is solely dependent on the financial resources of individuals who request it, the result is likely to be that the affluent can afford the preservation of their language while the less privileged would have to accept the educational decline of theirs. Their children would likely be instructed in a second or third language, potentially perpetuating a cycle of increasing inequality.

---

[5] For a critical assessment of the response to the policies adopted in South Africa concerning the rights of language, cultural and religious communities, see the De Klerk Foundation. (De Klerk Foundation 2023)

[6] Kriegler J observes, perhaps somewhat unsympathetically, that a community that desires to pursue its own cultural, language or religious identity can fund it themselves: 'Dit staan hul vry om eendragtig die erwe van hul vaders vir hul kinders te behou. Daar is egter 'n prys, naamlik dat so 'n bevolkingsgroep daarvoor die hand in eie sak moet steek. In 'n sin gaan die huidige geskil dus nie om volksgoed nie maar om geld.' (Gauteng Education Bill case 1996, para 42) (freely translated: 'They are free to consent to retaining the traditions of their fathers for their children. However, there is a price, namely that such a population group must pay for it. In a sense, the current dispute is therefore not about the public good but about money.') While this may be a very pragmatic approach, it does not recognise (as the Canadian and Indian courts have done) that budgetary allocation and the exercise of administrative discretion should be informed by the benefits of mother-tongue education.

9.1.3 In the best interests of children

Arguably therefore it is in the best interests of the South African state, as well as the country's children, to fund and support mother-tongue education as much as possible and for as long as is feasible. Where possible jurisprudence should give effect to this objective since it is consistent with the constitutional rights to culture, family, association and self-determination. This approach aims to improve and enhance educational performance, particularly for impoverished and marginalised communities, as well as to reassert recognition of the rainbow nature of the society by means of education. This ought to be a transformative value embraced by all organs of government, including the judiciary. The appreciation and celebration of diversity should not only be evident on the streets and sports fields, but also in classrooms, lecture halls and courts. As was said in the case of Canada, the same applies to South Africa about the role of government to commit to the promotion of mother-tongue education:

> [I]t then becomes a political choice: do the various governments [of Canada] truly believe that the French language and the communities who speak it deserve a special place within Canada? This is a question to which law and rights alone cannot provide an answer. (Foucher 2023, 474)

While the South African courts have repeatedly emphasised the importance of non-discrimination and equality in education, they have arguably not given adequate weight to how these rights can be harnessed through providing mother-tongue education. The pathway to equality may, in fact, be to mandate greater regard for mother-tongue teaching as a means to foster higher literacy rates, enhance social mobility and promote personal self-determination. If ever Ubuntu (Chapter 6) with its sense of community finds application, it could be in the field of mother-tongue education and cultural rights since those are so important to the self-being of a child within the context of their community. The failure to provide children with education in an official language of their understanding may in effect breach the substance of their right to education. (Boulais, Marinkovic, and Palomares 2023, 607) Note, for example, the Cyprus case, in which the ECtHR found that the decision of the Turkish authorities to discontinue secondary teaching in Greek and thereby requiring children to be sent away from home for Greek teaching, violated the right to family life. (Cyprus case 2002) In India the following has been observed about the impact of non-home-language teaching on educational outcomes:

> It [absence of mother-tongue teaching] causes educational failure, negative psycho-social consequences, socio-economic marginalisation, forcible loss of linguistic

> and cultural diversity, and amounts to linguistic genocide. (emphasis added) (Mohanty 2023, 563)

These dimensions, where the imposition of English as a form of 'linguistic imperialism' (Woldeyes 2023, 394) is having an impact on the cultural and other rights of children, have not been explored by the South African courts.

The survival and intergenerational transmission of a language as a medium of instruction inevitably rely on financial and other support from the state, including training teachers and providing and funding educational facilities. Schools do not operate in isolation; they require infrastructure, transportation, learning materials and utilities to function effectively.[7] While this economic reality is widely acknowledged, this chapter examines whether there is a legal entitlement for minority language communities to receive state support for their education. It also explores whether an individual has a justiciable right to state-funded mother-tongue education. Most relevantly for the purposes of this book, it delves into how the South African Constitution and courts respond to these questions.

9.1.4 Mother-tongue education: legal and practical considerations

The answer to these questions is simple in legality, but nuanced in practicality. *Legally*, there is no universal right to state-funded mother-tongue education. The principles of equality and non-discrimination prevail.[8] *In practice*, various

---

[7] Note, for example, that in 2023 it was estimated that around 239 schools in South Africa had no access to electricity, and more than 700 000 students had to walk *daily* more than 5 kilometres to school because of a lack of transport facilities. (Le Cordeur 2023, 22) Berger proposed in 2003 that the Constitutional Court declare the current 'education system as unconstitutional' because of the failure to allocate adequate resources for eradicating inequality. (Berger 2003, 615) The unexplored question is to what extent poor governance, corruption and maladministration have contributed to the lack of adequate educational facilities. While the courts have correctly focused on the country's apartheid history and its role in creating unequal access to education, there has been a notable lack of consideration from judges regarding ongoing issues of poor governance and maladministration as contributing factors to educational deficiencies.

[8] Sachs J observes as follows: 'It should be added that the central theme that runs through the development of international human rights law in relation to the protection of minorities, is that of preventing discrimination against disadvantaged and marginalised groups, guaranteeing them full and factual equality and providing for remedial action to deal with past discrimination.' (Gauteng Education Bill case 1996, para 87) While this statement is correct, one could add that substantive individual self-determination is also facilitated and enhanced by the full recognition of the individual's language, cultural and religious rights. Equal treatment relates not only to the absence of discrimination, but also to the constructive recognition of and support for identity rights. An argument can be made that the predominant funding of education in English

arrangements exist worldwide, both territorial and non-territorial, wherein states comprised of plural populations fund and support mother-tongue education, whether in private or public institutions. (Smith, Dodovski, and Ghencea 2023a) Territorial arrangements refer to decentralised systems where regional and local educational facilities teach in the language of the local community. Examples of these can be found in South Africa, Switzerland, Nigeria and Indonesia. On the other hand, non-territorial personalised arrangements refer to special government grants that support minority languages in schools. Examples of such arrangements can be found in South Africa also, as well as South Tyrol (Italy),[9] India,[10] Hungary,[11] Russia and Schleswig-Holstein (Germany).[12]

9.1.5 Constitution-drafting process

The right to state-supported mother-tongue education was a primary concern of particularly the Afrikaans community during the constitutional negotiations leading to the enactment of the 1996 Constitution. It was acknowledged that implementing a system of provincial government, whereby the provision of education at primary and secondary levels would be a provincial competency, would provide most of the major African language communities a territorial

is in itself a form of discrimination and unequal treatment since it fails to acknowledge the cultural and linguistic diversity of South African children and the identity rights recognised by the Constitution.

[9] Extensive power-sharing and other pragmatic arrangements exist in South Tyrol for the three main language communities, German, Italian and Ladin. These include the provision of mother-tongue education to children in state schools, even though members of the respective communities often live intermingled with other members of society. (De Villiers 2017)

[10] See below, the examples of how state-supported education in minority languages has been recognised and mandated by Indian and Canadian courts.

[11] In Hungary the ethnocultural self-government arrangements for national minorities include the provision of state-supported mother-tongue education through funding allocated to schools within the respective nationality communities. (De Villiers 2022f) For an overview of comparative non-territorial education and other self-governing arrangements, see Smith et al (Smith, Dodovski, and Ghencea 2023b) The definition of 'national minority affairs' also includes 'the provision of specific public services to persons belonging to a national minority', and equal opportunities, social inclusion and social welfare are included among the national minority rights. (Balogh, Halász, and Pap 2025) The nationality councils are therefore not restricted to only cultural affairs.

[12] Special autonomy and self-government arrangements exist in the German federal state of Schleswig-Holstein whereby children of the Danish minority community may receive education in their mother tongue. (Malloy and Salat 2021) Similar arrangements exist on the Danish side of the border for the German minority residing outside their homeland.

basis for teaching their mother-tongue language in state schools, particularly in the early years of education. For example, it was obvious that in a province such as KwaZulu Natal, the teaching of students in isiZulu would be a priority. The Afrikaans community, however, was concerned that, because of its lack of territorial concentration, provincial government (other than in the Western Cape and Northern Cape) would not provide members of the community with an adequate basis for state-supported Afrikaans language education.[13]

Despite the Afrikaans community's concerns, *any* form of constitutional recognition of single-medium teaching was resisted by the liberation parties. In fact the Afrikaner demands for some form of acknowledgement of mother-tongue educational language rights nearly 'derailed' negotiations. (Malherbe 2004, 20) The scepticism and resistance to grant any special educational language rights to minority communities were understandable in light of South Africa's history. Moseneke DCJ observed some years later, in 2010, that the 'most abiding and debilitating legacy of our pact is the unequal distribution of skills and competencies acquired through education'. (Head of Department, Mpumalanga Department of Education case 2010, para 46) The assumption was, perhaps an oversimplification, that teaching predominantly in English was the gateway to addressing educational inequality. This assumption in its simplicity was not realistic in light of the multilingual composition of the population and the proven benefits of mother-tongue education.

The negotiations did not result in an unqualified individual right to state-funded mother-tongue education. Instead, a pragmatic approach was adopted, recognising private funding of education as an individual right. Meanwhile, state-funded support for education in an official language was acknowledged as a legal entitlement pursuant to s 29, but subject to reasonable practicability. (Malherbe 2000)[14] In principle this is not an unreasonable limitation since

[13] Currie and De Waal observe that in practical terms 'the larger the number of speakers of a language in a particular area, the greater the obligation to provide mother-tongue education in that language in the area.' (Currie and De Waal 2013, 639)

[14] **29. Education**

1. Everyone has the right
   (a) to a basic education, including adult basic education; and
   (b) to further education, which the state, through reasonable measures, must make progressively available and accessible.
2. Everyone has the right to receive education in the official language or languages of their choice in public educational institutions where that education is reasonably practicable. In order to ensure the effective access to, and implementation of, this right,

providing education in a mother tongue inevitably depends on considerations such as demand, resources, equality and non-discrimination. The inclusion of s 29 in the Constitution was the result of a 'hard-fought battle', as described by Malherbe, who had close involvement with that part of the constitution-drafting process. (Malherbe 2004, 12)

The compromise reflected in s 29 sat 'uncomfortably' with the liberation parties (Malherbe 2000, 20), but such was the nature of the constitutional negotiations that neither side was ever going to fully secure their objectives. This outcome (again) reflected what the parties involved were able to agree to, not what they aspired to.

9.1.6 Debate complications due to the status of Afrikaans

The constitutional debates surrounding language rights were immensely complicated by the historical status of Afrikaans, in particular the perception of it as the language of the 'oppressor'. The Afrikaans language was seen as a symbol of apartheid, discrimination and inequality. It was practically impossible to discuss language rights dispassionately and objectively. It was always loaded with historical baggage. Internationally, minority language rights are typically associated with disadvantaged ethnocultural and indigenous communities seeking recognition. However, the situation in South Africa was the opposite. The Afrikaans community was considered advantaged, leading to scepticism about its pursuit of special cultural and linguistic rights under the new democratic Constitution. This was perceived as an attempt to safeguard the benefits and privileges the community had acquired during apartheid, and thus did not sit well with the liberation parties. Note in this respect the controversy surrounding the teaching of Russian in post-Soviet states of central and eastern Europe, where

---

the state must consider all reasonable educational alternatives, including single medium institutions, taking into account

(a) equity;

(b) practicability; and

(c) the need to redress the results of past racially discriminatory laws and practices.

3. Everyone has the right to establish and maintain, at their own expense, independent educational institutions that
   (a) do not discriminate on the basis of race;
   (b) are registered with the state; and
   (c) maintain standards that are not inferior to standards at comparable public educational institutions.
4. Subsection (3) does not preclude state subsidies for independent educational institutions.

the language remains to be widely spoken but yet in many respects detested due to the Russification of those countries under Soviet rule.

The perception of Afrikaans had a significant impact on the entire discourse surrounding ethnocultural rights during the negotiations. In effect it discredited any form of collective recognition of rights during the constitutional deliberations. (Chapter 3) Furthermore, the fact that no other language community during the negotiations expressed as much concern as the Afrikaners about language entitlements only added to suspicions that the Afrikaans negotiators intended to utilise language rights to perpetuate an indirect form of racial inequality, discrimination and exclusivity.[15] These issues continue to challenge the educational debate.

Although the lack of demand at the time of negotiations by other language communities for greater protection of the right to mother-tongue education can be attributed to various reasons, Moseneke DCJ noted in 2010 that many African parents choose to educate their children in English, regardless of the benefits of early-school mother-tongue education. (Head of Department, Mpumalanga Department of Education case 2010, paras 46–49)[16] While the 'flood-tide of English' poses risks to other official languages (University of Stellenbosch case 2019, para 48), the converse is also true: the English language opens doors that may otherwise be closed to those who are not literate in it. Maziwisa's observation – that transformative constitutionalism can protect the language rights of communities, but the importance of English in an international context, as well as its status as a lingua franca in South Africa, presents challenges to the promotion of mother-tongue education – thus seems quite reasonable. (Maziwisa 2022, 21)

Put simply, for the Afrikaners, who came from a privileged social, economic and political background, the focus during negotiations was on maintaining mother-tongue education in single-medium facilities. Conversely, for the liberation parties emerging from a disadvantaged background the primary emphasis was to achieve equality and non-discrimination in education, with little attention given to mother-tongue instruction.

---

[15] The 2024 Afrikaner Declaration issued by a group of Afrikaans organisation seems to perpetuate those suspicions of race being clothed in a cultural dress because of the purported distinction between Afrikaners and other Afrikaans-speaking persons based on their racial backgrounds. (Afrikaner Declaration 2024)

[16] Note also the concerns expressed by Woldeyes with reference to education language policy in Ethiopia, when he observes that, although English is the language of education, it is not widely spoken at a local and household level; thus educational outcomes are poor and home language is often perceived as inferior. (Woldeyes 2023, 401)

9.1.7 Advantages of mother-tongue education overlooked?

It is against this historical background that the potential advantages of mother-tongue education as a mechanism to facilitate equality and non-discrimination were 'overlooked' during negotiations. (Malherbe 2004, 20) Regardless of the historical complexities involved, s 29 nevertheless guarantees the right to mother-tongue education, subject to certain limitations. Indeed, I would suggest that s 29 *exceeds* the normative standards set out in international instruments such as the ICCPR, ICESCR, European Convention on Human Rights, and the African Charter concerning mother-tongue education (see below).

While this chapter does not intend to address these historical legacies, it is essential to recognise that one cannot analyse the educational language rights debate in South Africa without considering the historic role and status of the Afrikaans language. (Cameron et al 2022) Cameron et al summarise the complex status of Afrikaans in South Africa as follows:

> Language was both an implement of subordination and a marker of racial humiliation. Afrikaans became damagingly and deeply linked to white supremacism and the enduring injuries of exclusion and deprivation. (Cameron et al 2022, 265)

The historic status of a dominant language or the language of an oppressor has also been relevant in central and eastern Europe, where, as discussed below, the use of Russian during the era of Communism for the purpose of the 'Russification' of societies in central and eastern Europe has been considered by the ECtHR as a pertinent factor justifying the introduction of new, non-Russian national languages in various states to replace Russian. (Palermo and Constantin 2021) While Russian remains widely spoken in central and eastern Europe, several legal initiatives have been undertaken to replace Russian with local languages. In case law discussed below concerning eastern European countries, several efforts to remove or restrict Russian as a language of education have been upheld regardless of the large number of persons still speaking Russian. This highlights the complexity of dealing with a language that, on the one hand, is widely spoken, but on the other hand symbolises a previously oppressive system.

While Cameron et al described a widely-held perception of Afrikaans as principally a language spoken by white persons, the Constitutional Court in the UNISA case adopted an arguably more balanced historical assessment of Afrikaans. The court recognised that the history of the Afrikaans language is more complex and, most importantly, more representative of contributions from different races than is often acknowledged. The court observed that, viewed historically, Afrikaans is not a language of only white persons. In fact, some of the most disadvantaged people in the provinces of Western Cape and Northern Cape are Afrikaans-speaking. The court provided a very useful overview of the history and development of Afrikaans, noting as follows:

> The history of Afrikaans is multi-faceted. The establishment and existence of the language cannot be attributed to a single race. Afrikaans speakers were of different languages, races, nationalities and social classes. This black history teaches us that Afrikaans is more than just the language of racists, oppressors and unreconstructed nationalists, but instead that it bears the imprint of a fierce tradition of anti-imperialism, anticolonialism, of an all-embracing humanism and anti-apartheid activism. Afrikaans evolved mainly from Dutch, Malay, Portuguese, Khoi languages, and Arabic-Afrikaans. (emphasis added) (UNISA case 2021, para 21)

Historically, state funding for mother-tongue education had never been guaranteed in South Africa. Since 1996 the state has principally, though not exclusively, opted to fund English-language teaching as the most affordable common denominator to serve the largest cohort of students.[17] Public demand often favours English-language teaching because of its international and commercial status.[18] While the move towards English teaching is economically understandable, culturally

---

[17] The then national Minister of Education, Angie Motshekga, acknowledged in 2022 that the emphasis on English-language education since 1996 has worked to the detriment of students, that educational standards were below expectation, and that greater emphasis must in the future be placed on state funding of mother-tongue education. The Minister said: 'The bottom line is that we need to adopt mother-tongue instruction in South Africa.' (Motshekga 2023b) This statement reflects the views of UNICEF that to improve educational standards in South Africa a greater emphasis on mother-tongue education is needed. The UNICEF report concludes critically that the '*rush to English* in lower grades only widens the learning gap, since it further decreases the child's learning time in a language he or she speaks'. (emphasis added) (UNICEF South Africa 2016) However, it is also important to note that many parents, particularly black parents, elect to send their children to schools where English is the primary language of instruction. Furthermore, even in those instances where an African language is offered, the language or dialect in question is not necessarily the mother language or dialect of the child attending the class.

[18] De Wet and Niemann made the following observation, soon after the enactment of the 1996 Constitution, regarding the apparent dichotomy between the educational merits of mother-tongue instruction and the preference of many parents for their children to be educated in English even though it is not their home language:

> From the research it becomes clear that the majority of educational staff and academics are in favour of mother-tongue education and the development of IALs as MOI. The language demographics, however, reflect that the majority of learners and/or their parents prefer education through the medium of a foreign language (English). At the core of this discrepancy is the fact that the educated elite's (academics and educational staff) language preferences may be based on sound educational principles, while bread-and-butter issues

and educationally it is not necessarily in the best interest of children. Meanwhile, for those who can afford it in the Afrikaans community, privatised education is increasingly become the preferred option in what has been termed a form of 'functional autonomy', or what I have referred to as 'self-do' self-determination. (De Villiers 2023c, 362–7)

Although the educational value of mother-tongue education is widely accepted,[19] it is also relevant to consider the converse: children principally taught only in their mother tongue in a linguistically diverse society may lack the social abilities and skills needed to integrate into a broader multilingual society if they are not literate in the dominant or majority language.[20] This notion is exemplified in some of the judgments of the ECtHR regarding the introduction of a single national language to the exclusion of Russian. In these cases, of which some are discussed below, the court acknowledges that achieving the benefits associated with having a common language is a valid and reasonable objective of a state, and proportionate to the aim of building national unity, regardless of the presence of other minority languages.[21]

---

and old political feuds dictate the preferences of the masses and the student-teachers. (De Wet and Niemann 1999, 92)

[19] Note, for example, how the UN Committee on the Elimination of Discrimination 'welcomed' the commitment by Botswana to expand mother-tongue education to all primary school children. (Mackay 2022, 31)

[20] Note in this regard how within the European context in general, but particularly in countries such as the Netherlands, Belgium and Germany, English is taught from a young age as a second language. Moreover, in many respects English has become the scientific language of choice for international cooperation and publication. Furthermore, there are proposals under way to introduce English as a commercial language in the context of litigation in Germany. This would arguably enable German commercial courts to conduct their proceedings in English. (Glucroft 2023)

[21] Note, for example, the discussion by Maziwisa on the difficulty for government departments in South Africa at all levels to deal with the purportedly equal status of the 12 official languages. In practice English is becoming the most commonly used language in governance and administration, albeit not the most widely spoken language among households. (Maziwisa 2022, 15) It is not unusual for parents and students to choose English-language instruction for their children, while simultaneously continuing to use their mother tongue as a spoken language. Moseneke DCJ has questioned the assumption that teaching in English is the obvious pathway to better education. (Head of Department, Mpumalanga Department of Education case 2010) In fact, the empirical evidence suggests that the emphasis on English-language instruction 'has not served South African learners well'. (Woolman and Fleisch 2014, 157) In reality the use of language in schools involves many layers and nuances. There is 'no easy algorithm' to determine the language options available for any school. (Woolman and Fleisch 2014, 160)

9.1.8 Chapter outline

This chapter reflects on the constitution-drafting process concerning mother-tongue education, the development of international human rights instruments and standards in response to demands for mother-tongue education, and the manner in which jurisprudence in South Africa has addressed s 29 of the Constitution.[22] As explained in Chapters 3 and 4, the courts are empowered to consider international law when interpreting the nature and scope of fundamental rights. Additionally, courts may consider developments in foreign case law. South African courts have surprisingly not reflected noticeably on international approaches to mother-tongue education. In many respects they have adopted a black letter approach supported by respect for the exercise of discretions by government educational departments. Consideration of international law and selected foreign cases may have assisted courts to assess South African jurisprudence in the mother-tongue education debate. Likewise, the approaches adopted by South African courts may contribute to the development of international case law. Courts across the world are increasingly receptive to foreign municipal judgments and developments in international law – a concept referred to as '*Volkerrechtfreundlich*' (international-law-friendly) by German theorists – demonstrating an element of reciprocity in jurisprudence.

9.2 CONSTITUTIONAL DEBATES ABOUT THE 'RIGHT' TO MOTHER-TONGUE EDUCATION

The topic of language of education in South Africa has historically been informed by a variety of factors such as colonisation, ideology, politics, practical considerations and power, rather than being guided primarily by fundamental

[22] At the time of finalising this part (March 2025) no litigation had been commenced pursuant to the BELA Act. The BELA Act seeks to provide greater power of oversight to provincial educational authorities over the language of instruction adopted by a public school. President Cyril Ramaphosa signed the Basic Education Laws Amendment (BELA) Bill into law on 13 September 2024. (BELA Act 2024) Sections 4 and 5 were not made operational at the time, but those have since become operational. These two sections require school governance bodies to submit their language policy to the relevant government department for approval. In setting a language policy a board is required to take into consideration the language interests of the broader community. Regardless of the outcome of these amendments the case law discussed in this chapter remains relevant for purposes of the discussion about mother-tongue education. Veriava is of the view that the BELA Act is needed to effect transformation of educational services since school boards have 'continued to maintain patterns of apartheid spatial geography' and those must be removed. (Veriava 2024, 158)

rights and the best interests of the child. Prior to 1993 there had never been a 'right' to education, nor a right to mother-tongue education. In that period the principal languages of teaching in public schools were Afrikaans and English, while African languages were mainly used for teaching at early primary school levels, particularly in rural 'homeland' areas. The common contemporary practice in South Africa is to use local African languages through to around Grade 3, with a transition to English around Grade 4. This is a practice also widely followed in Africa. (UNICEF South Africa 2016)

9.2.1 1993 Constitution

The 1993 Constitution sought to elevate the nine principal African spoken languages to the same official status as Afrikaans and English. Additionally, it took the first step in eradicating both discrimination against individuals based on the language they speak and the differential treatment of languages. (Constitution 1993, s 3) However, it was obvious during the drafting of the Constitution that while 11 languages (sign language was added later as an official language) could be equal in legal status, in practice there would inevitably be a first among equals. The irony recognised at the time of drafting was that the more languages were declared as 'official', the less likely it was that they would receive equal treatment in practice, and the higher the likelihood that English would dominate as the common denominator language. Cynics may conclude that this was a premeditated agenda, while others might argue that it was simply an outcome of pragmatism informed by limited resources.

Within the legal setting of equality among the official languages introduced by the 1993 Constitution the reality was that it would be impossible to treat all the languages as equal, both in practice and substance, for the purposes of general administration and especially in education. In the words of Heugh, the purported equality of the languages was a 'momentary illusion'. (Heugh 1999, 67)

It is particularly in the field of education that the limited resources of the state must be used to achieve the greatest possible outcome. This implies that language funding in education inevitably must be structured in a manner that brings about the greatest benefit for the widest section of the community. It is a simple matter of economics and pragmatism. The 1993 and 1996 Constitutions therefore contained a built-in stress fracture – the struggle between funding of language *diversity* based on mother-tongue education versus the funding of *equality* and accessibility of teaching to the largest possible community of children, even if it meant teaching them in their second or third language – which generally is English.

While the practical rationale for this approach adopted by the Constitution may be reasonable, the poor education outcomes achieved since its enactment reflect the reality that students are often taught in a language that is not their first, or even second, choice. This in turn impacts on the support they receive at home in their learning. For example, it has been found that children at year 3 level 'whose home language is not English found it particularly difficult to write a sentence in English' (Spaull 2016, 16), which puts them at least a year, or even two years, behind the required level.[23]

In policy terms the limited state resources have led to an increase in funding for education in the English language. This skewed funding allocation has not been viewed as discrimination against other official languages. The South African courts have generally endorsed government educational policy, with the emphasis being on equality and non-discrimination rather than funding of diversity and respect for cultural rights, even if this meant that the predominant language of teaching gravitates towards English.[24] It is worth noting, however, that in contrast to South Africa the courts in India have adopted a more critical approach to efforts by governments to limit or reduce the scope of availability of state-supported mother-tongue teaching. As shown below, the Indian courts have taken greater account of the importance of mother-tongue education than their South African counterparts.

The question arises whether the South African courts, in their transformative capacity, have adequately considered the importance of mother-tongue education to realise individual rights, eradicate poverty, recognise dignity and facilitate

---

[23] It is acknowledged that language proficiency is not the only factor contributing to delayed educational development. Other environmental factors such as class size, teaching environment, social circumstances, training of teachers and the home circumstances of a child also impact educational progress. For example, in 2023 it was estimated that around 86% of state schools did not have a laboratory and 1 800 schools did not have a library. (Le Cordeur 2023, 22) Berger proposed in 2003 that the Constitutional Court declare the current 'education system as unconstitutional' owing to the failure to allocate adequate resources for the eradication of inequality. (Berger 2003, 615) The courts have effectively acknowledged and focused on the impact of past injustices in providing education. However, the courts have been reluctant to critically analyse the impact of ongoing poor administration and corruption on the provision of education in general, as well as the lack of resources to support education in official languages other than English.

[24] The challenges faced by the South African education system are likened by Chürr to the folktale about a tree-climbing competition in Animal Land between a leopard, an elephant, a tortoise and a monkey. Some of the competitors could not even succeed in reaching the lowest limbs of the tree, while others excelled in scaling it. This highlights the failure to take into account different aptitudes, skills and talents. (Chürr 2015, 2439)

equality.[25] Note in this respect the Fosen case in Norway, where the court read the individual right to enjoy culture of a member of an indigenous community in the context of the right being exercised by the entire community to maintain their customs and identity. (Fosen case 2021)[26] Figone expresses the concern that the emphasis on English as the *de facto* preferred language of teaching has ironically prejudiced children whose mother tongue is an African language, in turn perpetuating their inequality. She concludes:

> One manifestation of this inequality is language, and especially the role of language in education. As indigenous African languages have been suppressed by English hegemony in public education, many indigenous African language-speakers have been thwarted in their efforts to succeed in school. (Figone 2012, 79)

Prinsloo also observes that the lack of funding for mother-tongue education is producing socio-economic consequences, including an unskilled workforce, low levels of functional literacy and poor productivity. (Prinsloo 2009, 29)

The approach adopted by government to the languages of education, which has generally been endorsed by the courts, is open to criticism – legally, socially, economically and educationally.

While the 1993 Constitution recognised the importance of state-supported mother-tongue education, it did so within the limits of what was considered 'reasonably practicable'. (Constitution 1993, s 32*(b)*) The education clause in the 1993 Constitution was silent about state funding of mother-tongue education, neither mandating nor precluding it. The Constitution allowed for the establishment of self-funded educational facilities by language communities, provided these facilities did not discriminate on the basis of race. (Gauteng Education Bill case

[25] Note, for example, how Cameron et al observe that in its approach to identity rights the Constitutional Court has 'trodden warily, but not so in its approach to Afrikaans as medium of instruction and place names where the court has "barged right in"'. (Cameron et al 2022, 263) This observation is perhaps reflected in the statement of Jafta J that 'cultural traditions rooted in the past' cannot be recognised under the Constitution. (City of Tshwane case 2016, para 174) This reflects in turn the strong anti-Russian approach prevailing in some of the central and eastern European countries against the teaching of language of the oppressor. One can of course ask which language, especially English, is not potentially tainted by its past. Noteworthy is Majiedt J, who observes that Afrikaans in itself is a rainbow language with more black people than white people speaking it. (UNISA case 2021, para 21)

[26] This approach reflects the Kichwa case, in which it was held that the right to a cultural identity is a fundamental and collective right of indigenous communities and must be respected in a multicultural, pluralistic and democratic society. (Kichwa case 2012, para 217) The same principle arguably applies to ethnocultural communities.

1996) Pursuant to the 1993 Constitution, the state had the inherent power to grant funding to private educational institutions, but there was no legal obligation for it to do so. (Malherbe 1995) These provisions at the time of drafting of the Constitution (Dlamini 1994, 591) reflected the status of international law. (de Varennes 2008) But not much came from the plurality of the population in the provision of education. Heugh observed in 1999 that what was hoped to be a 'vibrant and linguistically diverse' educational arrangement reflecting the diversity of the country had turned out to be 'disappointing'. (Heugh 1999, 70)

South Africa was not unique in seeking to respond to challenges related to mother-tongue education during the Constitution-drafting process. De Varennes, who later became special rapporteur of the United Nations on the rights of minorities, stated in 2008 as follows: 'It was never intended in international law that the right to education include the right to education in one's own language.' (de Varennes 2008, 133) In 2023 the European Court of Human Rights also observed that 'the principle of instruction in one's mother tongue is far from being the rule among the member States [of the Council of Europe]'. (Valiullina case 2023, para 210) Nonetheless, Zmyvalova highlights, by reference to international binding and non-binding instruments, that, although there may not be a justiciable right to mother-tongue education, there do exist strong encouragements, recommendations, and soft-law provisions in favour of it. (Zmyvalova 2024)

9.2.2 Constitutional Principles

The Constitutional Principles enshrined in the 1993 Constitution (Chapter 3) included some general principles related to language rights. For example, the diversity of language was acknowledged, protected and encouraged[27] (Constitutional Principle XI), and the formation of linguistic associations was recognised and safeguarded[28] (Constitutional Principle XII). However, the Constitutional Principles did not prescribe a right to mother-tongue education, be it state or privately funded.

One can only speculate why the Constitutional Principles did not contain greater detail about such a sensitive and important topic as mother-tongue education. I would suggest the following as possible reasons: (i) the Constitutional Principles by

---

[27] Constitutional Principle XI: 'The diversity of language and culture shall be acknowledged and protected, and conditions for their promotion shall be encouraged.'

[28] Constitutional Principle XII: 'Collective rights of self-determination in forming, joining and maintaining organs of civil society, including linguistic, cultural and religious associations, shall, on the basis of non-discrimination and free association, be recognised and protected.'

their nature only dealt with general design requirements of a future Constitution and did not enter the fray of specifics about the content of the Bill of Rights or any other details; (ii) there was an assumption that the scope of rights pertaining to education in the final Constitution would not be dissimilar to that in the interim Constitution, and thus the possibility of discretionary state-funded mother-tongue education and self-funded private education would be retained in the 1996 Constitution; (iii) the emphasis in the Constitutional Principles was principally on political participatory rights and the general design of institutions, rather than on details concerning the content of individual rights; (iv) the constitutional debates were principally rights-driven and did not consider in any depth the potential of mother-tongue education to serve the best interests of children and contribute to substantive equality; and (v) various concessions had to be made by all sides in areas such as power sharing, decentralisation, three-tier government, community rights, property rights and indigenous rights. The Constitutional Principles in essence reflected the level of detail on which parties were able to reach agreement. Realistically one should acknowledge that no sensible constitution can guarantee mother-tongue public teaching in a country with at least 11 major languages without limiting the right by way of considerations such as practicality, financial affordability and availability of resources.

9.2.3 1996 Constitution

The 1996 Constitution retained the approach adopted by its 1993 predecessor by recognising the right to education. It also acknowledged the opportunity for state-funded mother-tongue education where it is 'reasonably practicable' and recognised that the state was obliged to adopt policies that address 'past racially discriminatory laws and practices' (Constitution of South Africa 1996, s 29) Importantly, the right to self-funded educational institutions is recognised, provided such institutions do not discriminate on grounds of race and they are subject to the general limitation clause. (Constitution of South Africa 1996, s 29(3))

The point is often lost that securing a right to publicly and privately funded mother-tongue education was a major breakthrough (or concession, depending on how it is viewed) and *exceeded* the standards set at the time by international law.

9.2.4 Certification cases

In the Certification cases the Constitutional Court observed that only two objections had been received to the proposed s 29 of the new Constitution, which dealt with education rights. This paucity of substantive objections underlines the extent of the agreement regarding this section at the time of negotiations. The court noted that neither of the two objections explained in any level of detail the reasoning behind it (Certification case 1996, para 79), thus declaring that no Constitutional Principle had been breached by the text of s 29. It observed as follows:

> In any event, the various factors set out in New Text 29(2)(a) to (c) are the basis on which the state is directed to take positive action to implement the right to receive education in the official language or languages of choice; they impose a positive duty on the state which does not exist under the Interim Constitution. (emphasis added) (Certification case 1996, para 81)

Section 29(2) provides, in essence, that a child is entitled to receive education in an official language in a publicly funded institution subject to what is deemed 'reasonably practicable'. Ultimately, it falls to the courts to determine whether the state has failed to meet the constitutional standard of 'reasonably practicable' in each situation. This question is answered by referring to all relevant information, including the number of students demanding the service, availability of funds, suitability of facilities, access to alternative venues and presence of adequately trained teaching staff. Meanwhile, when considering educational alternatives, broader societal issues must also be taken into account, such as the need to achieve equity and redress the results of past racially discriminatory laws and practices. (Chürr 2013, 295)

It is worth noting that, in the context of the prevailing debates in international law at the time of the negotiations, the 1993 and 1996 Constitutions reflected *and improved* on international law standards concerning the right to mother-tongue education. The interim and final Constitutions were consistent with provisions found in other constitutions dealing with educational rights, such as ss 21A and 30 of the Constitution of India. Furthermore, there was never any likelihood, in a political, legal and financial sense, of a constitutional guarantee being inserted into the new Constitution that would legally obligate the state to fund single-medium mother-tongue education without any qualification.

The inclusion of s 29 in the Constitution, which took place only at the end of negotiations having been seen as a potentially 'insurmountable' hurdle, was regarded as the outcome of a 'hard fought battle'. (Malherbe 2004, 12)

9.2.5 Section 29 in the international context

Section 29 advanced the right to mother-tongue education, but in its practical operation and transformative potential, as well as in the philosophy espoused by the courts, the section may not yet have reached its full potential. Contrary to what may have been suggested by critics, s 29 of the Constitution, particularly in its reference to the right to education in an official language, moved beyond international norms in the sense that education in an official language is recognised in the Constitution as a justiciable right unless there is an 'objective justification' for its restriction. (Gauteng Education Bill case 1996, para 41) However, in its practical operation economic realities have taken precedence over language diversity considerations. The economic reality has clearly trumped the cultural and linguistic benefits of mother-tongue teaching. This notwithstanding, s 29 at worst complies or at best exceeds the provisions of international law, as international instruments do not recognise the right to mother-tongue education, particularly in publicly funded educational institutions. Nevertheless, the operation of the right to education in an official language in South Africa has inevitably been shaped by ideology, politics, history, policy measures, resource allocation and pragmatism.

The 1996 Constitution of South Africa is advanced in its recognition of *individual* cultural, linguistic and educational rights (e.g. Constitution of South Africa 1996, ss 29(2); 30; 31), as well as *collective* self-determination rights for cultural and linguistic communities.[29] These collective rights include the possibility for communities (encompassing indigenous communities) to establish cultural councils and pursue self-determination. (Constitution of South Africa 1996, ss 185; 235; De Villiers 2018a) Section 29(2) of the Constitution guarantees the right to education in an official language provided it is reasonably practicable. While there is a legal duty on the state, the practical discharge of this duty depends on factors such as feasibility, affordability and practicality. At a practical level the government's ability to fund and assist with the realisation of these collective rights is limited by various factors. These include: a scarcity of resources;

[29] The Constitution of South Africa uses the term 'community' rather than the term 'minority'. In doing so it attempts to avert the debate about the definition of a minority that has for so long preoccupied international and public law. (Chapter 4) However, the use of a different word to describe a minority has not substantially resolved the definitional issues; instead, it has given rise to the question of who is a community since the Constitution does not define the term. (De Villiers 2020c)

the apartheid history of the country, which has resulted in resistance to the promotion or funding of state-funded separate ethnocultural identities; the overwhelming need for basic educational services for the poor and marginalised; and demands for equality in areas such as education, housing and primary health. (De Villiers 2023c, 315) This juxtaposition highlights the tension between the progressive text of the Constitution, including the recognition of population pluralism, and the complex realities of South Africa's historical context, its status as a developing economy, resource constraints, struggles and failures in state-provided service delivery, and the overwhelming government priority of *funding of equality before funding of diversity*. Underlying these complexities is government corruption and ineptitude, which have seen the building of new schools fall way behind population growth. The irony, as pointed out by UNICEF, is that one of the most urgent and effective ways to address the inequality endured by disadvantaged communities is through state-funded mother-tongue education for the children of such communities. (UNICEF South Africa 2016)

9.2.6 State support pursuant to art 27 of the ICCPR

An essential question arising from s 29 of the Constitution is whether there is an obligation on the state to actively support and fund the provision of teaching in one of the official languages. In this regard it may be useful to reflect on the provisions of art 27 of the ICCPR, which places an obligation on the state not to deny ethnocultural communities the right to enjoy and practise their culture.

It remains a live policy issue for ethnocultural and indigenous communities in South Africa to ascertain to what extent, if any, the state is constitutionally obliged to support individuals with the protection and promotion of their culture, religion, traditions or language. As illustrated below by jurisprudence arising from India, there are often discretionary considerations involved to decide the language of instruction at a particular school and the exercise of such a discretion is justiciable. Even without an absolute guarantee for mother-tongue education the provisions of the South African Constitution offer a basis for language communities to argue that legislative allocation and administrative discretion in funding must consider not only financial aspects but also identity rights such as the right to use language, to practise culture, and to accomplish self-determination. The transformative nature of the Constitution arguably includes consideration of how legislative and administrative measures can promote and protect identity rights, including the promotion of education in an official language.

The following question of principle underlying art 27 of the ICCPR[30] presents itself in South Africa: What obligation, if any, rests on the state to take active steps to assist and fund individuals in order to protect and promote their language and culture? (Taylor 2020)

Ethnocultural and indigenous communities often find themselves in a situation where they are too poor and marginalised to privately fund activities and initiatives aimed at preserving their culture, language and traditions. Meanwhile, financially privileged individuals, typically more mobile, can pay their way to an education of their choice. In a country like South Africa, where marginalisation encompasses both racial and linguistic dimensions, educating children in an official language is essential to raise educational standards and foster a sense of self-worth and equality. Education in mother tongue is also an essential element of the rights to culture, language and community. At the same time, proficiency in a widely used language such as English, beyond one's mother tongue, offers benefits for social integration, employment opportunities, nation-building and enhanced mobility.

Any language policy in South Africa must therefore acknowledge the importance of preserving one's own identity through mother tongue while also embracing a shared identity for the collective good.

Article 27 of the ICCPR has been the subject of extensive literature and diverse opinions regarding the state's role in tolerating or promoting cultural diversity. (ICCPR 1966) It is widely accepted that art 27 does not legally obligate the state to provide funding and support to minorities in their collective capacity to exercise and enjoy their rights as a community. (Taylor 2020) Article 27, as explained by Sachs J, protects the rights of individuals belonging to ethnic, religious and linguistic minorities within a country to enjoy their own culture, practise their own religion and use their own language, but it places no legal obligation on the state to fund or actively support such activities or to recognise collective rights. (Gauteng Education Bill case 1996, para 62) While this analysis by Sachs J of art 27 is correct, the South African Constitution goes beyond the scope of art 27 by the recognition it gives in s 29 of the Constitution to the right to education in any of the official languages.

[30] 'In those States in which ethnic, religious or linguistic minorities exist, persons belonging to such minorities shall not be denied the right, in community with the other members of their group, to enjoy their own culture, to profess and practise their own religion, or to use their own language.'

Although the state is not legally obligated pursuant to art 27 of the ICCPR to assist or support minorities, any support it provides must be implemented without discriminating against individuals from different communities. (Waldman case 1996) Furthermore, the right to culture in the ICCPR and the Bill of Rights in South Africa potentially has a collective element since an individual can only effectively enjoy culture in association with other individuals who share the same culture. Note in this respect the Fosen case in Norway, where the court held that the individual right of a member of an indigenous community to enjoy culture must be read *in the context* of the right being exercised by other members of the community to maintain their customs and identity. (Fosen case 2021) The Fosen case highlights the ongoing development of understandings of individual identity rights *within* the context of some rights only coming to true fruition when exercised in association with others of the same community. The Fosen approach reflects the Kichwa case in South America, in which it was held that the right to a cultural identity is a fundamental and collective right of indigenous communities and must be respected in a multicultural, pluralistic and democratic society. (Kichwa case 2012, para 217) In this content the Daniel Billy case is also notable, where the UN Human Rights Committee for the first time declared that a state (Australia) had violated its obligations under art 27 of the ICCPR by its failure to ensure that members of an indigenous community could enjoy their culture because of the impacts of climate change. (Daniel Billy case 2022) [31]

Article 27 of the ICCPR and s 29 of the Constitution do not explicitly recognise a collective right, but leave open the possibility for effect to be given to exercising an individual right, considering that the right only comes to fruition when exercised with other individuals of the same community. This approach was also evident in the drafting of the European Framework Convention for the Protection of National Minorities (FCNM), in which justiciable rights are

---

[31] The Committee found that 'the climate impacts mentioned by the authors represent a threat that could have reasonably been foreseen by the State party' and that the failure to take adequate steps amounted to a breach of art 27. (Daniel Billy case 2022, para 8.14) This finding compelled the government to take mitigating steps to reduce the impacts of climate change on the community. However, specific remedial actions and budget allocations were not prescribed, nor was a time frame within which specific orders had to be met. A similar argument to that outlined above could be made regarding the importance of mother-tongue education in the context of the right to culture, namely, that the state has neglected its obligations, pursuant to art 27 of the ICCPR and s 29 of the Constitution, by not allocating adequate support for education in an official language.

conferred upon individuals rather than language communities. Thus governments cannot be legally obligated to fund specific linguistic or cultural activities of individuals or communities. (Hofmann, Malloy, and Rein 2018c)

While it is correct to state that governments cannot be obligated to fund collective activities of communities, it is open for courts to find that government, in its funding discretion, ought to have considered the collective nature of an individual right since certain rights only come to fruition if exercised with others. In short: the education, culture and religious rights in the South African Constitution ought to be interpreted within the context of the importance attached by the Constitutional Assembly to the protection and promotion of the ethnocultural and indigenous diversity of South Africa.

A distinction must be drawn between the state's inability to *fund* identity rights and the potential *discrimination* against a language community. The absence of funding does not, in itself, constitute discrimination. In the Nkosi case the Constitutional Court determined that it was justifiable to discriminate based on the requirement for students to accept education in English for admission purposes. However, the different status accorded in the same school to Afrikaans and isiZulu was deemed unjustified discrimination. (Nkosi case 2008) In the UNISA case the court emphasised that the university's decision to downgrade Afrikaans as a language of instruction, despite its previous use in certain subjects, was discriminatory and unconstitutional. (UNISA case 2021) The case focused on UNISA's decision to discontinue university courses that had previously been offered in Afrikaans. The court found in essence that the university's decision to stop using Afrikaans as a teaching language lacked factual support. It noted that there was still significant demand for teaching in the Afrikaans language at the time the decision was made to downgrade it. (UNISA case 2021, para 77) The court declared that, while it cannot compel a university to offer a course in a specific language, it can intervene to prevent a university from discontinuing teaching in a particular language if such action is deemed discriminatory.

The debate about state funding – or lack thereof – of ethnocultural and indigenous communities resonates not only in South Africa, but also in international law and in the constitutional law of many countries. (Molos 2013) For example, in the context of the FCNM Roter makes the following pertinent observation about the importance of state funding for identity rights in the European context:

> Sufficient funds are of the utmost importance to enable persons belonging to national minorities to be able to maintain, protect and develop their culture and identity. . . .

> Whereas private resources can be used to achieve the aims of Article 5,[32] private donors cannot and should not replace the state, which has a primary duty to create the necessary conditions for the preservation and development of the cultural heritage of persons belonging to national minorities. (Roter 2018, 134)

9.2.7 Trend since 1996

In the South African context the following trend in jurisprudence under the 1996 Constitution has been evident: while the identity rights of individuals are acknowledged as essential to recognise, protect and promote the plural tapestry of ethnocultural identities in South Africa, the primary focus of the state when allocating resources for education should be on eradicating inequality, combating discrimination and reducing poverty to ensure substantive equality for individuals. One practical outcome of this trend is that teaching in English has increased at all levels.

The rationale underlying this trend is principally informed by pragmatism: English, as the most widely used language despite not being the most spoken at home, is seen as best suited to help uplift children out of poverty in light of the scarce resources available to the state. While single-medium education in a mother tongue such as Afrikaans is permitted by the Constitution, the prevailing funding trend is not in its favour. The predominant emphasis, driven by practical but also perhaps ideological considerations, is on English as the preferred medium of instruction. However, this policy also reveals a weakness, as educating children, particularly at the primary level, in a language other than their own may not be the most effective method for addressing inequality. It is thus perhaps not surprising that severe inequality in educational performance persists three decades since the 1996 Constitution came into effect. (Sayed et al 2020, 9) This lingering inequality is admittedly not solely attributable to the government's focus on English-language instruction but also stems from various other factors, including resource scarcity, inefficiencies, corruption,

[32] Article 5 of the FCNM: '1 The Parties undertake to promote the conditions necessary for persons belonging to national minorities to maintain and develop their culture, and to preserve the essential elements of their identity, namely their religion, language, traditions and cultural heritage. 2 Without prejudice to measures taken in pursuance of their general integration policy, the Parties shall refrain from policies or practices aimed at assimilation of persons belonging to national minorities against their will and shall protect these persons from any action aimed at such assimilation.'

unequal facilities and misappropriation of funds.[33] What is often referred to as 'state capture' constitutes a vast system of corruption in various forms that have directed state funds away from where they are most needed. (Zondo 2022) It is arguable that corruption and maladministration have significantly eroded the country's capacity to fund essential services, one of which is education.

Identity rights are essentially considered in international law and South African law as passive rights, meaning that the state cannot impede their exercise. However, the state is not constitutionally obligated to fund or actively support the realisation of those rights, albeit the state must create an environment within which the rights can be freely exercised.[34] In contrast, the state is legally obligated to fund, support and promote equality and equal access rights. If a choice is to be made between competing legal provisions that cannot be harmonised, the

[33] It was estimated that in 2023 around 86% of state schools did not have their own laboratory; 239 schools did not have electricity; 2 700 schools did not have effective sewage disposal; 1 800 schools did not have a library; and 10 000 schools had no sports facilities. (Le Cordeur 2023, 22) While the South African state is struggling under the weight of limited resources, it is important to acknowledge the significant impact of serious mismanagement, wastage, corruption, state capture and ineptitude, all of which contribute to poor educational outcomes. For example, in the province of Gauteng students numbers since 2009 had increased by 725 000, but in the past ten years only five new public schools were built. (FEDSAS Teaching in Numbers 2024) Had it not been that private schools constitute 31% of all schools in Gauteng, the crisis in facilities would have been even bigger. It is reasonable to pose the question whether the courts should, in a similar vein to the reasoning laid out in the Grootboom case, demand greater accountability from the state to adhere to the constitutional obligation of education in an official language. The courts have declined, arguably in error, to acknowledge a causal link between the right to education in an official language and the realisation of cultural and self-determination rights.

[34] The question may arise whether the state may be obligated to demonstrate greater commitment to take positive action in the field of mother-tongue education, consistent with precedents such as the Daniel Billy case (Daniel Billy case 2022) and Grootboom case (Grootboom case 2000), in which the duty to take positive steps was emphasised (albeit in the context of housing in Grootboom). Note, for example, the 2011 judgment handed down by the Constitutional Court of Romania in which it was recognised that 'positive measures may be necessary to protect the identity of a minority and the rights of members of that group to enjoy and develop their own culture and language, and practice their religion'. (Romania Constitutional Court case 2011) This statement was made *obiter* and did not specify the nature of such positive measures. These judgments, read in conjunction with judgments in the Indian and Canadian courts, underscore the potential for South African courts to arguably play a more active role to promote teaching in and support for mother-tongue education. Note in this respect the Fosen case in Norway, where the court read the individual right to enjoy culture of a member of an indigenous community *in the context* of the right being exercised by the entire community to maintain their customs and identity. (Fosen case 2021) This approach reflects the Kichwa case, in which it was held that the right to a cultural identity is a fundamental and collective right of indigenous communities and must be respected in a multicultural, pluralistic and democratic society. (Kichwa case 2012, para 217)

emphasis is on prioritising funding for equality rights over funding for identity rights. Mubangizi aptly summarises the challenge as follows:

> Protecting human rights can be a daunting challenge in a country like South Africa where about half of the population is considered poor and the gap between the rich and poor is among the largest in the world. The challenge is aggravated by the fact that South Africa is a society of unprecedented diversity. Such diversity manifests itself in terms of race, colour, gender, language, ethnicity, religion, culture and disability. This challenge also has to be seen against the background of South Africa's unique history, which was characterized by gross violations of human rights, institutionalized racism, denial of access to social and economic resources and political disenfranchisement of the majority. As a result, before 1994, inequality was a defining feature of the South African society and was given expression through a variety of forms that were inconsistent with human rights. (Mubangizi 2008, 131)

The implication of the approach adopted by the courts is that, although the equality rights and identity rights in the Constitution should, as far as possible, be harmoniously interpreted, if an irreconcilable conflict or incompatibility arises, then the equality rights are given precedence within the context of the overall objectives of the Constitution. (Gauteng Education Bill case 1996) In essence the judgment in the Gauteng Education case, as described by Kriegler J, was 'about money' and the affordability of official language educational services in a language other than English. (Gauteng Education Bill case 1996, para 42)[35] Sachs J summarised the interaction between equality and diversity as follows:

> The very first fundamental right to be specified, preceding even the rights to life and dignity, is the right to equality. We are further enjoined to interpret the whole of Chapter 3, including section 32 [of the 1993 Constitution], in a way which promotes the values of an open and democratic society based on freedom and equality. The theme of diversity has markedly less constitutional pungency. . . . Thus, the dominant theme of the Constitution is the achievement of equality, while considerable importance is also given to cultural diversity and language rights, so that the basic problem is to secure equality in a balanced way which shows maximum regard for diversity. (emphasis added) (Gauteng Education Bill case 1996, para 52)

---

[35] The brutal reality of what Kriegler J said was reflected in the events of the week starting 16 December 2024: in that week two momentous events happened that will deeply impact on the Afrikaans community in years to come and both events were caused principally by scarcity of money. The first is that the BELA Act was signed into law, with one of the principal motivators being the provision of education to the widest possible community of children but in the context of limited funding. This is likely to lead to the diminishing of publicly funded Afrikaans single- and dual-medium schools. The second event of the week was the decision of MEDIA24 to close several Afrikaans-language newspapers because of declining profitability. Both events highlight the inescapable reality of financial challenges to funding diversity.

In practice, the approach adopted by the courts implies, as elaborated on in this chapter, that while public funds may be allocated to mother-tongue public education, in cases where resources are limited and children do not have equal access to educational institutions, the available public funds should be prioritised for education in a language in public schools that facilitates the broadest access for, and most equal treatment of, all children. This approach reflects the following statement made by the Constitutional Court in the Hugo case: '[E]quality . . . means nothing if it does not represent a commitment to recognising each person's equal worth as a human being. . . . Equality means that our society cannot tolerate legislative distinctions that treat certain people as second-class citizens . . . or that otherwise offend fundamental human dignity.' (Hugo case 1997, para 41)

Education in an official language is indeed a laudable objective and a justiciable right. However, its scope is constrained by practical considerations, financial affordability, the best interests of the child, principles of equality and non-discrimination.

The practical implication of art 27 of the ICCPR for South Africa is that the predominant language in public schools, particularly secondary schools (and almost exclusively at tertiary levels), is increasingly English, as it serves as the largest common denominator language for children and it is the most affordable approach to allocation of scarce resources. (Mkhize and Balfour 2017) While the rationale adopted in South Africa may have merit, the Indian courts have demonstrated how governments can be held accountable to discharge their constitutional obligations toward minorities by providing funding for mother-tongue teaching, despite facing similar challenges of inequality and resource constraints. (Kerala Education case 1959) The same cannot be said of South African jurisprudence, where the courts have tolerated what Malherbe calls the 'indiscriminate targeting' of Afrikaans-medium public schools. This trend has led many single-medium schools to transition to become dual-medium and ultimately single-medium English schools. (Malherbe 2004, 22)[36] The Canadian courts, meanwhile, have endorsed a sliding scale

[36] The following statistics may lend credibility to Malherbe's statement, but they also highlight the complexity of language policy and the reality faced by non-English-speaking parents in opting for English-language education despite speaking a different language at home: Between 1989 and 2006 the number of schools using English as the language of primary instruction increased from 2 921 to 4 342. In 2018 there were around 1 270 public schools teaching in Afrikaans out of a total of 23 700 public schools. It is estimated that the number of Afrikaans state-funded schools has declined by around 30% since 2002. (De Villiers 2023c, 330) To further complicate

approach to mother-tongue instruction, allowing public facilities to be shared by language communities of the two official languages to maximise resources, but within the context of single-medium parallel teaching. Importantly, this approach does not obligate children to attend schools in a different language from their language of choice. (CSF case 2016) The right also does not apply to other language communities or to indigenous people.

The primary focus of South African courts has not necessarily been to determine the language of instruction that is in the best interests of the child from an educational perspective. Instead, the approach has been more narrowly focused on how to maximise accessibility to education in the most common language for the largest group of students at the most affordable price. An economic rationale, rather than a recognition and encouragement of diversity, therefore characterises South African judgments. This means that, although the 11 official languages of South Africa theoretically have equal status at law, in practice English is effectively the *de facto* first among equals when it comes to the funding of public education at all levels.[37]

---

the educational picture it is worth noting that even in those schools where black children in their formative years receive education in an official African language, the language or dialect in question is not necessarily one they use at home. In 2020 there was a total of 8 096 single-medium schools, the main languages of which were as follows: Afrikaans (1 261); English (6 483); IsiXhosa (163); IsiZulu (31); and isiNdebele (85). (School Language Statistics 2020) The FW De Klerk Foundation critically analysed the trend under s 29, concluding as follows: '[T]he right of Afrikaans-speaking South Africans to education in the language of their choice at university level has been almost extinguished, while their right to education in Afrikaans at school level is under growing threat.' (De Klerk Foundation 2023) It is estimated that out of approximately 23 719 public schools in South Africa, only around 1 900 schools use Afrikaans as the language of instruction in single, dual or parallel mediums. (Motshekga 2023a; FEDSAS Teaching in Numbers 2024 slide 87) Of those, around 985 are single-medium Afrikaans teaching. (FEDSAS Teaching in Numbers 2024 slide 86) It is estimated that between 2021 and 2024 around 17% of Afrikaans single-medium schools had become dual-medium.

[37] The UNISA judgment emphasised, however, that where there is an established demand for and use of the Afrikaans language in the teaching of a course, the university cannot merely downgrade or abolish the teaching of that language for the course. Conversely, the university cannot be obligated to commence courses in a language other than English, or to initiate courses that were not previously offered in Afrikaans. (UNISA case 2021, para 18) This approach, where the language choice of *students* is relevant, does not seem consistent with the funding of public schools, where the interests of the broader *society* must be considered. The broader society test inevitably favours English.

9.3 STANDARDS IN INTERNATIONAL LAW CONCERNING MOTHER-TONGUE EDUCATION

The recognition and protection of the rights of minorities in general, and the right to education in mother tongue in particular, are topics that have attracted attention in international law for a long time.[38] One of the first international instruments to formally recognise the rights of minorities was the Polish Minority Treaty (1919),[39] which provided that minorities, most notably Jewish communities, residing in Poland had the right to establish, manage and control, at their own expense, charitable, religious and social institutions, schools and other

[38] One of the most notable earlier arrangements for minority self-government was enacted during the Ottoman empire (c 13–1923), when the millet system was used to grant to communities, principally religious (Greek Orthodox, Armenians and Jews) but also ethnic (the Kurds also had a Millet (Tas 2013, 168)), a form of self-government whereby they could, within the highly centralised empire, arrange their community and religious affairs consistent with their own traditions, customs and beliefs. The communities did not live separately in a territorial sense and, despite intermingling with the rest of the population, they had their own institutional and autonomy arrangements for aspects of their faith and traditions. (Tamanaha 2021, 37) In contemporary terms this amounted to a form of non-state law pluralism. (Chapter 2) These communities not only self-governed, but also raised taxes from within the community and provided it with social services such as education, family law, dispute resolution, medical treatment and elderly care. (Cakal 2020) The millets had what is nowadays described as a 'non-territorial' jurisdiction focusing on the needs of their members, regardless of their living intermingled with other people. (De Villiers 2022a, 44) Another early instrument of minority protection worth noting is the Edict of Nantes, signed on 30 April 1598, recognising the rights of the Protestant minority in Catholic dominated France. (Sutherland 1987) Additionally, the 1648 Peace of Westphalia, consisting of the Treaty of Münster (signed on 24 October 1648) and the Treaty of Osnabrück (signed on 15 May 1648), which concluded the religion-inspired Thirty Years' War, was particularly focused on the protection of religious (Christian) minorities. (Reus-Smit 2013)

[39] On 28 June 1919 (Fink 1998), 14 countries (Albania, Austria, Bulgaria, Czechoslovakia, Estonia, Greece, Hungary, Iraq, Latvia, Lithuania, Poland, Romania, Turkey and Yugoslavia) adopted similar treaties aimed at the protection of minorities within their national boundaries. These were ad hoc arrangements, primarily driven by concerns about the disruptive potential of unmet minority demands. They often arose from the pressure exerted by kin-states whose citizens resided in other countries. The role of kin-states in promoting the interests of members of their community residing in other countries remains relevant in contemporary society. (Hofmann, Malloy, and Rein 2018a, 21) As seen in European history, the activism of a kin-state may heighten the risk of conflict (the most notable current example being Russia's invasion of Ukraine). In contrast, a minority without a kin-state (for example, the Roma in Europe) may find that their interests are not adequately advocated for or taken seriously. (Undrea, Constantin, and Djordjević 2023) However, there are also many other instances where the foreign policy of states is influenced by the plight of their cultural citizens in other countries. See, for example, the relationship between Turkey and the Turks living in North Macedonia. (Gözübenli 2023)

educational establishments, and the right to use their own language and exercise their religion freely therein.[40] In addition to providing the right to establish privately funded educational institutions, the Polish Treaty also foreshadowed that in local areas where a 'considerable proportion' of the population belonged to minority an 'equitable share' of *public* funds should be allocated for the purpose of their education. (Minority Treaty 1919, art 9)[41] Several other European-based treaties aimed at protecting minorities were also concluded around the time.[42]

The following section provides an overview of the evolution of the right to mother-tongue education since the League of Nations, through to the United Nations and the European Convention on Human Rights. It also includes a few selected case studies from India, Belgium, Canada, Ukraine, Romania and Latvia.

---

[40] Article 8: 'Polish nationals who belong to racial, religious or linguistic minorities shall enjoy the same treatment and security in law and in fact as all other Polish nationals. In particular, they shall have an equal right to establish, manage and control, at their own expense, charitable, religious and social institutions, schools and other educational establishments, with the right to use their own language and to exercise their religion freely therein'.

[41] In general the approach to state funding for schools in South Africa, especially primary schools, also considers the most common language(s) in a local area when determining the language of instruction in the school. However, the situation in South Africa is complicated as language communities often do not reside in their own distinct enclaves but are rather intermingled. Determining language policy in a specific school is often a complex decision, primarily left to the discretion of the local school board. In retrospect, it might have been beneficial to include a clause in the 1996 Constitution to provide greater security for linguistic minorities to ensure that public funding would be available for single-medium mother-tongue education in areas where community members live concentrated and in sufficient numbers (as per the Canadian Charter of Rights (s 23)). However, such a geographical funding approach may have had the unintended consequence of encouraging persons of the same linguistic community to flock together, to the exclusion of others. School governing bodies are responsible for setting the language policy of a school (Mikro Primary School case 2006, para 22), but their functions can be altered by the legislation that created them. (Serfontein and De Waal 2013, 52) This was reflected in the controversy arising from the 2024-enacted BELA Act, which in ss 4 and 5 seeks to restrain the autonomy of school governing bodies to determine the language of education by granting expanded powers to the provincial education minister as final decision-maker about the language of education in a particular school. The minister of education expressed the opinion in the leadup to the legislation that some school governing bodies were encouraging students from a specific language community to attend a particular single-medium school, even if the students did not reside in the local area of the school. This practice was seen to exclude others who would otherwise have attended the school if not for the language policy set by the school governing body.

[42] See, for example, treaties between the Allied and Associated Powers involving Poland (28 June 1919); Serbia, Slovenia and Croatia (10 September 1919); and Greece (10 August 1920).

9.3.1 League of Nations

Established in 1919, the League of Nations faced the challenge to address the implications of new international borders, particularly concerning members of ethnocultural minorities who found themselves residing in states other than their own kin-state. Extensive arrangements were made to recognise population diversity within the respective states, driven by the fear that ignoring diversity could lead to new instability within the broader European context. There was concern that kin-states might interfere in the domestic affairs of another state to protect the interests of their ethnocultural members.[43]

The principal mechanisms employed by the League of Nations to protect minorities included decentralisation, localised minority rights and country-specific autonomy and power-sharing arrangements. (Rosting 1923; Scheu 2020) The minority arrangements primarily focused on the right to practise one's culture, language and religion, as well as the right to speak one's own language. The League was less concerned with designing institutions for self-government or power-sharing purposes. (Åkermark 1927) Furthermore, recognition of minorities was often prompted by the intervention of a kin-state owing to concerns about the security and safety of its cultural citizens residing in another state.[44]

One of the commonly recognised rights was the right to mother-tongue education, generally expected to be self-funded or, in some exceptional cases, supported by a kin-state. In some instances informal obligations rested on states to support minority schools where the concentration of people or the size of

[43] Notably, minorities could bring complaints to the League of Nations, but they did not have standing in the Permanent Court of International Justice. Only sovereign states had such standing, thus obliging them to take up a minority complaint in order for it to be heard. (Lissitzyn 1951)

[44] The interaction between kin-states and states where members of an ethnocultural minority culturally belong to the kin-state remains a challenge in Europe (and beyond). Undrea et al observe as follows: 'In the last two decades, the multiplications and diversification of kin-state actions have challenged the norms and principles regulating the relations between a kin-state and its kin minority groups, exposing the challenges of multilateralism in Europe. It has been shown that the European minority rights regime continues to promote the interests of state actors over those of minorities. Four issues dominate the current political science debates over kin-state – kin minorities relations in Europe: a) the instrumentalisation of kin-state engagement; b) the securitisation of kin minorities; c) the externalisation of kin-state citizenship; and d) the impact on the accommodation of kin minority groups as national minorities in their home states.' (Undrea, Constantin, and Djordjević 2023, 18) Also note how in light of the ongoing Ukraine–Russian conflict, the status of Russians in other parts of Europe has given rise to security concerns in the context of minority rights, including teaching in the Russian language. (Csergő, Kallas, and Kiss 2025)

the group justified it.[45] Other techniques of decentralisation on a territorial and non-territorial basis were also used to accommodate minority rights through self-governing arrangements, whereby minorities were granted various forms of autonomy to self-administer their cultural, linguistic and religious affairs. (Ermacora 1983; De Villiers 1989)

The status of the minority arrangements under the auspices of the League of Nations essentially required an adequate system for minority protection to rest on two pillars: first, non-discrimination and equal protection of members of the relevant minority; secondly, the recognition of special collective minority rights in certain instances (the content of which was determined on a state-by-state basis), such as mother-tongue education. The League of Nations is often regarded, as articulated by Sachs J, as the 'effective beginning' of the international protection of human rights. (Gauteng Education Bill case 1996, para 56)

In the Albania case the Permanent Court of International Justice declared that the right of an ethnocultural community to establish and manage its own schools is '*indispensable* to enable the minority to enjoy the same treatment as the majority, not only in law but also in fact'. (emphasis added) (Albania case 1935, para 67) However, the court did not mandate state funding for community schools. (Albania case 1935, para 79) As to the funding of educational facilities, the court declared as follows:

> Albanian nationals belonging to racial, linguistic or religious minorities [had] the right to maintain, manage and control at their own expense or to establish in the future charitable, religious and social institutions, schools and other educational establishments, with the right to use their own language and to exercise their religion freely therein. (emphasis added) (Albania case 1935 para 79)

9.3.2 United Nations

Since its inception the United Nations has sought to place emphasis on the protection of individual rather than collective rights.[46] The UN initially focused on what were

[45] Refer, for example, to art 9 of the Polish Minority Treaty, which provided as follows: 'Poland will provide in the public educational system in towns and districts in which a considerable proportion of Polish nationals of other than Polish speech are residents adequate facilities for ensuring that in the primary schools the instruction shall be given to the children of such Polish nationals through the medium of their own language.'

[46] According to Sachs J, the 'main trend after World War II was to eliminate the concept of minorities rather than to protect them'. (Gauteng Education Bill case 1996, para 59) The word 'eliminate' is arguably too strong and possibly reflects an ideological bias. The thought at the

regarded as 'first-generation' or 'passive' rights, whereby the state was prevented from interfering in the lives of individuals. Consistent with this approach, the state was not primarily seen as an enabler of rights, but rather as a power that needed to be constrained to protect individuals' rights to freely exercise their fundamental freedoms. Meanwhile, so-called second- and third-generation rights were seen as programmatic in nature, requiring active government involvement to be realised. Over time the purported distinction between first-, second- and third-generation rights has lost credibility, with rights being regarded as having the same status and to be interpreted harmoniously (Moosa 2002, 39). However, it is worth noting that some constitutions, such as Botswana's, have chosen not to include 'socio-economic rights',[47] thereby suggesting an ongoing distinction between the different categories of rights. (Dinokopila and Kgoboge 2021, 342)

The principles of non-discrimination and equal treatment of individuals form the backbone of the United Nations human rights regime. Article 26 of the Universal Declaration of Human Rights recognises the right to education, but does not impose a justiciable obligation on the state to provide education or to fund mother tongue instruction. The International Covenant of Economic, Social and Cultural Rights (ICESCR) also recognises the fundamental right to education but, likewise, makes no mention of any obligation on the state to fund mother-tongue instruction. (ICESCR 1966, art 13)[48] The same applies to the International Convention on the Rights of the Child (1989), which recognises the importance of education, but is silent on mother-tongue instruction other than to acknowledge that a child shall not be denied the right enjoy his or her

---

time was that minority rights could best be protected by means of individual rights, but the suggestion that collective rights were being eliminated is excessive. This is illustrated by the UNDRIP recognising the collective rights of indigenous minorities, and the United Nations, through the Declaration on the Rights of Persons Belonging to National or Ethnic, Religious and National Minorities, actively encouraging and supporting various forms of ethnocultural protection arrangements as part of democratisation. (UN Declaration on Minorities 1992) As discussed in Chapter 3, the United Nations has also been instrumental and supportive of various minority-institutional arrangements in emerging democracies. The relevance of ethnocultural minorities is far from having been 'eliminated'.

[47] The following was declared in Botswana: 'It is generally accepted, particularly in developing countries, that the courts have no role to play in dictating to the Executive or to the Legislature on issues of policy or on budgetary matters involving the use or distribution of public funds . . . This is particularly so in a Constitution such as ours which does not provide for judicially enforceable socio-economic rights . . . '. (Tapela case 2015, para 69)

[48] Sachs J refers to the ICCPR in general, and art 27 more particularly, as the 'emergence' of minority rights. (Gauteng Education Bill case 1996, para 60)

own culture, to profess and practise his or her own religion, or to use his or her own language. (Convention on the Rights of the Child 1989, art 30)

As far as the rights of indigenous people are concerned, there seems to be greater receptiveness in international law for their right to be taught in their mother tongue. For example, ILO 169 recognises the right of indigenous people, where practicable, to be taught in their mother tongue (ILO 169 1989, art 28(1)), while the UNDRIP recognises the right of indigenous people to establish and control their own educational institutions and for states to take 'effective measures' to provide indigenous children with an 'education in their own culture and provided in their own language'. (UNDRIP 2007, art 14)[49] The special treatment sought for indigenous communities may be justified because of their historic marginalisation.

International instruments do not guarantee state-funded education, but recognise the right of individuals to be educated. There is no legal obligation arising from international law for states to support or provide funds for mother-tongue education, although it is widely recognised that the best educational outcomes are achieved through mother-tongue education.

Under the auspices of the United Nations and other regional human rights bodies the importance of mother-tongue education is increasingly recognised as a valid objective for state policies, albeit without being enshrined as a fundamental 'right' in international law. To the extent that mother-tongue education is referred to in the literature as a 'right', it is often seen as little more than a 'noble inspiration'. (de Varennes 2008, 121) For example, the United Nations' Declaration on the Rights of Persons belonging to National or Ethnic, Religious and Linguistic Minorities places an obligation on the state to 'take measures' to encourage the knowledge of language,[50] but this falls short of providing a right to mother-tongue education. Moreover, the Declaration on Minorities is, like UNDRIP, not a binding instrument of international law.

The European Charter for Regional and Minority Languages recognises the obligation of the state to fund and support mother-tongue education, but

[49] As mentioned above, ILO 169 is binding in international law, but South Africa is not a party to it. Conversely, the UNDRIP is not binding in international law, but South Africa does subscribe to it.

[50] Article 4(4) provides as follows: 'States should, where appropriate, take measures in the field of education, in order to encourage knowledge of the history, traditions, language and culture of the minorities existing within their territory. Persons belonging to minorities should have adequate opportunities to gain knowledge of the society as a whole.'

this obligation is not justiciable. (European Charter for Languages 1992, art 8) The Hague Recommendations regarding the Educational Rights of National Minorities also recognise the importance of mother-tongue education to the survival of a language. However, it only imposes a vague and unenforceable obligation on the state 'to actively implement minority language education rights to the maximum of their available resources'. (The Hague Mother Tongue Education 1996, art 4) The right to establish and manage privately funded educational institutions is recognised by the Hague Recommendations (art 8), as is the importance of mother-tongue education from primary to secondary levels, but on terms whereby the state is obliged to facilitate rather than fund or support such endeavours. The African Charter on Human and Peoples' Rights recognises the right to education, but makes no mention of state-supported mother-tongue education or the right of minorities to self-fund education. (African Charter 1981, art 17)

9.3.3 Council of Europe

The Council of Europe seeks, by way of the Framework Convention for the Protection of National Minorities (FCNM), to expand and reinforce the recognition of minority languages in education, but without creating a justiciable right to mother-tongue education.[51] The FCNM is formulated in terms similar to the Indian Constitution's directive principles of state policy (De Villiers 1992), whereby certain objectives regarding the teaching of and respect for minority languages are adopted, but without those constituting justiciable rights.[52]

---

[51] Smith puts it as follows: 'It is concluded that though the law can throw a lifeline to such a language, it cannot force the policy-makers and native speakers to take positive remedial action.' (Smith 2003, 129)

[52] Sachs J correctly observes as follows: 'It will be noted that this framework Convention [FCNM], sensitive as it is to the rights of minorities, *does not impose positive obligations on states to establish or maintain minority schools.* Instead, it confirms the right to learn and be instructed in a minority language, and the freedom to set up educational institutions.' (emphasis added) (Gauteng Education Bill case 1996, para 89) Article 12(1) of the FCNM clearly states that the establishment of minority educational institutions 'shall not entail any financial obligation' on the state. Nonetheless, it is worth noting that, while not a justiciable right, the practices of European states, as in the case of the Roma as a disadvantaged community, are often to support and even fund special programmes, including schools, to improve educational outcomes. (Thornberry 2005, 392) Also, note how in Hungary the Roma community strives, by way of the cultural autonomy arrangements in place, to place greater emphasis on special programmes to assist their children in improving educational performance. (De Villiers 2022f) The definition of 'national minority affairs' also includes 'the provision of specific public services to persons belonging to a national minority', and equal opportunities, social inclusion and social welfare are included

For example, art 12 of the FCNM encourages research into minority languages; art 13 recognises the right to self-fund minority educational institutions; and art 14 encourages the state to 'endeavour' to fund minority education facilities in areas where members of the community are concentrated. These objectives can potentially be powerful if governments and courts utilise them to develop policies and guide the interpretation of human rights, as has happened to some extent with the directive principles of state policy in India. In particular, the objectives can inform and enrich the meaning and scope of civil, cultural and political individual rights. Note in this respect the Fosen case in Norway, where the court read the individual right to enjoy culture of a member of an indigenous community *in the context* of the right being exercised by the entire community to maintain their customs and identity. (Fosen case 2021) In the Sámi mining case it was emphasised that human rights treaties are 'living instruments' and therefore their interpretation is influenced by evolving approaches to the rights of indigenous people. (Sámi mining case 2024, para 13) The right to practise culture pursuant to the ICCPR can therefore be read in the context of the reindeer herding of the community and their right to be consulted about activities that may impact on the expressions of their culture. (Sámi mining case 2024, para 14.1)

In summary, there is no justiciable right in international law to mother-tongue education. However, several international instruments and policies recognise the importance of mother-tongue teaching as a sound policy measure. The international instruments acknowledge that efforts should be made by states to encourage, facilitate, provide and promote mother-tongue education. There is recognition that providing mother-tongue education is subject to financial resources and practical measures. Moreover, there is recognition that the fulfilment of the self-determination, identity, culture and respect of individuals and their community is closely linked to the right of their children to be educated in their mother tongue and to use their own language in public.

9.3.4 India

India is one of a few states that seeks to recognise state-funded mother-tongue education in public schools, albeit subject to the caveat of reasonably practicability. (arts 29, 30, 350A Constitution of India)[53] Useful jurisprudence has arisen from

among the national minority rights. (Balogh, Halász, and Pap 2025) The nationality councils are therefore not restricted to only cultural affairs.

[53] Article 350A specifically deals with the right to mother-tongue education at a primary level, and not secondary or tertiary levels.

the Indian courts about the right to state-funded mother-tongue education and the nature of reasonable restrictions that may be imposed. The Indian courts have, arguably, been more sympathetic than the South African courts to demands by minority language speakers for mother-tongue education. While in South Africa the principles of equality and non-discrimination have taken precedence over language and cultural entitlements, in India courts have been mindful of the legal entitlement of individuals to be educated in their mother tongue in public schools.

The following are some pertinent examples of judgments dealing with mother-tongue education arising from India:

In the Kerala Education case the Supreme Court held that maintaining and protecting language, religion and culture, while also upholding the importance of general secular education, are important objectives to ensure the eradication of inequalities affecting children of linguistic minorities. (Kerala Education case 1959, para 23)

In the Linguistic Protection case the court declared that the administrative order issued by government to declare one language the sole medium for education in public schools was unconstitutional because it deprived minorities of the right to be educated in their mother tongue. (Linguistic Protection case 1989)

In the English Schools Association case the court explained that the term 'mother tongue' implies the language that the child is brought up with and is most comfortable speaking. (English Schools Association case 2000)

In the Associated Managements case, the court emphasised the importance to consider the choice of the student, as they are best positioned to say the language they understand best. (Associated Managements case 2008)

The Supreme Court has acknowledged the fundamental right to be educated in one's mother tongue, subject to reasonable restrictions that may be imposed. (State of Karnataka case 2014)

The High Court of the state of Rajasthan declared that the right to education in one's mother tongue is a fundamental right protected under art 19(1)*(a)*, but it is subject to reasonable limitations under art 19(2), which can only be imposed by a law and not merely an administrative order. (Rajasthan case 2022) In the Rajasthan case the state had decided to change a public school's medium of instruction from Hindi to English. The court acknowledged the right of the state to determine language policy, but ruled that a change to the language of instruction must be approved by the court, rather than by mere administrative action.

In the Bhai Parmanand case the question arose whether the constitutional right to free education could be enforced against a privately funded school.

The court declared that, although the Constitution guarantees the right to education, it does not provide that this right can be unconditionally enforced against a private unaided school. The court also remarked that if the petitioner could not afford the fees of a private unaided school, they were free to seek admission to a state-funded school. (Bhai Parmanand case 2022)

In the Janhit Abhiyan case the Supreme Court declared that private schools must set aside 10% of their capacity for disadvantaged communities. (Janhit Abhiyan case 2022)

9.3.5 Belgium

In the Belgian Linguistic case it was alleged that legislation enacted by Belgium concerning the language of education in schools infringed the European Convention on Human Rights since the legislation discriminated against French speakers. (Belgian Linguistic case 1968) The French-speaking complainants resided in a Dutch-speaking region. The legislation stipulated that the language of education would be geographically defined, meaning Dutch in a Dutch-speaking region, French in a French-speaking region and German in a German-speaking region. The regions are therefore in effect monolingual, while the capital Brussels is considered multilingual. (Van der Jeught 2017)

Underlying the dispute was the constitutional power of each language region within the decentralised Belgian state (now called a federation) to operate its schools on the basis of unilingual subsidies aimed at promoting the language of the region. The complainants took issue with what they considered the inadequate support they received for teaching in the French language, resulting in some instances in children having to attend Dutch-speaking schools because of their locality of residence.

The ECtHR assessed the complaint considering the 'consociational' arrangements in place in Belgium, whereby one of the state's objectives is to protect and enhance the cultural and language identity of the respective communities. These arrangements were deemed essential to retaining the territorial integrity and unity of Belgium. (McCrudden and O'Leary 2013, 48)

The ECtHR dismissed the proposition that the language policy was discriminatory, emphasising that the distinction between the rights of language communities had been supported by an objective and reasonable justification, pursued a legitimate aim and was proportionate to the aim pursued. (Belgian Linguistic case 1968, para 6) No right to mother-tongue education was guaranteed by either European instruments or the Constitution of Belgium.

This judgment has become a keystone application for the concept of the margin of appreciation in Europe. This concept allows sovereign states a high degree of discretion to organise their internal affairs, including language policy in education, in a manner consistent with the unique demands of the particular state. (McCrudden and O'Leary 2013, 55) The court accepted that 'inevitable imperfections' may arise from striking a compromise between liberty and social values. Nonetheless, it found that the territory-based unilingual educational policy was rational, proportionate and consistent with the objective of providing each language community with a homogeneous region for the teaching of its language. (Belgian Linguistic case 1968, para 5)

9.3.6 Canada

The Canadian Charter of Rights and Freedoms, under s 23, offers protection to the English- and French-language communities regarding the education of their children in public schools. These rights do not extend to other linguistic minorities or to the indigenous peoples of Canada. The section essentially provides that parents of a child can opt for the child to receive formal government-funded education at a primary and secondary school in either the English or French language, on condition that the number of children seeking to attend such a facility justifies the provision of the service. The purpose of the Canadian bilingual education system is to preserve and promote the equality of the country's two official languages (Mahe case 1990, para 31), thus recognising the importance of language in the development of culture and national identity.

This arrangement acknowledges the partnership between the English- and French-language communities. The protection provided by s 23 also aims to ensure economic mobility, enabling parents and students to relocate to different parts of Canada in the knowledge that there is a reasonable chance, depending on educational demand, that their child will receive education in either French or English. (Solski case 2005, para 2) Furthermore, the section is intended to actively encourage the use of the two languages in public. (Mahe case 1990, para 35)

Section 23 has been described as a mechanism to combat assimilation, in that it seeks to protect the separate and unique identities of children until such time that they may decide as adults to assimilate or to retain their own identity. (CSF case 2016, para 343) It is regarded as a cornerstone of Canada's commitment to bilingualism. (Mahe case 1990, para 2)

Section 23 is structured as a right rather than a freedom or discretionary option. Unlike s 29 of the South African Constitution, the restrictions on the right to mother-tongue education in one of the official languages in Canada are limited. The right to education in either of the two languages is justiciable, provided that student demand justifies the service. (CSF case 2016, paras 411, 419) The section has been interpreted purposively in a 'manner consistent with the preservation and development of official language communities in Canada'. (Beaulac case 1999) The rights must therefore be interpreted in a remedial manner to extend protection to both languages. (CSF case 2016, para 134) Notably, the protections do not include pre-school, day-care, or tertiary levels. (Yellowknife case 2015, para 81)

The right to receive education in a public school in one of the two official languages is essentially qualified only by the demand for such a service. However, there is scope for a sliding scale of services depending on the size of the demand. For example, sharing of facilities is allowed, provided that the status of the minority language is not diminished as a result of pragmatic compromises. (Yellowknife case 2015, paras 121, 270)

9.3.7 Ukraine

In 2019 the Constitutional Court of Ukraine was called upon to adjudicate certain aspects of the Education Law of 2017. (Ukraine Constitutional Court 2019) The court affirmed the prioritisation of Ukrainian as the primary medium of instruction in public schools, while still allowing opportunities for teaching in minority languages.[54] The court accepted the state's policy objectives regarding

[54] The complexity Ukraine faces in dealing with Russian, which is widely spoken by both Russian and non-Russian communities, is to some extent comparable to the status of Afrikaans in South Africa. While Afrikaans is regarded as the language of apartheid, it is also widely spoken by people other than white Afrikaners. Prina and Pentassuglia summarise the complexity of dealing with the legacy of Russian as follows: 'As a "nationalizing state", Ukraine has sought to divest itself of Soviet legacies (and Russian influence) and address previous imbalances in both the linguistic and (geo)political spheres. At the same time, the Russian language has occupied a unique position in Ukrainian society. On the one hand, it has been widely spoken by many persons belonging to national minorities, including non-Russians as well as ethnic Ukrainians, often as a first language. On the other, it is now a language associated with foreign aggression, and there has been a significant shift towards the use of Ukrainian among much of the population.' (Prina and Pentassuglia 2023, 927) Also note Henrard's analysis, which discusses the complexity and sensitivity surrounding a language that, on one hand, carries the baggage of oppression, but, on the other hand, has speakers whose mistreatment may lead to instability and conflict. (Henrard 2023)

the use of Ukrainian, namely to facilitate full integration into Ukrainian society, unify the nation's citizens and enhance their ability to carry out professional activities, observing the following about the status of the language:

> The Constitutional Court notes that the Ukrainian language is the language of official communication between officials and officers in the performance of their official duties, in the work and in the documentation work of the bodies of state power and bodies of local self-government, in the proceedings, as well as in the educational process in the public and communal educational establishments of Ukraine. The state should ensure the comprehensive development and functioning of the Ukrainian language in all spheres of public life throughout Ukraine. . . . The Law guarantees the national minorities and indigenous peoples of Ukraine the right to study their native language and envisages them studying the Ukrainian state language, which is one of the conditions for their full integration into Ukrainian society. (emphasis added) (Ukraine Constitutional Court 2019 Summary)

9.3.8 Romania

In 2020 the ECtHR had to consider whether a requirement in Romania for members of a minority to write an exam in their mother tongue as well as in the national language was discriminatory. This was due to the concern that they had less time available to prepare compared to those who only had to write in the national language. (Ádám case 2020) The ECtHR acknowledged the wide discretion of states to organise their own curricula and languages of instruction. The court noted that there is 'an emerging international consensus among the Contracting States of the Council of Europe recognising the special needs of minorities and an obligation to protect their security, identity and lifestyle'. (Ádám case 2020, para 94) Despite this the court concluded that the scheduling of the exams was not discriminatory.

9.3.9 Latvia

In Latvia the ECtHR had to consider the legality of legislative amendments that had the effect of increasing the proportion of subjects taught in public schools in the only state language, Latvian, and thus reducing the use of Russian as the language of instruction. The court noted that, historically, the teaching of Russian had been a consequence of the unlawful occupation of Latvia by Russia and was part of an effort by Russian authorities to 'Russify' Latvia, which also included the mass migration of Russians to Latvia. (Valiullina case 2023, paras 11–20)

The ECtHR acknowledged that, under the European Convention, opportunities to teach in minority languages might vary according to the specific parameters of local situations. It emphasised the need to strike a balance between proficiency in the official language of the state and competency in minority languages. (Valiullina case 2023) The court also noted that there was no European consensus with respect to the rights of minorities in the field of education (Valiullina case 2023, para 210), asserting that differential treatment does not imply discriminatory treatment, provided that the differences can be 'objectively and reasonably' justified. (Molla Sali case 2020, para 135) The court further noted that under the Framework Convention states do not have a positive duty to ensure the preservation and development of language, ethnic and cultural singularity through the provision of education in the minority language. The court also accepted that one of the objectives of teaching in Latvian was to eliminate the consequences of educational segregation that had existed under the Soviet regime. (Valiullina case 2023, paras 21–31)

Among the other policy objectives of teaching exclusively in Latvian was to promote national unity and integration, uniformity and equal access. (Valiullina case 2023, para 199) Advancing the Latvian language as the sole official language of Latvia was accepted by the ECtHR as a legitimate aim of the government. It deemed this approach proportionate to the objective sought, particularly in light of the previous dominance of Russian.

The ECtHR noted that states enjoy a wide margin of appreciation to regulate the language of their educational system, and in this case the measures adopted by Latvia were both legitimate and proportionate. (Valiullina case 2023, para 212) The complaint was therefore dismissed. Kascian raises the question whether diversity is to be regarded as a threat in light of geopolitical circumstances and the rationale of Latvia that 'homogenisation is seen as a tool to achieve equality and social cohesion, and the existence of minority schools is perceived as segregation'. (Kascian 2024, 101)

9.3.10 Indicia about the 'right' to mother-tongue education arising from international law and foreign municipal law

The following indicia relevant for this chapter emerge from the foregoing overview of developments in international and municipal law regarding the right to mother-tongue education:

(a) There is no justiciable right to mother-tongue education in international law.

(b) There is no justiciable right to state-funded mother-tongue education in international law.

(c) Any specific rights to mother-tongue education, whether in public or private education, are bound to individual countries and associated with the statutory and policy arrangements of each particular country.

(d) The right to mother-tongue teaching – whether considered a justiciable right or a policy objective – does not necessarily imply single-medium education. Mother-tongue education can also be provided in multi-language or shared school settings.

(e) Case law arising from countries such as Belgium, Canada and India, as well as from the ECtHR, must be read in the context of the relevant specific legislation of the location and should not be interpreted as constituting universal legal norms or general legal principles.

(f) Mother-tongue education is not only relevant as a rights-based equality measure. It also concerns the best interests of the child, improvement of educational standards, empowerment of children to engage society and enhancement of their ability to contribute socio-economically as adults. In essence, it gives effect to various fundamental rights such as rights to language, culture, family, self-determination and an own script.

(g) Mother-tongue education is universally seen as an empowering tool that may contribute, in the broadest sense, to an individual's right to self-determination.

(h) International law and practice encourage mother-tongue education where practically feasible and financially affordable since it enhances educational potential, facilitates individual self-determination, protects and promotes cultural and linguistic rights, and protects against discrimination and unequal treatment.

(i) In multilingual societies the equal status of languages may be simple to guarantee through statute, but complex and costly to operationalise in practice. Providing equal educational access in public schools to individuals from multiple-language communities is likely to exceed the budgetary capacity of most, if not all, states.

(j) Despite the benefits of mother-tongue education, parents and students from minority-language communities, particularly in a developing country such as South Africa, often prefer English as the medium of instruction owing to perceptions of its elevated commercial, scientific, and international status.

(k) International law, as demonstrated by judgments handed down by the ECtHR, allows for a high degree of regard for the margin of appreciation, whereby the particularities, objectives and policy motivations of individual countries in the field of education are considered and respected. Essentially, there is no universal norm or emerging jurisprudence about the recognition of a *right* to mother-tongue education.

(l) Mother-tongue language schools often serve as focal points for community cultural activities, training, associations, sport, recreation, media, advocacy and leadership development.

(m) Caution must be exercised to ensure that the distinct nature of mother-tongue educational facilities does not become a basis for separatism or a hindrance to the development of national shared values and a common sense of patriotism.

(n) A distinction is made between state-funded and community-funded mother-tongue education. Generally, communities are entitled to establish and operate private educational facilities, including but not limited to home teaching. However, in practice this option is limited in scope because of the cost and operational demands to establish and manage such facilities without state support.

(o) Block grants and other forms of state support may be made available to language minorities for use in private education.

(p) The judiciary plays a vital role in delineating the obligations of the state regarding mother-tongue education.

(q) Courts in India and Canada have adopted a purposive approach to statutory interpretation. This approach aims to recognise the multilingual nature of society, encourage the protection of diversity as a strength of society, and obligate the state to give due regard to the importance of mother-tongue education. This is done to enhance individual rights, combat discrimination and reduce inequality.

9.4 JURISPRUDENCE ARISING FROM SOUTH AFRICA

The following section considers essential principles arising from South African jurisprudence as part of the evolving understanding of s 29 of the Constitution. These principles will be identified based on themes rather than through a case-by-case discussion, as there are numerous scientific works available that do the latter. This theme-based analysis is intended to offer a fresh and practical perspective on the judgments looked at and provide insight into the impact of judicial thinking in South Africa regarding the mother-tongue language debate. The judgments must be read within the context of the Constitution and education legislation, but I strive to draw general principles that may assist with comparative studies and offer insight into the reasoning of the courts.

9.4.1 Non-discrimination and equality

The guiding principles by which fundamental rights under the South African Constitution are given effect are those of equality and non-discrimination. Non-discrimination and equality are universal rights that form the backbone of international legal and municipal law instruments. While all provisions of the Constitution must, as far as practicable, be harmonised in their interpretation, the principles of non-discrimination and equality hold special status, since no language, religious, cultural or customary rights can be upheld if they discriminate against people or treat them unequally, based on their race.

Sachs J summarised the thread of the principle of equality that runs through international human rights instruments as follows:

> It should be added that the central theme that runs through the development of international human rights law in relation to protection of minorities, is that of preventing discrimination against disadvantaged and marginalised groups, guaranteeing them full and factual equality and providing for remedial action to deal with past discrimination. (Gauteng Education Bill case 1996, para 87)

Kriegler J added the following:

> [T]here may be no discrimination on the basis of race. The Constitution therefore does not protect racial prejudice within education. A common culture, language or religion that upholds racism as an element has no constitutional right to separate educational institutions. The Constitution protects diversity but not racial discrimination. (Gauteng Education Bill case 1996, para 40)

9.4.2 Differentiation does not amount to discrimination

Differentiation between individuals on account of their language, religion, gender, culture or customs is protected by the Constitution, provided that those characteristics are not used to unfairly discriminate, treat individuals unequally or serve as a veil for what otherwise may constitute racial or gender discrimination. In the Nkosi case the court found that it was reasonable to differentiate by requiring that students accept English-language teaching for the purposes of admission to a school. However, it also found that according a different status to

Afrikaans and isiZulu as secondary languages within the same school amounted to unjustified discrimination. (Nkosi case 2008)

Sachs J expressed the rationale for differentiation as a lawful policy measure as follows:

> There might, for example, be good educational or administrative reasons for having a girls-only school in a certain area, or for having a unilingual school in another. These would be questions of state policy and practice, subject to judicial review in the ordinary courts undertaken with due regard to fundamental rights guaranteed in the Constitution. They would not be matters of constitutional rights inhering in and enforceable by cultural, language or religious communities. (Gauteng Education Bill case 1996, 79)

Kriegler J put it succinctly:

> The Constitution protects diversity but not racial discrimination. (Gauteng Education Bill case 1996, para 40)

Furthermore, a school governing body is entitled to establish a single-medium language policy for its school. However, this policy is contingent upon 'the right which every South African has to education in similar institutions'. In cases where there is a 'clearly proven need to share education facilities' single-medium education must make way for a more just and equitable arrangement. (Laerskool Middelburg case 2003, 166)

9.4.3 Justification for differentiation must be objectively ascertained

If education in one of the official languages is provided to a part of the society that excludes other members of the society, the rationale for the exclusion and its application must be objectively defendable and ascertainable by fact. It is not the subjective intention or motivation of those providing the service that is conclusive, but the objective assessment of the service, the rationale, the practical impact and the constitutional provisions. Sachs J explained that any deviation from equality should be limited and must be objectively defendable, stating as follows:

> The deviation from the normal non-discrimination principles is therefore a highly qualified one. Firstly, it is limited to the spheres of culture, language or religion; secondly, the running of the school must be practicable insofar as it implicates the State in guaranteeing education of appropriate standard; thirdly, there shall be no discrimination on the grounds of race, and fourthly, the community concerned must itself be responsible for the setting-up and running of such a school. All these qualifications conform to criteria widely accepted in international instruments. (Gauteng Education Bill case 1996, 79)

9.4.4 Language as a criterion for admission to a public school

The Constitution provides for the right to education in an official language in state schools. Therefore, a child must either accept the language of instruction in a particular school or demonstrate why they are being discriminated against by the school's failure to offer an additional language, as per s 29(2) of the Constitution. Although the school governing body is statutorily entitled to set the language policy for its school, the actual administering of the policy is not the responsibility of the governing body but rather that of the principal and the relevant department. In this respect Mohammed J declared as follows:

> Language proficiency testing, as an admission requirement, was certainly competent, but was clearly in the hands of the state in terms of this statute. This was not a function of any parent body or of any governing body in which parents were represented. It was the principal who determined the mother tongue of the child admitted to school for the first time. (Gauteng Education Bill case 1996, para 23)

In the Mikro Primary School case the principal was instructed by the Department of Education to change the school's language of instruction policy from single medium (Afrikaans) to dual medium (Afrikaans and English). He refused to comply with the directive, explaining that English-language teaching schools were available in the immediate vicinity and that the Afrikaans single-medium school was filled to capacity. The refusal was upheld based on the following reasoning:

> The right of everyone to receive education in the official language or languages of their choice in public educational institutions where that education is reasonably practicable is a right against the State. The Constitution recognizes that there may be various reasonable educational alternatives available to the State to give effect to this right and has left it to the State to decide how best to do so. In order to ensure the effective access to, and implementation of, this right, the State must in terms of the provision consider all reasonable educational alternatives, including single medium institutions.... This is a clear indication that in terms of s 29(2) everyone has a right to be educated in an official language of his or her choice at a public educational institution to be provided by the State if reasonably practicable, but not the right to be so instructed at each and every public educational institution subject only to it being reasonably practicable to do so. It follows that the 40 learners in question had a constitutional right to receive education in English in a public educational institution provided by the State if reasonably practicable but, even if it was reasonably practicable to provide such education at the second respondent, they did not have a constitutional right to receive education in English at the second respondent. (Mikro Primary School case 2006, para 31)[55]

[55] Woolman and Fleisch described the Mikro Primary School case's outcome as a 'temporary relief' for the ability of school governing bodies to maintain a single-medium Afrikaans language policy. (Woolman and Fleisch 2014, 155)

9.4.5 Practicality of teaching in one of the official languages

The lack of recognition of a 'right' to mother-tongue education in international law is grounded in practical considerations, including the cost of such an arrangement, among others. While mother-tongue education has educational merit, the multitude of languages worldwide and within states complicates the recognition of a right to state-funded mother-tongue education. Guaranteeing a right without the practical means to give effect to it erodes not only the right itself but also public confidence in government and the judiciary. The inclusion of the condition 'where reasonably practicable' in s 29(2) is thus legally, scientifically and practically justified. Mohammed J observed as follows:

> The state has a positive interest in ensuring that the right is being asserted in circumstances where it is practicable. Otherwise this might engage the resources of the state quite unjustifiably in dealing with hopelessly impractical ventures eventually aborted or abandoned. Prospective students invited to such institutions might in those circumstances also be prejudiced. The state has a positive interest in ensuring that the execution of the right which is being asserted is practicable in the circumstances. (Gauteng Education Bill case 1996, para 11)

Sachs J added that,

> from a purely practical point of view, the financial and administrative implications of granting to each language or cultural group a claim, as of right, on the State to establish schools, exclusive to themselves, not to speak of the extreme educational fragmentation involved, seem to be insuperable. (Gauteng Education Bill case 1996, para 81)

9.4.6 Parental preference for English-language education

The pervasive and persuasive influence of English, attributed to its perceived value as an international language in commerce, science, media and advertising, among other areas, as well as the local and international mobility it facilitates, prompts many parents, particularly from African-language communities but also from the Afrikaans community, to opt for English-language education for their children. (FEDSAS Teaching in Numbers 2024) While this may not necessarily result in the best educational outcomes, especially in the early school years, the proverbial power of the market often compels parents and students to choose English-language education.[56] Moseneke DCJ critically described this phenomenon as follows:

---

[56] This trend towards English-language teaching, particularly within the tertiary sector, has been described as a 'threat' to indigenous languages. (Munyani and Phooko 2021, 326)

> Learners whose mother tongue is not English but rather one of our indigenous languages, together with their parents, have made a choice to be taught in a language other than their mother tongue. This occurs even though it is now well settled that, especially in the early years of formal teaching, mother-tongue instruction is the foremost and the most effective medium of imparting education. (Head of Department, Mpumalanga Department of Education case 2010, para 50)

9.4.7 Does the right to culture imply a right to mother-tongue education?

The Constitution contains various provisions related to the cultural diversity of the South African population. Specifically, s 30 recognises the right to use language and participate in cultural life. This prompts the question of whether the right to use language, when read together with the right to mother-tongue teaching, strengthens the obligation on the state to provide single-medium education. The answer, however, has been (erroneously in my view) in the negative.[57] Mohammed J explained as follows:

> I am not persuaded, however, that a positive obligation on the state to establish educational institutions based on a common culture, language or religion can necessarily be inferred from the fact that the right of every person to use the language and to participate in the cultural life of his or her choice is expressly protected. . . . (Gauteng Education Bill case 1996, para 12)

9.4.8 Meaning of the limitations criteria

The limitations criteria set out in s 29 consist of three categories. First, the right to education in an official language in public schools is granted if it is 'reasonably

[57] Note, however, the approach adopted by Norway in the Fosen case, where the individual right to culture by a member of an indigenous community was given content by reference to the collective exercise of the right by the entire indigenous community. (Fosen case 2021) This approach reflects the Kichwa case, in which it was held that the right to a cultural identity is a fundamental and collective right of indigenous communities and must be respected in a multicultural, pluralistic and democratic society. (Kichwa case 2012, para 217) The South African courts have not been open to recognise the link between the right to equality and the right to culture and the way the rights come to fruition through collective exercise. In the Sámi mining case it was emphasised that human rights treaties are 'living instruments' and therefore their interpretation is influenced by evolving approaches to the rights of indigenous people. (Sámi mining case 2024, para 13) The right to practise culture pursuant to the ICCPR can therefore be read in the context of the reindeer herding of the community and their right to be consulted about activities that may impact on the expressions of their culture. (Sámi mining case 2024, para 14.1)

practicable'. Secondly, to ensure effective access, all reasonable educational alternatives must be considered, considering equity, practicability and the need to redress past discrimination. And, thirdly, private educational institutions may not discriminate on the basis of race, must be registered with the state and must maintain educational standards that are not inferior to public institutions. The condition of being reasonably practicable contains a factual and a normative element, both of which must be satisfied. (University of Stellenbosch case 2019, para 37) Moseneke DCJ explained what falls within the scope of 'reasonably practicable':

> When it is reasonably practicable to receive tuition in a language of one's choice will depend on all the relevant circumstances of each particular case. They would include the availability of and accessibility to public schools, their enrolment levels, the medium of instruction of the school its governing body has adopted, the language choices learners and their parents make and the curriculum options offered. In short, the reasonableness standard built into section 29(2)(a) imposes a context-sensitive understanding of each claim for education in a language of choice. An important consideration will always be whether the state has taken reasonable and positive measures to make the right to basic education increasingly available and accessible to everyone in a language of choice. (Head of Department, Mpumalanga Department of Education case 2010, para 52)

Kriegler J observed that the concept of 'reasonably practicable' is flexible (in Afrikaans 'rekbaar') and allows for a wide variety of circumstances to be considered. However, the test for it is objective, which means that the exercise of government discretion is subject to review by the courts. (Gauteng Education Bill case 1996, para 41) Overall, the most eminent fundamental right is to be treated equally, as elaborated by Sachs J:

> The very first fundamental right to be specified, preceding even the rights to life and dignity, is the right to equality. We are further enjoined to interpret the whole of Chapter 3, including section 32 [of the 1993 Constitution], in a way which promotes the values of an open and democratic society based on freedom and equality. The theme of diversity has markedly less constitutional pungency. . . . Thus, the dominant theme of the Constitution is the achievement of equality, while considerable importance is also given to cultural diversity and language rights, so that the basic problem is to secure equality in a balanced way which shows maximum regard for diversity. (Gauteng Education Bill case 1996, para 52)

In the Head of Department, Mpumalanga Department of Education case, the flexibility of discretion was explained as follows:

> What would constitute reasonable grounds will have to be determined on a case-by-case basis. This will require full and due regard to all the circumstances that actuated the HoD to bypass the governing body in relation to the specific power withdrawn. In this

> regard, a reviewing court will have to consider carefully the nature of the function, the purpose for which it is revoked in the light of the best interests of actual and potential learners, the views of the governing body and the nature of the power sought to be withdrawn as well as the likely impact of the withdrawal on the well-being of the school, its learners, parents and educators. And all these factors would have to be weighed within the broad contextual framework of the Constitution. (Head of Department, Mpumalanga Department of Education case 2010, para 74)

In the University of Stellenbosch case the court considered factors such as the cost of providing teaching in Afrikaans and English, the burden on staff and the ability of Afrikaans students to study in English compared to the lack of ability of non-Afrikaans students to study in Afrikaans. The court concluded that the university was entitled to adopt a single-medium English policy because of the enormous and prohibitively expensive cost of dual-medium instruction. (University of Stellenbosch case 2019, para 33)

9.4.9 Private single-medium schools guaranteed, but at a cost

There are two constitutional avenues to single-medium language schools under the Constitution: the first is by way of s 29(2), which provides for education in a language of choice when 'reasonably practicable'. The second is by way of s 29(3), which provides for language-of-choice teaching in an independent privately funded facility, provided it does not discriminate based on race. Sachs J observed as follows:

> It [s 29(3) of the Constitution] acknowledges that constitutionally guaranteed space should be made available for private individuals to set up and maintain [establish] their own schools if they feel that their special cultural, language or religious needs are not being sufficiently catered for in the state system. (Gauteng Education Bill case 1996, para 78)

Kriegler J added to this that language-of-choice teaching in private facilities has to be paid for, and thus the issue of mother-tongue education is principally about affordability. (Gauteng Education Bill case 1996, para 42)

9.4.10 Can education in *any* official language be demanded at *any* school?

Since s 29 guarantees the right to be educated in an official language, the question arises whether this right enables a student to demand that education must be provided in any of the official languages at any public school. The answer is no.

The condition of being reasonably practicable also applies to those who do not constitute adequate numbers and those who have other educational opportunities within the same area available to them. In the Mikro Primary School case it was emphasised that the general right to education in an official language does not imply that *every* school must offer the full range of official languages:

> This is a clear indication that in terms of s 29(2) everyone has a right to be educated in an official language of his or her choice at a public educational institution to be provided by the State if reasonably practicable, but not the right to be so instructed at each and every public educational institution subject only to it being reasonably practicable to do so. (Mikro Primary School case 2006, para 31)

9.4.11 Status of Afrikaans as a language of instruction and its general use in education

As explained above, the Afrikaans language carries significant historic, social and political baggage. Yet Afrikaans is an official language and is to be treated equally with other official languages. South African courts have been careful to elucidate why, in certain cases, single-medium Afrikaans education must make way for dual-medium education, without thereby diminishing the importance of Afrikaans or the right of children to receive their education in it. Sachs J observed as follows:

> [T]he Afrikaans language is one of the cultural treasures of South African national life, widely spoken and deeply implanted, the vehicle of outstanding literature, the bearer of a rich scientific and legal vocabulary and possibly the most creole or 'rainbow' of all South African tongues. Its protection and development is therefore the concern not only of its speakers but of the whole South African nation. (Gauteng Education Bill case 1996, para 49)

In the University of Free State case the court critically reviewed the role of Afrikaans in the tertiary sector, noting that the university had decided to adopt a policy of English-only teaching by phasing out Afrikaans 'to advance a constitutionally inspired transformational agenda'. (University of Free State case 2017, para 7) The court pointed out that, whatever language model for education is chosen, it

> must be informed by among others the constitutional obligation to make education accessible to all so as to free the potential of all our people.... It would be unreasonable to wittingly or inadvertently allow some of our people to have unimpeded access to education and success at the expense of others as a direct consequence of a blind pursuit of the enjoyment of the right to education in a language of choice. (emphasis added) (University of Free State case 2017, paras 48, 49)

The decision to introduce a single language of instruction at the university was upheld on the basis that 'reasonable practicability therefore requires not only that the practicability test be met, but also that considerations of reasonableness that extend to equity and the need to cure the ills of our shameful apartheid past, be appropriately accommodated'. (University of Free State case 2017, para 53) Froneman J delivered the minority view that leave to appeal should have been granted for the dispute to be fully ventilated, expressing his concern as follows:

> Like the Supreme Court of Appeal, the main judgment accepts the University's assertion that it is impossible to provide education in a language of choice without indirectly discriminating on the basis of race. This has enormous implications beyond the confines of the University's campus. It sanctions an approach that deprives speakers of one of our official languages of the constitutional right to receive education in the language of their choice. This is not an issue that has been dealt with authoritatively by this Court before. (emphasis added) (University of Free State case 2017, para 83)

In the UNISA case the court concluded, after an extensive overview of the history of Afrikaans, that:

> It bears emphasis that, to simplistically style Afrikaans as having a one-dimensional history and existence as 'the language of the whites', and as 'the language of the oppressor', is entirely misconceived and flies in the face of the true history of its origins and development sketched above. . . . While Afrikaans originated out of oppression and continued to be a tool of oppression, its subsequent development into a heterogeneous, 'rainbow' language, spoken today by more black people than white people, is a marvellous paradox of human ingenuity and creativity. Recognising the major role played by lowly indigenous peoples and enslaved people in its history and development is crucial. . . . To conclude under this rubric: the disturbing tendency of the one-dimensional portrayal of Afrikaans as a 'white language', and as 'the language of the oppressor', is manifestly misconceived, as I have attempted to show. (emphasis added) (UNISA case 2021, paras 19–23)

9.4.12 Prospects for single-medium Afrikaans instruction in public schools

As mentioned above, the inclusion of s 29 was a major breakthrough (or concession, depending on one's perspective) during negotiations. The provision was primarily included as a concession to the Afrikaans-speaking community, who were concerned about the potential diminishment of the educational and scientific status of Afrikaans under the democratic constitution.[58] The constitutional space

[58] This concern is to some extent acknowledged by Froneman J in his minority judgment in the University of Free State case: 'For some people, particularly white Afrikaans speakers, the

was therefore created for state-supported *and* private education in the official language of Afrikaans (and others). As discussed earlier, s 29 went beyond the requirements of international law by granting individuals the right to state-funded education in one of the 11 official languages. Therefore the challenge for the Afrikaans community lies not in the legal basis for teaching their language in schools, whether public or private. The challenge is primarily twofold: first, in public schools the qualification of 'reasonably practicable' and, secondly, in private schools, the qualification of 'at their own expense' present serious hurdles to Afrikaans mother-tongue education.

Current demographics and the impact on public finances will likely result in the continued decline of single-medium publicly funded Afrikaans-language education over the long term in public schools. Meanwhile, in private schools the cost of single-medium teaching is prohibitive, with the average Afrikaans speaker unable to afford private education. One option that remains open for the government is to provide block grants, as a gesture of respect for plurality and diversity, to private schools that teach in an official language other than English, subject, of course, to s 29(3).[59] Such grants may diffuse much of the controversy surrounding the language debate in education.

In public schools the high demand for school places, the scattered residential patterns of the Afrikaans community and the high regard in which Afrikaans teaching culture are held all contribute to the demand for dual-medium teaching. Sachs J put it as follows:

> At the same time, there is nothing in these principles to guarantee the exclusivity of Afrikaans in any school. On the contrary, the promotion of multi-lingualism, even leaving out the factor of equal access to schools, would encourage the establishment of dual- or multiple-medium schools. (Gauteng Education Bill case 1996, para 74)

result in this case – the loss of the right to receive tertiary education in Afrikaans – *may be seen as a betrayal of their expectations about the Constitution's guarantees in respect of their home language.*' (University of Free State case 2017, para 119)

[59] I was co-author of a report in 2018 in which the decline of government funding for Afrikaans teaching in public schools had been anticipated. We recommended that the Afrikaans community place greater emphasis on private teaching supported by an annual block grant from government in an exchange to refrain from the public criticism of government funding arrangements for public schools and downscaling of litigation against government school funding and organisational policies. (De Villiers, Geldenhuys, and Matthee 2018)

Sachs J also observed:

> Any claim of Afrikaans community groups to have the State subsidise what, objectively speaking, are privileges in terms of exclusive access to affluent schools, would therefore be weak. (Gauteng Education Bill case 1996, para 83)

As far as tertiary education is concerned, in a unanimous judgment in the Stellenbosch University case Froneman J noted that in practice 'near-universally, brown and white-Afrikaans-speaking first-year entrants to the University are able to be taught in English. Conversely, though most entrants are able to receive tuition in Afrikaans, a significant minority cannot.' (University of Stellenbosch case 2019, para 26)

If the practicality test is applied, it follows that the decision to provide university teaching solely in English was sound, since retaining Afrikaans as a language of teaching 'created an exclusionary hurdle' for non-Afrikaans students. (University of Stellenbosch case 2019, para 28)

9.4.13 Sliding scale of cost and benefit

The Stellenbosch University case also saw the disadvantages of reducing instruction in a particular language, in this instance Afrikaans, at the tertiary level weighed against the benefits of education in English, given the latter's status as an international language with broader application which offers greater opportunities for mobility and social justice for university students. Froneman J put it as follows:

> This is to say that the exclusion of non-Afrikaans speakers from full participation in tuition and other institutional benefits seems to me a legitimate basis for upgrading English, while continuing to offer significant tuition in Afrikaans, even while sacrificing the previous primacy of Afrikaans. In this, a sliding scale of what is lost in language terms, and what is retained, as against the social justice objective sought to be attained, weighed together, where appropriate, with cost considerations, seems to me constitutionally justified. (emphasis added) (University of Stellenbosch case 2019, para 41)

9.4.14 Role and status of school governing bodies

Under South African legislation school governing bodies have a high degree of autonomy in setting policies for the control and management of public schools.[60]

[60] President Cyril Ramaphosa signed the Basic Education Laws Amendment (BELA) Bill into law on 13 September 2024. (BELA Act 2024) Sections 4 and 5 were not made operational at the time. Those sections, which have since become operational, require school governance bodies to submit their language policy to the relevant provincial government department for approval.

Education legislation sets out the functions of these bodies within the context to provide education to their community. Pertinently, school governing bodies can establish language policies for their respective schools, but such decisions are typically subject to oversight by the head of the department. (Serfontein and De Waal 2013)

Several disputes have emerged regarding matters such as the status of school governing bodies, their interactions with education department heads and oversight of their policies. The school governing bodies exist separately from the state and are in effect self-governing institutions. (Mikro Primary School case 2006, paras 20–22) Nonetheless, their functions and powers are derived from statute and are therefore subject to change. The school governing bodies are not part of a 'sphere' of government, and therefore the constitutional obligations pertaining to cooperative government do not apply to them. (Mikro Primary School case 2006, para 22) Despite this, school governing bodies and government authorities must work together in the interests of the child by consulting, coordinating and, if possible, averting litigation.

In the Head of Department, Mpumalanga Department of Education case the court emphasised that while school governing bodies have devolved powers and functions, this does not imply that they operate independently or without oversight, declaring as follows:

> It would, however, be wrong to construe the devolution of power as absolute and impervious to executive intervention when the governing body exercises that power unreasonably and at odds with the constitutional warranties to receive basic education and to be taught in a language of choice. The Constitution itself enjoins the State to ensure effective access to the right to receive education in a medium of instruction of choice. (Head of Department, Mpumalanga Department of Education case 2010, para 78)

9.4.15 Role of school governing bodies in determining language of instruction

School governing bodies have the authority to determine the language of instruction in a public school, among other functions. However, this determination is subject to the constitutional provision that it must be 'reasonably practicable'

In setting a language policy a board is required to take into consideration the language interests of the broader community. At the time of writing (March 2025) no litigation had yet been initiated pursuant to these sections. Veriava is of the view that the BELA Act is needed to effect transformation of educational services since school boards have 'continued to maintain patterns of apartheid spatial geography' and those must be removed. (Veriava 2024, 158)

and the state must also consider equity, practicability and the need to redress past racial discrimination to ensure effective access to education. While school governing bodies wield significant power to set the language policy of their school, any legal victories affirming their autonomy 'only bring relief in the short run'. (Serfontein and De Waal 2013, 46) This is because the prevailing policy, legal and social pressures on these bodies to accommodate English as the language that provides the broadest access to education are often overwhelming.

In the Mikro Primary School case the court declared that the school governing body is 'in so far as the determination of a language and admission policy is concerned, not subject to executive control at the national, provincial or local level and can therefore, like the Electoral Commission, in so far as the performance of those functions is concerned, not be said to form part of any sphere of government'. (Mikro Primary School case 2006, para 22)

Four relevant aspects arise from this categorisation: (a) governing bodies are created by statute but function independently, not subject to general executive directives; (b) practical realities often necessitate governing bodies to consider dual-medium instruction over single-medium instruction; (c) dual-medium instruction often proves unsustainable over the long term because of the burden it places on teachers, leading schools to transition towards English as the primary language of instruction; and (d) when setting policies, governing bodies must consider the interests of the broader community, not solely the community of parents that elected them.

9.4.16 Interaction between language policy and its administration

The powers and functions of school governing bodies are comparable to few international examples because of the extensive involvement and control parents have over school admission policies and setting the language of instruction in South Africa. This raises the inevitable question of how to regulate the relationship between school governing bodies and the relevant educational department under which the school operates. It is acknowledged that, while school governing bodies set general policy, those policies are subject to judicial review and the implementation of the policies is an educational responsibility carried out by the school principal. The principal, in turn, operates under the supervision of the relevant department of education. In the Rivonia Primary School appeal this relationship was described as follows:

> Thus, while the school governing body determines admission policy, individual decisions on admission are taken only provisionally at school level, by the principal acting under the authority of the head of department. (Rivonia Primary School appeal 2013, para 44)

9.4.17 Interaction between school governing bodies and the education department

The school governing body and the educational department respectively have defined functions, but there are overlaps in their exercise, leading to potential disagreements. While the school governing body may set language policy, such policies are subject to administrative oversight and judicial review. The head of the department, for instance, may intervene in the discharge of a function of a school governing body on reasonable grounds and in pursuit of a legitimate purpose. The interaction has been described as follows:

> It is therefore clear that the determination of language policy in a public school is a power that in the first instance must be exercised by the governing body. The power must be exercised subject to the limitations that the Constitution and the Schools Act or any provincial law laid down. Even more importantly it must be understood within the broader constitutional scheme to make education progressively available and accessible to everyone, taking into consideration what is fair, practicable and enhances historical redress. (emphasis added) (Head of Department, Mpumalanga Department of Education case 2010, para 61)

9.4.18 Importance of a cooperative relationship between school governing bodies and the education department

School governing bodies and the department of education share the responsibility to provide education, serving the same clients but with distinct functions, duties, and responsibilities. Both entities operate in accordance with the Constitution, which necessitate cooperation, liaison, and coordination. In essence, they form a partnership to fulfil their respective educational mandates. In the Rivonia Primary School appeal this close interaction was elucidated as follows:

> In this case there is particular reason to emphasise the duties of co-operative governance and the impact they might have on the children concerned. The duty on the parties to cooperate and attempt to reach an amicable solution is intimately connected to the best interests of the child. . . . Both parties could and should have done more to prevent the need for litigation. . . . But one organ of state cannot use its entrusted powers to strong-arm others. All sides are required to work together in partnership to find workable solutions to persistent and complex difficulties – and resorting to court in every skirmish is not going to help in that process. (emphasis added) (Rivonia Primary School appeal 2013, paras 77–78)

9.4.19 Obligation on school governing bodies to consider the interests of the wider community

When setting admission and language policies school governing bodies are required to consider not only the interests of the students attending the school or their parents, but also those of the broader community in which the school is located. This often favours English-language instruction. Moseneke DCJ declared as follows about the obligation of a governing body to consider the wider community's demands for access to education and the school's capacity availability:

> It must act, recognising that there is a great demand for the admission of grade 8 learners who prefer English as a medium of instruction. (Head of Department, Mpumalanga Department of Education case 2010, para 100)

9.4.20 Overarching principles for school governing bodies

In summary the following overarching principles, as outlined in the Rivonia Primary School appeal, may serve as useful guidelines for school governing bodies in fulfilling their duties:

> Distilling the core of these judgments, the principles that have emerged from the case law can be set out as follows:
>
> (a) Where the Schools Act empowers a governing body to determine policy in relation to a particular aspect of school functioning, a head of department or other government functionary cannot simply override the policy adopted or act contrary to it. This is so even where the functionary is of the view that the policies offend the Schools Act or the Constitution. But this does not mean that the school governing body's powers are unfettered, that the relevant policy is immune to intervention, or that the policy inflexibly binds other decision-makers in all circumstances.
>
> (b) Rather, a functionary may intervene in a school governing body's policymaking role or depart from a school governing body's policy, but only where that functionary is entitled to do so in terms of powers afforded to it by the Schools Act or other relevant legislation. This is an essential element of the rule of law.
>
> (c) Where it is necessary for a properly empowered functionary to intervene in a policy-making function of the governing body (or to depart from a school governing body's policy), then the functionary must act reasonably and procedurally fairly.
>
> (d) Further, given the partnership model envisaged by the Schools Act, as well as the co-operative governance scheme set out in the Constitution, the relevant functionary and the school governing body are under a duty to engage with each other in good faith on any disputes, including disputes over policies adopted by the governing body. The engagement must be directed towards furthering the interests of learners. (Rivonia Primary School appeal 2013, para 49)

9.4.21 Single-medium mother-tongue education other than in English

The Constitution acknowledges the right to education in an official language, but it does not imply that this right is to be realised through single-medium education. As discussed earlier in the context of Canada, there exists in effect a sliding scale of educational services which can be offered in an official language in single medium, parallel medium, dual medium and through shared facilities, among other options. The choice of approach ultimately hinges on practical considerations in their broadest sense. Although double and parallel medium seems feasible, the pressure on teachers often causes the second teaching language to fall away and for English to become the dominant or sole teaching language.

In the Laerskool Middelburg case the court emphasised that the provision of single-medium education depends on its practical feasibility. Additionally, the court noted that a well-administered dual- or parallel-medium school cannot be regarded as a diminishment of the right to receive education in one's mother tongue. The court concluded that 'the right to single-medium education is clearly subject to the right of each South African to education' and 'must give way if there is a clearly established need to share educational facilities with other cultural communities'. (Laerskool Middelburg case 2003)

In the Head of Department, Mpumalanga Department of Education case the school governing body essentially determined that Afrikaans would be the sole language of education for the school. The body defended its policy by reasoning that race was not used as a basis for exclusion. Moseneke DCJ declared the following to explain why the language policy set by the school governing body was open to review:

> The power to determine a school's language policy vests in the governing body. The legislation devolves the decision on the language of instruction onto the representatives of parents and the community in the governing body. It accords well with the design of the legislation that, in partnership with the state, parents and educators assume responsibility for the governance of schooling institutions. A governing body is democratically composed and is intended to function in a democratic manner. Its primary function is to look after the interest of the school and its learners. It is meant to be a beacon of grassroots democracy in the local affairs of the school. Ordinarily, the representatives of parents of learners and of the local community are better qualified to determine the medium best suited to impart education and all the formative, utilitarian and cultural goodness that come with it. This does not, however, mean that the function to decide on a medium of instruction of a public school is absolute or is the exclusive preserve of the governing body. (emphasis added) (Head of Department, Mpumalanga Department of Education case 2010, para 57)

9.4.22 School language policy as a veil for discrimination

There is an acknowledged potential for school governing bodies to rely on their authority to determine the language policy or maximum student capacity of a school as a means of indirectly discriminating against individuals of other races. There is a risk of fostering segregation and discrimination disguised within the objective to promote linguistic uniqueness.

In the Matukane case it was determined that what initially seemed like the promotion of language and culture in fact amounted to discrimination aimed at excluding black children from the school:

> The fact that no pupils of colour have been admitted to the school notwithstanding the number of applications received by the respondent, not only for this year but also for the previous year, is a strong indication in this direction [discrimination]. . . . The respondent failed to establish that there was no unfair discrimination against the black children. Even if their applications had been rejected because they had elected to receive their schooling through the medium of English, it would still constitute unfair discrimination. (emphasis added) (Matukane case 1996)

The assessment of the rationale for a specific language policy must therefore be objective, considering all relevant considerations. In the Rivonia Primary School case the court observed as follows:

> Leaving schools to determine their admission policy, including the power to determine their capacity, and subject only to appeals in individual cases, one unwittingly creates space privileged schools can use and manipulate that power to fortify rather than dismantle existing inequalities. Schools such as the applicants could thus craft admissions policies that allow them to continue to offer a premium education to their learners, while ignoring the increased demand their action places on other schools in the area that are already operating with fewer resources and higher learner-to-class ratios. (emphasis added) (Rivonia Primary School case 2012, para 73)

However, the education department must also consider the rationale that causes a school governing body to adopt a certain policy. The department cannot override a policy simply because it disagrees with it or seeks a different outcome.

In the Rivonia Primary School appeal the court elucidated as follows:

> [T]he suggestion that the Gauteng HOD was rigidly bound by a school's admission policy when exercising that power is untenable. . . . If there were good reasons to depart from the policy, it was always open to the principal or the Gauteng HOD to do so. . . . However, a decision to overturn an admission decision of a principal, or depart from a school admission policy, must be exercised reasonably and in a procedurally fair manner. (emphasis added) (Rivonia Primary School appeal 2013, paras 54–58)

9.4.23 Best interests of the child

All those involved in providing education must ultimately be guided by what is in the best interests of the child. Sachs J put it as follows:

> The Constitution therefore requires us to take into consideration not only the interests of the parents, which may be unduly rooted in the past, but to give paramount place to the interests of the child, which may require looking more to the future. Each child is unique, and each child is entitled to a good education, independently of what might in any particular case be the motives or passions of his or her parents or of the parents of other children. (Gauteng Education Bill case 1996, para 53)

When ascertaining the best interests of the child the court does not only consider the interests of the child who is already in a school or a child who seeks access to a particular school – all relevant information is considered. In the Rivonia Primary School case, while the court acknowledged that the school governing body's intention to reduce the number of pupils per class was commendable and had a sound educational objective, it noted that the interests of the wider community were better served by having bigger classes to accommodate a greater proportion of the community's children. The court declared that 'while the [school's] desire to offer the best possible education for its learners is laudable, the constitution does not permit the interest of a few learners to override the right of all other learners in the area to receive a basic education'. (Rivonia Primary School case 2012, para 72)

In the Juma Musjid case it was held that the High Court had failed to give due consideration to the interests of the children affected by an eviction order. Nkabinde J stated as follows:

> It is evident that the High Court failed to give consideration to the impact that the eviction order would have had on the learners and their interests. Had the High Court considered the character and nature of the occupants and the mechanism in terms of which the school obtained occupation of the private property, considerations which the High Court regarded as irrelevant, it would not have ordered the eviction. (Juma Musjid case 2011, para 68)

9.4.24 Relevance of international law and foreign municipal law

As discussed above (Chapters 3 and 4), the Constitution empowers courts to consider international law and foreign law when interpreting the Bill of Rights. Although the courts may consider foreign municipal law and jurisprudence, in the educational fields the courts have primarily relied on the text of the Constitution along with enabling legislation and policies in mother-tongue cases.

Their references to international law have typically been in passing, without in-depth analysis of foreign case law, selective and arbitrary. The benefits that could have been gained from case law arising from, for example, the ECtHR, India and Canada have remained unexplored. What is particularly striking is the little regard the courts have had to the importance of mother-tongue education and its interaction with other identity rights such as cultural and language rights as well as the right to individual self-determination.

The following are relevant excerpts from the respective judgments, with the judgment in the Gauteng Education Bill case making the most extensive reference to international law and foreign municipal law:

> *Applicability of Canadian Law, according to Mohammed J:* 'The language and structure of s 23 of the Canadian Charter are wholly distinguishable from s 32*(c)* of our [interim] Constitution. Section 23 of the Canadian Charter is clearly concerned with the obligation of the Government to provide education in the official languages of Canada to linguistic majorities and minorities. It is analogous to s 32*(b)* of our Constitution, but very different from s 32*(c)*. The interpretation accorded to it by the Canadian courts can therefore be of scant assistance in the proper interpretation of s 32*(c)* of our Constitution.' (Gauteng Education Bill case 1996, para 15)
>
> *Overview of literature concerning the rights of minorities, according to Sachs J:* 'A review of literature by leading authors in the field suggests that over the years there has been a firm movement from the concept of tolerance of religious and other minorities, to that of protection of national groups, to that of guaranteeing rights of individuals.' (Gauteng Education Bill case 1996, para 55)
>
> *Compliance with s 29 of international human rights law, according to Cameron J:* 'At the outset, it is important to note two salient features of the right to language. One is that respect for language preference, where appropriate and reasonable, entails no special concession or privileged treatment. It flows from fundamental rights and values. It is an embodiment of the right to be treated equally and without discrimination, which inheres in everyone. It requires no special pleading for its recognition. Second, *it is established in international human rights law* that the way in which that respect is practically realised must depend on what is appropriate and reasonable. Section 29(2) of our Bill of Rights recognises this. It accords the right to receive education in public educational institutions in a language of choice 'where that education is reasonably practicable'. In this, the Constitution accords with international instruments.' (emphasis added) (University of Stellenbosch case 2019, paras 21–22)
>
> *Does art 27 of the ICCPR protect the right to mother tongue education, according to Sachs J:* 'Thus, even on their most benevolent interpretation, it [art 27 of the ICCPR] falls far short of imposing a firm duty on the state to promote the separate development of minorities (as opposed to the duty of preventing discrimination against them, where there is a high level of responsibility). *It comes nowhere near supporting a State duty to establish separate schools*, as argued for by the Petitioners in this case. On the contrary, legislative

history at the United Nations suggests that such an obligation was expressly considered and expressly rejected.' (emphasis added) (Gauteng Education Bill case 1996, para 65)

Relevance of international law, according to Sachs J: 'I would merely add one further reason, influenced by my explorations of international human rights law, but derived directly from the text of the Constitution, as to why I consider that it makes best sense to regard this paragraph as concretising rights to a certain measure of cultural/linguistic autonomy in the private sphere, rather than as imposing an express duty on the State to establish single-medium community based schools.' (Gauteng Education Bill case 1996, para 75)

Sachs J then continues: 'The literature to which I have referred, however, suggests that there is *little hard international human rights law to back a generalised claim on State resources for the promotion of cultural, linguistic and religious diversity,* and none at all to support a legal entitlement to separate state-funded schools.' (emphasis added) (Gauteng Education Bill case 1996, para 83)

Support for special treatment in international law of minority languages, according to Froneman J: 'There is a total lack of appreciation in the main judgment that Afrikaans remains a minority language and that there is *considerable foreign and international authority in support* of the proposition that minority languages deserve special measures for their protection.' (emphasis added) (University of Free State case 2017, para 124) Froneman J does not, however, address the conclusions drawn by Sachs J in the Gauteng Education case, which asserted that there is no justiciable right to mother-tongue education in international law or foreign municipal law.

9.5 CONCLUSION

In conclusion the following can be said about developments concerning the right to mother-tongue education in international law, foreign municipal law and s 29 of the Constitution:

First, an individual right to state-funded mother-tongue education is not recognised in international law. However, the importance of mother-tongue education in the self-development and effective learning of a child is widely acknowledged in international law and educational policy. Added thereto, democratisation theory and practice acknowledge and promote the recognition of identity rights as a necessity for peace-building in deeply divided plural societies.

Secondly, in those instances where hard and soft international law recognise the right to mother-tongue education the funding of such education is not the responsibility of government unless explicitly so provided by state law. Minority language communities do, however, implicitly have the right to self-fund mother-tongue education.

Thirdly, it is widely acknowledged in contemporary international law and practice that policies should aim to offer mother-tongue education from as early as possible and for as long as practically possible. This not only enhances educational outcomes for children but also contributes to their self-determination and self-esteem.

Fourthly, the 1996 Constitution of South Africa stands as an advancement over other constitutions drafted in the 1990s and the standards set in international law in its recognition of the right to state-funded education in any of the 11 official languages, subject to practical considerations. Additionally, the Constitution acknowledges the right to privately established mother-tongue educational facilities and does not prohibit state funding for private education institutions. It is noteworthy that there were no substantial objections to s 29 of the Constitution during its drafting or certification process. However, it was apparent, even at the drafting stage, that South Africa's resource constraints would over time present a major obstacle to maintain single- or even dual-medium teaching, with English likely to emerge as the most widely state-funded language of instruction.

Fifthly, the limitations in the Constitution on the right to education in an official language are assessed objectively and determined by fact. There is no right to single-medium education in state-funded schools, but if warranted by circumstances, single-medium education in an official language is consistent with the Constitution. Similarly, dual-medium or parallel-medium education is not as a matter of principle inconsistent with the Constitution. However, in the operation of two languages practical considerations may often give rise to a gradual transition towards predominantly English-language instruction.

Sixthly, school governing bodies are responsible to determine the language policy of a school. In setting this policy the governing body must consider the broader needs of the community, beyond just the interests of current students or the parents who elected them. While educational authorities may exercise administrative oversight over the language policy, such oversight must be fair, reasonable and rational. Additionally, the language policy is subject to judicial review, as the governing body operates within the framework of the Constitution.

Seventhly, in practice South Africa's limited resources, coupled with the imperative to address historical injustices and achieve greater equality and non-discrimination, have led courts to prioritise funding for educational equality over funding of diversity. This approach, while accepted in South African jurisprudence, may invite criticism when compared to the jurisprudence of a country such as India, where greater emphasis has been placed on the state's obligation to fund and support mother-tongue education within the context of equality and non-discrimination.

Eighthly, jurisprudence arising from regional instruments like the European Convention on Human Rights recognises a high degree of autonomy for states to determine their language policy in schools. This provides states with the discretion to establish their own domestic language policies, including and especially those concerning education. Moreover, the ECtHR has shown sympathy towards arguments asserting that the use of a single language in state education may contribute to national integration and individual mobility, as well as serve as a mechanism to rectify past injustices. However, the ECtHR is also sympathetic to the protection and preservation of minority languages and traditions. This shows the challenge to strike a balance between pluralism and uniformity.

Ninthly, the right to mother-tongue education is intrinsically linked to other identity rights such as culture, language, association, religion, self-determination, identity and script. These rights are interrelated and collectively represent identity rights aimed at acknowledging, protecting, and promoting societal plurality. *Differentiation* among children based on language, culture or religion in education is tolerated, and even encouraged, by international law and jurisprudence in South Africa. However, if such differentiation results in unequal access to educational facilities or is used to segregate children, it is considered unjustified and regarded as *discrimination.*

CHAPTER 10

RECOGNITION OF CUSTOMARY LAW: HARMONISING TRADITION WITH MODERNITY (OR THE OTHER WAY AROUND?)

The epoch of customary law, and of its custody by a privileged order, is a very remarkable one.

– James Sumner Maine

10.1 INTRODUCTION

Customary law is arguably *the* most pertinent practical example (in addition to religious pluralism) of legal pluralism in contemporary society. To those living in countries where customary law intersects with contemporary constitutional law the topic of this chapter is a lived reality – there is nothing theoretical about it. Legal pluralism permeates the daily affairs of customary communities and individuals from within those communities in nuances that are too many to list, too dynamic to be confined by definition, and too refined, layered and complex to describe. A person who excels as a highly accomplished barrister in one context may in another setting adhere to and honour an uncodified tradition, norm or rule of customary law. A man or woman who serves in Parliament, where contemporary laws about equality and non-discrimination are legislated, may also engage in the practice of lobolo (bride wealth),[1] paying homage to traditional customs surrounding marriage, or subscribe to customary rules governing succession.[2] Parents whose son attends an exclusive private school may also allow him to be initiated in compliance with ancient traditions. A tribal chief who rules with authority over his people may have to accept the decisions of an elected local government whose jurisdiction overlaps with his territory in functional areas that traditionally would have been his exclusive domain, and vice versa. A person who no longer lives in compliance with *The Law*, may still sing the song of a waterhole in outback Australia in accordance with a millennia-old tradition. A nurse who was part of the stolen generation may refrain from gazing at the stars when in the Outback bush out of fear of the Feather Man and in obedience

[1] The Recognition of Customary Marriages Act defines lobolo as 'the property in cash or in kind, whether known as *lobolo*, *bogadi*, *bohali*, *xuma*, *lumalo*, *thaka*, *ikhazi*, *magadi*, *emabheka*, or by any other name, which a prospective husband or the head of his family undertakes to give to the head of the prospective wife's family in consideration of a customary marriage'. (Recognition Act 1998, s 1) Bronstein observes that even persons who get married in a church may continue to subscribe to the tradition of lobolo and the customary practices arising from it. (Bronstein 1998, 391)

[2] Note, however, the criticism expressed by Osman to the Reform of Customary Law of Succession and Related Matters Act 11 of 2009, namely that the manner in which the Act approaches 'families' may not be consistent with the 'myriad ways' in which families are nowadays formed and that greater discretion should be given to determine the beneficiaries of an estate. (Osman 2023) Rautenbach also points out that women who find themselves in certain domestic partnerships that are not recognised may be treated differently because of their cultural background. (Rautenbach 2023a) The same issue arises in the case of Muslim marriages. (Chapter 8) Rautenbach puts the question about what remains of the uniqueness of customary law in light of state intervention in the law of succession? (Rautenbach 2024)

to ancient traditions that dictate such behaviour of women.[3] Aboriginal Elders may oppose the building of weirs in a riverbed based on their customary beliefs of a pre-ancestral snake having created and using the river and their obligation to adhere to those beliefs. (Forrest case 2023)

The intersections of state law, customary law and the authority of traditional leaders are numerous, yet at the grassroots level there often exists no clear practical hierarchy, only various modes of accommodation and tolerance.

Ironically, the liberal democracies of the northern hemisphere are not immune to the influence of customary law, as migrants increasingly bring their rules and traditions with them to these countries. This phenomenon is also observed in South Africa, where migration patterns mean new forms of customary law are finding their way into the country. It remains to be seen how courts in South Africa (and the ECtHR and CJEU) respond to disputes arising from customary law that originates beyond the country's borders. As will be further elaborated, customary law is not always territorial in nature, but also personal; it can apply to persons wherever they reside. The authority of customary law is not declared by a Parliament, but rather emanates from conduct that grants it legality and legitimacy. Customary law is 'legitimated across sub-Saharan Africa [and beyond] through historically sedimented layers of authorities in complex and changing environments'. (Huizenga 2018, 12)

Unlike the authority of contemporary governments, customary law is fundamentally not confined by territorial jurisdiction. It may follow individuals, extending beyond national boundaries and persisting even when they relocate to an urban area.[4] While individuals have the option to deviate or withdraw from customary law, those who choose to adhere to its traditions find that it follows them like a shadow. This explains why Aboriginal people in Australia often refer in reverence to *The Law*, which encompasses their traditional rules and customs and governs every aspect of their interaction with their surroundings. It serves as a constant spiritual, practical and directional guide that applies regardless of location.

[3] I pay my respects to Auntie Rita Elliot (deceased) with whom my family and I spent such precious time in the Australian Outback listening to ancient stories. She, along with so many other Aboriginal elders whom I represented in native title proceedings, opened my eyes to a history that far precedes all records, to traditions that have survived thousands of years despite being unwritten, to beliefs that continue to influence their daily lives as living law, and to the *The Law* that commands and directs them similar to a contemporary sovereign legal system.

[4] Note, for example, in Canada and the USA the ongoing efforts of indigenous people to exercise some form of autonomy and self-administration outside traditional reserve areas, particularly in urban areas. (Mathieu-Bedard 2017)

Customary law may be seen as an extension of the general genus of cultural rights, yet it also functions as a distinct system of norms with the effect of law to those who subscribe to it. Just as customary law emerges from culture, culture itself is shaped by customary law. International law and the Constitution distinguish between customary rights as collective rights to be exercised by a community, and cultural rights which are generally individual in nature. Nonetheless, in practice the right to culture is exercised with other members of the same cultural community. This was acknowledged by the Norwegian Fosen case, which linked the collective cultural practice of reindeering with the individual right to culture. (Fosen case 2021)

The recognition of customary law is consistent with the principles outlined in the UNDRIP, which acknowledge the right of indigenous people to maintain and strengthen their distinct, collective legal and cultural institutions. (UNDRIP 2007, art 5) Customary law extends in some respects beyond what are ordinarily seen as cultural rights of individuals, such as the right to practise their culture, speak their language, organise festivals, display symbols and commemorate historic events without state interference. Cultural groups rarely have a set of ancestral laws with institutional arrangements and governance that are comparable to customary-law arrangements. It is rare for cultural norms to attain the status of non-state *law*.

Not every indigenous custom, tradition, habit or practice can, however, be equated to a legal norm.[5] Ascertaining what constitutes a legal norm is a matter of origin, degree, adherence, universality (within the group), consistency, enforcement and sanction. It is community legitimacy that supports non-state customary law, not just its legality. Customary law is not written and hence its contents must be ascertained though evidence of customs that continue to be practised as if law. (Zwane case 2024, para 43) The court must strive to recognise and give effect to 'actually observed customary law'. (Mabuza case 2002, para 17) As stated in the Van Breda case, for a custom – in the general sense of the word in civil law – to be declared as a source of law, three requirements must be met: the practice must be certain uniformly observed for a long period of time, and reasonable. (Van Breda case 1921, para 334)[6] One must also note, however,

[5] Note, for example, that customary requirements for a valid customary marriage may include customs and rituals that are not necessarily part of customary law, but rather constitute customary practices or habits. There is no simple test to ascertain when a customary *habit* become a customary *law*.

[6] In the Shilubana case the court noted that the Van Breda test may not be entirely suitable for the development of customary law, but made no decision on it. (Shilubana case 2008, para 56;

how challenging it can be to develop an in-depth understanding of indigenous customs. Waboose, a Canadian indigenous legal scholar, admits how even for her it was a 'struggle' to write from an indigenous perspective. (Waboose 2021, 295) Note also the Chief Avhatendi Ratshibvumo Rambuda case, in which a dispute arose about the appointment of a new headman or headwoman. Notably, there was no mention of Ubuntu or its potential applicability or reason for its non-applicability to an intra-tribal dispute of this nature. (Chief Avhatendi Ratshibvumo Rambuda case 2024)

Customary law is both ancient and dynamic, existing in its own right as a legal system, regardless of how it is classified or viewed by the state legal system. (Alexkor case 2004) In essence, customary law does not require recognition by another legal system to prove its existence. It exists irrespective of how other legal systems may perceive it. For example, customary marriages were before 1988 not recognised as marriages but rather as 'contracts between families' and effect given to relationships with that in mind, with the property collectively owned by the family head for the benefit of all. (Zwane case 2024, para 28) Note, for example, how in the Australian Forrest case it was emphasised that the concept of 'sacred' should be viewed from the perspective of the community who asserts the sacredness, not from the view of other communities. (Forrest case 2023) As declared in the Mabo case, while common law does not create native title, common law recognises native title as a distinct legal system. (Mabo case (2) 1992) Similarly, in the Canadian Delgamuukw case, it was emphasised that an indigenous community makes decisions collectively in accordance with its laws and customs, without interference by government. (Delgamuukw case 1997) The self-determination of indigenous people includes the right of the community to decide pursuant to their customary law to what use land is put to and what priorities apply to the use of land. (Borrows and Rotman 2023, 143)

However, this general statement prompts many questions, such as: How are the customary law rules applicable to a dispute at any given moment ascertained if customary law is not codified? Whose version of customary law prevails in relation to a specific complaint? What is the legal effect on a rule in customary law if it does not comply with the Constitution: is the rule merely rendered

---

Oninku 2024) The test applied in Van Breda is not dissimilar to the definition in the Evidence Act of Nigeria, 2011, of a traditional custom as a 'rule which, in a particular district, has, *from long usage*, obtained the force of law'. (emphasis added) Sachs suggests the following: 'By common law is meant that body of law that has been regarded as common law; by custom is meant that body of practices, rules, institutions, and values that has been treated as customary law.' (Sachs 2012, 313)

irrelevant to the resolution of the dispute but allowed to continue to exist within a community; is it legally abolished due to its unconstitutionality; or can it be criminalised?[7] Can a person opt in and out of the scope of customary law based on free association? What is the appropriate response to forum shopping, where a person seeks relief under the legal system that best suits their desired outcome?[8]

The debates among European countries concerning the development of a *modus vivendi* that seeks to accommodate the contemporary constitutional law of those liberal democratic states and the religious pluralism that exists there are viewed by many in Africa, Asia and the Americas with a sense of bemusement. To those from the southern hemisphere, legal pluralism, legal dualism and a diversity of legal systems – whether customary, indigenous, cultural or religious in origin – are facts of life. Legal pluralism characterises daily life in many parts of the global south, where individuals live within and under multiple legal systems simultaneously.[9] This experience shapes and informs their identity, enhancing and even optimising individual self-determination by recognising identity rights. That said, navigating these diverse legal systems is never simple, as norms of modernity and custom may compete for obedience within the same societal context.[10]

Living under the dual influences of custom and modernity entails a complex existence marked by nuance and degree. However, it also offers a profound sense

---

[7] Note in this regard the declaration by the Supreme Court of Nigeria in the Okonkwo case, in which it stated as follows about the effect of a declaration of repugnancy on a traditional custom: '[A] declaration by the courts that a particular custom is repugnant to natural justice, equity and good conscience, *does not necessarily imply that such customary law is illegal. . . .*' (emphasis added) (Okonkwo case 1994, para 344) Nhlapo suggests that many of the new arrangements facilitated by statutes in South Africa 'are being ignored wholesale in traditional communities'. (Nhlapo 2017, 11)

[8] Note, for example, the Makholiso case, in which siblings sought by way of different avenues to claim inheritance from the deceased: one approaching the claim via the civil rites adhered to when the marriage had been concluded, the other approaching the claim based on the customary law adhered to. (Makholiso case 1997)

[9] Note, for example, in Indonesia how communities must navigate up to three distinct legal systems at a local level – customary, Islamic and Indonesian. (Dahwal and Fernando 2024)

[10] Note, for example, how the Constitutional Court of Indonesia has had to respond to a traditional custom in a part of the country where in elections the so-called Big Man casts the vote of an entire community on behalf of those under his jurisdiction. While this custom, known as the Noken system, has ancient roots, it clearly offends the principle of universal franchise. The court has nevertheless upheld the electoral practice in repeated elections. (De Villiers 2023b, Noken case 2009) A similar approach has been adopted in Mexico, where the indirect election of members of an indigenous community at municipal level has been held to be consistent with the Constitution. (Indirect election case 2023)

of belonging, fostering a connection to society and the experience of Ubuntu in the context of community-caring rather than the *solitaire* of pure individualism-aloneness. Nevertheless, navigating life within two systems can be challenging, necessitating a balance between the enduring power of tradition, time and culture with the rationality, authority, jurisprudence and codification inherent in modern legal frameworks. Placing customary law on equal footing with other legal systems may, on the one hand, be a simple exercise in legal prescription, but on the other it does not necessarily change cultural and customary practices within communities. For example, striking a balance between male and female regarding access to and control of land in Africa remains problematic and often gives rise to females being discriminated against, subject to greater poverty than men, and socially locked into arrangements that may not be in their best interests. (Mubecua and Nojiyza 2022)

The quasi-scientific notion of *state law* and *non-state law* (Chapter 2) does not come close to encapsulating the complexity that characterises customary law in contemporary society. Similarly, the categorisation of *official law* versus *living law* (Bhe case 2005) does not provide sufficient clarity to understand the complexity of customary law being stable and dynamic.[11] To those adhering to customary law it has the status of state law. Even to those who view customary law as non-state law the question arises whether a customary norm evolves into state law when it is recognised and given effect by a court of law, legislation or an administrative arrangement. In other words, does customary law gravitate toward becoming state law when recognised, or does the genus of adaptability of customary law remain intact?[12]

The distinction between *official* customary law and *living* customary law appears to be a desperate yet unscientific effort to impose order on an undefined realm characterised by both stability and change, nuance, and ongoing adaptation of customary law.[13] As argued below, the distinction does not withstand the test

---

[11] Werbner and Werbner suggest with reference to Botswana that customary law 'in practice' or customary law 'in context' may be a better reflection on the dynamic nature of customary law than 'living' customary law. (Werbner and Werbner 2022, 255)

[12] Badejogbin suggests that recognition of non-state customary law by state law 'bestows on it [customary law] the status of state law'. (Badejogbin 2022, 254) At the same time, however, he acknowledges that 'living customary law is not certain', (Badejogbin 2022, 263) which highlights the risk of trying to encapsulate customary law in a state of permanency.

[13] Badejogbin goes so far as to propose that all references to 'official' customary law automatically exclude 'living customary law'. (Badejogbin 2022, 253) As argued below, such a rigid and inflexible distinction is not supported by legal or scientific scrutiny. Customary law

of legal or scientific scrutiny.[14] Customary law as a legal system is both official and living: 'official' in the sense that there is always an element of codification, recognition, scientific analysis, observation, recording and judicial precedence; 'living' in the sense that it is always dynamic, undocumented, evolving and subject to change. This is consistent with the approach adopted in the Australian Yorta Yorta case, in which the High Court held that it would be an error to adopt a 'frozen in time' approach to indigenous law as if it had ceased to develop at some historic point. Nonetheless, the dynamic nature of customary law does not suggest that historic laws of custom or materials should be disregarded, as 'sometimes it may well be possible to start with the present and look backwards to see whether the former is in truth a current manifestation of the latter'. (Yorta Yorta (HCA) case 2002, para 190)[15] Moreover, as observed by Langa DCJ in the Bhe case, the challenge is not so much to accept the notion of living customary law, 'but in determining its content and testing it'. (Bhe case 2005, para 109)

As with many aspects of law, the reality of legal pluralism is more complex than social or scientific definitions can offer. It is a complicated and multifaceted phenomenon that cannot be fully encapsulated or described by mere categorisations. In short:

> Customary law in Africa is pervasive and it has significant impact on the lives of Africans in the area of family law, especially with respect to the laws of marriage and divorce. (Ojogbo and Edu 2022, 252)

---

includes, among other sources, documented and undocumented sources, which in effect are often regarded as official customary law.

[14] Note that Manthwa seeks to draw a distinction between indigenous law and customary law: 'It must be stated that customary law differs from indigenous law as customary law emerges from the latter. Customary law is people's adaptation of indigenous law to socio-economic changes.' (Manthwa 2023, 662) The Constitution of South Africa does not draw a similar distinction. To the extent that Manthwa purports that adaptations to indigenous law should be seen as customary law, I take issue with the proposed approach since my view is that all laws, including indigenous law and customary law, are by nature dynamic, living and open to adjustment. Indigenous law is therefore open to be living and adjustable in similar ways as any other legal system.

[15] Determining whether a purported custom indeed persists within a community is a question of fact. For example, in the Yorta Yorta case Callinan J commented *obiter* that he might question whether the use of a motorboat for the purposes of fishing remained in accordance with traditional law and custom, 'particularly one [custom] of alleged totemic significance'. (Yorta Yorta (HCA) case 2002, para 187) This observation was made in reference to the Australian Yanner case, in which the court found that the hunting of two juvenile crocodiles using a motorboat was consistent with the exercise of indigenous law and custom. (Yanner case 1999)

This chapter provides a brief overview of customary law in South Africa and highlights both the territorial and non-territorial nature of its jurisdictional reach.[16] It reflects on how the courts have responded to the official and dynamic (living) nature of customary law, recognising the weaknesses of such a binary distinction. A bird's eye view is then taken of the relevance and role of customary law in the constitution-drafting and certification process. The attempts to give statutory effect to customary law and to modernise it, such as through the Recognition of Customary Marriages Act, are considered. Finally, relevant jurisprudence from South Africa along with a few international case studies are analysed, aided by a set of questions that may help distil the core of jurisprudential thinking on the topic.

10.2 BACKGROUND OF CUSTOMARY LAW IN SOUTH AFRICA

Customary law has been rooted in South Africa for as long as humans, including hunter-gatherers and tribal groups, have lived in some form of collective community.[17] The primary sources of customary law, and the intergenerational

---

[16] Jones observes, correctly, that while indigenous rights are often associated with tribal lands or traditional areas, the right to self-determination of indigenous people is not restricted to their traditional lands. Some indigenous communities may have been hunter-gathers with no settled territory, while others may have been displaced from their land, or others may have lands that straddle international borders. Some may be dispersed and even integrated with other communities. The notion of non-territoriality is therefore consistent with collective self-determination. (Jones 2024, 22)

[17] Note the findings of the groundbreaking case of Mabo (2) in Australia, where it had been presumed since European settlement in 1788 that the hunter-gatherer Aboriginal people of the continent lacked sophistication and social organisation, to the extent that the area had been regarded as *terra nullius* (no person's land) without any form of organised customary legal system or traditional ownership of land. (Milirrpum case 1971) This proposition was overturned in Mabo when it was declared that a sophisticated system of traditional native title holding and social and law organisation, based on traditional customary laws and traditions, had existed at the time of settlement and continues to exist in the case of the applicants. (Mabo case (2) 1992) The relevance of this finding for the purposes of the discussion about living customary law in the current chapter is that the legal and anthropological understandings of indigenous law and customs may change. Allowance should therefore be made not only for traditional customs themselves to be dynamic and open to change, but also for scientific observations and understandings of those customs to adjust and for scientists to identify such changes in a timely manner. The way in which customary law is observed at a specific point in time by outsiders should therefore not be frozen, as if no ongoing developments or better understandings can occur. One should also be mindful that those making observations about customary law may only understand a language or a customary practice in part. The risk also exists, as recently found in Australia, that contemporary scientific

mode of transferring its rules, are oral. The moment of birth of customary law cannot be ascertained, nor can its original permutations and varieties be traced, or its adaptations mapped with any accuracy. By the time the first codes of customary law had been observed and written down by outsiders, those rules and traditions had been in existence for countless generations. In a contemporary world which places so much emphasis on the clarity and certainty purportedly offered by positive law and codification, customary law appears like an anachronism. It does not easily fit into the mould of modernity. Yet, it survives and thrives. This phenomenon is not unique to South Africa. The landscape of the African continent (and beyond) is covered like a *lappieskombers* (patchwork blanket) with customary law systems that combine with modern systems to form legal reality.

10.2.1 Customary law: territorial and non-territorial

The jurisdiction of customary law has territorial and non-territorial elements. Although customary law is usually associated with a specific territorial or tribal area, its jurisdiction is not necessarily limited by territory.[18] In several respects, customary law serves as a contemporary example of non-territorial self-determination, allowing individuals to opt out of a system of law, custom, and authority through freedom of association rather than being subject to a territorially imposed jurisdiction. (De Villiers 2014b)[19]

'understandings' of indigenous law and custom may be influenced by the personal agendas and preferred outcomes of non-indigenous parties (perhaps similarly to past anthropological practices). In a headline case in Australia the Federal Court was scathing about the expert opinion given by an expert since it was not grounded in fact. In the Munkara case expert evidence about the existence of an Aboriginal storyline had been found to be unreliable (Munkara case 2024), with the court expressing criticism that indigenous witnesses may have been exposed to 'subtle coaching' to give evidence favourable to the arguments put forward by one side of the dispute against the laying of an undersea pipeline. (Munkara case 2024, para 1135) The presiding judge described the expert evidence as 'so lacking integrity that no weight can be placed on them'. The court ultimately awarded A$9 million legal costs against the Environmental Defenders Office, who supported and financed the proceeding. (Rauso 2024; Munkara consent orders cost 2024)

[18] Notably, the Evidence Act of Nigeria, 2011, defines a 'custom' as a 'rule which, *in a particular district*, has, from long usage, obtained the force of law'. This clearly links custom to territory, an approach that has not been adopted by the South African legislature.

[19] Note below that objections were lodged against the proposed text of the 1996 Constitution on the basis that traditional authorities had not been recognised as a distinct *sphere* or level of government. The Constitutional Court rejected the objections and concluded that the Constitutional Principles did not mandate the recognition of traditional authorities as a separate sphere of government in the Constitution. (Certification case 1996)

In contrast to the territorial jurisdiction of state law, where everyone within a territory is bound to the laws of the state institution (whether national, regional or local government), customary law operates in a more nuanced manner for two reasons relevant to this chapter: firstly, in traditionally held tribal areas under direct control of a tribal authority, the rules may apply to all those within the entire territory; but, secondly, even if members of an indigenous community live outside the traditional area, they could still be bound by customary law (in areas such as personal, succession, criminal and family law) if they so choose. An example of this are those individuals who adhere to Zulu customary laws and customs despite residing in provinces such as Mpumalanga, Western Cape, and Gauteng.[20] In the same way that religious communities may take their beliefs with them when they migrate, so persons under customary law may continue to adhere to those legal norms even in new places of residence.

In this way customary law has territorial and non-territorial applications,[21] as is particularly evidenced in customary systems in Oceania, Asia, Africa and the Americas. This explains how migrants may sometimes take their customary law systems with them to urban areas, and to new countries of residence.

---

[20] Note the efforts in northern Canada and the Russian Federation to accommodate indigenous self-determination by way of territorial and other forms of autonomy. (Wilson and Fondahl 2024)

[21] The notion of non-territorial autonomy (NTA) implies in short that the jurisdiction of an autonomous legal entity of an ethnic, religious, indigenous or cultural community can be exercised by reference to *persons* rather than *territory*. (De Villiers 2016a) Freedom of association, rather than residence in an area, attracts the authority of the self-administration body. Typical categories of functions that often form part of NTA are aspects of education, culture, religion, language, recreation, media and historic commemorations, as well as traditions and customs that impact on the unique identity of the community. (Malloy, Osipov, and Vizi 2015) Those individuals who associate with the community therefore fall within the jurisdiction of the cultural or religious council or tribal authority (or whatever the decision-making body is called) through their free association, rather than them residing within a specific territory. In Chapter 2 reference is made to one of the first documented systems of NTA, called the millets in the Ottoman empire, whereby religious minorities enjoyed a degree of self-government on a non-territorial basis. Examples of different contemporary forms of NTA in liberal democracies can be found in the institutional arrangements in Brussels (Belgium); South Tyrol (Italy); Kosovo; Hungary; Schleswig-Holstein (German); and Estonia. It is also worth noting the non-territorial element of the Aboriginal corporations in Australia, the most notable example being the Noongar settlement. (De Villiers 2020a)

10.2.2 Changing nature of customary law

The first settlers to South Africa brought with them European norms and legal systems. Although these became the predominant state law, customary laws nevertheless persisted. Over time customary systems were variously suppressed, ignored, tolerated, informally enforced and even codified. However, even after several centuries there remains work to be done to harmonise the relationship between state law and customary law. In the face of many failed democratisation efforts in the southern hemisphere, customary systems have often proved resilient and enduring. Several international instruments, notably ILO 169 and UNDRIP, seek to recognise the continued relevance of indigenous laws and customs.

Since customary law is not codified, it is not always straightforward to determine what specific rule applies, at a specific point in time, to a dispute. Sometimes it may be plain to ascertain the relevant customary rule because of the longevity and clarity of a particular practice. However, complexities may also arise since customs may change or fall into disuse, or there may be disagreements within the community about what they entail. Customs may be challenged by some within the community, or may suffer on account of an urban–rural divide, generational shifts away from adherence to ancient rules, or increasing resistance from women against subservient roles.[22]

The right to equality is not to be understood in abstract terms, but instead within its social context. (Hugo case 1997, para 41) This statement applies to the interface between state law and non-state law. This contextual understanding may lead to the invalidation of customary-law provisions that discriminate against women, for example. Some customs may be acknowledged, but only as historic relics and practices rather than as binding laws. There is no specific demarcation between what is a *customary practice* and what is *customary non-state law*. What one person perceives as a legal customary norm may be regarded by another simply part of social life or a habit, but not as *law*. What is a customary law in space in time may through changes in practices or non-use erode from a living legal code of conduct to a mere memory. Customs may come to be complied with by only a part of the community. Or customs may be remembered with nostalgia without being adhered to. As customs evolve the new norms that emerge may take time

[22] Note, for example, the Adeleke case in Nigeria, in which it was held by a customary court that a woman who got divorced was not entitled to maintenance since 'such an allowance is contrary to native law and custom'. The rationale here was that the woman is free to remarry and hence the previous husband should not be burdened with maintenance. (Adeleke case 1976)

to be fully defined or recognised as law. In short, in the absence of codification it is hazardous for an outsider to declare the precise nature of customary law.

It is trite to state that not all social habits and practices can be construed as laws. (Diala 2017) Individuals may argue that they were forced against their will into a particular customary arrangement, or that circumstances have changed and they no longer wish to be bound by a customary legal norm. Customs that benefit one side of a dispute, in some cases the male-dominated hierarchy, may be emphasised or selectively cited. A custom may be officially recognised (in laws, judgments or scientific works) but no longer be adhered to by a community in its living practice. A contemporary romantic and idealistic view of a customary practice may exist which is influenced by what it is supposed to imply, not necessarily what it does imply. Some customary law may fly in the face of contemporary understandings of fundamental rights. Osman correctly cautions against idealising customary law 'assuming it gives effect to human rights'. (Osman 2019) Indeed, changing contemporary human rights standards, encompassing principles such as equality and non-discrimination, may lead to customary-law principles being challenged and even criminalised.

Codification of customary law carries the risk of ossifying existing customary practices into written form. This may stifle the spontaneous development of customary laws. On the other hand, relying solely on oral customary law as conveyed by tradition exposes it to vagueness, potential abuse, reinforcement of existing power dynamics, selective recollection and a lack of clarity. Furthermore, so-called living customary law places a burden on the person relying on a customary norm to prove that the norm exists and to clarify its terms. This poses challenges to accessing justice because of the evidentiary and financial burden that may arise from attempting to prove the existence or non-existence of a particular custom within the context of living law. Maimela seeks what he calls 'genuineness within the interpretational context' whereby courts demonstrate a real concern and interest in cultural customs as practised. (Maimela and Morudu 2024, 415) But the burden to prove a custom and the binding nature of the custom can remain a challenge for the person seeking to rely on it, as was highlighted in the Sengadi case, in which an important custom for the conclusion of a customary marriage was not upheld by the court. (Sengadi case 2019)[23] Conflicts or inconsistencies may arise between documented and oral customary law, as described by Sinclair:

[23] Davies raises concern that by attempting to reduce indigenous laws to writing by way of a form of codification or simplification may end up 'freezing it in time, downgrading it, filtering it in some way, and only partially listening, if at all'. (Davies 2024)

> Codification of certain systems of customary law, moreover, has stultified its development. And there is an acknowledged wide gap between customary law crafted by professional lawyers and expressed in text books, the case law, and the legislation, on the one hand, and current African social practice, on the other. Customary law is seen by many to have been deeply alienated from its community origins. (emphasis added) (Sinclair 1994, 560)

While it may seem straightforward to task courts with the duty to ascertain customary law pertaining to a specific dispute, the difficulty lies in courts hearing adequate and sufficiently representative evidence to enable them to authoritatively declare a customary legal norm at a specific point in time. After all, courts can only declare facts and interpret how the law applies to a set of facts based on the evidence before them. Judges cannot conduct public inquiries or rely on their own knowledge or understanding of a customary system, thereby effectively supplementing the evidence presented by witnesses.[24]

10.2.3 Judicial notice of customary law

The Law of Evidence Amendment Act of South Africa in s 1(1) states, relevantly, that a court may take judicial notice of a well-known customary-law norm, provided the norm can be ascertained readily and with sufficient certainty. The challenge to ascertain a norm 'readily and with sufficient certainty' is that even long-held customary rules may be subject to change, and a judge may not be aware of these subtleties.[25] While the Act encourages judicial notice of customary

[24] Note, for example, the criticism expressed by Zondo J in the Mayelane case against the calling of additional witnesses from the community to assist the court to ascertain the currency of a particular custom. Zondo J is of the view that such an invitation by a higher court opens the door to contradictory evidence, with the court not being able to resolve the conflict. Furthermore, as an appeal court, the court was supposed to decide the appeal based on the same facts as those heard in the lower court. However, by inviting new affidavit material the appeal court exceeded its appellate function. Finally, the parties had enjoyed adequate opportunity to present their case and evidence to the lower court. (Mayelane case 2013, paras 112–116)

[25] In a similar vein to the concerns raised in the discussion of Ubuntu (Chapter 6), the consideration of customary law pursuant to judicial notice raises some interesting questions: if official customary law is at risk of not adequately reflecting customary law, on what basis may a judge utilise their personal knowledge of customary law to supplement evidence or to develop customary law? In light of South Africa's cultural diversity, are some judges better 'equipped' to take judicial notice of customary law than others who do not come from the same cultural, tribal or racial background? Furthermore, must a judge put their understanding of the customary law of a particular indigenous community to the parties so they can respond to it pursuant to the rules of natural justice and procedural fairness? Note, for example, how Ubuntu has been relied on by

law, this notion also lends credibility to so-called official customary law, as the custom sought to be relied on may get documented and thus considered settled by a judge.

The question arising from juridical notice is obvious: even if a custom is well known, how does a court ascertain if a purported practice, as it relates to the specific community and as understood by the court, continues to be the *actual practice* of the community? Courts cannot conduct their own inquiries or call witnesses regarding contemporaneous rules of customary law.[26] Nor can they ascertain by their own inquiries whether those rules continue to be adhered to by a community or have been subject to change. It is also possible that customary rules among indigenous communities, or even within communities, pertaining to the same matters may differ, such as those related to property or land rights. (Ojogbo and Edu 2022, 236) Furthermore, parties to a dispute may call witnesses that suit their respective dispositions, without the leadership of the community even being aware of the dispute. Ironically, by acknowledging an established norm or by declaring that a specific customary rule applies in a dispute, the court may contribute to customary law becoming 'official' since such a declaration of a customary norm will inevitably be relied upon in future as a precedent.

There may be different views within an indigenous community about the nature of a customary rule or its application to a specific dispute. The South African Law Commission observed in 1999 that 'no community is so culturally homogeneous that only one system of law can express the attitudes and lifestyles of all its members'. (South African Law Commission 1999, 27) In view of this the South African Parliament has undertaken various initiatives under the 1996 Constitution to codify aspects of customary law – including those related to matters such as customary marriages, customary law of succession and the organisation of customary institutional arrangements – for the sake of consistency and to relieve individuals from burdensome evidentiary requirements.

---

courts without the pleadings of a case reflecting either its relevance or applicability or without witnesses being called to give evidence about the applicability of Ubuntu to a dispute. A case in point: Ubuntu has in some cases been relied on to justify a refusal to issue an eviction notice, while in other instances eviction notices have been issued without any reference to Ubuntu or explanation as to why it does not apply to the case. (Chapter 6)

[26] Even if experts are called to give evidence, the opinion of experts must be supported by evidence of the traditional customs and beliefs. Note the Munkara case in Australia, where it was found that the opinion of the expert of traditional customs and beliefs was not reflective of the facts before the court. (Munkara case 2024) This raises the concern – who checks the experts and those external to a community who purport to 'know' traditional customs and practices?

While the enactment of customary law may be useful by providing certainty, it also undermines the scientific credibility of the purported distinction between official and living customary law. Indeed, the enactment of certain customary laws in legislation emphasises the inappropriateness of categorising official customary law and living customary law, regardless of how appealing this may be.

In short: customary law, akin to any legal system, encompasses elements of official law that are codified and written, alongside living law that evolves and adjusts over time.[27]

Although the settlers brought to South Africa their European-based domestic legal systems and laws, reality dictated that those foreign systems could not be adopted and enforced in all respects across the entire territory of the colony. Pragmatism had to prevail, particularly in rural areas where traditional customs, chiefs and tribal authorities had existed before settlement and continued to hold sway. Therefore lower courts were often called upon to take note of, recognise and even administer customary law. (Brooks 1927, 181) Courts were, however, restricted by what was generally referred to as the 'repugnancy proviso', whereby customary law could only be applied if it did not offend European standards of moral and justice.[28] Although the High Court historically refused to apply customary law in disputes between Africans (Ngqobela case 1893), lower courts often acknowledged and applied customary laws, when applicable, for the sake of pragmatism and public order at a local level, especially in rural and tribal areas.

Ironically the repugnancy proviso prevails under the Constitution in the form of the Law of Evidence Amendment Act 45 of 1988. This provides that indigenous law shall not be 'opposed to the principles of public policy or natural justice', and furthermore that the custom of lobola shall not be declared by any court to be 'repugnant to such principles'. (s 1(1)) An arguable case can be made that the

---

[27] Note in this respect the conversation in South Africa about the codification of Muslim marriage arrangements and the different views *within* the Islamic community whether their religious customs should be codified by Parliament or left for flexible development, adjustment and application outside the state law system in accordance with their holy book and interpretations thereof. (Chapter 8) At the time of writing (March 2025) the objective of creating a Marriage Act to regulate Muslim marriages had not yet been achieved, with an extension of time granted to June 2026. (Speaker of the National Assembly and Another case 2024)

[28] Note, for example, practices of initiation in South Africa and criminal punishment by way of traditional spearing in traditional Aboriginal communities in Australia, where authorities must often navigate a delicate line between accepting, tolerating, noticing and endorsing acts of bodily harm that in other circumstances might be regarded as criminal. (Australian Law Reform Commission 1986)

repugnancy test ought no longer to be relevant or applicable to South African law since the constitutionality of customary law is measured not by reference to a European moral or ethical standard, but rather by the terms of the Constitution. (Chuma 2023, 41) Since the word 'repugnant' implies a condescending value judgment of a legal system, it would be preferable to use the phrase 'inconsistent with' the Constitution.

10.2.4 Equality of customary law as a legal system

The 1996 Constitution introduced a new era for customary law in South Africa. For the first time customary law became recognised and elevated as a legal system in its own right. (Bhe case 2005, para 41) Customary law is now recognised, at law, as being on an equal footing with other legal systems.[29] For the first time since colonial settlement in South Africa customary law is viewed as a legal system that 'lives side by side with common law and legislation'. (Gumede case 2009, para 22) One condition, however, applies: the supremacy of the Constitution prevails over all other laws and legal systems, including customary law, thus ensuring that the universal liberal democratic values enshrined in the Constitution are ultimately upheld. (Constitution of South Africa 1996, s 211(3)) This highlights the challenge faced by the judiciary when addressing customary law. Even within the new democratic milieu a hierarchy of legal orders exists, with the legal order outlined in the Constitution and given effect by judges taking precedence in the event of any inconsistency, as encapsulated by Langa DCJ:

> It bears repeating, however, that as with all law, the constitutional validity of rules and principles of customary law depends on their consistency with the Constitution and the Bill of Rights. (emphasis added) (Bhe case 2005, para 46)

The South African Law Commission cautioned in 1999 that since the provisions of the Bill of Rights also have horizontal application into the private affairs of indigenous (and ethnocultural and religious) communities, those indigenous and cultural practices could fail the test of the Constitution. The private, customary, religious or cultural activities of a community may in some cases be considered inconsistent with the Constitution. (Freedom of Religion case 2019, para 69;

[29] Diala is critical of the notion that customary law, with its ancient roots, is recognised as equal to other legal systems but at the same time subservient to the Constitution, statutes by Parliament that regulate customary law, and the common law. The Constitution makes a 'mockery of indigenous law's parity with the common law' and perpetuates the repugnancy clause in a different way. (Diala 2019, 16)

Gaum case 2019; Bhe case 2005)[30] This constitutional supremacy could thus in due course have the effect that 'the constitutional recognition given to customary law in 1996 would be an empty gesture' (South African Law Commission 1999, 23), as ultimately the Constitution would prevail in the event of any inconsistency with privately held customs (and religious practices).[31] As a result, there may as time passes be little left of a unique customary law system because customs may offend the constitutional standards, which in turn are informed by universal understandings of fundamental rights.[32]

Note in this respect the Shomang case, where the court had to strike a balance between the ownership of property under common law with the ownership of property under customary law. The court emphasised that customary law must be understood with reference to customary law and not by reference to another legal system. (Shomang case 2022, para 57) This includes taking account of the 'fluidity' of customary law (para 60). The way that common law views ownership

---

30 Note in this respect how judges dealing with the legal system of the Roma in the Nordic countries have responded to the relevance of Roma law to proceedings. According to Nafstad, judges tend to take note of Roma law to better understand a dispute, but when the law is applied the uniform laws of the country are enforced. She says: 'Knowledge about Roma and about Roma law is of importance for several of the judges, but mostly as a basis for understanding the case and the involved persons better, as a tool to solve a problem. It does not imply that their cases should be treated in any other way than other cases. Among the judges, whether they had knowledge about Roma law or not, there is a strong emphasis and consensus on formal equality before the law.' (Nafstad 2018, 110)

31 It is worth noting, for example, how critics have pointed out shortcomings in Botswana's jurisprudence, arguing that the courts' failure to accommodate customary law should be 'condemned'. They contend that the courts have 'effectively rendered customary laws and practices that ordinary citizens consider as important and relevant to the order in their lives, inapplicable'. (Dinokopila and Kgoboge 2021, 354) This criticism is echoed in the opinion of Faris, who says that it 'is becoming evident that African customary law is being "recolonised" – deconstructed – to fit into the mould of a predominantly Western legal system, and in the process once more losing its identity'. (Faris 2015, 176)

32 Bronstein cautions that the right to equality does not need to imply 'progressive Westernization'. (Bronstein 1998, 410) The notion of equality can serve to modify customary law, to bring it into the 21st century and to adjust its practices within the context of its continued status as customary law. In this respect it is worth repeating how the Constitutional Court of Indonesia has had to respond to a traditional custom in a part of the country where in elections the so-called Big Man casts the vote of an entire community on behalf of those under his jurisdiction. While this custom, known as the Noken system, has ancient roots, it clearly offends the principle of universal franchise. The court has nevertheless upheld the electoral practice in repeated elections. (De Villiers 2023b, Noken case 2009) A similar approach has been adopted in Mexico, where the indirect election of members of an indigenous community at municipal level has been held to be consistent with the Constitution. (Indirect election case 2023)

of property does not necessarily correlate with the customary holding of property (para 73). Property law must therefore develop in a manner consistent with the recognition of customary law (para 77). The house that was the subject of the proceeding was therefore declared a 'family house' rather than a house belonging to an individual (para 81).

10.2.5 Ascertaining a customary legal norm

One of the challenges for judges is that a customary-law principle may not always be easily ascertainable, or what appears to be an established principle of customary law may be subject to nuance or change. Therefore the customary law as interpreted by judges or as codified in statutes like the Recognition Act may not necessarily align with the customary law as lived by a community, or as claimed by the parties involved in the dispute. Such potential discrepancies underline the importance of ascertaining 'living' customary law by way of evidence rather than relying solely on official customary law. (Bhe case 2005, paras 81, 152) According to the Constitutional Court, 'true customary law will be that which recognises and acknowledges the changes which continually take place'. (Bhe case 2005, para 86) For instance, in contemporary society the phrase 'household' may not necessarily reflect the same dynamics as those in the past, with females playing more prominent roles and even acting as the head of the household.[33] Determining with certainty the terms of a customary-law norm can be a delicate balancing act. As noted by Van der Westhuizen J, it requires consideration of all relevant circumstances, both historical and current. (Shilubana case 2008, paras 42–49)

Despite the reality of living customary law, there are also distinct benefits to codify it. Codification contributes to certainty and consistency in understanding and application of customary law, but codification runs the risk of falling out of date with what is actually happening in communities. Codification can also be a blunt instrument to encapsulate something that is nuanced and subject to change. While, on the one hand, courts should endeavour to respect the 'sanctity of customary practices' (Maimela and Morudu 2024, 417), practices may also

[33] Criticism has been expressed that in the Bhe case the court struck down customary provisions rather than using its constitutional powers to develop customary law in a way that better reflects contemporary standards. (Church and Church 2007, 60) However, it is also worth noting that for the court to develop customary law the judges need to be 'well versed in the norms of indigenous law to be able to ascertain the principles or jural postulates which underpin the law or norm'. (Church and Church 2007, 62)

through effluxion of time become remnants of a tradition rather than ongoing law. In Africa, for example, many aspects of customary law have been successfully codified, but there are also examples where communities have not complied with the codified version of their customary laws. This highlights the fact that a custom is sought to be codified, but then it becomes frozen and not adequately 'living'. In this respect Sachs highlights both the living part of customary law but also its ability to adjust to contemporary human rights norms. (Sachs 2024) Additionally, consider the South African Law Commission's observation that the practices developed by courts under the discriminatory Black Administration Act[34] – nowadays recognised as official customary law in literature – provide a 'useful foundation' for ascertaining when customary law should be applied to a dispute, with appropriateness and reasonableness being essential elements in the decision to apply it. (South African Law Commission 1999, 28) Also notable is Rautenbach's suggestion that declaring customary law in a specific dispute may require expert evidence. (Rautenbach 2023b, 31) However, ironically, such expert testimony may partly rely on official or documented customary law and observations made by the expert. Furthermore, expert evidence or opinions may be biased in favour of a particular outcome. This happened in the Australian case of Munkara when an expert witness was criticised for lacking a factual basis for their opinion. (Munkara case 2024)

The courts are empowered and obligated, pursuant to the 1996 Constitution, to apply and, if necessary, develop customary law, provided the relevant legal norm complies with the Constitution and the parties involved in the case agree that their dispute is to be determined by reference to customary law.[35] The

[34] The Black Administration Act of 1927 recognised, for the first time, customary law throughout South Africa. In the Motaung case the court described the purpose of the Act as 'to meet the needs of the Native who has emerged from the tribal state to the wider and more enlightened one of western civilisation and to systems of legal jurisprudence'. (Motaung case 1930) In the Moseneke case Sachs J described the Act as being 'in conflict with the establishment of a non-racial society where rights and duties are no longer determined by origin or skin colour'. (Moseneke case 2001, para 21)

[35] While it is unlikely that a court would declare a person bound to customary law against their will, a more pertinent question is whether persons can mutually consent for customary law to apply to an arrangement to the exclusion of other legal provisions, including those in the Constitution. The answer to this has yet to be provided, but would surely be in the negative. On the one hand, personal autonomy, freedom of association and the right to contract allow adults to enter into an agreement on terms that are mutually acceptable, including consenting to have their arrangement governed by applicable customary law. However, on the other hand, circumstances may have changed since the agreement was made, leading to challenges regarding

application of customary law to a particular dispute must be just, appropriate and proportionate.[36] Although the repugnancy provision has not been cited in contemporary jurisprudence, the South African Law Commission has nevertheless expressed concern that a court could potentially 'subordinate' customary law by invoking repugnancy in light of uniform human rights principles. (South African Law Commission 1999, 40) Even if the term 'repugnancy' is not used, the effect under the Constitution could be similar in that the application of the universality of individual rights pursuant to international law may over time render inconsistent customary practices unconstitutional.

As observed above, striking a balance between upholding a constitutional value and giving recognition to a customary law may be complex. For example, while some initiation procedures, on the one hand, may be open to criticism to the violence against the person, on the other hand courts have accepted the reality and applicability of those events. Note, for example, how in the Bulelwa case the applicant relied on the processes of initiation and seclusion as a valid defence for failure to comply with court procedures. (Bulelwa case 2022) In the case Mathenjwa J recognised the customary concept of ukuthwasa to allow a stay

---

the constitutionality of the original agreement. Similarly to other religious and cultural norms, the Constitution takes precedence over customary law. Therefore, parties cannot use customary law to circumvent the Constitution or be deprived of their constitutional rights. In this regard, consider Chapter 2, where the issue of forum shopping was addressed in the context of the ECtHR. Forum shopping refers to a situation where an individual seeks to pursue a claim according to a normative system – whether religious or constitutional – that offers the best likelihood of achieving the desired outcome. The fact that many people live under multiple systems of law enables them to potentially attempt to apply rules in a manner that best suits their desired outcome. Diala, for example, observes that it is not unknown in South Africa and Nigeria for persons to display 'dual observance' and hence engage in 'remarkable *forum shopping* in issues such as land and marriage contracts'. (Diala 2017, 157)

[36] Concerning the questions of when and to whom customary law applies, Moseneke DCJ observed as follows: 'Difficult questions may surface about the reach of customary law, whom it binds and, in particular, whether people other than indigenous African people may be bound by customary law. *Happily, that matter will have to stand over for decision on another day.*' (Gumede case 2009, para 23) An essential question of fact to consider before recognising living customary law is whether the parties in a dispute had agreed – explicitly or tacitly – for customary law to regulate their arrangement. The answer to this question is to be determined by reference to the evidence of the circumstances surrounding the dispute, such as the customs followed, lobola paid, ceremonies adhered to or conduct of the parties. The voluntary nature of adherence to customary law is likely to weigh heavily on the mind of any court, especially if an outcome associated with the application of a customary norm appears prejudicial to the party who denies that customary law should be applied. See, for example, the Maisela case, in which it was held that the concept of 'voetstoots' (buy as is) is not known in customary law. (Maisela case 2000)

of execution since the ancestral spirits have called a person into isolation and away from family. Manthwa describes the judgment as 'refreshing' since it was accepted that a traditional custom could be relied on in defence of a civil claim. (Manthwa 2023, 669) In each case customary law is sought to be relied on in defence of an action that may appear to be inconsistent with the Constitution; fine balancing is required to ensure, on the one hand, that constitutional principles are upheld, but on the other hand that customary law as a system of non-state law is recognised.

10.2.6 Defining customary law

The Constitution does not define customary law. Furthermore, customary law does not imply a single legal system that commands adherence from all indigenous communities or all individuals who form part of a particular community. Customary law does not necessarily bind all individuals who associate culturally with an indigenous community. There are several systems of customary law, with some overlaps and common practices, as well as separate and autonomous traditions. The same customs may appear in different communities under different names or there may be variations to a custom or nuances in the way it is applied. For example, in the Mabena case the court accepted that lobolo negotiations could take place only with the mother of the prospective wife since this gender-neutral approach was consistent with the 'spirit, purport and objects' of the Bill of Rights. (Mabena case 1998, paras 1074–1075) This does not necessarily mean that the same standard applies to all indigenous groups that use a form of lobola. Furthermore, the rights arising under the Constitution must be interpreted purposively. For example, in the Maneli case, where the term 'adoption' was used in a statute, it was held that the term must encompass its customary-law interpretation. (Maneli case 2010)

The Recognition of Marriages Act defines customary law as 'customs and usages traditionally observed among the indigenous African people of South Africa and which form part of the culture of those people'. (Recognition Act 1998, s 1) Despite the clarity sought to be achieved by the Act, each concept it introduces prompts additional inquiries into the definition of customary law. For instance, questions arise regarding which customs and usages are encompassed by the Act, whether all customs and usages qualify as 'law', when a usage is traditionally observed, who qualifies as indigenous, the extent of adherence by a community or substantial part of a community required for a custom to be recognised, whether an individual's association with a community also implies acceptance of customary laws, the meaning of 'culture', and the legal status of customary law for migrants who have relocated to South Africa.[37]

It is also notable that the terms 'indigenous law' and 'customary law' are used interchangeably in statutes and literature in South Africa. (Certification case 1996, footnote 142) Another question to emerge is whether the protections accorded by the Recognition of Marriages Act extend to same-sex marriages. If not, the issue arises of how, if at all, customary law or statutory law should be developed to address this gap. (Osman and Baase 2022)[38] These illustrate that, even if certainty is sought to be given by codifying customary law, new questions are likely to arise.

In the Bhe case the Constitutional Court referenced certain inherent characteristics of customary law, including its flexibility, emphasis on consensus, obligation toward family, community care and ethos of preventing disputes. (Bhe case 2005, para 166)[39] In many respects the values embedded in Ubuntu

---

[37] Above, I raised the question of how courts might respond to new customary laws introduced to South Africa through immigration. The Recognition of Marriages Act stipulates that only customary marriages of 'indigenous people of South Africa' may be recognised. Considering the transformative and Ubuntu-driven character of the Constitution, it is possible that a future Constitutional Court may also consider indigenous customs originating from outside South Africa when those arise in a dispute between immigrants.

[38] Note, for example, that many customary marriages in South Africa are not registered, albeit that those marriages can be registered pursuant to legislation that seeks to regulate customary marriages (Recognition Act 1998). Because of the complexities that often arise from the non-registration of customary marriages, Sibisi recommends that traditional leaders should play a greater role in officially recording and registering marriages over which they officiate. (Sibisi 2023, 531) The same challenges are likely to arise under any statutory arrangement to regulate Muslim marriages.

[39] This may be a rather idyllic view of customary law. As Bronstein observes, there are many examples in customary law of the controlling power of men over women and children, control of the productive power of men and women, conflict and absence of harmony, and groups with opposing interests. (Bronstein 1998, 395) The irony is that if those elements were removed, customary law may become a reflection of contemporary laws, with its uniqueness eroded. The descriptions of customary law in general, and Ubuntu in particular, in terms that evoke the peace of the original Garden of Eden are somewhat romanticised, portraying an idealised state of affairs. It has been observed, with reference to Botswana, that 'it seems customary law rules inherently continue to perpetuate unacceptable inequalities of gender, age, and lineage'. (Dinokopila and Kgoboge 2021, 348) In Botswana protections against discrimination can be limited by legislation aimed at accommodating customary law in areas such as adoption, marriage, divorce, burial, property and 'other matters of personal law'. (Constitution of Botswana s 15(4)*(c)*). Note in this respect the recognition of the Noken electoral system in Indonesia, as previously mentioned. A similar approach has been adopted in Mexico, where the indirect election of members of an

(Chapter 6) permeate customary law. (Bhe case 2005, para 74) Ubuntu is referred to as a 'dominant value in African traditional culture' (Bhe case 2005, para 163), although the way it is applied to a particular dispute must be ascertained by way of evidence.

It is widely acknowledged that the way customary law was observed and regarded in the past by anthropologists, politicians, social scientists and lawyers, as well as by the courts, was invariably influenced by their respective background and prejudices. Historically, customary law was typically described from an external perspective, using terms, values and norms purportedly comparable to those originating from other legal and social systems. Diala refers to this as the 'pigeon-holing' of customary law, where a customary normative value is forced to fit into a familiar Western value for the purposes of comparison and explanation. (Diala 2017) This ultimately led to legislation aimed at encapsulating and codifying customary law. However, this approach carried the risk that the legislation defined customary law based on what it was *thought to be* by reference to other legal systems, rather than reflecting its true nature. (Rautenbach 2023b, 30) Ngcobo J, for example, observed how difficult it can be to draw a distinction between 'living customary law and . . . its distorted version'. (Bhe case 2005, para 154) This discrepancy is at least partly attributed to the emphasis placed on the patriarchal elements of customary law, criticised by Langa DCJ as a 'major distortion'. (Bhe case 2005, para 89)

In addition to the possible imperfections in historical understandings of customary law, the South African Law Reform Commission observed that judicially applying living customary law remains challenging because of the difficulty in ascertaining its meaning in practice. (South African Law Commission 1999, 21) Furthermore, the Commission cautioned that the principle of constitutional supremacy may ultimately undermine customary law:

> Because many rules of customary law reflect, directly or indirectly, the patriarchal traditions of African culture, large parts of the law could be declared invalid for infringing the right to equal treatment. If that were allowed, the constitutional recognition given to customary law in 1996 would be an empty gesture. (South African Law Commission 1999, 23)[40]

---

indigenous community at municipal level has been held to be consistent with the Constitution. (Indirect election case 2023)

[40] Note, for example, how in the Bangindawo case, the question arose about the arrangement that legal representation was not allowed in customary courts. While this seems to be in obvious breach of constitutional rights, the court emphasised that customary courts could not simply be

10.3 CUSTOMARY LAW IN CONSTITUTIONAL NEGOTIATIONS

The future status of customary law, including the recognition of traditional leaders and institutions, presented serious challenges during the constitutional negotiation processes. On the one hand, customary law and traditional leaders were tainted by the legacy of apartheid, homelands and intra-discriminatory practices particularly towards women. On the other hand, proponents of customary law and the recognition of traditional institutions enjoyed substantial support within the liberation movements, exemplified by organisations like CONTRALESA (Congress of Traditional Leaders of South Africa). The liberation parties had to politically accommodate traditional leaders and customary law to garner support, particularly in rural areas. Moreover, traditional leaders and their customary systems still exerted influence over large parts of South Africa's rural (and to a certain extent urban) population. Their significance could not be overlooked during the constitution drafting process. Even as the homelands were legally to be abolished, traditional tribal areas frequently overlapped with these territories. Thus, a delicate balance had to be struck between dismantling apartheid structures while preserving tribal institutions and their authority.

The status of women, in particular, required serious discourse. Holomisa, during the drafting period, recognised the need for traditional leaders to reassess the role of women, acknowledging that women could no longer be considered as 'minors', as they had been traditionally perceived. In similar vein other indigenous customs that may be inconsistent with contemporary democratic standards may also have to be revisited. However, he also emphasised the importance of addressing the role of traditional leaders in a 'politically honest way if negative tribalistic emotions are to be controlled'. (Holomisa 1997)

Donkers and Murray expressed the challenge facing the Constitution's drafters as follows:

> The general notion that all traditional authorities are stagnant institutions incapable of accommodating social and political change should be countered through the adaptation of those features that are still contentious. Any endeavour to create a fully democratic society in South Africa must utilize the intrinsic strengths of traditional leaders. Traditional leaders and authorities are essential political, social and economic structures for maintaining the sociopolitical order that is a prerequisite for rural development. (Donkers and Murray 1997, 55)

---

compared to magistrates' courts, and that allowance should be made for the different value system of customary law. (Bangindawo case 1998)

10.3.1 1993 Constitution

The 1993 Constitution established the following benchmarks about the recognition of customary law: first, customary law cannot be relied upon to limit the scope of fundamental rights as contained in the Constitution (s 33(2)); secondly, the entrenchment of fundamental rights in the Constitution cannot be construed as denying rights under customary law, nor the equality of customary law as a separate legal system (s 33(3)); thirdly, when interpreting any customary law the courts shall have due regard to the spirit, purport and objects of the chapter on fundamental rights (s 35(3)); fourthly, traditional authorities are recognised (s 181(1)); and, fifthly, indigenous law is to be subject to regulation by law (s 181(2)).

Many questions, however, remained unresolved in the 1993 Constitution, leading Sinclair to observe that 'the future of customary law is uncertain'. (Sinclair 1994, 559) It was particularly in the area of gender equality under customary law that Sinclair was concerned that the 'value of traditional custom relegates them [women] to a status of subordination to men'. (Sinclair 1994, 560; Ojogbo and Edu 2022) There were also concerns that since legislating over customary matters was a shared competency between the national and provincial governments, it could lead to overlap, duplication and uncertainty. Meanwhile, traditional leaders argued that their role and status in the final Constitution should be clarified as a distinct sphere of government, effectively making them a fourth level of government.

10.3.2 Constitutional Principles

Constitutional Principle XIII recognised the institution, status and role of traditional leadership, providing, relevantly, that:

> The institution, status and role of traditional leadership, according to indigenous law, shall be recognised and protected in the Constitution. Indigenous law, like common law, shall be recognised and applied by the courts, subject to the fundamental rights contained in the Constitution and to legislation dealing specifically therewith. (emphasis added)

10.3.3 Certification case

The question arose during the Certification case whether the new Constitution had to make provision for and regulate the role of traditional leaders as an institution of government, similarly to national, provincial and local government, or whether the proposed constitutional provision stating that those matters would be regulated by legislation in due course was adequate.

Objections against the text of the draft Constitution had been received, arguing that the proposed recognition of traditional leaders and institutions, without greater protection afforded to them, was inconsistent with Constitutional Principle XIII. (Certification case 1996, para 189) The Constitutional Court rejected the proposition, declaring that the recognition, functioning, powers and functions of traditional authorities had always been dependent upon national legislation. The court found that the 'umbrella' clause of the proposed Constitution, in which provision was made for traditional leaders and customary law, was 'wide' and that ultimately 'no one exercised power or authority outside of the constitution'. (Certification case 1996, para 194) The court was satisfied that the proposed constitutional text not only guaranteed the continued existence of traditional leaders but also 'the survival of an evolving customary law'. (Certification case 1996, para 197) Finally, the court emphasised that, when developing customary law, every court must 'promote the spirit, purport and objects of the Bill of Rights'. (Certification case 1996, para 202)

This reasoning illustrates how the Constitutional Court made a value judgment in applying a Constitutional Principle (see the discussion in Chapter 3). While the court had adequate scope to use its discretion to direct greater recognition of traditional leaders as a distinct sphere of government within the constitutional text, it chose a less prescriptive approach. Instead of directing greater specificity about the status of indigenous leaders as a level of government, the court endorsed the recognition of traditional leaders and customary law, deferring the clarification of specifics to legislation.

10.3.4 1996 Constitution

The 1996 Constitution contains several provisions dealing with the institution of traditional leaders and the recognition of customary rights. First, s 31 recognises the rights of persons belonging to cultural, religious or linguistic community to enjoy and practise their culture; secondly, s 39(2) mandates that any court developing customary law is required to promote the spirit, purport and objects of the Bill of Rights; thirdly, s 39(3) provides that the Bill of Rights does not deny the existence of customary law to the extent that those norms are consistent with the Bill of Rights; fourthly, ss 211 and 212 recognise the institution of traditional leaders 'according to customary law', and matters associated therewith; and, fifthly, s 211(3) determines that 'the courts must apply customary law when that law is applicable, subject to the Constitution and any legislation that specifically deals with customary law'.

Importantly, customary law is elevated to the same status of other laws; customary law norms are subject only to the Constitution; and customary law and norms are impacted upon by the horizontal application of the Bill of Rights (s 8(2)). Essentially, pursuant to the 1996 Constitution, the courts are placed in a position to ascertain 'an accurate picture of the social reality' concerning the relevant customary law that applies to a dispute, including the constitutionality of the customary law in question. (Chuma 2023, 43)

10.4 THE CHALLENGE OF RECOGNISING AND CODIFYING CUSTOMARY LAW: THE EXAMPLE OF THE RECOGNITION OF CUSTOMARY MARRIAGES ACT

A challenge that faced the new Parliament was whether customary law should remain oral and uncodified, or whether for the sake of consistency legislation should be enacted to codify and regularise customary law. Parliament opted for a dual approach whereby certain aspects of customary law are codified by way of legislation, while other parts are left to be ascertained when the need arises.

The Recognition of Customary Marriages Act is an example of legislation enacted by Parliament under the new Constitution aimed at regularising, standardising, harmonising and codifying certain features of customary law. (Recognition Act 1998)[41] As the Recognition Act sought to remove aspects of discrimination pertaining to customary marriage that had previously existed within customary law (Chuma 2023, 47), it created a lawful, statutory option for couples to be married pursuant to customary law – thereby ironically highlighting the benefit of customary law being 'officially' codified by way of legislation.[42] Notably, couples getting married in accordance with customary law are not obligated to record their marriages under the Act.

---

[41] The Preamble states as follows about the objectives of the Recognition Act: 'To make provision for the recognition of customary marriages; to specify the requirements for a valid customary marriage; to regulate the registration of customary marriages; to provide for the equal status and capacity of spouses in customary marriages; to regulate the proprietary consequences of customary marriages and the capacity of spouses of such marriages; to regulate the dissolution of customary marriages. . . .'

[42] Notable elements are that spouses must be over the age of 18 years; the must consent to marry each other; they must consent to marry pursuant to customary law; and the marriage must be negotiated and celebrated according to customary law. The marriages are in community of property and they must be registered under the Recognition Act. (ss 2, 3, 4, 7).

The Recognition Act harmonises customary law and fundamental rights, while also protecting the non-discriminatory elements of customary law. (Ramatsekisa 2008, 41) The irony, however, is that the Recognition Act seeks to do the same as the previous official law had done, namely to codify customary law. This to some extent perpetuates the 'typical representation' that the validity of law is 'founded on clear rules emanating from a central authority'. (Diala 2017, 147)

The Recognition Act was an 'ambitious effort to remedy the historic humiliation' of persons who had been married under customary law but who did not enjoy the same recognition and protection offered to those married pursuant to statutory law. (Gumede case 2009, para 16) The Act sought to acknowledge the dynamic nature of customary law and facilitate its development as a legal system, akin to the evolution of common law. An example of such an evolution is that the contemporary role of the husband in customary law marriages differs from the historic role. Meanwhile, greater equality between spouses and the recognition of children's rights in society and pursuant to the Constitution can further influence the manner in which customary law adapts to contemporary circumstances. In line with this, the Recognition Act sought not only to recognise customary marriages, but also to modify such relationships in a manner consistent with the Constitution. (Recognition Act 1998, para 21) Importantly, the Recognition Act also aimed to modernise customary law by 'jettisoning gendered inequality within marriage'. (Gumede case 2009, para 24) The enactment of the Recognition Act placed courts in a position where they could recognise and develop customary law to ensure it 'aligns with constitutional dictates'. (Gumede case 2009, para 29) In the Zwane case the court explained why three wives, two who were married under customary law and one married in accordance with civil law, had to be treated equally by the estate of their deceased husband. (Zwane case 2024, para 42)

In the Gumede case, however, the issue at stake did not involve an unwritten customary norm but rather a statutory provision, the constitutionality of which was challenged. Moseneke DCJ expressed the view that courts should be slow to 'develop' uncodified living customary law since Parliament may be better suited to perform such a task by way of legislative intervention. (Gumede case 2009, para 30) This is consistent with the reservation expressed in the Mthembu case that the court must be mindful and respectful of the doctrine of separation of powers whereby Parliament is better equipped to legislate after having heard public opinions. (EB case 2024) Developing customary law holistically is a task Parliament is arguably more adept at carrying out. (Mthembu case 1997)[43]

This seems to be a sensible approach since Parliament may be better equipped than a court to hear submissions and obtain evidence, including by way of community meetings, on the actual status of a customary law within a community, any shortcomings it may have and how it can be improved consistent with the Constitution. It is also important to bear in mind that living customary law may develop very slowly, in an ad hoc manner and without uniformity. (Ramatsekisa 2008, 44) But linked to this uncertainty is also the strength of living customary law and its ability to adapt and adjust. (Sachs 2024) Finally, any interpretations provided by a court must be aligned with the primary purpose of the Constitution and relevant legislation, namely to ensure that the values of non-discrimination and equality are accorded to all. (Gumede case 2009, para 43)

In the Ramuhovhi case, where the constitutionality of s 7(1) of the Recognition Act was contested, the court ruled that the provision was unconstitutional. Interim orders were issued to give Parliament an opportunity to rectify the statutory shortcomings. The applicants contended that s 7(1) excluded pre-Act polygamous marriages from the protections provided by the Act. Both parties agreed that Venda customary law does not confer property rights or control over property to wives in polygamous marriages. (Osman and Himonga 2017, 171) The Constitutional Court confirmed the invalidity of the subsection and gave Parliament two years to rectify it. (Ramuhovhi case 2017 order 4)

Relevant to this chapter is the question of which forum, the courts or Parliament, is better suited to develop a customary law to bring it into alignment with the Constitution. In the Ramuhovhi case the court declared that 'it is best to leave it to Parliament to finally decide how to regulate the proprietary regime of pre-Act polygamous customary marriages'. (Ramuhovhi case 2017, para 50)

The statutory recognition of customary law raises three pertinent questions for this chapter: How does a court determine the applicable legal system for a marriage? What happens in cases, not atypical nowadays, where couples incorporate a mix of legal and customary systems and symbolism into their marriage? How does the legal system address situations where one party denies the applicability of customary law to their marriage or claims coercion into such a union?

---

[43] Note the criticism of the Mabena case expressed by Nhlapo (Mabena case 1998), when she stated that the court '*contrived* to find some evidence to support the view that a new customary practice had evolved'. (emphasis added) (Nhlapo 2017, 15)

The general principle likely to be adopted by courts is that all relevant information, circumstances, evidence and material must be considered to ascertain the legal system under which the parties had intended to be bound (Gumede case 2009, para 44); the rationale why customary law should be applied to resolve a specific dispute; the different remedies that may be available under different legal systems; what is just, equitable and reasonable in the current dispute; whether the parties elect for customary law to apply; and whether the customary norm sought to be relied on by one party is consistent with the Constitution.

10.5 PERTINENT QUESTIONS TO ANALYSE JURISPRUDENCE

In this section some of the pertinent questions that have emerged from the foregoing literature review are addressed by referencing judgments handed down by South African courts:

10.5.1 Which is the supreme law of the land?

During the colonial era in South Africa customary law was often disregarded or, if recognised, it was considered subordinate and inferior to laws imposed by the colonial authorities. An established hierarchy existed whereby customary laws could be adhered to informally, as long as this was not done to the exclusion or limitation of the laws of the sovereign. In Africa in general, and South Africa in particular, customary law received some limited official recognition by state law and local courts, especially in tribal areas. However, over time customary law and traditional institutions also became tools of control, dominance and corruption. Eventually, the system of traditional authorities became tainted by discrimination and unequal treatment of women and children. The institutions of traditional leaders were often used by colonial authorities to exert control over communities, to secure political backing, to reward supporters and to marginalise dissenting voices. Regrettably, an examination of contemporary politics in South Africa and beyond would suggest that the politicisation of traditional institutions persists.[44]

[44] A notable example was the 2023 dispute over the appointment of the Zulu monarch (Zulu case 2023), affected by the lack of transparency and proper community consultation that marred the Traditional and Khoi-San Leadership Act 2019. (Khoisan Act appeal 2023) The question arising in the case was whether the Zulu king had been correctly appointed pursuant to Zulu custom. The decision of President Ramaphosa to recognise Misuzulu kaZwelithini was set aside because of the former's failure to comply with statutory provisions that regulate how a complaint of this nature should be dealt with. (Zulu case 2023, para 62)

The constitutions of 1993 and 1996 changed the presumption of pre-eminence of parliamentary laws vis-à-vis customary laws. The 1996 Constitution acknowledges the inherent equality of customary law as a legal system, subject only to the Constitution. The Constitution thus became the supreme law, recognising and endorsing legal pluralism but providing that all laws, including parliamentary, customary, traditional and religious laws, are aligned with the fundamental norms outlined within the Constitution.

The Constitutional Court in the Alexkor case broke new ground by recognising for the first time the new status of customary law as it relates specifically to rights to land. (Alexkor case 2004; Barrie 2021) The Alexkor case reflected an increasing trend in African jurisprudence (and beyond) towards better recognition and accommodation of indigenous and customary rights in relation to their lands in particular. This was particularly evident in cases concerning land rights and the right to be consulted when land interests are affected. (Endorois Welfare Council case 2003; De Villiers 2023c) The Constitutional Court, much like in the Australian cases of Mabo, Yorta Yorta and Wik, and the Canadian case of Delgamuukw, acknowledged the existence of indigenous law in its own right as a legal system of substance. While common law may recognise indigenous rights, it does not dictate the content of indigenous law. The operation of indigenous law therefore does not arise from common law, but from indigenous law itself. Previous approaches that sought to interpret indigenous customs through the lens of common law have therefore been replaced by efforts to understand indigenous law within its own framework.

When this approach as set out in the Alexkor case is applied to land rights, it suggests that indigenous land ownership could have survived despite colonial settlement. (Mabo case (2) 1992) It then becomes a question of evidence whether, pursuant to indigenous law rather than common law, the indigenous community claiming native or indigenous title to the land still exists and functions as a cohesive society with ongoing connection to the land in question, and in accordance with their own laws and customs. (Yorta Yorta (HCA) case 2002) The yardstick used to ascertain ongoing indigenous connection to land is the rules of the customary legal system under which the community operates. (Alexkor case 2004, para 51) The same approach can be adopted to determine whether an indigenous custom continues to apply to a particular dispute. The court's role is to determine which indigenous *law* custom is being invoked and whether the community continues to adhere to it.

In the Alexkor case the Constitutional Court declared that the Richtersveld community retained their rights to land, including mineral rights. (Alexkor case 2004, paras 64, 82) The court adopted an approach similar to jurisprudence emanating from Australia, Canada and New Zealand. With this approach, primary consideration is given to the legal system under which the indigenous community functions to ascertain the nature of indigenous rights, thereby embracing the concept of legal pluralism. An indigenous community may possess a bundle of indigenous rights, the content of which is determined by referencing their customary law *as it continues to be adhered to.* For example, in the Ward case in Australia, the court endorsed the reasoning that native title is to be understood as a bundle of rights rather than a simple title to land. (Ward case 2002)[45] The content of this bundle of rights for each community is established through various forms of evidence, including documents, judicial precedents, written records and oral testimony. Once the elements of the bundle of rights for a particular community are determined, the court can assess how a specific legal norm concerning native title within the bundle interacts with contemporary legislation, including the Constitution. The US Supreme Court has adopted a similar approach, describing each property right of indigenous peoples under treaty as a 'stick in the bundle' that collectively comprises the rights of a reservation. (Arizona case 2023) Consequently, the bundle of rights exercisable by different indigenous communities may vary depending on their particular customs, traditions, and practices, as well as the extent to which traditional rules have been modified, abandoned or affected by acts that extinguish native title. (De Villiers 2022h)[46]

The following principles stemming from the Alexkor case are relevant to the question of the supremacy of legal systems:

---

[45] The majority reflected on the utility of the concept of a bundle of rights as follows: 'The metaphor of "bundle of rights" which is so often employed in this area is useful in two respects. It draws attention first to the fact that there may be more than one right or interest and secondly to the fact that there may be several *kinds* of rights and interests in relation to land that exist under traditional law and custom. Not all of those rights and interests may be capable of full or accurate expression as rights to control what others may do on or with the land.' (Ward case 2002, para 95)

[46] The approach adopted by the Constitutional Court regarding indigenous land rights has, perhaps surprisingly, not given rise to broader indigenous native title claims to land in South Africa. However, the principles established by the court concerning the supremacy of the Constitution, and the implications thereof for indigenous law and customs, are relevant for the purposes of this chapter.

First, indigenous laws are not set in stone – they evolve over time. Moreover, not all customs or traditions can be regarded as law, nor are the laws contained in a 'fixed body of formally clarified and easily ascertainable rules. Indigenous law is subject to changes and patterns of living adjustments.' (Alexkor case 2004, para 52)

Secondly, since customary law is not written, its content and application must be ascertained by reference to facts as they arise in a particular situation and in accordance with the beliefs of the community concerned.[47] As an evolving system, the scope of rights, interests and obligations at a specific time must be ascertained through evidence of ongoing adherence and practice by a community. In this respect various forms of evidence, such as published materials, scientific works, academic observations and jurisprudential examples, may be cited, but oral evidence may also be necessary to determine whether a particular custom continues to be applied as law or has been modified or abandoned. (Alexkor case 2004, paras 53–54)

Thirdly, when citing published works and historic jurisprudence it is important to recognise that they may have been written during a time when customary law may have been viewed as subordinate to other legal systems. It is crucial to consider that contemporary perspectives on customary law may have evolved, providing greater insight into the details and functioning of traditional customs. Customary legal systems are now regarded as legal systems in their own right, rather than

[47] Note, for example, the finding of the State Administrative Tribunal of Western Australia concerning the belief held by an indigenous community that the building of weirs in a river would upset the snake that spiritually resides there, adversely impacting the community in turn: 'We have found that the River occupies a central role in the belief system of the Thalanyji people. We are satisfied that the Thalanyji people's deep connection to the River, and their belief in its healing properties, is such that the Thalanyji people's relationship to the River is properly regarded as deeply spiritual. We have also found that the Thalanyji people's beliefs in the water snake, which lives in the River, and which controls the natural flow of the River, are a central part of their spiritual beliefs in relation to the River. . . . We have found that, *from the Thalanyji people's perspective*, the implementation of the MARS project, which will affect the natural flow of the River, risks killing or harming the water snake, or causing the water snake to become angry, and that that would have a significant adverse impact on the Thalaynji people. This may occur in the form of fear or concern that the water snake may act in anger and cause harm to them, in the form of emotional harm that they will be held responsible to the water snake, in the form of spiritual harm flowing from action which interferes with one of the central tenets of their spiritual beliefs, and in the form of emotional harm in a sense of shame or failure in their personal responsibility, as custodians of the River, to prevent the MARS project from proceeding.' (Forrest case 2023, paras 603–607)

subject to evaluation from the standpoint of another legal system. (Alexkor case 2004, para 54) Conversely, historical materials may have depicted customary law as subservient or uncivilised, potentially influencing the portrayal and assessment of the customary-law system. However, contemporary understandings of customary law may also get it wrong, which means caution must be displayed to uncritically accept contemporary explanations of customary law.

Fourthly, the ongoing validity and applicability of a customary norm as law depend on its consistency with the Constitution. As the supreme law of the land the Constitution serves as the standard against which all laws, regulations, customs and traditions are measured. Any found to contradict it may be deemed unconstitutional or rendered inoperative. In essence:

> While in the past indigenous law was seen through the common-law lens, it must now be seen as an integral part of our law. Like all law it depends for its ultimate force and validity on the Constitution Its validity must now be determined by reference not to common law, but to the Constitution. The courts are obliged by section 211(3) of the Constitution to apply customary law when it is applicable, subject to the Constitution and any legislation that deals with customary law. In doing so the courts must have regard to the spirit, purport and objects of the Bill of Rights. . . . It is clear therefore that the Constitution acknowledges the originality and distinctiveness of indigenous law as an independent source of norms within the legal system. At the same time the Constitution, while giving force to indigenous law, makes it clear that such law is subject to the Constitution and has to be interpreted in the light of its values. Furthermore, like the common law, indigenous law is subject to any legislation, consistent with the Constitution, that specifically deals with it. In the result, indigenous law feeds into, nourishes, fuses with and becomes part of the amalgam of South African law. (emphasis added) (Alexkor case 2004, para 51)

In short, the Constitution stands as the highest law of the land, taking precedence over any other legal norm, whether indigenous, cultural or religious. Any conflicting non-state law or customary or religious norm may duly be declared inconsistent and not given legal effect. Critics may be concerned by the standardisation espoused by the Constitution since it may erode customary law to remove all its uniqueness as a separate legal system.

10.5.2 Is there a distinction between official customary law and living customary law?

In literature and jurisprudence a common distinction is made between *official* customary law and *living* customary law. The former implies customary law as recognised and recorded by colonial and settler regimes, often portrayed as stagnant and fixed in the past. On the other hand, the latter refers to customary law as a dynamic legal system with rules and practices evolving over time. The content of living customary law is ascertained by contemporary evidence rather than relying solely on historical documentation.

Diala characterises this distinction as 'fashionable' yet somewhat ambiguous. (Diala 2017, 143) In his view the concept of living customary law has not 'benefited from a detailed legal theoretical explanation'. This perspective aligns with Claassen and Weeks, who observe that living customary law resembles official customary law in some respects. (Claassens and Weeks 2009, 516) Meanwhile, in the Bhe case and other subsequent cases the purported distinction between the two has been approached non-critically.

The risk in seeking to establish a separation between official and living customary law is that court judgments, which in effect reflect official customary law, may diverge from community developments or, even worse, communities may simply ignore court determinations altogether. When definitively pronouncing on a customary norm, courts may face similar criticism to that expressed about pre-1993 codifications and expert views of customary laws. Furthermore, courts attempting to develop customary law consistently with the Constitution may encounter resistance from communities who consider such changes to be 'modernisation' and Eurocentric and ignore them. It is not entirely surprising that Nhlapo comments that 'it would be fair to conclude that we are no closer to a uniform guideline as to when and how development of customary law should be approached by the courts'. (Nhlapo 2017, 19)

At face value the distinction between living and official customary law is noteworthy, but it does not survive legal or scientific scrutiny.

Although the reliance on a purported distinction between official and living customary law has grown in popularity, its efficacy as a scientific or legal tool for categorising or analysing customary law in all its facets, in both its historic and modern application, remains open to challenge. The principle of customary law being flexible, dynamic and adaptable has long been acknowledged. However, the understanding of customary law pre- and post-1996 is also informed by research, documentation, recording and expert opinions. It is through considering the totality of this evidence that a comprehension of customary law is gained. For example, in the Lewis case of Nigeria Osborne CJ observed as follows:

> [I]n nearly every case [of customary law] I have found that there are general underlying principles not difficult to understand, and obviously based on the primitive requirements of the community. In some instances those principles have been modified, and even

> departed from, as the result of contact with European methods; indeed, one of the most striking features of West African native custom, to my mind, is its flexibility; it appears to have been always subject to motives of expediency, and it shows unquestionable adaptability to altered circumstances without entirely losing its individual characteristics. The great danger in applying it in this Court is that of crystallising it in such a way that it cannot be departed from in cases where expediency demands, and where natives themselves would depart from it; and I therefore preface my findings with the remark that they are intended as findings of the general principles which govern native custom in Lagos at the present day, and not as hard-and-fast findings of immutable native law. (Lewis case 1909)

This chapter does not aim to engage in a detailed debate on the validity of distinguishing between official customary law and living customary law. It is sufficient to observe that, regardless of its source or codification, customary law, like any legal system, is dynamic and susceptible to change. Just as ordinary laws, whether statutes or common law, are dynamic or living and subject to legal interpretation, so does customary law also evolve over time. Even if its rules, customs or procedures are reduced to writing or recognised in jurisprudence at a particular moment, customary law retains its dynamic nature. Declaring the content of customary law at a particular point in time does not crystallise or freeze it, nor does it halt its evolution. Documenting a custom, as seen in the Recognition of Marriage Act, merely reflects a legal norm as it exists at a specific time.

Any legal system, whether based on contemporary legislation, common law, customary law or religious rules, is inherently 'living' and subject to change. But there also hides danger in the fold of the living system. As Strauss cautions regarding the 'living' nature of the US Constitution, while the concept of living law may be appealing, it also poses the risk of uncertainty and manipulation by those tasked with interpreting current legal content who may bring to the court their own perspectives, prejudices and bias. Conversely, rigidity with regard to legal norms offers certainty, but risks resulting in diminishing relevance over time. (Strauss 2010) Ultimately, in any dispute concerning customary law both lay oral and expert evidence may have to be heard to ascertain what, in the context of the dispute, the applicable provisions of customary law are to a specific community. This is consistent with what the Botswana Court of Appeal has referred to as the 'prevailing societal ambience of the concerned community'. (Ramantele case 2013, para 677)[48] Although the phrase 'living customary law'

---

[48] Weinberg explains how the court in the Ramantele case was open to societal evidence and expert views of contemporary society in order to 'destabilise' the traditional approach whereby

has not been widely used in the jurisprudence of Botswana, judges nevertheless 'interpret the law according to changing ideas about gender and generation' (Werbner and Werbner 2022, 14)[49]

The proposition that a watertight distinction can be drawn between so-called official (documented) customary law (which has been written down in some form) and living (oral) customary law (which is principally verbal) is somewhat romantic and overly simplified. It fails to acknowledge that any investigation into customary law inevitably results in declaring its content as it exists at a particular moment in time, effectively rendering it 'official'.

In the Certification case the Constitutional Court acknowledged that customary law is always evolving and subject to 'social evolution' and future 'legislative deliberation' as well as 'judicial interpretation'. (Certification case 1996, para 197) In a dispute arising from customary law a court may be called upon to ascertain what the exact content of the customary law is as it relates to a particular situation. There is, of course, a risk that codifying customary law through legislation or defining it through judicial interpretation or scientific observation and research may be a blunt instrument that does not accurately capture the true essence of customary law within a community. Moreover, such codification or interpretation could stifle the development of indigenous law, creating the perception that the customs have become static. (Alexkor case 2004, footnote 54) The court in the Certification case stated:

> The [Constitutional Assembly] cannot be constitutionally faulted for leaving the complicated, varied and ever-developing specifics of how . . . customary law should develop and be interpreted, to future social evolution, legislative deliberation and judicial interpretation. (Certification case 1996, para 197)

In the Alexkor case, while the court also acknowledged the dynamic nature of customary law, it did not seek to draw a rigid line between official customary law and living customary law. The court recognised that customary law

---

courts seek specific norms and rules on which to base their judgments. (Weinberg 2016, 187) She concluded that 'social science research' can broaden the basis for the admissibility of evidence that may otherwise be 'contested and uncertain'. (Weinberg 2016, 202)

[49] Note, for example, how in Botswana courts have adjusted their approach to sensitive social topics in a customary context such as adultery, polygamy, extra-marital relationships and parental responsibility to reflect changing community values. Werbner and Werbner conclude that from the perspective of 'living law' the approach of customary courts in Botswana 'are embedded in considerations of equity that also inform wider ideological, critical movements and processes of judicial innovation'. (Werbner and Werbner 2022, 170)

may be ascertained by referencing published works and other sources such as jurisprudence, but that 'caution must be exercised when dealing with textbooks and old authorities because of the tendency to view indigenous law through the prism of legal conceptions that are foreign to it'. (Alexkor case 2004, para 54) The court also acknowledged that customary law may have changed and that there may be differences within a community about which customary law or version of customary law is applicable.

It is important to highlight that in the Alexkor case the court did not outright reject existing published works and jurisprudence solely because they were deemed 'official' and thus not representative of living or relevant customary law, as some literature suggests. Rather, the court appropriately cautioned that it may be necessary to look beyond published materials to accurately ascertain the current status of customary law. The irony is, however, that once a court engages in such an exercise and issues a finding or declaration regarding a rule in customary law, that declaration becomes 'official' and serves as a source for future citation.

This underscores the tenuous nature of a rigid distinction between official customary law and living customary law. It is worth noting, for example, how the court in the Alexkor case reflected on historic observations and documents to support its finding that the Richtersveld community had always regarded the land in question as theirs and that the content of their rights must be ascertained by 'reference to history and the [historic and current] usages of the community of Richtersveld'. (Alexkor case 2004, para 60) The court stated, correctly, that 'indigenous law may be established by reference to writers on indigenous law and other authorities and sources, and may include the evidence of witnesses if necessary'. (Alexkor case 2004, para 54)

In the Alexkor case the court furthermore noted the caution expressed by Bennett (Bennett 1991, Preface (vi)), in which he warns against attempting to ascertain customary law *solely* by reference to existing historic material. The court endorsed the proposition that the contemporaneous content of customary law is to be ascertained by referencing the official body of law employed in the courts and by the administration, customary law as used for the purposes of education and teaching, *and* evidence of customary law as practised and observed on a daily basis. (Alexkor case 2004, footnote 51) Ultimately, the existence of a provision in customary law is to be established by 'adducing evidence', whether from written records, oral testimony or a combination of sources. (Alexkor case 2004, para 52)

In the Alexkor case the Constitutional Court cautioned against the 'tendency' to view customary law through the 'prism of legal conceptions that are foreign to it'. (Alexkor case 2004, para 54) There is thus a distinction between what is meant by official and living customary law, as opposed to assessing and understanding customary law on its own terms and merits. While the former is theoretically weak, the latter is more defensible. As a legal system customary law must be evaluated for what it truly is, rather than through the lens of another legal system's perceptions.

In brief, the distinction sought to be made between official and living customary law is fragile; it does not withstand scientific, legal or practical scrutiny. Moreover, it overlooks the fact that all legal systems contain elements that are living, dynamic, codified and recorded.

10.5.3 Is customary law frozen in time?

Customary law is not frozen in time. Longevity should not be mistaken for immutability. While rooted in the past, customary laws can be adjusted to suit contemporary conditions. Changes in customary law may occur slowly over generations or rapidly because of evolving circumstances. This does not imply, however, that every customary rule or norm is in flux, nor does it suggest that every custom, rule or practice carries the force of law. The tradition upon which customary law is based gives it certainty but, like any custom or tradition, it is susceptible to adjustment and modification. Ultimately, it falls upon the courts to determine whether a customary law sought to be relied upon is current and whether it constitutes an enforceable legal norm, or merely an unenforceable custom or practice lacking binding force.

Moseneke DCJ explained in the Gumede case how past attempts to record customary law had made it appear fossilised. This was due to efforts to codify it in an overly rigid manner and simplify it to fit the common-law framework. For example, the richness and deeper value of marriage under customary law was reduced to 'crude and gendered forms of inequality'. This resulted in 'fossilised rules and codes that displayed little or no understanding of the value system that animated the customary law of marriage'. (Gumede case 2009, para 17)

An example of the fossilised approach to customary law is the proposition that common law has failed to fully comprehend the bond that customary marriage constitutes between the families of the couple, not just between the individuals getting married. Further to this it is asserted that women have historically played a significantly greater role in customary marriages than assumed, as subsequently recognised through various observations, academic works and judicial rulings. Essentially, the consent of women 'was indispensable to all crucial family decisions'. (Gumede case 2009, para 18) Despite these realities, the dominance of husbands has become entrenched over time as the fossilised approach to customary law has hindered its ability to adapt to changing societal norms, thereby impeding progress towards greater equality for women and non-discrimination. Consequently, 'official customary law' has been left 'unreformed and stone-walled by static rules and judicial precedent'. (Gumede case 2009, para 20)

The assertion that customary law should be allowed to adapt like any other legal system ought not be controversial. However, the question for South African courts is which forum is best suited to align customary law with the Constitution. Should customary law be allowed to reform by itself through different practices being adopted by the community, or should courts or Parliament intervene by attempting to bring customary law into the fold of the Constitution? When considering this question, it is important to bear in mind the risk of non-adherence to court determinations, particularly when community practices do not align with legislative or judicial interventions.

In the Gumede case Moseneke DCJ sought to differentiate between the role of the court and that of Parliament as forums tasked to modernise customary law, particularly focusing on the distinction between official customary law and living customary law. In this case the issue specifically related to a statutory official provision of the legislation in respect of customary law. The court was satisfied that it could develop the *statutory* position by reference to the Constitution. (Gumede case 2009, para 29) However, there was a concern that developing living customary law might prove more challenging because of the court's limited functions and its focus on specific disputes and related evidence. Therefore it was considered more suitable for Parliament to develop living customary law through statutes. (Gumede case 2009, para 30) A similar approach was adopted in the Ramuhovhi case, where the court deferred to Parliament to establish suitable legislative arrangements to safeguard the rights of women in polygamous marriages. The court acknowledged that the relief it ordered was 'fraught with imponderables', underscoring its limited capacity to develop customary law. (Ramuhovhi case 2017, para 65; EB case 2024)

There is a risk that as courts seek to develop customary law they might become prescriptive and fail to accurately reflect the essence of customary law. Instead, they may reformulate customary law based on perceived ideals rather than its actual practices. Courts may thus become a new forum of dominance and prescription to the detriment of customary law. This does not imply, however, that courts are incapable of developing customary law, but rather highlights their functional limitations with regard to the specific customary norms arising in individual disputes.

If customary law is not codified, the question arises how its norms are determined within the context of a dispute. As a point of departure, any determination of customary law must be evidence-based. There is, however, a risk that individuals purporting to give effect to changing customary law may be influenced by their own predispositions and limited understanding, leading them to err similarly to how anthropologists and practitioners of other sciences did in the past. Rather than accurately reflecting what customary law is, they may declare what they believe a customary norm is or should be, resulting in misconceptions. While there was no need in the Gumede case for the court to ascertain and determine the provisions of living customary law, Moseneke DCJ observed that a court should 'carefully examine all the circumstances relevant' to determine what a 'just and equitable' outcome would be. (Gumede case 2009, para 44)

Evolving over time, the twin notions of living customary law and official customary law have walk a shared path. South African courts, through various judgments, have showcased the dynamic and adaptive nature of customary law in areas such as marriage, land access and utilisation, succession, inheritance and rights of dissent and association. These developments seek to reflect not only changing customary norms, but also efforts to bring customary law into compliance with the Constitution.

Essentially, akin to developments in common law, customary law is subject to change. While historic and existing published records, literature and jurisprudence may sometimes adequately reflect community customary standards, courts will demand oral and written evidence if those standards are challenged. Having ascertained contemporary provisions of customary law, the court then assumes responsibility to develop customary law by way of declaration consistently with the Constitution.

10.5.4 When is a customary custom, habit or practice equated to customary law?

The question what constitutes 'law' was identified in Chapter 2 as fundamental to any attempt to distinguish between non-state laws and other non-legal societal and cultural norms, habits, customs and practices. This chapter does not aim to propose a definitive answer to this deeply philosophical and practical question.

The distinction between state law and non-state law acknowledges that the state is not the sole author of law. (Ehrlich 1936, 493)

There is no universally established definition for law, and even less agreement on the concept of non-state law. Nonetheless, consistent with the theme of this book the following can be postulated: first, not all cultural norms, customs, habits and practices can be equated to legal norms; secondly, a legal norm must possess a common understanding, clarity, universality (within the group), adherence and associated sanction that distinguishes it from an ordinary custom; and, thirdly, if an individual seeks to rely on a customary legal norm, the burden of proof rests on that individual to demonstrate that it is indeed an obligatory legal norm and not merely a voluntary custom, practice or habit.

This distinction is not straightforward, as simply identifying various categories of human conduct such as norms, customs, practices and habits is not necessarily sufficient to elevate a custom to the level of non-state law. As the court emphasised in the Mabena case, living law is 'law actually observed by African communities'. (Mabena case 1998) The court, having heard evidence that the payment of lobolo to the mother of the bride was not an isolated event in the community concerned, accepted that this was a typical example of customary law which had been developed in a manner consistent with the equality and non-discrimination provisions of the Constitution.

Ultimately, the pivotal issue is whether the community in question views a customary practice as customary law. This entails a sense of obligation to adhere to the practice, potentially accompanied by sanctions for non-compliance with it. In the Shilubana case the court emphasised the significance of consistently applying and adhering to customary law. (Shilubana case 2008, paras 54–55) In this case the issue was whether the Valoyi community should be able to develop their customary law in a manner that would end, or at least reduce, gender discrimination in accordance with the new Constitution.[50] Specifically, a female had been appointed to the chieftainship position for which she had previously been ineligible because of her gender. Van der Westhuizen J held that it is essential to recognise the right of indigenous communities to 'amend and repeal' their

[50] Note, in contrast, the case of Masupha in Lesotho, in which it was held that a law prohibiting a woman from succeeding to the chieftainship was within the limits imposed by the Constitution of that country. (Masupha case 2013) Also of note is the Zimbabwean case of Magaya (Magaya case 1999) and the Kenyan case of Mukindia Kimuru (Mukindia Kimuru case 2000), in which limitations on equality were upheld within the context of the inequality being consistent with customary law.

customary laws since they form part of a 'constantly evolving system'. (Shilubana case 2008, para 45) Sometimes a custom may develop gradually, while at other times it may do so with greater immediacy. Allowing a community time to develop a custom while requiring more expeditious outcomes can be a 'balancing act'. (Shilubana case 2008, para 47) The court acknowledged that the community can by conscious decision bring their customs into line with constitutional requirements. (Shilubana case 2008, para 85)[51]

The risk, however, for courts to adjust customary law to comply with the normative standard of the Constitution is that customary law as a legal system may be eroded, with only non-legal practices or habits remaining. Diala is of the view that the power of the courts to develop common law could ultimately cause its demise as a distinct legal system. (Diala 2019, 17–18)

The question whether a customary legal norm exists is usually not answered in the abstract, but by reference to all evidence about the origin, status, compliance, clarity, community adherence, duration, adaptions and sanctions associated with the purported legal norm. This may, however, prove to be a 'herculean' task, as 'courts are often confronted with more than one version of customary law'. (Badejogbin 2022, 264) In the Mayelane case Zondo J explained that the individual who alleges customary law applies bears the onus of proof. (Mayelane case 2013, para 108) In that case a woman had to prove that her marriage had been in accordance with the customary law of the community to which she belonged. Zondo J was also critical of a court of appeal's decision to invite additional evidence about community practices, asserting that it is the duty of lower courts to make findings of fact. (Mayelane case 2013, para 118) The majority in the Mayelane case were of the view that to ascertain customary law is a question of law rather than a question of fact.

The debate over whether the determination of customary law is a question of fact or a question of law may itself be inappropriate, representing yet another instance of customary law being viewed from the perspective of a different legal system. Essentially, two types of questions arise: firstly, a *question of law* concerning the content of the law being relied upon; and, secondly, a *question of fact*, namely whether the law is adhered to by those seeking to invoke it. Zondo J, in the minority, emphasised this aspect by stating that to ascertain customary law is a question of fact, not law. (Mayelane case 2013, para 98) It is

[51] Oninku draws from the Shilubana case to make recommendations in respect of recognition of customary law in Ghana. (Oninku 2024)

important to consider that 'there is no singular living customary law that applies to all communities and at all times' (Budlender 2021, 328), and therefore the customary law applicable to a specific community in a particular dispute must be ascertained by the court.

In summary, determining whether a custom exists in customary law which has the effect of law is a question of fact, with the answer determined by evidence from various sources such as laypersons, traditional leaders, publications, documents and expert testimony. The onus rests on those who assert that the customary law applies to the dispute, to prove it. While lower courts may invite further submissions and evidence, higher courts of appeal typically refrain from conducting their own inquiries, aiming to rely on the same facts established by the lower court to determine an appeal, except in exceptional circumstances where new evidence previously unavailable to the lower court emerges. Distinguishing between custom, practice, habit and law is often nuanced, involving considerations of degree, general observance, sanction and community belief in the mandatory nature of a norm as if it were a law.

10.5.5 What evidence is required to ascertain 'living' customary law?

There are essentially two pathways for a court to declare that a customary legal norm applies to a dispute. First, according to s 1(1) of the Law of Evidence Amendment Act, a court may take judicial notice of a well-known customary law norm if it can be readily ascertained with sufficient certainty. Secondly, a party wishing to rely on a customary legal norm must present evidence and call upon lay witnesses and experts to testify regarding the law, its terms, its application to a specific community and why it should be considered a binding legal norm rather than merely a practice, cultural tradition or habit.

The Evidence Amendment Act speaks about the 'substance of a legal rule' having to be established (s 1(2)). The evidence relied upon may include testimony from laypersons, individuals within the traditional authority hierarchy and expert witnesses. In essence, as explained by Van der Westhuizen J, all relevant circumstances, both historical and current, must be considered. (Shilubana case 2008, paras 42–49) Importantly, evidence must support the law as it exists rather than how it may have existed historically. This is where the notion of living law arises. In the Nigerian case of Oyewunmi the court usefully stated that customary law is 'organic in that it is not static' and it 'controls the lives and transactions of the community subject to it'. (Oyewunmi case 1990)

In the Shilubana case the court endorsed the practice, as established by evidence within the particular community, to identify the rightful heir to the chieftainship of the community. (Shilubana case 2008) The court accepted that the practice had developed within the community yet, contrary to some assertions, it did not introduce uncertainty into customary law in general concerning the law of chieftainship succession. (Nhlapo 2017, 8) It was ultimately the facts of the dispute that gave rise to the judgment, rather than a general change of course about traditional customs concerning chieftainship succession. Meanwhile, in the Mayelane case it was held that, within the particular community, there was no established requirement to obtain the consent of a wife before marrying another customary wife. However, the court, considering the Constitution, expanded the community's customary law to include this rule. (Mayelane case 2013)

In the Mayelane case Zondo J elucidated as follows on the evidence required to ascertain the existence of a customary law and its applicability to a particular dispute:

> The result of the exercise referred to above will be the customary law of that group of people on that issue. That can be established by way of evidence from a person or persons who have knowledge of the relevant custom or customs and usages as contemplated in the definition of 'customary law'. A person who gives evidence about such matters need not be an expert witness nor does such a person need to occupy a particular position of authority in the relevant group of people. Anyone who has knowledge of the relevant custom or customs and usages may give evidence about them. (Mayelane case 2013, para 98)

Referencing South African jurisprudence, Nhlapo succinctly summarises the circumstances under which evidence is likely to be required to ascertain a customary legal norm and the types of evidence needed. These circumstances include: when a living law aligns with the Bill of Rights; when the court is compelled to rectify historical distortions; when promoting a constitutional right; and when seeking to minimise interference with customary law. On the other hand, courts have shown reluctance to invite additional evidence in certain circumstances. These include: when justices believe that the matter is more appropriately addressed by Parliament; when inadequate evidence has been presented and the court refrains from running the case for the applicant; and when the dispute can be resolved without reference to living customary law. (Nhlapo 2017, 19–20)

In the Sengadi case the court had to consider several aspects of customary practices regarding the marriage and burial sites of the parties. (Sengadi case 2019) The applicant contended that she was the customary wife of the deceased and she cited several customs that had been complied with to confirm their customary marriage. The respondent denied that a customary marriage had taken place since the required customary formalities had not been completed. The court found that, regardless of any shortcomings in adherence to traditional customs, in substance a customary marriage had been concluded. (Sengadi case 2019, paras 36–38) Essentially the court declared that the traditional hand-over of the bride to the bridegroom's family was not 'an essential prerequisite for the lawful validation and the lawful existence of a customary marriage' under the Recognition Act. (Sengadi case 2019, para 42) Maimela expresses criticism at the court for not giving effect to an essential custom of the relevant community. In doing so the court has 'diminished' the normative nature of customary law. Maimela cautions against a positivist approach whereby statutory provisions are given precedence over 'daily experiences' of communities. (Maimela and Morudu 2024, 401) Customary law as lived may not reflect customary law as legislated. The legislature has despite best attempts been unable to 'capture the essence of customary law'. (Maimela and Morudu 2024, 402) Sibisi says that culturally the process of marriage is not complete without this ceremony and that empirical evidence does not support the finding that the important step can be waived. (Sibisi 2024, 935)

Put briefly, all relevant material, including documents, observations, input from laypersons, community leadership and expert opinions, may be utilised to ascertain a customary legal norm.

10.5.6 How is membership of an indigenous community determined?

The jurisdiction of customary law over the affairs of an individual is in essence determined by the association of the individual with the community that subscribes to customary law. Even in traditionally governed areas customary law typically only applies to individuals who belong to the traditional community, accept, adhere and subscribe to its customs, and seek dispute resolution by reference to customary law. Merely identifying with a specific cultural or religious group, such as being iZulu or Jewish, does not necessarily imply that the customary or religious laws of that community apply to the individual concerned. Individuals can associate with a particular indigenous, religious or cultural group without regarding its customary legal system as applicable to and legally binding on them. Indeed, individuals are free to participate in the culture or religion they choose. (Chuma 2023, 45) The extent of their association, whether close or distant, is determined by the individual and, in the event of a dispute, it is for the court to determine whether a customary rule applies. Added thereto, municipal law may require biological linkage to a group other than mere association or acceptance. (Kapeli case 2024, para 232)

The obvious question is how to ascertain whether a person accepts customary law to regulate their affairs. Demonstrating *disassociation* from an indigenous community may be easier than proving *association* with one. Disassociation can be ascertained in many ways, from an explicit declaration by an individual that customary laws are not recognised, to evidence of living a life without regard to customary law. It is ultimately a question of fact whether customary law can be applied in a particular dispute. The proof of association with an indigenous community is more complex. To claim association and seek resolution according to a customary norm, evidence must establish entitlement, under customary law, to be recognised as part of the community in question. In this way and others association may be more challenging to establish than disassociation.

South African courts have not had to deal extensively with disputes about membership of an indigenous community, but case law emanating from Australia may, in this respect, be instructive. The courts in Australia have devised a three-pronged test to determine the legitimacy of an individual's claim to belong to the Aboriginal community. (De Villiers 2023f, 41–52)[52] Firstly, *descent* is considered, which includes factors such as ancestry, adoption, kin-relations, family ties, and other foster arrangements. Secondly, the *self-identification* of the individual with a particular community is assessed. And, thirdly, the *acceptance* of the individual as a member of the community by others within that community is evaluated. These elements were expressed as follows in the Mabo case:

---

[52] The context within which these disputes have arisen does not necessary relate to the application of customary law to a specific dispute between parties. However, it may, for example, affect whether a person can participate in indigenous community deliberations, represent a part of the country that traditionally belongs to the indigenous community, access indigenous community benefits, qualify for government programmes for Aboriginal people, or avoid criminal prosecution for activities like hunting or fishing pursuant to traditional laws and customs. For example, observe how in Australia legislation has been enacted in different states to accommodate the traditional rights of Aboriginal people, particularly concerning fishing and hunting. These laws exempt Aboriginal people from certain restrictions in these activities that apply to the rest of the population. As an illustration, in the state of Western Australia the Fish Resources Management Act 1994 (WA) exempts Aboriginal people from the requirement to hold a recreational fishing licence when catching fish in accordance with the *continuing* Aboriginal tradition, provided that the fish are caught for personal and/or family purposes and not for commercial use. (Fish Resources Act 1994, s 6)

> Membership of the indigenous people depends on the biological descent from the indigenous people and on mutual recognition of a particular person's membership by that person and by the elders or other persons enjoying traditional authority among those people. (Mabo case (2) 1992, para 70)

No single factor is conclusive, as the court must consider all circumstances, including the 'interplay of social responses', both positive and negative, that 'creates self-perception and identify'. (Shaw case 1998, para 223) While the primary consideration of courts tends to be self-identification pursuant to the individual right to freedom of association, concerns have been raised by indigenous communities, such as the Sámi in Finland, that individuals not widely accepted as part of the community may attempt to associate with it in order to influence its decision-making or to gain benefits not ordinarily available to them. (De Villiers 2021b) The UNHRC has also weighed in on the debate by advocating for greater self-determination of indigenous communities like the Sámi to determine their membership, viewing this as an expression of sovereignty. (UN Expert Mechanism 2021) In Canada the Supreme Court has upheld a requirement that, for the purposes of the elections of self-determination bodies of an indigenous community, residence within the area of self-government is a valid requirement to be elected. (Dickson case 2024)

In short, the determination of community membership typically involves both subjective and objective criteria, with the right to freedom of association seeming to emphasise personal choice, while the recognition of indigenous sovereignty seemingly favours community self-determination.

10.6 CONCLUSION

It is fitting that the final theme chapter of this book addresses the legal pluralism embodied by customary law. The 1996 Constitution heralded a new era, recognising customary law as a legal system on par with other legal systems in South Africa. However, customary law remains subject to and regulated by the Constitution and legislation enacted pursuant to it, creating a hierarchy within the framework of equality.

Giving effect to this new status of customary law is not simple. There is a possibility that over time substantial elements of customary law may become weakened or eroded as the liberal democratic values espoused by the Constitution and international law are applied to traditional laws and customs. Such an evolution would not be dissimilar to the way European legal systems developed from unwritten customary and religious legal norms to parliamentary enactments, codification and constitutionalism. Over time the individual-centric principles enshrined in the Constitution may increasingly take precedence over the communal collectivism inherent in customary law. This also mirrors the efforts of other countries that have attempted to strike a balance between preserving customary law while ensuring the protections associated with contemporary human rights standards are accorded to all individuals.

The fundamental challenge to reconcile customary law with contemporary constitutionalism can be distilled into a simple question: Why should unequal treatment, discrimination or unjustified differentiation of individuals be tolerated just because it stems from customary law? For example, why should an entire community in Indonesia be disenfranchised under the Noken system, given that the country's constitution guarantees equality and universal franchise?[53] On the other hand, if customary law is entirely beholden to liberal democratic constitutional values, which in turn draw from universal human rights norms, does this not suggest that eventually customary law will regress to the *status ante*, becoming a *de facto* secondary customary system entirely subservient to the Constitution and legislation enacted by Parliament aimed at regulating it? The ultimate consequence would be the erosion of customary *law* to the point where little, if anything, remains of it. In such a scenario, customary habits and practices may survive, although not as part of a distinct legal system.

In this chapter I did not set out to provide definitive answers to this question, but rather to facilitate analysis and discussion of the challenges and progress made by South African courts in disentangling complex issues related to customary law. The following conclusions can be drawn from the case law discussed in the chapter:

1. Customary law is a substantive legal system on an equal footing with other legal systems in South Africa.
2. Customary law needs to be analysed and understood within its own context, rather than by reference to or through the lens of another legal system.

[53] As previously explained, the Constitutional Court of Indonesia has accepted as consistent with the Constitution an indigenous arrangement whereby the so-called Big Man votes on behalf of an entire community, without any individual votes being cast or counted. (De Villiers 2024, Noken case 2009) A similar approach has been adopted in Mexico, where the indirect election of members of an indigenous community at municipal level has been held to be consistent with the Constitution. (Indirect election case 2023)

3. The supremacy of the Constitution is not a function of customary law, but rather an outcome of the democratic constitution-drafting process. Customary law does not necessarily recognise a superior constitutional system external to itself.
4. It is the role of the judiciary to ascertain and apply customary law. Where necessary and possible, the courts may develop customary law to ensure its consistency with the Constitution.
5. Not every ordinary custom, practice or habit can be equated to a legally binding customary legal norm. No objective standard exists to ascertain the difference between a non-legally binding custom and a legally binding customary norm. This is ultimately for a court to determine, having heard evidence whether a specific practice is regarded by the community as a legal norm.
6. The evidence to ascertain the existence of a customary legal norm can take a variety of forms. These include the following: historic documents, practices and recordings; expert evidence and opinions; contemporary research and publications; statutory provisions; and oral evidence. All relevant evidence – whether historic or contemporary, written or oral, lay or expert – must be considered.
7. The application of customary law to a specific dispute involves both a question of law and a question of fact. It is a question of fact in the sense that the adherence of the parties to customary law and their intention to be bound by it must be ascertained and confirmed. It is a question of law in the sense that the customary law provision applicable to the dispute must be declared. Notably, however, the methodology used for questions of fact and questions of law may in itself be foreign to customary law.
8. The distinction between living and official customary law is weak and serves little practical, scientific or legal purpose. All legal systems, including customary law, display elements of being official and being living alike. It is ultimately for a court to declare, on the basis of all the evidence before it, what rule, if any, of customary law applies to a dispute at a specific point in time.
9. A declaration that a customary law norm is inconsistent with the Constitution does not necessarily imply that the norm is no longer adhered to by an indigenous community. Courts may seek to develop customary law, yet the ultimate test of adherence to customary law and

the implications of such development lie in the actions and practices within the community to which the customary law applies.

10. An inconsistency may arise between customary law as developed by courts and customary law as practised by communities. A declaration by the court of what customary law ought to be pursuant to the Constitution does not necessarily imply that community practices would follow.
11. The sovereignty of the Constitution, and its infusion with universal human rights values, may over time cause the erosion of customary law to the status of *customary practices* rather than *customary laws*. In this scenario customary law may become transformed into cultural customs, akin to many unique and special ethnocultural practices that do not constitute laws.
12. Because of their function, courts serve as a blunt instrument to develop customary law, considering that their jurisdiction is enlivened by a specific dispute and by reference to specific facts. Courts are not equipped to undertake broad inquiries into the terms and functioning of customary law, as their role is to adjudicate disputes based on the evidence before them. A court may give leave for additional witnesses to be called, but it cannot manage the case of the applicants and judges may not supplement evidence by their own understanding of customary law.
13. The reality of legal pluralism is that many individuals reside, figuratively speaking, in both legal systems, subject to common law and customary law. There may not always be neat distinctions in their minds about which legal norm applies in each situation. When disputes arise, individuals may choose the legal system that best suits their desired outcome. This phenomenon, referred to as forum shopping, is not unfamiliar in plural legal systems.

CHAPTER 11

THE BILL OF RIGHTS AND PLURALISM: REFLECTION ON SOUTH AFRICAN JURISPRUDENCE

Minorities are always better off in a culture which protects dissent than in a culture which protects us from dissent.

– Jonathan Rauch

11.1 INTRODUCTION

South Africa's journey to respond to its population diversity by way of internationally credible and acceptable standards started in seriousness with the 1990–1996 constitution-drafting process and then meandered through various judgments handed down by the courts over the past three decades, dealing with ethnocultural and indigenous diversity in the rainbow nation. It is prudent to commence an analysis of the response to diversity challenges with the constitution-drafting process because South Africa's jurisprudence dealing with identity rights and legal pluralism cannot be assessed in isolation from the Great Settlement. This Settlement set the scene for the judicial reasonings that followed over the next three decades. The *grundnorm* set the direction, the standard, and reflected the philosophy of unity and diversity.

The Constitution cannot be understood, interpreted, analysed, appreciated or criticised in a vacuum. The Constitution is set within a context of compromise and nation-building, of give and take, of working together for the sake of the greater whole, of being a birth certificate of a new nation. The Constitution must be interpreted with its nation-building and transformative purpose in mind – not merely as a black letter document. The success of nation-building depends on transformation, and transformation cannot occur if diversity is not appreciated. Transformation does not imply that the rainbow loses its colours. Many international post-1990 constitutions elsewhere failed because they were imposed. They were not home-grown. They failed to harmonise diversity and unity. This Constitution survived because it was built on compromise. There was no winner and no loser.

The lawfare that has arisen from the Constitution is testimony of its relevance, its legitimacy, the reliance by the public on the separation of powers, the value of independent institutions and the trust in the judiciary.

The Constitution is intended to transform society. It is not a *status quo* constitution. The transformation includes the importance to accommodate diversity, to create greater equality, to foster non-discrimination, to bring about socio-economic change, and to promote nation-building and respect for the law. The courts must speak those values. The courts must balance those values.

In my view the courts have done remarkably well to give effect to the spirit of the Constitution. The standard of accountability to which courts have held government and Parliament under the Constitution is unprecedented in South Africa's history and arguably unparalleled in Africa and other emerging democracies. But one must be mindful that the powers of courts are limited.

Ultimately courts can only be successful if other organs of government are successful. Lawfare can only achieve so much. The scepticism often displayed towards Parliament can easily spill over and negatively affect the judiciary. The law-making powers of courts must be approached with great circumspection.

The Constitution is, importantly for the topic of this book, intended to respect, reflect, accommodate and celebrate the plurality and diversity of the South African people. I therefore focused through the eyes of the courts on pluralism, both within the context of legal pluralism, which signifies accommodating different legal systems (e.g. religious and customary) within the same country, as well as recognising ethnocultural and indigenous pluralism (e.g. mother-tongue education, freedom of speech, duty of consultation, Ubuntu) that reflect the rainbow cultural diversity of South Africa. I attempted to put South African jurisprudence against a comparative background of some other plural nations to ascertain how the responses of the South African courts compare to international jurisprudence. I did so in the knowledge and awareness that comparative law is susceptible to many caveats, but the South African courts are empowered to 'consider' international jurisprudence. I thus took liberty to also consider foreign judgments.

The South Africa courts have on balance and under the guidance of the Constitutional Court been remarkable in their efforts to strike an equilibrium between national uniformity and accommodation of ethnocultural and customary diversity. The identity-based judgments emanating from South Africa have made a notable contribution internationally to discourse in social sciences in general and legal science in particular. Some issues that are at the centre of ongoing European legal challenges seem to have been navigated well by South African courts.

The South African courts do not always get it right, but courts never do. Comparative international jurisprudence highlights how challenging it is for courts to accommodate uniformity and diversity. One may disagree with some judgments of the South African courts because the essence of tolerance is that reasonable minds may disagree. But generally one cannot deny their effort to get things right. The courts are in a never-ending endeavour to achieve their goals. Their interpreting of the Constitution is at best a journey that unfolds and not a task completed. The jurisprudence of South Africa nevertheless makes for fascinating reading and the country has, as much as it had gained from international experiences during the drafting of the Constitution, also contributed during the past 30 years to international jurisprudence through its interpretation of the Constitution. I would suggest there is no emerging democracy of the 1990s of which judgments have been so often cited by foreign courts and foreign scientists.

Various themes have crystallised from South African and foreign jurisprudence about the essence of legal, cultural, religious and customary plurality. In this chapter I respond to the themes I have identified as particularly relevant for the South African context.

11.2 LEGAL PLURALISM AS A SCIENTIFIC PROPOSITION

Legal pluralism is a relatively recent scientifically coined concept with varied applications. Attempts to define it remain vague and ambiguous. In practice legal pluralism has existed as a social phenomenon since the formation of the first organised communities with their respective ancient rules and customary laws, predating the modern state with its fixation on sovereign territory and unified supreme law. Legal pluralism in its origin was personal. The focus was on community. Territory only became relevant at a later stage of state organisation. Legal pluralism has been part of human society for longer than records exist. Nonetheless, only recently have social scientists attempted to define the concept of legal pluralism, to explore it, to develop a thesis for its consistent and harmonious application, and to find sustainable approaches to multiple legal systems within the same territorial space. The awareness of legal pluralism has travelled hand in hand with the greater attention given to the rights of ethnocultural minorities and indigenous people. The uniformity of the modern state is no more. The scientific focus on legal pluralism is as if we are revisiting history to make sense of it all.

Legal pluralism reflects in many respects the efforts to give greater recognition to minority systems of law, custom and practice. Legal pluralism in effect challenges the notions of universality of norms and the generality and blandness of globalisation. Legal pluralism seeks to recognise and accommodate the legality and legitimacy of locally based community systems of law. It is open to living norms whereby cultures and customs adapt. The political uniformity of the state is challenged by the legal pluralism of its communities.

Legal pluralism in essence aims to describe an existing social condition whereby more than one legal system operates within the same territorial jurisdiction, called a sovereign state. The legal systems may complement each other or may contradict each other. A *modus vivendi* and *modus operandi* are required for the systems to coexist. The challenge is how to exist together and yet to function separately. In the foregone age of power, the police powers of governments supported by parliamentary sovereignty determined which legal system prevailed, but in the contemporary age of accommodation and respect for pluralism supported by constitutionalism and international instruments, a live and let live approach is preferred where pluralism is as far as possible accommodated.

The multiple legal systems are, however, not equal in their source, scope, authority, enforcement or jurisdiction. There is inevitably a hierarchy of legal systems and laws within the same territorial space. The notion of sovereignty of the state implies there exists a sovereign legal system for the entire state. Even in the case of South Africa, where legal systems are treated equally under the Constitution, the principle of constitutionalism applies whereby constitutional norms contained in the Constitution are supreme to the norms of any other legal system, be it parliamentary, religious, cultural or customary. The challenge is, however, that constitutional norms are not neutral – they reflect values. And hence some would argue that the values reflected by the South African Constitution are not always consistent with those of the African continent. Critics would see the Constitution as a Trojan horse whereby liberal norms trump customary norms.

Thus, within the accommodation of legal plurality in South Africa (and other liberal democratic states) a hierarchy is nevertheless constitutionally enshrined. Ultimately, it is the role of judges to declare which legal norm, state or non-state, applies to a particular dispute.

11.3 STATE LAW AND NON-STATE LAW

I refer in the book to the laws emanating from the principal, or dominant, legal system of a country as state law since it derives its authority from the Constitution, sovereignty of Parliament and common law. State law has application to the entire territory of the state and its resident population. State law is enforced by the organs of state. State law is tolerant of other customs and practices but only to the extent that those do not offend state law. I have denoted other legal systems as non-state law because their legal character emanates from tradition, custom or holy book and are only applicable to a specific community through longstanding culture, customs, habits, practices, religion and traditions.

A non-state legal system applies principally to those individuals who freely associate with each other in a community, rather than to territory (although there may be tribal areas where customary law principally applies to all within the tribal area, but even then the tribal area is subject to national sovereignty). Adherence to non-state law is principally voluntary, the community is formed through freedom of association, a person can (theoretically) opt out of or elope from non-state law, and enforcement of non-state law primarily occurs through community traditions, sanctions, censures and customs rather than by state organs.

While state law applies to all persons within a territorially defined space (such as a country, region or local government), non-state law applies primarily to persons who associate with a community. A person cannot therefore opt out of state law (unless they physically relocate), but a person can opt out of or refuse to comply with non-state law, for example by disassociating from the community concerned or refusing to comply with its rules. Opting out of non-state law may have social consequences for the person, but not legal consequences under state law.

11.4 RECOGNITION OF LEGAL PLURALISM: DEEPENING OR WEAKENING DEMOCRACY?

Pluralism is a social reality. Legal pluralism does not necessarily accompany all forms of social pluralism. For example, not all cultural or religious communities have non-state *laws* that apply to them. They may have habits, customs, traditions and practices, but those do not necessarily constitute a distinct legal system. But some communities, particularly indigenous and religious, may live and abide by a separate legal system in some respects of their intra-group social interaction. The system is regarded by them as a binding legal system and not mere customs or practices. The acceptance of customary norms *as actual laws* equates to legal pluralism since there is an autonomous legal system in existence additional to the state legal system.

The question is how do states and courts respond to legal pluralism? Is a non-state legal system relevant for purposes of jurisprudence, or are those non-state 'laws' regarded as unenforceable practices, habits and customs of a community with no legal consequence in civil law?

The South African Constitution does not refer to the concept of legal pluralism, but it does recognise the presence of other legal systems in the country, be those religious, cultural or indigenous. In the Certification case, however, it was emphasised that those separate legal systems are not to constitute a basis for the exercise of separate political rights. The effect of the non-state legal system is therefore to regulate the relationships in a specific social field between members of the community in their private affairs, but not to serve as a basis for political collective rights that could undermine national unity. In this respect the legal pluralism and minority protection debates emphasise different aspects – the former seeks recognition of the unique *legal* system, the later seeks *political* participatory rights that may include various forms of power-sharing and autonomy, albeit within the same legal system.

Recognising legal pluralism can deepen democracy, enhance individual rights and freedoms, expand individual self-determination, protect minorities and indigenous people, and promote the principles of subsidiarity. It is within the comfort of the community that an individual may feel most at home, free, valued and acknowledged. Pure individualism where one becomes a statistical element is mitigated by legal plurality through the person's interaction with others of the same religion, tradition, culture or language. Ubuntu, for example, reflects this spirit of feeling at home within a community.

However, if taken to its extreme, legal pluralism that implies competing legal systems can weaken democracy, undermine national unity, erode social integration, cause deterioration of community cohesion, challenge the legitimacy of state law, cause balkanisation of communities, politicise identity, lock individuals into an imposed identity, authorise discrimination and unequal treatment, and even lead to violence or the breakup of the state. Separate legal systems may also gravitate towards separate political participatory rights.

There seem to be competing forces at play – centrifugal and centripetal: those of globalisation and its implied universality and standardisation, and those of pluralism, ethnocultural community rights and individual and community self-determination that imply localism with resultant complexity. Caution should therefore be exercised that the universality of rights and its intended uniformity based on the individual do not negate social plurality and the importance and value of non-state law, cultures and practices to the individual in community with others. Conversely, legal pluralism should not be recognised at the cost of social cohesion, equality and legal uniformity.

Courts do not create legal pluralism; legal pluralism inherently exists within the social fabric as a fact. However, courts may determine whether a non-state legal system or a non-state legal norm is recognised; what those rules are; the relevance of non-state law to a proceeding; the contribution of a non-state legal norm in dispute resolution; the enforcement or implementation of non-state legal norms; and the consistency of non-state law with the Constitution.

11.5 WHAT IS 'LAW'?

A threshold question arising from legal pluralism is what constitutes 'law'. Where runs the invisible threshold for a custom or practice to become a legal norm, or when does an historic legal norm fall into disuse by becoming a mere custom or practice but no longer a law? I do not purport to answer this question. Like beauty, the legal nature of a custom is perhaps in the eye of the beholder. Persons from the same community may hold different views about their community practices. One could suggest that law in its widest sense is what is being perceived and adhered to by a community as legally binding norms – be it codified, customary or traditional.

If law is only understood as the enactments of a sovereign parliament, the answer to the question is simple – only state law constitutes law. If, however, law includes customs and traditions that are perceived by those who adhere to them as laws that have binding force on their conduct, then the scope of law becomes much wider. If rights can emanate from conduct through long use in civil law, then why could some cultural and religious customs not similarly be recognised as right-giving through conduct and acceptance?

However, not all customs, practices, habits and beliefs of an ethnocultural or indigenous community can be elevated to the status of 'law'. Many customs are respected, noted, remembered or adhered to informally and with flexibility by communities without those being regarded as binding laws. There may even be disagreement within a community about the content or the binding nature of a custom. This is evidenced in the ever-evolving discourse within religious groupings about the binding nature of their dogma and a proper understanding of their respective holy books. For example, neither in Islam, Christianity nor Judaism is there internal agreement in all respects on dogma. In fact, wars have been fought on the preferred approach to dogma. To therefore suggest that a religious or indigenous customary norm is adequately clear and specific to be regarded as a binding legal norm can be open to intra-community disagreement. Codification may assist to bring certainty about the content of a legal norm, but codification may also be rigid and deprive a community of living law.

While state law applies to all individuals within a territorial space regardless of their understanding or knowledge of the law, non-state law has an element of awareness, acceptance and choice, although in practice the choice may be more theoretical than practical.

For simplicity, I refer to non-state law in the context of a rule of conduct, whether written or unwritten, that impacts the rights and interests of those *who accept it as law*. It is a subjective test in contrast to state law. Non-state rules are treated by individuals belonging to an ethnocultural, religious or indigenous community as if it is a legal power. The content of the non-state law must be ascertained by reference to the customs and evidence of the community, not through the prism of another legal system. The non-state laws are capable of being enforced, either formally or informally, by the community from which they originate through means other than state sanction.

South African and foreign case laws and jurisprudence acknowledge that the binding nature of indigenous law is not determined by what other legal systems think of it, but how indigenous people view their own legal system. The same can be said of religious non-state law. Religious non-state law is par excellence non-factual but based on belief and faith.

11.6 HOW TO DETERMINE WHEN A CUSTOM BECOMES A LEGAL NORM

There is no precise demarcation between a custom being collectively adhered to informally as a mere practice and a custom that has attained the force of law that is binding. In fact, there may be disagreements within a religious or indigenous community whether a particular custom is merely to be adhered to informally or whether it has the force of law. It may ultimately be for courts to determine, based on relevant lay and expert oral and documentary evidence, whether a custom is so widely adhered to within the community *as if law* that it is recognised by the court as a non-state legal norm. A court may also find that a customary law that had previously existed has fallen into disuse and is no longer regarded a law but is rather categorised as a custom or a practice.

South African courts are in essence required to make four determinations when called upon to apply a purported non-state law to a dispute: first, to determine whether there is a non-state legal system being adhered to by a community; secondly, what the relevant legal rule is arising from the non-state legal system sought to be relied on in the proceeding; thirdly, whether the parties to the dispute intend to be bound by the non-state legal rule; and, fourthly, whether the non-state legal rule is consistent with the Constitution.

11.7 HOW TO COHABITATE STATE LAW AND NON-STATE LAW

If state law is regarded as the sole, primary and sovereign legal system of a country, then all other community practices or customs are of a private civil nature with no relevance to the resolution of disputes in the municipal legal system. However, if it accepted that communities adhere to customs as if those have the force of law to the community and that courts may legally consider and even give effect to those non-state laws, then courts must in the event of an inconsistency between state law and non-state law declare which of the norms shall prevail.

The following four principles are proposed to harmonise legal pluralism in the context of the interaction between state law and non-state law: (a) individuals must elect whether or not they submit to the authority of a non-state law since state law can be imposed because of residence but non-state law requires voluntary adherence or acquiescence; (b) the non-state law norm sought to be invoked must be consistent with the Constitution; (c) courts, ultimately, determine the validity, relevance, appropriateness and application of non-state law to a dispute; and (d) the enforcement of law and the application of a sanction in the event that a law was breached is a function of state organs.

11.8 ETHNOCULTURAL AND INDIGENOUS RIGHTS IN THE CONSTITUTION

The 1996 Constitution embodies a negotiated outcome. The process leading to its formulation benefited from contributions of some of the world's foremost legal minds in the field of individual, ethnocultural and indigenous rights. While the text of the Constitution can be critiqued by suggesting retrospectively the insertion, deletion or reformulation of specific clauses, a negotiated outcome inevitably carries the DNA and the weight of compromise. A negotiated outcome represents what parties *were able to agree to*, not what they *aspired to achieve*. The Constitution reflects *consensus*, not *demands*. It is the very consensus arising from the inclusive processes of constitution-drafting in the first half of the 1990s that has ensured the survival of the Constitution while many constitutions of the 1990s have failed.

The Constitution generally complies with contemporary liberal democratic constitutional theory and legal standards and, more specifically, with provisions of international law regarding the rights of ethnocultural communities and indigenous people. In some respects the Constitution leads the way, for example the recognition of self-determination rights, right to mother-tongue education in public schools and the recognition of customary indigenous rights.

The Constitution does not contain explicit political participatory rights for minorities in their collective capacity, but there is no obligation in international law for collective political rights to be recognised. The recognition of collective rights arises from political compromise and pragmatism (as under the 1993 Constitution) within a nation, rather than through universal legal prescription.

Added thereto, collective rights are often informally accommodated by way of territorial arrangements such as local, regional and tribal governments.

International norms relevant to pluralism, ethnocultural minorities and indigenous rights principally relate to the rights of the individual. The identity individual rights, such as rights to culture, religion, language and identity, only come to fruition when exercised with others of the same identity. Although communities do not have a legal identity or personality, the individuals making up the community can claim a class or collective right. This is reflected in the Constitution by recognition of identity individual rights, collective indigenous rights, potential for collective rights and self-determination of cultural communities, as well as several aspects of the design of institutions to accommodate pluralism, such as a proportional electoral system, decentralisation to provincial and local governments, recognition of traditional leaders and demarcation of provinces on the basis, among others, of language considerations.

The individual identity rights usually come to practical effort through the exercise of the right, e.g. the right to culture or religion, with other individuals of the same identity; but the right bearer remains the individual, not the community, since it is not a legal entity. Courts may, however, when interpreting an identity right, take into account that the nature of the right only becomes substantially operative when it is exercised with others who are also bearers of the same right. This is why individual rights of freedom of association, self-determination, culture, language, religion and education are interrelated and intimately joined. This is consistent with the interrelated nature of fundamental rights as adopted by the ECtHR, namely that the rights to identity and private life include and are related to integrity, identity, personal autonomy, sexual orientation and culture. (Ciubotaru case 2010) It can be argued that 'all individual human rights could be interpreted in a minority-sensitive way' (Chronowski and Nagy 2024, 23) The nature of Ubuntu also recognises the interrelatedness of the rights of the individual in their interaction with community.

11.9 DEFINITIONAL CHALLENGES OF THE CONCEPTS OF COMMUNITY AND INDIGENOUS PEOPLE

The outcomes of the constitutional debates about the rights of ethnocultural and indigenous communities were relatively simple: the term 'community' was preferred to the term 'minority'; the rights attributed to a community are protected through the individual members of the community rather than as collective rights for a community as if it were a legal entity (which it is not);

the potential of a collective right of self-determination of cultural communities is recognised in s 235 but, for it to be operationalised, enabling legislation is required; and special collective rights are foreshadowed for indigenous people in addition to individual rights.

The terms 'community', 'indigenous', 'traditional' and 'tribal' are not defined in the Constitution and neither are those terms defined in international law. South African courts have adopted a broad meaning of community whenever consultation rights are affected without becoming entangled in the definitional issues about dividing lines that separate tribe, indigenous and community. An essential prerequisite of community is the individual right to freedom of association, equality and non-discrimination.

11.10 WHAT IS THE UTILITY OF S 235 OF THE CONSTITUTION?

The questions arise, what was intended with the purported collective right to self-determination of ethnocultural communities pursuant to s 235, and does the section hold any contemporary relevance or is it an anachronism?

Section 235 was at the time of drafting of the Constitution a symbol of accommodation of plurality of South Africa. It reflected in substance, not in detail, international efforts to accommodate the political participatory rights of ethnocultural minorities, particularly in respect of various forms of community autonomy. It was a major breakthrough for the Constitution to recognise the potential of collective political participatory rights, particularly in response to concerns of the Afrikaans community of being permanently politically marginalised. But because of the failure of the Afrikaans community to come to an internal agreement about what they sought in terms of self-determination, coupled with the persistency of some within the Afrikaans community to pursue a race-based outcome that seeks to distinguish between Afrikaners (white) and other Afrikaans-speaking persons,[1] and also the worsening political climate to consider special collective community rights, the practical operation of s 235 has

[1] The Afrikaner Declaration of 2024 issued by some Afrikaans organisations highlights the persistence of race as the basis on which some in the Afrikaans community seek to pursue collective rights. (Afrikaner Declaration 2024) This is problematic for three reasons: first, discrimination on the basis of race to define a language community is inconsistent with the Constitution and international law; secondly, restrictions on freedom of association on the basis of race is inconsistent with the Constitution and international law; and, thirdly, the emphasis on race as a characteristic to define the Afrikaner ignores the historic and contemporary reality that Afrikaans is not only a language of white persons.

perhaps fallen into the 'too hard' basket. I asked the question in 2014 whether at that stage it was too early or too late to operationalise s 235. (De Villiers 2014a) The question remains valid.

When elucidating the meaning of 'community' in s 235 of the Constitution the following, arising from approaches in international law, may assist:

Akin to definitional challenges in international law of 'minority,' there exists no legally binding definition in South African law for 'community'. It is therefore equally difficult to ascertain who is a community as it is to work out who is a minority since these are sociological phenomena rather than legal concepts.

The concepts of 'minority' and 'indigenous' are not terms of art and their meanings must be deduced in the specific context of the country in which the term is employed – the same principle applies to 'community' – its definition is local and circumstantial, not universal. This may explain why some countries (e.g. New Zealand, Hungary) have opted to specifically mention the communities that are the subject of special collective political participatory rights rather than rely on the vagueness of definition of indigenous, minority and community.

Individuals, as the right-bearers of identity rights, may act together pursuant to their right to free association to promote and protect their rights collectively, but such joint action does not bestow collective rights onto the community as if the community is a legal subject with separate collective political participatory rights. A community is in essence a sociological phenomenon, not a legal concept, which explains why international law does not recognise any rights of an ethnocultural community as a distinct legal entity.

Special statutory arrangements may be made in the design of institutions to recognise the collective status of an ethnocultural or indigenous community, for example by creating a cultural council for communities (e.g. cultural communities in Hungary);[2] by establishing an advisory body for a community (e.g. Sámi indigenous people in the Nordic countries, Aboriginal bodies in Australia); by allocating reserved seats to a community (e.g. Māori in New Zealand); by facilitating the establishment of a legal corporation for the community for a form of functional autonomy (e.g. Aboriginal people in Australia); or by allowing some autonomy arrangements for communities (e.g. South Tyrol, Brussels, Serbia, Kosovo, Estonia).

[2] The definition of 'national minority affairs' in Hungary also includes 'the provision of specific public services to persons belonging to a national minority', and equal opportunities, social inclusion and social welfare are included among the national minority rights. (Balogh, Halász, and Pap 2025) The nationality councils are therefore not restricted to only cultural affairs.

The typical fundamental rights of individuals that are exercised in the context of their community relate to language, religious, customary and cultural rights. These rights attain their full realisation through intra-community interaction. This underscores the principle that it is the individual, not the community, who bears these rights, but the identity rights attain substantive meaning when exercised with others of the same community. Therefore, courts may consider that certain individual rights only come to their full realisation when exercised with other members of the community. This is consistent with the understanding of Ubuntu, which recognises the relationship between individual and community. A court may therefore declare that an individual right was breached on the basis that the full realisation of the right requires it to be exercised in association with other members of an ethnocultural or indigenous community (e.g. mother-tongue education, exercise of culture, protection of an interest in land).

11.11 DIFFERENCE BETWEEN AN ETHNOCULTURAL COMMUNITY AND AN INDIGENOUS COMMUNITY

While international law and jurisprudence arising from municipal law acknowledge in principle the collective nature of indigenous communities based on their historic sovereignty with an own distinct legal system, it is important to note that an ethnocultural community typically lacks the attributes of a 'society' with its own legal systems akin to an indigenous community. Indigenous collective rights are grounded in them originating from a pre-settlement sovereign society with its own legal system and institutions of authority.

If an indigenous community seeks to be the beneficiary of contemporary collective rights, it must demonstrate that it is related to the ancestral community, that it continues to function as a society and that the legal norm sought to be relied on remains in practice as a law within the community.

An ethnocultural community usually does not usually have an own legal system associated with pre-settlement land as commonly observed in the case of indigenous peoples. Indigenous people are therefore regarded by (soft) international law as the bearers of individual *and* collective rights based on their previous sovereignty, while ethnocultural communities are principally seen by (soft) international law as the bearers of individual rights, albeit that the rights may be exercised collectively. This explains why in the Certification case the Constitutional Court emphasised that the protection of individual identity rights and diversity does not imply recognising collective political rights of self-determination.

Two caveats apply to the above statement. First, indigenous people must demonstrate that they continue to exist as a society in accordance with their traditional laws and customs because if they no longer function as a society they are regarded as an ethnocultural community since their historically distinct legal system had fallen into disuse. Secondly, ethnocultural communities may benefit from ad hoc institutional arrangements to secure their collective participation of governance processes such as power-sharing, autonomy and self-determination because of their risk of being permanently marginalised by the majority.

11.12 STATE SUPPORT FOR ETHNOCULTURAL AND INDIGENOUS COMMUNITIES

The protection of identity rights, encompassing cultural, linguistic, educational, traditional, religious and customary rights, resonates universally but only to the extent that these rights are attached to the individual. Pursuant to freedom of association, individuals may exercise these rights with others from the same community and a court may find that an individual right had been encroached in the context that the right can only be substantively exercised in association with other individuals of the same community. Furthermore, the diversity of individual rights are primarily exercised within the context of civil rights. This implies that the identity rights do not imply any special collective political rights and privileges in public law, such as self-government or autonomy, unless explicitly provided for by municipal legislation.

There is no legal obligation in international law or in the Constitution of South Africa on the state to fund or support the realisation of identity rights, for example by funding cultural events, promotion of language or education in mother tongue. The giving effect to identity rights largely hinges on the private resources available to individuals and the circumstances of each country. Consistent with international law, the South African state is not legally obliged to fund the realisation of mother-tongue education or the exercise of cultural, religious or indigenous rights. The right to mother-tongue education in public schools is conditional upon pragmatic considerations such as funding and teacher resources. The reason is obvious: the primary attention of the state is towards its individual citizens, not to communities or associations that may be formed by them. The state may of course make grants available to ethnocultural, indigenous and religious associations, but it is not legally obligated.

Pragmatism rather than legal prescription guides funding of ethnocultural and indigenous communities. For example, in the South African context the controversy surrounding Afrikaans mother-tongue education may to some extent be circumvented by making available a special annual grant to language communities for them to provide mother-tongue education to their children. The debate thus far has been one-dimensional with the focus solely on the funding of state schools. A trade-off may be for special grants to also be made available to language communities for private education.

The predicament posed by self-funding is that minority languages and cultures may become endangered because of a lack of public funding. This in turn may result in ethnocultural and indigenous communities and their members being treated procedurally equal under law, while in substance they experience inequality and marginalisation since the funding of their identity rights remain unmet. Courts may in their review of administrative actions by government consider the fairness and justness of a government action in light of the importance attached by the Constitution to identity rights and Ubuntu. Thus far the courts have been reluctant to read the right to mother-tongue education in association with other rights, such as the right to culture, self-determination and language.

In this respect the courts in India have arguably shown greater awareness of the importance of state-supported mother-tongue education to give content and substance to individual cultural and educational rights, compared to their South African counterparts.

11.13 CONSIDERATION OF FOREIGN MUNICIPAL LAW

A notable aspect of the 1996 Constitution is the importance it places on consideration of international law and foreign state jurisprudence to potentially provide insight, meaning and effect to the Bill of Rights. The Constitution in essence stipulates that courts *must* consider international law when interpreting South African law for consistency, *may* consider foreign jurisprudence, and *must* recognise the binding nature of international agreements approved by Parliament. This interpretation guide is intended to assist courts to consider developments in both international and foreign municipal law concerning the rights of ethnocultural communities and indigenous peoples and to develop the South African Bill of Rights pursuant to those international standards.

The evidence suggests, however, that South African courts are not consistent in their approach to the consideration of international law and foreign law. For example: (a) there is no consistency *when* foreign law is considered; (b) it is unpredictable *which* cases or country studies are considered; (c) it is unclear what *weight* is attached to international or foreign jurisprudence; (d) there is generally a lack of consideration of the different responses adopted by foreign courts to the same subject-matter; and (e) there is a *risk* that foreign case law may be selectively cited to justify a particular outcome or to hide an undisclosed bias, rather than to objectively inform and assist the court in the process of making a finding pursuant to the Bill of Rights.

Consideration of foreign case law has been shown to be highly discretionary, selective and inconsistent, and its utility outside the context of scientific work and narrow legal topics can be questioned since legal systems, history, policies, population composition and circumstances of countries are so different.

11.14 INDIVIDUAL RIGHTS ARE THE CORE OF ETHNOCULTURAL AND INDIGENOUS RIGHTS

The protection of ethnocultural and indigenous rights focuses on individual rights. The point of departure is equal treatment of all individuals and protection against discrimination against an individual for reason of their ethnocultural, religious or indigenous identity.

This individual-centred approach notwithstanding, in specific circumstances international soft law and practice encourage institutional design and political processes within states to provide enhanced protection for and participation by marginalised minorities and indigenous people in political processes by way of special participatory measures and funding. Such measures may include power-sharing, autonomy, guaranteed seats, vetoes and advisory bodies. Special funding arrangements may, for example, be made for education, with private schools receiving a state subsidy to promote mother-tongue education.

Courts may also consider the nature of an individual right within the context of it being ordinarily exercised in association with other members of the same ethnocultural, religious or indigenous community. For example, the right to mother-tongue education can be read with the rights to language, self-determination and culture when administrative reviews take place of government budget allocations or the exercise of administrative discretions about the language of education for a school.

The legal effect of minority rights in international law is based on the rights of the individual as a universal norm, while political participatory rights of ethnocultural and indigenous communities and special funding may be accommodated by way of ad hoc institutional design and grants on a case-by-case basis.

11.15 COLLECTIVE RIGHTS ARE OPTIONAL

International law places an obligation on the state to protect and respect the rights of individuals belonging to ethnocultural, religious and indigenous communities to associate and practise and enjoy their culture, traditions, religion and language. I referred to these rights as *identity rights* because they are so closely related to personal identity and individual right to self-determination.

There is no legal obligation in international law for states to recognise collective rights whereby an ethnocultural or indigenous community is regarded as a separate legal entity that has collective rights of self-government or power-sharing distinct from the individual rights of its individual members. States may nevertheless, consistent with international law and foreign precedents, design special institutions or enact policies to accommodate ethnocultural and indigenous communities collectively, provided that the principles of equality of individuals and non-discrimination are respected.

Courts may also consider the nature of identity rights within the context of those rights being substantively exercised in association with other members of the same ethnocultural or indigenous community. Exercising individual rights in association with others does not elevate the right to a collective right of the community, but it does emphasise that identity rights only come to true value when exercised collectively. This is arguably consistent with Ubuntu, where the individual comes to full realisation through association with community.

11.16 LEGAL PLURALISM AND ETHNOCULTURAL RIGHTS

The rising international interest in and recognition of legal pluralism as a social reality coincide with the ongoing discourse about the suitable protection of ethnocultural, religious and indigenous rights in plural societies. Legal pluralism tends to place an emphasis on the recognition of separate *legal* systems, while the minority protection debate tends to focus on the necessity of measures aimed to ensure effective *political participation* because of the political marginalisation of a community.

This dichotomy between an own legal system and political participatory rights was and remains exemplified in South Africa, where some religious and indigenous communities seek their legal systems to be recognised, while some ethnocultural communities, such as parts of the Afrikaans community, seek some form of collective rights but not within the context of a separate legal system. In both instances, however, the underlying motivation of the communities is that the modern state, with its emphasis on uniform norms and institutions, does not adequately accommodate or reflect the pluralism of the population.

With this in mind, special measures may be required to ensure that non-dominant communities, whether ethnocultural, religious or indigenous, are accorded adequate recognition, protection, funding and support to maintain and sustain their unique identity, customs, practices and non-state laws.

11.17 WHAT CONSTITUTES HATE SPEECH?

Hate speech is generally found in the facts of specific speech rather than by way of definition or analysing speech in the abstract. Several indicia can be identified arising from the approaches in international law and comparative constitutional law about what constitutes hate speech.

Among all forms of objectionable speech, hate speech is the most stringent threshold to satisfy since it is the most extreme form of speech. Even if hate speech is defined by legislation, the practical circumstance in which the speech is used determines whether speech meets the legal threshold of hate speech. The difficulty to prove hate speech has caused some countries to ban the display of certain symbols or the singing of certain chants, rather than to attempt to prove that speech in a particular context was hate speech.

In one circumstance speech may be regarded as hate speech, but the same speech may be regarded in another context as dislikeable, inappropriate, offensive or part of academic discourse. Furthermore, what is regarded socially as hate speech may not meet the legal threshold for hate speech.

There is a risk of bracket creep in the restrictions placed on freedom of expression, where the boundaries of lawful expression become so fluid that objectionable, dislikeable or offensive speech may drift into what is (incorrectly) regarded as hate speech.

In essence, speech we hate is not to be equated with hate speech.

11.18 TEST FOR HATE SPEECH

The test to be applied for hate speech is objective from the perspective of the reasonably informed onlooker, rather than subjective from the mind of the speaker or the person exposed to the speech. The circumstances of the speech, the intention of the speaker and the perceptions of the complainant are nevertheless relevant factors to be considered by the fictional reasonable person.

This test of objectivity is complex in its application and arbitrary because the sensitivity of the general community towards speech may not be the same as the sensitivity of the community at which the speech is directed. In fact, the general community may be insensitive or unaware of how a member of the targeted community experiences speech. The test of a reasonable person therefore becomes fictional and highly discretionary. This raises the question of what evidence is required for a judge who is called upon to ascertain the opinion of the reasonable person to declare how a reasonable person would perceive speech.

An objective assessment of hate speech is not as simple as the case of the reasonable person test in delict or torts, where a general societal assessment about conduct is made. When the hate speech test is applied one must be satisfied that the reasonable person in the wide community would understand how the community that is the subject of the speech perceives the speech. Speech may have different meanings, of which *only one* meaning may be regarded as hate speech by a complainant. If any of the potential meanings of speech meet the threshold of hate speech, the speech may be curtailed.

Determining whether speech meets the threshold of hate speech depends on all the relevant circumstances. Account must also be taken of all the possible meanings of speech, not only the predominant meaning or the meaning most obvious or most preferred by the judge. If any of the meanings of speech constitutes hate speech, then the speech must be so declared.

Speech that may be hate speech in one circumstance may not be hate speech in another circumstance. Speech may also as time passes become hate speech or lose its hate speech effect. The banning of certain speech renders the speech a criminal offence, but hate speech must be assessed in each circumstance and any finding of the court or order of the court only relates to the specific incident.

Importantly, if freedom of expression is to be curbed, the curtailment should be proportionate, retrospective by reference to the event and narrow rather than broad.

11.19 HOW PRACTICAL IS THE 'REASONABLE PERSON' TEST TO DETERMINE HATE SPEECH?

The duty that rests on a court to establish the perception of a reasonable person towards speech is a fictional and potentially highly unreliable exercise, especially in deeply divided societies where judges might introduce their own biases and subjective views of history and opinions of socio-political events into their formulation of the imaginary reasonable person's view. The minority that turns to the court for protection against hate speech may find that the court becomes another forum of marginalisation and insensitivity, or the courts may become an extension of political dominance with the sensitivity of one community treated with greater respect than those of other communities.

It may be challenging for a judge who is not part of a community that is the subject of purported hate speech to ascertain how such a community experiences the speech, especially if speech is open to multiple meanings.

A court in essence faces at least three threshold-tests: first, to investigate *all* possible meanings of speech, not only the most obvious or predominant meaning; secondly, to hear adequate evidence to ascertain how the person or community that is the subject of the speech perceives the offending speech and the reasons for it alleging that the speech is hate speech; and, thirdly, to hear adequate evidence about how the general community perceives the speech on the assumption that a reasonable person in the community has a fair grasp on how the community that is the target of the speech perceives it. The court may also hear expert evidence about the meaning or effect of speech, but expert opinions may also be subject to personal bias. It therefore becomes a highly discretionary test, particularly if no element of threat or potential violence is required for hate speech. This explains why in some foreign jurisdictions courts have required some form of intimidation, threats of violence or actual violence for a finding of hate speech.

All relevant evidence should be considered by a court in the light of the fundamental importance of freedom of expression to a free and open democratic society. If the evidence presented is not adequate to declare speech as hate speech, judges may not supplement the evidence with their own understandings of the topic, history or circumstance. A judge must be guided by the evidence, including adequate evidence to form an opinion of what a reasonable person would conclude about each of the meanings of the speech.

The Kill the Boer and Old Flag cases highlight the complexity involved in applying an objective assessment to the reasonableness of speech. This is particularly true in a deeply divided society, where the history of the respective communities, as well as their perceptions of history and their response to speech, are multidimensional, nuanced and complex. If ever speech was susceptible to various meanings, it was in these cases.

The approach adopted by the courts regarding the Old Flag and the Kill the Boer chant seems to place a higher value on the experiences, fears, sensitivities and perceptions of one community over those of another. In both cases the courts seem to emphasise the *predominant* meaning of speech from the view of the majority community, rather than to consider *all* possible meanings of speech.

Hence it is not surprising that the courts in both instances based their findings on the opinion of the black community towards the speech. One can argue that in similar way that the Old Flag has as *one* of its meanings an element of hate speech, so the Kill the Boer chant as *one* of its meanings has an element of hate speech. However, in both cases the courts opted for the view of the majority of society: the Old Flag was categorised as hate speech while the Kill the Boer chant was not regarded as hate speech. The courts adopted a predominance test where the perception of one community of the speech was given greater weight than the perception of another community.

These judgments underscore the inherent complexities to ascertain objectively *all* the potential meanings of speech and then to determine if the threshold of hate speech is met by *any* of the meanings of the speech.

The judgments also bring attention to the challenge of weighing the different histories of peoples and communities, the difficulty of distinguishing between literal and figurative meanings and interpretations of speech, the possibility that the offensive nature of speech may change over time, the different meanings of speech, and the intricacies arising generally from the so-called objective test.

11.20 HATE SPEECH IN COMPARATIVE PERSPECTIVE

The lack of consistency evident in comparative jurisprudence between states and even within states about the application of the hate speech test affirms the propositions that:

- the declaration of speech as hate speech and the consequent curtailment of speech should be reserved for the most extreme forms of speech;
- any restriction on speech should be proportionate to the speech in question;
- courts shall take into consideration where and when the speech was expressed and by whom; and
- a restriction on speech shall be directed at only the specific incident concerned rather than imposing a broad restriction on speech into the future.

In their application of these criteria courts have, at best, been inconsistent.

International theory and jurisprudence suggest that unless Parliament or the executive restricts or bans certain speech or insignia, a declaration of hate speech should be directed at the specific incident and at the person involved in the event. Comparative jurisprudence emphasises that a declaration of hate speech applies retrospectively to a specific incident and not as a future restriction on speech.

11.21 KILL THE BOER AND OLD FLAG CASE STUDIES

The judgments arising from the Kill the Boer and Old Flag case studies highlight the following pertinent aspects of the application of any hate speech test in practice:

- First, adequate evidence must be available for a finding of fact to be made about *all* the possible meanings of speech, as well as the circumstance, the speaker and the context in which it was made. Furthermore, adequate evidence must be available of the opinions, perceptions or observations of the person or community who is offended by the speech or one of the potential meanings of the speech.
- Secondly, judges may not rely on their own perceptions of speech or their personal knowledge, opinions or understandings of historical or social events to categorise speech or supplement evidence.
- Thirdly, of all offensive speech the categorisation of hate speech is the highest and hence the most difficult to achieve. Speech should not easily be declared hate speech. Offensive or inappropriate speech may also serve as a basis to educate the community, to stimulate debate and to marginalise speech that offends community values.
- Fourthly, if a constitutionally implied term such as Ubuntu is relied on to weigh speech, it must be done consistently and not be used or ignored at the sole discretion of a judge.
- Fifthly, the categorisation of speech is objective, but it takes into account *all* the possible meanings of speech as well as all the circumstances in which the speech was uttered, including the intention and identity of the speaker, the forum where the speech was made and the circumstances in which the speech was uttered.
- Sixthly, if *any* of the possible meanings of speech can reasonably be construed in the circumstances as hate speech, it must be so declared.
- Seventhly, where the display of a cultural or religious symbol or speech is being complained about, the protection against hate speech must also be assessed within the content of the right to practise culture and religion.
- Eighthly, any finding that speech is restricted must be proportionate to the speech, the event in question and by reference to the speech in a particular circumstance, not a general restriction of the offending speech (or display of an emblem) into the future. A general ban or restriction on speech or an emblem is a matter for Parliament, not for the courts.

11.22 UBUNTU AS AN IMPLIED TERM OF THE CONSTITUTION

The term 'Ubuntu' has been relied upon by the South African judiciary as an embedded term of customary law to be utilised when the Constitution is interpreted. The use of Ubuntu by courts to approach the Constitution as a living organism that reflects changing community values is highlighted by the width and depth of jurisprudence citing Ubuntu. There is arguably no other foreign law case study where an implied customary term has been so widely used in jurisprudence as Ubuntu.

In a deeply divided pluralistic society like South Africa, where a balance between individual and community rights is sought, Ubuntu serves to inspire and guide the judiciary with its emphasis on respecting diversity, appreciating cultural differences and fostering the promotion and survival of unique identities. Ubuntu recognises the importance of community in the well-being of an individual. The South African reliance on the term 'Ubuntu' underscores the unique interaction between the humanity of the individual, the customary use and application of non-state law, the recognition of non-state law by state law and the collectivism of the community.

Ubuntu has become a widely used term in South Africa, exceeding the traditional customary meaning of the word. In the application of Ubuntu courts have adopted a creative way to link the legalities of the Constitution with the soul of African values and traditions. Consequently, the courts have used Ubuntu in various contexts such as fundamental rights, criminal law, law of contract, employment rights, property rights and law of defamation. By citing the inherent qualities of Ubuntu the legal pluralism of South Africa has been given further visibility, credibility and legitimacy.

Ubuntu is accepted, without much analysis or critique by courts, as an implied norm of the Constitution that is derived from African customary law. Ubuntu is also treated as an interpretive tool, a source of law and an explanatory aid.

11.23 DEFINITIONAL CHALLENGES OF UBUNTU

Ubuntu as a term of customary law does not appear in the Constitution. It remains undefined. Ubuntu is described, rather than defined. Judges often seem to use poetic licence to add liberally to the meaning and application of Ubuntu.

Ubuntu was neither cited during the 1994–1996 constitutional debates nor referred to in scholarly works or committee proceedings leading to the adoption of the 1996 Constitution. Ubuntu did not appear as an essential value-laden term in publications leading up to drafting of the Constitution. The term was briefly referred to in the 'post-amble' of the 1993 interim Constitution, but with reference only to reconciliation and not as part of the Bill of Rights. No mention was made of Ubuntu in the Certification cases. This low profile of Ubuntu under the 1996 Constitution-drafting process comes as a surprise since such high value has since been place by the courts on Ubuntu as an implied norm of the Constitution. Added thereto is the lack of scientific attention given to Ubuntu as a term of law prior to 1996.

In retrospect the exclusion of Ubuntu from the Constitution was an opportunity lost. All efforts by the courts to clarify the term for legal application have been descriptive of its character with a sense of judicial knowledge, rather than definitive of its legal meaning. Ubuntu remains therefore open-ended, dynamic, vague, discretionary and inconsistent in its interpretation and application.

11.24 UBUNTU AS SOURCE OF HOME-GROWN JURISPRUDENCE

The meaning of Ubuntu in African tradition is not primarily legal, but rather relational. The Constitutional Court has nevertheless elevated Ubuntu to a state law legal term that can imply a source of law, a mechanism for statutory interpretation or a useful way to explain the rationale of a judgment to the population. By relying on the term the courts have developed a home-grown jurisprudence with Ubuntu at its core.

Ubuntu in many respects reflects the legal meaning of equality, equity, proportionality and fairness – terms that are prevalent in foreign jurisprudence. Those terms, frequently relied on in foreign legal systems, are equally as undefined and flexible as Ubuntu, and yet they are regularly cited by courts to balance competing interests and to develop as societies change. It is therefore not unknown for a non-constitutional term or phrase to be adopted and adapted by courts.

Note should, however, be taken that Ubuntu is not consistently cited by courts as is the case with principles of equity, proportionality and reasonableness. It appears that judges are at liberty to use or ignore Ubuntu or not to explain why Ubuntu is not relevant in one case but relevant in another. This discretionary approach heightens the risk of Ubuntu being cited selectively, subjectively, inconsistently and unpredictably.

11.25 UBUNTU HAS MANY APPLICATIONS

The overview of jurisprudence highlights how Ubuntu is applied to various disputes, often with an element of romanticism, without an exegesis of how a specific meaning within the context of the specific dispute is ascertained. The term is often approached as if it has a precise legal definition with a meaning that seems to arise from judicial knowledge. There is even to some extent a quasi-religious use of the meaning of Ubuntu.

The reality is, however, that there are few cases, if any, where expert evidence is heard to justify the specific meaning attached to Ubuntu and to explain why Ubuntu ought to be applied or not applied to the dispute. Courts generally cite each other without providing an in-depth explanation that attaches a particular meaning to the term. Judges tend to add liberally and poetically through what appears to be their personal understanding of the term.

In general Ubuntu is relied on in three principal ways: as a source of law, an instrument for statutory interpretation and an explanatory term.

The risk is that Ubuntu, with its origins entrenched in African tradition, is being employed to resolve disputes arising across a multicultural community such as South Africa. Not all communities may display an affinity or understanding of Ubuntu and, even if different persons use the same word, their cultural understanding of the meaning of the word may vary. It remains unexplained why Ubuntu has become such a go-to term while other equally meritorious terms or phrases arising from religious and cultural contexts have not received equal status or attention.

The use of Ubuntu by the Constitutional Court has demonstrated how a non-state law term pertaining to a specific community may be elevated to a state law term applicable to an entire population. The utility of Ubuntu lies particularly in its legitimising impact. It aids courts to establish contours by which powers and functions are to be exercised in accordance with a term that resonates 'South Africa'. Political realism, legal pragmatism and the transformative objectives of South Africa are served by the values represented by Ubuntu.

Given that Ubuntu is principally used as an explanatory tool to provide the rationale behind a judgment, rather than constituting a legal right in itself, the application of the term has generally speaking gained acceptance and credibility among the wider society.

11.26 UBUNTU AT RISK OF BECOMING AN IDEOLOGICAL TOOL?

It is important to acknowledge the ambiguity and lack of consistency surrounding the invocation and application of Ubuntu by courts. This ambiguity and inconsistency pose the risk of Ubuntu becoming an ideological tool used to enforce a form of hegemony under the guise of being authentically African. The selective, discretionary and inconsistent reliance on Ubuntu potentially erodes its value as an implied constitutional term. The inconsistency also raises the spectre of Ubuntu being used to justify an outcome, rather than being utilised as a legal principle that assists and guides courts methodically to declare the law.

It is furthermore not clear whether judges with a particular cultural Ubuntu background, black judges for example, have greater freedom and discretion to cite and interpret Ubuntu based on they may see as judicial knowledge, than judges who cannot first-hand speak about its inherent cultural meaning, considering their different cultural background. For example, if non-black judges apply Ubuntu, are they restricted in their discretion by only citing previous applications of Ubuntu? Or can they expand the application of the term without some form of expert evidence? It seems as if Ubuntu has become a lexicon or thesaurus term that lends itself to any virtuous expression.

The above observation is illustrated by the Old Flag and Kill the Boer cases, where in only the 2011 Kill the Boer case the court, constituted by a white judge, cited Ubuntu. In none of the other proceedings was Ubuntu cited nor explanation given why Ubuntu was not cited or why it was not relevant. The same can be said of the Qwelane case, in which no mention was made of Ubuntu. One would have thought that if ever Ubuntu had a message, it would be found in the context of potential hate speech and equal treatment. The question thus arises: has Ubuntu become a non-racial term or is it deeply embedded into race?

The use of Ubuntu illustrates how application of a non-state, customary law term by persons who do not share the customs from which the term originates may be more complex than it seems at first glance. Ubuntu has indeed become a repository of many meanings. And the term may become an unfortunate cloak to disguise judicial bias.

11.27 WHEN IS UBUNTU CITED?

The use of Ubuntu has become so widespread in South Africa that it may give rise to a somewhat romantic and poetic approach to dispute resolution, which, in turn, may be marred by inconsistencies and biases in its application and meaning. While Sachs observed critically the rigidity of the rules of interpretation, Ubuntu on the other hand also opens the door to judicial creativity and interventionism but with unpredictability and lack of consistency.

It is reasonable to be critical about some discrepancies that prevail when Ubuntu is applied in practice by the courts. For example, one court cited Ubuntu to stay an eviction, while another granted an eviction without reference to Ubuntu. One court relies on Ubuntu to declare Kill the Boer hate speech, while the other does not cite Ubuntu, does not explain why Ubuntu is not applicable and finds that the chant does not constitute hate speech. Furthermore, no mention is made of Ubuntu in the Qwelane case, in which personal respect, integrity and dignity were so important. The same question arises in the Chief Avhatendi Ratshibvumo Rambuda case, in which no mention is made of Ubuntu or its potential applicability or lack of applicability to an intra-tribal dispute about the election of a tribal leader. (Chief Avhatendi Ratshibvumo Rambuda case 2024)

The meanings ascribed to Ubuntu often emerge without expert evidence to explain the relevance of the term to the particular dispute, relying instead on one judge citing another judge and relying on their own understandings and scientific papers. While Ubuntu may play a useful role to rationalise judgments, it prompts the question whether courts are obligated to cite Ubuntu, when Ubuntu must be cited, when it must be explained that Ubuntu is not relevant, or if reliance on Ubuntu is entirely discretionary and haphazard.

While the inherited rules of statutory interpretation may be old and perhaps uncompromising, highly technical and unwieldy, Ubuntu brings a freshness and flexibility but also unpredictability that may lead to a lack of consistency and heightened arbitrariness.

Generally, reference to and reliance on Ubuntu have imbued South African jurisprudence with a distinctly African character that enhances its legitimacy and popular understanding.

As a legal term Ubuntu is vague. However, as a soulful concept underpinning the Constitution it represents the values and aspirations cherished by the broader community, such as fairness, neighbourliness, restoration, kindness, mutual dependence and reasonableness. These values are not restricted to Ubuntu since they also arise from the value systems of other cultures and religions. Ubuntu, however, has become the term that encapsulates those multi-meanings.

As a term of law Ubuntu lacks precision, but as a spiritual value it adds life and purpose to the Constitution. Ultimately, the use of the term Ubuntu illustrates how a constitution can be interpreted in a relevant customary manner by recognising non-state law to give effect to the societal values of the nation that the constitution is intended to serve.

11.28 DOES UBUNTU SUPPORT OR ERODE LIBERAL DEMOCRATIC VALUES?

The values promoted by Ubuntu may reflect universal elements, but, given its association with African value systems and religions, the use of the term may be alienating to some segments of the community, especially if it is applied selectively or cited at the unpredictable discretion of judges.

Africanists have been concerned that Ubuntu as an African customary concept is being colonised by applying it to non-African customary disputes and attributing meanings to it that derive from individualism and universality of international law. By such expanded application of Ubuntu, critics say the customary value of Ubuntu is weakened by diluting the collective cultural and customary nature of the concept as it is known in Africa. On the other hand, the concept has been effectively used as a vehicle to bring into South African law universal concepts underlying dispute resolution and human rights protection.

Critics have also noted that the concept of community or group solidarity arising from Ubuntu may be at odds with individualism as expressed by liberal democratic principles in the Constitution. In African customs and traditions there is often an emphasis on the subservient role of the individual to the community. This hierarchical relationship that underpins Ubuntu may potentially erode liberal democratic understandings of fundamental individual rights and freedoms. As living law Ubuntu may become a tool for modernisation or it may be a Trojan horse that introduces foreign concepts to African custom.

Given that Ubuntu is a culturally informed concept lacking in precise definition, it could potentially be applied to disputes to which it may not be appropriate.

11.29 UBUNTU IN CONTEXT OF NON-AFRICAN ELEMENTS OF THE CONSTITUTION

The use of Ubuntu in dispute resolution is not inconsistent with the way foreign legal systems have developed concepts such as equity, fairness, proportionality and reasonableness. Those concepts had taken many generations to develop through common law and tradition, and they continue to evolve. While the South African Constitution draws inspiration from Western liberal democratic values, the criticism often heard since 1996 is that the Constitution does not adequately reflect an African culture, identity or fingerprint. This criticism is to some extent addressed using and relying on Ubuntu.

Ubuntu provides the Constitution with an African soul, serving as a source of rights, enhancing a purposive approach to interpretation and presenting as a mechanism to explain judgments in a manner that resonates with the public. Therefore Ubuntu lends credibility and legitimacy to judgments that otherwise would have to rely on foreign concepts, rights, obligations and precedents as rules for interpretation.

11.30 DEFINITION OF 'CONSULT' AND 'FREE, PRIOR AND INFORMED CONSENT'

The rights to be consulted and to give free, prior and informed consent (FPIC) to an activity that affects rights and interests are particularly relevant to indigenous communities in matters related to their traditional lands. Consultation rights also benefit the wider South African community but, for purposes of this book, the emphasis of consultation is on the rights of indigenous people.

Neither the right to consultation, nor the right to FPIC is defined, prescribed or set out in detail in international law. The right to FPIC does not, regardless of the use of the word 'consent', imply a veto unless specifically so determined by municipal statute or international treaty. An example is the Informal Land Rights Act (1996), which grants a veto to a community when their rights in land are affected.

The rights to consultation and FPIC are to be given practical content in each country depending on the circumstances, the nature and scale of the project or measure in question, the local regulatory scheme and the rights and status of the indigenous people involved. Importantly, FPIC represents an objective and an endeavour to seek consent, rather than a right of veto by withholding consent. FPIC does not imply co-decision-making and it does not substitute the regulatory authority of the state.

In international law there are no legally defined pro forma requirements or conditions resembling a checklist that must be strictly followed to meet the criteria for good faith consultation. In foreign and South African jurisprudence useful indicia of good faith consultation have been identified, but those do not form a closed list.

Evaluating compliance with good faith consultation and FPIC typically involves assessing the overall *process*, *conduct* and *attitude* of the parties, rather than adhering to specific institutional or procedural tick-the-box requirements.

11.31 GOOD FAITH IS THE KEY FOR CONSULTATION TO ACHIEVE FPIC

The processes of consultation and FPIC must be conducted in good faith. This involves participating in consultations and negotiations with an open mind, providing sufficiently detailed information about the proposed project or measure in a timely manner, explaining the reasons for objecting to a proposal, demonstrating a willingness to compromise, responding to communications, presenting proposals in a format that is understood by the community, and sincerely considering the position adopted by the other party.

The obligation of good faith applies to all parties involved in the consultation, including the indigenous people.

Good faith brings obligations to both parties. There is, unless specified by law, no time limit to good faith negotiations. It depends on context if adequate time had been allowed for consultation. Importantly, the absence of a reached agreement does not necessarily indicate a failure in good faith or a refusal to comply with processes arising from FPIC. International and domestic law acknowledge that parties can engage in good faith negotiations and participate in FPIC without arriving at an agreement. Essentially, the requirements of FPIC can be satisfied without a mutually agreed outcome. Herein lies a risk for indigenous people because, on the one hand, their participation in consultation may grant legitimacy to the process even if their views are not heeded, while, on the other, if they refuse to participate in consultation, a court may declare that they did not act in good faith.

South African jurisprudence often provides greater clarity about consultation standards than is found in the general standards suggested by international law. The concept of FPIC has not been incorporated into South African statutory law and hence there is not an expectation of 'consent' in South Africa when in fact only good faith 'consultation' is intended. The use of the word 'consent' in the UNDRIP may cause unrealistic expectations.

South African legislation is generally unequivocal about the nature of the duty when consultation is required, specifying either the obligation to obtain consent or to engage in consultation. If there is no specific statutory obligation, the courts have accepted that under the rules of procedural and administrative fairness and in common law the affected person or community should have a reasonable opportunity to be heard and make inputs when their rights and interests are affected. The right to be consulted in South African law does not, however, imply a right of veto.

11.32 CONSIDERATION OF INTERNATIONAL LAW TO ASCERTAIN MEANING OF CONSULT

The content given to the terms 'consult' and 'consent' in South Africa is principally determined by the interpretation given to the originating relevant statute according to which consultation is mandated. Although South African courts may consider international jurisprudence, disputes in South Africa about the adequacy of consultation are resolved by reference to South African law and statutes, with international jurisprudence either not being cited or, if cited, only by way of remarks made *obiter*. International standards about consultation have informed South African law, but courts have been careful not to read 'consent' when 'consult' is intended.

Although in the Baleni case mention was made of FPIC in the context of international law, this was also done *obiter* since the right to veto of the community in that case arose from the relevant statute and not from consideration of or an application of international law.

Courts consider all relevant factors to determine if those whose rights and interests are affected had a reasonable opportunity to be consulted and to effectively participate in the process.

11.33 WHEN TO CONSULT?

Unless otherwise specified, consultation is required about administrative, environmental, developmental and legislative measures that may affect a community in general, and indigenous people in particular, in a direct or disproportionate way. Consultation with indigenous people as a special category of community is not mandated for general socio-economic matters, public policies or legislation that impact on the entire population. Consultation is often, albeit not exclusively, related to interests of indigenous people in land or the environment associated with their traditional lands.

In South African jurisprudence the obligation to consult with tribal communities or informal land occupiers generally arises from specific statutory and common-law entitlements related to their local rights and interests in land. The right to be consulted does not imply a right to be consulted in policy and governance issues of a general nature. The test to be applied, generally speaking, is if the interest of an indigenous or tribal community is so directly or uniquely affected that consultation with it ought to take place.

Good faith consultation standards also apply to legislative processes where legislation have been declared invalid because of a lack of procedural fairness and inclusiveness in the public consultation during the legislative process (e.g. Khoisan Act). This South African legal standard for legislative procedural fairness is advanced in comparison to many liberal democracies.

11.34 INDICIA OF CONSULTATION

Consultation within the context of FPIC must occur in a manner that provides timeous information about a measure to the indigenous community if their rights or interests are potentially affected, presented in a format understandable to the community and is supported by disclosure about the nature, extent, impact and duration of the proposal as well as rehabilitation of land.

Consultation is not to be regarded as merely informing a community about a predetermined outcome. The consultation must take place at a stage before a measure is finalised so the outcome may be affected by the process of consultation. If relevant, information must also be provided about the rehabilitation of land or other steps to mitigate the impacts of a proposed measure. Although the process of consultation is open-ended in the search for agreement, it does not imply that a party must change its position to prove that it had consulted in good faith.

The sharing of information is subject to the degree and reasonableness necessary to enable the indigenous community to make an informed decision. Commercially sensitive information or culturally sensitive information may be withheld or shared with only a core group of negotiators.

Consultation neither implies an obligation to compromise nor a veto power for the indigenous community, but it does require a willingness and commitment of both parties to strive to reach agreement, to keep an open mind, to allow the community time to consider and to make counterproposals. In essence, it is the *attitude* and *style*, not the outcome, that determine if legal obligations for consultation had been fulfilled.

11.35 WHO SHOULD PARTICIPATE IN CONSULTATION?

The indigenous community involved in consultation is entitled to nominate the mechanism or forum through which they prefer their leaders or elders to represent them. The representative forum may be based on hereditary considerations, nomination, election or a combination of mechanisms. In areas where land access is often sought, for example for mining, a community may opt for a permanent negotiation committee and adopt a negotiation protocol whereby their community consultation processes are set out.

The process to nominate negotiators is itself an extension of the right of self-determination for indigenous people and must be decided by them, rather than prescribed by an external party. External parties must be cautious not to interfere with the representative process of a community or to contribute to internal division since it may be viewed as a lack of good faith consultation if the proponent seem to favour parts of the community.

The indigenous community must, however, ensure that its internal processes are transparent, representative and fair to the various subsegments of its community. It is essential that third parties have confidence in the preferred negotiating mechanism of an indigenous community, including in the way the community deals with dissenting opinions in their midst. It may be very challenging and costly for a proponent of a measure to consult with a community that does not speak through a unified negotiation process.

Dealing with various subgroups or factions may complicate FPIC, but an effort should at least be made to do so. That said, neither international law nor South African law mandates consultation with or agreement by all subgroups. It is accepted that indigenous communities may have internal disagreements about the position to be adopted by the community.

In essence: a reasonable effort must be made to consult widely and a reasonable opportunity granted for subgroups to participate in consultation. If a community fails to participate in consultation as a cohesive unit or if a community is splintered into feuding groups, the community may fall short of its obligation to engage in good faith consultation.

11.36 CONSULTATION AS AN INDIVIDUAL RIGHT BEING EXERCISED IN COMMUNITY WITH OTHERS

The right to be consulted arises not only from international instruments such as ILO 169 and UNDRIP. The right to be consulted also originates from fundamental individual rights such as the right to self-determination, human dignity, equality, non-discrimination, culture, property and a safe and secure environment, as embodied in international legal instruments such as the ICCPR and the ICESCR.

The right to be consulted therefore finds its origin in various sources. While the processes associated with FPIC typically have a collective nature, an individual may also initiate action or demand consultation based on their individual rights and freedoms. This expansion of individual rights is acknowledged in South African jurisprudence, the principle of a participatory democracy implying consultation when interests are affected, be it the interests of an individual or those of a community.

The right to consultation under the Constitution is therefore not limited to indigenous or tribal communities but extends to all communities and individuals. This does not necessarily grant to each individual the right to be separately consulted. Context, distinct interest, practicality and proportionality determine the extent to which an individual or community ought to be consulted.

11.37 UNIVERSALITY OF RIGHTS AND MAJORITARIANISM

Rights generally regarded as universal, for example religion, culture, association and speech, are often subject to restrictions that may reflect the realities of the country in which those rights are sought to be exercised. As a general principle limitations may be imposed on a right in a manner that is fair and reasonable in a democratic society. For example, judgments arising from the ECtHR show how in different countries in the European sphere the practical content given, and limitations imposed on, rights such as freedom of religion may vary between states. The universality of a right may therefore be given different practical content depending on the country in which the right is exercised.

Rights that are purported to be 'universal' often lack the practical effect and legal certainty of real 'universality' in their operation. Limitations may be imposed on rights by majoritarianism, the constitution, by courts or by non-state law customs and beliefs. The ECtHR, for example, has relied on the so-called margin of appreciation to allow restrictions on fundamental rights based on majoritarian considerations within states, thereby potentially eroding the very concept of universality of a right across all of Europe.

The same applies to South Africa, where the control exercised by the majority over political processes and the appointment of judges may cause the arms of majoritarianism to extend deep into civil liberties and restrictions on pluralism.

11.38 INTERFACE OF STATE LAW AND RELIGIOUS NON-STATE LAW

The separation of state and religion must be assessed within the context of the history of Europe and Western liberal democratic thought, while acknowledging that there are ongoing discussions in liberal democracies about how this separation is to be given practical effect. In Europe, for example, public and legal opinions are divided especially in response to the growing number of followers of Islam who seek to live in accordance with Islamic law in the context of legal plurality, in contrast to state law that may demand uniformity and secularism based on universal human rights standards.

The balance sought to be achieved between religious freedom and protection of other rights is not limited to European interaction with Islam. There are many other examples where conduct arising from the dogma of a religion may potentially be inconsistent with state laws. For example, in Christianity, Judaism and indigenous customary law the treatment of females and children may not be consistent with the state law principle of equality and non-discrimination.

The current challenges being experienced by Europe, with the arrival of large numbers of immigrants from countries where Sharia plays a key role in all respects of their daily life, are testing the ability of the ECtHR to maintain a consistent balance between protecting and respecting universal human rights norms as enshrined in the European Convention on Human Rights, and to respect the prerogative of sovereign states to formulate policies suited to their specific state-based circumstances. There is widespread agreement that European jurisprudence, along with democratic norms and standards, have some way to go to respond successfully to the challenges associated with religious diversity in general, and particularly issues concerning Sharia non-state law and its interaction with state law.

While the concept of the separation of state and religion is generally accepted as a principle of liberal democratic theory, its application differs in democratic states, and even among European democracies there are different approaches on how to operationalise the principle.

In South Africa and internationally, religion remains an important source of non-state law; hence its influence on public policy remains clearly discernible and its potential conflict with state law often draws the attention of courts.

11.39 COURTS AND RELIGIOUS DOGMA

In the discharge of their functions, courts strive to avoid becoming entangled in disputes about the constitutionality or lawfulness of religious dogma or doctrine. Given that religions organise themselves internally on the basis of systems of thought and spiritual beliefs, disputes about the interpretation of their spiritual beliefs are not for courts to resolve.

The separation of state and church implies that religions may adhere to and promote their beliefs, but the conduct of persons, religious or secular, must be consistent with state law.

It is not unusual for courts to be drawn into the lawfulness of conduct pursuant to religious or customary dogma when a person, for whatever reason, relies on religious or customary teaching to defend specific action that may seem to be inconsistent with state law. The courts, when called upon, must determine whether conduct sought to be protected under freedom of religion is indeed protected by the Constitution or whether it offends the provisions of the Constitution. In this sense religion is treated similarly to customary law, where the Constitution has an egalitarian effect.

The principle emphasised by South African jurisprudence is that a person is not entitled to preferential treatment, nor should they endure unequal treatment, because of their religious beliefs.

11.40 UN-FREEDOM DUE TO RELIGIOUS NON-STATE LAWS

South Africa's diverse population provides evidence of how rights to religion, culture, language, custom and identity are interwoven. Culture is clearly informed by religion and religion is informed by culture. Clear lines of demarcation do not exist. Culture and religion are simple words that seek to encapsulate different aspects of the complexity of human existence. For those who profess a faith, their religion often forms the core of their existence. Some who have eloped from religion may still regard themselves as culturally religious. One cannot simply 'opt out' of religion, especially if one is socially, culturally and practically deeply integrated with a closely knit religious community.

In addition to the religious commands of obedience, religious communities often impose their own obligations, sanctions and pressures on those of the same faith. Religious sanctions can be controlling and harsh – exclusion from their religious community can leave a person isolated, vulnerable, and possibly without legal recourse. While freedom to practise religion is on the one hand an extension of the individual right to self-determination, on the other hand, the inability to dissociate from a religious community may cause despair and entrapment, particularly for women and children.

Freedom to practise religion may become un-freedom to withdraw from a religious community. South African courts have acknowledged that respect for legal plurality cannot allow non-state law to remove basic human rights protection from an individual. Practising a faith or being part of an indigenous community does not imply a person contracts out of basic human rights protections of the Constitution. This applies to religious communities as much as it does to customary communities. Religious beliefs or customary adherence does not imply contracting out of protections of the Constitution.

Courts are the protectors of pluralism, but also a bulwark against non-state law norms, customs or practices that encroach on fundamental rights.

11.41 WHEN RELIGIOUS DOGMA AFFECTS FUNDAMENTAL RIGHTS

There is a fine balance for courts to assess the actions of a religious group without, when doing so, becoming involved in disputes about the constitutionality of the doctrine or core dogmatic teachings of the religion.

In various disputes, such as the approach of a church to same-sex marriages, the defence of corporal punishment of children, the different treatment of men and women in customary law, the slaughter of animals, or the rights of individuals in Muslim marriages, South African courts have tested the constitutionality and practical application of the rules, practices, and effects of religious dogma and practices. The courts have done so without conducting an inquiry into the constitutionality of the religion itself or the soundness of its teaching. Indeed, the judgments handed down by courts may assist religious groups to review their dogma and practices in light of contemporary civil and democratic standards, or religions may ignore judgments of the courts and persist with their teaching. In this respect religious and customary norms are living since they adjust with community standards.

While religious groups may, collectively and individually and without state interference, teach and adhere to their own non-state rules and prescriptions, it is when an action arising from a non-state religious law potentially offends the Constitution that the courts must proclaim on the constitutionality of the religious rule or practice in question.

11.42 FAITH VERSUS RIGHTS

Various cases highlight the delicate line of separation between religion and the Constitution, whereby the privacy of religion is respected, but within the public sphere the values of equality, dignity and non-discrimination for all individuals must prevail regardless of their religious beliefs.

The Constitution is not a neutral document without an inherent rationale. The Constitution is a social compact of the terms whereby a populace consents to be governed. That is why the conception events and birthing processes of the South African Constitution are so important to understand. Not only were the words of the Constitution subject to detailed consideration, but the philosophy of the Constitution also permeates those words.

The essence of the South African Constitution is that a person who professes a faith cannot be expected to be treated preferentially to a person who does not profess a faith, unless such a differentiation can be justified pursuant to constitutional criteria. The right to religion does not grant to the believer a constitutional right to undertake an action or an obligation to endure treatment that would in another circumstance be unconstitutional or unlawful. By the same token the Constitution provides safeguards for individuals irrespective of their religious belief.

When religious practice enters the public arena it is treated in accordance with the civil standard as found in the Constitution. If religion is sought to be relied upon to defend an action under the Constitution, such an exemption must be consistent with the exceptions permitted under the Constitution. The same applies to customary law.

11.43 NO RIGHT TO MOTHER-TONGUE EDUCATION IN INTERNATIONAL LAW

There is no justiciable right to mother-tongue education in international law. That said, the merit and importance of mother-tongue education as a sensible policy measure is widely acknowledged in international law and practice. It is also accepted that the right to self-determination of individuals and the fulfilment of other rights, such as the right to culture, can be enhanced by educating students for as long as possible in their language and recognising their language for public use. Added thereto, in democratisation theory and practice state support for ethnocultural and indigenous communities is often seen as a necessity for peacebuilding in deeply divided plural societies.

While logic dictates the benefits of mother-tongue teaching, those benefits have not evolved internationally into a justiciable right because of practical and financial considerations. Even in those instances where, within municipal law, mother-tongue education is a right, the exercise of the right is subject to financial and other restrictions. Minority language communities do, however, have the right to self-fund mother-tongue education pursuant to the individual right to free association and self-determination.

South Africa is one of only a few countries that formally recognises, in the Constitution, the right to state-funded education in any of the official languages, albeit within relatively narrow parameters.

11.44 BENEFITS OF MOTHER-TONGUE EDUCATION

It is widely acknowledged in contemporary international law and practice that policies should aim to offer mother-tongue education to children from as early as possible in their formal schooling for as long as practically possible. This not only enhances educational outcomes for children, but also contributes to their self-determination, self-esteem and realisation of other individual rights.

The 1996 Constitution of South Africa stands as an advancement over many other constitutions and the standards set in international law since the Constitution recognises the right to state-funded education in any of the official languages, subject to practical considerations. Additionally, the Constitution acknowledges the right to privately established mother-tongue educational facilities. The Constitution furthermore does not prohibit state funding for private education institutions. The possible funding of private mother-tongue teaching by way of block grants by government is arguably an unexplored avenue in the education language debate. The state may consider an annual block grant to, for example, the Afrikaans community and other language communities, to run private teaching.

It is noteworthy that there were no substantial objections to s 29 of the Constitution during its drafting or certification process. However, it was apparent, even at the drafting stage, that South Africa's resource constraints would over time present a major obstacle to maintain large numbers of schools with single or even dual-medium teaching, with English likely to emerge as the most widely, albeit not the only, state-funded language of instruction. With the predominance of English teaching the language colours of the rainbow in schools are fading – perhaps the right of a child to be taught in their own language was, like a rainbow, just a mirage.

11.45 COURTS UNCRITICALLY ENDORSE A GRADUAL TRANSITION TO ENGLISH FUNDING

The limitations in the Constitution on the right to education in an official language are assessed objectively and determined by fact. There is no absolute right to single-medium education in state-funded schools but, if warranted by circumstances, single-medium education in an official language is consistent with the Constitution. Similarly, dual-medium and parallel-medium education is in principle also consistent with the Constitution. Practically, dual- and parallel-medium teaching has proven to be difficult to sustain, often giving rise over time to predominantly English-medium teaching.

An overview of South African judgments indicates a trend where practical (principally financial) considerations are often accepted by the courts to allow and even mandate a transition of public schools towards predominantly English-language instruction. Financial considerations seem to trump all other rights or entitlements. Courts have generally been uncritical of the anglicisation of teaching, with the emphasis on equality and non-discrimination, without due regard to the importance of identity rights such as cultural and linguistic rights in addressing socio-economic disadvantage. Financial considerations informed by ideology under the veil of transformation opens the door whereby the richness of South Africa's language history will decline in education. The courts have generally failed to take government to task for the lack of building of new schools, with current facilities becoming overwhelmed by rising student numbers. Is it not a reasonable question to ask from government, when it considers the language policy of a school board, what government has done to provide additional educational facilities to serve the interests of the community? Courts have even sought to delink the right to education from the right to culture, while the opposite approach is preferred by international legal developments, namely that the realisation of education and cultural and socio-economic rights are closely linked.

The philosophy of the Constitution with its respect for plurality, its acceptance of Ubuntu and community, and recognition of diversity arguably allows for greater scope for the courts to critically assess budget allocations and exercise of administrative discretions to ascertain if the right to education in a mother tongue as well as the importance of the right to culture and socio-economic development have been adequately considered by decision-makers when they ascertain the best interests of society.

11.46 RESPONSIBILITIES AND DISCRETION OF SCHOOL GOVERNING BODIES

School governing bodies are pursuant to statute responsible to determine the language policy of a school. In setting its language policy the governing body must consider the broader needs of the community beyond just the interests of current students who attend the school or the parents who elected the governing body. While educational authorities may exercise administrative oversight over the language policy of a school, such oversight must be fair, reasonable and rational. Additionally, the language policy is subject to judicial and administrative review, as the governing body operates within the framework of the Constitution. The practical changes to be brought about pursuant to the BELA Act and any litigation arising from the Act are yet to be seen.

11.47 LANGUAGE OF EDUCATION INTRINSICALLY LINKED TO OTHER IDENTITY AND SOCIO-ECONOMIC RIGHTS

The right to mother-tongue education is intrinsically linked to the realisation of other identity rights such as culture, language, association, religion, self-determination, identity and script. This dimension has escaped the attention of courts. These rights are interrelated and collectively represent a bundle of identity rights intended to acknowledge and protect societal plurality. Mother-tongue education is also linked to the realisation of socio-economic rights when the full ability of individuals becomes realised by them being able to enter the economic arena in their preferred language.

So far, the South African courts have not adequately considered the interaction between mother-tongue education and the realisation of other identity and socio-economic rights. Generally, the courts have uncritically emphasised financial and administrative arrangements to facilitate English as language of education, but without critically accessing alternative options available to educational authorities. While the approach adopted by the courts is understandable in light of South Africa's background, the trend of judgments has also operated to the detriment of other official languages.

Differentiation among children based on language, culture or religion in education is tolerated, and even encouraged, by international law and jurisprudence in South Africa. However, if differentiation results in unequal access to educational facilities and restricted opportunities for children of some ethnocultural minorities, it is considered unjustified and regarded as *discrimination*.

11.48 CUSTOMARY LAW ON PAR WITH OTHER LEGAL SYSTEMS

Customary law is according to the Constitution a substantive legal system placed on equal footing with other legal systems in South Africa. Customary law must be analysed and understood within its own context, rather than by reference to, or through the lens of, another legal system.

It is the role of the judiciary to ascertain and apply customary law to a specific dispute based on relevant evidence. Where necessary and possible, the courts may develop customary law to ensure its consistency with the Constitution.

In fulfilling their mandate to develop customary law, however, courts must be mindful that communities may at a grassroot level continue with their practices regardless of judgments of courts. Courts must therefore be slow in their attempts to change customary law like a Parliament since judicially imposed changes may, on the one hand, render courts complicit in treating customary law as a subservient system of law, and, on the other hand, communities may simply disregard developments sought to be imposed by courts.

11.49 WHEN IS AN INDIGENOUS CUSTOM TREATED AS A LEGAL NORM?

Not every ordinary indigenous custom, practice or habit can be equated to a binding customary *legal* norm. Unfortunately no objective standard exists to ascertain the difference between a non-legally binding custom and a legally binding customary norm. This is ultimately for a court to determine, having heard evidence, whether a specific practice is regarded by the community as a legal norm; has been practised for a substantial period; is widely adhered to within the community; and whether there is compliance with it by the community as if a law.

The evidence to ascertain the existence of a customary legal norm can take a variety of forms. These include the following: historic documents, practices and recordings; expert evidence and opinions; contemporary research and publications; statutory provisions; and oral evidence. All relevant evidence – whether historic or contemporary, written or oral, lay or expert – must be considered.

11.50 CUSTOMARY LAW: A QUESTION OF LAW OR A QUESTION OF FACT?

The application of customary law to a specific dispute is both a question of law and a question of fact.

It is a question of fact in the sense that the adherence of the parties to customary law and their intention to be bound by it must be ascertained and confirmed by evidence.

It is a question of law in the sense that the customary law provision applicable to the dispute must be declared after considering whether the custom sought to be relied on is indeed regarded as a customary legal norm by the community.

Notably, however, the methodology used to distinguish between a question of fact and a question of law may be foreign and inappropriate to be applied to customary law.

11.51 WEAKNESS OF DISTINCTION BETWEEN OFFICIAL AND LIVING CUSTOMARY LAW

The distinction sought to be made between living and official customary law is scientifically weak and serves little practical, scientific or legal purpose. All legal systems, including customary law, display elements of being official (rigid, documented) and being living (dynamic, flexible). It is ultimately for a court to declare, based on all the evidence before it, what rule, if any, of customary law applies to a dispute at a specific point in time.

Because of their functions and constraints, courts serve as a blunt instrument to develop customary law. This is because, first, their jurisdiction is only enlivened by a specific dispute; secondly, the dispute is to be resolved on the basis of specific facts; and, thirdly, only the parties to the dispute and their witnesses are heard. Courts generally only have a very limited view of social reality.

Courts are also not well equipped to undertake broad inquiries into the terms and functioning of customary law because their role is to adjudicate disputes based on the evidence before them. A court may give leave for additional witnesses to be called, but it cannot manage the case of the parties, and judges may not supplement evidence by their own understanding of customary law unless so authorised by statute.

The doctrine of separation of powers limits the role of the courts to declare law as it arises in a dispute or otherwise to adjourn to Parliament an issue that requires legislative intervention.

11.52 WILL CUSTOMARY LAW ULTIMATELY WITHER AWAY UNDER THE WEIGHT OF THE CONSTITUTION?

The sovereignty of the Constitution and its infusion with universal human rights values may over time cause the erosion of customary law to the status of *customary practices*. This is not dissimilar to what has happened with many legal norms of religious dogma in liberal democracies. For example, the role of the church as a lawgiver and a law enforcer has become negligible since parliaments, the executive and judiciary have over many years taken over those functions. Many religious laws that applied previously are now mere customs, traditions or relics.

Similarly, constitutionalism may contribute to customary laws being transformed into nothing more than cultural customs. This would lead to indigenous people being in a similar position as ethnocultural communities who may have unique and special cultural practices, but those do not constitute laws.

A final word

This brings me to the end of my overview and assessment of South African case law in response to pluralism, diversity and identity rights. The topics of identity and diversity rights have always fascinated me. Is ethnocultural identity a prison caused by DNA, is it a sentence handed down intergenerationally, is it a voluntary choice, is it a lie that binds? Or is it so complex that we simply do not have a way of encapsulating it?

I conclude this book with the words of Appiah about identity, its complexity, its impact and its multifaceted presentation in his book *The Lies that Bind – Rethinking Identity*:

> There is a liberal fantasy in which identities are merely chosen, so we are all free to be what we choose to be. But identities without demands would be useless to us. Identities work only because, once they get their grip on us, they command us, speaking to us as an inner voice; and because others, seeing who they think we are, call on us, too. . . . We all have many things to 'do out there'. And the problem is not the walls as such but walls that hedge us in; walls we played no part in designing; walls without door and windows; walls that block our vision and obstruct our way; walls that will not let in fresh and enlivening air. (emphasis added) (Appiah 2018, 217–18)

BIBLIOGRAPHY

1 BvR 471/10. 2015. 1 BvR 471/10 and BvR 1181/10, January 27, 2015.

AB case. 2017. AB and another v Minister of Social Development (Centre for Child Law as amicus curiae) 2017 (3) BCLR 267 (CC).

ABC case. 1995. Public Sector Union v Australian Broadcasting Commission (1995) 36 AILR 372.

Abduroaf, M., and N. Moosa. 2023. 'A Brief Analysis of the Judgment in Women's Legal Centre Trust v President of the Republic of South Africa 2022 (5) SA 323 (CC)'. *PER/PELJ* 26. https://doi.org/DOI http://dx.doi.org/10.17159/1727-3781/2023/v26i0a14595.

Acharya, M. 2023. 'Will India Embrace the Uniform Civil Code and Finally Have a Single Common Law for Its 1.4 Billion Citizens?' *ABC*, 1 July 2023.

Ackermann, L.W.H. 2005. 'Constitutional Comparativism in South Africa: A Response to Sir Basil Markesinis and Jorg Fedtke'. *Tul. L. Rev* 80:169–85.

Ádám case. 2020. Case of Ádám and others v Romenia, ECH-2020-3-021 81114/17, 49716/18, 50913/18 et al. 13.10.2020.

Adeleke case. 1976. Adeleke v Yinka Suit No M/559/76 of 5/11/76 (Customary Court, Mapo, Ibadan).

African Centre for Biodiversity case. 2024. African Centre for Biodiversity NPC v Minister of Agriculture, Forestry and Fisheries and Others (934/2023) [2024] ZASCA 143 (22 October 2024).

African Charter. 1981. 'African Charter on Human and Peoples' Rights (Adopted 27 June 1981, OAU Doc. CAB/LEG/67/3 Rev. 5, 21 I.L.M. 58 (1982), Entered into Force 21 October 1986)'. https://www.achpr.org/public/Document/file/English/banjul_charter.pdf.

African Climate Alliance case. 2024. African Climate Alliance and others v Minister of Mineral Resources and Energy and others 56901/2021 High Court Gauteng 4 December 2024.

African Congress for Transformation case. 2024. African Congress for Transformation v Electoral Commission of South Africa; Labour Party of South Africa v Electoral Commission of South Africa and Others; Afrikan Alliance of Social Democrats v Electoral Commission of South Africa [2024] ZACC 7.

AfriForum Research Institute. 2020. 'Farm Attacks and Farm Murders in South Africa'. Pretoria: AfriForum.

Afrikaner Declaration. 2024. 'Afrikaner Declaration'. https://afrikanerverklaring.co.za/en/#tab-mediastatement.

Agbor, A. 2024. 'Preface'. In *Prosecuting 'Hate Speech' in International Criminal Law*, edited by A. Agbor, vii–ix. Springer.

Ahmed, F. 2020. 'Pluralism and Personal Laws in India'. In *Constitutions and Religion*, edited by S. Mancini, 415–32. Cheltenham: Edward Elgar Publishing Limited.

Ahmed, T. 2011. *The Impact of EU Law on Minority Rights*. Oxford: Hart Publishing.

Ahren, M. 2023. 'An Unsettled Liberal Democratic Order and Indigenous Peoples' Rights'. In *Minority Rights and Liberal Democratic Insecurities*, edited by A. Biro and D. Newman, 171–88. Oxon: Routledge.

Åkermark, A. 1927. *Justifications of Minority Protection in International Law*. Marthinus Nijjhof.

Al Midani case. 1999. Al Midani and Another v Al Midani and Others [1999] 1 Lloyd's Rep. 923 Queen's Bench Division (Commercial Court). Commercial Court.

Albania case. 1935. Minority Schools in Albania, Advisory Opinion. Permanent Court of International Justice.

Alexkor case. 2003. Alexkor Ltd and Another v The Richtersveld Community 2004 (5) SA 460 (CC). Constitutional Court.

Alfredsson, G. 2019. 'The Rights to Self-Determination in International Law'. In *Minority Self-Government in Europe and the Middle East*, edited by O. Akbulut and E. Aktoprak, 3–31. Leiden: Brill.

Alkiviadou, N. 2022. 'Liberating Expression: Contemporary European Challenges'. *Int J Semiot Law* 35:2193–2209. https://doi.org/10.1007/s11196-022-09891-9.

Ally, N., and M.J. Murcott. 2023. 'Beyond Labels: Executive Action and the Duty to Consult'. *Law, Democracy and Development* 27:93–122.

Almanza, M.C., and J.C. Salazar. 2022. 'Limitations on Democracy in Multilateral Policies to Regulate the Political Participation of Indigenous and Tribal Peoples'. *Colombia Internacional* September:111–33.

Al-Nuaimi, A.R. 2024. 'When History Cripples the Future for Muslims in Europe: The Struggle between Two Notions of Constitutionalism'. In *Islam, Religious Liberty and Constitutionalism in Europe*, edited by M. Hill and L. Papadopoulou, 31–42. Oxford: Hart Publishing.

Alva-Arevalo, A. 2021. 'A Critical Evaluation of the Domestic Standards of the Right to Prior Consultation under the UNDRIP: Lessons from the Peruvian Case'. In *The United Nations Declaration on the Rights of Indigenous Peoples: A Contemporary Evaluation*, edited by D. Short, L. Lennox, J. Burger, and J. Hohmann, 233–47. London: Routledge.

Amin, A. 2021. 'A Teleological Approach to Interpreting Socioeconomic Rights in the African Charter: Appropriateness and Methodology'. *African Human Rights Law Journal* 21:204–26.

Amish Devgan case. 2020. Amish Devgan vs Union Of India on 7 December, 2020.

Amnesty International. 2020. 'Freedom of Expression'. Amnesty International. https://www.amnesty.org/en/what-we-do/freedom-of-expression/.

Amod case. 1999. Amod v Multilateral Motor Vehicle Accidents Fund (Commission for Gender Equality Intervening) 1999 (4) SA 1319 (SCA).

Anaya, S.J. 2004. *Indigenous Peoples in International Law.* Oxford: Oxford University Press.

Anaya, S.J. 2009. 'Report of the Special Rapporteur on the Situation of Human Rights and Fundamental Freedoms of Indigenous People'. A/HRC/12/34. Geneva: UNHRC.

Anaya, S.J. 2010. 'Expert Mechanism on the Rights of Indigenous Peoples, Statement of the Special Rapporteur on the Situation of Human Rights and Fundamental Freedoms of Indigenous People'. Geneva: Human Rights Council. unsr.jamesanaya.org/statements/statement-of-special-rapporteur-on-the-right-toparticipation- to-the-emrip-2010.

Andeva, M., B. Dobos, L. Djordjević, B. Kuzmany, and T.H. Malloy, eds. 2023. *Non-Territorial Autonomy: An Introduction.* Cham: Palgrave Macmillan.

Aneme, G.A. 2015. 'Ethiopia: Legal and Judicial Plurality and the Incorporation of Traditional Dispute Resolution Mechanism within the State Justice System'. In *Non-State Justice Institutions and the Law: Decision-Making at the Interface of Tradition, Religion and the State*, edited by M. Kötter, T. Röder, G. Schuppert, and R. Wolfrum, 80–96. Hampshire: Palgrave Macmillan.

Anggraeni, D. 2023. 'Islamic Law and Customary Law in Contemporary Legal Pluralism in Indonesia: Tension and Constraints'. *AHKAM* 23:25–48.

An-Na'im, A.A. 2020. 'Islam, Sharia and Comprative Constitutionalism'. In *Constitutions and Religion*, edited by S. Mancini, 172–83. Cheltenham: Edward Elgar Publishing Limited.

Appiah, K.A. 2018. *The Lies That Bind – Rethinking Identity.* London: Profile books.

Arizona, Y., and M. Cohen. 2024. 'The Recognition of Customary Land Rights at the Constitutional Court of Indonesia: A Critical Assessment of the Jurisprudence'. In *Courts and Diversity: Twenty Years of the Constitutional Court of Indonesia*, edited by B. De Villiers, S. Isra, and P. Faiz, 173–94. Leiden: Brill.

Associated Managements case. 2008. Associated Managements of Primary and Secondary Schools in Karnataka v The State of Karnataka by its Secretary, Department of Education and Others I.L.R. 2008 (Kar.) 2895.

Austen-Baker, R. 2023. *Implied Terms in English Contract Law.* Cheltenham: Elgar.

Australian Capital Television case. 1992. Australian Capital Television Pty Ltd & New South Wales v Commonwealth [1992] HCA 45; (1992) 177 CLR 106 (30 September 1992).

Australian Law Reform Commission. 1986. 'Recognition of Aboriginal Customary Laws'. Australian Law Reform Commission 31. Canberra: Australian Law Commission. https://www.alrc.gov.au/publication/recognition-of-aboriginal-customary-laws-alrc-report-31/.

Awas Tingni case. 2001. The Mayagna Awas Tingni v Nicaragua, Inter-American Court of Human Rights, (2001).

Aziz, H. 2023. 'The Struggle for Transformative Constitutionalism Continues'. *De Rebus* May. https://www.derebus.org.za/the-struggle-for-transformative-constitutionalism-continues/.

Azrapart case. 2024. Azrapart (Pty) Limited v Huseyin (Pty) Ltd t/a Dufy and another [2024] JOL 66766 (GJ).

Badejogbin, R.E. 2022. 'Judicial Discretion: Problematizing the Ascertainment and Application of Customary Law by Formal Courts and Relevant Theories (Nigeria and South Africa)'. *Legal Pluralism and Critical Social Analysis* 54:252–77.

Baleni case. 2019. Baleni v Minister of Mineral Resources 2019 (2) SA 453 (GP).

Balogh, L., I. Halász, and A.L. Pap. 2025. 'Minority Rights, Minority Protection, and Diaspora Policy in Hungary, 2010–2018'. In *The Resilience of the Hungarian Legal System since 2010: A Failed Resilience?*, edited by F. Gárdos-Orosz, 57–72. Cham: Springer.

Baloro case. 1995. Baloro and Others v University of Bophuthatswana and Others 1995 (4) SA 197 (B).

Bangindawo case. 1998. Bangindawo and Others v Head of the Nyanda Regional Authority and Another; Hlantalal v Head of the Western Tembuland Regional Authority and Others Case No's 2185 95, 312/96; 1998 (3) SA 262 (Tk).

Baranyai, N. 2024. 'Non-territorial and Territorial Objectives of Central and Eastern European Ethnoregional Parties'. *Journal of Urban and Regional Analysis*.

Barelli, M. 2012. 'Free, Prior and Informed Consent in the Aftermath of the UN Declaration on the Rights of Indigenous Rights: Developments and Challenges Ahead'. *International Journal of Human Rights* 16:1–24.

Barendt, E. 2005. *Freedom of Speech*. Oxford: Oxford University Press.

Barkey, K, and G. Gavrilis. 2017. 'The Ottoman Millet System: Non-Territorial Autonomy and Its Contemporary Legacy'. In *Non-Territorial Autonomy in Divided Societies – Comparative Perspectives*, edited by J. Coakley, 25–42. London: Routledge.

Barkhuizen case. 2007. Barkhuizen v Napier 2007 (5) SA 323; 2007 (7) BCLR 691 (CC).

Barngarla case. 2023. Barngarla Determination Aboriginal Corporation RNTBC v Minister for Resources [2023] FCA 809. FC.

Barrie, G.N. 2000. 'Ubuntu Ungamntu Ngabanye Abantu: The Recognition of Minority Rights in the South African Constitution'. *Journal of South African Law*, 270–309.

Barrie, G.N. 2013. 'The United Nations Declaration on the Rights of Indigenous People: Implications for Land Rights and Self-Determination'. *Journal of South African Law* 22:292–305.

Barrie, G.N. 2018. 'Land Claims by Indigenous People – Litigation Versus Settlements? Observations on the Richtersveld Litigation Route Followed in South Africa Versus the Noongar Settlement Route Followed in Western Australia'. *Journal of South African Law*, 344–65.

Barrie, G.N. 2021. 'The Mabo-Decision and the "Discovery" of Native Title in Australia and Beyond'. In *Litigating the Rights of Minorities and Indigenous Peoples in Domestic and International Courts*, edited by B. De Villiers, J. Marko, F. Palermo, and S. Constantin, 7–51. Leiden: Brill.

Barrie, G.N. 2024a. 'The Introduction of "free, Prior and Informed Consent" to the Land Reform Legal Lexicon'. *Obiter*, 900–912.

Barrie, G.N. 2024b. 'The "Right" to Free, Prior and Informed Consent: Evolving Customary International Law'. In *Courts and Diversity: Twenty Years of the Constitutional Court of Indonesia*, edited by B. De Villiers, S. Isra, and P. Faiz, 195–227. Leiden: Brill.

Barten, U. 2015. 'Article 27 ICCPR'. In *The United Nations Declaration on Minorities: An Academic Account on the Occasion of Its 20th Anniversary (1992–2012)*, edited by U. Caruso and R. Hofmann, 46–65. Leiden: Brill.

Bartlett, R. 2020. *Native Title in Australia*. Australia: LexisNexis Butterworths.

Batwa case. 2021. Constitutional Petition 3 of 2013 19 August 2021, Constitutional Court, Uganda.

Bauer, H. 1992. *Die Bundestreue*. Tubingen: Mohr.

Bayar and Gürbüz case. 2012. Bayar and Gürbüz v Turkey App. No. 37569/06. ECtHR.

BBC Old Flag, dir. 2017. 'South Africans Hold Black Monday Protests Over Farm Murders'.

Beadica case. 2020. Beadica 231 CC and Others v Trustees for the time being of the Oregon Trust and Others (CCT109/19) [2020] ZACC 13; 2020 (5) SA 247 (CC); 2020 (9) BCLR 1098 (CC) (17 June 2020).

Beaulac case. 1999. R v Beaulac [1999] 1 SCR 768.

Bektashi Community case. 2018. Bektashi Community and Others v The Former Yugoslav Republic of Macedonia (Applications nos. 48044/10, 75722/12 and 25176/13).

BELA Act. 2024. *Basic Education Laws Amendment Act, 2024.* https://www.parliament.gov.za/storage/app/media/Acts/2024/Act_32_of_2024_Basic_Education_Laws_Amendment_Act.pdf.

Belgian Linguistic case. 1968. Case 'Relating to Certain Aspects of the Laws on the use of Languages in Education in Belgium' v Belgium (Merits). ECHR.

Belgium Headscarf case. 2023. ECJ-2023-3-017.

Belkacem case. 2017. Belkacem v Belgium ECHR 253 (2017).

Bengwenyama Minerals case. 2011. Bengwenyama Minerals (Pty) Ltd and Genorah Resources (pty) Ltd (CCT 39/10) [2010] ZACC 26; 2011 (4) SA 113 (CC).

Bennett, T.W. 1991. *A Sourcebook of African Customary Law for Southern Africa.* Cape Town: Juta.

Bennett, T.W. 2011. 'Ubuntu: An African Equity'. *Potchefstroom Electronic Law Journal* 14:30–61.

Benvenisti, E. 2008. 'Reclaiming Democracy: The Strategic Uses of Foreign and International Law by National Courts'. *American Journal of International Law* 102:241–74.

Beretka, K., and B. Dobos. 2023. 'The Legal and Institutional Context of NTA'. In *Non-Territorial Autonomy: An Introduction*, edited by M. Andeva, B. Dobos, L. Djordjević, B. Kuzmany, and T.H. Malloy, 147–63. Cham: Palgrave Macmillan.

Berger, E. 2003. 'The Right to Education under the South African Constitution'. *Columbia Law Review* 103:614–61.

Bernauer, J., and A. Vatter. 2024. 'Power Concentration and Power Diffusion: A New Typology of Political-Institutional Patterns of Democracy'. In *Handbook of Comparative Political Institutions*, 410–28. Edward Elgar Publishing Limited.

Berman, P.S. 2020. 'Undertanding Global Legal Pluralism: From Local to Global, from Descritive to Normative'. In *The Oxford Handbook of Global Legal Pluralism*, edited by P.S. Berman, 1–35. Oxford: Oxford University Press.

Bhai Parmanand case. 2022. Master Divyam Bhateja through father Mr Vinod Bhateja v Bhai Parmanand Vidya Mandir and Others WP(C) 8466/2022; 2022 LiveLaw (Del) 563.

Bhe case. 2005. Bhe v Khayelitsha Magistrate (Commission for Gender Equality as Amicus Curiae); Shibi v Sithole; South African Human Rights Commission v President of the Republic of South Africa [2004] ZACC 17; 2005 (1) SA 580 (CC); 2005 (1) BCLR 1 (CC).

Bhuiyan, J.H., and A. Black. 2022. 'Religious Freedom in a Secular State: An Introduction'. In *Religious Freedom in Secular States*, edited by J.H. Bhuiyan and A. Black, 3–20. Leiden: Brill.

Bhuiyan, J.H., and C.M. Zoethout, eds. 2023. *Freedom of Religion and Religious Pluralism*. Leiden: Brill.

BIH-2024-1-001. 2024. BIH-2024-1-001.

Black, A. 2010. 'Legal Recognition of Sharia Law: Is This the Right Direction for Australian Family Matters?' *Family Matters* 84:64–67.

Black, A. 2024. 'Religious Rights: Testing the Limits of Tolerance'. In *Courts and Diversity: Twenty Years of the Constitutional Court of Indonesia*, edited by B. De Villiers, S. Isra, and P. Faiz, 145–72. Leiden: Brill.

Blokker, P. 2024. 'How Religious Conservatism is Redirecting the European Project'. IACL Blog. 19 November 2024.

Bober, S. 2019. 'Does Regional Development Matter in Minority Politics? Regional Development in the Recent Electoral Activity of Three National Minorities'. Flensburg. chrome-extension://efaidnbmnnnibpcajpcglclefindmkaj/https://www.ecmi.de/fileadmin/redakteure/publications/pdf/WP__116_Does_Regional_Development_Matter_in_Minority_Politics.pdf.

Bornschlegl, Z., D. Ocampo, and I. Urrutia. 2021. 'Free Prior Informed Consent (FPIC) in the Mining Sector'. Hannover: Federal Institute for Geosiences and Natural Resources. https://rue.bmz.de/en/releases/publications_new/topics/human_rights/FPIC_in_the_Mining_Sector.pdf.

Borrows, J.J., and L.I. Rotman. 2023. *Indigenous Legal Issues, Cases, Materials and Commentary*. Ontario: LexisNexis.

Bottoni, R. 2022. 'The Constitutional Principle of Secularism in the Member States of the Council of Europe'. In *Religious Freedom in Secular States*, edited by J.H. Bhuiyan and A. Black, 147–72. Leiden: Brill.

Bottoni, R. 2023. 'Gender Equality in Ethiopia: The Interaction of Secular, Religious, and Customary Law'. In *The Rights of Women in Comparative Constitutional Law*, edited by I. Spigno, V.R. Scotti, and L.P. Da Silva, 191–210. Oxon: Routledge.

Boulais, A.G., A.U. Marinkovic, and G.C. Palomares. 2023. *A Practitioner's Guide to the European Convenion on Human Rights*. 7th ed. London: Sweet and Maxwell.

Bowen, J.R. 2016. *On British Islam: Religion, Law and Everyday Practice in Sharia Councils*. Princeton: Princeton University Press.

Brandenburg case. 1969. Brandenburg v Ohio 395 U.S. 444 (1969). US.

Brechin, J. 2013. 'A Study of the Use of Sharia Law in Religious Arbiration in the United Kingdom and the Concerns That This Raises for Human Rights'. *Ecclesiastical Law Society* 15:293–315.

Breuer, M., ed. 2019. *Principled Resistance to the ECtHR Judgements – a New Paradigm?* Heidelberg: Springer.

Breyer, S. 2018. 'America's Courts Can't Ignore the World'. *The Atlantic*, October. https://www.theatlantic.com/magazine/archive/2018/10/stephen-breyer-supreme-court-world/568360/.

Bronn case. 1860. Bronn v Frits Bronn's Executors [1860] 3 SC 313. Supreme Court.

Bronstein, V. 1998. 'Reconceptualizing the Customary Law Debate in South Africa'. *South African Journal on Human Rights* 14:388–410.

Brooks, E.H. 1927. *The History of Native Title Policy in South Africa from 1830 to the Present Day*. Johannesburg: Nasionale Pers.

Brown, A. 2017. 'What Is Hate Speech? Part 1: The Myth of Hate'. *Law and Philosophy* 36:419–69.

Brown, A., and A. Sinclair. 2023. *Hate Speech Frontiers: Exploring the Limits of the Ordinary and Legal Concepts*. Cambridge: Cambridge University Press.

Brown case. 1954. Brown v Board of Education 347 US 483 (1954).

Brownley case. 1999. Brownley v Western Australia (no 1) [1999] FCA 1139.

Bruce, D. 2023. 'Murder Trends in South Africa's Deadliest Provinces'. Pretoria: Institute for Security Studies. https://issafrica.org/research/policy-briefs/murder-trends-in-south-africas-deadliest-provinces.

Bryan, Michael, and Vicki Vann. 2012. *Equity and Trusts in Australia*. Cambridge: Cambridge University Press. https://doi.org/10.1017/CBO9781139194013.

Büchler, A. 2016. *Islamic Law in Europe? Legal Pluralism and Its Limits in European Family Laws*. Routledge.

Budlender, G. 2021. 'Afterword Searching for the Constitutional Living Customary Law'. *Journal of Southern African Studies* 47:327–32.

Bulelwa case. 2022. Bulelwa Ndamase v Development Bank of Southern Africa Limited D8073/2020 [2022] (ZAKZDHC) (30 May 2022).

Burgess, M. 2012. *In Search of the Federal Spirit*. Oxford: Oxford University Press.

Burns case. 2015. United States v Burns. Supreme Court.

Burnside, S. 2009. 'Negotiations in Good Faith under the Native Titlte Act: A Critical Analysis'. *Land, Rights, Laws: Issues of Native Title* 4:1–16.

BVerfGE 1 56 see ch 6 n 2.

BVerfGE 7 198 case. n.d. BVerfGE 7 198.

BVerfGE 74 case. 1987. BVerfGE 74, 358, 370 (1987).

BVerfGE Case No 1 BvR 2150/08 see ch 5

Cairo Declaration. 1990. 'Cairo Declaration on Human Rights in Islam, Aug. 5, 1990, U.N. GAOR, World Conf. on Hum. Rts., 4th Sess., Agenda Item 5, U.N. Doc. A/CONF.157/PC/62/Add.18 (1993)'. http://hrlibrary.umn.edu/instree/cairodeclaration.html.

Cakal, Ergun. 2020. 'Pluralism, Tolerance and Control: On the Millet System and the Question of Minorities'. *International Journal on Minority and Group Rights* 27(1): 34–65. https://doi.org/10.1163/15718115-02701004.

Calma-Langton Report. 2021. 'Indigenous Voice Co-Design Process Final Report to the Australian Government'. Canberra: Indigenous Voice. https://voice.niaa.gov.au/sites/default/files/2021-12/indigenous-voice-co-design-process-final-report_1.pdf.

Cambou, D. 2019. 'The UNDRIP and the Legal Significance of the Right of Indigenous Peoples to Self-Determination: A Human Rights Approach with a Multidimensional Perspective'. *The International Journal of Human Rights* 23:34–50.

Cambou, D. 2024. 'The Significance of the Fosen Decision for Protecting the Cultural Rights of the Sámi Indigenous People in the Green Transition'. In *The Significance of Sámi Rights*, edited by D. Cambou and O. Ravna, 52–70. Oxon: Routledge.

Cameron, E., E.S. Cheng, R. Gore, and E. Webber. 2022. 'Rainbows and Realities: Justice Johan Froneman in the Explosive Terrain of Linguistic and Cultural Rights'. *Constitutional Court Review* 12:261–87. https://doi.org/10.2989/CCR.2022.00010.

Canada case. 2012. 'UN Doc. CERD/C/SR.2142, 2 March 2012, Para.39.' Geneva: UN Committee on the Elimination of Racial Discrimination (CERD).

Canada UNDRIP Act. 2021. United Nations Declaration on the Rights of Indigenous Peoples Act S.C. 2021, c. 14, Assented to 2021-06-21.

Capeta, T. 2021. 'The Weiss/PSPP Case and the Future of Constitutional Pluralism in the EU'. In *Exploring the Social Dimension of Europe*, edited by G.G. Sander, A. Poscic, and A. Martinovic, 145–60. Hamburg: Kovac.

Capotorti, F. 1979. 'Study on the Rights of Persons Belonging to Ethnic, Religious and Linguistic Communities'. E_CN.4_Sub.2_384_Rev.1. New York: Subcommission on prevention of discrimination and protection of minorities.

Carrasco, S.H. 2019. 'The Rights of Indigenous Peoples in the Jurisprudence of the Inter-American Court of Human Rights'. In *Critical Indigenous Rights Studies*, edited by G. Corradi, K. De Feyter, E. Desmet, and K. Vanhees, 160–77. London: Routledge.

Carstens, M. 2016. 'Sami Land Rights: The Anaya Report and the Nordic Sami Convention'. *Journal on Ethnopolitics and Minority Issues in Europe* 15:75–116.

Carstocea, A. 2011. 'Ethno-Business – The Manipulation of Minority Rights in Romania and Hungary'. In *Perpetual Motion? Transformation and Transition in Central and Eastern Europe and Russia*, edited by T. Bhambry, T. Griffin, and T. Hjelm, 16–28. UCL: SSEES.

Cassese, A. 1995. *Self-Determination of Peoples: A Legal Reappraisal.* New York: Cambridge University Press.

Castellino, J. 1999. 'Order and Justice: National Minorities and the Right to Secession'. *International Journal on Minority and Group Rights* 22:402–29.

Catch the Fire case. 2006. Catch the Fire Ministries Inc v Islamic Council of Victoria [2006] VSCA 206 284; (2006) 206 FLR 56 (2006).

CATSI Act. 2006. *Corporations (Aboriginal and Torres Strait Islander) Act 2006, No 124 of 2006.* https://www.legislation.gov.au/Details/C2017C00055.

CATSI Act: Register. 2020. 'Steps to Register'. ORIC. https://www.oric.gov.au/start-corporation/steps-register.

CEACR. 2011. 'General Observation (CEACR) – Indigenous and Tribal Peoples Convention, 1989 (No. 169)'. ILO Office. https://www.ilo.org/global/standards/subjects-covered-by-international-labour-standards/indigenous-and-tribal-peoples/WCMS_305958/lang--en/index.htm.

Census. 2011. 'Census 2011'. Pretoria. http://www.statssa.gov.za/census/census_2011/census_products/Census_2011_Census_in_brief.pdf.

Census 2022. 2023. 'Census 2022'. Statistics South Africa. chrome-extension://efaidnbmnnnibpcajpcglclefindmkaj/file:///C:/Users/devillib/Downloads/Census%202022%20Statistical%20Release.pdf.

Centre for Child Law case. 2019. Centre for Child Law and Others v Media 24 Limited and Others (CCT261/18) [2019] ZACC 46; 2020 (3) BCLR 245 (CC); 2020 (1) SACR 469 (CC) (4 December 2019).

CERD General Recommendation. 1997. 'CERD, General Recommendation 23, Rights of Indigenous Peoples (Fifty-First Session, 1997), UN Doc A/52/18, Annex V at 122 (1997) Para 4(d), 5'. CERD.

Certification Amended text case. 1997. In re: Certification of the Amended Text of the Constitution of the RSA, 1996 1997 (1) BCLR 1 (CC), 1997 (2) SA 97 (CC).

Certification case. 1996. In re: Certification of the Constitution of the RSA, 1996 1996 (10) BCLR 1253 (CC), 1996 (4) SA 744 (CC). Constitutional Court.

Cesari, J. 2010. 'A Cultural Conundrum: The Integration of Islamic Law in Europe'. *Harvard International Review* Winter:12–15.

CESCR. 2009a. 'Concluding Observations of the Committee on Economic, Social and Cultural Rights on Brazil 12/BRA/CO/2 12 June 2009'. Geneva: UNCESCR.

CESCR. 2009b. 'Consideration of Reports Submitted by States Parties under Articles 16 and 17 of the Covenant: Concluding Observations of the Committee on Economic, Social and Cultural Rights: Cambodia, 12 June 2009, E/C.12/KHM/CO/1'. E/C.12/KHM/CO/1. Geneva: UN Committee on Social, Economic and Cultural Rights. https://www.refworld.org/docid/4af181b20.html.

CESCR. 2015. Concluding observations on the fourth periodic report of Paraguay. Committee on Economic, Social and Cultural Rights.

Charnell Commando case. 2024. Charnell Commando and Others v City of Cape Town and Another (CCT 49/23) [2024] ZACC 27.

Chief Avhatendi Ratshibvumo Rambuda case. 2024. Chief Avhatendi Ratshibvumo Rambuda and Others v Tshibvumo Royal Family and Others [2024] ZACC 15.

Chronowski, N., and N. Nagy. 2024. 'Minority Identity in the Making? Conceptualization and Operationalization of National and Ethnic Minorities in the Case Law of the European Court of Human Rights'. *Hungarian Journal of Legal Studies*, 1–27. https://doi.org/DOI: 10.1556/2052.2024.00554.

Chuma, H. 2023. 'Recognition, Application, and Ascertainment of Customary Law'. In *Introduction to Legal Pluralism in South Africa*, edited by C. Rautenbach, 6th ed, 37–64. Cape Town: LexisNexis.

Church, J., and J. Church. 2007. 'The Constitutional Right to Culture and the Judicial Development of Indigenous Law: A Comparative Analysis of Cases'. *Anthropology South Africa* 30:56–64.

Church of Jesus Christ of Latter-Day Saints case. 2014. The Church of Jesus Christ of Latter-Day Saints v the United Kingdom – 7552/09 Judgment 4.3.2014. ECtHR.

Church of Scientology case. 2007. Church of Scientology Moscow v Russia. Application no. 18147/02. ECtHR.

Chürr, C. 2013. 'The Right to Mother-Tongue Education: Practicable or Not?' *Obiter*, 274–304.

Chürr, C. 2015. 'Realisation of a Child's Right to Basic Education in the South African School System: Some Lessons from Germany'. *Potchefstroom Electronic Law Journal* 18:2405–55.

City of Tshwane case. 2016. City of Tshwane Metropolitan Municipality v Afriforum and Another (157/15) [2016] ZACC 19; 2016 (9) BCLR 1133 (CC); 2016 (6) SA 279 (CC) (21 July 2016).

Ciubotaru case. 2010. Ciubotaru v Moldova, App. no. 27138/04, judgment of 27 April 2010. ECtHR.

Claassens, A., and B. Matlala. 2014. 'Platimun, Poverty and Princes in Post-Apartheid South Africa: New Laws, Old Repertiores'. *New South African Review* 4:116–32.

Claassens, A., and S. Weeks. 2009. 'Rural Women Redifining Land Rights in the Context of Living Customary Law'. *South African Journal on Human Rights* 25:491–615.

Clark, B., and B. van Heerden. 2024. 'Recent South African Marriage Reform Proposals: Confused and Conflicted?' *SALJ* 141:467–82.

Clyde River case. 2017. Clyde River (Hamlet) v Petroleum Geo-Services Inc., 2017 SCC 40 (CanLII), [2017] 1 SCR 1069.

Coakley, J., ed. 2017. *Non-Territorial Autonomy in Divided Societies – Comparative Perspectives.* London: Routledge.

Cockrell, A. 1996. 'Rainbow Jurisprudence'. *Journal on Human Rights*, 1–38.

Coco case. 1994. Coco v The Queen (1994) 179 CLR 427.

Coleman, T.E. 2024. 'Re-Assessing the African Principles on the Law Applicable to International Commercial Contracts through the Prism of African Traditional Values'. *Journal of South African Law*, 76–95.

Columbia Constitutional Court. 1997. Ruling SU-039/97, Proponent Magistrate Antonio Barrera Carbonel. Translated in: R Roldan, 2000, Indigenous Peoples of Colombia and the Law, A Critical Approach to the Study of Past and Present Situations Gaia Foundation/COAMA/ILO, Colombia (1997).

Commission on Demarcation. 1993. 'Report of the Commission on the Demarcation/Delimitation of States/Provinces/Regions'. Johannesburg: CODESA. http://wiredspace.wits.ac.za/handle/10539/17987.

Communist Party case. 1957. Communist Party of Germany v The Federal Republic of Germany, European Commission of Human Rights, No 250/57.

Constitution 1993. 1993. *Constitution of the Republic of South Africa 200 of 1993.* https://www.gov.za/documents/constitution/constitution-republic-south-africa-act-200-1993.

Constitution Alteration Act. 2023. *Constitution Alteration (Aboriginal and Torres Strait Islander Voice) 2023.* https://www.legislation.gov.au/Details/C2023B00060/Html/Text.

Constitution ofHungary. 2011. *Constitution ofHungary, 2011.* https://www.constituteproject.org/constitution/Hungary_2011.pdf.

Constitution ofMalaysia. 1957. 'Constitution ofMalaysia'. https://www.constituteproject.org/constitution/Malaysia_2007.

Constitution of South Africa. 1996. *Constitution of the Republic of South Africa, 1996.* https://www.gov.za/documents/constitution/constitution-republic-south-africa-1996-1.

Convention on the Rights of the Child. 1989. *Convention on the Rights of the Child, General Assembly Resolution 44/25.* https://www.ohchr.org/en/instruments-mechanisms/instruments/convention-rights-child.

Cornell, D., and N. Mavangua. 2012. 'Introduction'. In *uBuntu and the Law: African Ideals and Postapartheid Jurisprudence*, edited by D. Cornell and N. Mavangua, 1–32. New York: Fordham University Press.

Coutsoudis, A., and M. Du Plessis. 2020. 'We Are All International Lawyers; Now What? Taking Seriously the Constitutional Injunction to Integrate International Law Obligations into South African Law.' *Constitutional Court Review* 10:155–95.

Craig, E. 2016. 'Who Are The Minorities? The Role of the Right to Self-Identify within the European Minority Rights Framework'. *Journal on Ethnopolitics and Minority Issues in Europe* 15:6–30.

Croce, M., and M. Goldoni. 2020. *The Legacy of Pluralism: The Continental Jurisprudence of Santi Romano, Carl Schmitt, and Constantino Mortati*. Stanford: Stanford University Press.

Csergő, Z., K. Kallas, and T. Kiss. 2025. 'Kin-State Intervention and the Securitization-Minority Policy Nexus: Hungarians and Russian-Speakers in Central and Eastern Europe: Minorities Caught between States and the Effects of Kin-State Involvement on the Securitization-Minority Policy Nexus'. *Journal of Global Security Studies* 10. https://doi.org/10.1093/jogss/ogae035.

CSF case. 2016. CSF de la C-B v British Columbia 2016 BCSC 1764.

Cultural Survival and First Peoples Worldwide. 2023. 'Securing Indigenous Peoples Right to Self-Determination: A Guide to Free, Prior and Informed Consent'. Cultural Survival and First Peoples Worldwide. https://static1.squarespace.com/static/62cd7860272be4335685de88/t/650b105c830dca28a4ee35ff/1695223916300/FPIC+guide+sm_compressed.pdf.

Cumper, P. 2014. 'Multiculturalism, Human Rights and the Accommodation of Sharia Law'. *Human Rights Law Review* 14:31–57.

Currie, I., and J. de Waal. 2013. *The Bill of Rights Handbook*. 6 ed. Cape Town: Juta.

Cyprus case. 2002. Cyprus v Turkey (25781/94) [2001] 5 WLUK 291; (2002) 35 EHRR 30; 11 B.H.R.C.

Dahlab case. 2001. Dahlab v Switzerland Application No. 4293/98, 15 February 2001. ECtHR.

Dahwal, S., and J. Fernando. 2024. 'The Intersection of Customary Law and Islam: A Case Study of the Kelpeak Ukum Adat Ngen Ca'o Kutei Jang in the Rejang Tribe, Bengkulu Province, Indonesia'. *Cogent Social Sciences* 10:1–14.

Dakir case. 2017. Dakir v Belgium (Application no. 4619/12). ECtHR.

Dalisile case. 2018. Dalisile v Mgoduka ((5056/2018) [2018] ZAECMHC.

Damons case. 2022. Damons v City of Cape Town (2022 10 BCLR 1202 (CC).

Daniel Billy case. 2022. Daniel Billy et al. v Australia (Communication No. 3624/2019).

Daniel case. 2002. Western Australia v Daniel [2002] NNTTA 230.

Daniels case. 2003. Daniels v Campbell N.O. and Others 2003 (9) BCLR 969 (C).

Daniels case. 2004. Daniels v Campbell N.O. and Others 2004 (5) SA 331 (CC). CC.

Davies, M. 2024. 'Legal Pluralism and the Limits of Law'. *Res Publica*. https://doi.org/10.1007/s11158-024-09697-5.

Davis, D. 2023. 'Autocratic Legalism: The South African Experience'. *IACL-AIDC Blog*. https://blog-iacl-aidc.org/autocratic-legalism/2023/6/6/autocratic-legalism-the-south-african-experience.

Davis, D., and M. le Roux. 2019. *Lawfare: Judging Politics in South Africa*. Johannesburg: Jonathan Ball Publishers.

Davis, D.M. 2018. 'Is the South African Constitution an Obstacle to a Democratic Post-Colonial State?' *South African Journal on Human Rights* 34:359–74.

Davis, D.M., and K. Klare. 2024. 'Two Cheers for Transformative Constitutionalism'. *Law and Critique*. https://doi.org/10.1007/s10978-024-09404-6.

Dawood case. 2000. Dawood and Another v Minister of Home Affairs and Others; Shalabi and Another v Minister of Home Affairs and Others; Thomas and Another v Minister of Home Affairs and Others 2000 (8) BLCR 837.

De Angelo, A., and S. Tolino. 2017. 'Introduction: Defintions of Minority'. *Journal of Arabic and Islamic Studies* 17:143–55.

De Gaetano, V.A. 2024. 'Islamic Headgear: The Case Law of the European Court of Human Rights'. In *Islam, Religious Liberty and Constitutionalism in Europe*, edited by M. Hill and L. Papadopoulou, 141–52. Oxford: Hart Publishing.

De Klerk Foundation. 2023. 'Cultural, Religious and Language Rights'. Cape Town: FW De Klerk Foundation. chrome-extension://efaidnbmnnnibpcajpcglclefindmkaj/https://fwdeklerk.org/wp-content/uploads/2023/09/CRLRC2023.pdf.

De Varennes, F. 2008. 'International Law and Education in a Minority Language'. In *Encyclopedia of Language and Education*, edited by S. May and N.J> Hornberger, 121–35. London: Springer.

De Varennes, F. 2021. 'Minority Issues: Report of the Special Rapporteur on Minority Issues'. A/HRC/46/57. Geneva: Human Rights Council of the United Nations.

De Varennes, F. 2022a. 'Closing Statement'. Presented at the Fifteenth session of the Forum on Minority Issues, Geneva, December 3. https://hrcmeetings.ohchr.org/HRCMechanisms/ForumMinority/Pages/15th-session.aspx.

De Varennes, F. 2022b. 'Conflict Prevention through the Protection of the Human Rights of Minorities'. A/HRC/49/46. Geneva: Human Rights Council.

De Villiers, B. 1989. 'Estland: Kopseer vir die USSR, maar Lesse in Minderheids-akkommodasie?' *Tydskrif vir die Suid Afrikaanse Reg*, 55–68.

De Villiers, B. 1992. 'Directive Principles of State Policy and Fundamental Rights: The Indian Experience'. *South African Journal on Human Rights* 8:29–49.

De Villiers, B. 1993. *Regionalism: Prospects and Problems*. Pretoria: HSRC Press.

De Villiers, B, ed. 1994a. *The Birth of a Constitution*. Cape Town: Juta.

De Villiers, B. 1994b. 'The Content and Significance of the Constitutional Principles'. In *The Birth of a Constitution*, edited by B. De Villiers, 37–49. Cape Town: Juta.

De Villiers, B. 1995. 'Federalism in South Africa: The Debate Unfolds'. In *Towards a European Constitution Institute for Federalism*, edited by T. Fleiner and N. Schmitt, 185–222. Fribourg: Institute of Federalism.

De Villiers, B. 2008. 'Principles Underlying Demarcation: Implication for Provincial Boundaries'. In *Review of Provinces and Local Governments in South Africa: Constitutional Foundations and Practice*, edited by B. De Villiers, 29–45. Johannesburg: Konrad Adenauer Foundation.

De Villiers, B, ed. 2009. *Crossing the Line – Dealing with Cross-Border Communities*. Johannesburg: Konrad Adenauer Foundation.

De Villiers, B. 2012a. 'Creating Federal Regions – Minority Protection versus Sustainability'. *Heidelberg Journal of International Law* 72:310–51.

De Villiers, B. 2012b. 'Language, Cultural and Religious Minorities: What and Who Are They?' *University of Western Australia Law Review* 36:67–89.

De Villiers, B. 2012c. 'Protecting Minorities on a Non-Territorial Basis – Recent International Developments'. *Beijing Law Review* 3:170–83.

De Villiers, B. 2014a. 'Section 235 of the Constitution: Too Early or Too Late for Cultural Self-Determination in South Africa?' *South African Journal on Human Rights*, 458–83.

De Villiers, B. 2014b. 'The Protection of Dispersed Minorities: Options for Aboriginal People in Australia'. *Heidelberg Journal of International Law* 74:105–40.

De Villiers, B. 2016a. 'Community Government for Minority Groups: Revisiting the Ideas of Renner and Bauer towards Developing a Model for Self-Government by Minority Groups under Public Law'. *Heidelberg Journal of International Law* 76:1–40.

De Villiers, B. 2016b. 'Divided Together: Asymmetrical Autonomy of Muslim Communities in Aceh and Bangsomoro and Possible Lessons for Accommodating Minorities within Sovereign Borders'. *Journal of Oriental and African Studies* 25:145–74.

De Villiers, B. 2017. 'Power-Sharing Options in Complex Societies – Possible Lessons from South Tyrol for Young Democracies on Ways to Protect Ethnic Minorities at a Regional Level'. *Journal on Ethnopolitics and Minority Issues in Europe* 16:1–31.

De Villiers, B. 2018a. 'Managing Diversity in Deeply Divided Societies: The Quest for Self-Determination by the Afrikaans Speaking Community in South Africa'. *Journal on Ethnopolitics and Minority Issues in Europe* 17:47–76.

De Villiers, B. 2018b. 'The Recognition Conundrum – Is an Advisory Body for Aboriginal People Progress to Rectify Past Injustices or Just Another "Toy Telephone" '. *Journal on Ethnopolitics and Minority Issues in Europe* 17:24–28.

De Villiers, B. 2019. 'The Duty on Organs of State to Cooperate: *Bundestreue*, Cooperative Government and the Supply of Electricity in a Culture of Non-Payment'. *Journal of South African Law*, 605–18.

De Villiers, B. 2020a. 'Chasing the Dream – Self-Determination on a Non-Territorial Basis for the Noongar Traditional Owners in the South West of Australia'. *International Journal on Minority and Group Rights* 27:171–93.

De Villiers, B. 2020b. 'Chasing the Dream – Self-Determination on a Non-Territorial Basis for the Noongar Traditional Owners in the South West of Australia'. *International Journal on Minority and Group Rights* 27:171–93.

De Villiers, B. 2020c. 'Is it Possible to Define the Impossible – What is a "Community" for Purposes of s 235 of the Constitution of South Africa?' *International Journal on Minority and Group Rights* 27:826–54.

De Villiers, B. 2021a. 'Striking a Balance Between Free Association and Regulating Membership of a "Community": Exploring s 235 of the Constitution of South Africa'. *International Journal on Minority and Group Rights* 28:91–116.

De Villiers, B. 2021b. 'The Elephant in the Room – Resolving Disputes about Membership of a Minority or Indigenous Community'. In *Litigating the Rights of Minorities and Indigenous Peoples in Domestic and International Courts*, edited by B. De Villiers, J. Marko, F. Palermo, and S. Constantin, 52–80. Leiden: Brill.

De Villiers, B. 2022a. 'A Promise Not to Keep? Lessons from Central and Eastern Europe to Establish Cultural Councils and Relevance to the Afrikaans Community of South Africa'. In *Navigating the Unknown – Essays on Selected Case Studies about the Rights of Minorities*, 38–72. Leiden: Brill.

De Villiers, B. 2022b. 'Breaking New Ground for Indigenous Non-Territorial Cultural Self-Government: The Noongar Settlement in Australia'. In *Navigating the Unknown – Essays on Selected Case Studies about the Rights of Minorities*, 138–62. Leiden: Brill.

De Villiers, B. 2022c. 'Does a Constitution Have a Soul? The Role of Bundestreue in Germany and Ubuntu in South Africa to Give Life and Identity to a Constitutional Text'. In *Navigating the Unknown – Essays on Selected Case Studies about the Rights of Minorities*, 163–214. Leiden: Brill.

De Villiers, B. 2022d. 'Flying a Flag for Freedom of Expression: When Does a Historic Symbol of a Minority Turn into Hate Speech? The Case of the Old Flag of South Africa'. In *Navigating the Unknown – Essays on Selected Case Studies about the Rights of Minorities*, 215–50. Leiden: Brill.

De Villiers, B. 2022e. 'Freedom of Expression and Hate Speech: When Values Collide in Divided Societies'. *Constitutional Review* 8:184–214.

De Villiers, B. 2022f. 'Non-Territorial Self-Government and Socio-Economic Empowerment: The Roma of Hungary'. In *Navigating the Unknown – Essays on Selected Case Studies about the Rights of Minorities*, 73–103. Leiden: Brill.

De Villiers, B. 2022g. 'The Design of Institutions in Response to Diversity: A Shot in the Dark or a Fine Art?' In *Navigating the Unknown – Essays on Selected Case Studies about the Rights of Minorities*, 1–37. Leiden: Brill.

De Villiers, B. 2022h. 'Using Control over Access to Land to Achieve Self-Government (of Some Sort): Reflecting on the Experiences of Aboriginal People with the Right to Negotiate in Australia'. In *Navigating the Unknown – Essays on Selected Case Studies about the Rights of Minorities*, 104–37. Leiden: Brill.

De Villiers, B. 2023a. 'Breathing Life into the Constitution: The Transformative Role of Courts to Give a Unique Identity to a Constitution'. *Constitutional Review* 9:109–41.

De Villiers, B. 2023b. 'Dithering between Consultation and Consensus – Whereto with Advisory Bodies for Indigenous Peoples?' *Journal of Ethnopolitics and Minority Issues in Europe* 22:32–63. https://doi.org/10.53779/HBKA3992.

De Villiers, B. 2023c. 'Going It Alone – Privatised, Cultural Self-Government for Afrikaners in South Africa: Insights from a Non-Indigenous Community in Functional Self-Determination'. In *Indigenous Rights in the Modern Era: Regaining What Has Been Lost*, 314–70. Leiden: Brill.

De Villiers, B. 2023d. 'Modernism versus Traditionalism: A Reflection on the Noken Electoral System of West Papua'. In *Indigenous Rights in the Modern Era: Regaining What Has Been Lost*, 297–313. Leiden: Brill.

De Villiers, B. 2023e. 'Quotas in the Modern Era – the Reserved Māori Seats in New Zealand'. In *Indigenous Rights in the Modern Era: Regaining What Has Been Lost*, 201–40. Leiden: Brill.

De Villiers, B. 2023f. 'Recognising Indigenous Sovereignty – Sort Of Essential Principles in International Law to Operationalise the Right to Self-Determination of Indigenous Peoples'. In *Indigenous Rights in the Modern Era: Regaining What Has Been Lost*, 14–67. Leiden: Brill.

De Villiers, B. 2023g. 'Regaining What Has Been Lost: The Art of the Possible'. In *Indigenous Rights in the Modern Era: Regaining What Has Been Lost*, 371–96. Leiden: Brill.

De Villiers, B. 2023h. 'Right to Be Consulted, but the Frustration of Being Ignored: The Ongoing Efforts in International Law to Give Practical Meaning to Free, Prior, and Informed Consent'. In *Indigenous Rights in the Modern Era: Regaining What Has Been Lost*, 68–130. Leiden: Brill.

De Villiers, B. 2023i. 'Speaking, but Does Anyone Listen? The Path of Progress and Frustration with Indigenous Advisory Bodies of the Sámi, Aboriginal People, and the Khoisan'. In *Indigenous Rights in the Modern Era: Regaining What Has Been Lost*, 131–200. Leiden: Brill.

De Villiers, B. 2024a. 'Collective Decision-Making versus Individual Rights: A Reflection on the Noken Electoral System of Papua and the Operation of Native Title in Australia'. In *Courts and Diversity: Twenty Years of the Constitutional Court of Indonesia*, edited by B. De Villiers, S. Isra, and P. Faiz, 228–59. Leiden: Brill.

De Villiers, B. 2024b. 'Life after the Failed Voice: Options for Aboriginal Self-Determination and Consultation in Australia'. *International Journal on Minority and Group Rights*, 1–32.

De Villiers, B. 2024c. 'The Rejection of the Voice for Aboriginal People in Australia – a Postmortem of Causes of Failure'. *Constitutional Review*, 266–306.

De Villiers, B. 2024d. 'The Rejection of the Voice for Aboriginal People in Australia – Do Indigenous Advisory Bodies Have a Place in Modern Society?' *Verfassungs Und Recht in Übersee*.

De Villiers, B., and J. Sindane. 2011. *Cooperative Government – The Oil of the Engine*. Johannesburg: Konrad Adenauer Foundation.

De Villiers, B., D. Geldenhuys, and H. Matthee. 2018. 'Afrikaans: Visie vir 2030 / Afrikaans: Vision for Afrikaans 2030'. 1 September 2018. https://docplayer.nl/107167406-Afrikaans-n-visie-vir-2030.html.

De Villiers, B., S. Isra, and Z. Mochtar. 2019. 'Asymmetry in a Decentralised, Unitary State: Lessons to Be Drawn from the Experiences of Decentralisation to the Special Regions of Indonesia'. *Journal on Ethnopolitics and Minority Issues in Europe* 18:43–71.

De Wet, C., and S. Niemann. 1999. 'The Status of Mother Tongue Education in South Africa: A Comparative Perspective'. Cape Town: UNESCO Regional Office for Education in Africa (Senegal). https://unesdoc.unesco.org/ark:/48223/pf0000117579.

Deagon, A. 2023. *A Principled Framework for the Autonomy of Religious Communities*. Oxford: Hart Publishing.

Delcamp, A. 1994. 'Definition and the Limits of the Principle of Subsidiarity'. Local and regional authorities in Europe, No. 55. Strasbourg: Council of Europe.

Delcker, J. 2020. 'Germany's Balancing Act: Fighting Online Hate While Protecting Free Speech'. *Politico*, 1 October 2020. https://www.politico.eu/article/germany-hate-speech-internet-netzdg-controversial-legislation/.

Delgamuukw case. 1997. Delgamuukw v British Columbia, [1997] 3 SCR 1010.

Delport, D. 2022. 'SA 19de Op Lys van Lande Met Ergste Georganiseerde Misdaad'. *Netwerk24*, 24 September 2022. https://www.netwerk24.com/netwerk24/nuus/misdaad/sa-19de-op-lys-van-lande-met-ergste-georganiseerde-misdaad-20220923.

Delport, D. 2024. 'RNE "Taktiese Besluit om ANC te Laat Seëvier" '. *Die Burger*, 31 December 2024.

Design Principles. 2023. 'Design Principles of the Aboriginal and Torres Strait Islander Voice'. First Nations Referendum Working Group. chrome-extension://efaidnbmnnnibpcajpcglclefindmkaj/https://voice.gov.au/sites/default/files/2023-06/design-principles-aboriginal-torres-strait-islander-voice.pdf.

Diala, A. 2017. 'The Concept of Living Customary Law: A Critique'. *Journal of Legal Pluralism and Unofficial Law* 49:143–65.

Diala, A. 2019. 'Our Laws are Better than Yours: The Future of Legal Pluralism in South Africa'. *Revista General de Derecho Público Comparado* 26:1–23.

Dickson case. 2024. Dickson v Vuntut Gwitchin First Nation, 2024 SCC 10.

Diko, M. 2024. 'Anthems of Oppressed Voices: A Postcolonial Deliberation of the South African Apartheid Phrase Dubul'ibhunu (Kill the Boer or Shoot the Boer)'. *Cogent Social Sciences* 10:1–16. https://doi.org/10.1080/23311886.2024.2395662.

Dikoko case. 2006. Dikoko v Mokhatla 2006 (6) SA 235 (CC).

Dinokopila, B.R., and B. Kgoboge. 2021. 'Customary Law and Limitations to Constitutional Rights in Botswana'. *Nordic Journal of Human Rights* 39:339–57.

Dinstein, Y., and M. Tabory, eds. 2023. *The Protection of Minorities and Human Rights*. London: Marthinus Nijjhof.

Dladla, N. 2025. 'Not yet Ubuntu: A Philosophical Essay on the History of Government and the (Ab)Use of Ubuntu in Conqueror-South Africa'. In *Beyond Mimicry: Re-Imagining Public Governance*, edited by A.M. Iye and A. Holl, 159–84. Berlin: De Gruyter.

Dlamini, C. 1994. 'Culture, Education, and Religion'. In *Rights and Constitutionalism: The New South African Legal Order*, edited by D. Van Wyk, J. Dugard, B. De Villiers, and D. Davis, 573–98. Cape Town: Juta.

Dobos, B. 2016. 'The Minority Self-Governments in Hungary'. Online Compendium: Autonomies of the World. Bolzano. www.world-autonomies.info.

Doctors for Life case. 2006. Doctors for Life International v Speaker of the National Assembly [2006] ZACC 11; 2006 (6) SA 416 (CC); 2006 (12) BCLR 1399 (CC).

Dogru case. 2009. Dogru v France (Application no. 27058/05). ECtHR.

Domingo, R. 2023. 'The Right to Religious Freedom: Extension or Erosion?' In *The Cambridge Handbook of Natural Law and Human Rights*, edited by T. Angier, I.A. Benson, and M.D. Retter, 418–31. Cambridge: Cambridge University Press.

Donkers, A., and R. Murray. 1997. 'Prospects and Problems Facing Traditional Leaders in South Africa'. In *The Rights of Indigeous People: A Quest for Coexistence*, edited by B. De Villiers, 39–57. Pretoria: HSRC Publishers.

Dorfling, C. 2024a. '14 Dood in Oos-Kaapse Inisiasies Die Winter'. *Netwerk24*, 1 August 2024.

Dorfling, C. 2024b. 'Inisiasie-Dodetal: "Om Skok Uit Te Spreek Is Nie Genoeg" '. *Netwerk24*, 28 December 2024.

Doyle, C. 2014. *Indigenous Peoples, Title to Territory, Rights and Resources The Transformative Role of Free Prior and Informed Consent*. London: Routledge. https://www.taylorfrancis.com/books/mono/10.4324/9781315780665/indigenous-peoples-title-territory-rights-resources-cathal-doyle.

Doyle, C. 2022. 'Free Prior and Informed Consent and Indigenous Rights: A Bulwark against Discrimination and Platform for Self-Determination'. In *Research Handbook on the International Law of Indigenous Rights*, edited by D. Newman, 96–128. Cheltenham: Edward Elgar Publishing Limited.

Du Plessis case. 1996. Du Plessis v De Klerk 1996 (5) BCLR 658 (CC). Constitutional Court.

Du Plessis, J. 2022. 'Fairness in the Law of Contract: Reflections on Beadica'. *Constitutional Court Review* 12:197–222.

Du Plessis, L. 1994. 'A Background to Drafting the Chapter on Fundamental Rights'. In *The Birth of a Constitution*, edited by B. De Villiers, 89–100. Cape Town: Juta.

Dube, F. 2022. 'The Ethos of Tolerance of Diversity in Post-Apartheid Jurisprudence'. *Obiter* 43:124–41.

Dumisa, S., and O. Amao. 2015. 'The Utility of Moral Philosophy and Professional Ethics in the Fight Against Corruption in South Africa: Any Role for Ubuntu?' *Ubuntu: Journal of Conflict and Social Transformation* 4:85–111.

Dunlap, A. 2018. ' "A Bureaucratic Trap:" Free, Prior and Informed Consent (FPIC) and Wind Energy Development in Juchitán, Mexico'. *Capitalism Nature Socialism* 29:88–108.

Duy, I.N. 2020. 'The Limits to Free Speech on Social Media: On Two Recent Decisions of the Supreme Court of Norway'. *Nordic Journal of Human Rights* 38:237–45.

Dyani-Mhango, N. 2024. 'South Africa and the "Othering" of the "Non-Euro-Christian" Religions'. *AJIL* 118:124–28.

EB case. 2024. EB (born S) v ER (born B) and others and a related matter 2024 (1) BCLR 16 (CC).

Ebrahimian case. 2015. Ebrahimian v France App. No. 64846/11, 26 September 2015.

Economic Freedom Fighters case. 2020. Economic Freedom Fighters and Another v Minister of Justice and Correctional Services and Another (CCT201/19) [2020] ZACC 25; 2021 (2) BCLR 118 (CC); 2021 (2) SA 1 (CC); 2021 (1) SACR 387 (CC) (27 November 2020).

Egli, P. 2010. *Bundestreue: Eine Rechtsvergleichende Untersuchung.* Baden Baden: Nomos.

Ehrlich, E. 1913. *Grundlegung Der Soziologie Des Rechts.* Berlin: Duncker and Humblot.

Ehrlich, E. 1936. *Fundamental Principles of the Sociology of Law.* (Translated W. Moll) Cambridge: Harvard University Press.

Eichler, J. 2019. *Reconciling Indigenous Peoples' Individual and Collective Rights Participation, Prior Consultation and Self-Determination in Latin America.* London: Routledge.

Elazar, D.J. 1994. 'Form of State: Federal, Unitary, Or . . .' In *The Birth of a Constitution*, edited by B. De Villiers, 29–36. Cape Town: Juta.

Eloff, T. 1994. 'The Process of Giving Birth'. In *The Birth of a Constitution*, edited by B. De Villiers, 12–19. Cape Town: Juta.

Emelianenko, E. 2022. 'The Role of Ubuntu in South Africa's Foreign Policy'. *FRESKA* 1:197–205.

Enarsson, T. 2024. 'Navigating Hate Speech and Content Moderation under the DSA: Insights from ECtHR Case Law'. *Information & Communications Technology Law* 33:384–401. https://doi.org/10.1080/13600834.2024.2395579.

Endorois Welfare Council case. 2003. Centre for Minority Rights Development (Kenya) and Minority Rights Group (on behalf of the Endorois Welfare Council), 273 of 2003.

English, R. 1996. 'Ubuntu: The Quest for an Indigenous Jurisprudence'. *South African Journal on Human Rights* 7:641–48.

English Schools Association case. 2000. Tamil Nadu Tamil & English Schools Association v The State of Tamil Nadu rep. by its Secretary to Government School Education Department 2000 (2) C.T.C 344.

Enslin, P., and K. Horsthemke. 2004. 'Can Ubuntu Provide a Model for Citizenship Education in African Democracies?' *Comparative Education* 40:545–58.

Epple, S., and G. Assefa, eds. 2020. *Legal Pluralism in Ethiopia: Actors, Challenges and Solutions.* transcript Verlag.

Equality Act. 2000. *Promotion of Equality and Prevention of Unfair Discrimination Act 4 of 2000.* https://www.justice.gov.za/legislation/acts/2000-004.pdf.

Erez, L., and A. Banai. 2024. 'Self-Determination and the Limits on the Right to Include'. *Political Studies*, 1–17.

Erkizia Almandoz case. 2021. Erkizia Almandoz v Spain ECHR 197 (2021).

Ermacora, F. 1983. *The Protection of Minorities before the United Nations.* Leiden: Brill.

Erueti, A. 2022. *The UN Declaration on the Rights of Indigenous Peoples: A New Interpretive Approach.* Oxford: Oxford University Press.

European Charter for Languages. 1992. 'European Charter for Regional or Minority Languages Strasbourg, 5.XI.1992'. Council of Europe.

European Framework Convention. 1998. *European Framework Convention for the Protection of National Minorities, 1998.* H (95) 10. Strasbourg: Council of Eurppe. https://www.refworld.org/docid/3ae6b36210.html.

Everfresh case. 2012. Everfresh Market Virginia (Pty) Ltd v Shoprite Checkers (Pty) Ltd [2011] ZACC 30; 2012 (1) SA 256 (CC).

Eweida case. 2013. Eweida and Others v the United Kingdom – 48420/10, 36516/10, 51671/10 et al. Judgment 15.1.2013. ECtHR.

Expert Report Provinces. 1993. 'Regions in South Africa: Constitutional Options and Their Implications for Good Government and a Sound Economy'. Johannesburg: Expert Report.

Explanatory Report on FCNM. 1995. 'Explanatory Report to the Framework Convention for the Protection of National Minorities'. Council of Europe.

Eze, M.O. 2008. 'What Is African Communitarianism? Against Consensus as a Regulative Ideal'. *South African Journal of Philosophy* 27:106–19.

Ezeani, N., and D. Newman. 2022. 'Definitional Complexities and the Boundaries of the Concept of Indigenous Peoples'. In *Comparative Election Law Research Handbooks in Comparative Law Series*, edited by J.A. Gardner, 438–58. Massachusetts: Elgar Online.

FA Picture case. 2005. FA Picture International v Central Board of Film AIR 2005 Bom 145, 2005 (1) BomCR 5, 2005 (2) MhLj 869.

Fáber case. 2012. Fáber v Hungary ECHR 310 (2012).

Falconer case. 2024. Falconer v Commissioner of Police [No 2] [2024] WASCA 47.

Faris, J.A. 2015. 'African Customary Law and Common Law in South Africa: Reconciling Contending Legal Systems'. *International Journal of African Renaissance Studies* 10:171–89.

Farzan, A. 2023. 'Islam in the Jurisprudence of the European Court of Human Rights (ECtHR): An Analysis of Selected ECtHR Cases to Evaluate the Court's Approach and Its Consequences : Refah Partisi and Others v Turkey, Molla Sali v Greece, E.S. v Austria'. University of Strassbourg.

Faurisson. 1996. Faurisson v France Communication No 550/93 views adopted 8 November 1996.

Fedotova case. 2023. Case of Fedotova and Others v Russia, Applications nos. 40792/10, 30538/14 and 43439/14, 2023.

FEDSAS Teaching in Numbers. 2024. 'FEDSAs: Teaching in Numbers / Onderwys in Syfers'. Pretoria: FEDSAS.

Fenner, F. 2024. 'End of the Road for "racist" Street Name'. *West Australian*, 30 October 2024.

Féret case. 2009. Féret v Belgium, application No. 15615/07 (ECHR 16 July 2009). ECHR.

Ferrari, A. 2022. 'Human Rights and the Osmosis between Secular and Religious Legal Systems'. In *Religious Diversity, State, and Law*, edited by J. Marko, M. Lakitsch, F. Winter, W. Weirer, and K. Wonisch, 23–53. Leiden: Brill.

Ferrari, S. 2020. 'Constitutional Models of Law and Religion Relations in Western Europe'. In *Constitutions and Religion*, edited by S. Mancini, 96–110. Cheltenham: Edward Elgar Publishing Limited.

Figone, K.E. 2012. 'The Hegemony of English in South African Education'. Scripps Senior Theses. Paper 43. chrome-extension://efaidnbmnnnibpcajpcglclefindmkaj/https://scholarship.claremont.edu/cgi/viewcontent.cgi?article=1044&context=scripps_theses.

Filippova, E., and V. Filippov. 2015. 'National-Cultural Autonomy in Post-Soviet Russia over Two Decades: Concept and Institution'. *Ethnicity* 13:50–61.

Fink, C. 1998. 'The Minorities Question at the Paris Peace Conference: The Polish Minority Treaty, June 28, 1919'. In *The Treaty of Versailles: A Reassessment after 75 Years*, edited by G. Boemeke, G. Feldman, and E. Glaser, 249–74. London: Cambridge University Press.

Fish Resources Act. 1994. *Fish Resources Management Act 1994 (WA)*. https://www.legislation.wa.gov.au/legislation/statutes.nsf/law_a283.html.

Flemmer, R. 2022. 'The Implementation Paradox Ambiguities of Prior Consultation and Free, Prior, and Informed Consent (FPIC) for Indigenous Peoples' Agency in Resource Extraction in Latin America'. In *The Routledge Handbook of Indigenous Development*, edited by K. Ruckstuhl, I.A. Velásquez Nimatuj, J. McNeish, and N. Postero, 126–42. London: Routledge.

FMG case. 2009. FMG Pilbara Pty Ltd v Cox [2009] FCAFC 49.

Food and Agriculture UN. 2016. 'Free Prior and Informed Consent: An Indigenous Peoples' Right and a Good Practice for Local Communities'. Geneva: Food and Agriculture Organisation of the United Nations. https://www.fao.org/3/i6190e/i6190e.pdf.

Forrest appeal case. 2024. Forrest and Forrest Pty Ltd v Minister of Aboriginal Affairs [2024] WASCA 96.

Forrest case. 2023. Forrest and Forrest Pty Ltd v Minister for Aboriginal Affairs 2023 [WASAT] 28.

Fortman, B. 2011. 'Minority Rights: A Major Misconception?' *Human Rights Quarterly* 33:273–92.

Fose case. 1997. Fose v Minister of Safety and Security (CCT14/96) [1997] ZACC 6; 1997 (7) BCLR 851; 1997 (3) SA 786 (5 June 1997). CC.

Fosen case. 2021. Supreme Court of Norway, HR-2021-1975-S.

Foster, J. 2011. 'The Use of Foreign Law in Constitutional Interpretation: Lessons from South Africa'. *University of San Francisco Law Review* 45:79–131.

Foucher, P. 2023. 'Court Challenges and Linguistic Human Rights: The Canadian Case'. In *The Handbook of Linguistic Human Rights*, edited by T. Skutnabb-Kangas and R. Phillipson, 469–76. Hoboken: John Wiley.

Foulkes, I. 2024. 'Swiss Parliament Defies ECHR on Climate Women's Case'. *BBC News*, 13 June 2024.

Fraser case. 1997. Fraser v Children's Court, Pretoria North, and Others 1997 (2) SA 261 (CC). CC.

Freedom of Expression ECtHR. 2022. 'Guide on Article 10 of the European Convention on Human Rights: Freedom of Expression'. Strasbourg: European Court of Human Rights.

Freedom of Religion case. 2019. Freedom of Religion South Africa v Minister of Justice and Constitutional Development and Others [2019] ZACC 34.

Fruhstorfer, A., and A. Hudson. 2022. 'Majorities for Minorities: Participatory Constitution Making and the Protection of Minority Rights'. *Political Research Quaterly* 75:103–17.

Fujitsu case. 2023. Fujitsu Services Core (Pty) Limited v Schenker South Africa (Pty) Limited (CCT 32/22) [2023] ZACC 20; 2023 (9) BCLR 1054 (CC); (2023) 44 ILJ 2391 (CC); 2023 (6) SA 327 (CC) (28 June 2023).

Gaffney, F. 2021. 'Indigenous Land Use Agreements in Australia: A Vehicle for Economic Prosperity or an Empty Gesture?' In *Indigenous–Industry Agreements, Natural Resources and the Law*, edited by T. Odumosu-Ayanu and D. Newman, 229–45. London: Routledge.

Galanter, M. 1981. 'Justice in Many Rooms: Courts, Provate Ordering, and Indigenous Law'. *Journal of Legal Pluralism* 19:1–47.

Gargarella, R. 2006. 'Theories of Democracy, the Judiciary and Social Rights'. In *Courts and Social Transformation in New Democracies*, edited by R. Gargarella, P. Domingo, and T. Roux, 13–34. Hampshire: Ashgate.

Gatis Kovaļkovs case. 2012. Gatis Kovaļkovs v Latvia (Application no. 35021/05). ECtHR.

Gaum case. 2019. Gaum and others v Van Rensburg NO and others (Commission for Gender Equality and another as amici curiae) [2019] 2 All SA 722 (GP).

Gauteng Education Bill case. 1996. Gauteng Provincial Legislature In re: Gauteng School Education Bill of 1995 (CCT39/95) [1996] ZACC 4; 1996 (4) BCLR 537; 1996 (3) SA 165 (4 April 1996).

Gehman, J., L. Lefsrud, and S. Fast. 2017. 'Social License to Operate: Legitimacy by Another Name?' *Canadian Public Administration* 60:293–317.

Gelber, K. 2012. 'Political Culture, Flag Use and Freedom of Speech'. *Political Studies* 60:163–79.

Geldenhuys, D. 2020. 'Autonomy Initiatives of the Afrikaner Community in South Africa'. In *Non-Territorial Autonomy and Decentralization*, edited by T.H. Malloy and L. Salat, 91–114. London: Routledge.

Gibbs case. 1995. Desmond Gibbs v Lyle Capewell, Australian Electoral Commission and Minister of Aboriginal and Islander Affairs [1995] FCA 1048; (1995) 128 ALR 577 (1995) 54 FCR 503 (3 February 1995). Federal Court.

Ginsburg, T., ed. 2012. *Comparative Constitutional Law*. London: Edward Elgar Publishing Limited.

Glenister case. 2011. Glenister v President of the Republic of South Africa & Others [2011] ZACC 6, 2011 (3) SA 347 (CC).

Glucroft, W.N. 2023. 'English Language Use Gets a Boost in Germany'. *DW*, 26 August 2023. https://www.dw.com/en/english-language-use-gets-a-boost-in-germany/a-66633711.

Goldstone, R.J. 2008. 'The First Years of the South African Constitutional Court'. *Sup. Ct. L. Rev* 42. https://digitalcommons.osgoode.yorku.ca/cgi/viewcontent.cgi?article=1148&context=sclr.

Gorzelik case. 2004. Gorzelik and Others v Poland, App. No. 44158/98, judgment of 17 February 2004. ECtHR.

Gözübenli, A.S. 2023. 'New Turkey's Other Turks Abroad: A Brief Critical Reading of the Erdoğan Regime's Kin-State Policy toward Turks of North Macedonia'. *SocArXiv Jngv3*. https://ideas.repec.org/p/osf/socarx/jngv3.html.

Greater Tzaneen Municipality case. 2024. Greater Tzaneen Municipality v Bravospan 252 CC [2024] ZACC 20.

Griffiths, J. 1986. 'What Is Legal Pluralism?' *The Journal of Legal Pluralism and Unofficial Law* 18:1–55. https://doi.org/10.1080/07329113.1986.10756387.

Grootboom case. 2000. Government of the Republic of South Africa and Others v Grootboom and Others (CCT11/00) [2000] ZACC 19; 2001 (1) SA 46; 2000 (11) BCLR 1169 (4 October 2000).

Gül case. 2000. Gül and Others v Turkey App. No. 22676/93. ECtHR.

Gumede case. 2009. Gumede v President of the Republic of South Africa 2009 (3) SA 152 (CC).

Gunther, K. 2020. 'Normative Legal Pluralism: A Critique'. In *Jurisprudence in a Globalized World*, edited by J. Fabra-Zamora, 84–99. Cheltenham: Elgar.

Gutan, B. 2024. 'Are Rights of Judges Becoming Rule of Law Standards in Europe?' MPIL Research Paper Series. Heidelberg.

Gutierrez. 2019. 'Compatability of Sharia Law with the European Convention on Human Rights: Can State Partis to the Convention to Signatories to the "Cairo Declration"?' Doc 14787 and Resolution 2253 (2019). Strasbourg: Council of Europe: Parliamentary Assembly.

Habib, A. 1995. 'The Transition to Democracy in South Africa: Developing a Dynamic Model'. *Transformation* 27:50–73.

Hagan case. 2000. Hagan v Trustees of the Toowoomba Sports Ground Trust [2000] FCA 1615 (2000). FCA.

Hagan case. 2003. Stephen Hagan v Australia, Communication No. 26/2002, U.N. Doc. CERD/C/62/D/26/2002 (2003). CERD.

Haida Nation case. 2004. Haida Nation v British Columbia (Minister of Forests) [2004] 3 SCR 511.

Hailey, J. 2008. *Ubuntu: A Literature Review.* London: Tutu Foundation.

Hamidović case. 2018. Hamidović v Bosnia and Herzegovina (Application no. 57792/15). ECtHR.

Handbook ILO. 2013. *Understanding the Indigenous and Tribal Peoples Convention, 1989 (No. 169).* Geneva: ILO Office. https://www.ilo.org/wcmsp5/groups/public/---ed_norm/---normes/documents/publication/wcms_205225.pdf.

Handyside case. 1976. Handyside v UK App no. 5493/72 (ECHR, 7 December 1976). ECtHR.

Hannum, H. 2023. *Documents on Autonomy and Minority Rights.* Leiden: Martinus Nijhoff Publishers.

Harare Declaration. 1989. 'Harare Declaration'. Organisation of African Unity.

Harris, B. 2024. *Indigenous Peoples and Constitutional Reform in Australia.* Singapore: Springer.

Hart, H. 1961. *The Concept of Law.* Oxford: Oxford University Press.

Hasan and Chaush case. 2000. Hasan and Chaush v Bulgaria (Application no. 30985/96).

Hassam case. 2009. Hassam v Jacobs NO and Others 2009 (5) SA 572 (CC). CC.

Hate Speech Act. 2024. *Prevention and Combating of Hate Crimes and Hate Speech Act, 2024.*

Head of Department, Mpumalanga Department of Education case. 2010. Head of Department, Mpumalanga Department of Education and another v Hoerskool Ermelo and another [2009] ZACC 32, 2010 (2) SA 415 (CC), 2130 (3) BCLR 177 (CC).

Heidemann, K. 2024. 'Citizen's Assemblies in Germany'. *IACL-AIDC Blog* (blog). 28 November 2024.

Heinämäki, L., C. Allard, and S. Kirchner. 2017. 'Actualizing Sámi Rights: International Comparative Research'. Publications of the Government´s analysis, assessment and research activities 4/2017. Helsinki: Office of the Prime Minister of Finland. https://valtioneuvosto.fi/documents/10616/3866814/4_Saamelaisten+oikeuksien+toteutuminen+kansainv%C3%A4linen+oikeusvertaileva+tutkimus/e765f819-d90c-4318-9ff0-cf4375e00688?version=1.0.

Heinze, E., ed. 2024. *Criminalising Hate Speech: A Comparative Study.* Heidelberg: Springer.

Henrard, K. 2002. *Minority Protection in Post-Apartheid South Africa: Human Rights, Minority Rights, and Self-Determination.* Westport: Praeger.

Henrard, K. 2007. 'The Interrelationship between Individual Human Rights, Minority Rights and the Right to Self-determination and Its Importance for the Adequate Protection of Linguistic Minorities'. *Global Review of Ethnopolitics* 1:41–61.

Henrard, K. 2010. ' "The EU, Double Standards and Minority Protection": A Double Redefinition and Future Prospects'. In *Double Standards Pertaining to Minority Protection*, edited by K. Henrard, 21–70. Leiden: Brill.

Henrard, K. 2013. 'Introduction'. In *The Interralation between the Right to Identity of Minorities and Their Socio-Economic Participation*, edited by K. Henrard, 1–17. Leiden: Marthinus Nijjhof.

Henrard, K. 2015. 'How the European Court of Human Rights' Concern Regarding European Consensus Tempers the Effective Protection of Freedom of Religion'. *Oxford Journal of Law and Religion* 4:398–422.

Henrard, K. 2023. 'Minority and Language Rights in the Eventual Peace Settlement after the Russian-Ukrainian War'. *International Journal on Minority and Group Rights* 30:821–53. https://doi.org/10.1163/15718115-bja10142.

Henrico, R. 2019. 'Proselytising the Regulation of Religious Bodies in South Africa: Suppressing Religious Freedom?' *Potchefstroom Electronic Law Journal* 22.

Henrico, R. 2023. 'Judicial Review in South Africa and India: Advancing Constitutionalism or Undue Activism?' *Obiter* 43:797–811.

Heritage Council. 2021. 'Free, Prior and Informed Consent in the Work of the Australian Heritage Council'. 2021. https://www.dcceew.gov.au/sites/default/files/documents/free-prior-informed-consent-work-of-australian-heritage-council.pdf.

Herrera, J.C. 2019. 'Binding Consent of Indigenous Peoples in Colombia: An Example of Transformative Constitutionalism'. In *The Prior Consultation of Indigenous Peoples in Latin America: Inside the Implementation Gap*, edited by C. Wright and A. Tomaselli, 41–57. London: Routledge.

Herz, M., and P. Molnar, eds. 2012. *The Content and Context of Hate Speech: Rethinking Regulation and Responses*. Cambridge: Cambridge University Press.

Heugh, K. 1999. 'The Promise of Multilingualism and Education in South Africa: Mirage or Reality ?' *Languages and Education* 18:64–82.

Heunis, J. 1994. 'Transitional Executive Council'. In *The Birth of a Constitution*, edited by B. De Villiers, 20–28. Cape Town: Juta.

Higgins, N. 2023. 'Cultural Expertise and Indigenous Rights'. In *Cultural Expertise, Law and Rights: A Comprehensive Guide*, edited by L. Holden, 201–14. Oxon: Routledge.

Hilpold, P. 2007. 'UN Standard Setting in the Field of Minority Rights'. *International Journal on Minority and Group Rights* 14:204–22.

Himonga, C. 2013. 'The Right to Health in an African Cultural Context: The Role of Ubuntu in the Realization of the Right to Health with Special Reference to South Africa'. *Journal of African Law* 22:165–95.

Himonga, C., M. Taylor, and A. Pope. 2013. 'Reflections on Judicial Views of Ubuntu'. *Potchefstroom Electronic Law Journal* 16:372–614.

Hoekema, A. 2017. 'The Conundrum of Cross-Cultural Understanding in the Practice of Law'. *The Journal of Legal Pluralism and Unofficial Law* 49:67–84.

Hofmann, R. 2018. 'Commentary on Article 1 of the Framework Convention for the Protection of Minority Rights'. In *The Framework Convention for the Protection of National Minorities*, edited by R. Hofmann, T.H. Malloy, and D. Rein, 84–87. Leiden: Brill.

Hofmann, R., T.H. Malloy, and D. Rein, eds. 2018a. 'Introduction'. In *The Framework Convention for the Protection of National Minorities: A Commentary*, edited by R. Hofmann, T.H. Malloy, and D. Rein, 1–21. Leiden: Brill.

Hofmann, R., T.H. Malloy, and D. Rein, eds. 2018b. *The Framework Convention for the Protection of National Minorities*. Leiden: Brill.

Hoffmann case. 2001. Hoffmann v South African Airways 2001 (1) SA 1 (CC); 2000 (11) BCLR 1235 (CC).

Hohmann, J., and M. Weller, eds. 2018. *The UN Declaration on the Rights of Indigenous Peoples: A Commentary*. Oxford: Oxford University Press.

Holl, A. 2025. 'Early Human Social Organizations and Ancient Forms of Governance in Africa'. In *Beyond Mimicry: Re-Imagining Public Governance*, edited by A.M. Iye and A. Holl, 19–42. Berlin: De Gruyter.

Holomisa, S.M. 1997. 'Foreword'. In *The Rights of Indigeous People: A Quest for Coexistence*, edited by B. De Villiers. Pretoria: HSRC Publishers.

Hooker, M.B. 1975. *Legal Pluralism: An Introduction to Colonial and Neo-Colonial Laws*. Durham: Clarendon Press.

Horowitz, D.L. 1990. 'Ethnic Conflict Management for Policymakers'. In *Conflict and Peacekeeping in Multiethnic Societies*, edited by J. Montville, 115–34. New York: Lexington Books.

Horowitz, D.L. 1991. *A Democratic South Africa? Constitutional Engineering in a Divided Society*. San Francisco: University of California Press.

Horowitz, D.L. 1993. 'Democracy in Divided Societies'. *Journal of Democracy*, no. 4, 18–38.

Horowitz, D.L. 2021. *Constitutional Processes and Democratic Commitment*. Stanford: Yale University Press.

Hotz case. 2017. Hotz v University of Cape Town [2016] ZASCA 159, 2017 (2) SA 485 (SCA); [2016] 4 All SA 723 (SCA).

Howard, E. 2022. 'Bans of the Wearing of Burqas, Niqabs and Hijabs, Religious Freedom and the Secular Nature of State'. In *Religious Freedom in Secular States*, edited by J.H. Bhuiyan and A. Black, 73–94. Leiden: Brill.

Howard, E. 2024. *Headscarves and the Court of Justice of the European Union: An Analysis of the Case Law*. London: Routledge.

HR-2020 case. 2020. HR-2020-185-A case no. 19-111561STR-HRET. SC.

HRC. 2000. 'Concluding Observations of the Human Rights Committee: Australia. 28/07/2000. CCPR/CO/69/AUS.(Concluding Observations/Comments)'. Geneva: UN Human Rights Committee.

HRC. 2014. Concluding observations of the Human Rights Committee: Chile.

HRC Lubicon Lake Band. 1984. Lubicon Lake Band v Canada, Communication No. 167/1984 (26 March 1990), U.N. Doc. Supp. No. 40 (A/45/40) at 1 (1990). UNHRC.

Hugo case. 1997. President of RSA v Hugo 1997 (6) BCLR 708 (CC), 1997 (4) SA 1 (CC).

Huizenga, D. 2018. 'Articulations of Aboriginal Title, Indigenous Rights, and Living Customary Law in South Africa'. *Social and Legal Studies* 27:3–24.

Hungary Nationalities Act. 2012. *Act on the Rights of Nationalities of Hungary Act CLXXIX of 2011. CDL-REF(2012)014.* chrome-extension://efaidnbmnnnibpcajpcglclefindmkaj/https://www.venice.coe.int/webforms/documents/default.aspx?pdffile=CDL-REF%282012%29014-e.

Huntington, S.P. 1991. 'Democracy's Third Wave'. *Journal of Democracy* Spring:12–34.

Husain, S., N.P. Ayoub, and M. Hassmann. 2024. 'Legal Pluralism in Contemporary Societies: Dynamics of Interaction between Islamic Law and Secular Civil Law'. *SYARIAT: Akhwal Syaksiyah, Jinayah, Siyasah and Muamalah* 1:1–17.

ICCPR. 1966. 'The International Covenant on Civil and Political Rights'. United Nations office of the High Commissioner for Human Rights. https://www.ohchr.org/en/professionalinterest/pages/ccpr.aspx.

ICCPR Comment Minorities. 1994. 'ICCPR General Comment No. 23: Article 27 (Rights of Minorities)'. Adopted at the Fiftieth Session of the Human Rights Committee, on 8 April 1994 CCPR/C/21/Rev.1/Add.5, General Comment No. 23. (General Comments). Geneva: UN Human Rights Committee. https://www.refworld.org/docid/453883fc0.html.

ICESCR. 1966. 'International Covenant on Economic, Social and Cultural Rights, Adopted and Opened for Signature, Ratification and Accession by General Assembly Resolution 2200A (XXI) of 16 December 1966 Entry into Force 3 January 1976, in Accordance with Article 27'. https://www.ohchr.org/en/professionalinterest/pages/cescr.aspx.

Ikhwan, H., and F. Aidulsyah. 2020. 'Sultanates and the Making of Nationhood in Indonesia and Malaysia'. *Asian Journal of Social Science* 48:339–52. https://doi.org/10.1163/15685314-04803008.

ILO 169. 1989. 'Indigenous and Tribal Peoples Convention, 1989 (No 169)'. https://www.ilo.org/dyn/normlex/en/f?p=NORMLEXPUB:12100:0::NO::P12100_ILO_CODE:C169.

ILO Argentina. 2008. 'Report of the Committee Set up to Examine the Representation Alleging Non-Observance by Argentina of the Indigenous and Tribal Peoples Convention, 1989 (No. 169), Made under Article 24 of the ILO Constitution by the Education Workers Union of Río Negro (UNTER), Local Section Affiliated to the Confederation of Education Workers of Argentina (CTERA)'. ILO. https://www.ilo.org/dyn/normlex/en/f?p=1000:50012:0::NO:50012:P50012_COMPLAINT_PROCEDURE_ID,P50012_LANG_CODE:2507187,en:NO.

ILO Brazil. 2009. 'Report of the Committee Set up to Examine the Representation Alleging Non-Observance by Brazil of the Indigenous and Tribal Peoples Convention, 1989 (No. 169), Made under Article 24 of the ILO Constitution by the Union of Engineers of the Federal District (SENGE/DF)'. ILO. <http://www.ilo.org/dyn/ normlex/en/f?p=1000:50012:0::NO:50012:P50012_COMPLAINT_PROCEDURE_ID,P50012_LANG_CODE:2507317,en:NO.

ILUA/Right to Negotiate. 2020. 'ILUA or the Right to Negotiate Process? A Comparison for Mineral Tenement Applications'. National Native Title Tribunal. http://www.nntt.gov.au/Information%20Publications/ILUA%20-%20The%20Right%20to%20Negotiate.pdf.

Incorporations Act. 2015. *Associations Incorporation Act 2015 (WA)*. chrome-extension://efaidnbmnnnibpcajpcglclefindmkaj/https://www.legislation.wa.gov.au/legislation/prod/filestore.nsf/FileURL/mrdoc_28811.pdf/$FILE/Associations%20Incorporation%20Act%202015%20-%20%5B00-b0-02%5D.pdf?OpenElement.

Indirect election case. 2023. MEX-2023-2-005.

Inman, R.P., and D. Rubinfeld. 2013. 'Understanding the Democratic Transition in South Africa'. *Am. L. & Econ. Rev* 15:1–38.

International Convention on Discrimination. 1965. 'International Convention on the Elimination of All Forms of Racial Discrimination: Adopted and Opened for Signature and Ratification by General Assembly Resolution 2106 (XX) of 21 December 1965 Entry into Force 4 January 1969, in Accordance with Article 19'. United Nations. https://www.ohchr.org/en/professionalinterest/pages/cerd.aspx.

Investigating case. 2001. Investigating Directorate: Serious Economic Offences and Others v Hyundai Motor Distributors (Pty) Ltd and Others In re: Hyundai Motor Distributors (Pty) Ltd and Others v Smit NO and Others (CCT1/00) [2000] ZACC 12; 2000 (10) BCLR 1079; 2001 (1) SA 545 (CC) (25 August 2000).

Isa, F.G. 2019. 'The UNDRIP: An Increasingly Robust Legal Parameter'. *The International Journal of Human Rights* 23:7–21.

Isa, F.G. 2021. 'The UNDRIP: An Increasingly Robust Legal Parameter'. In *The United Nations Declaration on the Rights of Indigenous Peoples: A Contempary Evaluation*, edited by D. Short, L. Lennox, J. Burger, and J. Hohmann, 7–21. London: Routledge.

Islamic Convention case. 2002. Islamic Unity Convention v Independent Broadcasting Authority and Others 2002 (4) SA 294 (CC). CC.

Ismail case. 1983. Ismail v Ismail 1983 (1) SA 1006 (A). AD.

Isra, S., and P. Faiz. 2024. 'The Indonesian Constitutional Court: An Overview'. In *Courts and Diversity: Twenty Years of the Constitutional Court of Indonesia*, edited by B. De Villiers, S. Isra, and P. Faiz, 55–95. Leiden: Brill.

Jackson, V.C. 2013. *Constitutional Engagement in a Transnational Era*. London: Oxford University Press.

Jacobs, B. 2021. 'Indigenous Justice in Oceania and North America'. *Criminology and Criminal Justice*. https://doi.org/10.1093/acrefore/9780190264079.013.627.

Jakóbski case. 2011. Jakóbski v Poland (Application no. 18429/06). ECtHR.

Jamneck, J. 2014. 'The Problematic Practical Application of Section 1(6) and 1(7) of the Intestate Succession Act under a New Dispensation'. *Potchefstroom Electronic Law Journal* 17. http://www.scielo.org.za/scielo.php?script=sci_arttext&pid=S1727-37812014000300005.

Janhit Abhiyan case. 2022. Janhit Abhiyan v Union of India Writ Petition (Civil) No. 55 Of 2019.

Jegede, A.O., and M.C. Stoffels. 2022. 'Climate Change Protests and a Liberal Rights Approach in South Africa: Pitfalls and Potentials'. *Stellenbosch Law Review* 33:285–309.

Jehovah's Witnesses of Moscow case. 2010. Jehovah's Witnesses of Moscow and Others v Russia (Application no. 302/02). ECtHR.

Johardien case. 1990. S v Johardien 1990 (1) SA 1026 (C).

Jones, N. 2024. *Self-Determination as Voice: The Participation of Indigenous Peoples in International Governance*. Cambridge: Cambridge University Press.

Joppke, C. 2013. 'Double Standards? Veils and Cruxifixes in the European Legal Order'. *European Journal of Sociology* 54:97–123.

Joppke, C. 2020. 'Constitutional Law and the Integration of Islam in Europe'. In *Constitutions and Religion*, edited by S. Mancini, 383–98. Cheltenham: Edward Elgar Publishing Limited.

Juma Musjid case. 2011. Governing Body of the Juma Musjid Primary School and Others v Essay NO and Others (CCT 29/10) [2011] ZACC 13; 2011 (8) BCLR 761 (CC) (11 April 2011).

Ka'a'Gee Tu First Nation case. 2007. Ka'a'Gee Tu First Nation v Can. (A.G.) (2007), 315 F.T.R. 178 (FC).

Kalina and Lokono case. 2015. Kalina and Lokono Peoples v Suriname (Merits, Reparation, Costs) IACHR No. 309 (25 November 2015).

Kamga, S.D. 2018. 'Cultural Values as a Source of Law: Emerging Trends of Ubuntu Jurisprudence in South Africa'. *African Human Rights Law Journal* 18:625–49.

Kapeli case. 2024. Kapeli v Secretary, Department of Home Affairs [2024] FCA 1246.

Karaduman case. 1993. Karaduman v Turkey App no 16278/90 ECtHR 3 May 1993.

Kascian, K. 2024. 'Latvia's Ambiguous Attitude towards the Framework Convention for the Protection of National Minorities: Is Diversity a Threat?' *Public Governance, Administration and Finances Law Review* 9:91–104.

Kaushal Kishor case. 2023. Kaushal Kishor v State of Uttar Pradesh Special Leave Petition no 34629 of 2017.

Kayange, G.M. 2023. *Meaning of Justice in African Philosophy*. Cham: Springer.

Kaye, A. 2025. 'Jewish Legal Pluralism: A Historical Approach'. In Jewish Law: New Perspectives, edited by S.L. Stone and Y. Brafman, 85–102. Berlin: Walter de Gruyter.

Keegstra case. 1990. R v Keegstra [1990] 3 SCR 697. SCR.

Keevy, I. 2009. 'The Constitutional Court and Ubuntu's "Inseparable Trinity" '. *Journal of Juridical Science* 34:62–87.

Kelly, T. 2023. 'What Ever Happened to the Africa in African Human Rights?' *Rutgers International Law and Human Rights Journal* 4:83–138.

Kelsen, H. 1945. *General Theory of Law and State.* Cambridge: Harvard University Press.

Kemp, G. 2023. 'From Apartheid to Democracy in South Africa'. In *Dictatorship, Democracy, and Transitional Justice in Global Legal History*, edited by I. Czeguhn and J. Thiessen, 153–76. Berlin: Duncker and Humblot.

Kerala Education case. 1959. The Kerala Education Bill [1959] 1 SCR 995.

Khan case. 2005. Khan v Khan 2005 (2) SA 272 (T).

Khanyile, X, D. Iyer, and T. Matadi. 2024. 'Decolonising the Reasonable Person Test: A Transformative Constitutional Imperative'. In *Management, Business, Administration and Legal.* Aberdeen.

Khoisan Act. 2019. *Traditional and Khoi- San Leadership Act, 2019.* https://www.gov.za/sites/default/files/gcis_document/201911/4286528-11act3of2019tradkhoisanleadership.pdf.

Khoisan Act appeal. 2023. Mogale and Others v Speaker of the National Assembly and Others [2023] ZACC 14.

Khumalo case. 2019. SAHRC v Khumalo 2019 (1) SA 289 (GJ).

Kibet, E., and C. Fombad. 2017. 'Transformative Constitutionalism and the Adjudication of Constitutional Rights in Africa'. *African Human Rights Law Journal* 17:340–66.

Kichwa case. 2012. Kichwa Indigenous People of Sarayaku v Ecuador, Merits and Preparations, Judgment, Inter-Am. Ct.H.H. (ser. C) No. 245 (June 27, 2012).

Kill the Boer appeal case. 2024. AfriForum v Economic Freedom Fighters and Others (1105/2022) [2024] ZASCA 82 (28 May 2024).

Kill the Boer case. 2011. Afriforum and Another v Malema and Another (20968/2010) [2011] ZAEQC 2; 2011 (6) SA 240 (EqC); [2011] 4 All SA 293 (EqC); 2011 (12) BCLR 1289 (EqC) (12 September 2011).

Kill the Boer case. 2022. Afriforum v Economic Freedom Fighters and Others 2022 (6) SA 357 (GJ) EQ 04/2020. Equality Court.

King case. 2021. King NO and Others v De Jager and Others [2021] ZACC 4.

Kiviorg, M. 2014. 'Collective Religious Autonomy versus Individual Rights: A Challenge for the ECtHR?' *Review of Central and East European Law* 39:315–41.

Klare, K. 1998. 'Legal Culture and Transformative Constitutionalism'. *South African Journal on Human Rights*, 146–88.

Klug, H. 2008. 'South Africa's Constitutional Court: Enabling Democracy and Promoting Law in the Transition from Apartheid'. *Journal of Comparative Law* 3:174–93.

Klug, H. 2010. *The Constitution of South Africa: A Contextual Analysis*. Oxford: Hart Publishing.

Kokkinakis case. 1993. Kokkinakis v Greece, ECtHR Appl. No. 14308/88, judgement of 25 May 1993.

Korkeakivi, A. 2018. 'Beyong Adhocism – Advancing Minority Rights through the United Nations'. In *The Framework Convention for the Protection of National Minorities: A Commentary*, edited by R. Hofmann, T.H. Malloy, and D. Rein, 22–48. Leiden: Brill.

Kosonen, K., and C. Young. 2009. 'Mother Tongue as a Bridge Language of Instruction: Policies and Experiences in SouthEast Asia'. Bangkok: World Bank.

Kotze, L.J., S. Adelman, and F. Dube. 2023. 'The Problem with Sustainable Development in the Anthropecene Epoch: Reimagining International Environmental Law's Mantra Principle Thorugh Ubuntu'. In *The Routledge Handbook of Law and the Anthropocene*, edited by P.D. Burdon and J. Martel, 3–17. Oxon: Routledge.

Kroeze, I.J. 2002. 'Doing Things with Values II: The Case of Ubuntu'. *Stellenbosch Law Review* 14:252–64.

Kryazhkov, V.A., and R.S. Garipov. 2021. 'ILO 169 Convention as a Vector for the Aboriginal Legislation Development in Russia'. *The International Journal of Human Rights* 25:1007–31.

Ktunaxa case. 2017. Ktunaxa Nation v British Columbia (Forests, Lands and Natural Resource Operations), (2017) SCC 54.

Kunz, J.L. 1954. 'The Present Status of the International Law in the Protection of Minorities'. *American Journal of International Law* 48:275–92.

Kuokkanen, R. 2011. 'Self-Determination and Indigenous Women – "Whose Voice It Is We Hear in the Sámi Parliament?" ' *International Journal on Minority and Group Rights* 18:39–62.

Kurnia, T.S., and N. Melatyugra. 2024. 'Universality of Rights as an Interpretive Principle for the Indonesian Constitutional Court'. *Constitutional Review* 10:474–504.

KwaZulu/Natal Certification. 1996. Certification of the Kwazulu-Natal Constitution (CCT15/96) [1996] ZACC 17; 1996 (11) BCLR 1419; 1996 (4) SA 1098 (6 September 1996).

Kymlicka, W. 1989. *Multicultural Citizenship: A Liberal Theory of Minority Rights*. London: Oxford University Press.

Kymlicka, W. 1995. *Multicultural Citizenship. A Liberal Theory of Minority Rights*. Oxford: Oxford University Press.

Kymlicka, W. 2008. 'The Internationalization of Minority Rights'. In *Constitutional Design for Divided Societies: Integration or Accommodation?*, edited by S. Choudhry, 94–115. Oxford: Oxford University Press.

Laerskool Middelburg case. 2003. Laerskool Middelburg v Departementshoof Mpumalanga Departement van Onderwys 2003 (4) SA 160 (T).

Lagerspetz, Mikko. 2014. 'Cultural Autonomy of National Minorities in Estonia: The Erosion of a Promise'. *Journal of Baltic Studies* 45 (4): 457–75.

Land Air Water Association case. 2001. Land Air Water Association vs Waikato Regional Council, Environment Court Decision No 110/01.

Larkin, S., and K. Butler. 2019. 'Aspirational, Not Binding'. In *Conversations about Indigenous Rights: The UN Declaration on the Rights of Indigenous People in Aotearoa New Zealand*, edited by S. Katene and R. Taonui, 93–102. Massey University Press.

Laroia, A. 2022. 'Amish Devgan vs Union of India'. *Jus Corpus Law Journal* 2:74–79.

Lars-Anders Ågren case. 2020. Lars-Anders Ågren et al. vs. Sweden, CERD/C/102/D/54/2013. CERD.

Larsen, P.B. 2020. 'Contextualising Ratification and Implementation: A Critical Appraisal of ILO Convention 169 from a Social Justice Perspective'. *The International Journal of Human Rights* 24:94–111.

Lautsi case. 2011. Lautsi & Others v Italy [2011] ECHR Application No 30814/06 (18 March 2011). ECtHR.

Law Society case. 2019. Law Society of South Africa and Others v President of the Republic of South Africa and Others 2019 (3) BCLR 329 (CC).

Le Cordeur, M. 2023. 'Oorvol Skole, NELA and Leesprobleme'. *Beeld*, 30 December 2023.

Lehtonen, M., and M. Kojo. 2020. 'The Roles of the State and Social Licence to Operate? Lessons from Nuclear Waste Management in Finland, France, and Sweden'. *Energy Researchand Social Science* 61. https://www.sciencedirect.com/science/article/pii/S221462961930297X.

Lenis case. 2023. Lenis v Greece ECtHR 240 (2023).

Lenzerini, F. 2022. 'Declaration on the Rights of Indigenous Peoples (UNDRIP)'. In *Elgar Encyclopedia of Human Rights*, edited by C. Binder, M. Nowak, J.A. Hofbauer, and P. Janig, 452–58. Cheltenham: Edward Elgar Publishing Limited.

Leonardy, U. 2003. 'Territorial Reform of the Länder: A Demand of the Basic Law'. In *German Public Policy and Federalism: Current Debates on Political, Legal, and Social Issues*, edited by B. Gunlicks, 65–90. New York: Bergbahn.

Letseka, M. 2012. 'In Defence of Ubuntu'. *Studies in Philosophy and Education* 31:47–60.

Lewis case. 1909. Lewis v Bankole, Supreme Court of Nigeria, 12/7/1909.

Leyla Sahin case. 2005. Leyla Sahin v Turkey App no 44774/98 (ECtHR, 10 November 2005).

Liberty Group case. 2019. Liberty Group Limited and Others v Mall Space Management CC t/a Mall Space Management (644/18) [2019] ZASCA 142; 2020 (1) SA 30 (SCA).

Lijphart, A. 1969. 'Consociational Democracy'. *World Politics* 21:207–25.

Lijphart, A. 1977. *Democracy in Plural Societies: A Comparative Exploration*. New York: Yale University Press.

Lijphart, A. 1998. 'South African Democracy: Majoritarian or Consociational?' *Democratization* 5:144–50.

Lilliendahl case. 2020. Lilliendahl v Izeland, App. 29297/18 (2020). ECtHR.

Linguistic Protection case. 1989. Linguistic Protection Committee v State of Karnataka AIR 1989 Kant 226.

Lissitzyn, O.J. 1951. *The International Court of Justice*. New York: Carnegie Foundation of International Peace.

Litina, A., and K. Papastathis. 2024. 'Islamophobia, Xenophobia and Religion in the European Union: A Quantative Analysis'. In *Islam, Religious Liberty and Constitutionalism in Europe*, edited by M. Hill and L. Papadopoulou, 257–72. Oxford: Hart Publishing.

Ljubljana Guidelines. 2012. 'The Ljubljana Guidelines on Integration of Diverse Societies'. OSCE.

Local Government Municipal Systems Act. 2000. *Local Government Municipal Systems Act 32 of 2000*. chrome-extension://efaidnbmnnnibpcajpcglclefindmkaj/https://www.gov.za/sites/default/files/gcis_document/201409/a32-000.pdf.

Lund Recommendations. 1999. 'The Lund Recommendations on the Effective Participation of National Minorities in Public Life'. The Hague: Organization for Security and Co-operation in Europe. https://www.osce.org/files/f/documents/0/9/32240.pdf.

Luts-Sootak, M., I. Kull, K. Sein, and H. Siimets-Gross. 2018. 'Legal Pluralsm Scrutinised'. In *Legal Pluralism – Cui Bono?*, edited by M. Luts-Sootak, I. Kull, K. Sein, and H. Siimets-Gross. Tartu: University of Tartu Press.

Mabena case. 1998. Mabena v Letsoalo 1998 (2) SA 1068 (T).

Mabo case (1). 1988. Mabo v Queensland (No 1) (1988) 166 CLR 186.

Mabo case (2). 1992. Mabo v Queensland (No 2) [1992] HCA 23, (1992) 175 CLR 1.

Mabuza case. 2002. Mabuza v Mbatha 2002 (4) SA 218 (C).

Macatė case. 2023. Case of Macatė v Lithuania, Application no. 61435/19, 2023.

Machnyikova, Z. 2005. 'Article 8'. In *The Rights of Minorities: A Commentary on the European Framework Convention for the Protection of National Minorities*, edited by M. Weller, 225–61. Oxford Commentaries on International Law. Oxford, New York: Oxford University Press.

MacInnes, A., M. Colchester, and A. Whitmore. 2017. 'Free, Prior and Informed Consent: How to Rectify the Devastating Consequences of Harmful Mining for Indigenous Peoples''. *Perspectives in Ecology and Conservation* 15:152–60.

Macioce, F. 2016. 'A Multifaceted Approach to Legal Pluralism and Ethno-Central Diversity'. *The Journal of Legal Pluralism and Unofficial Law* 48:1–16.

Mackay, F. 2022. *A Compilation of UN Treaty Body Jurisprudence, Special Procedures of the Human Rights Council, and the Advice of the Expert Mechanism on the Rights of Indigenous Peoples Volume IX.* Indigenous Peoples Rights International.

Macklem, P. 2006. 'Militant Democracy, Legal Pluralism, and the Paradox of Self-Determination'. *International Journal of Constitutional Law* 4:488–516.

Macnab, A. 2020. 'Indigenous Law Expert Explains How UNDRIP Advances the Law of Consultation and Consent'. *Canadian Lawyer.* https://www.canadianlawyermag.com/practice-areas/indigenous/indigenous-law-expert-explains-how-undrip-advances-the-law-of-consultation-and-consent/330496.

Magaya case. 1999. Magaya v Magaya 1999 (1) ZLR 100 (SC).

Magazzini, T. 2024. 'When Ethnicity Is "National": Mapping Ethnic Minorities in Europe's Framework Convention for the Protection of National Minorities'. *Ethnic and Racial Studies* 47:1812–33.

Maharaj, M. 2008. 'The ANC and South Africa's Negotiated Transition to Democracy and Peace'. Berlin: Berghof Research Center for Constructive Conflict Management. file:///C:/Users/devillib/Downloads/transitions_anc.pdf.

Maharjan, S.K., J. Carling, and L. Sherpa. 2012. *Training Manual on Free, Prior and Informed Consent (FPIC) in REDD+ for Indigenous Peoples.* Chiang Mai: IWGIA. https://www.iwgia.org/images/publications/0593_FPIC-Manual-eb.pdf.

Mahe case. 1990. Mahe v Alberta [1990] 1 SCR 342.

Mahlangu and Another v Minister of Labour and Others (CCT306/19) [2020] ZACC 24 (19 November 2020) (Mahlangu case 2020)

Mahuika case. 2000. Mahuika v NZL (Human Rights Committee, UN doc CCPR/C/70/D/547/1993, 16 November 2000). UNHRC.

Maimela, C.A., and N.L. Morudu. 2024. 'Cherishing Customary Law: The Disparity Between Legislative and Judicial Interpretation of Customary Marriages in South Africa'. *Obiter* 45:400–417.

Maisela case. 2000. Maisela v Kgolane 2000 (2) SA 370 (T).

Makate case. 2016. Makate v Vodacom (Pty) Ltd 2016 (6) BCLR 709 (CC).

Makholiso case. 1997. Makholiso and Others v Makholiso and Others 1997 (4) SA 509 (Tk).

Makwanyane case. 1995. S v Makwanyane 1995 (3) SA 391 (CC).

Malan, K. 2014. 'The Suitability and Unsuitability of Ubuntu in Constitutional Law: Intercommunal Relations versus Public Office-Bearing'. *De Jure* 47:232–46.

Malan, K. 2023. 'The Disintegration of the South African Order'. *Politicsweb*, 7 January 2023. https://www.politicsweb.co.za/opinion/the-disintegration-of-the-south-african-order.

Maledu case. 2018. Maledu v Itereleng Bakgatla Mineral Resources (Pty) Limited (CCT265/17) [2018] ZACC 41; 2019 (1) BCLR 53 (CC); 2019 (2) SA 1 (CC) (25 October 2018).

Malepe, W.O., and K.O. Odeku. 2023. 'Perspectives on the Recognition of Male and Female Primogeniture in Post-1994 Democratic South Africa'. *African Journal of Gender, Society and Development* 12.

Malherbe, R. 1995. 'Die Onderwysbepalings van die 1993 Grondwet'. *TSAR*, 1–25.

Malherbe, R. 2000. 'A Fresh Start: Education Rights in South Africa'. *European Journal for Education Law and Policy* 4:49–55.

Malherbe, R. 2004. 'The Constitutional Framework for Pursuing Equal Opportunities in Education'. *Perspectives in Education* 22:9–28.

Malloy, T., A. Osipov, and B. Vizi, eds. 2015. *Managing Diversity through Non-Territorial Autonomy: Assessing Advantages, Deficiencies, and Risks*. London: Oxford University Press.

Malloy, T., and L. Salat, eds. 2021. *Non-Territorial Autonomy and Decentralization: Ethno-Cultural Diversity*. New York: Routledge.

Malloy, T.H. 2018. 'Commentary of Article 10 of the Framework Convention for the Protection of National Minorities'. In *The Framework Convention for the Protection of National Minorities: A Commentary*, edited by R. Hofmann, T.H. Malloy, and D. Rein, 205–19. Leiden: Brill.

Malloy, T.H. 2020. 'Non-Territorial Autonomy: Traditional and Alternative Practices'. In *Effective Participation of National Minorities and Conflict Prevention*, edited by W. Romans, I. Ulasiuk, and A.P. Thomsen, 105–22. Leiden: Brill.

Malloy, T.H. 2022. 'Territorial or Non-Territorial Autonomy'. In *The Routledge Handbook of Comparative Territorial Autonomies*, edited by B.C.H. Fong and A. Ichijo, 48–66. London: Routledge.

Malloy, T.H., and U. Caruso, eds. 2013. *Minorities, Their Rights, and the Monitoring of the European Framework Convention for the Protection of National Minorities: Essays in Honour of Rainer Hofmann*. Leiden: Marthinus Nijjhof.

Mancini, S. 2020. 'Introduction: Constitutionalism and Religion in the Age of Consolidaiton and Turmoil'. In *Constitutions and Religion*, edited by S. Mancini, 1–21. Cheltenham: Edward Elgar Publishing Limited.

Maneli case. 2010. Maneli v Maneli 2010 (7) BCLR 703 (GSJ).

Mangena, F. 2020. 'Hunhu/Ubuntu in the Traditional Thought of Southern Africa'. *Internet Encyclopedia of Philosophy*. https://www.iep.utm.edu/hunhu/.

Manthwa, A. 2023. 'The Infusion of African Jurisprudence on Legal Defences into Judicial Deliberations'. *Obiter* 44:661–70.

March, A.F. 2020. 'The Theoretical Framework of Modern Islamic Constitutionalism'. In *Constitutions and Religion*, edited by S. Mancini, 59–74. Cheltenham: Edward Elgar Publishing Limited.

Marglin, J., and M. Letteney. 2024. 'Legal Pluralism as a Category of Analysis'. *Law and History Review* 42:143–53.

Maria Alekhina case. 2018. Maria Alekhina and Others v Russia App. No. 38004/12. ECtHR.

Marin, A.A., T. Inatani, and M. Infantino. 2021. 'Comparative Law and Epistemologies of Ignorance in Chilean Constitutional Adjudication'. In *Decolonizing Law: Indigenous, Third World and Settler Perspectives*, edited by S. Xavier, B. Jacobs, J. Hewitt, and A. Bhatia, 181–95. Oxon: Routledge.

Marine Produce case. 2018. Marine Produce Australia Ltd and Western Australia v Mayala People [2018] NNTTA 28.

Marko, J. 2022a. 'Introduction'. In *Religious Diversity, State, and Law*, edited by J. Marko, M. Lakitsch, F. Winter, W. Weirer, and K. Wonisch, 1–20. Leiden: Brill.

Marko, J. 2022b. 'Is a Comparative History of Western and Islamic Political Thought Possible?' In *Religious Diversity, State, and Law*, edited by J. Marko, M. Lakitsch, F. Winter, W. Weirer, and K. Wonisch, 173–202. Leiden: Brill.

Maron, G. 2023. 'Legal Prohibition of Hate Speech in Jurisprudential Practice – between Judicial Discretion and Arbitrariness'. *Consilium Iuridicum* 8:48–74.

Marsal, S., and F. Palermo. 2018. 'Commentary on Article 3 of the Framework Convention for the Protection of National Minorities'. In *The Framework Convention for the Protection of National Minorities: A Commentary*, edited by R. Hofmann, T.H. Malloy, and D. Rein, 92–110. Leiden: Brill.

Martinez-Sanz, R., and P. Durantez-Stolle. 2024. 'Memes as Hate Speech'. *Visual Review* 16:1–16.

Martínez-Torrón, J. 2024. 'Hate Speech, Offences to Religion, and Public Morals in Strasbourg Case Law'. In *Fundamental Rights, Religion and Human Dignity: A Constitutional Journey*, edited by J. Martínez-Torrón and L. Thio, 129–64. London: Routledge.

Maseko, P. 2023. 'Recognising the Importance of Mother Tongue Education'. *The Herald*, 24 February 2023. https://news.mandela.ac.za/Opinion-pieces/Opinion-pieces-archive/Recognising-the-importance-of-mother-tongue-educat.

Massyn, J. 2022. 'The Maledu and Baleni Cases' Impact on Customary Communities' Vulnerability to Expropriation'. LLM, Cape Town: University of Cape Town.

Masupha case. 2013. Masupha v The Senior Resident Magistrate for the Subordinate Court of Berea and Others Lesotho Court of Appeal (CIV) 29/2013.

MAT Procedure Rules. 2015. 'Procedure Rules of Muslim Arbitration Tribunal'. Muslim Arbitration Tribunal. http://www.matribunal.com/rules.php#:~:text=The%20Procedural%20Rules%20which%20regulate,practice%20in%20England%20or%20Wales.

Matal case. 2017. Matal, Interim Director, United States Patent and Trademark Office v Tam 582 U. S. (2017). US.

Mathieu-Bedard, R. 2017. 'Non-Territorial Indigenous Self-Governance in Canada and the United States'. ECMI Working Paper #97. Flensburg: ECMI.

Matukane case. 1996. Matukane and others v Laerskool Potgietersrus [1996] 1 All SA 468 (T).

Maya Peoples case. 2021. Indigenous Maya Kaqchikel Peoples of Sumpango vs. Guatemala.

Maya Village case. 2007. Manuek Coy, Maya Village of Conejo v Attorney General of Belize, Supreme Court, 18 October 2007. SC.

Mayelane case. 2013. Mayelane v Ngwenyama 2013 (4) SA 415 (CC).

Maziwisa, M.R. 2022. 'The Politics of Language in Post-Apartheid South Africa'. Ottowa: Forum of Federations.

M'Bala case. 2015. M'Bala M'Bala v France ECtHR 354 (2015).

McCorquodale, R. 2022. 'Collective and Group Rights'. In *Elgar Encyclopedia of Human Rights*, edited by C. Binder, M. Nowak, J.A. Hofbauer, and P. Janig, 279–85. Cheltenham: Edward Elgar Publishing Limited.

McCreery, R. 2012. 'Promoting Indigenous-Led Economic Development: Why Parties Should Consult the UNDRIP'. *Indigenous Law Bulletin* 8:16–19.

McCrudden, C., and B. O'Leary. 2013. *Courts and Consociations*. Oxford: Oxford University Press.

McGoldrick, D. 2009. 'Accommodating Muslims in Europe: From Adopting Sharia Law to Religiously Based Opt Outs from Generally Applicable Laws'. *Human Rights Law Review* 9:603–45.

McKerracher, K. 2023. 'Relational Legal Pluralism and Indigenous Legal Orders in Canada'. *Global Constitutionalism*, 133–53.

MEC for Education case. 2007. MEC for Education: Kwazulu-Natal v Pillay 2008 (1) SA 474 (CC).

Medda-Windischer, R., C. Boutler, and T. Malloy, eds. 2020. *Extending Protection to Migrant Populations in Europe: Old and New Minorities*. New York: Routledge.

Medeiros, E., ed. 2018. *European Territorial Cooperation Theoretical and Empirical Approaches to the Process and Impacts of Cross-Border and Transnational Cooperation in Europe*. Cham: Springer.

Meel, B.L. 2010. 'Traditional Male Circumcision-Related Fatalities in the Mthatha Area of South Africa'. *Medicine, Science and the Law* 50:189–91.

Mensi, A. 2022. 'The South Africa High Court Baleni Judgment: Towards an Indigenous Right to Consent?' *African Human Rights Yearbook* 6:375–94. http://dx.doi.org/10.29053/2523-1367/2022/v6a17.

Metz, T. 2019. 'Reconciliation as the Aim of a Criminal Trial: Ubuntu's Implications for Sentencing'. *Constitutional Court Review* 9:113–34.

Meyer, Y. 2020. 'Baleni v Minister of Mineral Resources 2019 (2) SA 453 (GP): Paving the Way for Formal Protection of Informal Land Rights'. *PER/PELJ* 23:1–18.

Mhango, M. 2012. 'Recognising Religion: Emerging Jurisprudence in South Africa'. *Journal for the Study of Religion* 25:23–50.

Mhlungu case. 1995. S v Mhlungu 1995 (7) BCLR 793 (CC).

Michaela Community case. 2024. The King on the application of Ttt, by her mother and litigation friend Uuu) v Michaela Community Schools Trust v London Borough of Brent [2024] EWHC 843 (Admin), 2024 WL 01639385.

Mikisew Cree case. 2005. Mikisew Cree First Nation v Canada (Minister of Canadian Heritage), [2005] 3 SCR 388, 2005 SCC 69.

Mikro Primary School case. 2006. Minister of Education, Western Cape v Governing Body, Mikro Primary School 2006 (1) SA 1 (SCA).

Milirrpum case. 1971. Milirrpum v Nabalco Pty Ltd (1971) 17 FLR 141 (27 April 1971) Supreme Court (NT).

Military Service case. 2005. Movement for Quality of Government v Knesset HC 6427/02 (12 Dec 2005).

Mineral and Petroleum Act. 2002. *Mineral and Petroleum Resources Development Act 28 of 2002*.

Minority Rights Group. 1994. 'Education Rights and Minorities'. Florence: UNICEF.

Minority Treaty. 1919. 'Treaty of Peace between The United States of America, The British Empire, France, Italy , Japan, and Poland Signed at Versailles on June 28th, 1919'. chrome-extension://efaidnbmnnnibpcajpcglclefindmkaj/http://www.forost.ungarisches-institut.de/pdf/19190628-3.pdf.

Mitchell, T., C. Arseneau, J. Aylwin, and D. Thomas. 2021. 'The Right to Free, Prior and Informed Consent (FPIC): Reflections on Experiences of Two Indigenous Communities in Northern Regions of Canada and Chile'. In Decolonizing law: indigenous, third world and settler perspectives, edited by S. Xavier, B. Jacobs, V. Waboose, J. Hewitt, and A. Bhatia, 215–36. London: Routledge.

Mkhize, D., and R. Balfour. 2017. 'Language Rights in Education in South Africa'. *South African Journal of Higher Education* 31. https://www.journals.ac.za/index.php/sajhe/article/view/1633.

Mlambo, D. 2022. 'Transformative Social Change and the Role of the Judge in Postapartheid South Africa'. *Stellenbosch Law Review* 33:595–618.

MM case. 2019. MM v MM [2019] ZAWCHC 158.

Modiri, J. 2024. 'Narrating Constitutional Dis/Order in Post-1994 South Africa: A Critical Response to Theunis Roux'. *VRÜ Verfassung Und Recht in Übersee* 57:82–97.

Modood, T. 2007. *Multiculturalism. A Civic Idea.* Cambridge: Polity Press.

Mogale case. 2023. Mogale and Others v Speaker of the National Assembly and Others [2023] ZACC 14.

Mohamed case. 2020. Mohamed and Others v President of the Republic of South Africa and Others (21402/20) [2020] ZAGPPHC 120; [2020] 2 All SA 844 (GP); 2020 (7) BCLR 865 (GP); 2020 (5) SA 553 (GP) (30 April 2020).

Mohanty, A. 2023. 'Linguistic Human Rights in Education in India: Odisha's Partial Success Story'. In *The Handbook of Linguistic Human Rights*, edited by T. Skutnabb-Kangas and R. Phillipson, 561–75. Hoboken: John Wiley.

Mokgoro, Y. 1998. 'Ubuntu and the Law in South Africa'. *Potchefstroom Electronic Law Journal* 8:1–11.

Mokgoro, Y. 2011. 'Ubuntu as a Legal Principle in an Ever-Changing World'. In *Ubuntu: Good Faith and Equity*, edited by F. Diedrich, 1–2. Cape Town: Juta.

Mokgoro, Y. 2012. 'uBuntu and the Law in South Africa'. In *uBuntu and the Law: African Ideals and Postapartheid Jurisprudence*, edited by D. Cornell and N. Mavangua, 333–45. New York: Fordham University Press.

Mokwena, L. 2024. *Orania: Post-Apartheid South Africa's Bogeyman?* Cape Town: UWC Press.

Moleya, N.I. 2023. 'Reflecting on the Tension between the Development of the Common Law and the Doctrine of Separation of Powers in Paulsen v Slip Knot Investments 777 (Pty) Ltd'. *South African Law Journal* 140:170–96.

Molla Sali case. 2020. Molla Sali v Greece (Application no. 20452/14). ECtHR.

Molos, D.J. 2013. 'Underappreciated Resource or Inadequate Measure? Minority Protection under Article 27 of the International Covenant on Civil and Political

Rights'. Canada: Queen's University. https://search-proquest-com.dbgw.lis.curtin.edu.au/docview/1886371914?pq-origsite=primo.

Moon, R. 2022. 'Does Freedom of Expression Have a Future?' In *Dilemmas of Free Expression*, edited by E. Macfarlane, 15–34. Toronto: University of Toronto Press.

Moosa case. 2018. Moosa N.O. and Others v Minister of Justice and Correctional Services and Others [2018] ZACC 19; 2018 JDR 0915 (CC); 2018 (5) SA 13 (CC).

Moosa, N. 2002. 'Promoting Minority Rights in the Context of Economic, Social and Cultural Rights in South Africa'. *Codicillus* 43:37–51.

Morrow, W. 2007. *Learning to Teach in South Africa*. Pretoria: HSRC Press.

Moseneke case. 2001. Moseneke and Others v The Master and Another 2001 (2) SA 18 (CC); 2001 (2) BCLR 103 (CC).

Motaung case. 1930. Motaung v Philemon Dube 1930 BAH (N&T).

Motshekga, A. 2023a. 'Language Policy Conference'. July 21. https://www.gov.za/news/speeches/minister-angie-motshekga-language-policy-conference-27-jul-2023#:~:text=Out%20of%20approximately%2023%2C719%20public,standards%20of%20teaching%20and%20learning.

Motshekga, A. 2023b. 'South Africa Moves to Mother Tongue Education'. *Language Magazine*, 23 July 2023.

Mthembu case. 1997. Mthembu v Letsela 1997 (2) SA 690 (C).

Mubangizi, J.C. 2008. 'Protecting Human Rights amidst Poverty and Inequality: The South African Post-Apartheid Experience on the Right of Access to Housing'. *African Journal of Legal Studies* 2:130–46.

Mubecua, M., and I.S. Nojiyza. 2022. 'The Dichotomy of Land Laws in South Africa: The Challenges Faced by Women in Accessing Land'. *African Journal of Gender, Society and Development* 11.

Mugumbate, J.R. 2024. 'Understanding Ubuntu and Its Contribution to Social Work Education in Africa and Other Regions of the World'. *Social Work Education* 4:1123–39.

Mugumbate, J.R., and A. Nyanguru. 2013. 'Exploring African Philosophy: The Value of Ubuntu in Social Work'. *African Journal of Social Work* 3:82–100.

Mujib, J. 2023. 'The Evolutive Interpretation of the African Charter on Human and Peoples'

Mukaddam, F. 2024. *Muslim Women between Community and Individual Rights: Legal Pluralism and Marriage in South Africa*. Cham: Springer.

Mukheibir, A. 2022. 'Ubuntu and the Amende Honorable – A Marriage Between African Values and Medieval Canon Law'. *Obiter* 28:583–89. https://doi.org/10.17159/obiter.v28i3.13795.

Mukindia Kimuru case. 2000. Mukindia Kimuru and Another v Margaret Kanario (2000) JELR 104109 (CA).

Mukwevho, N. 2022. 'The Evolution and Development of the Principle of Free, Prior and Informed Consent in South Africa'. *South African Journal on Human Rights* 38:144–62.

Munkara case. 2024. Munkara v Santos NA Barossa Pty Ltd (No 3) [2024] FCA 9.

Munkara consent orders cost. 2024. Simon Munkara and others v Santos NA Barossa Pty Ltd VID907/2023 (28 November 2024).

Munyani, A., and M.R. Phooko. 2021. 'Is English Becoming a Threat to the Existence of Indigenous Languages in Institutions of Higher Learning in South Africa?' *Dejure Law Journal*, 298–327.

Munzert, S., R. Traunmuller, P. Barbera, A. Guess, and J. Yang. 2020. 'Citizens' Preferences for Online Hate Speech Regulation in the United States and Germany'. 13 June 2020. https://simonmunzert.com/meof/material/munzert-et-al-citizen-preferences-epsa.pdf.

Murauskas, D. 2023. 'Non-Compliance with the European Court of Human Rights Judgments'. In *Law, Culture and Identity in Central and Eastern Europe*, edited by C Cercel, A. Mercescu, and M. Sadowski. London: Routledge.

Muslims of Belgium case. 2022. Executief van de Moslims van België and Others v Belgium – 16760/22, 16849/22, 16850/22 et al. Judgment 13.2.2024 [Section II].

Mwipikeni, P. 2018. 'Ubuntu and the Modern Society'. *South African Journal of Philosophy* 37:322–34.

Nafstad, I. 2018. 'Roma Law, National Minority Rights and Equality before the Law in Norwegian and Swedish Courts'. *Justice, Power and Resistance* 2:96–116.

Nagy, N., and B. Vizi. 2024. 'Conceptualisation and Operationalisation of Minorities in International Law: Past Experiences and New Avenues'. *Hungarian Journal of Legal Studies*, 2–27. https://doi.org/10.1556/2052.2024.00546.

Nahimana case. 2007. Nashimana et al. v Prosecutor, Judgement, Case No. ICTR-99-52-A, 28 November 2007.

National Environmental Act. 1998. *National Environmental Management Act 107 of 1998*. chrome-extension://efaidnbmnnnibpcajpcglclefindmkaj/https://www.gov.za/sites/default/files/gcis_document/201409/a107-98.pdf.

National Native Title Tribunal. 2020. 'What Is the Right to Negotiate?' NNTT. http://www.nntt.gov.au/futureacts/Pages/Negotiation.aspx#:~:text=The%20right%20to%20negotiate%20is,future%20acts%20are%20lawfully%20done.&text=The%20right%20to%20negotiate%20gives,reaching%20agreement%20about%20the%20act.

National Union of Metalworkers case. 2019. National Union of Metalworkers of South Africa obo Nganezi and others v Dunlop Mixing and Technical Services (Pty) Limited and others (Casual Workers Advice Office as amicus curiae) 2019 (8) BCLR 966 (C).

Native Title Act. 1993. *National Native Title Act, 1993.* https://www.legislation.gov.au/Details/C2019C00054.

Native Title Map. 2024. 'Native Title Determinations and Claimant Applications'. NNTT. https://digital-classroom.nma.gov.au/images/national-native-title-tribunal-map-australia.

Naude, P. 2019. 'Decolonising Knowledge: Can Ubuntu Ethics Save Us from Coloniality?' *Journal of Business Ethics* 159:23–37.

Ndeunyema, N. 2021. *Re-Invigorating Ubuntu Through Water: A Human Right to Water under the Namibian Constitution.* Pretoria: Pretoria University Law Press.

Ndulo, M. 2021. 'International and Foreign Law in Domestic Constitutional Law: A Comparative Examination of the Practice in United States and Post-Conflict Countries'. In *Constitutionalism: Old Dilemmas, New Insights*, edited by A. Linares-Cantillo, C. Valdivieso-León, and S. García-Jaramillo. Oxford: Oxford Academic.

Needham, R. 1975. 'Polythetic Classification: Convergence and Consequences'. *Man* 10:349–69.

Nemeiksis, G. 2024. 'The Challenges in Application of Criminal Liability for the Spread of Hate Speech'. *Public Security and Public Order* 35:195–207.

Neo, J.L. 2020. 'State Legal Pluralism and Religious Courts'. In *The Oxford Handbook of Global Legal Pluralism*, edited by P.S. Berman, 879–900. Oxford: Oxford University Press.

Netshitomboni, S. 1998. 'Ubuntu: Fundamental Constitutional Value and Interpretive Aid'. Masters of Laws, Pretoria: University of South Africa.

Newman, D. 2023. 'Minority Rights Implications of Changing State Engagement with Religion'. In *Minority Rights and Liberal Democratic Insecurities*, edited by A. Biro and D. Newman, 156–68. New York: Routledge.

Ngadju case. 2013. WA v Graham (Ngadju People) [2013] FCAFC 143.

Ngobese, D. 2023. 'Apartheid Flag Politics in Democratic South Africa: A Case of Ncome and Blood River Museums'. *African Journal of Peace and Conflict Studies.* doi: 10.31920/2634-3665/2023/v12n2a3

Ngqobela case. 1893. Ngqobela v Sihele 10 SC 346 (1893).

Ngurrajuta Local Decision Making Agreement. 2024. 'Ngurrajuta Pmara/Ntjarra Local Decision Making (LDM) Agreement, Northern Territory Government'. The Chief Minister and Cabinet.

Nhlapo, T. 2017. 'Customary Law in Post-Apartheid South Africa: Constitutional Confrontations in Culture, Gender and "Living Law" '. *South African Journal on Human Rights* 33:1–24.

Nimni, E. 2007. 'Nationalist Multiculturalism in Late Imperial Austria as a Critique of Contemporary Liberalism: The Case of Bauer and Renner'. *Journal of Political Ideologies* 4:289–314.

Nishanthi, R. 2020. 'Understanding of the Importance of Mother Tongue Learning'. *International Journal of Trend in Scientific Research and Development* 5. chrome-extension://efaidnbmnnnibpcajpcglclefindmkaj/https://www.researchgate.net/profile/Rajathurai-Nishanthi-2/publication/345436020_Understanding_of_the_Importance_of_Mother_Tongue_Learning/links/5fa6aa3692851cc2869cfebd/Understanding-of-the-Importance-of-Mother-Tongue-Learning.pdf.

Nix case. 2018. Nix v Germany ECHR 131 (2018).

Nkondo, G.M. 2007. 'Ubuntu as Public Policy in South Africa: A Conceptual Framework'. *International Journal of African Renaissance Studies* 2:88–100.

Nkosi case. 2008. Nkosi v Vermark NO and Another 77/2007 [2008] ZAKZHC 83 (30 Sep).

Noken case. 2009. Constitutional Court No 47-18 / PHPU.A / VII / 2009. Constitutional Court.

Noongar Package. 2017. 'South West Native Title Settlement Package'. https://www.wa.gov.au/organisation/department-of-the-premier-and-cabinet/south-west-native-title-settlement#:~:text=South%20West%20Native%20Title%20Settlement%20Package,-Show%20more&text=The%20Settlement%20package%20is%20a,partnership%20with%20the%20WA%20Government.

Nortje case. 1995. Nortje v Attorney-General of the Cape 1995 (2) SA 460 (C).

Norval, A.J. 1998. 'Reinventing the Politics of Cultural Recognition: The Freedom Front and the Demand for a Volkstaat'. In *South Africa in Transition*, edited by D.R. Howarth and A.J. Norval, 93–110. London: Palgrave Macmillan.

Ntlama, N. 2019. 'The Centrality of Customary Law in the Judicial Resolution of Disputes That Emanate from It – Dalisile v Mgoduka (5056/2018) [2018] ZAECMHC'. *Obiter* 40:202–13.

Nyamakazi case. 1992. Nyamakazi v President of Bophuthatswana 1992 (4) SA 540 (B).

Observatory Civic Association case. 2023. Observatory Civic Association and another v Trustees, Liesbeek Leisure Properties Trust and others 2023 (1) SA 583??? (WCC).

Occupiers of Erven case. 2017. Occupiers of Erven 87 and 88 Berea v De Wet NO and Another (Poor Flat Dwellers Association as amicus curiae) 2017 (8) BCLR 1015 (CC).

Odendaal, A. 2023. *Dear Comrade President: Oliver Tambo and the Foundations of South Africa's Constitution.* Cape Town: Pengiun.

OECD Guidelines. 2023. 'OECD Guidelines for Multinational Enterprises on Responsible Business Conduct (2023, OECD Publishing)'. https://api.research-repository.uwa.edu.au/ws/portalfiles/portal/336910632/southalan_2023_increasing.pdf.

OECD Guidelines 2011. 2011. 'Human Rights and Transnational Corporations and Other Business Enterprises' (6 July 2011) UN Doc A/HRC/RES/17/4." '

O'Faircheallaigh, C. 2016. *Negotiations in the Indigenous World, Aboriginal Peoples and the Extractive Industry in Australia and Canada.* London: Routledge.

O'Faircheallaigh, C. 2021. 'Negotiated Agreements, Indigenous FPIC, and Mine Life Cycle'. In *Indigenous-Industry Agreements, Natural Resources and the Law,* edited by T. Odumosu-Ayanu and D. Newman, 63–78. London: Routledge.

Ogunde, J., ed. 2019. *Ubuntu and the Reconstituting of Community.* Indiana: Indiana University Press.

Ojogbo, S.E., and O.K. Edu. 2022. 'Comparing Maintenance and Property Rights in Marriage under Customary Law and Statutory Law in Africa'. *Oxford University Commonwealth Law Journal* 22:229–52.

Okonkwo case. 1994. Okonkwo v Okagbue [1994] 9 NWLR (pt 368) 301 (SNC).

Old Flag appeal case. 2023. Afriforum NPC v Nelson Mandela Foundation Trust and Others (Case no 371/2020) [2023] ZASCA 58 (21 April 2023). Supreme Court of Appeal.

Old Flag case. 2019. Nelson Mandela Foundation Trust and Another v Afriforum NPC and Others (EQ02/2018) [2019] ZAEQC 2; [2019] 4 All SA 237 (EqC); 2019 (10) BCLR 1245 (EqC) ; 2019 (6) SA 327 (GJ) (21 August 2019). Equality Court.

Oliva, J.G., and H. Hall. 2022. 'Religious Footprints in Secular Sand – the Imprint of Religious Culture in Civil Law'. In *Religious Freedom in Secular States,* edited by J.H. Bhuiyan and A. Black, 125–46. Leiden: Brill.

Oninku, E.A. 2024. 'A Review of the Decision of the Constitutional Court of South Africa in the Shilubana Case: Lessons for the Development of Customary Law in Ghana'. *Comparative and International Law Journal of Southern Africa* 57:1–24.

Orissa Mining case. 2013. Orissa Mining Corporation v Ministry of Environment and Forest and Others. Supreme Court.

Ormaza, M. 2017. *The Requirement of Consultation with Indigenous Peoples in the ILO.* Leiden: Brill.

Osipov, A. 2015. 'Non-Territorial Autonomy in the Post-Soviet Space'. In *Managing Diversity through Non-Territorial Autonomy: Assessing Advantages, Deficiencies, and Risks,* edited by T. Malloy, A. Osipov, and B. Vizi, 208–29. London: Oxford University Press.

OSJI Report. 2022. 'Restrictions on Muslim Women's Dress in the 27 EU Member States and the United Kingdom'. Open Society Justice Initiative.

Osman, F. 2019. 'The Ascertainment of Living Customary Law: An Analysis of the South African Constitutional Court's Jurisprudence'. *The Journal of Legal Pluralism and Unofficial Law* 51:98–113.

Osman, F. 2023. 'The Reform of Customary Law of Succession Act in Contemporary South Africa'. *Acta Juridica.*

Osman, F., and M. Baase. 2022. 'The Recognition of Same-Sex Marriages under South African Customary Law'. *South African Journal on Human Rights* 38:1–23.

Osman, F., and C. Himonga. 2017. 'The Constitutionality of Section 7(1) of the Recognition of Customary Marraiges Act: Ramuhovhi v President of the Republic of South Africa'. *The Journal of Legal Pluralism and Unofficial Law* 49:166–82.

Osman-Hyder, M. 2022. 'Termination of Muslim Marriages in the South African Legal Context: Understanding the Challenges'. *Stellenbosch Law Review* 33.

Osmanoğlu case. 2017. Osmanoğlu and Kocabaş v Switzerland (Application no. 29086/12). ECtHR.

O'Sullivan, D. 2022. 'Fiji and the UN Declaration on the Rights of Indigenous Peoples: Indigeneity and the Right to Self-Determination in a Majority-Indigenous Context'. In *Research Handbook on the International Law of Indigenous Rights*, edited by D. Newman, 397–412. Cheltenham: Elgar.

Otto Preminger case. 1994. Otto Preminger Institut v Austria, application 13470/87 judgment 20 September 1994.

Oyewunmi case. 1990. Oyewunmi and Another v Ogunesan (1990) 3 NWLR (part 137) 207E–F.

Oyowe, A.O. 2013. 'Strange Bedfellows: Rethinking Ubuntu and Human Rights in South Africa'. *African Human Rights Law Journal* 13:103–24.

Ozoemena, R., G. Wara, and K. Ramarumo. 2024. 'Balancing Customary Practices and Human Rights in the Proposed Single Marriage Bill'. In *Reimagining Legal Pluralism in Africa: Balancing Indigenous, State, and Religious Laws*, edited by A. Diala and C. Rautenbach, 93–120. Leiden: Brill.

Palermo, F., and S. Constantin. 2021. 'Litigating Linguistic Rights of National Minorities in Central, Eastern and South-Eastern Europe'. In *Litigating the Rights of Minorities and Indigenous Peoples in Domestic and International Courts*, edited by B. De Villiers, J. Marko, F. Palermo, and S. Constantin, 179–218. Leiden: Brill.

Panzano, G. 2018. 'Ethnic Dominaiton in Deeply Divided Places: The Hegemonic State in Israel and Estonia'. Corso di Laurea Magistrale, Firenze. https://www.academia.edu/39847246/ETHNIC_DOMINATION_IN_DEEPLY_DIVIDED_PLACES_THE_HEGEMONIC_STATE_IN_ISRAEL_AND_ESTONIA?email_work_card=view-paper.

Papillon, M., J. Leclair, and D. Leydet. 2020. 'Free, Prior and Informed Consent: Between Legal Ambiguity and Political Agency'. *International Journal on Minority and Group Rights* 20:223–32.

Paradise Park case. 2023. Residents of Paradise Park v Magna Business Services (Pty) Ltd and another 2024 JDR 0141 (WCC).

Pascale, G., and S. Tonolo. 2022. 'The Vienna Convention on the Law of Treaties: An Introduction'. In *The Vienna Conventon on the Law of Treaties*, edited by G. Pascale and S. Tonolo, 1–20. Napoli: Edizioni Scientifiche Italiane.

Pastor, E.R. 2019. 'Recognizing Religious Minority Rights – A Key Tool to Managing Pluralism in the European Court of Human Rights'. *European Yearbook of Minority Issues* 18:3–32.

Pastörs case. 2019. Pastörs v Germany ECHR 331 (2019).

Paterson, A. 2022. 'Protected Areas, Community Rights and Affirmative Action: The Plight of Uganda's Batwa People'. *African Human Rights Law Journal* 22:290–318.

Pavel, C.E. 2021. *Law Beyond the State*. Oxford: Oxford University Press.

PCIJ-Greco-Bulgarian case. 1930. Greco-Bulgarian 'Communities'. Permanent Court of International Justice.

Perinçek case. 2015. Perinçek v Switzerland App no 27510/08 (ECHR, 15 October 2015). ECtHR.

Pesurnay, A.J. 2018. 'Pancasila Ideology as A Field of Interpretation'. *Social Sciences and Humanities* 1:161–70.

Petane case. 1988. State v Petane, Supreme Court decision, 1988 (3) SA 51 (C), ILDC 1348 (ZA 1987), 3rd November 1987, South Africa; Supreme Court of Appeal [SCA]. Supreme Court of Appeal.

Phillips, A. 2015. 'Historical Background on the Declaration'. In *The United Nations Declaration on Minorities: An Academic Account on the Occasion of Its 20th Anniversary (1992–2012)*, edited by U. Caruso and R. Hofmann, 3–18. Leiden: Brill.

Phillips, T. 2005. 'Britain "sleepwalking to Segregation" | Race | The Guardian'. *The Guardian*, 19 September 2005. https://www.theguardian.com/world/2005/sep/19/race.socialexclusion.

Pieterse-Robertson, D. 2019. 'The Implications of the Traditional Khoisan Leadership Bill of 2025'. Online and amend to 'Bill of 2019'.

Pirie, F. 2023. 'Beyond Pluralism: A Descriptive Approach to Non-State Law'. *Jurisprudence* 14:1–21.

Planitex case. 2006. Platinex v Kitchenuhmaykoosib Inninuwug First Nation (2006), 272 DLR (4th) 727 (Ontario SCJ).

Polavarapu, A. 2023. 'Myth-Busting Restorative Justice: Uncovering the Past and Finding Lessons in Community'. *UC Irvine Law Review* 13:949–92.

Poleshchuk, V. 2015. 'Russian National Cultural Autonomy in Estonia'. In *Managing Diversity through Non-Territorial Autonomy: Assessing Advantages, Deficiencies, and Risks*, edited by T. Malloy, A. Osipov, and B. Vizi, 230–49. London: Oxford University Press.

Poma Poma case. 2009. Ángela Poma Poma v Peru, CCPR/C/95/D/1457/2006.

Port Elizabeth Municipality case. 2005. Port Elizabeth Municipality v Various Occupiers 2005 (1) SA 217 (CC).

Porter, B. 2009. 'The Reasonableness of Article 8(4) – Adjudicating Claims from the Margins'. *Nordic Journal of Human Rights* 27:39–53.

Powell, D.M. 2024. 'The Idea of Power-Sharing in South Africa's Transition from Apartheid to Constitutional Democracy (1983–1993)'. In *Power-Sharing in the Global South: Patterns, Practices and Potentials*, edited by E.W. Aboultaif, S. Keil, and A. McCulloch. Cham: Palgrave Macmillan.

Praet, P. 2018. 'From Legal Pluralism towards Plural (Il)Legalities'. In *Legal Pluralism – Cui Bono?*, edited by M. Luts-Sootak, I. Kull, K. Sein, and H. Siimets-Gross, 30–53. Tartu: University of Tartu Press.

Prasetyo, T. 2016. 'Pancasila The Ultimate of All the Sources of Laws (A Dignified Justice Perspective)'. *Journal of Law, Policy and Globalization* 54:103–9.

Pravasi Bhalai Sangathan case. 2014. Pravasi Bhalai Sangathan v UOI and Others 12 March 2014. Supreme Court.

Premier, Eastern Cape and Others v Ntamo and Others 2015 (6) SA 400 (ECB) (Cala Reserve case 2015)

Prina, F., and G. Pentassuglia. 2023. 'Ukraine's Law on National Minorities and "Effective" Participation: Expanding or Diluting Standards?' *International Journal on Minority and Group Rights* 30:880–830. https://doi.org/10.1163/15718115-bja10138.

Prince case. 2002. Prince v President of the Law Society of the Cape of Good Hope (CCT36/00) [2002] ZACC 1; 2002 (2) SA 794; 2002 (3) BCLR 231 (25 January 2002).

Prinsloo, D. 2009. 'The Right to Mother Tongue Education: A Multidisciplinary, Comprative Perspective'. *Southern African Linguistics and Applied Language Studies* 25:27–43.

Promotion of Administrative Justice Act 2000. *Promotion of Administrative Justice Act 3 of 2000*. https://www.justice.gov.za/legislation/acts/2000-003.pdf.

Pulver, F. 2022. *The Implementation of Free, Prior and Informed Consent and Indigenous People's Rights under the OECD Guidelines for Multinational Enterprises*. Zurich: EIZ Publishing.

Qwelane case. 2021. Qwelane v South African Human Rights Commission and Another [2021] ZACC 22. Constitutional Court.

R case. 2008. R (on the application of E) v JFS Governing Body [2008] EWHC 1535 (Admin); [2008] ELR 455. EWHC.

Radebe, S.B., and M.R. Phooko. 2017. 'Ubuntu and the Law in South Africa: Exploring and Understanding the Substantive Content of Ubuntu'. *South African Journal of Philosophy* 36:239–51.

Rajasthan case. 2022. School Development Management Committee, Shri Hari Secondary School v State of Rajasthan and Another. Civil Writ Petition No. 16367/2021, 2022 LiveLaw (Raj) 3.

Ramantele case. 2013. Ramantele v Mmusi and Others [2013] 2 BLR 658 (CA).

Ramaphosa National Dialogue. 2024. 'President Cyril Ramaphosa: National Reconciliation Day 2024'. Western Cape, December 16. https://www.gov.za/news/speeches/president-cyril-ramaphosa-national-reconciliation-day-2024-16-dec-2024.

Ramatsekisa, T.G. 2008. 'Pre-Constitutional State of Customary Law in South Africa'. *US–China Law Review* 5:39–46.

Ramcharan, B.G., T.C. Van Boven, A.G. Koroma, and I. French, eds. 2023. *The Universality of Human Rights: A Handbook*. Leiden: Brill.

Ramuhovhi case. 2017. Ramuhovhi and Others v President of the Republic of South Africa and Others [2017] ZACC 41.

Rao, P.V. 2020. 'After Supreme Court Judgment, We Must Combat Hate Speech at Social and Political Levels'. *The Leaflet*, 8 December 2020. https://theleaflet.in/after-supreme-court-judgment-we-must-combat-hate-speech-at-social-and-political-levels/.

Rauso, A. 2024. '$9 Million Green Wipeout'. *West Australian*, 29 November 2024.

Rautenbach, C. 2016. 'The South African Constitutional Court's Use Of Foreign Precedent In Matters Of Religion: Without Fear Or Favour?' *Potchefstroom Electronic Law Journal* 18:1545.

Rautenbach, C. 2020. 'The Influence of Foreign Judgments on the Development of Post-Apartheid Constitutional Law in South Africa: Judicial Law-Making in Action?' *Journal of International and Comparative Law* 7:99–125.

Rautenbach, C. 2021a. 'Key Judgements on the Accommodation of Muslim Law in South Africa'. In *Litigating the Rights of Minorities and Indigenous Peoples in Domestic and International Courts*, edited by B. De Villiers, J. Marko, F. Palermo, and S. Constantin, 82–124. Leiden: Brill.

Rautenbach, C. 2021b. 'The Phenomenon of Legal Pluralism'. In *Introduction to Legal Pluralism in South Africa*, edited by C. Rautenbach, 6th ed., 3–18. Durban: LexisNexis.

Rautenbach, C. 2023a. 'Cultural Vulnerability and Judicial Recognition of Heterosexual Life-Partnerships in South Africa'. *Acta Juridica.*

Rautenbach, C. 2023b. 'Nature and Sphere of African Customary Law'. In *Introduction to Legal Pluralism in South Africa*, edited by C. Rautenbach, 6th ed., 19–35. Cape Town: LexisNexis.

Rautenbach, C. 2024. 'State Intervention in the Customary Law of Succession in South Africa: What Remains of Customary Norms in the "Rainbow Nation"?' In *Reimagining Legal Pluralism in Africa: Balancing Indigenous, State, and Religious Laws*, edited by A. Diala and C. Rautenbach, 21–61. Leiden: Brill.

Rautenbach, I.M., and R. Malherbe. 2004. *Constitutional Law.* Johannesburg: LexisNexis Butterworths.

RAV case. 1992. RAV 386 v City of St Paul 505 U.S. 377 (1992). SC.

Ravna, O. 2022. 'The Fosen Case and the Protection of Sámi Culture in Norway Pursuant to Article 27 ICCPR'. *International Journal on Minority and Group Rights* 30:156–75.

RB case. 2016. RB v Hungary App. No. 64602/12, (Apr. 12, 2016). ECtHR.

Recognition Act. 1998. *Recognition of Customary Marriages Act Act 120 of 1998.*

Reddell case. 2022. Reddell and Others v Mineral Sands Resources (Pty) Ltd and Others 2023 (2) SA 404 (CC).

Refah Partisi case. 2003. Refah Partisi (the Welfare Party) and Others v Turkey [GC] – 41340/98, 41342/98, 41343/98 Judgment 13.2.2003 [GC]. ECHR.

Repucci, S., and A. Slipowitz. 2022. 'Freedom in the World 2022: The Global Expansion of Authoritarian Rule'. Freedom House. https://freedomhouse.org/sites/default/files/2022-02/FIW_2022_PDF_Booklet_Digital_Final_Web.pdf.

Restriction on funding case. 2023. BEL-2023-2-006.

Reus-Smit, C. 2013. *Individual Rights and the Making of the International System.* London: Cambridge University Press.

Reynolds, J. 2018. *Aboriginal Peoples and the Law: A Critical Introduction.* Vancouver: UBC Press.

'Richard Dawkins: I'm a Cultural Christian'. 2024. LBC. https://www.youtube.com/watch?v=COHgEFUFWyg.

Richardson, J.T. 2019. 'Religious Freedom in Flux: The European Court of Human Rights Grapples with Ethnic, Cultural, Religious, and Legal Pluralism'. *Changing Societies and Personalities* 3:303–18.

Rio Tinto Alcan case. 2010. Rio Tinto Alcan Inc. v Carrier Sekani Tribal Council 210 SCC 43.

Rita Dempster case. 1999. Rita Dempster on behalf of the Southern Noongar People v Western Australia [1999] NNTTA 235.

Rivonia Primary School appeal. 2013. MEC for Education in Gauteng Province and Other v Governing Body of Rivonia Primary School and Others (CCT 135/12) [2013] ZACC 34; 2013 (6) SA 582 (CC); 2013 (12) BCLR 1365 (CC) (3 October 2013).

Rivonia Primary School case. 2012. Governing Body, Rivonia Primary School v MRC for Education, gauteng Province [2012] 1 All SA 576 (GSJ).

Roberts, J.V. 2023. 'Sentencing Reform in Tanzania: Moving from Uhuru to Ubuntu?' *Journal of African Law* 67:97–116.

Robinson, A.M. 2020. 'Governments Must Not Wait on Courts to Implement UNDRIP Rights Concerning Indigenous Sacred Sites: Lessons from Canada and Ktunaxa Nation v British Columbia'. *The International Journal of Human Rights* 24:1642–65.

Röder, T., and N. Shinwari. 2015. 'Pakistan: Jirgas Dispensing Justice without State Control'. In *Non-State Justice Institutions and the Law: Decision-Making at the Interface of Tradition, Religion and the State*, edited by M. Kötter, T. Röder, G. Schuppert, and R. Wolfrum, 25–46. Hampshire: Palgrave Macmillan.

Romania Constitutional Court case. 2011. Constitutional Court of Romania, Decision number 2/2011 of 4 January 2011.

Rombouts, S.J. 2014. *Having a Say: Indigenous Peoples, International Law and Free, Prior and Informed Consent.* New York: Wolf Legal Publishers.

Rombouts, S.J. 2017. 'The Evolution of Indigenous Peoples' Consultation Rights under the ILO and U.N. Regimes'. *Stanford Journal of International Law* 53:167–92.

Rombouts, S.J. 2018. 'Consultation and Consent Norms under ILO Convention No. 169 and the UN Declaration on the Rights of Indigenous Peoples Compared'. Presented at the EMRIP expert seminar on free, prior and informed consent, Tilburg. https://www.ohchr.org/Documents/Issues/IPeoples/EMRIP/FPIC/RomboutsSJ.pdf.

Rosenfeld, M. 2003. 'Hate Speech in Constitutional Jurisprudence: A Comparative Analysis'. *Cardozo Law Review* 24:1523–67.

Rosting, H. 1923. 'Protection of Minorities by the League of Nations'. *American Journal of International Law* 17:641–60.

Roter, P. 2018. 'Commentary of Article 5 of the Framework Convention for the Protection of National Minorities'. In *The Framework Convention for the Protection of National Minorities: A Commentary*, edited by R. Hofmann, T.H. Malloy, and D. Rein, 126–47. Leiden: Brill.

Roucek, J.S. 1929. 'The Working of the Minorities System under the League of Nations'. PhD, New York: New York University.

Rules Beth Din. 2018. 'Rules and Procedures Beth Din of America'. chrome-extension://efaidnbmnnnibpcajpcglclefindmkaj/https://bethdin.org/wp-content/uploads/2018/04/BDA118-RulesProcedures_Bro_BW_02.pdf.

Ryan, E. 2020. 'Federalism as Legal Pluralism'. In *The Oxford Handbook of Global Legal Pluralism*, edited by P.S. Berman, 491–531. Oxford: Oxford University Press.

Ryland case. 1997. Ryland v Edros 1997 (1) BCLR 77 (C). Constitutional Court.

Sachs, A. 1990. *Protecting Human Rights in a New South Africa*. London: Oxford University Press.

Sachs, A. 1992. *Advancing Human Rights in South Africa*. Cape Town: Oxford University Press.

Sachs, A. 1999. 'The Creation of South Africa's Constitution'. *New York Law School Law Review* 41:669–702.

Sachs, A. 2009. *The Strange Alchemy of Life and Law*. London: Oxford University Press.

Sachs, A. 2012. 'Towards the Liberation and Revitalization of Customary Law'. In *uBuntu and the Law: African Ideals and Postapartheid Jurisprudence*, edited by D. Cornell and N. Mavangua, 303–38. New York: Fordham University Press.

Sachs, A. 2024. 'Epilogue'. In *Reimagining Legal Pluralism in Africa: Balancing Indigenous, State, and Religious Laws*, edited by A. Diala and C. Rautenbach, 474–94. Leiden: Brill.

Saeed, H.H. 2021. 'The Role of Mother Tongue in Early Childhood Education'. *International Journal of Pedagogy Innovation and New Technologies* 8:36–43.

Sajo, A., and R. Uitz. 2020. 'Individual Religious Freedom under the European Convention of Human Rights'. In *Constitutions and Religion*, edited by S. Mancini, 286–306. Cheltenham: Edward Elgar Publishing Limited.

Salah, O., and C. Rautenbach. 2015. 'Islamic Finance: A Collary to Legal Pluralism or Legal Diversity in South Africa and the Netherlands?' *CILSA* 48:488–515.

Salat, L. 2023. 'The Concept of Non-Territorial Autonomy: Origins, Developments, and Subtypes'. In *Non-Territorial Autonomy: An Introduction*, edited by M. Andeva, B. Dobos, L. Djordjević, B. Kuzmany, and T.H. Malloy, 1–26. Cham: Palgrave Macmillan.

Salat, L., S. Constantin, A. Osipov, and I. Szekely, eds. 2014. *Autonomy Arrangements around the World: A Collection of Well and Lesser Known Cases*. Cluj-Napoca: EURAC.

Sámi consultation case. 2024. Committee on the Rights of the Child CRC/C/97/D/172/2022: Views adopted by the Committee under the Optional Protocol to the Convention on the Rights of the Child on a communications procedure, concerning communication No. 172/2022.

Sámi mining case. 2024. E/C.12/76/D/289/2022: Views adopted by the Committee under the Optional Protocol to the International Covenant on Economic, Social and Cultural Rights, concerning communications Nos. 251/2022 and 289/2022.

Samir Chakma case. 2016. Samir Chakma v State of Tripura WP(C)(PIL) No.10 of 2016.

Samira Achbita case. 2017. Samira Achbita v G4S Secure Solutions NV, C-157/15, March 14, 2017. CJEU.

Samuel, O.S. 2023. 'Practicing Ubuntu'. *The Philosophical Forum*, May. https://onlinelibrary.wiley.com/doi/epdf/10.1111/phil.12338.

Sanchez case. 2015. Affaire Sanchez v France (Requête no 45581/15). ECHR.

Sanderson case. 1998. Sanderson v Attorney-General, Eastern Cape 1998 (2) SA 38 (CC). CC.

Sani, H.B.A. 2020. 'State Law and Legal Pluralism: Towards an Appraisal'. *The Journal of Legal Pluralism and Unofficial Law* 52:82–109. https://doi.org/10.1080/07329113.2020.1727726.

Sapignoli, M., and K. Hitchcock. 2013. 'Indigenous Peoples in Southern Africa'. *The Round Table* 102:355–65.

Saramaka case. 2007. Saramaka, Preliminary Objections, Merits, Reparations and Costs, Judgement, Inter-Am. Ct. H.R. (ser.C) No 172, (Nov. 28, 2007).

SAS case. 2014. SAS v France [GC] – 43835/11 Judgment 1.7.2014 [GC]. ECtHR.

Saskatchewan case. 2013. Saskatchewan (Human Rights Commission) v Whatcott, 2013 SCC 11 (CanLII), [2013] 1 SCR 467. Supreme Court.

Saugeen First Nation case. 2017. Saugeen First Nation v Ontario (MNRF), 2017 ONSC 3456.

Savva Terentyev case. 2009. Savva Terentyev v Russia (Application no. 10692/09). ECtHR.

Sawhoyamaxa Community case. 2006. Sawhoyamaxa Indigenous Community vs. Paraguay, Judgment of March 29, 2006. Inter-American Court of Human Rights.

Sayed, Y., S. Motala, D. Carel, and R. Ahmed. 2020. 'School Governance and Funding Policy in South Africa: Towards Social Justice and Equity in Education Policy'. *South African Journal of Education* 40. https://doi.org/10.15700/saje.v40n4a2045.

Schacht, J. 1983. *An Introduction to Islamic Law*. Oxford: Oxford University Press.

Scheu, H.C. 2020. 'The Heritage of the League of Nations' Minority Protection System'. *Hungarian Journal of Legal Studies* 61:356–71.

School Language Statistics. 2020. 'Question NW182 to the Minister of Basic Education'. https://pmg.org.za/committee-question/13419/#:~:text=Table%201%20indicates%20that%20there,483%20and%201%20261%20respectively.

Schuppert, G. 2015. 'From Normative Pluralism to a Pluralism of Norm Enforcement Regumes: A Governance Research Perspective'. In *Non-State Justice Institutions and the Law: Decision-Making at the Interface of Tradition, Religion and the State*, edited by M. Kötter, T. Röder, G. Schuppert, and R. Wolfrum, 188–212. Hampshire: Palgrave Macmillan.

Schweppe, J., and D. Walsh. 2008. *Combating Racism and Xenophobia Through the Criminal Law*. Limerick: Centre for Criminal Justice.

Schwimmer case. 1929. United States v Schwimmer, 279 U. S. 644, 655 (1929). US Supreme Court.

Secorun, L. 2018. 'South Africa's First Nations Have Been Forgotten'. *Foreign Policy*, 19 October 2018. https://foreignpolicy.com/2018/10/19/south-africas-first-nations-have-been-forgotten-apartheid-khoisan-indigenous-rights-land-reform/.

Seedat case. 1917. Seedat Executors v The Master (Natal) 1917 AD 302. AD.

Seinecke, R. 2018. 'What Is Legal Pluralism and What Is It Good For?' In *Legal Pluralism – Cui Bono?*, edited by M. Luts-Sootak, I. Kull, K. Sein, and H. Siimets-Gross, 13–29. Tartu: University of Tartu Press.

Sejati, A., and D. Kartono. 2024. 'The Urgency of Recognition the Rights of Indigenous Peoples in Asymmetric Decentralization in Papua and Papua Barat'. *Transformasi: Jurnal Manajemen Pemerintahan* 16:1–15.

Sengadi case. 2019. Sengadi v Tsambo 2019 (4) SA 50 (GJ) and Tsambo v Sengadi [2020] ZASCA 46.

Serfontein, E.M., and E. De Waal. 2013. 'The Effectiveness of Legal Remedies in Education: A School Governing Body Perspective'. *De Jure*, 45–62.

Sesana case. 2006. Sesana and Others v Attorney General (52/2002) [2006] BWHC 1.

Shaheed, F. 2010. 'Report on the Conceptual Framework of Cultural Rights'. Report of the independent expert in the field of cultural rights, Ms. Farida Shaheed, submitted pursuant to resolution 10/23 of the Human Rights Council A/HRC/14/36. New York: United Nations.

Shanahan, M. 2024. 'High Court Judge Warns of World's "Slide towards Autocracy" '. *Financial Review*, 6 November 2024.

Shaw case. 1998. Shaw v Wolf (1998) 163 ALR 205, 211–212. Federal Court.

Shilubana case. 2008. Shilubana and Others v Nwamitwa (CCT 03/07) [2008] ZACC 9; 2008 (9) BCLR 914 (CC); 2009 (2) SA 66 (CC) (4 June 2008).

Shomang case. 2022. Shomang v Motsose NO and Others (6990/2022) [2022] ZAGPPHC 441; 2022 (5) SA 602 (GP) (24 May 2022).

Sibisi, S. 2023. 'Registration of Customary Marriages in South Africa: A Case for Mandatory Registration'. *Obiter*, 515–33.

Sibisi, S. 2024. 'Problems With Waiving the Handing-Over of the Bride in Customary Marriages'. *Obiter*, 921–35.

Sidiropoulos case. 1998. Sidiropoulos and Others v Greece, App. No. 26695/95, judgment of 10 July 1998. ECtHR.

Sigcau case. 2018. Sigcau and Another v Minister of Cooperative Governance and Traditional Affairs and Others 2018 (12) BCLR 1525 (CC).

Simion, O. 2023. 'The Issue of Migration in the Context of the New Perfect Storm: Pact on Migration and Asylum'. In *The European Union and the New Perfect Storm: The Pandemics, Geopolitics, and Populism*, edited by D. Dungaciu and R. Iordache, 210–20. Newcastle: Cambridge Scholars.

Sinclair, J. 1994. 'Family Rights'. In *Rights and Constitutionalism: The New South African Legal Order*, edited by D. Van Wyk, J. Dugard, B. De Villiers, and D. Davis, 502–72. Cape Town: Juta.

Singh, A., and S. Tembo. 2022. 'Constitutionalism and Public Health Emergencies: Covid-19 Regulations in South Africa and the Constitutional and Human Rights Slippery Slope'. *Obiter* 43:152–66.

Sing'Oei, K. 2013. 'Engaging the Leviathan: National Development, Corporate Globalisation and the Endorois' Quest to Recover Their Herding Grounds'. In *The Interralation between the Right to Identity of Minorities and Their Socio-Economic Participation*, edited by K. Henrard, 373–401. Leiden: Marthinus Nijjhof.

Slavery and Trafficking Act. 2013. *Crimes Legislation Amendment (Slavery, Slavery-like Conditions and People Trafficking) Act 2013.*

Smith, D. 2019. 'From Little Things, Big Things Grow: Exercising Incremental Self-Governance in Australia'. In *Reclaiming Indigenous Governance*, edited by W. Nikolakis, S. Cornell, and H.W. Nelson, 130–54. Tucson: University of Arizona Press.

Smith, D.J. 2016. 'National Cultural Autonomy'. In *The Routledge Handbook of Ethnic Conflict*, edited by K. Cordell and S. Wolff. London: Routledge.

Smith, D.J. 2023. 'NTA as a Democratization Tool'. In *Non-Territorial Autonomy: An Introduction*, edited by M. Andeva, B. Dobos, L. Djordjević, B. Kuzmany, and T.H. Malloy, 65–83. Cham: Palgrave Macmillan.

Smith, D.J., I. Dodovski, and F. Ghencea, eds. 2023a. *Realising Linguistic, Cultural and Educational Rights through Non-Territorial Autonomy*. Switzerland: Palgrave Macmillan.

Smith, D.J., I. Dodovski, and F. Ghencea, eds. 2023b. *The Role of Law and Non-Territorial Autonomy Arrangements in the Implementation of Linguistic Rights: A Comparative Perspective.* Cham: Palgrave Macmillan. https://library.oapen.org/bitstream/handle/20.500.12657/60138/978-3-031-19856-4.pdf?sequence=1&isAllowed=y.

Smith, R.K.M. 2003. 'Mother Tongue Education and the Law: A Legal Review of Bilingualism with Reference to Scottish Gaelic'. *International Journal of Bilingual Education and Bilingualism* 6:124–45. https://doi.org/10.1080/13670050308667776.

Snyder case. 2011. Snyder v Phelps, 131 S. Ct. 1207 (2011). US Supreme Court.

Sodhi, R. 2023. 'Empowering Africa: The Importance of Mother Tongue Education'. *The Cornell Diplomat.*

Soetjipto, A.W. 2022. 'Journey to Justice: The United Nations Declaration on the Rights of Indigenous Peoples in the Context of West Papua'. *Journal of ASEAN Studies* 10:129–49.

Sokolovskiy case. 2024. Sokolovskiy v Russia 618/18.

Solski case. 2005. Solski (Tutor of) v Quebec (Attorney General) [2005] 1 SCR 201.

Sottiaux, S. 2023. 'Conflicting Conceptions of Hate Speech in the ECtHR's Case Law'. *German Law Journal* 23:1193–1211.

South African Law Commission. 1999. 'The Harmonisation of the Common Law and the Indigenous Law'. Pretoria: South African Law Commission.

South African Law Commission. 2000. 'Islamic Marriages and Related Matters'. 59. Pretoria: South African Law Commission. chrome-extension://efaidnbmnnnibpcajpcglclefindmkaj/https://www.justice.gov.za/salrc/ipapers/ip15_prj59_2000.pdf.

Southalan, J., and J. Fardin. 2019. 'Free, Prior and Informed Consent: How and from Whom? An Australian Analogue'. *Journal of Energy & Natural Resources Law* 37:365–88.

Sparrow case. 1990. R v Sparrow (1990) 1 SCR 1075.

Spatial Planning Act. 2013. *Spatial Planning and Land Use Management Act 16 of 2013.* chrome-extension://efaidnbmnnnibpcajpcglclefindmkaj/https://www.gov.za/sites/default/files/gcis_document/201409/367305-8act16of20.pdf.

Spaull, N. 2016. 'Disentangling the Language Effect in South African Schools: Measuring the Impact of "Language of Assessment" in Grade 3 Literacy and Numeracy'. *South African Journal of Childhood Education* 6:1–20.

Spaull, N. 2023. '2023 Background Report for the 2030 Reading Panel'. Cape Town: Reading Panel. https://www.readingpanel.co.za/_files/ugd/b385b7_7476724ee8a74ba8be8320a3be46b5cc.pdf.

Speaker of the National Assembly and Another case. 2024. Speaker of the National Assembly and Another v Women's Legal Centre Trust and Others [2024] ZACC 18.

Stajnko, J., and D. Siter. 2023. 'Discrimination, Freedom of Expression and Two Concepts of Liberty: Assessing European Legislation Criminalizing Hate Speech'. *Hungarian Journal of Legal Studies*, no. 64, 288–307.

State Forest case. 2012. State Forest case No. 35/PUU-X/2012.

State of Karnataka case. 2014. State of Karnataka & Another vs Associated Management of English Medium Primary & Secondary Schools & Others (2014) 9 SCC 485.

Stay case. 2023. Stay At South Point Properties (Pty) Ltd v Mqulwana and Others (UCT intervening as amicus curiae) (1335/2021) [2023] ZASCA 108 (3 July 2023).

Stepien, A., A. Petretei, and T. Koivurova. 2015. 'Sámi Parliaments in Finland, Norway, and Sweden'. In *Managing Diversity through Non-Territorial Autonomy: Assessing Advantages, Deficiencies, and Risks*, edited by T. Malloy, A. Osipov, and B. Vizi, 117–38. London: Oxford University Press.

Steuer, M. 2023. 'Cultural Expertise and Extreme Speech'. In *Cultural Expertise, Law and Rights: A Comprehensive Guide*, edited by L. Holden, 158–65. Oxon: Routledge.

Steuer, M. 2024. 'Cultural Expertise, Hate Speech, and the Far Right: The Slovak Mazurek Case'. *Legal Pluralism and Critical Social Analysis* 56:215–35.

Steytler, N. 2024a. 'A Century of South African Constitutional Identities'. In *Constitutional Identity and Constitutionalism in Africa*, edited by C.M. Fombad and N. Steytler, 139–65. Oxford: Oxford University Press.

Steytler, N. 2024b. 'South Africa's Government of National Unity: Power Sharing in a Fractured Society'. *ISCL-AIDC Blog* (blog). 14 November 2024.

Strategic Minerals case. 2003. Strategic Minirals Corporation NL/Allan Kyuna and Ors on behalf of Woolgar Group/Queensland [2003] NNTTA 83.

Strauss, D.A. 2010. 'The Living Constitution'. 27 September 2010. https://www.law.uchicago.edu/news/living-constitution.

Strickland case. 1998. Strickland v Minister of Lands (WA) (1998) 85 FCR 303.

Strydom, H.A. 1997. 'Minority Rights Issues in Post-Apartheid South Africa Symposium: Minority Rights'. *Loyola of Los Angeles International and Comparative Law Journal*, 873–914.

SUI-2024-1-001. 2024. SUI-2024-1-001.

Suleman, M. 2023. 'Muslim Personal Law, Yes and No: Religious Leader's Views on Its Legalization'. *Journal for the Study of Religion* 23. http://www.scielo.org.za/scielo.php?script=sci_arttext&pid=S1011-76012023000100001.

Sultan, M.S., N. Akhtar, and M. Imran. 2024. 'Balancing Freedom of Expression and Hate Speech Regulations: A Comparative Analysis of Pakistani and United Kingdom'. *Traditional Journal of Law and Social Sciences* 3:26–41.

Sürek (No. 1) case. 1999. Sürek (No. 1) v Turkey App. No. 23927/94. ECtHR.

Sustaining the Wild Coast case. 2024. Minister of Mineral Resources and Energy and Others v Sustaining the Wild Coast NPC and Others (Case no 58/2023; 71/2023; 351/2023) [2024] ZASCA 84 (3 June 2024).

Sutherland, N.M. 1987. 'The Huguenots and the Edict of Nantes 1598–1629 .' In *Huguenots in Britain and Their French Background, 1550–1800*, edited by I. Scouloudi, 158–74. London: Palgrave Macmillan.

T-129/11. 2011. T-129/11. CC.

Tagiyev case. 2020. Tagiyev and Huseynov v Azerbaijan ECtHR 419 (2019).

Taib, K.N., M. Sama, and S. Yusof. 2024. 'The Causal Nexus of Freedom of Speech and Hate Speech in Multiracial Society'. *International Journal of Law, Government and Communication* 9:129–42.

Tamanaha, B. 1993. 'The Folly of the "Social Scientific" Concept of Legal Plurality'. *Journal of Law and Society* 20 (February):192–215.

Tamanaha, B. 2015. 'Introduction: A Bifurcated Theory of Law in Hybrid Societies'. In *Non-State Justice Institutions and the Law: Decision-Making at the Interface of Tradition, Religion and the State*, edited by M. Kötter, T. Röder, G. Schuppert, and R. Wolfrum, 1–24. Hampshire: Palgrave Macmillan.

Tamanaha, B. 2021. *Legal Pluralism Explained: History, Theory, and Consequences*. Oxford: Oxford University Press.

Tapela case. 2015. Attorney General and Others v Tapela and Others, Court of Appeal Civil Case No. CACGB-096-14; Attorney General and Others v Mwale, Court of Appeal Civil Case No. CACGB-076-15.

Tark, T. 2022. 'Die Deutsche Kulturselbstverwaltung Und Die Änderung Der Volkszugehörigkeit in Estland in Den 1920er Jahren'. *Jahrbücher Für Geschichte Osteuropas* 70:131–58.

Tas, L. 2013. 'One State, Plural Options: Kurds in the UK'. *Journal of Legal Pluralism and Unofficial Law* 45:167–89.

Tas, L. 2016. *Legal Pluralism in Action: Dispute Resolution and the Kurdish Peace Committee*. London: Routledge.

Tauli-Corpuz, V. 2017. 'End of Mission Statement by the United Nations Special Rapporteur on the Rights of Indigenous Peoples, Victoria Tauli-Corpuz of Her Visit to the United States of America'. Geneva: United Nations. https://www.ohchr.org/EN/NewsEvents/Pages/DisplayNews.aspx?NewsID=21274.

Taylor, P.M. 2020. *A Commentary on the International Covenant on Civil and Political Rights The UN Human Rights Committee's Monitoring of ICCPR Rights*. London: Cambridge University Press.

Tazo, G. 2023. 'Constitutionalisation of Ethnicity and Decolonisation of African Constitutionalism: Towards an Authentic African Constitutional Identity?' *Journal of Comparative Law in Africa* 10.

Terminiello case. 1949. Terminiello v. Chicago, 337 U.S. 1 (1949). US.

Teubner, G. 2012. *Constitutional Fragments, Societal Constitutionalism and Globalization*. Oxford: Oxford University Press.

Teubner, G., and G. Bukovina. 1997. 'Legal Pluralism in the World-Society'. In *Global Law without a State*, edited by G. Teubner, 3–28. Dartsmouth: Aldershot.

Texas case. 1989. Texas v Johnson, 491 US 397 (1989).

The Hague Mother Tongue Education. 1996. 'The Hague Recommendations Regarding the Education Rights of National Minorities'. OSCE. https://www.osce.org/hcnm/hague-recommendations.

Thompson, S. 2020. 'Beadica 231 CC: An End to the Trilogy?' *South African Law Journal* 137:641–58.

Thornberry, P. 2005. 'Article 12'. In *The Rights of Minorities: A Commentary on the European Framework Convention for the Protection of National Minorities*, edited by M. Weller, 356–92. Oxford Commentaries on International Law. Oxford, New York: Oxford University Press.

Timber Creek High Court-appeal. 2019. Northern Territory v Mr A. Griffiths (deceased) and Lorraine Jones on behalf of the Ngaliwurru and Nungali Peoples [2019] HCA 7, 13 March 2019.

Tipakalippa case. 2022. Santos NA Barossa Pty Ltd v Tipakalippa [2022] FCAFC 193. Federal Court.

Tom, P. 2018. 'A "Post-Liberal Peace" via Ubuntu?' *Peacebuilding* 6:65–79.

Tomaselli, A. 2017. 'The Right to Political Participation of Indigenous Peoples: A Holistic Approach'. *International Journal on Minority and Group Rights* 24:390–427.

Tomaselli, A. 2019. *Indigenous Peoples and Their Right to Political Participation*. Baden-Baden: Nomos.

Tomaselli, A., and F. Cittadino. 2021. 'Land, Consultation and Participation Rights of Indigenous Peoples in the Recent Jurisdictions of the Inter-American Court of Human Rights: The Cases of Sarayaku v Ecuador and Kalina and Lokono v Suriname'. In *Litigating the Rights of Minorities and Indigenous Peoples in Domestic and International Courts*, edited by B. De Villiers, S. Constantin, F. Palermo, and J. Marko, 149–79. Leiden: Brill.

Tomuschat, C. 1983. 'Protection of Minorities under Article 27 of the International Covenant on Civil and Political Rights'. In *Volkerrecht Als Rechtsordnung, Nternationale Gerichtbarkeit, Menschenrechte: Festschrift Fur Hermann Mosler*, edited by R. Bernhardt, 114–42. Berlin: Springer.

Topidi, K. 2019a. 'Religious Pluralism in State-Centric Legal Spaces in Europe: The Legacy of the Molla Sali Case'. *European Yearbook of Minority Issues* 18:33–58.

Topidi, K. 2019b. *Words That Hurt (1): Normative and Institutional Considerations in the Regulation of Hate Speech in Europe*. Flensburg: ECMI. https://www.ecmi.de/publications/working-papers/118-words-that-hurt-1-normative-and-institutional-considerations-in-the-regulation-of-hate-speech-in-europe,.

Topidi, K. 2023. 'Minority Identity in Digital Governance and the Challenges of Online Hate Speech and Content Regulation'. In *Minority Rights and Liberal Democratic Insecurities*, edited by A. Biro and D. Newman, 135–54. Oxon: Routledge.

Topidi, K. 2024. 'Minority Cultural Governance through Autonomy Arrangements as a means of Exercising Agency'. *Annali Di Studi Religiosi*, 397–419. https://doi.org/10.53136/979122181466822.

Topidi, K. 2025. 'Introduction: Ethno-Cultural Minority Identities at War in Ukraine and Beyond'. In *Minorities at War: Cultural Identity and Resilience in Ukraine*, edited by E. Muratova and N. Zasanska, 1–19. London: Routledge.

Tsavousoglou, I. 2015. 'The Legal Treatment of the Muslim Minority Women under the Rule of Islamic Law in Greek Thrace'. *Oslo Law Review* 3:241–62.

Tsevas, C. 2023. 'Religious Diversity in Greece: Recent Developments and the Challenges of the Molla Sali Case'. In *Religious Minorities in Pluralist Societies*, edited by R. Medda-Windischer, K. Wonisch, and A.C. Bubabin, 124–52. Leiden: Brill.

Tshoose, C.I. 2023. 'The Role and Impact of Constitutional Values of Ubuntu, Equality, and Human Dignity in the Interpretation and Protection of the Right to Have Access to Social Security in South Africa'. *Journal of Juridical Science* 48.

Tsotetsi, C., and B. Omodan. 2020. 'Deconstructing Power Differentials in the Postgraduate Supervision Process: Mentoring in Ubuntu Praxis'. *Ubuntu: Journal of Conflict and Social Transformation* 9:105–26.

Tusseau, G. 2020. 'Debating Legal Pluralism and Constitutionalism: New Trajectories for Legal Theory in the Global Age'. In *Debating Legal Pluralism and Constitutionalism*, edited by G. Tusseau, 1–92. Cham: Springer.

Tutu, D. 1999. *No Future without Forgiveness*. New York: Doubleday.

Ubink, J., and J. Pickering. 2020. 'Shaping Legal and Institutional Pluralism: Land Rights,Access to Justice and Citizenship in South Africa'. *South African Journal on Human Rights* 36:178–99.

Ubuntu-software. n.d. 'Ubuntu for Desktops'. Accessed 25 May 2026. https://ubuntu.com/desktop.

Ujomu, P.O. 2024. ' "Ubuntu" African Philosophy or "Ubuntu" as a Philosophy for Africa'. *Институт По Философия и Социология При БАН*.

Ukraine Constitutional Court. 2019. Constitutional Court of Urkaine, Decision number 10-p/2019 of 16 July 2019.

UN Declaration on Minorities. 1992. 'United Nations Declaration on the Rights of Persons Belonging to National or Ethnic, Religious and Linguistic Minorities General Assembly Resolution 47/135'. United Nations. https://www.ohchr.org/EN/ProfessionalInterest/Pages/Minorities.aspx.

UN Declaration on Minorities. 1993. 'Declaration on the Rights of Persons Belonging to National or Ethnic, Religious and Linguistic Minorities :: Resolution /: Adopted by the General Assembly.' UN. https://digitallibrary.un.org/record/158458.

UN Expert Mechanism. 2021. 'Expert Mechanism on the Rights of Indigenous People: Country Engagement Finland'. Geneva: UN Expert Mechanism.

UN International Law Commission. 2018. 'Draft Conclusions on the Identification of Customary International Law, with Commentaries'. United Nations. https://legal.un.org/ilc/texts/instruments/english/commentaries/1_13_2018.pdf.

UN Resolution. 2004. 'Resolution Adopted by the General Assembly on 22 December 2003 A/Res/58/182'. United Nations General Assembly.

UN Strategy Hate Speech. 2019. 'UN Strategy and Plan of Action of Action on Hate Speech'. Geneva. https://www.un.org/en/genocideprevention/documents/advising-and-mobilizing/Action_plan_on_hate_speech_EN.pdf.

Undrea, A., S. Constantin, and L. Djordjević. 2023. 'Kin-State Engagement and its Impact on Minority Protection in Europe: Relevant Findings for Southeast Europe'. Council of Europe.

UNDRIP. 2007. 'United Nations Declaration on the Rights of Indigenous People'. https://www.un.org/development/desa/indigenouspeoples/declaration-on-the-rights-of-indigenous-peoples.html.

UNESCO collection. 2012. 'Archives of the CODESA (Convention For A Democratic South Africa) 1991–1992 and Archives of the Multi-Party Negotiating Process 1993'. UNESCO. https://en.unesco.org/memoryoftheworld/registry/316.

UNESCO mother tongue. 2022. 'Why Mother Language-Based Education Is Essential'. https://www.unesco.org/en/articles/why-mother-language-based-education-essential.

UN Experts. 2022. 'Comprehensive Anti-Discrimination Legislation Must Be a Priority, Say UN Experts Ahead of Universal Declaration Anniversary'. UNHRC. https://www.ohchr.org/en/statements/2022/12/comprehensive-anti-discrimination-legislation-must-be-priority-say-un-experts.

UNHCR. n.d. 'Minorities and Indigenous Peoples'. UNHCR. Accessed 15 May 2022. https://www.unhcr.org/en-au/minorities-and-indigenous-peoples.html.

UNHRC. 2010. 'Minority Rights: International Standards and Guidance for Implementation'. HR/PUB/10/3. New York: UNHRC. https://www.ohchr.org/documents/publications/minorityrights_en.pdf.

UNHRC. 2022. Comprehensive anti-discrimination legislation must be a priority, say UN experts ahead of Universal Declaration anniversary - https://www.ohchr.org/en/statements/2022/12/comprehensive-anti-discrimination-legislation-must-be-priority-say-un-experts.

UNICEF South Africa. 2016. 'The Impact of Language Policy and Practice on Children's Learning: Evidence from Eastern and Southern Africa'. chrome-extension://efaidnbmnnnibpcajpcglclefindmkaj/https://www.unicef.org/esa/sites/unicef.org.esa/files/2018-09/UNICEF-2016-Language-and-Learning-South-Africa-Case-Study.pdf.

Union of Refugee Women case. 2007. Union of Refugee Women v Private Security Industry Regulatory Authority 2007 (4) SA 395; 2007 (4) BCLR 339 (CC).

UNISA case. 2021. Chairperson of the Council of UNISA v AfriForum NPC [2021] ZACC 32.

University of Free State case. 2017. AfriForum and Another v University of the Free State (CCT101/17) [2017] ZACC 48; 2018 (2) SA 185 (CC); 2018 (4) BCLR 387 (CC) (29 December 2017).

University of Stellenbosch case. 2019. Gelyke Kanse and Others v Chairperson of the Senate of the University of Stellenbosch and Others [2019] ZACC 38.

UN–World Bank. 2018. 'Pathways for Peace Inclusive Approaches to Preventing Violent Conflict'. Washington DC: World Bank. file:///C:/Users/devillib/Downloads/9781464811623.pdf.

Updegrove, A.H., M.N. Cooper, and J.R. Dmello. 2021. 'Heritage Not Hate? Confederate Flag Supporters Less Likely to Perceive Criminal Injustice, More Likely to View Police as Friends'. *Race and Justice*.

Urrejola, A., and E.C. Neira. 2024. 'Indigenous Rights in the Inter-American System: The Application of Precautionary Measures from a Culturally Appropriate Perspective'. In *The Impact of the Inter-American Human Rights System: Transformations on the Ground*, edited by A. Von Bogdandy, F. Piovesan, E.F. Mac-Gregor, and M. Antoniazzi, 254–67. New York: Oxford Academic.

Vahed, G. 2022. 'Muslim Marriages, the South African State and the Courts: Between Limbo, Liberation, and the Spaces for Contestation in between'. *Contemporary South Asia* 30:44–57.

Vajnai case. 2008. Vajnai. 2008. Vajnai v Hungary App. No. 33629/06 ECtHR 8 July 2008. ECtHR.

Valiullina case. 2023. Valiullina and Others v Latvia – 56928/19, 7306/20 and 11937/20. ECtHR.

Van Breda case. 1921. Van Breda and Others v Jacobs and Others 1921 AD 330.

Van Coller, H. 2022. 'Religious Freedom in South Africa'. In *Religious Freedom in Secular States*, edited by J.H. Bhuiyan and A. Black, 217–33. Leiden: Brill.

Van Crombrugge, R. 2017. 'Belgium and Democratic Constitution-Making: Prospects for the Future'. *Netherlands Journal of Legal Philosophy* 46:13–28.

Van der Jeught, S. 2017. 'Territoriality and Freedom of Language: The Case of Belgium'. *Current Issues in Language Planning* 18:181–98. https://doi.org/10.1080/14664208.2016.1243883.

Van der Jeught, S Jiménez, M.J.O. 2022. 'Indigenous Peoples' Normative Orders and Restitution: Latin American Private International Law and Human Rights'. *Legal Pluralism and Critical Social Analysis*, 176–92.

Van der Schyff, G. 2014. 'Ritual Slaughter and Religious Freedom in Multilevel Europe: The Wider Importance of the Dutch Case'. *Oxford Journal of Law and Religion* 3:76–102.

Van der Stoel, M. 1993. 'Case Studies on National Minority Issues: Positive Results'. Warsaw, September 24. http://www.osce.org/documents/hcnm/1993/05/3688_en.pdf.

Van der Westhuizen, J. 2023. ' "Johann, Moenie Dit Opf*k!": Volkstaat-Klousule se Morsige Geboorte'. *Rapport*, 2 June 2023.

Van Schalkwyk, D. 2006. 'The Indigenous Law of Contract with Particular Reference to the Swazi in the Kingdom of Swaziland'. LLD, Pretoria: UNISA.

Van Vuren case. 2012. Van Vuren v Minister of Correctional Services 2012 (1) SACR 103 (CC).

Van Wyk, D. 1994. 'Introduction to the South African Constitution'. In *Rights and Constitutionalism: The New South African Legal Order*, edited by D. Van Wyk, J. Dugard, B. De Villiers, and D. Davis, 131–70. Cape Town: Juta.

Vejdeland case. 2012. Vejdeland and Others v Sweden – 1813/07. ECtHR.

Venice Commission. 1994. 'The Protection of Minorities'. CDL-STD(1994)009. Strasbourg: Venice Commission.

Venizelos, E. 2024. 'Religious Freedom for Muslims: A Challenge to the Historical Foundations and Recilience of European Constitutionalism'. In *Islam, Religious Liberty and Constitutionalism in Europe*, edited by M. Hill and L. Papadopoulou, 17–30. Oxford: Hart Publishing.

Veracini, L., and R. Verbuyst. 2020. 'South Africa's Settler-Colonial Present: Khoisan Revivalism and the Question of Indigeneity'. *Social Dynamics* 46:259–76.

Veriava, F. 2024. 'The Basic Education Laws Amendment Bill: A Case Study in Transformative Constitutionalism beyond the Courts'. *African Human Rights Law Journal* 24:153–78.

Viellechner, L. 2020. ' "Friendliness" towards Others: How the German Constitution Deals with Legal Pluralism'. In *Debating Legal Pluralism and Constitutionalism*, edited by G. Tusseau, 189–228. Cham: Springer.

Virginia case. 2003. Virginia v Black 538 US 343 (2003). US.

Waboose, V. 2021. 'Conducting Research from an Indigenous Lens'. In *Decolonizing Law: Indigenous, Third World and Settler Perspectives*, edited by S. Xavier, B. Jacobs, J. Hewitt, and A. Bhatia, 276–96. Oxon: Routledge.

Waldman case. 1996. Waldman v Canada, Comm. No. 694/1996, views (1999), UN Doc. A/55/40, CCPR/C/67/D/694/1996.

Walker, J.G. 2021. 'Should Afrikaans Be Declared South Africa's Indigenous Language?' *Universities South Africa* (blog). 30 September 2021. https://www.usaf.ac.za/should-afrikaans-be-declared-south-africas-indigenous-language/#:~:text=Afrikaans%20IS%20an%20indigenous%20South%20African%20language.,enriched%20by%20the%20local%20context.%E2%80%9D.

Walley case. 1996. Walley v Western Australia (1996) 137 ALR 561.

Ward case. 2002. Western Australia v Ward (2002) 213 CLR 1; 191 ALR 2.

WCCJ. n.d. 'World Conference on Constitutional Justice'. Accessed 8 March 2023. https://www.venice.coe.int/WCCJ/WCCJ_E.asp.

Weber, A. 2024. 'Minority Rights'. In *Writing Constitutions: Volume 2: Fundamental Rights*, edited by W. Babeck and A. Weber, 475–93. Cham: Springer.

Weinberg, T. 2016. 'Pushing the Boundaries of Customary Law Jurisprudence in Botswana: Social Science and the Law in the Case of Ramantele v Mmusi'. *The Journal of Legal Pluralism and Unofficial Law* 48:186–207.

Weller, M., ed. 2005. *The Rights of Minorities: A Commentary on the European Framework Convention for the Protection of National Minorities*. Oxford Commentaries on International Law. Oxford, New York: Oxford University Press.

Weller, M. 2007. 'Minority Consultative Mechanisms: Towards Best Practices'. *European Yearbook of Minority Issues* 7 (August):425–47.

Wellington International Airport case. 1991. Wellington International Airport Ltd v Air NZ [1991] 1 NZLR 671.

Werbner, P., and R. Werbner. 2022. *African Customary Justice: Living Law, Legal Pluralism, and Public Ethics*. Oxon: Routledge.

Western Cape Constitution. 1997. In re: Certification of the Constitution of the Western Cape, 1997 1997 (9) BCLR 1167 (CC), 1997 (4) SA 795 (CC).

Wieshaider, W. 2024. 'Hunting Grounds for Religious Slaughter: A Case Study from the Court of Justice of the European Union'. In *Islam, Religious Liberty and Constitutionalism in Europe*, edited by M. Hill and L. Papadopoulou, 153–66. Oxford: Hart Publishing.

Williams case. 1995. S v Williams 1995 (7) BCLR 861 (CC). Constitutional Court.

Williams, R. 2008. 'Civil and Religious Law in England: A Religious Perspective'. February 7. http://rowanwilliams.archbishopofcanterbury.org/articles.php/1137/archbishops-lecture-civil-and-religious-law-in-england-a-religious-perspective.html.

Williamson case. 2019. Williamson v Germany ECHR 046 (2019).

Wilmot-Smith, Frederick. 2023. 'Express and Implied Terms'. *Oxford Journal of Legal Studies* 43 (1): 54–75. https://doi.org/10.1093/ojls/gqac023.

Wilson, G.N., and G. Fondahl. 2024. 'Ethnofederalism and Indigenous Self-Determination in Northern Canada and the Russian Federation'. *The Polar Journal*, 1–21. https://doi.org/10.1080/2154896X.2024.2342120.

Wilson, R.A. 2021. 'Hate Speech on Social Media: Content Moderation in Context'. *Conn. L. Rev.* 52:1031–44.

Winks, B. 2023. 'Hate Hurts: Qwelane and the Lingering Obscurity in South Africa's Hate Speech Law'. *Constitutional Court Review*, 76–123.

WMC case. 1999. WMC Resources v Western Australia [1999] NNTTA 230.

Woldeyes, Y.G. 2023. 'English Linguistic Imperialism and Mother Tongue Medium Education in Ethiopia'. In *The Handbook of Linguistic Human Rights*, edited by T. Skutnabb-Kangas and R. Phillipson, 393–404. Hoboken: John Wiley.

Wolfrum, R. 2015. 'Legal Pluralism from the Perspective of Internaitonal Law'. In *Non-State Justice Institutions and the Law: Decision-Making at the Interface of Tradition, Religion and the State*, edited by M. Kötter, T. Röder, G. Schuppert, and R. Wolfrum, 216–32. Hampshire: Palgrave Macmillan.

Women's Legal Centre Trust case. 2018. Women's Legal Centre Trust v President of the Republic of South Africa 2018 (6) SA 598 (WCC).

Women's Legal Centre Trust case. 2022. Women's Legal Centre Trust v President of the Republic of South Africa and Others (CCT 24/21) [2022] ZACC 23; 2022 (5) SA 323 (CC); 2023 (1) BCLR 80 (CC) (28 June 2022). Constitutional Court.

Wood, P., and D. Rossiter. 2022. *Unstable Properties: Aboriginal Title and the Claim of British Columbia*. Vancouver: UBC Press.

Woolman, S., and B. Fleisch. 2014. 'The Problem of the "other" Language'. *Constitutional Court Review* 5:135–71.

Woolman, S., and J. Swanepoel. 2013. 'Constitutional History'. In *Constitutional Law of South Africa*, edited by S. Woolman and M. Bishop, Sections 2.1–2.6. Cape Town: Juta.

World Bank. 2016. 'Review and Update of the World Bank Safeguard Policies'. World Bank. https://consultations.worldbank.org/consultation/review-and-update-world-bank-safeguard-policies.

World Bank Environment and Social Framework. 2016. 'Environmental and Social Framework Setting Environmental and Social Standards for Investment Project Financing'. New York: World Bank. https://consultations.worldbank.org/sites/default/files/materials/consultation-template/review-and-update-world-bank-safeguard-policies/en/materials/the_esf_clean_final_for_public_disclosure_post_board_august_4.pdf.

Wright, C., and A. Tomaselli, eds. 2019. *The Prior Consultation of Indigenous Peoples in Latin America: Inside the Implementation Gap*. London: Routledge.

Xanathaki, A. 2022. 'Self-Determination Rights'. In *Research Handbook on the International Law of Indigenous Rights*, edited by D. Newman, 75–95. Cheltenham: Elgar.

Xucuru case. 2018. Xucuru Indigenous People and their members v Brazil [2018], IACtHR, Ser. C No. 346.

Yaker case. 2018. Yaker v France UNHRC CCPR/C/123/D/2747/2016, 17 July 2018.

Yanner case. 1999. Yanner v Eaton (1999) 201 CLR 351; 166 ALR 258.

Yellowknife case. 2015. Yellowknife (Northwest Territories (A.G.) v Association des parents ayants droit de Yellowknife 2015 NWTCA 2.

Yorta Yorta (HCA) case. 2002. Yorta Yorta v Victoria [2002] HCA 58; (2002) 214 CLR 422.

Yupsanis, A. 2011. 'The International Labour Organisation and Its Contribution to the Protection of the Rights of Indigenous Peoples'. *Canadian Yearbook of International Law* 49:117–76.

Yupsanis, A. 2013. 'Article 27 of the ICCPR Revisited – The Right to Culture as a Normative Source for Minority / Indigenous Participatory Claims in the Case Law of the Human Rights Committee'. *Hague Yearbook of International Law* 26 (January):345–83.`

Zana case. 1997. Zana v Turkey, App. No. 18954/91 (1997). ECtHR.

Zheng case. 2009. Zheng v Cai [2009] HCA 52.

Zmyvalova, E. 2024. 'The Right to Language in School: Russian Sámi'. *International Journal on Minority and Group Rights*, on-line.

Zoethout, C.M. 2017. 'Animals as Sentient Beings: On Animal Welfare, Public Morality and Ritual Slaughter'. *ICL Journal*. https://doi.org/10.1515/icl-2013-0303.

Zondo, R.M.M. 2022. 'Judicial Commission of Inquiry into Allegations of State Capture, Corruption and Fraud in the Public Sector Including Organs of State'. Pretoria: Judicial Commission. https://www.statecapture.org.za/site/files/announcements/649/Judicial_Commission_of_Inquiry_into_State_Capture_Report_Part_3-1.pdf.

Zulu case. 2023. Prince Simakade Ka-Zwelithini Zulu and the President of the Republic of South Africa No 38670/22 (High Court, Gauteng) handed down 11/12/23.

Zwane case. 2024. Zwane v Zwane and others [2024] JOL 63913 (MM).

INDEX

L

M

www.ingramcontent.com/pod-product-compliance
Lightning Source LLC
LaVergne TN
LVHW070905210926
848482LV00017B/993
* 9 7 8 1 4 8 5 1 5 3 8 5 6 *